Ellison "Tarzan" Brown

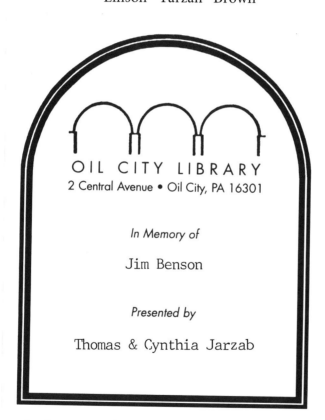

Ellison "Tarzan" Brown

Brown

The Narragansett Indian Who
Twice Won the Boston Marathon

MICHAEL WARD

with a foreword by JOHN J. KELLEY

McFarland & Company, Inc., Publishers
Jefferson, North Carolina, and London

LIBRARY OF CONGRESS CATALOGUING-IN-PUBLICATION DATA

Ward, Michael, 1954 May 11–
　　Ellison "Tarzan" Brown : the Narragansett Indian who twice
won the Boston Marathon / Michael Ward, with a foreword by
John J. Kelley.
　　　　p.　　cm.
　　Includes bibliographical references and index.

　　ISBN-13: 978-0-7864-2416-0
　　ISBN-10: 0-7864-2416-8 (softcover : 50# alkaline paper)

　　1. Brown, Ellison, 1913–1975.　2. Runners (Sports)—United
States—Biography.　3. Marathon running—United States.
4. Boston Marathon.　I. Title.
GV1061.15.B74W37　2006
796.42092—dc22　　　　　　　　　　　　　　　2006015635

British Library cataloguing data are available

On the cover: Ellison "Tarzan" Brown in the Providence 12-mile road
race, September 3, 1940 *(courtesy Providence Journal)*

Manufactured in the United States of America

McFarland & Company, Inc., Publishers
　Box 611, Jefferson, North Carolina 28640
　　www.mcfarlandpub.com

To three resplendent, loving wives:
Ethel (Ellison's), Ann (my dad's) and Bonnie (mine)

Acknowledgments

The town of Westerly, Rhode Island, and its environs, despite its relatively small size, has produced an impressive number of the nation's finest musicians, including drummer Neil Gouvin and bandleader, singer, and harmonica player Sugar Ray Norcia. In a fortuitous turn of events, our musical paths came together in 1978, beginning a twenty-seven-year span of association. Throughout that period, during travels to gigs all across America and overseas, I was introduced to the storied life and lore of Ellison "Tarzan" Brown. Gouvin and Norcia provided the perspective of the local area resident. At first I listened to some of Brown's exploits with skepticism. As a resident of the Boston area, I found that every April brought a plethora of marathon memories and more stories.

At some point, and without being sure exactly why, I felt a compelling need to find out more about Tarzan Brown. Over time, as computers and the Internet became an established modern-day presence, I tried to find some corroboration to the stories, but very little information was available. I decided to look into newspaper sources on microfiche. I was fascinated to read of Brown's athletic successes and the way the newspapers portrayed him.

This led to a search for more information. Cherie Haitz, librarian at Mount Auburn Hospital in Cambridge, Massachusetts, graciously accessed the *New York Times* index online for me and with her help I had a good start. To my surprise and chagrin, I was to discover that only the *Times* was indexed fully in the critical years I was searching. The sports pages of the various Boston and Rhode Island newspapers had to be viewed page by page on the microfiche reader, in a tedious search for pertinent articles. Many a time my heartbeat would increase as my eye focused upon the word "Brown" on a page. Disappointment would follow quickly as I discovered that the "Brown" of a headline, a subheadline, or a sentence tucked inside a paragraph of some otherwise easily-overlooked article referred to Brown University, the St. Louis Browns, or another individual with that same surname.

Though it was time consuming, I managed to view most of the sports pages from the years 1933 to 1946 in at least four major Boston newspapers (and two Rhode Island papers). I have the assiduous yet always cordial staff of the Microtext Department at the Boston Public Library to thank foremost for enabling this extraordinary effort to be undertaken with some semblance of efficiency.

The Print Department of the Boston Public Library deserves special mention. Aaron Schmidt, from first contact, was helpful beyond legitimate expectation. Jane E. Duggan, very knowledgeable about Tarzan Brown perhaps in part due to her Rhode Island roots, was especially generous with her time and encouragement. I cannot thank her enough for all her assistance. This book is without question markedly better because of the Boston Public Library's caring staff, with its obvious commitment and expertise.

I owe thanks to Michael Delaney, the managing editor for visuals at the *Providence Journal*. Mr. Delaney deserves plaudits for enabling me to acquire the historic photographs from that newspaper's archives to augment this work. I must also thank Linda Henderson of the *Journal's* library department. And, while I am extending thanks for photographs, Kevin O'Sullivan of AP/Wide World should be acknowledged here as well. When you cast your eyes upon that incredible photograph of the just-married, youthful couple, Ethel and Ellison, I am sure you will immediately understand.

Neil Gouvin was responsible for introducing me to the life of Tarzan Brown. He was also responsible for introducing me to Brown's wife, Ethel, although not literally. Gouvin made the initial telephone calls to Ethel on my behalf, but she rebuffed all overtures. Indeed, she wanted her husband's memory to be left alone, "left in peace." Ellison Brown's legacy had been subjected to reprehensible treatment — at the hands of some newspaper journalists, some nefarious "historians" (her scrapbooks and photographs were stolen from her), and others attempting to extort or exploit the name or memory of the man for personal gain. Not fully understanding the situation, I called Ethel myself and, although she played me very tough, purporting to be uncooperative, she finally agreed to an initial visit from me, but under the condition that I bring Bonnie, my wife, along. As it turned out Ethel opened up her home to us. That first visit and each since, time spent with both Ethel and Sis, her kind and supportive daughter, has been tremendously illuminating and always highly pleasant. Those visits have made this work vastly more complete. It has been my unvarying goal not to mishandle Ellison Brown's legacy — to restore his rightful place in the history of athletic achievement — and, at the same time, not to disinherit Ethel's trust.

Other family members supplied pieces of the overall picture. Former town policeman and expert on Narragansett native dance Byron Brown spoke by telephone of his memories. *Westerly Sun* writer John Hopkins' work deserves recognition for preserving his uncle's legacy.

Thanks to *Westerly Sun* president and publisher David Lucey are in order. I must also express my thanks to Donna Bains and Mary Jane Wilkinson of the *Boston Globe*, and retired *Globe* sportswriter Michael Madden. His written work and our conversations, always enlightening, added to this work.

Extraordinary human being John J. Kelley elevated this work with his spirit. "Tarzan was a remarkable person, and he deserves to have his life extended in literature," John e-mailed early on. I loved the way he put that, and, of course, I couldn't have agreed more, so you can imagine my exhilaration when John graciously agreed to write the foreword. His trust was gratifying and humbling; it added a dimension to the undertaking, elevating it. I have expressed it before but I wish to have it right here in print: my deepest gratitude is extended to you, John J. Kelley. Thank you.

I had hoped to get this book into print before the passing of Johnny A. Kelley, but that, alas, did not come to pass. Needless to say, speaking with him face-to-face was a cherished moment, and stimulating, to say the least. Kelley, a feisty ninety-five at the time, with evident joy reminded me numerous times during our talk: "Tarz would say, 'Kelley, my boy, you better get out of my way or I'll run right over you.'" This he would follow each time with an insuppressible chuckle. I thank his wife, Ginger DeLong. Without her care and assurance, our meeting may never have taken place.

Curator extraordinaire Dick Johnson of the New England Sports Museum deserves special mention for the selfless offering of his valuable time and resources. I want to thank Gloria Ratti and the organization for which she works, the Boston Athletic Association. Larry Hirsch, a boxer in his younger days under the supervision of Tarzan Brown's manager and first trainer, Tippy Salimeno, was gracious and generous with his memories, his historical items, and his time. His attitude constitutes the epitome of the best that small-town America had to offer in bygone years, an era sadly now past. Domingo "Tall Dog" Monroe, another former Rhode Island boxer, provided insight into life from the Narragansett point of view. Frank Genese shared recollections of what was at one time a very familiar sight, Tarzan running the streets of Westerly. Richard D. Comolli of the Comolli Granite Co. of Ashaway, Rhode Island, maker of monuments and headstones, helped me locate Brown's mother's grave. Comolli explained the distinctions of Westerly granite, and put me in touch with useful area sources, one of whom was Frank Limpert, proprietor of Frank's Trading Post, North Stonington, Connecticut. Frank furnished some color to the larger canvas; he knew Brown personally in Brown's later years. Park director Alan Peck, as trustworthy a guardian of Wilcox Park in Westerly as could ever be found, answered questions about the tree and stone that serve as a dedicated reminder of the greatest runner ever to come from the area.

My mother, Ann, and my father, Larry, were all-encouraging, but went way beyond parental moral support even to assist hands-on with some arduous microfiche scanning and research at critical junctures along the way. Without their help in uncountable ways, this project might not have seen the light of day; their love has always kept me going.

Speaking of love, the love of my son, Clay, and my wife, Bonnie, ever present, nourished this work at every stage. They deserve the highest praise for enabling me to devote such time and effort as it required to get this project off the ground and to pursue it until completion. Clay, serving as a sounding board for ideas, was invaluable. I am grateful. Only the families of the family of writers can really know the extent of the experience, the inherent ups and downs.

My brother, Peter, was instrumental in assisting me in securing certain difficult-to-obtain data and access passes as only an experienced newspaper reporter can. His continual love and support mean a lot. Sandy, Larry and Melissa Simon also warrant my gratitude and love; their backing is greatly appreciated. Alexander Ward, a young athlete in his own right; his mother, Esther Sanchez; and her husband, John Anderson, have each made contributions in spirit. Thank you all.

Mindy Koyanis, thank you for sharing generously of your knowledge and point of view during the critical early stages. For computer help and more, thanks go to Rebecca Maki, Tricia Doherty, and Doug Harris.

Written acknowledgments, by intrinsic design, must stand incomplete. The point of cutoff, like a finish line, can sometimes arrive too soon, like the few races Tarzan Brown failed to win because he ran out of course before his final spurt was complete. So, thank you, too, Ken Graczyk, supervisor, graphic artist and friend for nearly three decades. (You just made it under the wire.)

I have done my absolute best to see that this biography is accurate, honest and complete. Any departures from that, in keeping with the tradition of acknowledgments, are, of course, unintended and my responsibility alone.

Michael Ward
April 2006

Contents

Contents

Foreword:
I Remember Tarzan Brown
by John J. Kelley

On a blustery April afternoon in the mid-1950s, I met "Tarzan" Brown. We shared a handshake, over almost before it occurred.

I might have expected a figure of Rushmorean proportions. Instead, I found an unprepossessing fellow huddled in a trenchcoat, standing beside the Boston Marathon's old Exeter Street finish line.

The thought struck me that he was an "old man" of forty. Had to be. He'd been twenty-two when he won his first Boston back in '36. They said a hernia had ended his racing career.

Now, on this later Patriots' Day, I myself was twenty-two, recently married, and a Boston University student; and though I hadn't won, I'd completed my second Boston Marathon attempt (having dropped out of the '49 race as a high schooler), and I was elated to know that my fifth-place finish had earned me "First American" honors.

"You ran great," Tarzan said. Then I was steered away, into the BU Soden Building's cellar "recovery room" by my friend Johnny Semple. Nearly two decades would pass before I would see the man whose formal name was Ellison Myers Brown for what would prove the last time.

During our overlapping years on Earth, I was destined to spend but a few hours in his company. Next to nothing. But I would know that I shared those hours with a living legend.

The legend of Tarzan Brown, like all legends, loomed larger than life. Yet the man who took his nickname from Edgar Rice Burroughs's famous jungle hero would never settle for static stone. He reveled in the pleasures and pitfalls of the flesh.

In his prime, Ellison Brown's physique might have inspired a modern-day Praxiteles. His as-if-sculpted muscles riveted the eyes of his beholders. To print reporters covering his meteoric dash through the 1936 marathon's opening miles, he was "a superb physical specimen" and "a mahogany-hued marvel."

1

Rave coinages, to be sure. Ah, but there was a dark downside to such compliments. They were the judgments of men unused to witnessing raw talent trumping the products of "traditional" training methods.

So the young marvel was deemed a prodigy of nature, unsubmissible to evolved coaching techniques. Summarizing Tarzan's against-the-laws-of-probability victory, the *Boston Globe's* Jerry Nason wrote, "For his wild, undisciplined run ... [he] became known to the Marathon as 'Chief Crazy Horse.' In his second Marathon race, Brown took off in such a headlong flight at the outset that the press cars were unaware that he was out ahead and followed the wrong runners, mistaking them for the leaders for five miles...."

Mr. Nason was off on one point. The 1936 Boston wasn't actually Tarzan's second Marathon. He had finished in 32nd place in 1933 and again in 1934.

The press's take on the 1936 race's show-stealer imbued the emergent legend with an unsightly stain.

The gentlemen of Boston's press called him a "raw natural." They called him a "penniless redskin." They said he preferred a lazy hunting life on his Narragansett tribe's Ashaway, Rhode Island, reservation to one of regular employment in nearby Westerly. They photographed him lying abed flexing his biceps while making the Tarzan ape call on the morning following his BAA win. Seconds later, a more reflective Tarzan offered, "Maybe now the white man will take me seriously."

How the white man took him depended on the depth of the observer's prejudice.

You couldn't come into the running game, as I did, in eastern Connecticut during the late 1940s, and not have caught something of the legend.

Tarzan's racing days were already history. Whatever we kids knew of him had come to us as hearsay.

It came accompanied by chuckles and winks intended to let us in on a secret shared by our insider elders. The secret's transmission invariably began with the words, "Tarzan Brown could have been The Greatest Distance Runner of All Time."

Then came the secret: "Of course, Tarzan liked his good times." (Here, the chuckle and the wink.)

Oh yes, Tarzan indisputably liked his good times. They were times told over and over until the reciting of them outstripped the listing of his racing times.

Tarzan, all agreed, was a "free spirit." And like many another free spirit, he often seemed deaf to the meanspiritedness of those who seemed bent on enlarging the legend. Possibly, the man who proudly carried his tribal name, Deerfoot, secretly relished the reputation that grew as much from misrepresentation as from fact.

If they would believe he could run in defiance of their holy training rules, why not let them? If they were determined to believe he reckoned neither proper rest nor eating habits to be important, why not let them? A marathoner's fame is modest at best. During his brief time as a contender, Ellison Myers Brown won two Boston Marathons. His second victory, in 1939, must have yielded sweet vindication. This time he ran a perfectly paced race to set a new Boston course record and post the world's best marathon time for that year.

Despite the triumphs, his overall Boston record bears out the popular image of a wildly mercurial performer. Tarzan's 1936 win was followed by a 31st-place finish in 1937 and an even more lackluster 54th place in 1938. He started the 1936 Berlin Olympic Marathon with high hopes, only to drop out at nineteen miles.

When he was good, Tarzan was like the girl of the nursery rhyme. He was "very, very good. But..."

He raced heroically. He defied principles and odds alike. His failures sometimes proved as spectacular as his triumphs.

To readers in our era, an era used to corporate productions—corporate marathons and corporate marathoners—the story of an individual who rejected his society's unceasing attempts to typecast him, a man who was who he was in all circumstances, should exert a powerful appeal. Let's hope that your run through Michael Ward's life of Tarzan Brown will inspire you to be the person your heart knows yourself to be!

John J. Kelley won the Boston Marathon in 1957.

Introduction

Marathons (and shorter races) were sport and entertainment in the bleak Depression years of the 1930s. They could also be a means to fame, employment, self-esteem, escape, and glory for the mostly blue-collar, predominantly Caucasian, often unemployed men who determinedly competed in them, sometimes at astounding costs. A majority of the sportswriters of the daily newspapers at the time looked down upon these runners. The sports page scribes referred to them, usually derisively, as "plodders" and their sport events as "grinds." (Track runners from educational institutions, on the other hand, were universally respected.) In the view of Jock Semple, a marathoner of the era, in Boston, for one day each year, these resolute plodders were regarded not as oddballs or misfits or eccentrics or cranks but as serious athletes.

A handful of remarkable men stood apart from the ruck of runners that strove for the finish lines, and one man in particular achieved incredible successes in the running game for the few years until the arrival of World War II. That man was Ellison Myers Brown, well known in his day as Tarzan Brown.

A member of the Narragansett (situated in southeastern Rhode Island), Brown grew up in intense poverty. Early on he discovered he had a love for running and the outdoors. With little formal athletic training but blessed with an amazing combination of outstanding courage, strength, stamina, resolve and a magnanimous spirit, Brown managed to emerge into the consciousness of a downtrodden public with a thirst for spectacle, a citizenry existing in a realm veritably light years away from his impoverished tribal confines. His skills and talent carried him into that unfamiliar otherworld of electric refrigerators, elevators, underwear, collars and ties, the press corps and photographers with firecracker flashbulbs, telegrams from dignitaries, transportation wonders such as ocean liners and overnight Pullman railroad cars, the sounds of strange languages, and the tastes of foreign foods and beverages.

Lore developed, way before his death, surrounding the man with legendary actions that created a community of devoted admirers. Ask and on occasion you can still hear it, especially around Patriots' Day in New England, in a multitude of voices and timbres:

He jumped into Lake Cochituate — no, it was Fiske Pond, or wasn't it the Upper
Charles River — during the Boston Marathon.
Wasn't he the Indian who ran races wearing a big feathered headdress?
Tarzan Brown? Yeah, he was the one who ran races barefoot.
He used to eat tons of hot dogs and drink bottles of soda before marathons, didn't
he?
Tarzan'd stop during the middle of a race, go into a tavern and casually down
a few beers. Then, after seeing some of the racers pass the joint, he'd finish
his round, pay his tab and head out into the street where he'd get right back
into the race — and still manage to win by a quarter mile!
He was in the Olympics with the real Tarzan, the fellow in the movie; not Weiss-
muller — not Crabbe — the other one — you know, what's-his-name — Glenn
Morris.
The State of Rhode Island named a holiday after him — Tarzan Brown Day —
but he gave it to his people. It was changed to Indian Day.

The lore is rich and wonderful. It may reveal as much about us as it does about Tarzan Brown. It is not my intention to deflate the man by holding such stories up to the cold, harsh scrutiny of historical evidentiary standards. Firstly, it cannot be done. And secondly, I love the lore too. I don't want it to disappear. My aim is not to debunk but to magnify. At the same time, I want to determine, if possible, where the boundary line has been drawn between fact and embellishment.

In the days before accurate and precise methods of measurement, both of distance and of time, the outcome of a particular race could hinge as much upon the miscalculations of the race officials as upon the athletic abilities and perseverance of the competing participants. But what could not be controlled by event administrators, race authorities, referees, or municipal officials was the display of heart the athletes culled to the surface on the occasion of a race. Underpinning the hope and determination that comprised that show of heart was, in the case of distance runners, a love of running. Tarzan Brown loved to run.

For many, many years, the residents of Westerly and the small Rhode Island communities with American names of resonance and beauty — Alton, Bradford, Carolina, Charlestown, Hope Valley, Hopkinton, Peace Dale, and Wood River Junction — shared a common experience. They would occasionally see a familiar figure running along the streets or byways leading in or out of their towns. Whether looking out their windows, sitting on porches or front steps, or driving along the rural roads, it was a common sight to see Ellison Brown running by, perhaps loping ten miles on his way to buy a quart of milk to bring back to his resilient family. *"There goes Tarzan Brown,"* they might say or note silently to themselves.

And so, here goes the life story of Tarzan Brown.

Historical Note:
The Narragansett

The Narragansett can trace their lineage back to the Paleo-Indians from around 11,000 B.C.E., at the end of the last Ice Age, and some trace them back even further, to the very earliest inhabitants of the continent. By the White Man's reckoning, aided by archeological research, those earliest North America peoples figure to have been inhabitants of the region 20,000 years ago. According to the Narragansett, aided by oral history and clues from rock formations, those ancestors inhabited the area more than 30,000 years ago. The difference is 10,000 years. In what has been, especially in recent times, an uneasy coexistence, it is not surprising that there would be disagreement on any of the facts of history pertaining to the Narragansett.

In 1524, Italian explorer Giovanni da Verrazano, sailing for French interests, sailed along the Atlantic Coast from what is presently North Carolina to New York Harbor, and then continued east to Block Island and into Narragansett Bay, along what are now the eastern shores of Rhode Island. He anchored in today's Newport Harbor, and lived among the native peoples for fifteen days. He described the people as ones who "have the most civil customs that we have found on this voyage.... [T]heir manner is sweet and gentle."[1] The Narragansett lived under an organized system of leaders, and had relations with the neighboring tribes, in some cases providing protection for smaller bands. Methods of fishing and agriculture were well developed by the regional inhabitants that Verrazano observed. He departed in search of the Northwest Passage, but took notes of the fertile soil, woodlands, plentiful wild game and lavish fish stocks.

A limited trade between European settlers in Massachusetts and the Native American peoples, including the Narragansett, began in the 1620s. In 1635 the first European settlements in what is now Rhode Island were established. The following year the Massachusetts Bay Colony banished Puritan minister Roger Williams and a few of his followers from the community. The Narragansett sachem or traditional tribal leader at that time, Miantonomi, generously assisted Williams by giving land use rights for a homestead in what is now Providence.

In the Pequot War (1636–1637) the Narragansett allied with the English, having been promised a part of the Pequot lands as spoils in a victorious war. That promise was not kept. The Hartford Treaty signed at the conflict's end put the Narragansett legally under the jurisdiction of the colony of Connecticut. Soon thereafter, colonists seized the rights to some of the Narragansett lands. Miantonomi, with a high degree of sophistication in ecological matters, understood how the loss of land threatened the life of the people. "These English having gotten our land, they with their scythes cut down the grass, and their hogs spoil our clam banks, and we shall all be starved."[2] Around 1642, he made a pitch for Native American unity, to establish a confederacy, to fend off the growing threat posed by the European land thieves. He wanted the tribes to join in a coalition to wipe out the English colonists from the Native American lands in a one-day war, but intertribal squabbling could not be overcome.

A Mohegan chief, Uncas, informed the colonists of Miantonomi's plan. Uncas took Miantonomi into custody and turned him over to the colonists for a form of show trial where he was duly found guilty. Miantonomi was handed back to the Mohegan to face execution, in 1643.

A battle was staged against the collaborationist Mohegan in 1660. Four colonies—Connecticut, New Haven, Plymouth, and Massachusetts Bay—worked out a scheme whereby they assessed and applied an exorbitant fine to the Narragansett for the aggression against the Mohegan, but they would not accept payment; instead the consortium of colonies attempted to seize land as compensation.

When the Wampanoag Tribe attempted to reclaim their native lands from the colonists in Massachusetts, war broke out between King Philip's coalition of tribal forces and the united militias of the colonists. The Narragansett sachem, Canonchet, the son of Miantonomi, refused the colonists' demands to surrender Wampanoag refugees who had found safe shelter with the Narragansett.

In December 1675, well-armed colonial soldiers destroyed the winter camp of the Narragansett (in South Kingstown), massacring a majority of women, children and elderly men. The bloody episode became known as the Great Swamp Massacre. Three hundred women and children may have been burned to death that day along with an estimated six hundred Narragansett men killed. Hundreds of others were chained and sold into slavery. By the end of the war, the population of the Narragansett, which may have been 5,000 to 7,000 strong before the war, was reduced, by one estimate, to perhaps 200 survivors.[3]

Some of the surviving Narragansett merged with the Niantic, while others migrated to upstate New York or to Brotherton, Wisconsin. The 1700s were difficult years in terms of the survival and maintenance of the tribe. Pressures to lose or eschew tribal identity were strong. Town clerks throughout the state of Rhode Island, for example, attempted to make the Narragansett disappear, literally, by classifying tribal members in the town record rolls as "Mustees," and then transforming those into "mulatto," "Negro" and "black" persons.[4] An "Indian" category of classification did not exist. Furthermore, in concordance with a nationwide movement to make indigenous peoples melt into the mainstream, continuous efforts were made to convert Native Americans from their tribal religious beliefs to Christianity, "to bring the Indians under the civilizing influences of the gospel."[5]

In 1792, the state of Rhode Island overreached in its political authority and abolished the position of sachem in the tribe and installed a five-man council. Despite the interference, the Narragansett quietly kept the traditional leadership intact. Outright swindles and "legally incurred" debts reduced the Narragansett landholdings to 15,000 acres. The problem of theft of native lands was so drastic and widespread that the federal government had to intervene, with the Non-Intercourse Act, passed in 1790, which, among other things, attempted to preclude land-for-debt payments.

Nearly one hundred years passed before the state of Rhode Island "detribalized" the Narragansett. It did so without the legally necessary federal sanction. In 1880, the state legislature "purchased" the land. In some cases, some members of the tribe received less than $16 for their portion of the tribe's ancestral lands. The state acquired all but two acres in Charlestown.[6] Attempts to get relief in the Rhode Island state courts, not surprisingly, were unsuccessful.

Before the turn of the twentieth century, with the future of the very identity of the tribe in some doubt, Otis Byron Brown was born into the world. Raised among the rural tribesmen in a world without electricity or automobiles, telephones or radios, he and his siblings managed to grow into adulthood, eking out a living mostly by determination, perseverance, faith, and some luck. An uncle of Otis's named Louis Brown

> was once reported to have run a mile in four minutes flat on the track at the Kingston Fair Grounds. Thirty-five years ago the older Brown beat a fast field in the invitation mile. The timers were amazed to discover that he had covered the distance in exactly four minutes and for a few minutes a new record holder was a member of the Brown family. The time was thrown out on the grounds that the track had been measured wrong.[7]

That race would have taken place in 1901, nearly a half century before the achievement, a four-minute mile, was officially accepted.

Prologue: "What Kid Could Ever Run That Way from Westerly?"

Horatio S. Stanton, Jr., called "Chief" by those who knew him, was a respected and proud Narragansett runner. A strong distance runner, he enjoyed running marathons, races of 26 miles 385 yards in length. His combination coach, trainer, and manager was the inimitable Thomas "Tippy" Salimeno, a savvy but generous sports promoter of Italian heritage who recognized athletic talent when he saw it, and he saw it in Chief Stanton. In an era when very little cooperative interaction bridged the two worlds from whence the two men were raised and lived, these two very different men forged a viable working partnership. Tippy would handle the paperwork (entry forms and fees), transportation, and rubdown lotion, and Chief Stanton would handle the part from the blast of the starting pistol to the breaking of the tape span across the finish line. This arrangement worked out well, and together, Tippy and the Chief were each making names for themselves on the New England road race circuit. Chief Stanton was adding to his estimable reputation as a winning runner, and Tippy Salimeno was adding to his questionable reputation as a winning manager.

On one clear and breezy day in 1926, Chief Stanton was making preparations to commence his training, which usually involved running five or ten miles, either along the wooded trails that existed throughout rural Rhode Island or upon the poor rutted country roads. Just before beginning his regular practice run, Tippy Salimeno told the Chief that he was going up to Shannock to watch a baseball game.[1] In addition to viewing the game, there were some players there he wanted to scout. Shannock was a small town fourteen miles away from the town of Westerly, where they were. The two men agreed that Chief Stanton would run to Shannock, along country trails through the woods, and meet up with his manager there. Salimeno drove off in his trusty automobile as Chief Stanton began his day's training assignment, the fourteen miles on foot.

11

Over two hours later, Chief Stanton arrived at the baseball field where the ball game was still in progress. When he spotted Tippy, the still-wheezing runner signaled to him with his hand. Chief Stanton caught Salimeno's attention, and at that instant, Salimeno as trainer instinctively consulted his pocket watch to note the runner's time. Then Tippy sidled over to Stanton to find out how the workout had gone. Barely able to catch his breath, Chief Stanton pointed behind him.[2] Momentarily he spoke.

Tippy Salimeno remembered a puzzled Chief Stanton saying, "Some kid has been following me all the way from Westerly."[3] At first Salimeno had difficulty making sense of what Stanton was trying to tell him. In 1981, at the age of 81, he still recalled his response to the Chief.

"Kid?" I said. "What kid could ever run that way from Westerly?"[4]

Salimeno followed the Chief to the opening in the woods where the trail began. At first neither man could see any signs of any youngster present there. About ten minutes later, along the edge of the trail, against the backdrop of the trees, a twelve-year-old boy's outline emerged.

According to Tippy's vivid recollection, he summoned the boy over. The reticent youngster approached them. Tippy picked up the narrative.

I said to him: "Have you been following the chief all the way from Westerly?" Tarzan was a shy kid, very shy. He didn't say anything.[5]

Tippy Salimeno recognized a skillful athlete when he saw one, even one at such a young age. Tippy advised the boy to keep up the good running and to look him up as soon as he turned sixteen years old, the age one had to be to run in the official races at that time.[6]

Four years later, Ellison "Tarzan" Brown did exactly that.

1

"Helason Brown"—1933

Ellison Brown's parents, Otis Brown and Grace Ethel Babcock, had three daughters and four sons. None of the boys would die peaceably of old age. Franklin drowned. Elwin died when a gun discharged, a possible accident at the hands of a neighbor. Clifford, who had served time in prison for murdering his best friend and was later released, was stabbed to death in Providence in a fight.[1]

Ellison Myers Brown was born on September 22, 1913, in Potter Hill, Rhode Island. His father told Ruth Bodwell of the *Boston Post* for whom his son was named. "'The given name Ellison was for my boss, Ellison Tinkham, a Rhode Island mill owner, and the Myers is for Chief Myers [sic], once Indian catcher for the old New York Giants,' said Tarzan's father who admitted to being a baseball player of some local repute on the mill team where he worked from the age of 13 until he was close to 40 years old."[2]

Ellison received little formal schooling. He attended the Tomaquag School in Alton for at least three years, and did not complete his schooling beyond the seventh grade.[3] He was recognized in school for his drawing skills. Many years later Ellison's sister Grace (Spears) recounted how, on one particular occasion, her brother had created a sketch in charcoal to decorate a book cover. Their schoolteacher, Miss Merrill, highly praised the drawing and showed it to the school superintendent, a Mr. McCoy, who happened to be visiting the premises that day. McCoy was so taken with the drawing, he decided he had to own it. He handed a dollar to Miss Merrill to give to the young artist Ellison for the purchase of the artwork. It was a proud moment in the school for all. Grace recalled, "Now that was when a dollar was a lot of money. Tarzan went home and gave it to our mother."[4]

Ellison Brown learned to read and write, and became a very capable if not avid reader, especially of the newspaper accounts of races and reportage of his own exploits in particular. Scarce opportunities and suffocating poverty required that he leave school and work to make money, which he did at a young age, like many boys at that time in similar circumstances.

The nickname Tarzan, so the story goes, was attached to him very early in life. A natural outdoorsman with an athletic build and immense strength, Brown liked to climb trees, swing from branches and ropes. He possessed a daredevil type of personality; he was unafraid of dizzying heights and lofty perches that required an abundance of physical strength and good balance. He trusted his instincts and knew the extent of his abilities. What he may not have recognized were his limits. He saw none. If there was a kid that offered a dare requiring endurance, fearless composure, strength, or just complete recklessness and a disregard for bodily safety, Ellison Brown would take him on. That's just the way he was.

Many newspapers at that time carried Edgar Rice Burroughs's popular jungle hero in large, full-page comic strip format. When the motion pictures of Tarzan of the Jungle became available for commercial runs in theaters, the Tarzan character's exploits reached even greater numbers of the nation's population. Ellison, like most young people, loved the movies although he did not get to attend very often. He did manage to view the Hollywood Tarzan enough to take on some of the character's high-flying feats: swinging from ropes or tree branches, high diving into ponds, crossing streams of swift current, chasing (and catching) animals in the wild, and, of course, running like the wind through the woodlands.

"Indians as well as white people call him 'Tarzan' today," a reporter from Boston wrote, "a name he likes and one which he gave himself because he was a great admirer of the Edgar Rice Burroughs hero and he felt that he wanted to be like the real Tarzan."[5] More likely than not, the moniker was hung on the lad by playmates, and it stuck. Tarzan's aunt, Mrs. Mary Johnson, told K. S. Bartlett, a reporter, in 1939: "Ellison always liked to run and he used to like to climb and swing in the trees. That's why they called him Tarzan."[6]

Brown got hired in nearby Wood River Junction to work on the railroad beds for the New Haven railroad, doing manual labor with a pick and shovel. This lasted about two years.[7] Some time after that Brown went to work with an uncle, learning the traditional skills of a stonemason in the traditional Narragansett way. He started out as a helper, an apprentice, and he soon became a skilled wall and fireplace builder. Brown would resort to stonemasonry work when he could find it throughout his life. Fellow workers and tribesmen noted his incredible strength and his ability to lift the heaviest stones.

When the tribe would meet for its annual gathering with other tribes or on other occasions, Tarzan would take an active part in the athletic events. He was well-known as an incredibly fast runner, but he also quickly gained a reputation as being very formidable in competitive weight lifting, in fighting and wrestling, and in stunts such as lifting a full-sized man up by the belt in his clenched teeth. Brown continued to work as a mason, fished, and chopped wood during the winter months, and, by age sixteen, started training for races under the tutelage of Tippy Salimeno.

When Ellison sought Salimeno to handle his training, the young running prospect had little idea just what constituted professional training or what he was getting into. Salimeno, who trained a stable of amateur boxers and seemed more immersed in the promotion of fights and fighting rather than running, nevertheless saw in Tarzan Brown an unusually talented and trainable distance runner, and a very likeable young fellow. Salimeno was genuinely fond of the young athlete, and the Italian sports manager and the Narragansett athlete forged a friendship that would endure for more than four decades.

Salimeno had his own vision of how to best prepare physically for optimal shape and strength, whether for winning competitive races or for winning boxing bouts. (Running was an essential part of his training program for both his fighters and his runners.) John Ahern, a sportswriter with the *Boston Globe*, wrote of Salimeno's methods:

> Salimeno, with no true credentials as a trainer or coach, was ahead of his time. He was a believer in interval training, not jogging or dog trotting as he called it. He had the young Tarzan on interval training: a mile five or six times a day until he could run it regularly in five minutes or less. Then it was a two-mile routine until two miles could be covered in 10 minutes or less. Then three miles and 15 minutes; four miles and 20 minutes; five miles and 25 minutes.[8]

Brown, described as a natural runner, loved to run. He applied himself diligently to the training regimen Salimeno had set for him. "'He was a good worker,' the coach (Salimeno) remembered. 'He stuck at it, and we worked hard for months.'"[9]

Horatio S. "Chief" Stanton, Jr., a primary inspiration to the young runner Ellison Brown, competed in the annual B. A. A. Marathon[10] from 1923 to 1926, according to an obituary in the *Providence Journal*, marking his death over fifty years later in June 1981. Overlooked in the obituary was the fact that Stanton also ran the premier Boston race on at least three other occasions. In 1928, he finished 18th, with a very respectable time of 2 hours, 58 minutes, 33 seconds; he was 21 minutes and 26 seconds behind the famous Clarence H. DeMar, that year's repeat winner, who broke his old course record from the year before with a new record time of 2:37:07. In 1932, the *Boston Globe* reported "Chief" Stanton ran the B. A. A. Marathon and finished in the 28th position. The following year, among the officially entered runners again was Horatio S. Stanton, Jr., entrant number 218. And, entered for the 1933 contest along with Stanton, for his first time, was listed official entrant number 252, belonging to one "*Helason* Brown" of Westerly, Rhode Island.[11]

"*Helason* Brown" of Westerly, Rhode Island, was, of course, *Ellison* Brown. The nineteen-year-old-running novice and the thirty-six-year-old veteran runner arrived at Hopkinton, the starting line for the April 19 Patriots' Day race. That Wednesday was cold, unusually windy, raw, and heavily overcast. Among the competitors that afternoon were three past winners, four future winners, and two other notables. Paul deBruyn, a German-born sailor — now a laborer who shoveled coal in the cellar of the New York City Hotel Wellington — was first across the finish line the previous year of 1932. Jimmy P. Henigan, known as "Smilin' Jimmy," was a local favorite from Medford, Massachusetts. A father of four, he was employed at a corrugated box company. He had won in 1931, not a typifying April day as the thermometer reached 77 degrees. The next year, he placed second, as he had in 1928. The third past winner entered that day was the great Clarence H. DeMar, record-holding winner of seven B. A. A. Marathons—1911, 1922, 1923, 1924, 1927, 1928, and 1930. Perhaps the most famous resident of Keene, New Hampshire, at the time, DeMar was forty-one years old when he won his seventh time. A printer and teacher, he studied distance running not unlike the way Boston baseball star Ted Williams studied hitting. Like Williams, DeMar was not known for being easygoing, especially in his relations with the public. And, like Williams, he was an athlete and media star and a legend in his own era — respected, appreciated and idolized, even years after his final competitive sports event. DeMar often dreamed of his success prior to running an upcoming race. Although the dreams as premonitions always seemed to be an accurate indicator of how he would do, as a down-to-earth pragmatic though religious man, he relegated the whole dreaming experience to the realm of coincidence.

Also included among the runners that blustery afternoon of 1933 were four future B. A. A. Marathon winners. Leslie Pawson, a Pawtucket, Rhode Island, mill hand born in England, was an expert runner, "the speed man of our era," according to runner and later trainer as well as nuts-and-bolts marathon official Jock Semple.[12] Pawson, a talented athlete imbued with the true spirit of magnanimous sportsmanship, was a three-time winner of the Boston Patriots' Day marathon, including that year (1933), five years later in 1938 and three more beyond in 1941. Pawson competed magnificently against Brown throughout the 1930s and early '40s, and although a good friend to Ellison, he also was one of the fiercest, toughest of competitors, and when he ran, he meant business. On occasion, he would give Brown a ride to a race in his car, all friendly and buddy-buddy. But the moment the starting pistol reported, Pawson put personal friendliness aside and strove to leave Tarzan in the dust. Most often, it seems, Les Pawson would place second behind Brown, sometimes by just the barest few steps. No matter the outcome Brown could still expect a most pleasant return ride back with Pawson behind the wheel. Pawson would inevitably be just as friendly and conversant as he had been on the ride up, though he had expended all his energy minutes before to possess the first-place trophy or cup now being transported in the back seat, the one more often than not newly belonging to his passenger, Tarzan Brown, rather than to him.

The second future winner, Dave Komonen, a destitute Canadian resident emigrated from Finland, was an unemployed carpenter, former farmer and amateur cobbler, maker of his own special buckskin running shoes. On this wintry-like afternoon in April 1933, he placed second to Pawson, over five minutes in back of the leader, enabling Pawson to win with the largest gap between the first-place and second-place runners in the marathon's history. Komonen would improve to a first-place finish the very next year, 1934.

The third future winner participating that day was the remarkable John Adelbert Kelley, Boston's King of the Road and perennial local favorite, initially from Arlington, Massachusetts. In 1928 and in 1932, John Adelbert Kelley, referred to as Johnny Kelley the Elder (as he was sometimes called to eliminate identity confusion with another marathon runner named John J. Kelley — no relation — referred to as John Kelley the Younger) did not officially finish, dropping out before the finish line about 21.5 miles the first time and less the second try along the twenty-six mile course. In 1933, the first year for Ellison Brown to run in the B.A.A. Marathon, Johnny Kelley would manage to finish in only 37th place, but that was clearly improvement, since at least it *was* an official, quantifiable finish. Eventually Kelley would be victorious in 1935 and again one decade later in 1945. Seven times he would finish second. One of those times, in 1943, he ran his best ever time — an even two and one half hours, but it earned him only second place. Kelley finished in the top ten a record seventeen times. The scope of his marathon career would be most astonishing. Between 1928 and 1992, Johnny Kelley ran the marathon in Boston a record sixty-one times, and he holds the record for the most finishes — fifty-eight. He ran his last B. A. A. Marathon, in 1992 at the age of eighty-four, and he accomplished that one in 5 hours, 58 minutes flat![13] Johnny A. Kelley was Ellison Brown's most celebrated running rival, and the two will forever be tied together in the lore of the Boston Marathon, due to a hill, a gesture, a reporter's description of a moment, and the incredible desire that the greatest marathoners share. But that awaits the year 1936.

Competing that Patriots' Day in 1933 with Pawson, Komonen, and Kelley was a fourth future winner, a newcomer to the B. A. A. Marathon that year. He ran that day and finished thirty-second with little distinction or notice. Ellison Meyers Brown, called Tarzan by nearly everybody, arrived on the Boston running scene like most of the other marathon greats, not in the manner of a whirlwind but rather barely creating the faintest ripple.

Two notables, neither of whom was ever able to win Boston, were participants in the 1933 edition and deserve mention. John Duncan "Jock" Semple, the Scotsman who later nearly single-handedly managed the nuts-and-bolts operation of putting on the B.A.A. Marathon, was still a contender in those years, and he finished a very respectable thirteenth in 1933. The future chronicler's best finish, seventh in 1930, a year that Clarence H. DeMar finished first, may have been his proudest moment and "was the greatest day in my life."[14] He would compete against Tarzan Brown numerous times, a man Semple described as "a free spirit" and "certainly the most colorful" of the new generation of runners of the thirties and forties.[15] Jock Semple shared with most of his fellow plodders a great fondness for Ellison Brown. Time and again, Semple would witness Brown passing him by on Brown's way to the finish line. Undaunted Jock Semple would give it his all to finish, no matter how long it took.

Last but not least, a notable contemporary and tough competitor was the Baltimore runner of Welsh ancestry, Pat Dengis. Dengis, whose real name was actually Frank but who chose to go by Pat, won every major American marathon, including the prominent Yonkers (New York) marathon three times, but never Boston, though he did finish second behind Pawson in 1938. In the 1933 Boston race, he finished right behind Semple, in fourteenth place.

Brown would develop and perfect his racing technique and strategy, harness his physical gift, and become a threat to win each and every competition he entered. His efforts and achievements would be followed and reported in the newspapers. As word of his fabulous running ability increasingly spread, a core of appreciative fans made up of all races and from all social and economic classes began to attend events promoted with the promise of Tarzan Brown's appearance. In these days before television and mass marketing, road races were major spectator sporting events. Often taking place right on city streets, or connecting towns together, citizens would line the sides of the course and view the race. Usually a city or town dignitary would be on hand to award the winners' prizes. Much pomp and pageantry usually accompanied the event, especially during the prize-awarding ceremonies. On many occasions, some special commemorating event would control the selection of the date for the race. Centennials, bicentennials, etc. and annual Independence Day celebrations topped the list. Local chambers of commerce would often be tapped for donations to cover costs. Local merchants would take advantage of the attendant crowds to raise interest in the products and services they offered, seizing increased sales opportunities.

Local running clubs and sportsmen's collectives, an ever-present part of the landscape of urban life in those days, would usually partake in the sponsorship or organization of running events. They would also donate their club space for before and after preparations including showers, rubdowns, and snacks. In the races themselves, a team prize was offered, usually given to the running club with the three affiliated runners who placed the highest in the event. The runners when registering to enter a contest would be listed with their athletic club affiliation or they would be listed as unattached. The running clubs took great pride in the team prizes, and serious competition for the team prizes ensued, sometimes altering the very complexion of the individual runners' strategies. On occasion runners would change their membership. The B. A. A., or Boston Athletic Association, itself was a club, with the symbol of the unicorn. United Shoe Machinery A. A. and the North Medford Club were but two prominent, competitive running clubs from eastern Massachusetts that also sponsored noteworthy events.

Many small and large cities and towns had their own annual races, some five miles long, some ten, some half marathons of just over thirteen miles, and some twenty-mile events. National title races were, for the most part, delineated in kilometers, with fifteen-K and twenty-K runs being popular. Increasingly, it became incumbent upon the local organizers to see to it that Tarzan Brown was an invited guest to be on hand for their planned events, for his advertised presence greatly enhanced the event, ensuring its high quality in terms of the other participants, the level of competition, and the heightening of the excitement of the moment.

2

"Two of Them Trying to Run with One Pair of Legs" — 1934

In the year 1934, there was scant mention in news accounts of Ellison Brown. He had not yet captured the imaginations of the Boston sportswriters, for his visibility in hometown races was not yet established. But two races, one in the spring and one in the fall, are worthy of inclusion, though Brown won neither of them: the B. A. A. Marathon and the New England Title Marathon held in New Hampshire.

In 1934, Patriots' Day fell on a Thursday. Most of the great marathoners were in Boston to compete, including that terrific cast from the year before: Les Pawson (last year's winner and record holder), Dave Komonen (second place last year), Paul deBruyn, Clarence H. DeMar, James Henigan, Johnny Kelley, Jock Semple and Tarzan Brown. The Finnish-born Dave Komonen, a Canadian immigrant, ran a quick-paced race in homemade shoes. Beyond the seventeenth mile, it became a two-man race, the five-foot-six John Kelley being Komonen's only rival. The two men shared water as they competed. Between miles twenty-one and twenty-two, Komonen gradually began to put some distance between himself and Kelley, who ran out of his stash of special glucose pills and was losing strength. By the end, Komonen finished in 2 hours, 32 minutes, 53 seconds, nearly two minutes shy of Pawson's record, and Kelley registered the first of his seven second-place finishes, yet almost four minutes behind the winner. Semple finished twelfth, deBruyn finished thirteenth, and DeMar landed sixteenth. Ellison Brown repeated his position from the year before, finishing in an inconspicuous thirty-second place. He had completed the course in 3 hours, 13 minutes, 15 seconds. That was 13 minutes and 29 seconds slower than the previous year.

Two former winners did not finish in 1934. Henigan threw in the towel at mile seventeen, and Pawson, experiencing cramps, called it quits when he reached mile sixteen.

The fourth annual New England title marathon, sponsored by the Manchester and Concord councils of the Knights of Columbus, was held on October 12, 1934, and was a full length marathon routed from the town of Boscawen through the capital of Concord and onto Manchester. Jock Semple, from United Shoe Machine A. A. of Beverly, Massachusetts, was the favorite going into this marathon, having won each year since the marathon's inception. Veteran marathoner Clarence H. DeMar, a resident of Keene and thus regarded as a New Hampshire favorite son, had been narrowly beaten by Semple in the final stretch of the previous year's race. This year, the remarkable forty-six year old was once again considered the most likely to successfully challenge Semple's dynasty of first-place finishes.

Manchester, New Hampshire's newspaper of record, *The Leader*, on the day before the marathon, anticipated a repeat of the riveting, hotly contested battle between the two, with DeMar "on his [Semple's] heels" all the way.[1] Another competitive runner, 1931 B. A. A. Marathon winner "Smiling Jimmy" Henigan, was also singled out by *The Leader*. Henigan planned to give it all he had, for he had announced his intention of retiring from marathon competition following this Manchester run. "He chose to save his last big effort for the Granite State folks to claim," the newspaper proudly reported.[2] The next-to-last paragraph in *The Leader*'s prerace day article contained copy devoted to speculation about the chances of a little-known entrant, runner Ellison Brown. It stated:

> What many would like to know is whether or not "Tarzan" Brown, the 19-year-old Narragansett Indian boy from Pawtucket, R. I., will prove a dark horse. Brown has been running since he was 12 years old, although over the short route of from five to 10 miles. It is a question as to how he will stand up in the long grind, but the youth has dismissed any fears that he will drop out by saying that he expects to win. Brown usually walks to the race he is entered in, if it is not more than 40 miles from his home, so in this instance he will take some other means of getting to New Hampshire.[3]

How Brown managed to get to Boscawen for the 9:30 a.m. start of the marathon is not known. That he did get there is without question. On the front page of *The Leader*, published the same day of the race, were the results in black ink. *The Leader* proclaimed DeMar's victory and this subheadline: "STAGES NECK AND NECK BATTLE WITH BROWN ALL [THE] WAY." The article began, "Age and experience conquered youth today...."[4] Clarence H. DeMar beat Tarzan Brown by thirty seconds and two hundred yards. Moreover, being pushed as he was by the persistent Brown, DeMar shattered the two-year-old course record, set by Jock Semple, by nearly six minutes. Brown, in placing second, also trampled Semple's record. *The Leader* gave its readers the story:

> In the most thrilling race ever run on the course since it was inaugurated four years ago, DeMar and Brown ran close together the entire course. Twice the

youthful Brown passed DeMar only to relinquish the lead and finish 30 seconds behind the Keene schoolmaster…. The thousands along the highways cheered the pair as they jogged past, DeMar in his unorthodox short step style and Brown, a thick-muscled youngster, in slow, long strides.[5]

The *New York Times* sported the headline, "De Mar Clips A Record."[6] Though in an Associated Press dispatch, this marked the first instance of Ellison Brown being reported in the prestigious New York newspaper of record. At the start of paragraph two, it stated: "Tarzan Brown of Pawtucket, R.I., forced DeMar all the way, especially in the last half-mile, and finished only thirty seconds behind him. Cecil R. Hill of Lynn, Mass., was third, six minutes behind Brown."[7]

A few years later, Clarence DeMar wrote about this marathon, a race he considered one of the best of his life, in his 1937 autobiography *Marathon*. It was one of only three occasions, by his own admission, in which DeMar publicly made the pronouncement before the race that he would win. Incidentally, in all three instances he managed to substantiate his prediction, but in this case, just barely. DeMar described how the race looked from his point of view. "All the time Tarzan Brown, the Indian, was right with me," he wrote.[8] DeMar was perturbed by what he viewed as the completely useless, even damaging, assistance Brown was receiving from his manager, Tippy Salimeno. Wrote DeMar:

> His handler kept bossing him and refusing to let him run ahead. He could have rolled up one half mile lead early, but his boss said "not yet." The fact that there were two of them trying to run with one pair of legs gave me confidence that I should win and besides I had said I was going to, so continued to race hard with the Indian, who was very good indeed, even if he did have some one to spoil his concentration. At twenty miles which we did just under two hours his trainer began to urge Tarzan ahead. All he could get was one hundred yards lead at the most and I would close in frequently. Finally at twenty-three miles I passed him for the last time. But Tarzan didn't fall back much and coming down the home stretch I didn't dare to risk turning to see how close he was.[9]

This marvelous description by a highly determined man presented his competitor, Ellison Brown, as a runner commanding much of the bluff veteran's respect. In fact, DeMar claimed in his account to have crossed the finish line "with Tarzan Brown a few seconds back," not the thirty seconds reported by the Associated Press and by the *Leader*. Whether just a few seconds' difference or thirty, it certainly must have felt like just a few to the hard-running, forty-six-year-old DeMar that October day.

In DeMar's account, he referred to Tarzan's admirable ability despite the likelihood that his concentration may have been "spoiled." DeMar was a great believer in keeping one's concentration focused in order to achieve winning results. In *Marathon* the experienced veteran addressed the subject and its importance:

There is, however, one thing that I've always needed and which everyone else that I've ever known has needed, and that is concentration, both just before and during the race. Without concentration no one can do everything he is capable of in the contest. What printer, what business man, what editor, what schoolteacher wants distraction when he is working his hardest?[10]

Had Salimeno, Brown's handler, actually impeded the runner from doing better? There is no record of Brown being critical of the ramrod-straight-standing Salimeno. In fact, after Brown won his first B. A. A. Marathon (a year and a half later), he specifically praised Salimeno and the role the dapper trainer, a no-nonsense taskmaster, played in enabling the runner to finish first. Semple, in his autobiography, quoted Brown: "Trainer Salimeno deserves great credit. He kept encouraging me. He kept my pep up."[11] Maybe at this point, both Brown, the novice runner, and Salimeno, the very astute trainer, were learning—learning how better to work together, and learning to master the skills needed to triumph.

As a final comment on the New Hampshire marathon, The *Leader*, perhaps unwittingly, drew this prophetic conclusion: "Clarence's showing was expected," the newspaper asserted, "but the real sensation was young Brown."[12] That sentiment was clearly applicable in 1934 as it was intended, but it would be all the more so in just two years' time, at this very same event where marathon history would be made.

3

Even Without Shoes — 1935

The traditional opening of the season for runners in New England, beginning in 1932, was the North Medford Club 20-Mile Road Race, which was held in mid–March. All the great runners of the day usually took part. Pawtucket, Rhode Island, mill hand Leslie Pawson won the first two Medford races, and Johnny Kelley, a florist's assistant from Arlington, Massachusetts, won in 1934 ("the first big race I ever won."[1]). Clarence H. DeMar, Pat Dengis, Jim Henigan, Jock Semple and Biddie McMahon participated as well. Most of the Boston newspapers opened their sports coverage of the running season with the Medford race, treating it as a preview or warm-up to the B. A. A. Marathon which followed a month later.

Henry McKenna, sportswriter with the *Boston Traveler*, two days before the March 23 Medford road event in 1935, chose his pick to win and publicized it at the top of his article. McKenna wrote, "Every spring brings several 'dark horses' as contenders for top honors in the several local events and today we nominate Ellison 'Tarzan' Brown, running unattached from Westerly, R.I., a 19-year-old Indian, who has already been earmarked for greatness."[2] He went on to recall how Ellison Brown had "pushed" DeMar to record-breaking victory in the Manchester marathon the previous October. Brown's performance in that New Hampshire race had opened Henry McKenna's eyes to the abilities and potential of the young runner, and he was passing the word on to his readers every chance he got. It also got him thinking of another highly successful runner, also Native American, from a generation earlier.

Comparisons were made between Ellison Brown, a member of the Narragansett Indian Tribe, and Thomas Longboat, an Onondaga Indian from the Six Nations Reserve south of Brantford, Ontario, Canada, who had won the B. A. A. Marathon in 1907. Born June 4, 1887, Longboat was twenty when he competed in the Boston event, his first and only time. A huge favorite to win that year, Longboat overcame the twin interruptive obstacles of a slow freight train passing across the course and an intense snow squall to go on and smash the old record by twenty minutes, a record which had stood since 1901.[3] He completed the race in 2 hours, 24 minutes, 24 seconds.

Tom Longboat atypically achieved fame and fortune during his lifetime as a runner, running professionally in exhibitions, some held in large venues including Madison Square Garden in New York City. Later on, he served as a member of the Canadian army in France during World War I, working as a long-distance courier. At some point he was wounded, but was mistakenly listed as dead. Unfortunately, Lauretta, his wife back in Canada, remarried after learning the sad-but-false news. Eventually, Longboat returned to North America where he found out that he was no longer in the same marital situation he had been in before he went overseas. Reportedly, Lauretta was glad to discover that he was alive, but decided to continue on with her new marriage. Undaunted, Tom Longboat also remarried and fathered four children. A good many years later, he died from pneumonia, January 9, 1949, and was given a traditional native burial. Tom Longboat was by no means the only Native American marathoner to run in the B. A. A., but until the arrival of Ellison "Tarzan" Brown over a quarter of a century later, Longboat was and remained the best known.

1935's North Medford race belonged to Johnny Kelley. Not only did he repeat his victory but he did so in fine fashion, shaving five minutes off the record he had set the previous year, and crossing the finish line a half mile ahead of the second-place Bill Simons, according to the Boston newspaper accounts. The Associated Press, on the other hand, reported Kelley's lead over Simmons (sic) as "almost an eighth of a mile," not the half mile, a rather considerable difference. All accounts had McMahon third and Dengis fifth. Les Pawson managed only thirteenth. Ellison Brown finished fifteenth with Jock Semple right behind him at sixteenth, and Clarence H. DeMar finished twentieth. Henigan did not finish.

The newspaper coverage weighed in heavily on the local (Arlington) winner. Kelley was pleased about the weather ("It was one day you'd get in fifty years"), pleased about his condition ("I am about three pounds heavier than last year"), pleased about his warm reception from the spectators, and pleased about his new running shoes.[4] There was little coverage concerning the others, except for Pawson, whom they had expected to do better. "He looked strong as he ran shoulder to shoulder with Kelley for nearly 13 miles before he faded," noted the Globe's Jerry Nason.[5] Brown, for his part, ran in fifth position for about seven miles before eventually slipping back to fifteenth.

In the dissimilar account by the AP, carried in the Westerly Sun, Brown had run in fifth place for ten miles, not seven, a rather large discrepancy in the reporting, considering the reporters were witnessing the same event. According to the AP, Brown then had "suffered cramps which forced him far back over the final half," and he "failed to finish among the first 20."[6] This was absent from the Boston accounts; as far as the Boston newspapers were concerned, he was all but invisible. Only the Westerly paper devoted a paragraph to his efforts. Ellison Brown's finish was omitted altogether in Will Cloney's account in the *Herald*, which listed only the top fourteen finishers plus the nineteenth (Casano, a local Medford boy) and the twentieth (DeMar). Brown's fifteenth place finish, not mentioned in the *Herald*, did manage to find its way onto the list printed in the *Globe*.

Will Cloney included these four tidbits, three having to do with Kelley, and a fourth, the exposure of an alleged case of skullduggery: (1) "Kelley ran smartly, taking to the sidewalks when the opportunity presented." (2) "As he stepped over the finish line, Kelley was seized and stuck in the finger with a needle. It was not an attack or anything like that — just doctors from the Harvard fatigue research bureau making a test." (3) "The sound truck, which kept blaring orders to everyone, stopped on the top of one hill and blocked Kelley nicely." (4) "Martin Fitzgerald, a little man from the Jefferson Club, Cambridge, cantered joyfully toward the tape in fourth place. The officials walked out to meet him, however, and disqualified him for cutting corners — plenty of them. While Fitgerald claimed he ran every step of the way, he was not checked among the first 30 at any of the stations along the route."[7]

In attempt to gain every advantage, Kelley had participated in experiments at the Harvard Fatigue Laboratory. He was reportedly paid one dollar per hour, while both the scientists and the runner attempted to discover why he physically tired in the critical last few miles of a race. Partial results of the experiments resulted in the scientists' suggestion that Kelley carry and consume glucose pills in order to combat the late-race fatigue. Kelley followed their directives. He also received special treatments for his feet and spine massages and rubdowns under the direction of Angus McDonald, a massage therapist at McLean Hospital in Belmont, Massachusetts, who happened to be Kelley's neighbor in Arlington.

Being blocked "nicely" by a truck was an actual improvement over an incident that happened the year before. In his 1934 race in North Medford, the one hundred twenty-one-pound Johnny Kelley was brushed by an automobile on the course. Fortunately he avoided serious injury, but it slowed his overall winning time.

In the April 12 edition of the *Boston Traveler*, Henry McKenna's enthusiasm for Ellison Brown's talents had not diminished. Here he trumpeted the noteworthy entry of Brown to the upcoming B. A. A. Marathon:

INDIAN ENTERS

The field is now up to the 113 mark and the standout in the latest batch ... is Ellison "Tarzan" Brown of Narragansett Indian A.C., Westerly, R.I., who will be accompanied here by 10 Indians of his tribe, including three chiefs.

Brown, who will seek to follow in the footsteps of Tom Longboat, Indian from Toronto who won the B. A. A. marathon in 1907, is an up-and-coming plodder who first leaped into prominence last fall when he trailed Clarence De Mar [*sic*] when the latter won the New England A. A. A. U. marathon title at Manchester, N.H. Brown was only 100 yards back of the eight-times winner of the Unicorn grind.[8]

The *Globe's* same-day announcement that Brown was entering the marathon was not written by a sportswriter with as good an eye at spotting the talented though as-yet unproven marathoner. (No byline accompanied the *Globe* item.) The small headline stated "Tarzan Brown Enters, Marathon Field Now 113" but the opening line suggested that none of the latest lot of announced hopefuls contained any "tried-and-found-durable" types in it. After listing the most recent entries received, it specifically referred back to Brown, stating, "Brown, a Narragansett Indian, who was runner-up to Clarence H. DeMar by 100 yards in the New England Marathon at Manchester, N.H. in 1934 will be accompanied to Hopkinton by seven sturdy braves and three haughty chiefs."[9] The expectant spectacle of the ten-man entourage was deemed noteworthy.

Among the top ten names and numbers listed for the April 19 marathon were: 1 Komonen, 2 Kelley, 3 DeMar, 6 Pawson, 7 McMahon, 8 Henigan, 9 Dengis, and 10 deBruyn. For the first time, six past winners were to compete together in the event (deBruyn, DeMar, Henigan, Kennedy, Komonen, and Pawson). Listed as entrant 109 this year was Ellison "Tarzan" Brown, Westerly, R.I.

Sadly, Ellison's mother was very ill in the early spring of 1935. Of all the people—family members and tribe members—surrounding him, it was his mother who most encouraged the young boy to develop his natural running skills, his love of running, and to pursue his dreams of being a success in the racing field. She was his great inspiration. According to his wife, Ethel, Ellison's mother "had believed in his running when nobody else did. When they told her, 'You should put him to work instead of letting him run up and down the roads,' she encouraged him in his running. She had been the only one to encourage him when everybody else laughed at him."[10] Four days before the start of the B. A. A. marathon, on April 15, 1935, she died at age fifty-two. A funeral service for Grace Ethel Brown was held at the Gavitt Funeral Home, 46 Granite Street, in Westerly two days later. Ellison Brown's mother was laid to rest at the First Hopkinton Cemetery that Wednesday afternoon. "He was very close to his mother. I don't think he ever really got over it," Ethel Brown would remark nearly seventy years later.[11] Reportedly, among his dying mother's last wishes was the directive that Ellison go to Boston and compete in the marathon, despite her near-death condition at that time. He promised her (and himself) that he would.

Jerry Nason of the *Boston Globe*, writing in April 1985, claimed that it was at that time that Ellison Brown, the runner, first appeared on his radar screen. As Nason remembered, a Rhode Island colleague telephoned him with the tip:

> It was Joe Nutter of the *Providence Journal* who discovered Tarzan Brown. A press-boy contemporary and fellow track buff, he phoned me at the *Globe* a few nights before the 1935 Boston race, Brown's first Marathon.
>
> He said, "If you're around the Marathon this week, watch for an Indian kid from down this way, kid named Ellison Brown from Alton. Might be a story in it. It's his first race, and his mother died today. Made him promise to run and to finish the race."[12]

As mentioned before, it was not true that the 1935 B. A. A. Marathon was Brown's first. He had run in the 1933 and 1934 editions of that event. He had also run in other races, though not many and with perhaps little visibility. Nason's memory was not so keen in 1985. But evidently, Rhode Island-based Joe Nutter championed Brown, from his home state, well before Nason did. Jerry Nason, nevertheless, would carry the banner lifelong from that moment onward.

For the 1935 Boston Marathon, Tarzan Brown arrived with two pieces of very personal running apparel. One item was a beautiful multicolored jersey stitched by hand by family members. The material for this singlet had been the fabric of his mother's best dress, and it was woven full with sentiment and stitched replete with meaning. Wearing it during the race would spur the still-grieving son on. The other item, not of sentimental value, was his pair of very tattered primitive high-cut sneakers, running togs that were so worn and beat up they barely were able to hold together under the strain of use.

Track shoes, running shoes, sneakers, athletic footwear — all of these were in the very earliest stages of design in the 1930s. All runners, but especially impoverished ones, had great difficulty acquiring running shoes that did not impede their athletic success. Before 1935, most marathoners wore heavy-weighted, unventilated shoes of canvas or cowhide with thick leather or rubberized soles. Since the roads were often rutted and unpaved, it was thought that these heavy-duty pieces protected the feet best for the full distance. Unfortunately, many a marathoner's hopes were dashed by severe blisters, sores, and bloody cuts caused by the heat and friction of the unwieldy character of the materials, the stitches and the laces.

New England was the nation's home of shoe manufacturing, but running shoes were not a local product until 1933 when a sixty-eight-year-old designer from Peabody, Massachusetts, Samuel Thomas Albion Ritchings,[13] put his inventive mind to the task of designing an ideal running shoe, after seeing the disastrous condition of runners' feet after a race. He began with a careful examination of the many facets involved in running — heat, weight, durability, flexibility, the movement of the foot, sole, heel and toes. Ritchings came up with a model he eventually named S.T.A.R. Streamlines ("S.T.A.R." based on his initials) and word quickly spread among the athletes of this foot-friendly running shoe. Not inexpensive at $7.50 a pair, each pair required sixteen hours of labor to construct. S.T.A.R. Streamlines, superior to all other athletic footwear on the market at the time, were fraught with innovations. They were designed to be lightweight, only five and a half ounces, and came in white only, which was found to repel considerable heat. (The one exception was the first pair created, belonging to Les Pawson, whose S.T.A.R. shoes were black.) The shoes contained holes for purposes of ventilation on the uppers, which were mostly made of kidskin hide, which is very light and flexible but durable. A combination of crepe rubber and calf-skin made up the inner and outer sole, but there was no midsole. The design provided lots of freedom for the toes and enhanced support for the instep with a specially placed elastic strip. The laces were placed on the outside of the shoe, away from the foot.

Ritchings sent a pair of his design to the well-known marathoner Clarence H. DeMar just prior to the 1934 Manchester marathon. Ritchings received back a terse card that read, "Received shoes. They are wonderful. I will win."[14] He did. So taken with the shoes was DeMar that, according to Ritchings, DeMar felt he had had a big advantage over Tarzan Brown, who finished second. DeMar believed that the advantage was due to his custom-made running shoes, and, after winning that race, reportedly told Brown, "I beat you, Tarzan, but I wouldn't have, if you'd had these shoes."[15] Both DeMar and the ubiquitous Jock Semple were among the very first runners to try the shoes. They both highly recommended the shoes to their fellow runners, including John Kelley, who acquired a pair in time for the 1935 Boston Marathon. The shoes Ritchings created were sought after and in demand by most of the runners following their visibility in the 1935 B. A. A. Marathon, when nine out of the first eleven runners to finish wore them. Before Ritchings died in 1937, he had invented a mini industry, the athletic sports shoe, which thrives to this day. But Tarzan Brown was not one of the competitors running in S.T.A.R.s that April afternoon in 1935 — he would have to wait until the following April.

The Hopkinton starting line for the B. A. A. Marathon was crowded with marathoner heavyweights. Dave Komonen, the 1934 winner, was expected to repeat, according to one Boston newspaper, the *Post*. But Komonen was at a disadvantage. During his journey to Boston from Canada, he had gotten held up in a blinding snowstorm near Rochester, New York. Komonen had lost a valuable night's sleep in the ordeal.

Johnny Kelley, the number two man in 1934, was well prepared to give it all he had, having sustained careful, exacting training for the event. His confidence was high for a number of reasons. His feet, importantly, were comfortably situated inside a pair of S.T.A.R. Streamliners. As he had always been susceptible to painful, bloody blisters, the new running shoes inspired as much hope as they provided comfort. Two special items also added to his feeling of hopefulness. His aunt, a Miss Bessie Kilburn of Dorchester, had given a special handkerchief to her nephew to carry for good luck. And fifteen glucose pills for energy were placed in a lightweight pouch for supplemental energy during the twenty-six-mile haul. The glucose pills, recommended by the scientists at the Harvard Business School's Fatigue Laboratory headed by Dr. Bruce Dill, were one of Kelley's secret weapons. One further possession, not carried but held in his mind, additionally boosted Kelley's high hopes for victory. He had a plan by which to run.

At the noontime start, the weather was sunny and warm, with temperatures in the mid-sixties. Some light breezes abounded. As the afternoon developed, that Good Friday-Patriots' Day temperature rose.

Ellison Brown did not figure in the race, but he commanded some attention during the final five, six, or seven miles (depending on the source accepted). One version of the episode is that the old track shoes Brown was wearing when he began in Hopkinton gave out somewhere between mile nineteen and mile twenty-one. From that point to the Exeter Street finish line, Tarzan Brown continued his efforts barefooted. Even without shoes, on the warm pavement, he managed to finish the marathon in thirteenth place, with a time of 2 hours, 53 minute, 35 seconds, crossing the finish line ahead of such previous winners and strong contenders as Clarence H. De Mar (18th), Leslie Pawson (28th), and Bill Kennedy (23rd). Another version of the story is that his feet got uncomfortably hot by the time he got within seven miles of the finish line. Brown simply stopped momentarily and pulled off his shoes, preferring to go without them. "As early as the 15th mile he told Thomas Salimeno, his manager, that the shoes were troublesome, but it was not until the homestretch that they were removed," his supportive hometown press, the *Westerly Sun*, reported.[16] It continued, venturing, "While his showing was brilliant, inasmuch as this year marked only his third attempt over the gruelling course, he would have finished in an even better position, according to his followers, without having to discard his shoes."[17] According to the year-old recollection of sportswriter Arthur Duffey of the *Boston Post*, Brown continued to run the remaining seven miles barefoot and, more incredibly, "crossed the finish line without a blister."[18] The incident was an early piece of what has become a colorful part of the Tarzan Brown and Boston Marathon lore.

Pat Dengis ran a very strong race and gave Kelley the real run for his money. Kelley had taken the lead near the halfway point at Wellesley, having maintained the third spot up until then. A mile beyond, Dengis caught up to the leader and installed himself as head of the pack. All the while Kelley was imbibing his glucose pills. A mile further, Pat Dengis was halted by a sharp knifelike stab in his side, what runners call a stitch. At this point Kelley regained the front-runner's position. Dengis wasn't through, for as quickly as the pain had come, just like that it subsided. The two kept the pace, all the while Johnny Kelley stoking the running fires with the fuel of his sugary power pills. At Kenmore Square, mile twenty-five, this time it was Kelley who was halted. He doubled over, feeling very ill all of a sudden, possibly due to the ingestion of the pills without the benefit of enough water. Dengis appeared ready to take over the lead and very likely the victory. But Kelley was determined. And he came up with a quick solution. He put a finger down his throat, causing himself to vomit. Relief was almost instantaneous. He started moving again. Kelley maintained the lead, continued to head toward the finish line, and crossed it victorious, registering a winning time of 2 hours, 32 minutes, 7 seconds. Kelley finished without the lucky handkerchief his aunt had given him, for he had dropped it, actually in plain view of the finish line. He was sublimely overjoyed at his victory. Dengis crossed the line two minutes later, placing second.

Neither DeMar nor Pawson caused much of a stir in that year's contest. DeMar, who finished eighteenth, never was among the fast-paced leaders, but completed the race in under three hours. Pawson, a favorite and always a threat to win, was running with a painful stress fracture in one foot that was not completely healed. Still, he managed to finish at twenty-eighth. Bill McMahon and number ten-listed Paul deBruyn both failed to finish in the 1935 spectacle due to cramps. Henigan, who did not finish the year before, completed the run in the very respectable tenth place.

The youngest of the many competitors to run in Boston that year was seventeen-year-old Russell George, a member of the Onondaga tribe from Nedrow, New York, who was entered and given number 119. The high school sophomore, like Brown in the days preceding the marathon, was given press comparing him to Thomas Longboat. The *Boston Post*'s Arthur Duffey wrote under the headline this drop head: "Russell George May Prove Another Longboat in Classic Race on Patriots' Day" and described how the young runner had been making a name for himself in New York state. By no means a man beyond his times, Arthur Duffey used descriptions of the racist sort considered all right in the established (white) newspaper circles of those days. He wrote: "Resembling an Indian in every respect, George comes to the Boston race fully intent on winning the great honors and bringing the beautiful trophy back to his tribesmen.... All the natives swear by him as the coming champion. George first came into prominence by beating his brother redskins...."[19]

The 125-pound Russell George, who had finished second two weeks earlier in a Syracuse race of sixteen miles in length, disappointingly injured his ankle before the Boston race and was not able to live up to the high expectations of his early billing. As reported in the *Boston Traveler* the day after, columnist Jack Mulligan said George "was well up in the running, though he had no chance to beat Johnny Kelley after the straps, which bound his bad ankle, gave way at Boston College, and he had to limp the rest of the way in."

It was a game demonstration of courage, for the ankle swelled like a balloon, but he was determined to finish and did, though well back in the ruck."[20]

Although the *Boston Traveler* saw that George limped in late, two newspapers, the *Boston Post* and the *Boston Globe*, erroneously reported Russell George as finishing thirteenth in their lists of "official" marathon finishers, in place of Brown. Someone somewhere must have confused Russell George with Ellison Brown, both similarly lithe and muscular, young, and Native American, with dark-hued complexions. Both wore serious countenances while competing. Brown weighed 138 pounds, stood 5 foot 7 and was nineteen years old. George weighed in at a lighter 125 pounds, no height information was given, and he was two years younger, just seventeen. How much the two young men actually visually resembled each other is an open question.

4

Two National Titles in a Fortnight — 1935

Sometime after the 1935 Boston marathon, Ellison Brown and Tippy Salimeno discussed the need to fortify the training regimen in order to achieve more running success. A logical addition would be Jack Farrington of Pawtucket, Rhode Island, a trainer and a top official of the Rhode Island A. A. U. Jock Semple related how Farrington's talents were enlisted through Ellison Brown's ferocious letter-writing campaign: "After that race [B. A. A. Marathon] Tarzan wrote Jack Farrington, Pawtucket, R.I., who has been identified with A. A. U. sports the past 15 years and asked Jack if he would take charge of him, to which Jack replied that he didn't have the time, but Tarzan was just as persistent after Jack as he is after any lead runner that is in a race with him. After receiving many letters Jack sent for Tarzan and here started a combination that has had Tarzan clicking ever since."[1]

The desire to participate in officially sponsored races was shared by Ellison Brown and his loyal trainer, Tippy Salimeno, and this desire was heightened by the encouraging finish in the B.A.A. Marathon. Full-length twenty-six-mile marathons and shorter ten-mile, twelve-mile and 15-kilometer races were now the focus. Although a love of running and the satisfaction of being able to do something well were guiding Brown, the aim was to gain through experience the necessary stamina and knowledge required to enable a win at the next year's B. A. A. Marathon. This experience would be acquired, naturally, one race at a time.

The National A. A. U. 15-kilometer championship run at Elks Field in Norwich, Connecticut, was held on Memorial Day, May 30. This was Brown's second year in a row competing in Norwich for that national title. Over ten thousand people watched as Brown set a torrid pace in the first half of the event. That strenuous lead tripped him up, for he found he lacked the steam needed to stay ahead of the pack for the distance still ahead of him. In the final laps, he was surpassed by six other racers. The ultimate victor was the young Canadian athlete, Robert Rankine, who had hitchhiked to the event. The defending title holder from the previous year, Paul Mundy, finished second, just five yards behind the leader. Also close behind, ending up in third place, was Brooklyn, New York, runner Eino Pentti. Lou Gregory, another formidable New York athlete, was fourth. Familiar Rhode Islander Les Pawson finished fifth. A Northeastern University student, Andrew Hawk Zamparelli, finished in the sixth position. Then came Brown, finishing in the seventh spot, whereas he had finished fifth the year before. Brown once again had not managed his energy prudently; he had not left enough in reserve for the finale. The Norwich experience left him incrementally wiser.

The ten-mile road race in Pawtucket, Rhode Island, known as the Annual Valley Run, was held on Saturday afternoon, June 8. Les Pawson got to claim a victory over the year's B. A. A. Marathon winner, Johnny Kelley, by fifty-five seconds. "Right on the heels of the two leaders, Ellison Tarzan Brown, the colorful Indian star from Westerly, dashed home to finish third," the *Westerly Sun* reported. It described the action:

> The race was close over the entire distance, Kelley and Pawson matching stride for stride. Setting his pace a bit slower than usual, Brown trailed the two leaders for several hundred yards, keeping well ahead of the remainder of the pack. He allowed the leaders to get too far ahead of him, however, and a dashing sprint at the finish was not enough to nip the pair of Boston Marathon winners.[2]

This was an early look at what would become a successful strategy of Brown's—following behind the leaders rather than leading the pack, and then, at the right moment, letting rip a "dashing sprint at the finish." But just how to approach and execute that stratagem — that was what the young runner was developing. Through experience Brown was gaining valuable insight to be put to good use in the near future.

The Invitation Ten Mile Run in Bradford, Rhode Island, was scheduled to take place on Sunday afternoon, June 30, at Douglas Park, sponsored by the Bradford Athletic Association. Two years earlier, the B. A. A. Marathon winner Les Pawson had beat a young local runner, Ellison Brown, in an exciting contest. As the *Westerly Sun* brought this year's race into focus for its readers, it set its sights on a rematch of that contest between Pawson and Brown. Since John Kelley was unlikely to compete in the race, it was the *Sun's* determination that "There is no doubt that the man who Pawson will have to watch most closely and who worries him the most is none other than Westerly's own 'Tarzan' Brown."[3] Playing up the local challenger and the hometown support he was likely to be the beneficiary of, it continued:

> Displaying better form than ever before, the endurable young Indian lad is out to spoil Pawson's victory hopes. Ever since he was bested by the Pawtucket harrier in Bradford two years ago Brown has been waiting [for] a chance to turn the tables. He has run Pawson a number of very close races and now, with the local following bound to be behind him, he is primed to turn the trick. He is running in his own locality, the crowd for once will be with him and if "Tarzan" ever expects to outrun Pawson this is his chance.[4]

That afternoon turned out to be extremely humid and uncomfortable. A. A. U. commissioner Jack Farrington, in charge of administering the run, decided to reduce the distance to five miles because of the overwhelming humidity and unbearably hot temperatures. That decision, a sound one in terms of the athletes' health and safety, probably did not boost Brown's chances for a victory.

It may not have mattered. Leslie Pawson was in excellent form. He demonstrated terrific judgment in terms of deciding his pace. He completed the first mile before asserting himself and forging to the front of the pack. From that moment until the finish, he never relented. Brown, for his part, allowed Pawson to get too far ahead of him. "[Pawson] stepped out a good forty yards ahead of Brown and then set such a stiff pace until the finish that the Alton youth, strive hard as he did, was unable to overcome," observed the *Westerly Sun*.[5] The newspaper was generous with its account of its hometown hero. "Although he was forced once more to take the dust of Leslie Pawson, Tarzan Brown ran an equally brilliant race," it stated.[6] The crowd's support did not go unheeded by the young challenger. In pointing that out, the *Westerly Sun* said, "Responding to the entreaties of his local following the Indian lad from Alton was making a valiant bid to cut down that advantage of Pawson's, but always the leader stretched out with him and that same 40 yard space was still between them through the third and fourth miles."[7] By the time the last laps were run, Pawson had opened up a lead of more than one hundred yards, finishing with a time of 27 minutes, 24.6 seconds. The second-place Brown finished in 27 minutes, 51 seconds. Brown finished well ahead of the third-place runner, Bernard Malm.

One notable full-length marathon was held on the evening of July 14 in upstate New York. Beginning in Amsterdam and continuing to the finish line in Schenectady, Ellison Brown showed early signs of his soon-to-be-famous method of running for victory in these grinds. As reported in the sports pages of the *New York Times*, he was "content to keep in the middle of the pack for the first half of the race. Then he overtook the pacemakers and finished *twenty-five minutes ahead* (emphasis added) in 2:55:56."[8] It was described as an "easy victory."

Canadian runner Alfred Roberts was second across the finish line, in 3 hours, 22 minutes; Connecticut runner Frank Lalla was third; and Canadian Dick Winding finished fourth. The old veteran, "Bricklayer Bill" Kennedy, winner of the B. A. A. Marathon *eighteen* years earlier, back in 1917 when he was thirty-five years of age, ran behind the field in last place for most of this race, yet remarkably managed to pass all but four runners in time to capture the fifth-place prize. Young Russell George, who was limping with an ankle injury back in April, was forced to drop out of this race at the ten-mile marker.

The National A. A. U. 25-Kilometer championship race was held in Beverly, Massachusetts, on Saturday, August 24. Among the fifty-six[9] competi-

tors vying for the coveted national title were Johnny Kelley, winner of the
year's B. A. A. Marathon; Paul Mundy, the reigning national 15- and 20-K
champion; Eino Pentti, the defending champion of the title; Les Pawson, who
finished second in Beverly the previous year; and Biddie McMahon of Worcester, Massachusetts. Considered a tough course by most of the runners and
reporters of the day, the Beverly-to-Wenham-to-Danvers race had its share
of energy-taxing hills and some very rough surfaces in parts. Further com-
plicating the efforts of the combatants, the automobile and bicycle traffic was
particularly treacherous to runners on that course.

In those days, vehicular traffic was not prohibited from the course during races. The Massachusetts motorists of the thirties, the forebears of today's
drivers with their notoriously reprehensible driving reputations, were probably not much safer or skilled behind the wheel. Indeed, the only positive
point that might be offered on their behalf was that there were fewer of them
sharing the roads, perhaps improving their odds of a safe ride on any given
excursion.

The starting line was just outside the United Shoe Clubhouse (where Jock
Semple had found employment and organized a successful running team for
the company, a condition for his hiring). From the outset, Johnny Kelley ran
with the front-runners, and just beyond the three-mile point he managed to
assume the lead position. Paul Mundy, four-time winner of the national 15-
Kilometer title, kept relentlessly on Kelley's heels, constantly challenging him
and by doing so contributed to the heated pace. Eino Pentti, who set the
course record with his winning time the previous year, worked his way into
the front four, along with a fellow New Yorker, the always-competitive Lou
Gregory. This quartet appeared to be in a private race all their own. Ellison
Brown, on the other hand, was operating in accordance with his now-
signature strategic method, which he had used to fashion success before. In
the middle of the so-called ruck, he let the four speedy runners in the forefront set the pace. According to the *Herald*, "The stoical Indian was content
to stay in the background until the half way post, for he didn't break into the
first 10 until that stage."[10]

The *Globe* described the situation: "Kelley was watching Pentti, Paul
Mundy and Gregory, and all those three were watching Kelley, but none
thought of the dusky Brown striding smoothly along, nearly 200 yards
behind."[11] Then, slowly but with resolute determination, Ellison Brown made
his gains, one by one, on the men in front of him. He closed in on Pawson,
who was in sixth place. Sustaining the brisk pace, the first five runners maintained their positions as they careened over the hills and negotiated the turns
as thousands of spectators, lined along the sides of the road, watched and
cheered the runners on. Brown took advantage of the course's hills and his
ability to tame them. The Bridge Street Hill, beyond the ten-mile mark, was
where Lou Gregory began to slightly weaken. Brown passed him by, moving

into the fourth-place position. Now he was closing in within five yards behind Mundy, as "Pentti was matching Kelley stride for stride on the hill."[12]

Incredibly, the pace quickened. On the downgrade, Kelley gained some ground over the second-place Pentti and Mundy. Brown, running strong, was about to make his next move. He was approaching the Conant Street Hill. With an astonishing burst of energy, Tarzan charged up the hill, passing Mundy and Pentti, and blazed into second place, sixty yards behind Kelley. Brown continually closed the gap between himself and Johnny Kelley. Just twenty-five yards from the top of the long grade, he caught up with the by now tiring Kelley and overtook him, pushing forth to seize the front-runner's position for himself. From there he began to sprint toward the finish line, victory, and the national title. This awesome display of speed and power left Kelley one hundred yards (and twenty seconds) back. An estimated twenty thousand spectators, watching with excitement, loudly applauded Brown, the lone leading runner. As he snapped the tape, Ellison "Tarzan" Brown shattered the previous record by more than four minutes, with a time of 1 hour, 26 minutes, 42.8 seconds, winning his first national crown. By sustaining the torrid pace Kelley, as the pace-setting leader, had instituted, as it turned out, the previous record was actually broken five times that day—by the first-place winner, Brown; by the second-place winner, Kelley; and by the three runners in back of them, Mundy, Pentti, and McMahon. Pawson finished sixth, and Gregory held on to the seventh spot.

The headline in boldface across all eight columns of page twenty-five of the *Boston Globe* issued this message to its readers: "Full-Blooded Narragansett Indian Wins A. A. U. 25-Kilometer Championship Road Race at Beverly." The subheadline beneath that, in all uppercase letters, read: "BROWN SURPRISES DEFEATING KELLEY." *Globe* writer Ernest Dalton told the tale: "Today's race was a triumph for a comparatively unknown runner, who showed them how to run up hills…. It was Tarzon [*sic*] Brown's day today…. [He] ran a truly brilliant and talented field right into the ground."[13] Although the adjectives of praise were reserved for his opponents, the implication was perspicuous—Ellison Brown had arrived, and arrived in a big way.

The *Herald* headline, in boldface, put it simply: "INDIAN DEFEATS JOHNNY KELLEY." "Brown Captures National 25-Kilometer Run and Breaks Record."[14] A remarkable and beautiful two-column-wide photo showed two beaming athletes shaking hands with verve in front of a brick facade. Johnny Kelley and Ellison Brown were all smiles as they ignored the camera and gazed squarely into each other's eyes. The white-clad Kelley, still wearing his racing number eighteen and his shamrock logo, congratulated the dark-clad Brown, wearing a tilted number six. It was an exhibition of unmistakable genuine affection. The picture carried a title above it as well as a caption underneath. Above was quoted the curious "Top Hole, Top Row."

Tarzan Brown, now a national titleholder, had indeed arrived.

"Top Hole, Top Row": John A Kelley (left) congratulates Tarzan Brown for winning
the National A.A.U. 25-kilometer title in Beverly, August 24, 1935 (courtesy of the
Boston Public Library, Print Department).

The Valley Forge-to-Philadelphia marathon on a very chilly and rainy September 2 did not produce the results Ellison Brown wanted. Of the fifty[15] Labor Day starters, Pat Dengis of Baltimore managed a strong win by surging to the lead in the last two miles of the course. The thirty-three-year-old Dengis finished with a time of 2 hours, 38 minutes, 24 seconds, more than a minute and 500 yards ahead of the second-place Mel Porter of New York, who had led all until he suffered a cramp in his right thigh. Famed runners Paul deBruyn placed sixth and Clarence H. DeMar, forty-six years of age and carrying a stopwatch to adjust his pace during the run, took the twelfth spot, making the finish in 2 hours, 57 minutes, 36 seconds. Brown managed eighth place, with a time of 2 hours, 53 minutes, 11 seconds, one second better than ninth-place finisher and hometown hopeful Robert Willauer. But Brown's disappointment did not end nor remain there in the wet and chill of the City of Brotherly Love.

After his return to Rhode Island, Ellison Brown was to discover that he was being suspended from racing by the New England body of the Amateur Athletic Union, which called the shots at the official running events. The reason for the official suspension was technical and bureaucratic. Brown had violated N. E. A. A. U. rules by running in an out-of-state competition without first securing a "travelling permit" from the N. E. A. A. U. and by his failure to file "a return" when getting back to the home state. Jack Farrington, A. A. U. Rhode Island official, was notified of the indefinite suspension, a sanction making Brown ineligible to run in any of the official races. As soon as he found out about it, Tippy Salimeno, the runner's manager, challenged the New England officials' position in a letter. He claimed Brown had indeed "secured the traveling permit from the A. A. U ... two weeks ago" while in Boston, and "did not file his return with the race authorities until two days after the race," but that he had complied fully with the requirement, having mailed the return for filing as obligated.[16] An error yes, and not on our part, challenged Salimeno. The A. A. U. officers reported having received the return, and quickly reinstated the Rhode Island runner, just in the nick of time to participate in the national 20-K race in Newport, Rhode Island.

On the afternoon of September 8, 1935, a field of fifty runners competed in the national A. A. U. 20-kilometer event sponsored by the Newport Chamber of Commerce. In this race around Newport, speedy runner Les Pawson set the pace, and for eight of the twelve and a half miles, led the pack. Pawson was followed by fellow Rhode Islander Ellison Brown, who kept the leader in his sights at all times. The other runners were a considerable distance behind the two. At the approach of the ninth mile mark, Brown made his move and caught up to Pawson with a tremendous display of power. Over the next mile, the two matched each other stride for stride. A crowded line of spectators witnessed an incredible duel of heightened athletic performance. For the moment the runners were running even. Ellison Brown was going to alter that equilibrium. With an astonishing burst of supplementary effort, Brown edged ahead of Pawson, and managed to remain just a few feet in front of the unrelenting Pawson for the next mile. Only a foot or two behind, Pawson valiantly kept up the struggle to stay close to Brown. But inevitably the efforts of Pawson fell short, for the rapid pace he had originally set was finally about to take its toll.

Brown kept up his dizzying pace, and during the last two miles opened up what ended as a four-hundred-yard gap between himself and the second-place Pawson. He finished thirty-nine seconds ahead of Pawson with a record time of 1 hour, 5 minutes, 51 seconds, breaking the world mark by two minutes and thirty-three seconds. In fact, both runners finished well under the record. Biddie McMahon was a distant third. Only twenty-five of the fifty entrants even managed to complete the race.

For his magnificent performance, in a ceremony following the race, Ellison Brown was given a gold medal and he was also the recipient of a silver timepiece. It was his second national title in a fortnight; he now owned the 25-K and the 20-K national championship titles.

Six days later, Ellison Brown seized the time prize for the East Providence ten mile annual road race, breaking the course record Johnny Kelley had set in 1933. Brown covered the ten miles in 56 minutes, 20 seconds, the fastest time among racers. But he finished in seventh place. A handicap race, he had been assigned to run from scratch.

In races that employed the handicap model, and that included most of the short-distance races (not the full-length marathons or the title championship races), runners with an official history of times and wins were evaluated prior to each running event. Based upon the results of those past performances (sometimes supplemented by anecdotal or hearsay information), the faster runners were given disadvantages in order to equalize the slower runners' chances of winning. The slower runners were assessed handicaps or head starts. What this meant in practice was that the fastest, most successful runners had to wait at the starting line until a certain amount of time assigned them had elapsed before they could commence the race. In the meantime the other runners would have already started, thereby gaining an advantage in the competition. The start, then, was in actuality a series of starts, with different levels of runners commencing at differing times. Running from scratch meant being saddled with the largest limitation. The scratch runner or scratchman as he was called had the longest delay at the starting line, the scratch line, after the starting gun was fired (or the shouted "Go!" was hollered). The scratch times (the length of delay) were determined by the officials governing the event, generally but not always without input from the runner or his trainer or manager. A scratch assignment in the range of 5 to 5½ minutes was not unusual for a top-notch runner. A six-minute scratch was a serious hindrance for any athlete. Longer assessments, 6½ minutes, for example, were considered harsh by most observers. Some deemed them to be punitive.

The scratch runner would have the obvious delay at the start with which to contend, but that was just a part of the burden placed upon him. Once allowed to start, the scratchman would have the most runners in front of him to bypass on his way to the finish line. To pass other stragglers required extra valuable time. On top of that, often the police would clear a path for the runners at the head of the pack. The last ones to leave the starting line would frequently have the most traffic, both human and vehicular, through which to forge on the way to the finish line. Rarely did any officials ease the path for the scratchmen.

Two separate major prizes (among others) were offered in handicap races. One was presented to the runner who crossed the finish line first, the traditional first-place winner. (A scratch runner would have the most difficulty winning this prize due to his initial wait, especially if his assigned delay to start was a long one.) The other major prize awarded, called the time prize, was presented to the athlete who traversed the course in the shortest amount of time. Though an uncommon occurrence, one person could win both prizes. A very fast runner, for example, could beat all other opponents to the finish line, and do so in the shortest amount of time. But, as was usually the case, such a fast runner's previous track record would be known by the race officials, and they would attempt to minimize or diminish his advantage through the handicapping system. However, even a scratch runner, usually a proven speedster, although deliberately delayed at the starting line, might manage to beat the other contestants to the finish line, and, at the same time, also run the course in the shortest amount of time, not necessarily but most likely with the quickest pace as well.

In the East Providence handicap race, Tarzan Brown had been assigned to start the race from scratch. How long he had to wait at the starting line before being permitted to run was unreported, but the delay was substantial, for it "kept him far back in the race."[17] Despite the scratch assessment, Brown made up for lost time, for he was only two hundred yards in back of the first-place winner, Charlie Sabine, of Beverly, Massachusetts, when Sabine crossed the finish line. Five other runners, within that two hundred yards that separated Sabine from Brown, finished ahead of Brown. Brown was officially the seventh-place finisher, yet the runner with the fastest time over the course.

The Knights of Columbus of Concord and Manchester, New Hampshire, were in the throes of making preparations for their annual marathon event slated for the Columbus Day holiday. The organizers could only hope for as exciting a display as the previous year's extraordinary two-man contest, resulting in DeMar's slim thirty-second margin over Tarzan Brown. Two days before the event, the Manchester newspaper, *The Leader* reported a prospective "classy field of runners, embracing such stars as Clarence DeMar,

Tarzan Brown, Johnny Semple, Jimmy Henigan, Cecil Hill, and such strong local favorites as George Durgin and Honore St. Jean."[18] One day before the event, *The Leader* published the entry list of the field—forty runners, their assigned numbers, and their affiliations. DeMar headed the list at number one, Brown was in the second slot, and Semple third. An accompanying article featured this subheadline: "DeMar, Brown Certain to Continue Duel For New England Title Honors in Fifth Annual K. of C. Marathon." The third and fourth paragraphs, under the column divider "Indian Improves," follow:

> Tarzan Brown, 20-year-old Narragansett Indian from Pawtucket, R. I., who forced Clarence DeMar to run the race of his life last year, should be a greater threat Saturday to the Keene veteran. Brown finished 30 seconds behind DeMar in 1934 as the lead see-sawed between this pair. So great a stride did Brown hit that both he and DeMar shaved some five minutes off the previous record of two hours and 42 minutes. DeMar's time last year was 2:36:15 and Brown's 2:36:45.
>
> The fact that Brown recently defeated John Kelley of Arlington, Mass., 1935 B. A. A. winner, along with numerous other star runners, gives plenty of indication that the Indian runner will continue his duel with DeMar. Expecting a duplication of this great feat a larger gallery than usual will turn out and can fully expect to be rewarded.[19]

The newspaper article published two days after the Columbus Day marathon giving the marathon outcome did not show a result for Ellison Brown, nor did it give any explanation whatsoever for the omission of any reference to him. More likely than not, Ellison Brown did not ultimately participate in 1935. Whether Brown attempted to make it to New Hampshire and failed to get there in time to run, or did not even go is not known. If he had suffered an injury, no word of such was forthcoming. If he had been disqualified for any reason, even at the last minute, no report to that effect has surfaced.

Jimmy Henigan, listed on the published entry list, also apparently did not participate. In the newspaper coverage of the marathon, there is no mention of his name in any context, nor any explanation of its omission. In the papers the previous year, it was reported that the 1934 New Hampshire race would be his last marathon before retiring from athletic competition. Yet, in the newspapers this year prior to the event, his name appeared on the entry list.

Fifteen finishers and their official times were posted in the newspapers, along with a description of the race itself. Included in the coverage were the names of some runners who failed to reach the finish line and dropped out along the way. Since neither Brown nor Henigan were mentioned at all, it is unlikely that they were not able to complete the run. Had either one competed in any portion of the marathon, it is probable that his activity would have garnered some copy.

As it turned out, a United Shoe Machine A. A. runner, William Simons, twenty-eight years old, won first prize, registering a time of 2 hours, 46 minutes, 25 seconds. His teammate, Cecil Hill, finished in second place. Clarence H. DeMar finished third, six minutes behind Simons. Jock Semple, who finished fourth and thirty-two seconds behind DeMar, was happy to enable his United Shoe Machine A. A. to receive a cup for winning the team prize.

5

"This Human Powerhouse"—1936

At winter's end, 1936, extensive severe flooding created havoc over much of New England and parts of twelve states, especially Pennsylvania and Ohio. Torrential persistent rains joined with springtime thawing to raise area rivers to their highest levels ever. Rivers, overflowing their banks, caused immense damage in terms of lives ended and property ruined. Seven rivers in particular — the Connecticut, Ohio, Potomac, Susquehanna, Merrimac, Androscoggin and the Kennebec — caused major devastation. The high waters joined with ice, logs and wreckage to jam the riverways and threaten the supports of bridges spanning them. Many bridges and piers were destroyed by the ravaging waters. Martial law was declared in some cities, such as Nashua, New Hampshire, and "semi-martial law" was invoked in the hard-hit river cities of Lowell and Springfield, Massachusetts, and Hartford, Connecticut. Deaths totaled 133, and well over 150,000 people were left homeless. Property damages were estimated in the millions of dollars. Looting and disease (typhoid) were immediate problems, along with "the other horsemen of disaster — hoarding, profiteering and food shortages...."[1]

Against this backdrop, the North Medford Club 20-mile Road Race amazingly still managed to take place on Saturday, March 21. Fortuitously, flooded Medford areas had receded adequately. Although an early morning rain greeted race day, it gave way to a warm, partly cloudy afternoon. The course was in treacherous shape, due to the rains and recent flooding as well as normal springtime frost heaves, potholes and deep ruts. Yet, the course was reported to have "been viewed by the committee and described as being in 'wonderful' condition, despite the vigorous Winter."[2] Remarkably, so it seems, the race was on.

Reigning North Medford record holder and champion Johnny Kelley was looking to make it three straight. Les Pawson was looking for his third win overall, having won the event the first two times it was held. Kelley and Pawson were among a tough field of good runners for this, the fifth annual North Medford race. Other participants among the sixty-six that showed (seventy-eight entered) included Pat Dengis from Baltimore; Jimmy Henigan of the sponsoring North Medford Club; Worcester's Bill McMahon; Jock Semple, the undaunted Scotsman; the big husky youngster, Walter Ray, who was last year's Presentation Race winner; a Northeastern University student known as Hawk Zamparelli, first name Andrew; and, of course, Ellison "Tarzan" Brown.

In prerace hoopla, *Globe* sportswriter Jerry Nason wrote that Kelley was the expected winner, with Pawson being "the only man in the field Kelley really fears at this distance...."[3] He had this assessment of Ellison Brown: "Brown, national 20 and 25-kilometer titlist, is not a proved contender in races beyond 16 miles, albeit this young Indian is equipped with everything necessary to be a truly great Marathon runner."[4]

The pace was set and the pack was led by runners Bill McMahon and Bob Dirgin at the start. Behind them, falling back some two hundred yards, were Kelley; Pawson; Earl Collins of North Medford; Billy Simons, who finished second the year before; and Walter Ray. Dengis and Brown were just in back of this second grouping. Pawson kept pace with Kelley for eight miles, but then fell back, eventually finishing in tenth place. Kelley was content to stay behind the leaders for half the course, an atypical racing strategy for the lissome Arlington runner. By the halfway point he decided to challenge McMahon, who now solely led. Meanwhile Ray stayed right with Kelley, matching him stride for stride until the fifteen-mile mark when Kelley pulled ahead. Simons sputtered, began to fade, and ultimately was unable to finish. Ellison Brown, running in the fifth spot behind Collins, who had possession of fourth place, maintained a view of the back of Ray, who was third. Behind Brown, Pawson continued on. Dengis had managed to fall back to 17th place at one point but steadily made gains to recover ground.

At the start of a tough hill adjacent to the campus of Tufts College, at about the thirteen-mile mark, Johnny Kelley annexed the lead. From that point on, he never relinquished the front-runner position and put increasing daylight between him and the others. McMahon, who had run in an unfamiliar role as initiator of the pace, as a result of exhaustion began falling farther and farther back and eventually dropped out completely a mile before the finish line. Ray, running a strong second, was unable to catch up to Kelley, try as he might, but managed to hold onto the second spot, about two minutes of time separating them. Brown surpassed Collins, and was coming up fast behind Ray. Brown may have been able to overtake Ray had he not run out of course. If the race had been a little longer — a full-length marathon comes to mind — he may well have caught both Ray and Kelley. As it was, Brown spurted into third place, only thirty-two seconds behind Ray at the finish line. Dengis, it turned out, had accelerated remarkably enough to achieve the fourth-place prize. Collins finished fifth, Semple finished thirteenth, and Henigan was unable to finish at all, dropping out after eighteen miles of toil.

Kelley had won his third straight North Medford victory. His record set the year before was intact, although some observers seemed to think Kelley could easily have set a new one. What those observers did not know was that the pace and exertion had exacted a physical toll on Kelley during the last mile of the run. It was determined after the race that Kelley had suffered a pull to his "internal lateral ligament under the ankle of his right foot."[5] The *Herald* trumpeted the bad news in large headlines and subheadlines, like the following: "MARATHON KING PULLS LIGAMENT IN BEATING RAY." Sportswriter Will Cloney of the *Herald* did the momentous, locker-room reporting. Cloney wrote, "How serious the injury is could not be determined. Johnny himself was not particularly upset about it, as he stretched out on the rubbing table while both ankles were being taped, and although he did not promise to win the B. A. A. marathon on Patriot's Day, neither did he intimate that the *torn* ligament would hinder his bid"(emphasis added).[6]

The *Boston Post*, on the other hand, did not allude to the injury in any of the headlines adorning its coverage of the race. *Post* sportswriter Arthur Duffey wrote, "After the race Kelley was perfectly satisfied with his performance," and he quoted Kelley as saying, "'I felt good until the last part of the race when my legs began to bother me a bit.'"[7] In fact, Duffey did not divulge the injury until the sixth paragraph. Duffey minimized the scare to his readers in this way: "In the dressing room after the race, Kelley's legs were examined by Dr. Rush, who said he suffered from strained lateral ligaments, but figured this: the Boston Marathon champion will be right by April 19."[8] Only time would tell the extent of John Kelley's injury and its effect on his future running.

Ellison Brown's third-place finish and his impressive manner garnered notice. The Afro-American weekly, the *Boston Chronicle*, commended the runner, saying: "It was the best performance ever turned in by the colored runner to date. He finished very strong and his pre-race plan of running was such that he could have continued on for six more miles."[9]

Cloney was equally impressed by Brown's performance, though he had an odd way of expressing it. Cloney wrote: "Ellison 'Tarzan' Brown, the ethnological mystery man from Rhode Island, looked very strong in third place.... For Brown it was the best showing he ever made in a race over 17 miles, and the limber, deep-bronze youngster had plenty of strength as he cracked the worsted three minutes after Kelley."[10]

Cloney, perhaps motivated as some newspapermen are by trying to stir things up, seemed to lean in that direction regarding Pat Dengis vis-à-vis Ellison Brown. He first praised Dengis' worthy performance, especially the way Dengis managed to make up so much ground after trailing so far back during the first ten miles. Then, Cloney continued, but with this characterization, saying that Dengis "finished in fourth place, 27 seconds back of his particular nemesis, Brown."[11] Why Brown would be "his (or anyone's) particular nemesis" is unclear. Certainly Brown was a tenacious competitor, and he was obviously an obstacle to Dengis (or anyone) winning races, but so too were Kelley, Pawson, and many other great athletes at that time. Was the newspaperman here trying to frame a small drama within a drama, create a conflict within the context of the larger competition, for the sake of his sports audience, something Roone Arledge, in another medium (television), would develop into an art form a half century later for similar purposes?

Another columnist in the same newspaper carried the baton nearly three weeks later. Bob Dunbar placed this entry, the sixth of fifteen, in the middle of his April 10 column, a column composed of unrelated news and opinion pieces, each item a separate paragraph. He wrote: "Pat Dengis should be happy, now that Bill Steiner is in the B. A. A. marathoner [sic]. Pat doesn't like Bill any more than he likes Tarzan Brown, and if Pat gets worked up enough he'll win the race just out of spite."[12] No explanation was given, nor was Dengis' alleged sentiment attributed. The *Boston Chronicle* offered some insight with this March entry:

> "Tarzan" Ellison Brown won another victory in Medford when he crossed the tape ahead of the National Marathon champion, Pat Dengis of Baltimore, Md. The triumph over Dengis was especially gratifying to Brown, as a committee had tentatively selected four members to represent the United States in the Olympics—Kelley, Pawson, Dengis and Porter, despite the fact that Brown had defeated the latter three consistently during the past year. Only Kelley ranks ahead of Brown with a better mark.[13]

With an eye toward the Olympics to be held in Berlin, Germany, all the spring races carried an added possible prize for the winner. This year, the B. A. A. Marathon itself was going to be an official Olympic trial, and the general understanding was that the winner of the marathon would secure a berth on the U.S. team. Although the *Chronicle* and others were projecting ahead, that determination was a few weeks down the proverbial road at this juncture. Yet, by any measure, the 1936 edition of the North Medford 20-Mile Road Race, preview to the B. A. A. Marathon, had met expectations.

The Presentation 10-mile run, officially and formally a mouthful known as The Presentation Literary and Social Association 10-mile Handicap Road Race, frequently had some difficulty snaring quality name runners to its event because of the race's proximity to the B. A. A. Marathon just a few weeks later. Each runner's training regimen was personalized. Each man, alone or in consultation with his trainer if he had one, had to decide the precise amount of exertion sensibly expended in the upcoming days before the Boston Marathon in order to maximize his performance in that twenty-six-mile grind. If participation in a smaller race (both figuratively and literally) might hinder the optimum results in the grander marathon to come, then that participation was curtailed or nixed altogether. Saving one's strength for the Boston Marathon was the major consideration. When it came to training, the eye was on the goal, and the goal, if not the only goal for all the major marathoners, was winning the B. A. A. Marathon. North Medford was conceded by nearly everyone locally to be a good way to get the season started. The Presentation, on the other hand, could be a risky, even expensive undertaking.

The fifth annual Presentation race had 103 entrants for the Saturday afternoon event, held April 4. According to the prerace hype, two marathoners stood out as "leading entries" in the field: Les Pawson, who finished tenth the year before but still held the course record, and Ellison Brown, who did not compete in the 1934 event. Both men were assigned to run from scratch. The Presentation scratch limit was a full five minutes. This year, Walter Ray, Jock Semple and Hawk Zamparelli were among those in the running. Johnny Kelley and William McMahon each decided against competing but were on the sidelines as spectators. Smilin' Jimmy Henigan, who had signed up for the competition, was not permitted to participate on race day, as health officials quarantined him. No newspapers reported the reason. Team participation was represented by, among others, the United Shoe Machinery A. A., the North Medford Club, and the Fairlawn A. C.

The Brighton and Newton (Massachusetts) course began in front of the Presentation Club headquarters, 93 Tremont Street in Brighton. The runners headed first toward Newton Center, up Washington Street to Newtonville, further along toward West Newton, over to Commonwealth Avenue, then along Commonwealth Avenue over the Newton Hills (part of the same stretch as the B. A. A. Marathon course), to Chestnut Hill and back to the Brighton club building. The weather that day was described as ideal for running, cool but not cold with a slight breeze, and the road surface condition was dry. Mayor Frederick W. Mansfield was given the official chore of starting the runners, which was done in relays according to the handicaps issued. The last two runners to get the go-ahead to start were Brown and Pawson.

The best actual time of any athlete that day was turned in by Tarzan Brown, at 55 minutes, 58 seconds, which landed him the time prize, and, his second-place finish landed him a prize for that achievement as well. "Brown never showed finer form," Arthur Duffey of the *Post* observed. "He actually came from nowhere to land second prize.... This Narragansett Indian proved he is to be watched in the B. A. A. Marathon."[14] Duffey's favorable impression of Brown's chances was shared by *Herald* sportswriter Will Cloney, who wrote, "Brown ... now must be listed as a definite marathon threat...."[15] "The Indian boy, week by week [is] becoming a greater menace to the Boston Marathon favorites on April 20," concurred Nason in the *Globe*.[16] "This human powerhouse will enter the B. A. A. Marathon this year as a favorite after years of toiling upward through the ranks," stated the *Boston Chronicle*.[17] In agreement was Fred Foye of the *Boston Traveler*: "His chances to win the B. A. A. Olympic tryout now look very good."[18]

Foye's report from the locker room following the Presentation race was a strange mix of positive and negative observation. First, he covered Pawson, who, it turned out, had finished in sixth place yet had the second best time overall after Brown (and, like Brown, had done so from scratch.) Pawson informed Foye that he felt "in perfect shape" after the race and expected a winning result in the upcoming Boston Marathon. "I really feel that I'm ready to win it again," Pawson said. "At least I've got the same chance I had in 1933 when I actually did win," he quipped.[19] Contrasted with Pawson's satisfaction at his performance that afternoon and his very optimistic outlook, a very different picture of his fellow Rhode Islander was presented. Foye initially described Brown as "close-lipped to the point of surliness."[20] In answer to inquiries about how he felt he had done that afternoon or how he might do in the upcoming marathon, Ellison Brown, in the midst of getting a rub-down from two handlers, did not elaborate for the benefit of the reporters present. Instead he answered in brief sound bites, uttered like the following, as quoted by Foye: "the race was awright [sic]; yeh, I feel pretty good; I dunno—." But the portrayal Foye offered *Traveler* readers went well beyond a sketch of a man less than fully articulate after a physically challenging, size-able accomplishment. Under a column-wide, uppercase headline that stated "TARZAN THOUGHT HE HAD WON RACE," Foye continued:

> It was a strange sight to see him lying on his stomach, sobbing. The only answer could be the let-down of the terrific pace, or the fact that he had just discovered he had placed second instead of winning. As he raced down the stretch he thought he was the first man, but when there was no tape for him to break he learned that one Leo Giard, a high-handicap "dark horse" had been lost in the traffic far ahead and had finished first.[21]

In addition to the above passage, Foye described Brown as "sobbing softly to himself" and referred to him as "the mournful Indian." Negative and unflattering, to say the least, this was more than the depiction of either a very exhausted or a very disappointed athlete. Brushing across the realm of sportsmanship itself, Foye had painted Brown as a sore loser. Here was odd journalism indeed, since the athlete under discussion had handily won the time prize, and had done so having been saddled from the start with a five-minute handicap. Cloney, in the *Herald*, only briefly touched upon it in one sentence, when he reported, "After the race, Brown was a little per-turbed, although he would make no explanations."[22] No sobbing was men-tioned. Apparently no elaboration was deemed required. Cloney editorialized in his follow-up sentence: "Actually, his showing should have made him happy." That was the extent of it for the *Herald*. The *Travelers'* Duffey had nothing to say about it, nor did Nason of the *Globe*. Yet all the reporters unanimously praised Brown's racing performance that afternoon. Even Foye joined in the chorus of positive praises, with, "The [sic] 'Tarzan' had run the best race of the day" and "The national 20 and 25 kilometer champion

was superb over the short distance" and "His staying powers ... seem illim-
itable."[23] Cloney, too, was taken by Brown that afternoon: "It was sensational scratchman Ellison 'Tarzan' Brown who provided the real excitement
by picking his way through the pack to within 150 yards of the winner at the
tape."[24] Wrote Nason: "The blazing finish of Ellison Myers Brown, that fleet
Narragansett from Alton, R.I.... burning up the course from scratch and
rustling over the famed Newton hills in complete disdain of their reputation, was only 28 seconds off the course record in his run for second against
a stiff head wind...."[25]

Foye closed with this anecdotal snippet of Pawson and Johnny Kelley,
who had been present at the race but did not compete. Kelley was in the
locker room afterward, assisting Pawson.

Despite Ellison Brown's awesome abilities which he demonstrated that
afternoon, Foye wrote:

> Neither Kelley nor Pawson have any fear of him [Brown], however, and they're
> going ahead with their plans to finish one-two in the big race. "Who's going to
> be the number one?" somebody asked, and for answer the pair let out a great
> laugh. "Shall we flip a coin, Les?" asked Kelley with a smile.[26]

The first-place prize for the Presentation 10-Mile Road Race went to
thirty-three-year-old Leo O. Giard from Brocton, Massachusetts, an unemployed printer, who completed the distance with a corrected time of 53 minutes, 20.3 seconds. Giard had run in the Boston Marathon in 1928 and had
finished eighth that year. The following year, he was nearly four minutes
faster but only managed a fourteenth-place finish. Even though his running
prominence had been established before a six-year hiatus wherein he did not
compete in any races, Presentation officials considered Giard's past record in
determining his handicap, which was assessed at four minutes. His first-place
win was regarded as somewhat of an unexpected surprise, since he had not
run competitively for a significant number of years.

The handicapping was regarded as unusually well done, for runners in
positions three through nine finished within a thirty-five-second time span.
On top of that, according to Cloney, "every one of them [the runners] had
something left for the final spurt, too."[27] This indicated a grasp of the runners' abilities by the handicappers.

Third place went to Northeastern student Hawk Zamparelli. Melrose
High student Johnny Davidson finished fourth, Andre Brunelle was fifth, and
Pawson was sixth. Although sixth, Pawson finished with the second best time
record, only 43 seconds more time used than Brown.

Awarding the team prize was difficult, and involved a long and bitter
argument. It was at first reported as a tie, with the prize to be shared by
United Shoe Machinery A. A. (Jock Semple's gang) and by Fairlawn A. C.
(Pawson's affiliated outfit). But the referee of the race, Dick Walsh, follow-

ing the ensuing heated argument, decided in favor of Fairlawn after making a decision as to whether the A. A. U. rule regarding ties should govern. There was contention centered on whether to calculate points from elapsed or corrected times. Les Pawson had the fastest time for either club, and that fact became the deciding factor. But it once again called attention to the fact that determining times of runners, lengths of courses, and official race results was sometimes beyond the means of the available measuring tools or measuring skills of the race officials. For the most part it was accepted as sometimes unfortunate but a part of the racing sport.

The *Boston Chronicle* carried a picture of Brown alone in a white running outfit, left hand clenched in a fist and appearing very purposeful. The line under the photo declared, "TARZAN BROWN IN GOOD FORM."[28] In an article accompanying the photo, the newspaper stated, "The colored Indian ran a smooth race all the way and appeared to have much in reserve at the finish." It went on, "He has not yet unlimbered all of his power and this has won the curiosity of experts."[29]

In a news photo in the *Herald*, Mayor Mansfield was seen awarding a rather large trophy to a grinning Giard as Zamparelli looked directly into the camera while Tarzan Brown intently gazed at the mayor. The caption included this quotation from his honor: "I'm glad I was in my car instead of out there running."[30]

6

The Pre-Marathon
Buzz — 1936

The premarathon buzz was evident in the local newspapers well in advance of the April 20 race day.[1] Articles about the entrants featured their current running histories and their hopes and dreams about winning in Boston. Those who had won in the past and had hopes of repeating the glory were highlighted along with those without much of a chance. Speculation on various runners and how they would do was a major task of the sportswriters and filled their columns. Among the newspapermen, a big deal was made of their individual favorites and public betting on the outcome was a yearly event, like the race itself. Ellison Brown was a part of the prerace coverage like so many others.

A large cartoon by Bob Coyne, a semiregular feature in the *Boston Post*, was published April 9 that bore the title "The Vanishing American Reappears!"[2] It depicted a full, head-to-toe Tarzan Brown in his athletic running garb, looking very intent, hands loosely in fists, and ready to run. Perhaps the only unrealistic aspects of the sketch were his shoes and socks. In the drawing they appeared in fine condition, clearly not an accurate rendering of the pair he had worn in the marathon the previous year. The main caption, under Brown, announced: "TARZAN BROWN!—YOUNG NARRAGANSETT INDIAN FROM RHODE ISLAND NOW BEING GROOMED FOR THE B. A. A. MARATHON...."[3] Surrounding the figure of Brown were five Native American figures, four sports heroes and the fifth a stereotypical cartoon character making a comment to the reader. The upper left corner showed a shiny-haired, muscular runner in a rainstorm, with this caption: "We have to turn back the pages to 1907 to find the last great Indian marathoner—the colorful Tom Longboat—who set a new record in a blizzard of rain, sleet and snow!!"[4] In the upper right hand corner was a head inside a football helmet, adorned with an aura surrounding it. The face was smiling. The caption: "JIM THORP — The greatest of them all took years before he vanished!!"[5] Below Thorp's head was the figure of a man in a baseball uniform, looking as if he had just released a baseball. The caption read:

"CHIEF BENDER — Baseball's greatest redskin!!— Then there was Chief Meyers, Sockalexis, etc.— Today but one full blooded Indian is playing Major League ball ... Chief Hogsett of the Tigers."[6] The fourth portrayal was of a football player running with the football. The caption there read as follows: "Football had Metoxen, Thorp, Dillon, Mount Pleasant, Guyon, Hudson, Levi, etc... But the fame of the Carlisle and Haskell Indians is gone!!"[7] A cigar-smoking cartoonish figure in full headdress but Western business suit and tie, speaks to the reader, saying: "Even our Braves have been chased outta town by a flock of Bees!-Huh!!"[8] a reference to the National League baseball franchises which were located in Boston.

The *Boston Traveler* allowed some of the better-known runners to give a first-hand account of their training, past accomplishments, thoughts about their chances, and hopes. On April 10, "Ellison Brown" was the byline of an article titled: "'Tarzan' Brown Ready For Long B. A. A. Grind." (Under his name was the designation "written for United Press.") The article, presumably in his own words, follows:

> I have been doing road work for more than a month and a half and I think that I am in good condition for the Boston A. A. marathon. It's my ambition to win a place on the United States Olympic team. If I have to I will run in the national A. A. marathon at Washington, May 30.
>
> In my training I have been following a diet arranged for me by Dr. Edward F. Dougherty and my weight is much heavier. As a result, I feel lots better than I did before the B. A. A. race last year and lots stronger. Last year I finished 13th.
>
> I was in the North Medford Club 20-mile run about three weeks ago and finished third. Last Saturday, I placed second in the Presentation Club 10-mile run and won the time prize. I started from scratch.
>
> This will be my fourth try in the Boston A. A. marathon. On my first try in 1933 I was 32nd. In 1934 I finished 28th and last year I was 13th. After last year's B. A. A. marathon I won a marathon in Amsterdam, N.Y., and was eighth in a marathon at Philadelphia. I also won the National A. A. U. 20 and 25-kilometer races.
>
> It's very hard to say how the leaders will finish in the B. A. A. marathon. I would not attempt to pick them.[9]

In the passage Brown mentioned his training program which consisted of ongoing road work, coupled with dietary directives and careful attention paid to his weight. The regimen, a primary purpose of which was to increase his strength, also materially bolstered his confidence. Whereas "Tarzan" lore contained the conception that ascribed poor or absent efforts at training, evidently Brown was involved in training, expended effort toward it, and took it rather seriously, at least at this point in his running career. It may have fit the preconceived suppositions of white onlookers to see the Native American Ellison Brown as a child of (and out of) nature — being innately highly talented but with no hand in making himself a more improved athlete. In denying that Brown may have harnessed and directed his natural talents (like the white runners), by disallowing the possibility that he became a better competitor based on plain hard work, planning, and determination, springing from deep-seated desire — the Native American athlete remained something less than the human counterparts with whom he competed.

"We can only speculate how great he might have been had he been trained properly — trained at all, for that matter," wrote Jock Semple, who knew Brown and competed with him.[10] And, "Training is a haphazard affair for him at best."[11]

Jerry Nason wrote, "His greatest concession to training was to shut off the tap, so to speak. 'Quit beer and chop wood,' is the way he explained his basic training."[12]

His wife, Ethel, however, disputed that conception:

> As far as the stories of his not training regularly, I know differently. He always kept in good shape. He trained very hard a month or five weeks before the marathon, and about three weeks before any other race. It is true that he never ran the full 26 miles while training for the marathon; he ran only ten to twelve miles at one time.[13]

A double standard existed. Questions of inadequate (or nonexistent) training were raised every time Brown failed to meet prerace expectations in an athletic event. This questioning procedure did not occur in cases where other athletes failed to come through as expected.

In an article under the headline "BROWN LOOMS AS MARATHON CHOICE" in the *Boston Post*,[14] a mix of points of view concerning Brown's training was served up by writer Arthur Duffey. In one sentence alone, Duffey suggested Brown had no training and contrarily that he did in fact train: "Penniless and *without training in running*, except what he learned in actual competition, young Tarzan *has trained specially* and now has developed into one of the greatest of long distance runners, so common among the Red Men and will be a strong favorite to win the coming Boston run" (emphasis added).[15] Duffy supported the notion that Tarzan's talents were innate: "Ellison (Tarzan) Brown, a full-blooded Narragansett Indian, who inherited his natural skill at running from his savage ancestors along the southern trails of Rhode Island, has sent in his entry to the B. A. A. Marathon and will be one of the hottest contenders in the historic Marathon."[16] A picture with the article showed a smiling Ellison Brown standing, looking at Jack Farrington, his trainer. In the photo, Brown was wearing a beautifully crafted Native American vest, with an attachment to the floor, and an eagle feather in a band around his head. Jack Farrington, dressed in a traditional business suit, shirt and tie, was facing Brown, standing stiffly with his arms awkwardly by his sides. Farrington offered the following: "I wouldn't change his form for the world. He's a natural to win the B. A. A. Marathon this year, like Tom Long-

Tarzan Brown, in his traditional tribal costume, shares a premarathon photograph opportunity with his trainer, Jack Farrington, in his traditional costume in Providence, April 7, 1936 (*Providence Journal* photograph).

boat did in 1907. 'Tarzan' has a gliding gait, pressing forward all the time and does not waste any energy kicking up his heels."[17]

Just to what extent Ellison Brown had been training for the upcoming marathon was not commented upon publicly by Farrington. The sponsorship of Brown by the Providence Tercentennial A. C. put Jack Farrington squarely in charge of Brown's training regimen. In addition to providing funding for training for their contender, the tercentennial committee secured the use of William Waugh's summer cottage at Asawompett Pond in Middleboro near Lakeville in southeast Massachusetts as a training camp. This proved to be invaluable. Ellison Brown, Jack Farrington, and William Waugh resided at the secluded location for two weeks, their full concentration on training. Farrington, the Rhode Island A. A. U. commissioner, sought the advice and expertise of Dr. Edward F. Dougherty of Providence, who served as the New England A. A. U. commissioner. Dr. Dougherty, who moved in to the training camp, recommended a precise diet for the runner to follow. Brown partially described it:

> I went on a special diet prepared by Dr. E. F. Dougherty of Providence. It was practically a flesh diet with a little fish at times. But I think that a Marathoner needs a good steak under his belt when he goes into a Marathon or does any hard training.[18]

Reporters were more exacting when detailing food. Gerry Hern, referring to the diet, wrote in the *Post* that Brown "had bacon and eggs for breakfast, steaks and chicken for dinner. Nothing was too good for him."[19] He ate "plenty of meat and cereal (the latter with milk and sugar) and ...orange juice in generous doses," wrote the *Herald's* Art Walsh.[20]

Being secluded at the Waugh cottage enabled Farrington to keep tight control to ensure that Brown adhered to the strict diet. He was allowed three vanilla sodas each afternoon, not for his physical well-being per se but for that all important mental well-being. He was treated to a number of trips to the local movie theater during some of the afternoons to enjoy motion pictures, something he had experienced very rarely in his young life growing up among households with very little disposable income available for recreational purposes. Viewing movies helped fight the feelings of homesickness the young athlete experienced, having "never been separated [from his family] for more than a day at any other time in his life. He had never been so far from home, except in his trips to road races," reported Gerry Hern.[21]

Tercentennial committee funds were used to purchase custom-made running shoes by athletic shoemaker Samuel Ritchings of Peabody. The shoes were designed following a visit to Ritchings by Brown accompanied by Farrington. Ritchings paid attention to Brown's feet as he ran. Particularly careful scrutiny of Brown's feet as they made contact with the road surface revealed that the outer outside edge of his foot made contact with the ground first before the inner edge and the rest of his sole. With this in mind, Ritchings designed shoes for Brown that, for the most part, were similar to the S. T. A. R. Streamlines, but Ritchings incorporated some special modifications. "There was a special metatarsal arch and the sole was extended far back towards the heel on the outer side of each shoe to care for Brown's special stride wherein he lands on the outer side of his feet."[22] The "special pair of racing shoes [were constructed] for him to fit his peculiar method of running."[23] Brown had possession of them enough days to break them in.

A pair of new running trunks, a lightweight shirt, and socks—all white—were purchased for Ellison Brown with the committee's money. An unnamed *Globe* sportswriter took note of these items when they were seen as the runner sped past during the marathon. The observation as printed read, "Tarzan was wearing a pair of fancy white ankle socks and a white running suit which looked for all the world like his underwear."[24] Perhaps Farrington should have consulted the *Globe* fashion editor before making the sports apparel purchase.

Each day after a full breakfast, Brown would wash the dishes, one of his designated house chores. His exercise plan included running, and a daily walk of the four miles to town and back. He chopped wood. He worked out at the Middleboro Y.M.C.A., lifting weights and sparring with a punching bag. As the marathon day neared, the regimen was altered, including his food intake:

> During the last two days at Middleboro Tarzan was fed a diet of sugars in solution. Under the direction of Dr. Dougherty, who prepared the solutions, he took various doses of glucose to furnish him with the stamina to win the race.[25]

Ellison Brown described his running just prior to race day:

> They took me out to Hopkinton a few days before the race.... I was in great shape at Hopkinton and I'll tell you on the quiet than [sic] I ran a record trial just before the race from Natick to Boston, finished as strong as a bull and even didn't [sic] have a sweat up. My trainers then said I was a cinch for the B. A. A. Marathon. The time was one hour, 32 minutes—a record.[26]

By covering the expenses, Ellison Brown was given the opportunity to eat healthy food, exercise, and get plenty of sleep. The result was that by race day he was in excellent physical shape.

Ellison Brown awoke after a full eight hours of sleep on the morning of April 20 in Massachusetts.[27] Art Walsh reported that at 9:30 a.m. Brown "had a good half-pound sirloin steak, after orange juice and cornflakes, and just before the race he took orange juice and two lumps of sugar."[28] Jerry Nason reported the same breakfast but quoted Farrington as saying, "He didn't finish all of the steak."[29] Gerry Hern's report of that day's first meal differed slightly with the inclusion of a side dish. Hern reported, "At 9:30 Tarzan ate a steak and a few vegetables. When he had finished he was ready for the greatest race of his career."[30]

Reporting on the lives of various athletes as part of his premarathon coverage, Arthur Duffey painted a rustic picture of Brown's life, presumably very different from his readers' more urbane daily existences.

> The Indian lives in the outdoors most of the time. When he wants to breakfast he just goes down to the brook near his house and gets a couple of trout and

does not bother about a rod and line. He locates the trout in shallow water and heaves stones with such accuracy he stuns the fish. Then he picks 'em out and it is on the frying pan for 'em.[31]

Tarzan Brown was skillfully able to capture fish without store-bought fishing gear, as other handy outdoorsmen (and outdoorswomen) would, but that was neither his usual breakfast choice nor his routine morning ritual. By being portrayed as an exotic, albeit colorful personage, Brown was differentiated from the general field of plodders and was thereby noticed; indeed curiosity and interest were generated in the sports-page-reading public at large. This added attention enhanced the sportswriters, their respective newspapers, the runners, and the running events themselves. Everybody, so it seems, prospered from the additional interest spurred.

Arthur Duffey continued his premarathon remarks about Ellison Brown in an April 15 article that shared the space between two athletes, veteran runner Clarence H. De Mar and the relative newcomer Ellison Brown. The headline read: "DE MAR TO RUN 90TH MARATHON." The subheadline immediately underneath said: "Tarzan Brown Shapes as Favorite With Fans." After reviewing DeMar's impressive record of running the B. A. A. Marathon for his readers, Duffey predicted that DeMar, "the greatest Marathoner of 'em all," would complete the race and finish, and that he "will be among the first 15 at the worst."[32]

Focusing on Ellison Brown in the second part of the article, he was expected to "be one of the most dangerous contenders in the long journey."[33] Running the race for the first time under the auspices of the Providence (Rhode Island) Tercentenary Committee, Brown's entry documents arrived at the B. A. A. offices along with this official announcement from the committee (which Duffy quoted for the benefit of his readers):

> Inasmuch as the Narragansett tribe of Indians in the early days of the settlers along the east trail and in the neighborhood of Rogers Park were of exceedingly good friends to the white people, it is no more than befitting that Brown, a full-blooded Narragansett Indian, should represent our tercentenary celebration in the Boston Marathon.[34]

The historical understanding expressed in the Providence Tercentenary Committee statement was of the existence of a cordial mutuality between the early white colonists and the indigenous native people of what later became the state of Rhode Island. The amicable relationship and reciprocation that existed back in the 1600s, as expressed in 1936, made Brown's support by the Providence Tercentenary Association a natural, appropriate, even reasonable choice. But this muted, selective reading of history was by far grossly inaccurate to the spirit of the historical facts. The Great Swamp Massacre of 1675, which resulted in the deaths of many Narragansett — mostly women, children and elderly men living at their winter home — at the hands of white Puritan

Tarzan Brown poses with his trophies as he gets ready to represent the Providence Tercentenary Committee in the upcoming B. A. A. Marathon, April 1936 (*Providence Journal* photograph).

soldiers from Plymouth, Massachusetts Bay and Connecticut colonies, was but one bloody historical incident that was omitted from the Providence association's historical viewpoint. That tribal members were murdered or some sold into slavery, or that tribal property was seized and stolen by the colonial authorities were overlooked historical occurrences. As recently as fifty years prior to young Ellison Brown being invited to represent the committee whose very existence was designed to celebrate the incorporation of the capital city of Providence, the state government that was seated in that city had maneuvered to illegally "detribalize" the Narragansett Tribe without federal government sanction. Not during Ellison Brown's lifetime did the State of Rhode Island rectify the unlawful land confiscations it wrangled in the years before his birth. Yet the hope for success in the athletic achievements of one remarkable Narragansett runner (residing in the southern part of the state, not even in the city of Providence) was enough to qualify for the assistance of the official organization set up to commemorate the government whose very policies, if allowed to succeed, would have exterminated nearly the entire indigenous peoples within its borders, including Ellison Brown's own lineage. How the white power base of the 1930s in Rhode Island got to its *ostensibly* more enlightened level of consciousness in a matter of a few generations is an interesting question in itself, but beyond the scope of this book. I say *ostensibly* because by getting behind Brown, the tercentenary committee could have been more or less just crassly playing an opportunistic card, that is, supporting the athlete with the highest degree of likelihood of bringing a winner's trophy home to the city. But, if that were the case, perhaps a stronger argument could be made for Pawtucket, Rhode Island, resident Les Pawson being the best choice for bringing home the top prize. Unlike Brown,

Pawson had done it before, in record-breaking fashion (and would do it again — two times more, in fact.)

Getting back to the *Post* article on Brown (and DeMar), Duffey recalled Tom Longboat's heroics, reminded his readers of Brown's recent race results, and finished his article by reiterating that "Brown already has been named one of the real favorites to win the race."[35]

Bob Dunbar, columnist for the *Herald*, reported DeMar's entry into the race. "No one expects the Keene school master to do anything much," stated Dunbar, "but his name brings a glow to the faithful just the same." Dunbar continued:

> Strangely enough, DeMar's entry is announced at the same time as that of Tarzan "Ellison" Brown [*sic*], the most promising of the younger runners. Brown is a real threat, and the top notchers admit that he has them worried. The Indian is primarily a 15 or 20-miler, but he insists (as vigorously as a stoic can insist anything) that he will come through on the holiday.[36]

Jerry Nason provided Boston marathon hopeful Pat Dengis with an extensive platform (viz. the space of his entire personal column entitled "What About It?" in the April 16 edition of the *Boston Evening Globe*) to give his annual written "prognostications" under the self-serving headline: "Pat Dengis, Crystal Gazer Says Mr. Dengis Will Win, Pawson Second, Kelley Third."[37] Dengis offered the readers his inside view on the major marathon candidates. He began by discounting any John Kelley foot injury suffered in North Medford in March. Dengis also disavowed any power of a jinx to keep the last year's winner from repeating. "Johnny will be stopped, all right, this year but the jinx will not be the cause of it ... a lad from Baltimore [Dengis] will be the obstacle he will not be able to surmount."[38] Dengis next turned his attention to Leslie Pawson. "I rate him as the one man to beat," plainly stated Dengis, after considering the Pawson performance in North Medford and the lack of fatigue exhibited that day. He continued to review the field. In a short paragraph, he addressed runner Billy McMahon. Dengis suggested that McMahon was no longer a threat in a full-length marathon since he had now become "a 10 mile specialist.... I have an idea he will blow a fuse around Boston College." He considered Ellison Brown next and assessed his chances this way:

> With all the tribal chiefs and medicine men to cheer him on his way, Tarzan Brown will cut a pretty figure for a considerable part of the race. If the race finished in Auburndale he would most likely be the winner. By the time he has finished the hills at 20 miles the finish line will seem to him to be up near Lynn or Salem. And the evening papers will have to report that "another Indian bit the dust."[39]

He predicted Brown to finish "about seventh." He went on to handicap the Canadian runners ("I don't expect them to set the Charles River on fire"),

Mel Porter of New York ("Some think Mel Porter might win ... so might Mae West!"), Jock Semple ("afraid his knees will not stand the strain") and "dark horse" Walter Ray ("This lad Ray ... is an unknown quantity to me and may prove a surprise, but I don't think that a 'dark horse' will lead the parade at Exeter st.... look up your history books and you'll find the conqueror always rode a white horse.") Lastly, Dengis considered the possibility that *he* might not be the victor after all, for he closed with this line: "I have no alibis now, and if I am doomed to disappointment at Boston you still won't get one out of me except my old favorite ... 'I didn't run fast enough!'"

7

"A Pat on the Back"—1936

The temperature April 20 was in a comfortable range of 47 to 53 degrees Fahrenheit at midday and the sky was overcast, protecting runners and spectators from exposure to a burning sun. A light wind, estimated at fourteen miles an hour, was blowing easily, and the road surfaces were dry. Before the noon hour struck, the B. A. A. Marathon participants were making preparations for the fortieth annual edition of the Patriots' Day race. Lucky Rock Manor, also known as the Lucky Manor Inn, on the Tebeau Farm, headquarters and traditional race day mustering location for the runners, race officials, doctors, the large press contingent, and assorted onlookers, was bustling with activity. Some runners were stretching; some were making small talk; some were snacking; some were rechecking their shoelaces; some were saying their prayers. A thirty-room hostelry, the Lucky Rock Manor got its name, according to the matriarch of the household, Mrs. Alice Tebeau, "from a rock that used to be the rendezvous of sweethearts from Hopkinton, Ashland and wherever. The by-word of the smitten of heart, says Mrs. Tebeau, used to be 'Meet you at Lucky Rock.'"[1] The Tebeau farm was the subject of a rumor in 1936 that this would be the last year the B. A. A. had use of the place for its marathon participants. The rumor, which had circulated widely, had even been reported in the newspapers.

> Mary Tabeau, Hyde Park school teacher, and her mother tend to the needs of every one with a smile, but say that this is the last year they will hold open house. "It's too much," says Miss Tebeau. And it must be.[2]

The rumor, as it turned out, was somewhat premature. The Tebeau family generously continued providing their farm for B. A. A. use for a good many years more.

Official numbers were handed out as the athletes checked in with race administrators. Number 1, traditionally worn by the previous year's winner, was given to Johnny A. Kelley. Ellison Brown received number 147. Next the runners were required to submit to an examination by the marathon physicians for a prerace physical checkup. Pulse, blood pressure and weight were recorded for each entrant. No runners failed the health check that year. But two almost missed it altogether. The *Globe* reported:

Officials of the B. A. A. had near attacks of heart failure 15 minutes before the start of the race when a checkup revealed that neither Pat Dengis nor Gordon Norman had put in an appearance.

... Ten minutes before the gun was to be fired Dengis and Norman arrived, were hurriedly examined by physicians and toed the mark just as Brown was about to fire the shot. First reports had Dengis out of the race but with only a minute to spare he got off at Hopkinton and was on the road to Boston.[3]

At high noon, George Victory Brown fired his starting gun for the thirty-first time.[4] A field of 184 runners[5] commenced to race eastward, destination: Exeter Street in Boston. Sportswriter Joe Nutter reported the start of the marathon: "Tarzan was out with the gun. Leo Hickey of Waltham and Frank Vasic of Wright, N.Y. set the pace off the mark, but 'Tarzan' was right behind. After the first wild bid for places, Brown was ahead."[6]

John Hickey led the pack for 300 yards. He then faded fast, as did Vasic. The lead was immediately appropriated by Tarzan Brown. He was followed by Tom McDonough, a former New England ten-mile champion. A widening gap separated second and third places, with Mel Porter of New York in the latter position. Fourth place belonged to Lou Gregory. Bill Steiner was fifth, and Walter Ray of the United Shoe Machinery (Beverly, Massachusetts) was sixth. The trio of Pat Dengis, Les Pawson, and Johnny Kelley were in the next pack of runners, twenty in all bunched tightly together. Four hundred yards behind that large group were the two marathon veterans and former winners, Jimmy Henigan and Bill Kennedy, running side by side. Seven-time winner Clarence H. DeMar and Jock Semple were in the mix.

The B. A. A. Marathon was large enough to encompass both competitive runners determined to show their athletic prowess and all kinds of performers, show-offs, and a sundry of publicity seekers using the event as a ready-made public platform for purposes other than being awarded the victory laurel wreath. Two of these less serious racers but perennial spectacles, John "Cigars" Connors and a fellow known as "Cigars" Enos, made their annual official starts among the competitors. "Competing for the long-distance tobacco title, [they] were far back, just puffing along," reported Arthur Siegel.[7] Leonard Fowle also took note of one of the smoking joggers: "John 'Cigars' Connors was among the starters, as usual. When last seen, if these eyes do not deceive, he was plodding along toward Framingham with not one, but two stogies puffing smoke out like a steam engine."[8]

Front-runner Ellison Brown established a very rapid pace, more fitting for running a shorter dash than a grueling, long-distance marathon. He ran so fast, in fact, that the press corps, covering the runners as passengers in donated-for-the-day-in-exchange-for-publicity, showroom-new automobiles, followed what was in effect the *second* group of perambulators, mistaking *them* for leaders. Not until they reached the first checkpoint in Framingham did the pressmen discover their error. Incidentally, this was the first year a restriction was put on vehicular traffic on the course during the competition. Automobiles alongside the runners were limited to those carrying marathon officials, the press, and handlers, trainers, and coaches of the various individual runners. Regular passenger and commercial vehicles were temporarily diverted by police from the course's streets and roads.

The first checkpoint, 5.3 miles from the starting line in Hopkinton, was at Framingham. Brown set a new record for reaching this first checkpoint station. His time of 30 minutes, 23.4 seconds was nearly a minute faster than the previous record. At the moment he reached the Framingham station, Brown had put three hundred yards between himself and McDonough, who was two hundred yards ahead of Porter behind him. Kelley had managed to emerge into ninth place, but was a quarter mile in back of the front-running Brown.

Over the next four miles, Kelley managed to gain a position, eighth, behind the furiously paced, speeding Brown. Ellison Brown checked in at the second checkpoint, Natick, with another record time (50 minutes, 43 seconds). This was a minute and a half better than the old record set in 1932 by Nova Scotian Jimmy McLeod. Brown continued his record-shattering pace with McDonough still second, Ray third, Steiner fourth, and Gregory sixth. By that time Kelley had improved to fifth place. Two hundred yards behind Brown were Dengis, Pawson and DeMar. Kelley passed Steiner, moving into fourth place, trailing Ellison by .6 of a mile.

Ellison Brown passed by Wellesley College and received the traditional ovation and high-decibel encouragement the college women were famous for providing each year. The *New York Times* and the *Boston Post*, having photographers stationed steps apart at the same moment, published similar photos of Brown running past the line of college coeds who showed smiles of approval and some were clapping their hands. The *Times'* caption read, "Brown leading the field through the town of Wellesley."[9] The *Post's* photo had a headline and a caption. The headline stated: WELLESLEY GIRLS CHEERING BROWN.[10] The two-sentence caption read: "With the cheers of hundreds of Wellesley girls ringing in his ears, Tarzan Brown is shown showing the way to the Marathoners as he went by the famous school. Johnny Kelley, at that time fairly close behind Brown, also received loud applause as he plodded along."[11]

Brown maintained his unvarying race demeanor, looking straight ahead, turning his head neither right nor left — just keeping his body rhythmically moving and breathing steady, fists somewhat clenched. Brown showed no visible acknowledgment of the huge, boisterous crowds along the course. "He had speed to spare at this point," reported the *Globe*, "and showed no signs of breaking under the grueling and burning pace he had set for himself."[12]

At Wellesley Square, the approximate halfway point, Brown was two minutes ahead of McLeod's record for that checkpoint. His time was registered at 1 hour, 7 minutes, 31 seconds, and he was a full three minutes ahead of the others, ahead by nearly nine hundred yards. Ray overtook the fastly fading McDonough for second place. Meanwhile, in Wellesley, Les Pawson, who had set a similar record-breaking pace in 1933 on his way to victory, found that he too was unable to keep up with the extraordinarily torrid pace set by Brown this year. He dropped out and hitchhiked to B. A. A. headquarters on Exeter Street. Dengis had slipped to the twelfth spot. Kelley slightly increased own his pace.

The course through the Wellesley hills saw Kelley catch up to Ray. Ray picked up his pace and spurted ahead of Kelley, but the exertion inevitably caused him to slow back down, and the indomitable Kelley would catch up with him again. The two men ran side by side for a spell, and each led the other for short stretches. At about the fifteen-mile mark, "approaching the Newton Lower Falls, Fred Faller, his [Kelley's] trainer, dumped water over him and amidst a shower of spray, Kelley went past Ray and into second place."[13] Ray, unable to keep up with Kelley, never recovered and began a long slide away from the leaders toward the back. Meanwhile, Kelley's father, William, maintained his son's pace, not running but by vehicle, supplying the defending champion with water, wet towels, and oranges.

All along the course, spectators cheered Kelley as he passed. He received ovation after ovation as he was hailed and exhorted by the crowds. The front-running Brown, however, did not receive that kind of response early on. As Leonard H. Fowle of the Boston Globe noted: "The crowd could hardly believe Tarzan Brown could be in a race, so far ahead of the pack was he through Natick and Wellesley and they were reserved in their applause. Going into Auburndale, it was different."[14]

At about this time, Brown received some emotional support from some familiar people, people he hadn't seen since his long week of training. Ellison Brown and his trainer, Jack Farrington, had been guests at the summer cottage of William Waugh at Asawompsett Pond near Lakeville in Massachusetts. The seclusion during training had been beneficial to his training but Brown had been homesick for his family and friends. He had written to them, but that certainly wasn't the same thing as seeing (and hearing) them. Ellison Brown experienced a big emotional boost as he focused upon his father, Otis Byron Brown; his first running inspiration, Chief Stanton; Brown's two brothers, and other members of his extended family and fellow tribesmen — some dressed in traditional costumes including headdress and some playing tribal drums. They cheered exuberantly as they urged Brown on. The Globe's Leonard Fowle noticed, "a big delegation on hand to welcome him as he came up the hill from the bridge over the Charles [River]. One enthusiastic brave of this civilized tribe ran out fully clad in civies and began throwing kisses at the hero."[15] Fowle went on to report:

This first demonstration by fellow "native" Americans was surpassed just a little way farther on as the runners entered the happy "Woodland(s)" loaned for
the day to the Narragansett tribe. Here were braves and squaws in full
regalia — blood brothers of the hero! Chief Stanton was so overcome with joy
that he joined the race and ran along for half a mile with feathered headdress
flying to the winds as he encouraged his tiring warrior.[16]

Brown's father, brothers, and the other members of the Narragansett tribe
managed to get rides along the marathon course, stopping at various intervals to watch as their man, his Indian name *Deerfoot*, ran past. They voiced
heartfelt encouragement. Brown did not pause, but continued on his mission to the finish line. Farrington kept him focused on the goal at hand.

The check-in at Woodland Park in Auburndale, at about the seventeen-
mile mark, recorded Brown at 1 hour, 31 minutes, and 49.2 seconds. He had
shattered the checkpoint record by four minutes, and was a half mile ahead
of the second-place Kelley. Kelley checked in at a recorded time of 1 hour, 34
minutes, 31.6 seconds, showing that he was nearly three minutes behind the
unfaltering Brown. According to the station checks, Walter Ray was third,
Lou Gregory fourth, Bill McMahon fifth, Tony Paskell sixth, Leo Giard seventh, Mel Porter eighth, Earl Collins of North Medford ninth, and Pat Dengis
filled out the top ten.

So far, the course had been rather flat. The hills were ahead, the next
hurdle.

The roughly five miles between the Woodland check-in station and the
Lake Street checkpoint were crucial to the outcome of the race and proved
to be historic as well. In a most remarkable display of stamina and strength,
Johnny Kelley managed to accelerate over the Newton hills. Kelley, step by
step with undaunted determination and painful blisters, cut infallibly into
the half-mile lead of Ellison Brown, who was still running steadily — not slack-
ening his pace at all — and characteristically looking straight ahead. The
Globe's Victor O. Jones reported:

> Neither man seemed in any distress at this point and the Indian was running
> with great strength and power, albeit the hills had cut sharply into his speed.
> His lead looked safe until Newton's City Hall was reached. Then Kelley open
> the throttle for the run down to it while Brown was toiling up the hill on the
> other side of the valley, the Irishman caught his first glimpse of the Indian, the
> man he had to run into the ground.[17]

Ellison "Tarzan" Brown could hear individuals in the crowd informing him
of Kelley closing in, and he became audibly aware behind him of the spectators' cheers and shouts directed at Kelley as Kelley made his way by the thick
rows of people lining the sides of the grades. Jack Barnwell of the *Boston Post*
described the action at this juncture:

> Each of those three hills leading up to Boston College found Kelley getting
> stronger each stride. He had picked up more than a half mile during the course

of a little more than two miles of gruelling [*sic*] road. Brown was travelling [*sic*] along at his record-breaking rate, but Kelley was stepping along at the greatest clip ever known at that stage of the trip.[18]

Where Hammond Street and Wachusett Road run into Commonwealth Avenue, Johnny Kelley caught up with the man who had led the marathon all the way, for nearly twenty miles up to this point. The next instant, a special moment in marathon history, has been captured and recorded for posterity through an assortment of different accounts. As Kelley came up to Brown, Kelley reached out with his hand and "feebly tapped Brown on the shoulder," noted the *Boston Post*.[19] "The smiling Irishman who won a year ago, patted his Indian rival on the shoulder, then swept by," reported Joe Nutter for the *Providence Journal*.[20] "As he passed by, Johnny gave the flagging Tarzan a friendly pat on the shoulder as if to say, 'Nice try, kid, I'll take it from here,'" depicted Fred Lewis in *Young at Heart*.[21] Will Cloney observed a less-than-full-blown pat on Brown's western side, and a bit lower. He wrote:

Johnny caught Brown at the top all right, half patted him on the back as he went by, and set sail for his victory, but Brown was far from through.[22]

Author Joe Falls put the locale of the pat even lower:

Johnny Kelley put on one of the greatest runs ever staged through the hills and caught up to Brown. But Kelley made the mistake of patting the Indian on the backside as he was about to pass him, and that awoke Brown.[23]

Runner and chronicler Hal Higdon seemed to agree with Falls' placement of Kelley's palm:

In the 1936 race, John A. Kelley charged from behind to catch Tarzan Brown on the final Newton hill. As he pulled even, Kelley gave Brown a pat on the behind.[24]

Jerry Nason has written about that moment a number of times. He has redirected the scene numerous times. In 1936, two days after the marathon, Nason cast the epicenter of the contact at shoulder level. He was interested in giving readers a proper interpretation of John Kelley's unassailable intent:

Incidentally, when Kelley came to Brown's shoulder at B. C. [Boston College] after his hot pursuit, he patted the Indian's shoulder only as a friendly gesture, not an insolent acknowledgment that Kelley was the winner from there in.[25]

In 1966, Jerry Nason gave this description of Kelley's gesture in his compendium, *The Story of the Boston Marathon, from 1897*:

It was on the hills that brash Johnny Kelley set out to bring down the tiring Indian. This "Kel" did with one of the swiftest runs through the Newtons in history. At Boston College he caught Brown, patted him on the back as if to say "Nice running, Tarzan," and started to go by.[26]

Eleven years after writing the above passage for his "brochure," Nason used considerably more direct language describing the same event, an event he had personally witnessed forty-one years earlier. Jerry Nason's 1977 account moved the now-famous pat to the lowest specific locale it had ever been described at — at-the-time an unfit-to-print spot on the body. With assured certainty, he wrote:

> Old Johnny Kelley came on with a terrific rush from Wellesley, the halfway point, and he came up even with the Indian at the top of the hill at Boston College. I'll never forget it and I'm sure Johnny never will either. Just as Johnny was going by the Indian — in a friendly way, you understand — he patted the Indian on the botton of the ass, as if to say, "Nice run, pal. Nice try, boy." The Indian looked up and took off like a rabbit. It was like Johnny Kelley had put a pin up his ass.[27]

Ellison Brown told Nason after the race:

> When Kelley finally caught me near the end of the hills he patted my back as he started to go by. Maybe he thought he was going to go by, but I didn't.[28]

To Ruth Bodwell of the *Boston Post*, Brown reportedly related the incident this way, "When Kelley slapped me on the back in the run, he thought he was going by me, but I knew he wasn't."[29]

> "He patted me back, too," said Kelley [to Nason]. "It is merely road racing courtesy and I often do the same thing when passing or catching some opponent like Brown. I would never think of just trying to pass a leader without some sort of recognition."[30]

The gesture was returned? No other observer, press or fan, has given an account of any reciprocation by Brown, as far as I can ascertain. Johnny Kelley admittedly had the best view of his interaction with Brown, and, perhaps like a baseball umpire, perceived what others could not due to their lack of close proximity. On the other hand, Ellison Brown never reported a response on his part to Kelley.

Getting back to Kelley's gesture — whether Kelley patted or slapped Brown's shoulder, his upper back, his lower back or his backside made little difference as to the effect it had. Directly after the gesture, Kelley overtook the leader, and assumed the position of front-runner himself. Ellison Brown, perhaps slightly startled by the gesture itself or the turn of events overall, nevertheless kept on running and did not give in, as Kelley may have been anticipating. Barnwell wrote:

> After being divorced from the rest of the plodding pack for almost 20 miles, that one little tap would seem to be enough to take the starch out of any performer. But not Brown. He failed to lend any recognition to it, but just kept on bounding along with the lightness of a ping-pong ball.[31]

Brown kept up his pace, and he and Kelley found themselves in a spectacular two-man contest.

Every time the Indian went down the grade he whirled into the lead, only to lose ground once more when they hit another hill. Five times within a mile the lead changed hands in a nip-and-tuck struggle while the major part of the 500,000 who lined the course thrilled to the sensational battle.[32]

Brown and Kelley had kept alternating the leader's position on the way to the Lake Street checkpoint station. At one instant, Kelley opened up an eight-yard lead, the longest he would ever have, but Brown managed to close that gap just before the end of the downgrade to the Lake Street check-in. Ellison Brown gained the lead once more, and was the one recorded as the first runner at that checkpoint. His time was 1:59:43, nearly a minute quicker than the standing record. Second place at Lake Street belonged to Kelley. McMahon was recorded in third place there; in fourth was Gregory, Giard was fifth, followed by Burnside, Collins, Porter, Paskell and Ray, in that order.

It was at roughly this point in the course, at Boston College, that Kelley would later say he could smell the repeat victory he was after. He told the *Boston Post*: "I thought I'd won at Boston College. In fact, at that point I felt fine and figured that the rest would be easy."[33] But the still-burning pace and the exhaustive trek over the hills, not to mention the previous twenty-plus miles, were taking their toll. At Marion Street just before Coolidge Corner (approximately the 23.5-mile mark), Johnny Kelley began to walk. Brown continued onward, and so did McMahon, who overtook the walking Kelley at the Chestnut Hill reservoir. At that point Tarzan Brown led by about twenty-five yards. Kelley told Nason after the race:

> At Coolidge Corner I was dead. Blisters I had picked up in Wellesley pained terribly, but I didn't mind that so much. I was simply exhausted. On the hills Brown came back to me like he was on a rope. I tried to run him down and couldn't. I knew he'd have a sprint left.[34]

At the Coolidge Corner checkpoint, the last one required of the runners before the finish line, Ellison Brown registered a time of 2 hours, 16 minutes, 17 seconds, still under the old record, but by the barest one and four-fifths of a second. William McMahon registered in second place, having passed the faltering John Kelley, who had a shaky hold on the third position. Giard had moved into fourth place, Porter was fifth (up from eighth place at the previous checkpoint), Burnside was sixth, Collins was down a position to seventh, Paskell was up a position to eighth, Callard took ninth, and Gregory was still in the contest at tenth.

Brown had improved his lead over the second-place McMahon by nearly 250 yards at Kent Street. But then, in the vicinity of Audubon Circle, Brown stopped running. He was reeling. He was unable to see. Literally blinded, he was tottering from one side of the street to the other, unsteady on his weary legs. A dizzy spell accompanied the temporary blindness. Jack Farrington and Dr. Dougherty had been following closely in an automobile the entire journey. Farrington exited the vehicle and came to the rescue. Fred Knight wrote in the *Traveler*: "[Ellison Brown] had his dizzy spells and twice cried, 'I can't see, I can't see,' on Beacon street. An abbreviated shower bath cleared his head and set him on his way."[35] The *Post's* Jack Barnwell embellished the moment for his readers with the following dialogue, Hollywood-style:

> Farrington ... on the running board of a car rushed to his side.
> "What's the matter, Tarz?" shouted the frantic trainer.
> "I no see," gasped the plodding Indian.
> "You must go to town," shouted Farrington into his charge's ear.
> Brown nodded in ascent. "I go to town," he faintly whispered, and resumed his stride once again.[36]

Farrington's verbal push coupled with the cool water he splashed in Brown's face and in his hair seemed to energize Brown, for he instantly became alert. He started to jog, then quickly shifted gears and resumed running.

Otis Byron Brown had followed his son's progress, mostly from the sidelines, getting short automobile rides along the course as needed. He believed his shouts of encouragement had a positive effect on his son. The *Westerly Sun* reported Mr. Brown's description of his vocal participation:

> "Come on, Ellison, I'm here." He added, "I shouted and I knew that he was going to win because he waved to me and grinned. Then I said, "Only a few more miles to go, show your stuff."[37]

Biddie McMahon had slowed to a walk too, just after Brown had abandoned his running stride. In fact, the three top leaders of the Boston Marathon — Brown, McMahon and Kelley — were all walking, not running, within two miles of the finish line, an unusual sight indeed. Unlike Brown and Kelley, McMahon was a marathoner without a support entourage. No automobile full of trainers, doctors, and friendly supporters alongside McMahon followed his progress; no familiar faces exhorted him with instructions, encouragement, updates, or proddings. There were no offerings of fruit or water from the backseat window every step of the way. Only a lone press vehicle stayed nearby the second-place runner. According to Will Cloney, McMahon "pleaded for verbal goads that would keep him up," but his deepest pleas for such support fell on proverbial deaf ears. Cloney speculated in the next day's *Herald* about McMahon's predicament then:

> If McMahon had been bathed with water every time he needed refreshment, if he had been kidded into running, he would have been closer to Brown and perhaps would have won, for it was the Tarzan who stopped first, losing half of his 100-yard lead. But Bill later said, "If [Brown] had sat down at the curbstone, I probably would have sat down beside him."[38]

Two of Kelley's brothers and their father, riding an automobile alongside their walking boy, administered assistance. His father, William, supplied more water, pieces of oranges, and verbal encouragement. One of his brothers dramatically took off his coat, threw it in the car, and began jogging alongside his brother Johnny, verbally exhorting him to get reenergized, pick up the pace and run with him to Exeter Street, but Johnny, completely exhausted, was unable to comply though valiantly he tried. He alternated between walking and jogging, switching back and forth from one to the other, but without the energy to sustain a running motion he mostly resorted to walking.

> Johnny was walking like an intoxicated man, his legs pushing out to the sides. In the next half mile, Johnny stopped six times, definitely fading out of the winning picture but still having the chance to finish third.[39]

Meanwhile, Ellison Brown, approaching Kenmore Square, had to stop running a second time. The *Boston Globe*'s description of Brown resembling an inebriated person was nearly a match for the *Herald*'s strikingly similar account of the spent Kelley, who also stumbled as if he had had too much to drink. The scene was reported in the *Globe* as follows:

> Tarzan Brown ... wobbling and faltering, seemed to be on the verge of fainting as he hit the crowded square. His stumbling feet went crazily to the side as a drunken man might stagger. Toppling, he backed almost into an automobile and was missed by inches.[40]

Brown was at that moment very fortuitous, for he had narrowly avoided the certain injury that would have been his in what was a very close call. Again, Farrington at the scene resorted to his reserve of water, pouring it over the runner's head and splashing his face. "Only a mile to go," he shouted at Brown.[41] Once more, Brown seemed to reawaken, reactivating the unrested muscles necessary to break into a lope. The effort was enormous.

Ellison progressed about a quarter mile farther, running but in a less steadfast manner than before. On Commonwealth Avenue, in front of the Hotel Somerset, Brown was one turn away from Exeter Street, about three city blocks from the finish line. Yet once again he was forced to forgo the running gait. Brown came to a momentary stop. But he didn't remain halted. By sheer determination he resumed the slow, stumbling, faltering walk. He had submitted to a third case of the "blind staggers." Farrington, observing the situation, hastened to the rescue once more. "'Half mile to go,' he shouted. 'I go,' replied the Indian with considerable exertion. And he went."[42] This time Brown resumed his steady strong stride. Like a charm, Farrington's words and water had worked their magic a third time.

McMahon, who had been walking, began jogging, then running, but remained about a quarter of a mile behind the again-running leader, Brown. The front-runner was making strides of speed and strength, and in the very last stages of the course, had opened up an increasingly larger lead of nearly two minutes over McMahon and the rest of the pack. Kelley, incrementally farther back, was haltingly attempting to run, but mostly was fixed in a walking mode. Unable to get into a running pattern, he could not hold onto third place. Mel Porter, in a surge, had overtaken Leo Giard, and the pair passed by Kelley near the Harvard Club on Commonwealth Avenue.

Without delay or any more interruptions, Brown headed straight to the finish line demarcated by "the bright yellow worsted that was strung across Exeter Street in front of the old Boston A. A. clubhouse."[43] As he later told Arthur Duffey:

> When I got into Exeter street and saw that great crowd waiting to greet me, it gave me plenty of extra life. When I hit the tape I was so overjoyed that I do not remember just what happened. In fact, I was led away from the finish line by my friends, and it was some time afterwards before I really came back to my real self. My mind was in a whirl. If ever a guy was in a fog, I was that one.[44]

Ellison Brown crossed the finish line with a time of 2 hours, 33 minutes, 40.8 seconds. He had smashed all the checkpoint numbers, establishing new records for every one of them, except the very final one. Due to lapses in the final two miles, he did not break Leslie Pawson's 1933 standing course record (2 hours, 31 minutes, 1 second). But he had won the B. A. A. Marathon in one of its most thrilling editions.

The *Boston Herald's* Art Walsh was addressing the confidence of young runner and winner Ellison Tarzan Brown. Walsh asked aloud to Brown:

> You didn't even wonder when Kelley caught up with you? Did you think he'd beat you when he patted your back and then passed you?[45]

Said Brown, "He did, but I didn't."[46] Walsh reported Brown's terse reply, and remarked to his readers, "How are you going to beat a kid like that?"[47]

A laurel wreath literally grown and shipped from the historic marathon valley in Greece was placed in accordance with tradition upon the head of the marathon victor. In Boston, this ceremonial duty was in the reliable hands of George Demeter, a Greek-American and owner of the Hotel Minerva. It was Demeter's voluntary job to procure the laurel and make its annual presentation. As he did each year, Demeter would be poised at the finish line, awaiting the sight of the winning runner. He would place the laurel wreath upon the winner's head immediately after crossing the official finish line, clinching the victory. As he did so, Demeter would ceremonially utter the words "*Chairete nikomen*," or "All hail: we have conquered," which is what Pheidippides reputedly said, before fatally collapsing, according to the marathon legend of ancient Greece.[48]

A *Boston Globe* photograph showed a white-clad Ellison Brown crossing the finish line with Jack Farrington, in suit and tie, both hands clutching a sweatshirt, running a close second directly behind Brown. A smiling George Demeter is in the right foreground, in front of the police barricades, the victory wreath in his hands. A host of policemen and spectators lining the street are watching. The caption under the photograph in the morning edition read: "ELLISON 'TARZAN' BROWN CROSSING THE FINISH LINE A WINNER." "*His trainer, Jack Farrington, is behind him ready to place a sweater over his shoulders and George C. Demeter is starting out from the right to place the laurel wreath upon his head.*"[49]

Later on, when talking to reporters about the moment of victory, Brown admitted his memory of that instance was hazy. He is reported to have said:

> When that old tape broke over my chest, I didn't know any more. I was in a whirl. I was about ready to flop. I do not remember much until after I got over in the Lenox [Hotel] and they administered to my wants.[50]

"Across the finish line, he collapsed faintly into the arms of Jack Farrington, his trainer, utterly spent," wrote Victor O. Jones in the *Globe*.[51] Ellison Brown was immediately supported physically by a number of his handlers. "He would have fallen had not friends supported him while he was crowned by the wreath of laurel," observed Joe Nutter.[52] Then he was carried to an official post-race medical examination. *Westerly Sun* writer Ed Butler reported on the results of Brown's medical checkup. "After being taken into the B. A. A. rooms for a cursory examination, it was found his blood pressure was low but that his heart was all right. There was only a small blister on one foot and outside of intense fatigue, his general condition was good."[53] Where the *Westerly Sun* reporter was able to report on the "one small blister," sportswriter Leonard Fowle of the *Boston Globe* saw a completely different picture. He wrote: "Speaking of blisters, neither Tarzan Brown's nor Billy McMahon's feet showed hide nor hair of these troublesome annoyances after running 26 miles and 355 yards."[54] His *Globe* colleague Jerry Nason concurred, writing, "No blister or the cousin of one was on those sturdy extremities."[55] Suffering a blister or not, his feet were "burning him" at the race's conclusion, according to a lone report in the *Boston Traveler* by Fred Knight.[56] Brown reportedly claimed, "My feet got hot because I ran so fast in my new wings," his term for his specially made running shoes from Sam Ritchings.[57] Brown had never run the full distance of a marathon in that pair of shoes before. Whether the specially made Streamlines enabled Brown to set a more sweltering pace than he otherwise might have established is a matter of conjecture. Other variables—the results of his training, his physical conditioning, his mental attitude, the weather conditions, even the conditions of the course surface —certainly played a major part. But the shoes were instrumental in allowing Brown to run as he desired. They certainly didn't impede him. "If the ones [running shoes] I had today had not been custom-made—especially for my feet," Tarzan Brown said after the race, "I wouldn't have used them. If you remember, last year I got rid of my shoes several miles from the finish, and I did better than I would have done otherwise."[58]

It was noted by Jerry Nason that after his shoes and socks were removed,

Jack Farrington (left) watches Tarzan Brown cross the finish line to win the B.A.A. Marathon in Boston, April 19, 1936 (courtesy of the Boston Public Library, Print Department).

remarkably, the socks were completely dry — no perspiration there at all.[59] Ruth Bodwell reported that both his stockings and his special shoes "were as dry as a bone," and incredulously, "that there wasn't a drop of perspiration on [Brown]" at the race's conclusion.[60]

After his checkup, Ellison Brown was still not clearheaded amidst all the post-race activity. He requested some bottled lemon soda, but none was yet forthcoming. Butler continued the narrative:

> Staggering on his trembling legs, he was taken from the gymnasium to have a few pictures made and then, rushed across the street to the Lenox Hotel, where the A. A. A. U. official, Jack Farrington of Providence, had reserved a suite of rooms.
>
> Brown was dropped onto a bed and he fell sound asleep, just as if he had been hit on the head with a hammer. The door to the bedroom was closed and newspaper reporters and photographers congregated in the sitting room, waiting for him to have a 15-minute nap.[61]

Farrington permitted Brown a half hour of uninterrupted sleep before facing the exuberant print media anxious to debrief the runner, and the impatient cameramen wanting more pictures. Brown lay down on the bed in the separated bedroom of Suite 422. "One brother implanted a kiss on his cheek as he dropped into bed to lapse into a deep sleep," Joe Nutter reported.[62] Everyone was asked to wait in the suite's sitting room.

The overjoyed contingent of Rhode Islanders that had crowded into the hotel room included his trainer, Jack Farrington; his doctor and diet specialist, Dr. Edward F. Dougherty; Ellison's father, Otis Brown; his two brothers, Daniel Franklin Brown and Clifford Algeron Brown; his uncle on his mother's side, Charles Babcock; his original running mentor, Chief Horatio Stanton; and two distant relatives, Princess Red Wing and Princess Minnetonxa (Mrs. Marion W. Brown). In addition, thirty-five newspaper sportswriters and photographers from a host of media outlets were present. All were anxious for the slumbering marathon champion to awaken and speak.

> From the very start I knew I'd win. There never was any doubt in my mind. It's a grand feeling and I'm glad to have won.[63]

Farrington had opened the floodgates and the photographers and reporters rushed into the runner's hotel bedroom. Ellison Brown was still groggy as he faced the onslaught of newsprint practitioners along with the few family members, tribal members, and friends. Sportswriter Ed Butler described the scene for Ellison's hometown supporters:

> Flashlights popped like a bunch of firecrackers, and Brown sat propped up on his pillows, blinking and dazed. He still was fatigued and immediately after the pictures were taken, was allowed to resume his sleep. Before falling off again, however, he wanted to know where were those eight bottles of lemon soda he had asked for after the race.[64]

Many in the suite recessed to the hotel lounge for nearly an hour with Chief Stanton, who was dressed in "dramatic" native ceremonial attire. "The rush of men and women to the feather-crowned chief nearly swept him off his feet. Everybody in the place wanted to treat the chief, and he was agreeable," Butler observed.[65] Chief Stanton and others told tales and responded to ques-

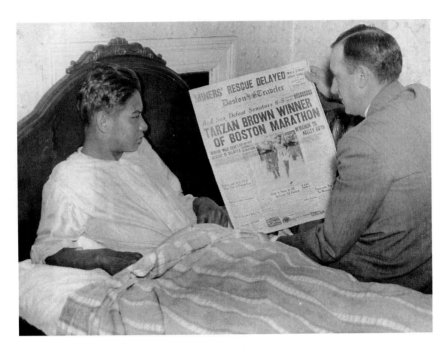

Top: Resting champion Ellison Brown (left) and trainer Jack Farrington view the latest news on the front page of the *Boston Traveler* in the Lenox Hotel, Boston, April 21, 1936 (courtesy of the Boston Public Library, Print Department). *Bottom:* A victory pose for press photographers in the Lenox Hotel, Boston, April 21, 1936 (courtesy of the Boston Public Library, Print Department).

tions about the Narragansett, their native lifestyle, and about Tarzan in particular. Said Stanton proudly, "I thought I was developing a Narragansett who would be as good as I was. He turned out to be a whole lot better."[66]

After an hour passed Ellison Brown awoke and was right away handed the first telegrams he had ever been sent. The first was from the governor of the state of Rhode Island, the Honorable Theodore Francis Green. The second was from Mayor James E. Dunne of Providence. Both were congratulatory. After reading them, Brown immersed himself in a shower. Next he was placed inside some brand new, unfamiliar clothing. Jerry Nason reported that Brown was

> dressed by Farrington and Dougherty. Until last week this appealing boy had never owned an undershirt or worn a collar. His new friends jack[ed] him into a fashionable grey suit, with blue pocket handkerchief; black shoes of taste. Dougherty knot[ted] the pale yellow polka-dotted tie for him.[67]

Fred Knight, for his *Traveler* readers, gave this description of Brown's new fashion look:

> In his new store clothes, a gray suit of the latest cut, a white shirt and collar attached, new shoes and top coat, the 22-year-old Indian was dressed to the minute. He actually wore an undershirt for the first time. And to top off the formality, he wore a bright-lined necktie. He even had pajamas. A dude, that's what he was.[68]

The dapper Ellison Brown was now ready to face the press. Firstly, how did he feel, most of the reporters wanted to know. "Good" was his one-word answer. The *Herald*'s Art Walsh suggested, from what came next, that Brown evidently had been rehearsed, since he was telling the reporters what they had already heard directly from Farrington himself, more or less in the same words. Walsh wrote of Brown: "He continued, obviously following script. 'I am glad I won and I want to thank the city of Providence tercentenary committee for sending me here and my trainer, Jack Farrington, for helping me win.'"[69] But shortly thereafter, the script, if there was one, was abandoned, and Ellison began replying to reporters' questions directly. Perhaps fatigue, perhaps limited ability — in any case, from here on out, "he was on his own," Walsh surmised. The sportswriter transcribed for his readers:

> The questions came rapidly. Did you think you wouldn't finish when you were so tired over the last few miles?
> "I knew I'd finish, for that was what my mother wanted."
> Whom did you worry about during the race? Was it Kelley or Pawson or Dengis or Porter?
> "I didn't worry about any of them — all I worried about was myself," with a laugh.[70]

Nason, also covering the extemporaneous press conference, reported the new B. A. A. Marathon champion's responses:

The hills? They weren't as tough as I thought they'd be. But they were tough enough. I knew I was slowing up on them, but I felt strong enough and knew I had the running left to finish....

At no time did I have any idea what time I was making. Somebody said I was far ahead of the record at one time, but I was out to win and didn't care how long it took me to do it.

I was feeling very strong when I finally started to go away from Kelley near the end and when I stopped that time near the finish. I had no warning of it. It came all of a sudden. My legs were tired, but I wasn't in trouble. Suddenly I stopped. Right then I wasn't worried about the other runners as much as myself. When Mr. Farrington doused that water on me I felt better right away.[71]

The questions posed were not only about the race and winning. They turned personal. Walsh reported it this way — question:

Have you a girl? Have you ever had a sweetheart?
[Answer] I'll think about girls after I forget how to run.[72]

Nason captured that exchange as follows:

"Girl friends?" Brown lifts an eyebrow to this one. "Nope, no women. They can come after I learn to really run."[73]

Otis Brown, Ellison's father, seized and elaborated upon the subject. In the *Post*, Ruth Bodwell reported his comments:

Ellison doesn't bother with girls. He is sort of bashful. But the girls like him. I have seen them pull him out of his seat at a dance and make him dance.[74]

Ellison's private life was getting an airing! Why fight it? Ellison reversed his previous statement on the subject and made this revelation even his father wasn't expecting:

Blushingly, Tarzan admitted that he'd like to get married.
"She's an Indian, just like me," he said proudly. "She lives just a little jog from my house at Alton, R. I.–seven miles to be exact.
Her name? Please don't embarrass either her or me now. I'll let you know about that later."[75]

Fittingly, Ellison related her house distance in terms of running ("a little jog") and he knew precisely how far away it was, being expert at estimating distances with exacting accuracy. After all, this was a crucial ability toward gaining an edge in some distance races, especially those of differing lengths. Yet, it was with relief that the subject was changed once more to the marathon. Ellison discussed his racing plan:

I had the race pretty well mapped out before hand. That is, I was to try to average about five and one-half minutes for the mile. When the race got started I guess I forgot all about the schedule I was feeling so good.
Right off the reel, I beat it for the head of the pack. I made up my mind

right then I was going to make a front race of it and they would have to keep running all the time. I do not know where the rest of the pack was. I didn't care. Someone told me Kelley, Dengis, Pawson, Steiner, Mel Porter and some of the cosey [sic] boys were away back, but that didn't make any difference to me. I just ran on my own and did not think of anyone else.[76]

Farrington expressed some uneasiness about the scorching pace Ellison had set. Of course he had considered the likelihood that it could backfire on the youngster. He had worried that it might come back to haunt Brown at a critical time much later in the race, wearing out the runner before he had completed the entire twenty-six miles. It almost happened. But despite those fears and concerns, Farrington professionally managed to stick to the game plan, which he had reiterated to Brown in Hopkinton that morning —"'run your own race' and Tarzan did exactly that."[77]

Part of Farrington's strategic advice to Ellison Brown involved keeping an eye out at all times for the whereabouts of Pat Dengis. As Brown told Arthur Duffey of the *Post*:

I only told myself, "I've got to lick Kelley." He got so much notice about being the favorite that I said to myself, "I'll lick that guy if nobody else."

My advisor, Jack Farrington, told me, "To heck with Kelley. Look out for Dengis. If Pat is running right, he'll give you plenty of trouble.... Stay with Dengis. Then if he gets too slow, go out on your own."[78]

Baltimore's Pat Dengis, as it turned out, dropped out by mile 17 in Auburndale.[79] Dengis suffered a ruptured blood vessel about mile seven. The bodily location of the vessel rupture was ascertained to be in the bladder, not in Dengis' kidney as first feared. The tough competitor continued onward for ten more miles in a condition of lethargy coupled with pain before being forced to concede.

At the fifteen mile mark he [Dengis] knew something was wrong with him. He wasn't moving along as fast as he wanted to. Trainer Jack Ireland wanted him to quit but he wouldn't, for he never had quit before.

"I went two more miles," stated Pat, "and fellows I never saw before were passing me."[80]

He had just registered in tenth place at the Woodland (Auburndale) checkpoint before finally acquiescing to the disappointing medical development and having to call it quits. His wife, Eva, and his trainer, Bill Ireland, both implored Pat to get into an available automobile and ride the rest of the distance to Exeter Street. He reluctantly complied. He later said:

At 12 miles I was heavy. I just couldn't get up there. Something was wrong. When they told me Brown was seven minutes ahead I couldn't believe it. I thought he was back of me somewhere. No alibis from Pat, though. I felt bloody weak at 17 miles, but I will defend my title at Washington.[81]

The *Globe* reported that Dengis collapsed two times. The first time was in the B. A. A. clubhouse following the marathon, during the ceremonial presentation of the prizes. Removed to the medical offices of Dr. Morris Cohen at the Boston Evening Clinic on Beacon Street, Dengis collapsed once again. He was taken to Massachusetts General Hospital and held until nine o'clock for observation. He and Eva departed for home as soon as he left Mass. General, against the advice of some of the attendant medical staff.

In the *Boston Herald*, the whole incident was described rather differently:

> Back in his hotel room after the race he did not want to bother with any examination, but he was coaxed to see a doctor. Then he went to the hospital and was supposed to stay there two days, but he grabbed his clothes last night and walked out.
> He met Dr. Dougherty and Farrington in the hotel, and the doctor gave him another examination and advised him to rest, but Pat wanted to be off for home and boarded a bus for New York. The doctor's last advice was to carry some ice cubes with him to use as a pack, but Pat refused to believe that he was seriously hurt.[82]

Pat and Eva checked out of their hotel at 11 o'clock that night. They headed to the bus station for the trip to Baltimore via New York City. He reportedly needed no additional medical attention.

Clarence H. DeMar finished sixteenth with a time of 2 hours, 48 minutes, 8 seconds. He quickly changed into his clothes in the clubhouse and hustled around the corner to the Boston Public Library. According to the *Herald*: "He explained he had a date at the Boston Public Library at 3:20 to get a ride back to Keene, N.H. 'I had to come in at 2:48 if I wanted to keep the date,' smiled the beloved veteran."[83] DeMar was right on time for his ride home.

Ellison, asked to comment on whether he was at the peak of his powers, answered with an uncannily predictive cast: "No, I do not think this is going to be my best Marathon race. I think I will be getting stronger and faster for the next three years, or until I'm 25 years old. When I can run through to the finish line like I did from the start to Lake st. I will be at my best."[84]

8

Nason and the Hill — 1936

Jerry Nason, the *Boston Globe* sportswriter most associated with the Boston Marathon and the sport of running, was a friend and supporter of Ellison Brown throughout his entire writing career at the *Globe*. Most of the sportswriters in the competing Boston newspapers would pick the runner they figured would win the marathon. In 1936, Nason stated in an afternoon column on the Saturday before Patriots' Day that Brown would win the race. His previous correct prediction was three years earlier, back in 1933, his first year covering the marathon for the *Globe*. Nason had picked Les Pawson, and Pawson had not disappointed Nason. (In 1934, Bill Steiner, a twenty-two year old from New York, was Nason's selection. He finished third. In the 1935 race, Nason had designated Pat Dengis for his winner. Dengis placed second to Johnny Kelley.)

In words meant to be humorous, Jerry Nason wrote:

> In keeping with our annual custom of not being able to name the winner of the Marathon in advance, your befogged recorder of the doings of the arch excursionists takes great pleasure in picking Ellison Tarzan Brown to go deliberately on the warpath from Hopkinton to Boston on Monday afternoon.
> The pleasure is mostly mine ... certainly Master Brown won't extract any from this stupendous announcement.... So we'll take Brown.... [1]

In the *Boston Daily Globe*, the early edition printed the morning of the marathon, an article on page one by Nason touted a Kelley-Pawson duel, with pictures of Kelley and Dengis, numbers one and two from the year before, under the line, "FAVORED IN MARATHON TODAY." On page 8 inside, though, Nason had written: "Brown has progressed so amazingly that his chances cannot be regarded as anything but favorable. He is the author's Blue Plate Special to win, and while his inexperience may prevent it, he has an abundance of physical requisites with which to accomplish what some consider impossible." [2]

In 1966, the *Globe* published Nason's *The Story of the Boston Marathon (from 1897)*, a paperbound booklet. Writing in the foreword of that publication, the unnamed editor of the *Boston Globe* characterized as "among his [Nason's] many startling predictions in advance of the event ... the '36 victory of 100-to-1 shot 'Tarzan' Brown."[3] Nason's prediction of Brown's win has remained a part of the retold lore of the B. A. A. Marathon to this day.

Jerry Nason's expertise in the annual event and his extensive knowledge of its participants were legendary. And it was really no wonder. According to Hal Higdon, "Nason missed the first dozen years of the race only because he had not yet been born."[4] When he finally did arrive into this world, he literally wasted no time beginning his observations of the B. A. A. Marathon, according to the lore (as augmented by the scribe himself). On April 14, 1909, Nason was born. It was Nason's positive luck that his mother had given birth in the old frame Newton Hospital, for it was situated overlooking the marathon course. At the ripe age of five days old, he was lifted to the window by a sympathetic nurse. From that caregiver's arms, Nason watched as the runners passed by on their way toward the Exeter Street finish line. According to author Joe Falls, Nason "doesn't remember who was leading, though he thinks it was the Frenchman Henri Renaud: 'My mother told me the story about being held up to the window and I'm not going to say anything against my mom.'"[5]

As a youngster he would ride his bicycle along the course, assisting with a canteen of water and some oranges to one of

> the lower-case runners who had no attendants. It was a big deal to carry a knapsack for one of the runners. We had to wear a corresponding number to his, so we always had a ten-cent bet, a little pool, to see who'd get the farthest down the course. I once had a guy who made it all the way to Cleveland Circle, within three miles of the finish, and don't think I didn't tell everybody that I held the world's record.[6]

The "wheelman," as the cyclist-handler was called, became obsolete over time, as automobiles replaced the bicycle as the conveyance of preference.

By the age of twelve, Nason had begun keeping handwritten records in leather-bound pocket notebooks of the yearly marathons, as well as other sporting events. He began collecting programs, schedules and other printed materials. Eventually he became employed as a sportswriter and as a cartoonist, becoming a famous and ubiquitous byline in the *Boston Globe*. Nason's writings stand as stunning examples of the language of sports writing as it developed, from the Great Depression, through the war years and the Cold War, to the Great Society. In his early days, he peppered his writing with racist descriptive words and phrases, well within the bounds of most newspaper standards at that time. Examples were these phrases: "the galloping redskin may, after all, scalp the Kelleys, the Dengises, the Pawsons, and the what nots;"[7] "won by an Indian who wouldn't bite the dust;"[8] and, "Ellison Meyers [*sic*] 'Tarzan' Brown, full-blooded Narragansett, stalked upon the warpath yesterday afternoon."[9] Let it be noted that Nason may have had Native American blood in his ancestry, a notion he suggested on at least one occasion.[10] The illustrious career of Jerry Nason has yet to be fully documented.

The prognosis of Ellison Brown's victory was but one distinction credited from the typewriter of Nason concerning that 1936 race. Another item of his looms even larger in the historic reporting and the lore of the B. A. A. Marathon.

The final Newton hill upon which Johnny Kelley caught up to, reached out and patted, and then temporarily passed Tarzan Brown in the race of 1936 will forever be known as *Heartbreak Hill*, so christened, according to legend, by none other than Jerry Nason. In describing Kelley's emotional loss following that seminal moment on that elevated incline, the geographical cause of Kelley's personal anguish and crushing disappointment was reputedly named by Nason, and the name stuck. The "heartbreak" in Nason's epithet was not generic, not a description of a universal discouragement that the difficult hill suffused in all hopeful runners. The heartbreak was personal. It was of a time and of a place. It belonged to one man. It was Johnny Kelley's.

Heartbreak Hill, at the start of mile 21 on the marathon course, is the last grade in a series,[11] with its highest peak at an elevation of 236 feet above sea level. But the hill, like the others before it, is not a gargantuan, enormously steep geological entity. In reality it is much more gradual in appearance, a rising slope. The long, upward ascent of Heartbreak Hill, its position as the climactic hill following a series of distinct rises coupled with its location in the overall race itself (roughly after three-quarters of the race is run) combine to make it a formidable obstacle with which to grapple. It has stymied many a contender. Arguably, it has influenced every annual outcome. Yet, odd as it may sound, some runners actually do not realize they are upon it at the moment they are encountering it. Runner Joan Benoit Samuelson of Maine, winner in 1979 and world record-setting winner in 1983, was unfamiliar with the course on her maiden Boston run and had uncertain expectations of the hills.

> All I kept hearing about was the Heartbreak Hills. So I asked somebody next to me, "Where are the Heartbreak Hills?" They said, "You've already gone by them."[12]

Jock Semple recollected to *Globe* writer Jackie MacMullan in April 1984 a pertinent, somewhat similar case as the former runner and the *Globe* writer drove over the marathon course in a car, rekindling the eighty-year-old Scot's memories along the way. The car approached the Newton hills. Semple recalled, "I remember one time the B. A. A. asked me to take some Japanese runners around the course before the race, and after I drove them all the way through, they turned to their interpreter and asked in Japanese, 'Where's the hills?'"[13]

To Jock Semple, the Newton hills themselves were not such a big deal. More important to him was the marathon itself. Said Semple just four years before he passed away, "They make too much fuss of the hills. Heartbreak Hill isn't all that tough — I've run a lot tougher than that — they just gave it that name because that was where Tarzan Brown passed Johnny Kelley one year."[14]

Despite unanimous agreement that Nason coined the name *Heartbreak Hill* for that notorious piece of elevated real estate that has ruined more than one Boston hopeful's chances of succeeding, there is one anomalous newspaper article that casts at least a shadow of a doubt on the claim. In the *Westerly Sun*, on the front page under the byline of Bill King, dated "Tuesday Evening, April 21, 1936," the following sentences appeared in an article describing the Boston event for the *Sun's* southern Rhode Island readers:

> Kelley had been trailing by three and one-half minutes until he pulled up on the steep Newton grade known as Heart Break hill [*sic*]. He pulled into the lead four different times, only to be out-footed by the Indian.[15]

The baffling aspect of this evidence is in the assertion that the Newton hill is "*known as* Heart Break hill" (emphasis added). Known by whom? Does King mean that hill was commonly referred to as "Heart Break hill?" Where would a *Westerly Sun* sportswriter get that impression if, up until that date, the hill had not yet been named that? That remains an unsolved conundrum.

The previous evening's edition of the *Westerly Sun*, dated Monday, April 20, 1936, trumpeted the success of the local winner, with the headline: Westerly Boy Wins Boston Marathon Defeating Field of 183 Expert Runners. In that postrace afternoon newspaper, front page articles attributed to the AP told the story of Brown's victory in the fortieth annual event. In that AP wire dispatch the following sentence appeared: "Once at Boston College on a hilltop overlooking the Lake Street Station, the heart breaking hill climbing is finished."[16] The adjective and common noun had not been transformed into a proper noun yet, but the nearly similar language was familiar and circulating.

In an article in Tuesday's *Boston Post*, Jack Barnwell referred to the beginning of that notorious Newton terrain as "the first of these heart-breaking humps of Mother Earth...."[17] The familiar image was circulating as well.

If Jerry Nason did in fact coin the name,[18] and no evidence contradicts the suggestion that he did, the question becomes exactly when he did so. That moment remains a mystery.

9

Marathon Aftermath — 1936

The headline across the first sports page of the *Boston Traveler* told the story: "Life Complete for 'Tarzan'— Sodas, Movies, Store Clothes." At the top of the page was a picture of Ellison Brown in his brand-new suit and tie, sitting between two very admiring and smiling young ladies from the stage show cast at RKO Boston. He appeared to be managing a smile and gazing forward. Both women's eyes were on the new marathon champion, and they appeared very pleased to be seated next to him. The alliterative title above the news photo read: "Bewildered but blissful."[1]

"A wild night" was how *Herald* writer Will Cloney described it.[2] It began after the nap, shower, the donning of new clothes and multi-interviews with the press and the business of having photographs taken. Then, accompanied by Jack Farrington, members of the Providence Tercentenary Committee, and a covey of reporters, the first official stop was tended at the home of Mr. Benjamin Levias, chairman of the Boston Olympic Committee. Both formality and politics required this visit for a show of appreciation and respect. The shared general understanding was that Brown's win had earned him a berth on the U.S. Olympic team. Off-the-record assurances were given to Farrington, but no judgment was proffered as to whether Brown would have to compete in the second trial in Washington, D.C., or whether the Boston victory alone was sufficient. Having just put the fortieth B. A. A. marathon and Olympic trial to bed a few hours earlier, perhaps it was really too soon for anyone to substantially say.

Next stop was the large RKO Theater to take in a Boston stage show and accompanying movie. As an honored guest, Ellison Brown was escorted backstage where he was introduced to some of the entertainers, many in glamorous show costumes. After mingling with the show people and being photographed, he was brought out front to be seated in a private box. "During the performance the spotlight was turned on him and he was introduced and the crowd gave him an ovation, which lasted for more than 15 minutes."[3] A trip to a nightclub continued the celebration of Brown's win. At every juncture, there were cheers, handshakes, and congratulations from folks out on the town. Everywhere, Tarzan Brown was received as a hero. "Men crowded into his party to shake his hand and a dozen times police were forced to hold

85

In new sartorial splendor, Tarzan Brown sits between two cast members of the RKO stage show backstage during his celebratory night out on the town. In the upper left Brown wears the laurel wreath of marathon victory. In the upper right he obligingly dons a headdress to indicate his heritage. Boston, April 20, 1936 (courtesy of the Boston Public Library, Print Department).

up traffic as thousands of well wishers rushed forward to glimpse the winner of one of the greatest marathon runs in history," reported the *Westerly Sun*.[4]

Fred Knight, like many of the newspaper reporters covering the post-race goings-on, relished the image of the uncivilized (savage) child thrown into the center of sophisticated, bustling city nightlife.

The receptions he was given from place to place he visited were almost too much to him. He could do little more than show a forced smile. All so new to him, all so different, this treatment he received and the places he saw, he could say nothing. His eyes bulged as he tried to take in everything in enjoying himself to the utmost.[5]

An ample supply of delicious ice cream sodas, vanilla sodas and lemon sodas were in constant easy reach throughout the evening. After all the nightlife thrills, he was taken back to the Lenox hotel[6] or to the Watertown home of William C. Waugh[7] for a night's rest.

A photograph in the *Traveler* showed a posing Brown the next morning in bed, his fists raised like a champion prizefighter, staring into the camera, and wearing a very new-looking pajama top. A line above the photo read: "The Morning After."[8] Whether the night had been spent at the Waughs' in Watertown or at the Lenox Hotel in Boston, early the next morning the familiar breakfasts of the training regimen were superseded by a giant breakfast of fried eggs, fried bacon and fried beans[9] and three bottles of soda[10] as training was temporarily suspended. After the morning meal, it was off to Providence, Rhode Island, from Watertown, Massachusetts, for ceremonies and celebrations in the state capital. Jack Farrington and Ellison Brown made a short stop in Pawtucket, Rhode Island, just a few miles to the north of Providence, so David Dorgan, the chairman of the council tercentenary committee, could join them on the rest of the way to the capital city. Once in the city center, the runner, the trainer and the key supporter, along with William C. Waugh, executive secretary of the tercentenary committee—plus reporters from Massachusetts and Rhode Island, friends, a few family members and fans—all made their way to the Tercentenary House, still unfinished, in the Mall by the Capitol, for the first official welcome led by the Honorable James E. Dunne, mayor of Providence. Standing along with the chief executive of the city were a host of city officials: Aldermen Frank Rao and Frank J. Duffy, Councilmen Joseph V. West and Edward F. Moran, Deputy City Clerk Earl Dodd, and Fire Chief Frank Charlesworth. Reporter Joe Nutter, covering the event for the *Providence Journal*, described the ensuing interaction:

After congratulating Brown on his great triumph, Mayor Dunne asked him how he felt.

"I feel fine," was the laconic answer.

"I hope," Mayor Dunne said, "that there is absolutely no question of your participation in the Olympics."

He was assured by Brown and Farrington that their understanding was that there was no question on that score.[11]

After the civic ceremony, a thrilled entourage worked its way toward the State House and eventually into the Executive Office of the governor, who was not present. Lieutenant Governor Robert E. Quinn stood in for his superior, Governor Theodore Green, and warmly greeted the marathon champion. The following exchange took place:

> (Brown) told Lieutenant Governor Quinn that the marathon grind "wasn't so tough" and expressed the hope that he would be successful in the Berlin Olympics. Lieutenant Governor Quinn recalled that he had shaken "Tarzan's" hand last week and wished him luck at Boston, and that "apparently it was a good gesture."
> "I'm going to shake again and wish you the best of luck in Berlin," Quinn said.[12]

Ellison Brown and the lieutenant governor deliberately shook hands, as if solidifying agreement on a wager. Flashbulbs exploded with momentary brilliant light. Brown spoke again, this time with a great deal of emotion, taking onlookers somewhat by surprise: "'It was grand,' said the youth, after shaking hands with Lieut. Gov. Robert E. Quinn, 'but it might have been better.' The plucky runner brushed aside the tears and told newsmen that his one regret was that his mother could not share in his triumph."[13] It was explained how Brown's mother had passed away before the 1935 marathon, and the words to her son giving him the resolve to keep running. Composure was restored all around. An attempt at levity came next.

The absent Gov. Green had been ceremoniously granted "chief" status "by a tribe of Western Indians years ago"[14] and at that time, allegedly was given the name "Chief White Buffalo." It was then that he was presented with a gift, a Native American full headdress made up of white and red eagle feathers. The headdress was "said to be one of three in existence, the other two having been presented to Alfred E. Smith and the late Calvin Coolidge, some years ago," reported Joe Nutter.[15] From an office closet, the lieutenant governor retrieved the governor's headdress for the office festivities. Whereas the *Providence Journal* reported that Quinn then placed it upon his own head, it was noted in the *Boston Herald* that the headdress was handed to Ellison Brown who put it on his head. According to Will Cloney: "Tarzan donned the affair to pose for pictures with about everyone, including State Senator Edward J. Fenelon of Westerly, Thomas A. Kennelly, state director of taxation; Attorney-General John P. Hartigan, Farrington, and Rep.V. Turce (*sic*-Dominic Turco of Westerly)."[16] Oddly but for no discernible reason, neither newspaper published the photographs taken that afternoon along with the story. Cloney recorded the proceedings after the impromptu photo shoot:

> In the broad expanse of the Governor's office the hero was suddenly missed. Then they found him, almost hidden behind an outspread newspaper, and sure enough, he was looking very closely at a group picture showing him with his two brothers in a Boston hotel after yesterday's race.
> "Sure, I have a scrapbook back home, and I got all the papers saved. Guess I may need another scrapbook now."[17]

The marathon champion "had a smile for every one, but very little to say to any one," Will Cloney observed.[18] "There is one thing certain, namely that the youngster will not annoy sports writers. Tarzan has but little to say," agreed its competitor, the *Boston Globe*.[19] Cloney turned his reportorial eye on the triumphant trainer:

> Trainer Jack Farrington was very nearly worn out. "Look at him" (he pointed to his pride and joy), "fresh as a daisy and he doesn't have to shave. I look like a bum, because I can't stop long enough to get cleaned up. If you want to see blisters, you should get a look at my feet."[20]

It had been an incredibly jam-packed day and a half—and an emotionally and physically draining couple of weeks to precede it. Farrington was showing signs of wear. Young Ellison Brown was excited, refreshed, and still raring to go.

At the close of the office visit, the entourage headed to the legislative side of the State House for yet another formal reception. As they left the governor's office, Cloney observed that Ellison Brown "made a bee-line for the elevator, but the party decided to walk down the one flight, so he didn't get his usual thrill."[21]

Prior to Speaker of the Rhode Island House William E. Reddy formally introducing Tarzan Brown to the state legislature, a joint resolution of congratulations had been introduced to both bodies of the General Assembly. In the Senate, Senator Edward J. "Happy" Fenelon was the sponsor, and in the House, Representative Dominic Turco. Both legislators were representatives of Westerly. The joint resolution, printed in its entirety in the *Providence Journal* and almost entirely so in the *Westerly Sun*, follows:

> "Of the General Assembly, extending to Ellison Meyers [*sic*] Brown, of the Narragansett Tribe of Indians, of Westerly, Rhode Island, the hearty congratulations of this honorable body upon his great fortitude and endurance in winning the 40th Boston Athletic Association marathon, thereby earning a place in the Olympics.
>
> "Whereas, When Roger Williams first rounded the headlands towards the site of these plantations, fleetfooted Indians, who inhabited these fields and forests, greeted him in friendliness three hundred years ago; and
>
> "Whereas, Upon April 20th, 1936, under a sky drab with blowing rain clouds, Ellison Meyers [*sic*] Brown, direct descendent of King Philip, born and reared upon the reservation of the Narragansett Tribe of Indians in Westerly, Rhode Island, won the 40th Boston Athletic Association Marathon, in a field of nearly [ ] one hundred and eighty-eight contesting runners; and
>
> "Whereas, This strong-hearted son of enduring spirit, the very embodiment of all those qualities which have made these Indian runners of the trail and hills [hill] an heroic part of our glamorous history, deserves the friendliest of greetings from this general assembly for thus bringing to Rhode Island in [on] her Tercentenary Anniversary year this high honor, with its placing at the assembly of the nations at the next Olympic:[Olympics:]

"Now, therefore, be it resolved, That every member of this general assembly unanimously applauding the splendid victory of this truly native son of our home soil, extends to Ellison Meyers [sic] Brown a [the] rightful acclaim for his will to win a [the] challenging race, as gruelling a marathon as ever faced his ancestors in those other [ever] memorable days; directing [and direct] the Secretary of State to transmit to him a duly certified copy of this resolution as the tribute of this honorable body to his sportsmanship."[22]

The Senate was in adjournment but the House was in session as Speaker Reddy introduced Ellison Brown to the members. "All of the members stood and paid the new marathon champion one of the finest ovations ever tendered a visitor," Joe Nutter reported.[23] Members lightheartedly debated just which district Brown hailed from, and various members claimed him as one of their own constituents. After these deliberations,

James H. Kierpan, Democratic floor leader, called on Speaker Reddy to ask Brown to tell the House how he did it. Brown, smiling at the enthusiastic reception as he stood on the speaker's stand, said in a very matter-of-fact tone, "I did it for Rhode Island." It was not a direct answer to the question but "Tarzan" stepped down satisfied that he had provided the answer to the question.[24]

An article by sportswriter Abe Soloveitzik in the *Westerly Sun* presented the identical quotation from Brown: "[Brown] then asked to speak, quietly said, 'I did it for Rhode Island.'"[25] Will Cloney reported the runner's utterance to the assembly in this way: "His address, word for word, unaltered for publicity purposes, was 'I done it for Rhode Island.'"[26] Just which reporter actually altered the text of the single-sentence speech is undetermined.

After leaving the legislative chamber, the champion runner and the trainer, along with two Boston reporters, continued the journey south to the town of Westerly, where they "made the complete round of relatives and friends."[27] Having been essentially sequestered during the training regimen for the marathon, Ellison had not seen members of his family for a few weeks and they hadn't seen him. They first arrived at his sister's residence at Wood River Junction, the home of Mrs. Alice Champlin. She was described in the press as "the sister who first lent encouragement to his marathoning efforts by pacing him for the first few miles of his longer training jaunts."[28] Despite the fuss that was being made over Ellison, he was apparently in an indifferent mood, somewhat preoccupied, during the visit and the accompanying commotion. It was reported that he was "thoroughly undemonstrative in the attention accorded him by his sisters and other relatives," preferring to look at newspaper accounts of his participation in the race and its aftermath "that they had assembled."[29] Getting him to pose for photographs with family members was difficult, requiring extensive coaxing from the attendant press corps. "He did object several times when they asked him."[30]

The second stop was at his own place of residence, which was the Alton,

Rhode Island, home of his uncle, Charles Babcock. Again, there was reluctance to having his picture taken. After a brief stay, the entourage traveled to the neighboring town of Bradford to greet his aunt, Mrs. Paul Babcock. "He completed the round of visits to his immediate family in a visit to Mrs. Myra Brown of 14 Wall street, White Rock, and there he also saw his younger sister, Grace. Myra is the sister who returned from the Westerly Hospital Monday after an attack of bronchitis and threatened pneumonia."[31] The newspaper noted her condition had improved upon seeing her brother.

Ellison Brown tried to contact his manager, Tippy Salimeno, but was informed that Salimeno was still in Boston.

> He then called on Abe Soloveitzik, a Westerly reporter who backed "Tarzan" for six long years before any talent was recognized to recommend him for the plaudits of an admiring world.
>
> Soloveitzik bought "Tarzan's" first running shoes, urged him to enter races, and saw to it that he found his way there. There the story came to light that Soloveitzik had worked overtime in recent weeks to raising [sic] a fund in Westerly to send "Tarzan" to Boston a day or two in advance of the race so that he might be amply prepared for the rigors of the marathon grind. The sum reached the figure of $37.00 but was never presented to Brown.
>
> When A. A. U. Commissioner heard of the contemplated presentation, he ordered the money held up. When the Tercentenary A. C. was formed and Providence officially took over the backing for the race, "Tarzan" expressed the wish that the money be divided between his sister, Myra, to pay a portion of her hospital bills, and his uncle, who has also been ill. No decision as to the disposal of the money has been reached.[32]

Keeping the amateur status of the runner was an important aspect of Farrington's duties. Buying the marathon runner running shoes or even a new suit of street clothes and innumerable dinners were apparently deemed all right within the limits of the rules, but any actual cash donations, even if for the purposes of purchasing those same items, were vigorously proscribed by the racing establishment. In this case of local money raised legitimately to assist the hometown runner, Farrington would have to take it up with others on the committee before anyone saw the dispensation of one nickel. For Farrington was going to err on the side of excessive cautiousness if need be, and not allow Brown to get snared in any bureaucratic entanglement, especially at this juncture with the official Olympic selections looming.

The only family member whose words were reported in the newspaper was Ellison's father, Otis. *The Westerly Sun* recorded the following:

> Otis Byron Brown, still thrilled at his young son's great victory, said that he was the happiest man in the world.
>
> "Oh gee, oh gosh," he said. "I just can't imagine that Ellison won this race. You know that Monday was the first time that I have ever been in Boston and I had the grandest time in my life.... You know, I never saw so many people in my life ... there were thousands of them around the finish line and I was

standing way back in about the 15th row. When I heard them hollering that Brown was coming I got up on the running board of a car to see the finish, but the man in the machine said something to me, and I became frightened and got off."[33]

As it turned out, Otis actually missed seeing the moment when his son officially became the marathon winner, his view obstructed by other spectators.

It was on to the Elm Tree Inn, across the river from Westerly in Pawcatuck, Connecticut, for a meal and to be greeted by some local well-wishers. Word was out that the local chamber of commerce was planning a celebratory banquet for Brown on the following Monday evening, their regular meeting night. Partly for that reason, "only a handful of Westerly people knew that he was here (at that moment) and they will have to wait until later to give him an official welcome."[34] Chamber of commerce president George Ben Utter invited Brown to the planned reception. Answering for his charge, "Farrington stated that 'Tarzan's' immediate plans are uncertain, but that he would communicate with Utter later."[35] The day before, "Mr. Farrington assured us [sportswriter Ed Butler of the *Westerly Sun*] he would be proud to be a guest on that occasion. He will be able to tell the inside story of Brown's training siege and his progress during the Patriots' Day race."[36]

In the dining room of the Elm Tree Inn, everybody ate well, including the hungry day's center of attention, who, according to the newspaper, devoured "two chicken sandwiches, two bottles of Moxie, and a 'lot of pickles.'"[37]

Ellison Brown made the suggestion that Farrington assist Les Pawson as Pawson's trainer, so Pawson could accompany them to Berlin as Olympic teammates. "'We'd be pals on the trip across if Les made the team,' Tarzan explained."[38] No response was recorded. Farrington never did undertake Pawson's athletic training, nor was Pawson selected for the team.

After dinner, Farrington and Brown were to return to Providence in order to be on hand for an early meeting the next day with the Tercentenary A. C. The purpose of the meeting was to "map out ... his [Brown's] immediate future in the hands of his new sponsors."[39] There was a lot of confusion to clear up. Once selected officially to the Olympic team, the presumption was that Brown's training would be under the jurisdiction of the National Long Distance Committee. Though only speculation at this point, Farrington felt that Brown was definitely going to be a U.S. team selection, and that he, Farrington, "had been assured of a place as trainer of the United States Olympic marathon team."[40]

At some point in the evening, before venturing back to Providence, Farrington was asked to express his opinion of Ellison Brown and his abilities. He enthusiastically responded: "'There,' Mr. Farrington said, pointing to Ellison, 'is the greatest runner in the world. Like all runners he is temperamental, but I knew he had the stuff and I knew he would win.'"[41]

The state government of Rhode Island's urge for honoring its worthy native runner was not sated the day it met personally with Ellison Brown. The day after his winning the marathon in neighboring Massachusetts, he had been honored with an invitation to the governor's office (by the lieutenant governor) and to the assembly chamber, where Brown was introduced to the members, given an ovation, and issued an official joint resolution of congratulations. A week later, they were still at it. The legislature passed a bill designating an annual holiday in honor of the marathon victor, and the governor was happy to sign it into law.

"'Tarzan Brown Day' Is New R. I. Holiday," announced the *Boston Traveler* in its sports pages. In the article that followed, apparently no effort was made to conceal a derisive tone, aimed, no doubt, at the legislative activities of its neighbor to the south. The article tried to lay it all out in perspective:

> There are those who thought Arlington's Johnny Kelley was overidolized after his victory in the B. A. A. marathon last year, but the state of Rhode Island has gone completely daffy over its new tercentenary B. A. A. champion, Ellison "Tarzan" Brown, the Narragansett Indian.
>
> They're treating him to a round of banquets and festivities which has him dizzy and only yesterday the Rhode Island Legislature went to the extreme with a tasty bit of tercentenary publicity. The boys passed a bill which forever establishes a Rhode Island holiday to be known as "Tarzan" Brown Day. They haven't decided the date yet. They're leaving that to the fathers of the Narragansett tribe.[42]

Governor Theodore F. Green signed the bill sponsored by State Senator Edward J. "Happy" Fenelon. The actual choice of the date for the official day was determined at a tribal meeting held Saturday night, April 25, at the Indian Church in Charlestown. Announcing the selection to the press was Chief Sachem Nighthawk Philip H. Peckham. He stated that the date chosen would be the third Monday in April, since Brown won the marathon on that particular day.

Right from the start, the name of what was planned to be an annual holiday was changed to *Indian Day in Rhode Island*, a change initiated by Ellison Brown as a gift to the tribe, according to his wife, Ethel.[43] While the *Providence Journal* was aware of the day's official designation in its April 27 edition, apparently word of the name had not reached the *Boston Traveler* by the time it went to press on April 28.

The City of Providence's urge to honor Brown also was not satiated with the personal meeting between the mayor along with city dignitaries and the runner that same Tuesday after the marathon victory. A testimonial dinner was organized by the Providence City Council Tercentenary Committee and the affair was held at the Narragansett Hotel. The program for the occasion was arranged by William C. Waugh, the executive director of the committee.

At the head table sat an elegantly attired Ellison Brown, in suit and tie.

Seated at that table of honor were Alderman David Dorgan, the committee chairman, and William A. Schlobohm, a member of the American Olympic Selection Committee and therefore considered a very important person at the present moment. Schlobohm was one of the guest speakers featured at the dinner. Invited along with Ellison Brown were two other winners of the B. A. A. Marathon, Rhode Islander Leslie Pawson and New Hampshire resident Clarence H. DeMar. Other invited guests in attendance included his trainer and A. A. U. commissioner for Rhode Island Jack Farrington, and 1908 Olympic marathon champion Johnny Hayes, the only American ever to win an Olympic marathon.[44] Arthur Duffey, the Boston sportswriter, was tapped to be another guest speaker. Dr. Edward F. Dougherty, Brown's nutritionist during his training regimen, was another special guest. Serving as toastmaster was Thomas J. Meehan. A host of municipal office holders and functionaries, both elected and appointed, including aldermen, councilmen, magistrates, clerks, deputy clerks, and other city employees shared in the fete. Also present were members of the Rhode Island press, to cover the occasion in the newspapers.

The highlight of the evening was the presentation to Ellison Brown of a trophy on behalf of the City Council Tercentenary Group. They could not contain their glee for they had placed their bets on a winner.

10

"That Man, Presuming That He Is an American": Olympic Team Selection — 1936

Selection to the United States Olympic Team was a process, and not everyone had the same understanding as to just how that process was supposed to work. There was evident confusion amongst the sportswriters of the various newspapers over what accomplishments were required to qualify for Olympic team selection. Just what was necessary for a runner to do or achieve in order to secure a berth on the U.S. team was never clearly defined. In fact, the layers of committees (an Olympic marathon committee, the higher-level Olympic committee, etc.) and officials added to the confusion. Moreover, without making much public comment about it, the Olympic officials quietly held onto their proprietary use of discretion. This was a matter of choice, and as far as they were concerned, they and they alone controlled the making of that choice. The one thing that all seemed to publicly agree upon, however, was that the 1936 B. A. A. Marathon and the 1936 A. A. U. Marathon (scheduled for later that spring) in Washington, D.C., were indeed Olympic trials. Beyond that, no one was clear what that really meant or whether winning either of these events guaranteed the winning athletes a chance to represent the country in the summer games in Berlin.

Some newspaper reports before the April 20 race suggested that the winner of the B. A. A. Marathon would automatically be the first selection to the U.S. team. Will Cloney conveyed this view in a front-page *Herald* piece, when he wrote of the winner, "That man, presuming that he is an American, will be No. 1 representative on the United States Olympic team."[1]

The *Boston Post* described the relationship between the Boston Marathon and the Olympic selection in this way: "This year the race has been officially designated as an Olympic tryout. The first three runners to finish will receive due consideration for their victory and no doubt will be named representatives of the U. S. A. in the Olympic Marathon in Berlin."[2] As the *Post* saw it, not only was the victor a shoe-in for selection (although not an automatic selection) but also the second- and third-place winners were likely candidates. The top three winners were guaranteed "consideration" only, which the paper then speculated would "no doubt" lead to their selection. But there was doubt.

The more cautious *Westerly Sun* ran a subheadline that stated: "Victory in jaunt from Hopkinton means chance at Olympics."[3] Perhaps their reporters understood better than most of their colleagues that if a Native American (or any non-Caucasian) won Boston, perhaps the selection would not be nearly so automatic.

From the moment Ellison Brown crossed the finish line securing victory in Boston, some of the various papers started hedging on whether the marathon winner had passed the tryout and earned a position on the Olympic team. Jerry Nason, for example, like his brethren, had regarded the B. A. A. Marathon as an Olympic tryout, and the winner as gaining a spot on the team. But after Brown's win, which he supported, he found it necessary to explain to his readers that the selection process was not a perspicuous one, and that as the winner, Brown had no lock on being chosen an Olympic competitor. In an article titled "Selection of Olympic Team Is Complicated" published the day after Brown's marathon win, Nason wrote that Brown's "victory had upset all the calculations of the Olympic Marathon committee."[4] According to Nason, the committee had all but forgone the public trials process, having perfunctorily selected Johnny Kelley, Pat Dengis, Mel Porter and Les Pawson based on their achievements in 1935. Nason claimed the committee had notified the four "to go ahead and train for Berlin." Ellison Brown's championship-winning ways—Boston, Newport, Beverly—had changed everything. As for Kelley, Dengis, Porter and Pawson, their 1936 results in the marathon in Boston were less than stellar: Kelley finished fifth, Porter finished third, Dengis ruptured a blood vessel and was forced to exit the race and enter Massachusetts General Hospital, and Pawson dropped out at mile twelve.

Nason suggested that the Washington race would now be a major factor. He continued:

> ... If you ask me, that spot [No. 1 Olympic selection] belongs to "Tarzan" Brown right now. The Indian boy will run at Washington if the Marathon committee demands it. I doubt it will demand it. After all he is not exactly a stranger to the A. A. U. big shots. Last summer he submerged the national 25-kilometer record and also the national 20-kilometer title, distances between 15 and 18 miles.
>
> His speed was never questioned, his staying powers in a race longer than 21 miles were. If skepticism reigned, then the skeptics were wetted in a shower of their own making yesterday ... Brown is on the threshold of greatness.[5]

Nason's sports-writing colleague at the *Globe*, John Lardner, also publicly proclaimed that by winning the Boston Marathon, "the most important distance event of its kind in the country," Brown earned the most serious consideration for selection, and was the "first Indian since Longboat [who] deserves to go to [the] Olympics."[6]

Ellison Brown responded to reporters inquiries about his Olympic prospects. Replied Brown with a certain amount of modesty, "The Olympics? Well, I don't know whether they'll send me as a result of winning today or not. If I have to I will run at the Washington tryout."[7]

The next day a Nason article appeared under the headline: "TARZAN BROWN NOT CERTAIN OF POST ON OLYMPIC TEAM." The subheadline underneath read: "But G. V. Brown, Chairman of U.S. Marathon Committee, Feels Winner of B. A. A. Grind Deserves Selection." In the first paragraph it was pointed out that Ellison Brown had not been officially named to the U.S. Team, despite his Boston heroics. George V. Brown (no relation) explained that his American Olympic Marathon Selection Committee did not choose the team members but only made recommendations to the Olympic committee, which alone had charge of the final decision. He did inform *Globe* readers that in his opinion Ellison Brown's "chances of being named are as good as anybody else's." He went on to assert that nothing would be decided until after the marathon in Washington, D.C. Then he made these revealing statements: "I would say offhand that the winner of the Boston A. A. trial would be a certain selection, however, and that the winner at Washington would also clearly win a place on the squad. Picking the third man will be quite a problem, not to mention the alternate selection."[8]

William Schlobohm of Yonkers, New York, a member of the American Olympic Marathon Selection Committee chaired by George Brown, was a guest at the testimonial dinner held in Ellison Brown's honor on May 2 in Providence, Rhode Island. At that celebratory affair, Mr. Schlobohm told the gathering that Ellison Brown "is as good as selected right now for the Olympic Marathon to be run in Berlin in August."[9] The committee official commented:

> I told George Brown, chairman of the committee, that "Tarzan" is the man to go to win the Olympics for Uncle Sam. His performance in the Boston meet was the most amazing I ever saw. I clocked "Tarzan" as going 11 miles in 55 minutes and 15 miles in an hour and 21 minutes. I am opposed to any more tryouts for this boy. He is as good as selected right now for the Olympics.[10]

Schlobohm was awestruck by Brown's performance. This man, by his own account, had witnessed "every B. A. A. Marathon since the year 1901," and he rated this most recent one as the most incredible of them all. He went on to express himself: "I am glad that by [*sic*— probably *my*] original selection for the marathon in Germany did not go through before I saw 'Tarzan' Brown go into action. If ever I had my eyes opened, it was in Boston, when

'Tarzan,' a 100 to 1 shot in the betting, ran off with that race, the most amazing thing that I have ever seen."[11] If Schlobohm was similar to other voting committee officials, it would appear that Ellison Brown's selection to the U. S. marathon team was in actuality a foregone conclusion. Schlobohm disclosed to those at the fete that "the six members of the committee are now balloting and their choice will be made known within a week."[12]

Whether Brown (and whether Kelley) should have to compete in Washington was debated by sportswriters and sports fans. Both Brown and Kelley had publicly resisted the suggested idea of racing in the Washington trial, but of course would do so if required to. As Nason put it, "The Indian will only run it if commanded to and the Olympic committee will pull a 'bloomer' [sic] if it ever issues such a command."[13] The suggestion was put forth that running twenty-six miles in Washington and in the Washington summer heat would take too large a physical toll out of these two competitors, who, for the most part, had already proven their worthiness for selection. Forcing them to compete in Washington would tax their bodies to the point that it would hurt their chances in Berlin if they were to be subsequently selected. The sense it made to hold the second tryout in the hot capital that late, so near the start of the summer Olympics, was a matter the Olympic overseers might have more closely examined long before April.

Brown in the end was not required to run the Washington, D.C., marathon, due to his selection by the committee. Kelley, McMahon, and Porter were not so fortunate; they were asked to participate in that second trial. Johnny Kelley believed strongly that his record over the previous two years should dictate his selection, and excuse him from the second trial. Moreover, he admitted to using bad judgment in the B. A. A. Marathon just run, but figured the Olympic committee decision-makers could understand his logic. As he explained to Nason:

> Some think I made a bad error in chasing after Brown over the hills. Maybe I did. I guess I lost my head and got frightened when they told me he was more than three minutes out front at nearly 20 miles. If I had just stuck to my normal pace, forgotten about his lead, I think I would have been at least second, maybe first.[14]

Had Kelley not accelerated over the furious hills, causing his eventual burnout, but instead had maintained his steady pace and adhered to his original game plan, he believed he would have achieved more favorable results, results the selection people certainly could compute with less consternation. Furthermore, Kelley intimated that he would ideally prefer to save his strength for the one last summer marathon performance that really counted, not the dress rehearsal. Kelley remarked: "I don't feel that I should run again [having run it in 1935] in Washington. I am certain I have one fine Marathon left for this Summer and I naturally would like to run it in Berlin."[15] Years later, he recalled his feelings about having to compete in Washington: "'I was a stubborn guy,' Johnny admits. 'I thought I deserved to be on the team. But they said I had to run the trial no matter what.' Half-heartedly, Johnny entered."[16]

Kelley would have his work cut out for him. Competition with Porter would be fierce. In three years running the Washington marathon, Porter had done well, having finished in third place the year before, and in second place his two previous starts. Mel Porter, in Nason's view at the time, was deserving of a spot on the team, "either as alternate or a regular."[17]

The Olympic tryout in the form of the National A. A. U. Marathon was held on May 30. The starting line was drawn at Mount Vernon, Virginia. The course traced the bank of the Potomac River, and marked the finish line at Capitol Hill. Although purported to be the standard twenty-six miles and 385 yards in length, some detractors claimed "the Washington course was fully a mile longer than the regulation one."[18] All agreed, however, that the last mile, the Capitol Hill district, was the most difficult segment, due to its hilly incline and the fact that it came late in the athletic grind.

As it turned out, Kelley's worries should have been directed at Worcester's Biddie McMahon, not the durable Mel Porter. McMahon won the national marathon championship and he won it decisively. According to the *New York Times*, "William T. McMahon, who has been knocking on the door to marathon championships for four years, finally hammered his way inside today with a record-breaking National A. A. U. victory that likely earned him a post on America's Olympic team."[19] McMahon beat Dave Komonen's official record for the course by more than five minutes, but more importantly, he beat Kelley by nearly two minutes or two hundred yards, with a time of 2 hours, 38 minutes, 14.2 seconds. Kelley's time was 2 hours, 40 minutes, 7 seconds.

Pat Dengis had set the pace and led for the first fifteen miles, but by mile eighteen was bothered by the same kidney ailment that caused his premature finish in the B. A. A. Marathon. The Baltimore runner, governed by pure determination and will, managed to continue running and complete the race this time, finishing in eighth place. At about the time Dengis faltered, McMahon and Kelley picked up the lead, and matched strides as they left Virginia and crossed the bridge into the District of Columbia. Through the city, Kelley and McMahon battled together, but in the homestretch, McMahon forged ahead for good. Johnny Kelley placed second and Porter finished third, a repetition of his outcome in Boston.

McMahon was selected to the Olympic team on the basis of his first-place performance in Washington and his second-place performance in Boston. In making its selection for the third spot, the committee was divided. How to compare the efforts of Kelley and Porter depended on how they were viewed and weighed.

To some committee members, Porter's two third-place finishes added up to an overall better total performance than Kelley's fifth-place finish and his second-place finish in the two trials. Mathematically, it could be argued that Kelley scored an average 3.5 compared to Porter's 3, the closer the number to 1, or first place, the more favorable (Kelley: 2+5=7, divided by 2 = 3.5; Porter: 3+3=6, divided by 2 = 3). But a look at the times involved cast a different light on the subject. "The average times for the two trials, 2:39:38 to 2:40:18, favored Johnny slightly."[20] Kelley recalled, "Overall, I had beaten Porter eleven of the twelve races we'd run. My record was even better than Brown's and McMahon's, never mind Porter's."[21] Kelley had beaten Porter to the finish line in two out of three full-length marathons.

In June the committee was still in deliberation, trying to decide which athletes would represent the United Sates in Germany. A vote by mail was required, according to sportswriter Arthur Duffey.[22] Late in June, the committee had finally made a decision. Committee chairman William J. Bingham of Harvard University made the official announcement. Bingham personally placed a call to the Anderson Florist Company in Arlington, Massachusetts, where Kelley was employed, to inform him of his selection. Kelley was overjoyed and vastly relieved. He described his mental state an hour after receiving the news:

> The moment I heard who was on the other end of that line I knew my worries were over. I don't know when I've ever been so happy. I've been a little worried for the past month, but you can bet I'm going to relax now. The first thing I did after hearing Bingham's words was call my mother. I don't need to tell you how delighted she was. You know, she's been as worried as I have. Yeh, and even more.[23]

Mel Porter, the odd man out, was selected as the alternate, which meant he would not sail to Berlin unless one of the other three suffered an injury before July 15. ("After that date Porter will automatically become ineligible," reported the *Boston Traveler*.)[24] As things turned out, the opportunity did not arise for Porter to replace Brown, Kelley or McMahon on the United States Olympic team.

Newport, Rhode Island, was the host of the New England A. A. U. 20-kilometer championship race, promoted by Jack Farrington as a part of his duties as A. A. U. commissioner of Rhode Island. Tarzan Brown was the defending champion, having won the event the previous year. His participation made this year's race an even bigger spectacle than the year before, since it offered fans two exciting opportunities at once: a chance to see a repeat victory by the reigning New England 20-K champion and the occasion to witness a genuine U. S. Olympic team member engaged in athletic competition.

The *Boston Post* headline told the story: "TARZAN BROWN WINS IN ROMP." The subheadline extolled: "Victory in N. E. A. A. U. Title Event

Easy." The AP reported that "Allison [*sic*] (Tarzan) Brown ... sped to an easy victory for the second time."[25] Brown's time for the 20-kilometer race was 1 hour, 7 minutes, 9 seconds. This winning "time was a good two minutes slower than last year" when he completed the race in 1 hour, 5 minutes, 51 seconds. The weather, which contributed to the slower pace, was very hot, a description that also applied to the "hard pavements."

A field of fifty runners sought the 20-K championship crown. At the gun, R. Campbell led by only a few yards for nearly two miles, according to the *Globe*. At that point Ellison Brown "sprinted into first place and kept the lead till the end."[26] The *Boston Herald* reported: "He drew out from the pack ... at the outset. Adopting the same tactics that won him the B. A. A. marathon, he moved with a piston-like stride into the lead and held his advantage until he broke the tape."[27] Brown was roughly two minutes ahead of the second-place runner, R. Campbell. Campbell, of Dorchester, finishing with a time of 1 hour, 9 minutes, 12 seconds, ran under the colors of the venerable unicorn, symbol of the B. A. A. Eight seconds behind was the third-place runner, Tony Medeiros of Lowell, Massachusetts, with a time of 1 hour, 9 minutes, 20 seconds. The team prize was won by the United Shoe Machinery club of Beverly, Massachusetts, with runners in 13th, 14th and 15th places. That fifteenth-place slot belonged to none other than Jock Semple, doing his part for the team honors with a time of 1:12:53.

Though not a twenty-six-mile marathon — 20 kilometers is about twelve miles — Ellison Brown's winning with such reported "ease" had to inspire confidence in both Brown and Farrington for what lay ahead overseas. If indeed this was the final competitive preparation of which Ellison Brown partook, the result had to be nothing short of positive and very assuring. But the Olympics were scheduled for early August; this race was held in early June. It was presumably Farrington calling the shots on Brown's training. The decision not to take part in any more competitive races before Berlin could be of great consequence for the runner.

Johnny Kelley's first competitive run since his official selection to the Olympic team was on Wednesday, June 17, at a ten-mile race held as a part of the festivities in celebration of Bunker Hill Day. Kelley handily beat all competitors in that one. Ellison Brown did not participate.

An earlier report in the *Globe*, published June 5, touted the Sacred Heart 10-miler between Haverhill and Bradford, Massachusetts, scheduled for June 26. The entrants as of June 5 had included the two Olympic teammates, Ellison Brown and Johnny Kelley. The third team member, Bill McMahon, hadn't signed up as of yet but was expected to do so. Other prominent participants of the more than one hundred expected included Clarence H. DeMar, Leo Giard, Anthony Medeiros, and defending title holder from the year before, Les Pawson. As it turned out, Ellison Brown did not show up. Whether by Farrington's direction cannot be uncovered. Johnny Kelley, on the other hand, did participate. He ran from scratch, taking the time prize with a time of 53 minutes, 56 seconds, and he placed second. First across the finish line was a relative newcomer, eighteen-year-old John Davidson from Melrose, Massachusetts. William McMahon, who had not signed up early for the event, did appear. He ran the race but with forgettable results. He finished 15th.

Johnny Kelley had run strongly in these two last opportunities to fine-tune the running mechanism before sailing overseas. Along with his continuous training, Kelley felt highly prepared for Berlin. He considered himself in fine mental and physical condition. He had wanted desperately to make the team, and now that he was given that honor, he planned to make the most of it. McMahon, the new title holder of the national marathon (the second trial for the Olympic team held in Washington, D.C.) may not have been as upbeat about his chances in Berlin, or as fully committed as Kelley to the endeavor. McMahon told reporters the day after his Washington victory:

> that he had two ambitions:
> 1-To get a job with salary sufficient to enable him to marry Margaret Beleulfine of his home town.
> 2-Win the Marathon race for the United States.[28]

"Which do you want most," asked reporters, "the Olympic championship or to marry your girl up in Worcester?" "'You fellows put me on a spot,' he said with a grin, 'but give me a job with a weekly pay check and my girl as a bride and I'll call it quits.'"[29]

11

Sailing to Germany: "Even Better Than Running" — 1936

Germany had been in preparation to host the Olympic Games back in 1916, but the VIth Olympiad was cancelled by the outbreak of World War I. In 1932, just before the start of the Olympic Games in Los Angeles, the International Olympic Committee announced that the XIth Olympiad would be held in Berlin, Germany. A year after that announcement, Adolf Hitler and the National Socialist German Workers Party, or Nazis, came to power, and it appeared once again that the games in Berlin might be threatened.

A military buildup and a crackdown on political freedoms domestically changed the atmosphere within Germany. Anti-Semitism, racism, and anti-intellectualism were promoted by government policies and enacted laws, and those attitudes were disseminated by the government-controlled media. Free speech was outlawed. Newspapers which did not support the Nazi party were forced out of business. Posters and billboards reminded the German public that the Nazis and Hitler were at one with the interests of the true German people. Large assemblies were organized and some were filmed exalting the glory of the Third Reich. A special Nazi salute was required of Germans. Banners with the emblem of the party, the swastika, were displayed everywhere, including every part of the Olympic Games multisports complex.

The Jewish people were the enemy of all Germans, according to the Nazis. They were blamed for any and all problems facing Germany, including the Great Depression, the reason Germany lost World War I, the reason they had to accept the terms of their defeat, high prices, and short supplies. Jews, along with political dissidents, intellectuals, Jehovah's Witnesses, Gypsies, black or dark-skinned peoples, labor organizers, socialists, communists, and homosexuals in time were taken into custody and many were eventually murdered, their property stolen.

To support the Nazi idea of the superiority of the Germanic race, the so-called Aryan master race, laws were passed that put certain German citizens on the German enemies list. Persons with mental or physical diseases and conditions thought to be inherited, like epilepsy, blindness, and deafness, were looked upon as a threat to the future health of the German people. The Nazis forced the sterilization of these mostly Aryan victims in an attempt to clear their genes out of the German gene pool.[1]

An "Aryans only" policy was set up restricting Jewish (or part-Jewish) and Gypsy athletes from being members of sports clubs or from using facilities such as gyms, playing fields, tracks, tennis courts and swimming pools, and, as a result, effectively excluding them from opportunities to practice for competition or compete in qualifying trials. In time, non-Aryans were cut from all German teams. Some were top-ranked athletes who could have won medals for Germany. In some cases they left Germany to compete for other countries' teams.

The ideal of international goodwill was a large part of what the Olympic organizers were publicly promoting. But the Nazi regime had no interest in that. (They were actually laying plans for taking over control of Europe at the time.) They did, however, have an interest in acquiring money, and foreign currencies especially, valuable particularly during the times of an ongoing worldwide depression. International events like expositions, world's fairs, and Olympiads usually turned out to be profitable to the host. They hoped to take advantage of that. But the Nazis had a greater overriding interest in hosting the games than just acquiring capital. The presentation of the Olympics would be used to glorify Hitler, the Nazi Party, and the German people. The Olympic Games were a perfect opportunity for the regime of Hitler and his Nazis to demonstrate to the rest of the world that Germany was a shining example of the modern state, that the government was efficient and popular with the people and not to be feared. Spectacular facilities for the games would enable the Germans to show off their talents in architecture and construction. Careful control would be cast over every aspect of the Olympic experience. Under the strict watch of the Nazi secret police, the visiting foreign journalists would spread the word around the world of the glories of Germany, its government, its athletes, and its people. Although not clearly acknowledged at the time, newspaper reports of Olympic events were screened and negative accounts of the German government were censored. Only positive accounts of the Nazi regime were approved for release back to the readers of foreign newspapers. The plan to orchestrate images and events to sway the foreign journalists to write favorably of the host country was very carefully developed and considered most important to Germany.

Because of the political climate in Germany in the 1930s, some people in the United States attempted to oppose any U.S. participation in the Olympic Games if they were held in Germany. A boycott was proposed. Supporters of the boycott, including some of the athletes, publicly decried the treatment of Jews and others inside Germany, and tried to ring an alarm concerning the

German army's increase in size and armament buildup. There was some official denial that these conditions prevailed. Opposition to the Berlin Games found pockets of support in Spain, France, England, Canada, Holland, Sweden, and Czechoslovakia. Alternative games were proposed and some athletes were unsure which course to take.

Under the strong guidance of Avery Brundage, the U.S. Olympic Committee was dead set against any cancellation of the games for any political reasons. Their position was that sports would bring antagonistic nations together in harmony, or at least it could lead in that direction. At the very least, battles for glory should be engaged on the playing field, not the battlefield. Partly in an attempt to bolster the committee's position against a boycott, Germany suddenly began to ease some of its restrictions against Jewish athletes, and toned down some of its most outlandish newspapers devoted to ridiculing and deriding Jews. One well-publicized episode involved the German fencing champion, Helene Mayer. She was a gold medal winner at the Amsterdam games of 1928, and in both 1929 and 1931 she won world championships. At the time she was arguably the number one female fencer in the world, and had represented her country, Germany, proudly and with much patriotism. Indeed Helene Mayer looked the "Aryan" part with her blond hair and tall figure.[2] She had remained in America following the Los Angeles Olympics, where she finished with disappointing results, due to her having health issues at that time. She enrolled in law school. She was intent on competing in Berlin as a part of Germany's fencing team as she had done in the two previous Olympics. But in 1933, she was astonished to learn that her membership had been voided from the Offenbach Fencing Club, which meant she would not be eligible to compete. The reason for her expulsion was that her father was Jewish. Her mother's Christianity made no relevant difference. Taking advantage of the situation as part of a ploy to remove the tarnish from their image and to strangle the Olympic boycott movement, the Germans publicly announced her reinstatement, inviting her once more to be a part of the German Olympic fencing team. She declared her acceptance in late 1935. In this case and in others, Germany successfully was able to paint a picture of an improved political climate, and effectively vanquished the boycott movement.

The day before Farrington and Brown sailed to New York City on their way to the Olympic Games, Ellison Brown had very important personal business to take care of—he had to formally make Ethel Wilcox his fiancée. Ethel cannot remember a time when she did not know Ellison Brown. He behaved brashly in their childhood days, once yanking a red-and-green necklace off her neck because he didn't like it. He would often act up around her, teasing her. When Ellison was given the Narragansett name Deerfoot in a tribal ceremony, Ethel was christened Morning Star. For a time their families lived next door to each other. The Browns had a dog named Teddy. Teddy was so well-trained and bright it seemed as if Tarzan could converse intelligibly with him. According to Ethel, Ellison could tell the dog to get some butter, and Teddy would enter the Wilcox family's kitchen, find the butter, and obediently bring some back to his master next door. On one occasion, Ethel got angry at that kind of pilfering teamwork and she threw a can of soup, the nearest item at hand, at the laughing Ellison, the man who put the dog up to the crime. She grew angrier and threw a few more cans. Ellison (and Teddy) gladly caught the unopened cans she pitched at them, and the two shared a meal from the contents with conspiratorial glee. Close to seventy years later, she could laugh about it.[3]

In 1934, Ethel's father passed away. Ellison's mother took ill; the following spring, she passed away. After that, Ethel recalled that her relationship with Ellison changed dramatically; they stopped "fighting." He started calling her by the shortened nickname "Et" with affection, and the affection grew.

Ethel and Ellison spent the warm summer evening of July 13, 1936, together on a Charlestown beach. Ellison lit a fire in the sand, legal in those days, and the couple cooked hot dogs and shared soda pop — picnic fare.[4] Their talking and laughing, the sounds couples make when together, could barely be heard above the sounds of the waves breaking upon the shore. Ethel and Ellison looked out in the direction he would soon be sailing. After a while they stood together silently, looking into each others' eyes, enjoying the slight ocean breeze on an otherwise hot and humid July evening. Things momentarily got solemn as Ellison addressed Ethel with a request. Ellison Brown asked the beautiful Narragansett young woman if she would be his loving wife. Ethel answered that she would. They discussed marrying later in the fall, after the excitement of the Olympics and the rest of the running season was over.

The day after he proposed to Ethel, Ellison "Tarzan" Brown and his trainer, Jack Farrington, traveled by boat from Providence, Rhode Island, to the harbor of New York City. This was the first sea leg of the trip — destination: Berlin, Germany. Brown had never journeyed by boat before but did not suffer any seasickness. In fact he thoroughly enjoyed the voyage. He told his trainer, "This is better than riding in an automobile. It is even better than running."[5]

The athletes' fares were paid by contributions collected by the U.S. Olympic Committee. Jack Farrington's ticket was another matter. His fare, $250, was raised by donations from a fund drive sponsored by the chamber of commerce in Westerly, Rhode Island, which proudly contributed the first $50 itself. In the midst of the Great Depression, raising this amount of money might have seemed like an inordinate task, yet it was reported to have been easy.[6] The townspeople had high hopes for their local hero, Tarzan Brown, and wanted to insure that his trainer accompany the young runner all the way to Germany for the following reasons. First, they wanted to be certain that he got to Berlin safely. Farrington could be relied upon to do that. Second, there was the likelihood that young Ellison would develop a severe case of homesickness. He had never been far from home, certainly not a continent away, separated from his friends, family, and the familiar ways and customs of the Narragansett tribe. There was a feeling expressed by "supporters of the Indian" (whomever that designation was purported to represent) that Tarzan might "fail to respond to the companionship of other members of the Olympic team."[7] The U.S. team was comprised of white and black athletes, but Ellison Brown was the only Native American to make the team. Interestingly enough, though, reported at the very same time was the prospect that Brown's "simplicity and his style are expected to make him one of the favorites of the Olympic representatives."[8] Certainly he was well regarded by the athletic community following his dynamic B. A. A. Marathon win three months earlier. Moreover, as the first choice for selection on the American marathon squad, his abilities were very well respected. A third reason why people wanted Farrington there with Tarzan was an obvious but crucial one: as trainer, his expertise would enable the young athlete to achieve the primary goal of the trip: winning the first-place medal. There was little doubt Ellison needed Farrington for coaching, providing a game plan, negotiating the German language, avoiding Nazi harassment, and ultimately, achieving success.

In New York City, some members of the U.S. Olympic team, including Ellison Brown, stayed at the Hotel Lincoln. Most teammates spent the few days in the city meeting each other, exercising, sightseeing, preparing for the time at sea, and anticipating the thrill that awaited them in Berlin. There were 384 athletes and 87 officials selected for the summer Olympics.[9] They were issued Olympic identification cards which were recognized from the day they boarded the ocean liner, the S.S. *Manhattan*, until the last day of August.[10] They were not required to carry passports. From New York City, Jack Farrington sent a note home to Westerly, Rhode Island, in care of the local newspaper, the *Westerly Sun*, to print so everyone could read it. It said:

> The boy sure enjoyed himself on the New York boat Sunday. He sure is in good shape. His short distance running is faster than when he trained in Boston. I want to get his weight down a bit. We sail Wednesday noon. Tell our friends in Westerly we thank them. We will do our part, they did theirs.[11]

On a scorching hot Wednesday, July 15, 1936, eight hundred passengers boarded the S.S. *Manhattan*, bound for Germany and the XIth Olympiad, with 383 Olympic athletes and officials among them.[12] Jock Semple wrote nearly fifty years later:

> I remember the day he [Brown] left with the Olympic team in 1936. He went down to the boat and began climbing up on the smokestack. I asked him why he did that. He said he wanted to see Germany. He didn't believe the boat could go there unless he could see the other side of the ocean first.[13]

The ship departed with much fanfare and excitement. They sailed for nine days, smoothly, according to reports. On board the ship, the athletes were able to do some training to keep in shape. "Most of us jogged on deck, but it was dangerous," Johnny Kelley recalled. "I always worried the ship might roll and I'd turn an ankle. But I did it just the same."[14]

Farrington and other personal trainers discovered that there were cumbersome restrictions put in place by the Olympic committee that strained their abilities to perform their roles of assistance to their respective Olympians. Farrington, for instance, was not permitted to eat at the table with Brown. This made it difficult for him to monitor Brown's food intake, an integral part of his training method. Newspaper correspondent Bill Cunningham, on the *Manhattan* with the U.S. team, observed that although evidently not "the worrying sort," Tarzan Brown was concerned "about his lack of control at the dinner table" and about his own inability to lay off those food items which had been temporarily restricted by Farrington's training regimen. Wrote Cunningham:

> Mr. Farrington, in normal times, sits by Mr. Brown, slapping such victuals as the Tarzan shouldn't eat out of his hand. I was on the boat when the Tarzan, almost with tears in his voice, confessed to Mr. Farrington that he had eaten three pickles and had washed them down with a glass of sweet milk. He knew it wasn't right. He just couldn't help it, he said.[15]

Johnny Kelley enjoyed the voyage over the Atlantic. He later would recall with fondness the climate on board that enabled a special bonding amongst the United States teammates. Kelley remembered:

> We went on the slow boat and we became one big, happy family. We put on shows for the whole boat. I sang some songs, and this shotputter, he did magic tricks. It was really something. When you'd walk into the dining hall, you'd be walking into a hall filled with champions.[16]

Another Kelley recollection of the trip, included in *Young At Heart*, gave this glimpse of Brown:

> We had a great time going over on the boat. Glenn Cunningham, the famous mile runner, was on the boat with us. Tarzan had brought an Indian headdress with him, so one day Cunningham went over and said, 'Hey Tarz, can I pose with you?' He put his arm around Tarzan and posed for pictures. Tarzan was the proudest guy on the boat.[17]

The *Manhattan* arrived in Hamburg, Germany, early on July 24. Formal official ceremonies greeted the athletes. They then boarded trains to Berlin. More official ceremonies met them in Berlin. The U.S. athletic contingent continued to travel by buses the dozen miles more to the Olympic village in Döberitz, a complex of 160 houses constructed of brick and stucco built especially for the international athletes on 139 acres partially in a birch forest near a few small lakes. More ceremonies still—"genial speeches, band music, and even a corridor of torch-bearing German youths" awaited the weary travelers.[18] It was at this juncture that Ellison Brown and his trainer, Jack Farrington, were separated, for Brown was housed with the athletes in the Olympic Village and Farrington was left to stay in Berlin.

It did not take long for the American athletes to settle into their new abode. Getting acclimated to the new surroundings took place under inclement weather conditions. Lots of rain and chilly temperatures marred the first week, causing muddy tracks and grounds, limiting some outdoor athletic training. Arthur Daley of the *New York Times* reported that the adverse weather conditions affected the Japanese athletes "even more than the Americans," but that they were "in far better condition because they have [had] a five-week advantage on the Americans, having been in Berlin that much longer."[19]

Daley reported on Brown's reaction to his new surroundings after having been in the athletes' village just three days. Wrote Daley, "The Olympic Village is such an impressive spot that Tarzan Brown, the Narragansett Indian marathoner, complained today that he was tired of staying in 'Berlin City' and wanted to get away from all such luxury and settle down in a 'village.'"[20] This iconoclastic entry about Brown (submerged, as it were, in the midst of an article evaluating the American swimming team's chances in contrast to those of the Japanese team's) is not altogether clear. The *Times*' correspondent may have simply detected a bit of homesickness on Tarzan's part; no doubt there had to be some. The alleged complaint, though, suggests that Brown may have experienced a certain amount of cabin fever, or restlessness, the result of staying put for three days in an unfamiliar place, without adequate opportunity to roam freely outside the village, unable to move about as he naturally had done his whole life. Access at this point may have been tightly restricted. Living under that kind of imposed restriction would have taken some getting used to. But there may be more to the quoted passage than that. If Daley's implication was that Brown would have been more at home in a native village rather than in a thoroughly modern urban setting, the passage may have revealed the writer's snobbish sensibilities and a lack of insight to some considerable degree; or, obversely perhaps, Daley may have very perceptively recognized the uniqueness of Brown and Brown's own natural preferences concerning his surroundings, preferences bolstered by a values system that would choose village over city. But, regardless of how Daley interpreted Brown's feelings, Ellison Brown was unquestionably a long way from home, a world away from the familiar rural, sparsely populated Rhode Island landscape he had known all his life.

Many of the sportswriters in Berlin to report on the Olympics, American ones included, sent features back home for the entertainment value or the educational benefit of their readers, often providing local color or foreign detail useful for conveying a more complete picture of the goings-on, especially in an era without television. Some items were unusual. For example, one of correspondent Frederick Birchall's dispatches to the *New York Times* addressed "the suspicion frequently voiced by Germans in private that some women athletes are really disguised men," and how a doctor was officially engaged to examine the private selective areas of those athletes whose publicly observable areas cast some doubt about his or her gender. Birchall included a piece about Ellison Brown, an athlete who obviously caught the reporter's attention. Birchall observed:

> Tarzan Brown, the lone Indian member of the American track and field team, has turned Hungarian. Tarzan was strolling around the Olympic Village yesterday in a new outfit. He wore a red, white and green striped jersey in which the Hungarians appeared in the track events, topping off this outfit with a feathered Tyrolean hat.[21]

Brown's sartorial appearance, particularly the mismatch of the traditional Hungarian print with the green hat native to the Austrian Alps, must have made an undeniable impression. For a young man who stood out in a crowd without trying, the vivid stripes and large side feather atop his head pointing skyward added considerably to his being noticed, and furnished an engaging introduction to his immensely playful persona.

Speculation in the American newspapers, in barbershops, in beauty parlors, in schools, in parks, in neighborhood bars—in fact, any place American citizens congregated—could be heard in the days preceding the official start of the Olympic Games. Americans were counting on the U.S. team to win a large share of the medals. The U.S. track and field squad, which included the extraordinary athlete Jesse Owens, provided especially high expectations of victories. The *New York Times* boasted that "the United States still ranked as the No. 1 power in track and field, the strongest numerically of the fifty-two nations and the strongest athletically as well."[22] It went on to presumptuously posit that "eight of the twenty-one individual championships may be reasonably allotted to America *in advance* [emphasis added], with eleven more uncertain and only two definitely beyond our reach. Those two are the javelin throw and the triple jump."[23] The marathon was squarely placed in the "uncertain" category, considered "absolutely unpredictable."[24] But it was pointed out that this year's marathoners (and walkers) were younger in age than previous teams, and that that factor could be a plus. Ellison "Tarzan" Brown was a ripe twenty-two years. The durable Johnny Kelley was twenty-eight. William McMahon's age was twenty-six, and alternate Mel Porter was the eldest at thirty-one.

Arthur Duffey, in the *Boston Post*, proudly touted the marathon team.

> The selection of Kelley, Brown and McMahon unquestionably represents the real Marathon strength of the country. No other runners have established a better record for speed, stamina and consistency. A glimpse into their records

proves that they are entitled to the award [selection to the U. S. team] and it is not beyond the pale of reasoning to think that one or the other may be first to cross the finish line in Berlin.[25]

When it reported that "The United States has three strong runners," the *Boston Globe* divulged its local bias, seeing that two of the three men were Massachusetts residents and also two of the three were the 1935 and the 1936 Boston Marathon winners. But, in sober assessment of the marathon at hand, it was compelled to overlook its local favorites, telling its readers that "the race generally is conceded to be fought out among Japanese and Finnish challengers of Argentina's champion, Juan Carlos Zabala, who has been training in Germany for five months and is primed to become the first Marathon repeater."[26]

The *Boston Post* saw it this way:

The British claim they have a sure winner in either Morris or Robertson. The Americans fear Son, a Jap with plenty of stamina; Coleman of South Africa, and Muinonen, a Finn, but Paavo Nurmi, coach of the Finns, says his charges are no good and selects Kelley to win the event.[27]

Arthur Duffy led off his *Arthur Duffey's Sports Comment* column with the words "I'M TELLING YOU" in uppercase type, followed by this noncommittal prediction: "If Ellison Brown, the Narragansett Indian, wins the Olympic Marathon today I won't be surprised a bit."[28] A paragraph later, he offered this candid assessment:

Brown, even though he probably was the most quickly forgotten B. A. A. Marathon winner we ever had, is a natural plodder, and, if he can stand the cobblestone course at Berlin, there is no reason why he shouldn't win. I saw "Tarzan" go over that Hopkinton to Boston course last April 20, and he is like a machine. Nothing bothers him, he's young and strong, and he loves to run. He may be our first Olympic victor since Johnny Hayes.[29]

Ellison Brown himself was very optimistic of his own prospects for winning. Looking back, he wrote:

Everything looked very bright going across to Germany on the *Manhattan*. I didn't get seasick and I was sure all the time that I was going to bring the title back to the United States.[30]

12

"Running for Uncle Sam"— 1936

Fifty-six[1] runners comprised the field on the afternoon of August 9, 1936. The weather, crucial to marathon runs, was uncomfortably hot and brightly sunny, around 71° F. The course began at the Olympic stadium, went through an underground passage under the stands out to the city streets, along the Havel River, past open-air beer gardens, and extended twelve miles until it reached the Avus racetrack. This was the halfway mark (at approximately 21K). The second half of the route was the return trip back to the finish line tape inside the stadium. Most of the course surface was hard macadam road. A reported 110,000 spectators were on hand at the stadium that hot August afternoon to watch the starting line excitement, and see the competitors run 750 meters around the cinder track inside the stadium (one and three-quarters laps) before making their way into the shaded tunnel that led outside the stadium. The sell-out crowd remained in the stadium to witness the reentry into the stadium of the runners as they emerged from the dark, sunless tunnel into the brightly sunlit stadium, making their way toward the finish line. In addition, more than a million other spectators lined the route to get two looks at the marathoners in action, literally going and coming.

At the start, the Olympic marathon title and record holder from the Los Angeles games, Juan Carlos Zabala of Argentina, wearing his famous white handkerchief on his head, led the field of runners on its way into the tunnel and out the stadium confines. With his rapid pace Zabala was setting time records at the three-, six-, ten- and even at the twenty-five-kilometer stations. At six kilometers, second place belonged to the Portuguese runner, Manoel Dias. Next, but not too close, were two runners who appeared to be conversing as they ran nearly side by side. They were the oldest contestant, British-born Ernest Harper, and Korean-born Son Kee-chung running as Kitei Son for Japan. Two Finnish runners followed, also running nearly side by side and most certainly talking.

By the ten-kilometer mark (almost one-quarter of the way) Ellison

Brown had managed to pass Harper and Son to claim third place. Zabala was still in front, followed by Dias. Now behind Brown were Harper, Son, the two Finns, and the rest of the field.

At fifteen kilometers, Juan Carlos Zabala was one hundred seconds ahead of Dias. Kitei Son and Ernest Harper had caught up to Brown and passed him. The twenty-two-year-old Korean and the thirty-five-year-old Englishman were now third and fourth. They were only thirty seconds behind the thirty-one-year-old Dias and incrementally closing the gap. Tarzan Brown was fifth, with Thore Enochsson, a twenty-seven-year-old runner from Sweden, next. A South African, Johannes Coleman, trailed Enochsson.

At the halfway mark, it was still Zabala, Son, Harper, Enochsson and Coleman, as Dias faded under the grueling pace and heat. The leaders reached the turnaround point of the Avus speedway and began the second half of the run, seeing, approaching and passing other contestants still completing their first half of the marathon. Brown had slipped behind, but started to regain his lost ground. At 25K, the first three positions remained unchanged, but Ellison Brown had retaken fourth place ahead of Coleman, Enochsson and Dias.

The 28-kilometer mark saw the undoing of two runners, Zabala and Brown. Zabala dropped to third behind Son and Harper, becoming sick to his stomach. He tripped and fell. He managed to get up and resume his running, but had lost crucial seconds as Son and Harper took advantage and surpassed the Argentine. Shortly before the 32K mark, Zabala had begun to walk, and was forced to sit. At 32 kilometers he dropped completely out of the running.

Tarzan Brown suffered a very severe cramp, located in the back of his right thigh. In a letter from John Farrington to the *Westerly Sun*, Farrington wrote, "His legs became knotted at this point (with eight miles to go) and a doctor forbid him to continue."[2] The *Sun* relayed to its readers a dispatch from Bill Cunningham of the *Boston Post*, in Berlin at the time, who elaborated on Farrington's terse description:

> It was the back of Tarzan's right thigh that got him. It knotted up so tightly that he could no longer move the leg. He stopped and was trying to rub it when a doctor came up — an official doctor.
> "Do you want me to rub that out for you?" asked the doctor. Tarzan said, "Yes."
> "If I do," said the doctor, "you can't start over. I'll be glad to do it for you, but you'll have to stop running."
> Tarzan isn't used to making important decisions and Farrington wasn't there. He took one look at the three leaders. They were bunched and no more than 50 yards ahead when he stopped.
> "Go ahead and rub it out," he said, "I can't run on it nohow the way it is." That wound up the Tarzan.[3]

A different slant on what happened, in an account by Brown, was written some years later by Jerry Nason:

They said I quit in the Berlin Olympics that summer. It wasn't true! I got disqualified at 18 miles because I stopped to rub out a cramped muscle and some
spectator helped me. This official with his big badge came up in a car just
then. He yelled, "You're disqualified! You got assistance. It's against the rules!"
    I didn't know then it was a rule, but later I found out it was. Anyway, there
was no point in finishing the race if I was disqualified.[4]

    Brown was observed by John Kelley, who had developed serious foot
blisters around the 16K mark. Running quite a distance behind the leaders
(he eventually finished 18th), Kelley passed by the spot where Ellison Brown
had stopped running. Kelley recalled:

    I remember seeing Tarzan Brown along the way. He was leaning against a tree
    with some German soldiers. He saw me coming and said, "Too tough, too
    tough."[5]

On another occasion, Kelley recollected the moment slightly differently: "'Too
tough for me today,' he said as I went by."[6]
    The Olympic marathon turned out this way: By the 33K mark (just over
three-fourths of the distance) the leader, Son, began to open up some room
between himself and the second-placed Harper. Two Finns, Vainö Muinonen
and Erkki Tamilia, now followed. Another Korean running for the Japanese
team, Shoryu Nan, surged from tenth place at 31K, to seventh place at 33K,
to third place at 35K. Nan would hold on for the more than seven kilometers
left to finish third. By the 37th kilometer, Son had a one-minute lead over
Harper. Son continued strongly, "picked up another minute in the last five
kilometers and finished as fresh as the proverbial daisy," reported Arthur
Daley.[7] Somewhere before the halfway point McMahon had quietly dropped
out. Said Kelley, "I never did see Billy McMahon."[8] McMahon, Brown and
Zabala were not alone. Only thirty-six athletes finished the race.
    And what a finish it was for Kitei Son, the 120-pound Korean-born stu-
dent. His record time of 2 hours, 29 minutes and 19.2 seconds had shaved
nearly two minutes off of Zabala's previous Olympic record set in 1932. In
second place came the British miner, Ernest Harper, two minutes, forty seconds and nearly 600 yards behind the victor, with a time of 2 hours, 31 minutes, 23.1 seconds. Harper's time, it should be pointed out, also broke Zabala's
previous record (2:31:36.0, by 12.9 seconds). Directly behind Harper came the
third-place winner, Shoryu Nan, with a time of 2:31:42.
    Of the three American runners, only Johnny Kelley managed to finish.
He recalled, "I finished eighteenth, which is no great shakes on my part, but
I gave it everything I had. I told my father and brothers I'd finish if I had to
walk in."[9]
    After the race, a matter-of-fact Son credited the British miner Ernest
Harper with helping him win the marathon. While matching strides alongside Harper, the blond-haired Harper apparently indicated to Son that the

Argentine front-runner, Zabala, would burn out at the pace he was setting in due time. This information evidently enabled Son to concentrate on his own performance and eventually it paid off for him.

Both Son (Son Kee-chung) and Nan (Nam Sung-yong), twenty-two and twenty-four years of age respectively, were Koreans who had spent their entire lives living in a country occupied by the militant Japan, which had ruled Korea since annexing it in 1910, after occupying the peninsula following the Russo-Japanese war. Neither Son nor Nan was proud to wear the rising sun symbol of his nation's occupiers on his jersey. Rather they were shamed and outraged. Son tried to draw attention to his nation's plight at every opportunity. Son signed his Korean name in Korean whenever called upon to write his signature. Next to his name he would draw a map of his native Korea. In the next decade he would play a role as a leader for Korean independence from Japan, and later on he became a track coach to teams proudly displaying the Korean national flag and colors.

John Kelley had this to say about Son: "It's a funny thing that the winner, Son, and I have become great pals in the village, and since an American couldn't win I am delighted he got it. He's a great kid and I can't wait to offer him my sincerest congratulations."[10]

What about John Kelley's efforts? His time of 2 hours, 49 minutes, 32.4 seconds placed him eighteenth overall, twenty minutes behind the winner, but he was the only American to finish. At the start Kelley found the going as he anticipated. After four miles, however, his impression drastically altered. He explained:

> I thought I had doped the race right and would set my own pace, but we hadn't gone five miles until I saw that Zabala and the rest were faster than I figured which forced me to put on extra steam too. When I tried to, I suddenly discovered that I could not get going. From the five to the 10 mile mark I gave it as much fight as I could and felt I was well placed and then I felt blisters forming on my right foot and it wasn't long before I was in very real agony.[11]

Kelley continued: "I must have stopped and walked 20 times and if it had been any other race but the Olympics I would have quit."[12] Patriotism played a role in keeping Kelley in the race despite much anguish. When he considered giving up, he considered his participation as an obligation. "I felt that since I had the honor of representing the United States it was up to me to finish even if I had to cross the line on my hands and knees."[13] He also said:

> It was just one of those days when everything went wrong. This isn't any alibi. We lost because the other boys were too fast, but even so everything seemed to go wrong for me. The day was blazing hot and my suit was too thick. After I got to running I knew what Tarzan Brown meant when he said "his shirt itched him."[14]

The runners' official jerseys were woolen, not fabricated from lighter, cooler cotton. They were not only hot but heavy, especially as they became soaked with perspiration. "Those shirts were like sandpaper," Kelley remembered years later. "On a hot day they chafed you all over."[15] Kelley's skin became seriously abraded and bloodied. "They rubbed my whole chest raw and my nipples were bleeding at the end," he recalled.[16] It was very painful. "Tarzan didn't want to wear his, but I was patriotic and I wanted to. Boy they were terrible."[17] Brown chose to run without the added burden.

Speaking of Tarzan Brown, his sheer formidable talent and surprising lack of success that hot August afternoon fueled much speculation as to "what really happened" in Berlin to cause his failure to win, let alone finish. This was the first instance of Brown failing to complete a race from beginning to end. "It marked the first time since he started to run that he was forced to surrender before the tape was reached," reported the *Westerly Sun*,[18] and it went on to offer the earliest explanation as to why. On the day after the marathon the *Sun* suggested that Brown had suffered an injury during training on Friday, two days before the race. The *Westerly Sun* reported: "The Westerly Indian strained the heel muscles in both legs while engaging in an informal match with one of the United States walking stars. The peculiar stride, used by walkers, moving along stiff-legged and jogging from the ball of the foot onto the heel is a considerable strain and injurious to persons not familiar with the walk."[19] It turned out not to be the case. Ellison did pull a ligament during training, roughly a week before race day. But that was neither an injury to his heel nor connected with any workout with the walking athletes. And, in any event, a heel injury as so described could not adequately explain how Brown had managed to run so well over the first half of the course.

Another explanation was sought. The very next edition of the paper displayed this front page headline: "Bath Blamed For Defeat. 'Tarzan' Brown Took One Before Race; McMahon Went Swimming." The article follows:

America's Marathon runners probably are wondering whether they traded Olympic gold medals for a bath.

It was disclosed today that … Brown got the idea that a hot bath (as hot as he could possibly stand it) would help him along the 26 mile path to glory. He had one just before starting Sunday's grilling [*sic*] race.

Meanwhile, William McMahon of Worcester, Mass. was seen listlessly breast stroking up and down the pool in the Olympic village to cool off before the run made him feel warm. Neither of them managed to finish the race.

This may offer an explanation of why the star spangled Marathoners failed to capture the Olympic crown.

Both Brown and McMahon were surprised when they felt worn out after this procedure.[20]

The "bath theory" has never been substantiated, and seems, on the face of it, to be rather absurd. Brown and McMahon both took advantage of swimming facilities in the days before the marathon. Kelley reported that one morning he saw Brown returning to the Olympic village while Kelley was on his way to breakfast. Kelley asked Brown, "'Where you been?' and he just kind of grunted and dove in the swimming pool."[21] Use of the swimming pool by the athletes was not uncommon, to be sure. To suggest that such water exercise would contribute to the detriment of either runner, Brown or McMahon, is farfetched.

A hint of a more sinister scenario, however, is embedded within Kelley's observation related above, with the suggestion that Brown was not in the Olympic village until the morning breakfast hour. Jock Semple, in his book *Just Call Me Jock*, wrote the following account of Brown's experience in Berlin. (The first paragraph is Semple's quotation of *Boston Globe* sportswriter Jerry Nason's words):

> When he was in Berlin in the 1936 Olympics just about all the Americans thought the Indian would make hash of the Japanese and the rest in the big Marathon race. Tarzan had a fondness for German beer, however, and on top of that he got into trouble. He picked on a couple of Nazi blackshirts and rapped together a couple of their heads.
> ... Tarzan only made the Olympic race after the Americans sprung him from jail following his fight with the Nazis. Asked why he got into a fight with them, he told me one time, "I didn't like them."[22]

Ellison Brown's great-nephew, John Christian Hopkins, writes for the *Westerly Sun*. In 1999, well over a half century after the Berlin Olympics, Hopkins wrote a tribute piece about Tarzan Brown for the newspaper. In it, he wrote the following:

> My father, the late John A. Hopkins Sr., said Brown told him ... Brown spent two days in jail, following a scuffle in a German beer hall. He barely got out in time for the race.
> He told my father he had a visitor in the jail warning him not to win the Olympic marathon.[23]

Beer drinking, fighting, being jailed, being released in time for the Olympic marathon, and intimidation — each component of this twentieth-century legend requires closer examination.

Consider the beer-drinking scenario. In later years, Ellison Brown abused alcohol, but the focus here is that narrow window of time in July and August 1936 while a member of the U.S. Olympic team. The U.S. athletes were under strict and clearly stated directives to "refrain from smoking and the use of intoxicating drinks and other forms of dissipation while in training,"[24] all spelled out in a handbook especially made up for each team member. By itself this may not have meant much.

But an incident occurred while sailing on the *Manhattan* that received

much publicity amongst the athletes and the American public at large. The
world recordholder in the backstroke for women at that time was Eleanor
Holm Jarrett, a member of two previous U.S. Olympic teams, and a team
member again in 1936. It was widely considered a done deal that she would
win the gold medal in Berlin, for the talented swimmer had not lost a race
in seven years. Many predicted that she would break the current record which
she had set. Her performance at the Los Angeles Olympics in 1932 winning
the gold medal for the 100-meter backstroke had made her very well known.
But beyond the celebrity she garnered as a successful athlete, she was additionally a celebrity of the stage and screen. Hollywood and the swimming star
took full advantage of the publicity shots featuring Eleanor Holm (not yet
Jarrett) in her competitive athletic garb, namely her swimsuits. In 1933 she
married a big-time singer and bandleader, Art Jarrett. Eleanor would often
tour with her husband as a guest singer. A woman with Hollywood trappings,
she was one who enjoyed the nightlife and the spotlight.

Eleanor Holm Jarrett was an older and "eminently worldly"[25] woman of
experience compared with the other younger women athletes on the 1936
team. During the voyage to Berlin, there were numerous occasions when she
was carousing at the bars onboard and reportedly inebriated on champagne.
The first incident, just two days into the voyage, occurred when she was
invited to the first-class deck for an all-night party with sportswriters and
revelers. Her drinking and conduct earned her an initial warning from the
Olympic committee members aboard. "Then during a stopover in Cherbourg,
France, she won a couple of hundred dollars playing dice with sportswriters
aboard the ship during the afternoon. That night, she attended another party
with them."[26] She was given warnings to adjust her deportment, but continued to party and publicly badmouthed the committee's rules and derided
their authoritative posture. She may have felt unduly singled out for she
always "maintained that many of her fellow athletes had also been drinking
on the voyage,"[27] a claim never corroborated nor contradicted.

One night after much partying, Jarrett accidentally crashed through the
cabin door of a matronly chaperone of the women swimmers on the way back
to her own cabin. The chaperone called the main deck, summoning the ship's
medical personnel. That was the last straw. Avery Brundage, the man in charge
of the U.S. team, under perceived pressure felt forced to hold an emergency
committee meeting on ship, which voted to suspend Jarrett from the swimming team. The decision was announced the day the ship reached Hamburg.
Newspaper reports enabled the country back home to follow every legal
maneuver that followed, the public and the sportswriters heavily supporting
the swimmer against what was seen as a drastically harsh penalty. Most of
the other athletes had sided with her as well, and petitions were drafted for
reconsideration but to no avail. Her suspension was not revoked. Yet Eleanor
Jarrett stayed on in Berlin. She attended the Olympics as a newly hired cor-

respondent for the International News Service[28] by day, and attended opulent receptions put on by Hermann Goering and other high-level German leaders by night. This infuriated Brundage. ("I was everything that Avery Brundage hated," she would recall.)[29] By an odd interpretation of the rules by the unrelenting Brundage, the last-minute employment cost her her status as an amateur and led to her ineligibility to participate in other sporting events later on.

In light of Eleanor Holm Jarrett's very public controversy, one might wonder: would a twenty-two-year-old Ellison Brown, overseas for the first time, representing the U.S. as the first selected member of the Olympic marathon team, probably knowing full well of Avery Brundage's unwavering response to the nationally famous Eleanor Jarrett, risk his participation in the race of his life for proscribed beer drinking? This is at a point during his training when he has not yet seen the marathon course, has had some adverse and strangely scary pains and unfamiliar sensations in his legs during some training drills, and has been immersed in such racist and pro-German propaganda that he wants to win the event more than ever for America and the free world.

Tippy Salimeno, a close associate and trainer of Brown although not in Berlin at the time, talked to John J. Kelley (the younger) about Brown's propensity to drink at that time: "People believe he was drinking while he was training. That is not true. Maybe he drank near the end of his career, but not from when he started in 1930 until 1940."[30] With all due respect to Salimeno, there is no possible way to affirm if his statement accurately described the behavior of his client overseas during the hot summer days of 1936. However, it was not unusual for Narragansett teens to drink beer.[31] In most parts of the world (then or now), early alcohol consumption was common; there was no legally explicit drinking age (and, by definition, therefore, no "underage drinking.") The United States has been the major exception.

Johnny A. Kelley, teammate, good friend and Olympic participant present in Berlin, has claimed that Tarzan Brown did in fact spend some time in the German beer gardens of Berlin, and has substantiated Semple's account of Brown in Berlin, although Kelley did not actually observe the altercation.[32] Whereas most of the U. S. athletes' travel was restricted to and from the athletic complex and the village where they were housed, Brown came and went from the village repeatedly, usually to meet with his trainer, Farrington. Jack Farrington, who was not officially permitted at the athletes' compound, stayed in an apartment in Berlin, not a regular destination for the American athletes who traveled between the Olympic housing village and the Olympic sports complex. There were plenty of evenings of no supervision for the Rhode Island youngster, traveling to and from Berlin in a strange environment (to say the least) of strange language, customs, and political postures. The opportunity existed for a young lad to sample some of the enticing indigenous malted beverages and appetizing culinary offerings, flavors never experienced by him in his twenty-two years of life.

Brown had the opportunity and perhaps the motive to imbibe illicit drink, risking removal from the team and perhaps greater personal humiliation than experienced by Ms. Jarrett, who always seemed to relish the publicity and public sympathy despite the punitive damages she was forced to accept.

Consider next Brown's ensuing fight with Nazi henchmen, described by Kelley as Tarzan having "got into some kind of trouble with the Police over there, in Germany."[33] Although that "kind of trouble" would have made all the newspapers, tabloids, the six and the eleven o'clock newscasts in our times, not one word of the alleged fight ever got mentioned in any of the international news reports of the Olympiad or even in subsequent reports in later years. Imagine a young Ellison Brown attempting to beat some Nazi thugs all by himself, well outnumbered. Any clash between beer-drinking Nazis and a dark-skinned, foreign young man isn't going to be a slight altercation or anything resembling a fair fight, but more likely a vigorous brawl probably involving nightsticks, blackjacks, barstools, or other objects. And if so, wouldn't Brown appear to have the body markings to show for having tried to single-handedly smarten up a company of uniformed fascists? Yet, there was no comment or mention made of anything out of the ordinary in Brown's physical appearance or condition in the final days before the marathon. Neither Jack Farrington, John Kelley, or any other teammates, not his roommate, nor his coaches—nobody apparently noticed anything different in his condition. And, if any one did so, not a single one of them reported such at the time or since. Was this fracas kept from the many sports reporters looking for a story? If Brown sported visible bruises, it must have taken a massive cover-up to keep a lid on the entire episode. Totalitarian societies do have the means and ends to control the media, both domestic and foreign.

Consider the part about being jailed. In particular, imagine an American Olympic athlete being jailed in the host city. Such an incident would create the very type of publicity the German government was trying to avoid while the eyes of the international community were cast upon it. Was the American consulate or the Olympic International Committee involved? It is conceivable that both sides could hush up any bad publicity that could be viewed as damaging or embarrassing to either party, especially in a totalitarian state in 1936, where the flow of information was under extremely tight control. A possibility is that reporters did get wind of the story, reported it, but the dispatches were prevented from leaving Berlin. A solitary reference to journalists being watched was noted in the *New York Times*.[34] An unnamed London reporter, not an American one, "alleged the copy he had written had disappeared from the box after he had been questioned about it by a stranger."[35] The journalist suggested that the foreign press was "being shadowed by secret police," and somehow his report of that fact did manage to reach his paper, The *London Daily Herald*. The *New York Times*, which characterized it as "a sensational story," offered no evidence or any further elaboration. None of the *Times'* own reporters reported on the topic, or if they did, their reports never managed to reach all the way back to the New York paper's pages.

Once back in the States, the fight and subsequent apprehension remained out of the public realm. No doubt it would have been looked upon as a major reason why Brown had to drop out of the event, and without a doubt it *would have been* the most compelling reason why such a star marathoner was unable to finish a race for the first time in his running career. On top of that, being beaten and jailed would have had to be considered an unparalleled breach of fair play and good sportsmanship. Could the U.S. Olympic Committee have condoned or accepted the occurrence of such an incident and then remained silent about it? Was the fact that Brown was a Native American and not Caucasian insignificant or not? Suppose Brown could have been, in fact, rescued from a local Berlin jail without any Olympic Committee members learning about it. What if someone aware of the incident had been able to get Brown released from his incarceration, perhaps by paying a fine for him, signing a statement (or not signing but) agreeing to deny that anything untoward happened, and promising that it wouldn't happen again — a release into the custody of some person connected with the American team under undisclosed circumstances? Again, the scenario is plausible, but another question is raised: just who would that "someone" have been?

Lastly, the intimidating visit in the jail cell: it certainly was plausible, especially in the fascist Nazi climate, but no revelations, details, or added information so far has ever come to light to support the incident. A suggestion that the late Jesse Owens possessed some knowledge of that circumstance could not be verified after his death.

Sixty years after the events in Germany took place, sportswriter Michael Madden wrote a story about Ellison Brown in the *Boston Globe*. In it, Madden wrote:

> In 1948, Brown admitting to some drinking and fighting at the Olympics, but said it happened after the marathon, not before it. "I had a jam in Berlin, Germany," he said, "and it was a day or so after I ran the Olympic marathon in '36. I got celebrating a little and some white coats tried to put me out of the place. They didn't do too good, and the next thing I knew, a half-dozen guys in black shirts were after me. I guess they took care of me."[36]

This passage by Madden raises more questions than it answers. It is the first (and only) description I have come across that puts any tussle with Nazi soldiers *after* the marathon had taken place. Though a fight after the athletic event was held would negate any explanatory value toward rationalizing Brown's poor showing, it conceivably could explain away how no one saw or reported Brown in the kind of shape that might be expected following a bruising physical encounter with uniformed Nazi thugs. The marathon took place on the final day of track and field competition. "A day or so after" that event would have been during the final week before the closing ceremony. A number of U.S. track team members had departed the Olympic Village for Cologne. It is certainly plausible that the sportswriters may have relaxed their news gathering during that last week. Some may have left the Olympic environs to travel with the track team or took a sightseeing jaunt for a number of days before the final official ceremony was scheduled to take place on August 16.

Exactly what Brown would have meant by "had a jam" and "they took care of me" is not defined or clarified with any more specificity than what is given. Madden did not provide attribution, claim or clue as to the source of the remarks from Brown.[37] To whom Brown made his 1948 admission is not stated, but it was not made directly to Michael Madden.

If Ellison Brown did have a scuffle with Nazi guardsmen (before or after the marathon), he was not the only member of the United States Olympic team to do so, nor was his incident the only one suppressed from the public's eye at the time. Louis Zamperini, a track and field runner, the University of Southern California record-setting single mile champion, and the 5,000 meters competitor in Berlin, was eighteen years of age at the time. He finished seventh in that Olympic event, and would have remained nearly invisible had he not hoisted himself up a flagpole and yanked a Nazi banner from its ropes up high. Nazi soldiers fired their weapons at him as he slid down the pole. He was not hit by their bullets. On the ground, he tried to run but could not elude the eight armed guards that apprehended him. The Nazi guards took the overpowered Zamperini into custody, and eventually he was brought before their commander, a General von Fritsch. Against expectations, the general "got him out of the difficulty by pleading it was a boy's prank."[38] Zamperini was allowed to go free and was returned to the U. S. team. Strangely, he even kept possession of the stolen flag, which for the rest of his life was one of his most prized possessions. The "rest of his life" turned out to extend for just seven years longer. Zamperini had joined the United States Army in September 1941, attaining the rank of lieutenant. He served as a decorated bombardier, stationed in the South Pacific. After his very first mission over Wake Island, he was quoted as saying, "Now I would like to return and bomb Berlin."[39] He never got the chance. Lt. Louis Zamperini was reported missing as of May 27, 1943. The AP dispatched the news during the first week of June.

The flag-snatching episode was not reported in any of the American newspapers at the time it occurred, and was not known by the public at large to have taken place. It was first publicly disclosed in reports at the time of Zamperini's disappearance, during the war. The incident has not been included in any of the historic accounts of the 1936 Olympics I have read. There may be a parallel here to Brown's apprehension and detention (if it occurred). Both athletes' incidents were not reported in the press at the time, and were quietly "handled" by the authorities without publicity. Perhaps if Brown had been killed in the war, his story too (if there was one to tell) would have been unveiled.

Brown's own admission of experiencing a severe leg cramp which forced him to quit the race is undisputed. Does it take more explanation than that to explain his inability to stay in the marathon and reach the finish line? (Even John Kelley admitted that he would have quit before the end had it not been the fact that it was the Olympics and he felt a strong patriotic obligation to finish.)

Did Brown suffer a hernia at the time? Good evidence supports this contention. *Globe* sportswriter Jerry Nason wrote:

> What Tarzan did not know then—but was to learn under perilous circumstances many weeks later—was that he competed in all three of those long events with a hernia. "Lots of times I'd been having some bad pain in the stomach during a race, but I thought it was because of something wrong I ate, so I kept on running," he revealed. "It wasn't until one day when I was out training, maybe 20 miles from Westerly, when all this pain hit me again, only this time I knew something was real bad. I was all doubled up at the side of the road when this guy in a car found me.
> "A half hour later I was on the operating table in the Westerly Hospital. I got me a strangulated hernia. I never even heard of one before, and I had been running 15, 16 races with one."[40]

In fact, it wasn't until October 28 that an emergency operation was performed.

Each athlete was given "an exhaustive physical examination" the day *before* the marathon. No adverse results were reported concerning Tarzan Brown's condition at that time. But, in his scrapbook[41] John Kelley made a reference to another physical, a quick check to which each runner was subjected on the day *of* the marathon, just before the event. Kelley mentioned that he was standing behind Brown, awaiting his own turn, when he overheard the physician asking Brown if something he was noticing had caused Brown any pain. According to Kelley, Brown retorted that whatever it was had not bothered him at all. He was told that he ought to have it looked into further, suggesting there was something that ought to be taken care of when he got back to the States. Presumably signs of the hernia were detected at that time. A similar account by Kelley was described briefly in *Young At Heart*. In that account, that Brown already had a hernia (in Berlin) was stated as a fact:

> Tarzan Brown ran the Olympic marathon with a hernia. "Tarz was just ahead of me getting his physical before the race, and the doctor told him, 'You'd better get this taken care of, son.' Tarz just said, 'Naw, doesn't bother me.'"[42]

It was Tippy Salimeno's position in 1979 "that Tarzan developed a hernia as a result of his running two marathons on successive days."[43] Those runs were in October, on the eleventh and twelfth, nearly two months *after* the Olympics of August.

As with many other contentious points in Ellison Brown's life story, even the doctor's October announcement of Brown's "strangulated hernia" operation was not sufficient to suppress rumors and alternative explanations that continually have cropped up, some even decades later. One example came to light as recently as 1995, when it was written as undisputable fact in the *Providence Journal Bulletin* that appendicitis was the cause of his cramps during 1936.[44] No confirmation of appendicitis could be verified.

A lack of proper training before the race is a plausible cause (or reason), in my view, why Brown may have suffered the sharp pain in his leg muscle that arrested him in his tracks in Berlin. He discussed it thirty years after the fact with Jerry Nason, who wrote of it nearly twenty years after that:

> Brown didn't begin training for the 1936 Olympic Marathon until his arrival in Berlin, nine days before the race. "I just loafed around all summer. Nobody told me better. If I know'd then what I know now, I would have kept on racin' those two months, keepin' sharp. But nobody told me there would be only nine days to train after we got there.
>
> "Nine days ain't enough for a big race like the Olympic. That's why I came up with a 'Charlie Horse' in one leg when I got the lead at 17, 18 miles, and figured I got this race won. I stopped, figurin' I could rub it out and get back racin' again.
>
> "That's what I was doin' when a man standin' there just watchin' the race— nice man, too—start helpin' rub that leg.
>
> "Just then is when this Olympic official comes along wearin' his big badge and he yells at me, 'You disqualified. Nobody can touch a runner during the race. That's the rule. You disqualified.'
>
> "I didn't know about that rule—and I learned about it the hard way that day. Disqualified in the Olympics! Weren't no point in runnin' any more that day."[45]

After his return from Berlin, it was Ellison Brown's stated intention to make up for his bad showing at the XIth Olympiad. He was determined to demonstrate his superior running skills to what he supposed was a disillusioned public back home. He sustained the brunt of the disappointment. "It's the biggest regret I ever had; I could have won that Olympic [marathon] in '36," he told Nason.[46] In a column in the *Westerly Sun* following his return to the States, Brown's regret was manifest. Brown wrote: "Running for Uncle Sam in the Olympic marathon gave me a great thrill but I didn't win it and I didn't even finish and I was very much disappointed. I had a good time, but because I didn't win the trip was a complete failure."[47]

The ceremony to close the XIth Olympiad took place on Sunday, August 16. United States Olympic hero and four gold medal-winner Jesse Owens, sprinter Ralph Metcalfe, and nine other American team members would miss it. They were required to leave Berlin for Cologne, Germany, on August 10. They were among a number of United States team members scheduled to further ply their athletic skills against competitors from the Continent and England, an effort designed to help recoup expenses incurred getting the athletes to the Olympics. Ellison Brown was reported to be among that first group scheduled for the track and field events in Cologne that Monday. Whether Brown actually made the trip, was able to run and actually did so is unrecorded.

On the following day, Tuesday, the U.S. athletes were scheduled to be in Prague. There they were joined by other American athletes traveling directly from Berlin. Most arrived about 4:30 in the afternoon and were expected to compete at six. Early the next morning they traveled back to Germany, this time to the city of Bochum. On the trip, Owens was painfully aware that he had no money and was unable to purchase lunch. A passenger bought the now-very famous American track star a sandwich and glass of milk. Though much appreciated, to Owens it did not feel right. The athletes were raising lots of money at the exhibitions but receiving no share of the proceeds, not even a small percentage. They received no per diems, no expense money. After competing in Bochum, Germany, Owens was scheduled to fly to London to run in the British Empire-United States Games on Saturday. Some of the other athletes traveled by land through France and by boat across the English Channel. Johnny Kelley, who had stayed behind in Berlin with his visiting father, William, and brothers Jimmy and Bill and Bill's newlywed wife, traveled to London and competed, before sailing back to the United States. Whether Brown participated is not clear.

Jesse Owens was exhausted ("so tired I felt sick to my stomach.")[48] He had lost fifteen pounds in the past two weeks under heavy competition and emotional strain. He was homesick to see his wife and child. Added to that, he had no cash in his pocket. On learning that the fund-raising tour was being extended to include at least a half dozen more track events in Sweden and Norway, he borrowed a few bucks from Larry Snyder, his friend and personal trainer. With the money he telegraphed the A. A. U. with the message:

SICK AND UNDERWEIGHT. CANNOT COMPETE IN STOCKHOLM. FAMILY WAITING FOR ME. GOING HOME. JESSE OWENS[49]

As Owens remembered, within two hours he received a reply sent by wire, informing him of his suspension from the Amateur Athletic Union and mandating that he "was never again to compete as an amateur athlete for the United States."[50] The harsh suspension effectively prohibited Owens from athletic competition anywhere. The A. A. U. was clearly miffed at his abandonment of the contracted Scandinavian exhibitions. Despite the intended pressure, Owens stuck to his decision; he quit the "post Olympic barnstorming tour" to return directly to the States.

The suspension was imposed on two distinct counts. The *Boston American* spelled out for its readers the two separate misdemeanors: "These [two counts] comprise (1) automatic suspension, for an indefinite period, for 'running out' on an agreement to compete with an American team of Olympic stars in Sweden, and (2) equally automatic suspension, for a period of one year, for publicly proclaiming his purpose to turn professional."[51]

The first count suggested that Owens and the A. A. U. had made a deal to do the barnstorming tour at some time prior to the end of the Berlin games, for if no agreement had been in place, there could be no "running out" on the deal. Owens maintained that he had never made such a commitment, nor had he signed on to such a mission. At the start of the barnstorming tour in Cologne, Germany, he was not yet aware of the upcoming Scandinavian leg. The grounds for the second count were also murky. Although much speculation about paying opportunities for Owens appeared in print at that time, Owens "denied flatly that he had [ever] signed a commercial contract [and] produced testimony to back up this assertion" in an appeal of his suspension.[52] The appeal was denied.

Avery Brundage, president of the A. A. U., president of the United States Olympic Committee and clearly the man in charge of the U. S. team in Berlin, had a considerable hand in Owens' suspension, yet, according to a report in the *Boston Herald*, as inconceivable as it may seem, publicly maintained that he "had nothing but praise for Jesse Owens."[53]

"For a time, at least, *I was the most famous person in the entire world*," Owens would write of his post-Olympic situation.[54] Even before his return to America, rumors had been circulating, and reported in some newspapers, of big-money offers from diverse members of the business and entertainment communities. One such offer, from the famous and respected radio personality Eddie Cantor, was mentioned in connection with a $40,000 deal, a huge sum in 1936. This deal was reputed to require a mere ten weeks of the athlete's time. But Owens soon discovered he was unable to cash in on the international fame he had garnered in Berlin. Promises vanished and grand offers were withdrawn from businessmen, entertainment moguls, and high rollers. The proposals turned out not to be genuine. An all-but-desperate Jesse Owens ultimately landed a position that paid and utilized his athletic acumen. He was hired to participate in exhibitions used to promote Negro baseball. Not playing the game, as he first believed he would, but running 100-yard races before the game got underway: footraces not against other men but against racehorses. "It was worse than sharecropping," he would write.[55] And, what made it even worse for Owens than the degradation implicit in the concept was the dishonesty involved.

> It was bad enough to have toppled from the Olympic heights to make my living competing with animals. But the competition wasn't even fair. No man could beat a race horse, not even for 100 yards.

Unless the race began on the man's terms, by the shooting off of a gun. A gun held very close to the horse's head. That would make the animal rear up for an instant, and take another second to come down and get into stride. Oh, that horse would be moving like a railroad train at the finish line, but it would be too late. The man — if he were the world's fastest human, anyway — would beat the horse by a handful of yards.

It made me sick. But I did it. Why did I do it? To survive — no, because I thought I had to do it in order to survive.[56]

It wasn't long before Jesse Owens decided he could no longer put up with what he felt was nightly humiliation. On a Saturday night, a half hour before the horse race was set to go, he informed the promoters that he had to quit. The threat of withholding his weekly money — admittedly pretty good money — could not and did not deter him. He tended his resignation, effective immediately. Thereafter, he lent his name to a dry cleaning business in the Cleveland area that started out hugely prosperous but by the end of 1939 ended up in dire bankruptcy. Jesse Owens was left personally responsible for an incredible $114,000.[57]

A study had been undertaken of Owens before he had left the States for Berlin. His great speed and winning methods were examined to determine why he was so able. The *New York Times* reported the results of the study, conducted by Dr. W. Montague Cobb of Howard and Western Reserve Universities. Under the headline "Owen's Speed Due to Courage and Industry, Not Racial Traits, Scientific Test Shows," the article claimed that the study

> reveals that industry, training, incentive and outstanding courage rather than physical characteristics are responsible for the young Negro sprinter's accomplishments.
>
> Dr. Cobb said a detailed physical examination of Owens has been made in the first of a number of scientific attempts to determine why some runners are so speedy.... After a preliminary examination, Dr. Cobb asserted he could not detect in the physique of Owens qualities which would stamp him as a record-breaking sprinter or jumper.... Dr. Cobb said racial difference was not a factor of speed or distance in running and jumping. He said it is conjecture that a longer heel bone, characteristic of Negroes, gives them greater leverage, but he said Owens does not have an exceptionally long heel.[58]

Jesse Owens, and by extension, every other nonwhite man of color (including Tarzan Brown) may have been gifted, but earned their athletic prizes through plain old hard work and sweat. In the thirties, that not-so-widely accepted precept was news.

Avery Brundage, on the day of his return to New York Harbor from Europe, was interviewed by the print media. Topics included Jesse Owens and Eleanor Holm Jarrett and the A. A. U. committee rulings still hugely unpopular and of continual discussion in the nation's newspapers, barbershops, beauty parlors, and bars.

Brundage defended his decision to remove swimmer and star Eleanor

Holm Jarrett from the team for what were termed "misconduct" charges. In Brundage's view, Ms. Holms got "what was coming to her." He was clearly on the defensive:

> "If you fellows," he told sleepy-eyed reporters who arose early to meet the Italian liner, *Vulcania*, "had been on that committee, you would have done the same thing. Except to say it was more than just a drink of champagne I'm not going into details. We warned her officially. We had her friends warn her of the consequences. We were as tactful as we could be but tact was useless. Stern action had to be taken. We took it."[59]

Some of the reporters were not satisfied with the breadth of this explanation and pointedly cross-examined the hard-nosed administrator further on the matter. Brundage continued, addressing and painting the decision-making process that led to the dismissal of the popular swimmer as entirely democratic rather than autocratic in nature. To reporters, Brundage

> shot back. "You may not know it but 20 of the finest amateur sportsmen of this country were on the committee that expelled her. All of them are tactful and fine men. They were at wits end. They voted unanimously for expulsion. Incidentally, I didn't vote because I was committee chairman, but if there had been a tie, I'd have voted for expulsion.[60]

Meanwhile, Eleanor Jarrett, already back in the States, was in Philadelphia, working an extremely well-paying "vaudeville engagement."[61] There she told reporters she hoped to run into Brundage. With some bravado, she asserted, "I'd sock the guy." She added a quick follow-up: "and run like the devil."[62]

13

Tarzan Brown's October Feat (and Feet)—1936

Ellison Brown was back home, back on familiar turf, and especially glad to see Ethel, the woman soon to be his bride. Brown returned to the United States emboldened with new resolve to show the world he was a winning distance runner. Wasting no time, he immediately began training for the upcoming Bridgeport Centennial Marathon, set for September 10. This would be the first competitive run for Brown since returning from overseas. With trainer Jack Farrington's assistance, Ellison worked and reworked those familiar roads throughout southeastern Rhode Island to regain the form he was unable to find in Berlin. Obstacles persisted. Along forest roads near Alton, he suffered a misadventure when he ran into a hornet's nest, receiving several painful stings. This was not a harbinger of things to come, both the runner and his trainer agreed—just the normal trials of a distance runner in the late summer.

Starting in the city of Danbury, Connecticut, and finishing just over twenty-six miles away in Seaside Park, in the city of Bridgeport, the highly competitive field of forty-five athletes included the Rhode Island star speedster Leslie Pawson, the ageless Clarence H. DeMar, U. S. Olympic team member William "Biddie" McMahon, the overlooked Olympic team alternate Mel Porter, Presentation winner Leo Giard, old "Bricklayer" Bill Kennedy, and the indomitable Jock Semple.

When the starting pistol pronounced the commencement of the road race at 1:35 p.m., Ellison Brown answered the call and set the pace, quickly moving to the fore of the fast-moving pack. For ten miles, Brown controlled the lead, marking those miles with a time a few seconds shy of an hour.

Then, Mel Porter passed Ellison Brown. Porter held the lead for the next ten miles, gaining as much as seventy-five yards over Brown and Pawson, holding down positions two and three respectively. But Brown and Pawson kept Porter within sight along the hilly course, and at Long Hill, with six miles left to go, Ellison Brown and Leslie Pawson caught up with the determined New Yorker. Over the next mile, they passed Porter by for good.

Now a dramatic four miles ensued, as Brown's powerful, rhythmic strides propelled him invariably forward, the resolute Pawson of Pawtucket "at Brown's elbow."[1] "From then on it was a hammer and tongs battle," exalted the *Boston Herald*, "with the actual result in doubt until the end."[2] With one last mile to traverse, Ellison Brown erupted with his famous power surge. That explosion — and it was all over! When he broke the tape at the finish line, Brown had managed to put four hundred yards between himself and the second-place Pawson, and two minutes and one second in elapsed time.[3] It wasn't even close, suggested the *Westerly Sun* in its subheadline: "Westerly Indian Outlasts Leslie Pawson To Win by Good Margin."[4]

Brown took the marathon with a time of 2 hours, 45 minutes, 46.4 seconds. Pawson registered 2:47:45, and the third-place struggle of Mel Porter ended at 2:52:30. Augustus Johnson was fourth, six minutes behind Porter! Leo Giard was fifth, DeMar sixth (3 hours, 6 minutes, 25 seconds), and Kennedy eleventh. Biddie McMahon, as in Berlin, was unable to finish.

Among the prizes awarded the winners was an unusual one — a new electric refrigerator. Ellison Brown won the appliance upon taking first place. Johnny Kelley, himself the recipient of a refrigerator in a race he won in Montreal (and who was not involved in the Bridgeport race), remembered, "Tarzan Brown won a refrigerator once down in Bridgeport, Connecticut, but he lived out in the woods and had no electricity, so he sold it."[5]

The reasoning in Kelley's recollection makes sense, but, according to Jerry Nason, the refrigerator was not actually sold at all. Instead it was used as a proverbial bargaining chip. Nason disclosed to his *Globe* readers, "'Tarzan' Brown won an expensive refrigerator in the Connecticut race two days before and, after pleading with Jack Farrington, his guardian angel, to be allowed to race yesterday [September 12th in Dedham, Massachusetts], offered the latter his prize."[6] If this were the case, it is unlikely Brown received any payment from Farrington for the appliance. As an A. A. U. official, Farrington was always acutely aware, especially in light of the recent suspensions of famous athletes Owens and Jarrett, of Brown's status as an amateur. Any circumstance of the runner receiving any money, even in exchange for a prize, was more than likely downplayed, discouraged, or proscribed altogether.

Did Brown have to plead with his trainer to let him compete in races scheduled to be held so close together? There is a suggestion that Farrington would not dissuade his young client from such unnecessary and grueling back-to-back exertion. Will Cloney wrote these two lines in the *Herald* following his coverage of the September 12 race in Dedham: "Brown will run again Saturday at St. John, N. B. He is being kept a little busy these days, and some track men think his schedule is somewhat heavy."[7] Cloney may have been attempting to alter what he perceived to be poor management on the part of Farrington, leading to excessive punishment on the body parts of Brown.

The Bridgeport victory behind him, Ellison Brown wasted no time delving again into the competitive mélange. Just a mere forty-eight hours after the full-length marathon in Connecticut, Brown was a late entry into the New England 15-Kilometer Championship Title Run, also known for its sponsor as the Oakdale A. C. Tercentenary Celebration Race, which took place principally in the town of Dedham, Massachusetts, September 12. This shorter race, roughly nine and a half miles, would involve a head-to-head match up with fellow Olympic teammate Johnny Kelley, the first since both men ran in Berlin, Germany. Having just outrun Pawson in Connecticut, Brown now intended to do the same to Kelley in Massachusetts. Kelley and fifty-one[8] other determined runners hoped to thwart that aspiration.

The race's 4 p.m. start was delayed almost a full hour in order to let a marching parade comprised of American Legionnaires get fully out of the way. That delay worked in Ellison Brown's favor, for it provided the time needed to officially process his entry, having arrived only a few minutes before the actual start. Arthur Duffey reported, "his entry was immediately accepted and more interest than ever was centered in the race with Kelley and Brown about to fight out their old B. A. A. and Olympic feud all over again."[9] Will Cloney described that robust enthusiasm for another Kelley-Brown contest, "the fight between the Olympians developing to such dramatic heights that the rest of the competitors were almost forgotten."[10]

An estimated 150,000 spectators viewed segments of the race. From the starting point in Oakdale Square, a group of runners including Kelley, last year's winner Andy "Hawk" Zamparelli, Walter Ray and Bill Simons both of United Shoe Machinery A. A., and Bob Campbell from Dorchester set the pace and led the pack. They "kept well bunched as they headed for Westwood."[11] Four miles in, Kelley had appropriated the front-runner position, with Simons some twenty yards back in second place. Campbell and Zamparelli were third and fourth, respectively. Ellison Brown, on the other hand, "stayed back, well back, for the first five miles, and let Kelly, Simons and Ray do the early running."[12] Tarzan Brown "was unable to loosen up," according to Nason.[13] That soon began to change.

From a position of 34th, Brown increased his tempo. This he did by "merely lengthening his stride a bit," wrote Cloney, making it sound so easy.[14] As the runners left the Dedham line heading west, Brown gained considerable ground. Into Westwood and before heading back east to Dedham, Kelley had maintained a comfortable lead, but:

> at the half way mark on Washington street, Kelley seemed to tire a bit and Simons came up and threatened him for the lead. They ran about a quarter of a mile together. Then Kelley got a good lead again as they raced down the hill.[15]

Ellison Brown, meanwhile, ran past the athletes in front of him one by one as he made an extraordinary push to the front of the pack. Cloney described it: "Through all this battle, Brown was a running machine, an expressionless stoic who just picked his feet up and set them down. He was not breathing heavily at any stage, and he scarcely developed a sweat."[16]

Zamparelli dropped out at the seven-mile mark with cramps in his legs. Brown passed Simons, and then he passed Campbell. Achieving second place, Brown relentlessly closed in on the leader, Johnny Kelley. Sportswriter Jerry Nason had to reach nearly three thousand miles from Boston to find the appropriate words to describe the action: "Brown had spotted him [Kelley] 400 yards, but when he opened the throttle, that vast gap melted like butter on a Mexico City pavement."[17] Repeatedly Kelley looked back over his shoulder, keeping mental tabulations on Brown's rapid approach. Then, with just twenty-five yards separating them, Kelley was forced to slow, then halt. He was feeling sick. He vomited. He had "nerved himself up into his sick condition," Cloney submitted.[18] Nonetheless, Brown passed Kelley and quickly built a lead, stretching it to nearly twenty yards. But Kelley had an astonishingly rapid recovery, and commenced his running ways. Within a two-hundred-yard stretch the resolute Kelley managed to catch up to the speedy, steadfast Brown. Kelley even surpassed Tarzan, but it was only momentary, as the two, running nearly shoulder to shoulder, swapped the lead back and forth.

With less than one mile left to go, the two Olympic runners were nearly even. As they turned onto Whiting Street for the final stretch to the finish line demarcated on the track at Stone Park, the final three hundred yards would determine the outcome. Ellison Brown ignited a turbocharged sprint, "going two yards for Johnny's one."[19] Wrote Nason: "Kelley met this challenge briefly, but he didn't have the hidden power of old 'Tarz.' He [Kelley] gave it everything he had. It wasn't quite enough."[20]

Ellison Brown won his second race in two days, winning this one by forty yards,[21] crossing the finish line in 51 minutes, 14 seconds (not threatening Zamparelli's time set the previous year.) Johnny Kelley finished second, his time, 51 minutes, 26 seconds, only twelve seconds behind Brown. Robert Campbell held onto third place, registering 52:11. Bill Simons took fourth place, with a time of 52:33.[22]

"Ellison Brown Is Easy Winner of Central Falls Race." This headline gave *Westerly Sun* readers the story about the race results of a ten-mile run sponsored by the James Stanton Post, American Legion of Central Falls, at Central Falls, Rhode Island, which took place in the afternoon of October 3, 1936.[23]

This event held the promise of being a veritable rematch of the contest between Ellison Brown and Leslie Pawson that transpired in Bridgeport, Connecticut, the month before, the only difference being the much shorter distance of the Central Falls course. With a strong field which included the veteran runners Clarence H. DeMar and Jock Semple, the race itself turned out, against all predictions, to be not much of a contest after all.

Over the first four miles, Brown and Pawson led the pack, running "shoulder to shoulder."[24] By mile five, the midpoint, Ellison took sole possession of the lead. He would never give it up and he never looked back. Brown crossed the finish line three-quarters of a mile and two minutes, five seconds ahead of the second-place Pawson, registering the win in fives with a time of fifty-five minutes, five seconds to Pawson's fifty-seven minutes flat. The third-place runner, Tommy Russell of Georgiaville, Rhode Island, was two minutes behind Pawson. DeMar placed sixth, his time a respectable 1 hour, 48 seconds. Jock Semple, having just recovered from a painful pulled tendon in recent weeks, came in twelfth in 1 hour, 5 minutes, 31 seconds. The previous month Semple had broken his magnificent string of nineteen consecutive years of completing every race entered. The pulled tendon had forced him to drop out for the first time. With this Central Falls run, Semple was initiating the start of a second streak.

Speaking of streaks, this win was Ellison "Brown's fourth consecutive"[25] since he returned from Berlin.

The eleventh and twelfth of October 1936 were made historic in the annals of marathon runners by Ellison Brown. In an extraordinary pair of performances, the *one* runner Brown successfully competed in *two* full marathons in *two* states (New York and New Hampshire) on *two* successive days. (Both races literally occurred within twenty-four hours.) That in itself would be one (or should I say *two*?) for the record books. Compound that with the fact that Tarzan Brown won both races!

The first of the two marathons took place in Westchester County, New York. The starting line for the course was drawn in Port Chester, where the runners assembled. They crossed into neighboring Connecticut, reaching the community of Greenwich. Making a large *U*, they then reversed direction as they headed back across the New York State line, but continued beyond Port Chester through Mamaroneck and Larchmont as far as New Rochelle, where they then turned back and returned to Port Chester. Very hilly in parts with multiple grades, this course was considered by knowledgeable observers to be a difficult one.

Among the notable entrants in competition were Baltimore's Pat Dengis; Mel Porter, listed from Newark, New Jersey; Leo Giard of Brockton, Massachusetts; and local heroes "Bricklayer" Bill Kennedy and August Johnson of Port Chester. To the sponsors' publicly expressed disappointment, the previous year's winner, Les Pawson, chose not to enter. Pawson revealed that he planned to run in the Yonkers Marathon the following month, and that it was his personal decision to run one or the other but not both.

Mayor William B. Banister set the field of fifty-two athletes on its way with a crack of the starter's pistol. Ellison Brown led the field in the early going and "set the pace the majority of the distance," reported *New York Times* sportswriter Emanuel Strauss.[26] He led until mile five. There Leo Giard assumed the position of front-runner with little discernable resistance by Brown. Giard's bid lasted but two miles as Tarzan retook the lead without visible strain. Giard's power seemed to be fading, but it was still early. For fifteen miles Brown maintained an even lope. The others followed like an obedient training squad.

The endeavor to beat Brown became the sole responsibility of Pat Dengis by default since none of the other runners appeared up to the task. But Dengis had to overcome a huge distance to do so, for he was running far behind for the entire first half. It took until the twenty-second mile mark for Dengis to get to Brown, but he did so and then installed himself as the front-runner. Dengis "continued to draw away and at one time led by 200 yards," Strauss observed.[27] But the hard pace and hilly course combined to take its toll on Dengis. He could not hold onto the lead, and Brown, who "took it all in stride,"[28] caught up to him and appropriated that front-runner spot with four miles left to go. Ellison Brown put two hundred yards[29] between himself and the second-place Dengis as Brown snapped the finish-line tape. With a recorded time of 2 hours, 36 minutes, 56.7 seconds, he had won the first of two weekend races. Pat Dengis placed second, about a half minute behind, with an official time of 2 hours, 37 minutes, 31 seconds. Although unsatisfied with his failure to come in first, Dengis could see a bright side. He was heartened to have run and completed a marathon that season without the medical matter of a bursting blood vessel recurring. (It had happened in both Olympic tryouts, in Boston and in Washington, D.C.) Mel Porter, clocked at 2:42:34, must have felt right at home with another third-place finish. Local hero August Johnson, five minutes in back of Porter, finished fourth. Giard's strong early efforts cost him, for he could manage only a seventh-place finish — his time: 2:54:32. "Bricklayer" Bill Kennedy, incidentally, finished eighteenth, with a time of 3:19:19.

Ellison Brown quickly showered, dressed, received his prizes and headed for the train station. His next destination was the Granite State — New Hampshire.

When the sixth annual Knights of Columbus Boscawen-to-Manchester marathon got underway at 10:17 a.m., Ellison Brown was there, ready to go. He had "hopped a sleeper," the *Westerly Sun* reported.[30] By riding the Pullman, Brown and Jack Farrington had deftly made workable what otherwise seemed to be an impossible plan. Rail travel from Westchester County in southeastern New York to the capital region of New Hampshire was obviously available, although how many stops, layovers, and changes the men were required to make is not known. A further complication may have been the fact that overnight it became Columbus Day, a holiday, which may have affected the train schedules. Once they got to New Hampshire there were still logistical considerations to untangle. The train carried them as far as the capital city of Concord, seventeen miles north of the city of Manchester, where the marathon's finish line was. Arriving Monday morning at the Concord train station, Farrington and Brown were still obligated to get to the race's starting point in the small town of Boscawen, eight miles to the north of where the train let them off. It is probable that they had to hitchhike the last leg of the way to Boscawen, their destination. Remarkably they were able to make all the connections necessary to complete the journey, and did so with some time to spare.

Although advertised for a 10 o'clock sharp start, the marathon commenced at 10:17 a.m. when starter Edward McCann fired the starting pistol. It was a cold October day with vigorous headwinds. A field of twenty-three runners, off with the handgun shot, attempted negotiation of "the hard hills of the Daniel Webster highway," as the *Boston Post* referred to the grade-laden course, and its very heavy vehicular traffic.[31] Brown did not lead the field, nor did he run with much intensity for most of the race, especially in the early going. The *Westerly Sun* described Brown as "a bit wan from his efforts of the previous day."[32] One member of Semple's United Shoe Machinery contingent, George Durgin[33] from Beverly, Massachusetts, arrogated the front-runner position for most of the marathon. Durgin set a pace to which all the runners seemed to acquiesce. He led by as much as a half mile during various points along the course, according to the *Manchester Leader*. Ellison Brown was biding his time, but he slowly started to gain some ground.

> At Concord the Indian was running seventh behind Kimball, Hill, Young, Pelkey, and Semple and nearly a mile behind the flying Durgin.
> Along the level airport road, Brown's light, full stride carried him past Pelkey and Semple and he caught Hill just south of Black Hill after the pack had rejoined the Daniel Webster highway. It was not until Brown and the faltering Kimball reached Pembroke academy, however, that he showed he was out to win.
> He passed the little United Shoe Machinery runner [Hill] in a burst of speed and went into second place a quarter of a mile behind Durgin. From that point into the home stretch it was only a matter of time before the relentless Indian, who looked neither to right nor left as he ran, caught up with the leader.[34]

After twenty-three miles, Ellison Brown asserted a challenge to George Durgin's hold of the lead. The *Manchester Leader* continued its coverage, focusing on what now became a veritable two-man battle with Durgin out in front:

> Once he [Tarzan Brown] bid for the lead prematurely as the two runners crossed the half mile of construction on the highway in Hooksett. At that point Durgin entered the gravel and sand covered road with a quarter mile lead. When he again struck his stride on the cement highway that margin had been cut to a scant 15 yards.

The spurt proved too much for the Indian, however, and he pulled up to a walk as he passed Mammoth road. While mounted [sic] motor vehicle officers and automobiles witnessed what appeared to be the end of the runner's almost superhuman bid for two victories in as many days, Brown ambled along the pavement for nearly a minute while his opponent opened up nearly 100 yards between them.

The bronzed figure resumed the chase again, however.[35]

With one final mile to go, as Ellison Brown crossed the city limits line, he narrowed the gap between Durgin and him. Exerting another one of his notably distinctive bursts of forceful speed, Brown managed to catch and then surpass Durgin. Soon thereafter, however, Tarzan Brown was back in a walking mode, where the Daniel Webster highway and Maple Street intersect. Durgin seized this opportunity, reconcentrated his efforts, and eventually positioned himself alongside Brown. "Just as Durgin drew up beside him, the laconic Indian hunched his shoulders and resumed the soft, relentless gait. From Webster street onward, he constantly increased his lead. Along Elm street he literally ran away from Durgin and Hill who was finishing strongly."[36]

A crowd of over one thousand spectators, duly apprised by the morning newspaper or word of mouth of the momentous historic achievement it was about to witness, cheered fervently as Brown came into view and crossed the finish line to victory. It was Brown all alone, loping at a fairly brisk clip, for he beat the second-place Hill to the end of the course by twenty-six seconds. Durgin, third, trailed Hill by fifty-nine seconds when it was all said and done. The final results proved to be a good day for United Shoe Machinery A. C. of Beverly. The club won the team prize; their affiliated members placed second, third, fourth, fifth, sixth (J. Semple), and tenth, out of the total field of twenty-three.

Brown's winning time, at 2 hours, 45 minutes, 52 seconds, may not have been such a fast time, but it was enough to win, and, in no way could it cast a shadow upon his overall accomplishment. He had run competitively over fifty-two miles within twenty-four hours to win two rigorous, full-length marathons back-to-back, an outstanding athletic display of stamina, courage, mental and physical strength, and gutsy determination.

Brown was physically weary as one might expect after more than fifty-two miles of intensive (and extensive) competitive effort, yet his feet apparently were in marvelous shape, with not a blister to be seen, according to the *Manchester Leader*.[37] From inside the clubhouse "where he lay exhausted and panting for the better part of an hour"[38] following his victory, Brown in time addressed the print media. He related how he had misjudged his standing in the marathon after nearly a third of the way through.

"I thought I had the race won about nine miles out," he said.

"You could have knocked me over with a feather when Jack (Brown's manager) told me that I had only one more man to catch and he was a half mile ahead. I didn't think I'd ever make it."[39]

The presentation of prizes—a collection of eight cups and trophies, ten medals, and a plaque for the team prize—took place in the Knights of Columbus' clubhouse. The top eight runners, dressed in suits and tie, received their awards. The Governor's Cup, described by the *Leader* as a "huge winner's cup," was bestowed upon the winner, Ellison Brown. He also received a solid gold "regulation" medal for his first-place finish in the A. A. A. U. New England championship event. Runners who finished in second through eighth place were awarded other cups of differing dimensions. Medals (gold for first place, sterling silver for second, and bronze for third) were presented to the top three runners. A plaque with an inscription was conferred on the United Shoe Machinery A. C., the team prize winner. A front-page photograph of the champion standing with his Governor's Cup facing Thomas J. King, state deputy, along with the grand knights of the Manchester and Concord councils, is situated under the headline "'Tarzan' Brown Tops Holiday Field to Win Second Marathon Honors in Two Days." Under the photo is this lengthy caption:

> "To the victor belongs the spoils." The spoils at yesterday's Knights of Columbus marathon from Boscawen to Manchester, incidentally, amounted to a huge cup for "Tarzan" Brown, Boston marathon winner and Olympic performer, and the honor of being the first man in the history of marathoning to win marathons on two successive days. The slim Narragansett Indian walked away with a race in Portchester, N.Y., Sunday and then came back again yesterday to win handily in New Hampshire. "Tarzan" is shown receiving the Knights of Columbus cup....[40]

Another photograph, of the eight winners—four crouching in front and four standing behind—was taken and ran in the *Manchester Leader*.[41] First row, left, squats Ellison Brown with his right arm resting on his winner's cup, and his left hand about his chin. The trace of a smile can barely be detected, but his expression of satisfaction is unmistakable.

Some caution—even suspicion—is requisite when reviewing some of the written material (and there isn't much) about Tarzan Brown's October feat. Even Jerry Nason was uncharacteristically guilty of some sloppy journalism, when he wrote, "On October 1936, he [Brown] even paused for a few beers between the two marathons he won on consecutive days at Yonkers, New York and Manchester, New Hampshire."[42] Nason confused the Port Chester, NY marathon with the annual one held at Yonkers raceway. The same error was committed by the runner Fred Brown (no relation) of North Medford, who was one of the competitors that day in the Boscawen-to-Manchester marathon, where, incidentally, he finished eleventh.

"Tarzan took a lot of kidding about the Olympics," recalled Fred Brown Sr.

"So what does he do? He enters two marathons on consecutive days, Saturday and Sunday. He won Yonkers, which was the New York championship, and then hitchhikes to Manchester, New Hampshire. He won that one too even though he didn't get there until 7 a.m."[43]

In addition to interposing the Yonkers race for the Port Chester event (as did Nason), Fred Brown did not correctly recall the days in which the marathons took place. They occurred on Sunday and Monday, October 11 and 12, of the year 1936. (October 12 was Columbus Day.) It should be noted that Ellison Brown did not run Yonkers that year. And, whether he arrived in Boscawen, New Hampshire, as early as 7 a.m. is unconfirmable, but he certainly managed to get there in time to make the race. The *Manchester Union* without elaboration reported Brown and Farrington's arrival "in Concord early yesterday morning."[44]

In the *Leader's* edition of Saturday, October 10, the newspaper ran the subheadline: "Tarzan Brown's Entry Uncertain Until Last Minute." The story went on to say:

> The entry list may be increased by one at the last minute and that would be Ellison "Tarzan" Brown, who won the last B. A. A. and then went on to the Berlin Olympics as a representative of Uncle Sam's long distance team.
> ... The obstacle is that Brown will run in the Portchester, N.Y. race on Sunday and will have to leave New York by Pullman Sunday night in order to reach Concord. Even with this close connection, Brown would probably not arrive until 8:43 o'clock Monday morning. His entry will not be considered after 9 o'clock, McCann has informed Farrington.[45]

According to this article published October 10, the expected arrival would have been the unrounded figure of 8:43 a.m., its selection most likely based upon prevailing train schedules. The following day, the 11th, the following article was published under the headline, "'GANSETT INDIAN IN RECORD TRY, Will Attempt Two Victories in as Many Days":

> The field of entries in the sixth annual Columbus Day marathon ... was increased by one last night by the "11th hour" entry of Ellison "Tarzan" Brown, Pawtucket, R. I., Narragansett Indian, who ... finished a good 300 yards ahead of his nearest competitor in yesterday's Portchester, N. Y. marathon.
> Brown and his manager, Jack Farrington, left New York last night by Sleeper and expect to arrive in Concord in plenty of time for the start of the 26 mile jaunt.[46]

How exactly his entry was registered that night is not known, nor how it could be accomplished "last night" (i.e. Sunday night) rather than in person Monday morning. In any event, Brown's entry was submitted before the 9 a.m. deadline, and his arrival to participate, as it turned out, was not a problem.

The *Westerly Sun* proclaimed the achievement of Ellison Brown's two successive victories to be "one of the greatest iron-man stunts in the history of American athletics."[47] Abe Soloveitzik, whose lengthy sports column was printed in the same paper a few days later, referred to Brown's two-state endurance ordeal also as "an iron-man stunt."[48] In the first half of his monograph, Soloveitzik marveled at Brown's incredible back-to-back efforts. He disclosed that he had been briefed of Brown's ambitious two-marathon-in-two-days plan by the runner himself and that the sportswriter had expressed his disbelief.

> He is a funny kid, this Indian lad who made racing history in that short space of time. Those who know the least thing about athletics know how harmful it is to overexert. I for one would have advised against him running in two marathons. In fact, when he told me he was going to attempt the trick I laughed and thought he was kidding.
>
> But he was serious. "Huh," he commented. "I can run in Portchester and then I can run in Concord the next day. I feel good. I never felt better in my life. There isn't anyone who can beat me now."
>
> And since he returned from Germany in his unsuccessful attempt to win the marathon title for Uncle Sam he has made good that boast.
>
> He has been entered in seven races, three of them full marathon events, and he has won them all. No one has been able to pass him on that home stretch and at the rate he is going, there doesn't appear to be a runner in the country today who can outstep him. I may [be] wrong, but I'm from Missouri and I've got to be shown.[49]

Despite his admiration for what Brown was able to do, the Westerly sportswriter did not believe, at first, that winning two marathons could seriously be done — by anyone. Now that it was a fait accompli (viz. one for the record books), he wanted to make clear how he decried the stunt on the grounds that it was harmful to the athlete and therefore should not be encouraged. He continued:

> But as I mentioned above I would not have approved of Brown's running in two marathons, and I don't think that his trainer, Jack Farrington did. He [Brown] wanted to do it and he did. Knowing Tarzan well, I know that when he sets his mind on anything it's like trying to stop the rising tide to switch his ideas.
>
> I am not the only one who frowned on the double marathon. This morning I received a letter from Ted Weall, who has had plenty of athletics, both in competition and as a trainer, in his lifetime. His note follows:
>
> "I see by the papers that our local boy and champion marathon runner Ellison Tarzan Brown has won two races in as many days, winning the last one after stepping off a sleeper, and running 52 miles in two days. Now I don't know much about running but I do know something about physical fitness and endurance, and I don't profess to know anything about training runners, but I do know that if I was handling the boy he wouldn't be running 52 miles in two days and burning himself out for the next big marathon. We don't see Kelly [sic], Pawson or McMahon doing it and I can't see Tarzan Brown lasting as a big-time runner if he keeps it up. Yours in sports, Ted Weall."[50]

Abe Soloveitzik's suggestion that Farrington was in opposition to the weekend running of both marathons was without corroboration, and flatly refuted in this passage published in the *Manchester Leader*.

> Jack Farrington, manager of the Narragansett Indian from Providence, is anxious to have Brown in the K. of C. race and has repeatedly informed Edward P. McCann, clerk of the entries, to this effect....
>
> It would be quite a stunt for a marathoner to compete in two long distance events in that many days *but Farrington wants his protege to do just that*—and win both events—so every effort will be made to get Brown in Concord in time to start the runners on their way [emphasis added].[51]

That Brown was, as Soloveitzik described, an obstinate, pertinacious individual has been, for the most part, substantiated. His very success over the weekend challenge was, on one level, confirming of the presence of these traits in the makeup of his personality. That unwavering determination to undertake and to win both marathons required tenacity rare in others, even among his fellow athletes. How else could Brown have staved off the competition to bring about the dual victories? How else could he have staved off the exhaustion that threatened to shut down his body, his leg muscles in particular?

His motivation? "Anyway, that's why I ran those two races in two days when I came home—just to show them Ellison Brown is no quitter!" he told Jerry Nason.[52] Despite all his racing wins and no losses since returning from overseas, Brown invariably felt he still had something to prove to somebody.

On the same Columbus Day Monday that Brown concluded his masterful victory, another race, a ten-miler, took place in Greenfield, Massachusetts. In that contest, the third annual Knights of Columbus Columbus Day Run, college runner Andrew "Hawk" Zamparelli beat a field of forty, including John Kelley (who finished fourth), Leslie Pawson (who finished sixteenth), and Clarence H. DeMar (who finished eighteenth). Why any of those participants chose to run the shorter distance race in Greenfield instead of the full marathon in New Hampshire is not recorded.

A third event, taking place on the same day, a 25-kilometer run in Fall River, Massachusetts, sponsored by the Eagles club, had advertised Tarzan Brown's participation. An October 4, 1936, item in the *Boston Post* announced in a headline: "TARZAN BROWN IN FALL RIVER RACE."[53] Whether this was purposeful, deceptive advertising employed to increase public interest and field a higher degree of competition in the cast of entrants or simply a journalistic error is unknown. Results of that event—indeed whether it actually transpired or not—were not reported in the Boston area newspapers.

Ted Weall's warning of injury ("burning himself out") in his letter to Abe Soloveitzik may be viewed as prescient in light of what Ellison Brown was about to face before the remainder of October had elapsed.

On the morning of October 28, 1936, a Wednesday, Ellison Brown left his home in Alton, Rhode Island, where he had been residing with his uncle Paul Babcock. He went to the nearby town of Westerly to visit some friends. By afternoon he returned to Alton, and underwent what was characterized by the *Westerly Sun* as "a light workout."[54] He was training for the difficult Yonkers (New York) Marathon, his next undertaking. Two other goals before the close of the runner's season remained after Yonkers—the New England A. A. A. U. 10,000-Meter Cross Country Championship held at Franklin Park, Boston, and the annual Thanksgiving Day run in Berwick, Pennsylvania. Three more victories would cap off a stellar string of successes[55], and that streak would in turn serve to relieve some of the humiliation Brown felt in not completing the Olympic marathon in August. Moreover, his public persona would not be forever tied to that one failed moment, the first and only time he had ever dropped out of a race before its completion in his athletic life, an occasion that troubled him his entire life. In the sporting world as linked to the public's perception, an athlete's solitary but important error, failure or boneheaded play could eclipse all previous (and future) success(es) generated or attained by that player, and the public's association of the athlete with that one dreaded moment could be forever melded together. Fans of the Boston Red Sox may be particularly sensitive to this phenomenon.

By afternoon's end Brown experienced some lower abdominal cramps. The severity of the pain increased to the point where he felt he needed to see a doctor. Ethel Brown remembered that her husband drove himself to the hospital. The local newspaper reported an initial visit to the offices of Dr. Johnson at six o'clock. It was there that Dr. Linwood H. Johnson examined Brown and decided that they repair in haste to the Westerly hospital for emergency surgery. By seven o'clock, he was being readied for the operating room.

The diagnosis was "acute strangulated inguinal hernia, ... the aggravation of a previous hernia."[56] Dr. Johnson, assisted by Dr. Hartford P. Gongaware, successfully performed the surgery, which they completed around ten o'clock.

A differing account of the afternoon leading up to the hospitalization and surgery was put forth by Jerry Nason over four decades later, in 1981. A description of his condition in a quote from Brown began Nason's passage:

"Lots of times I'd been having some bad pain in the stomach during a race, but I thought it was because of something wrong I ate, so I kept on running," he revealed.

"It wasn't until one day when I was out training, maybe 20 miles from Westerly, when all this pain hit me again, only this time it was tearing at me. I knew something was real bad. I was all doubled up at the side of the road when this guy in a car found me.

"A half hour later I was on the operating table in the Westerly Hospital. I got me a strangulated hernia. I never even heard of one before, and I had been running 15, 16 races with one."[57]

In an AP wire story carried by much of the New England press, Dr. Johnson said that the runner would be sidelined from competition for at least six months, and would in all likelihood remain hospitalized for a period of several weeks.[58] The minimum of six months for recuperation outlined by the surgeon, everyone who heard starkly understood, would preclude a run in the 1937 B. A. A. Marathon.

The man who gained prominence taking many steps in a hurry took a major step in what might be considered for many a hurry. Less than one month after undergoing emergency surgery, Ellison Brown was united in marriage to Ethel Mae Wilcox on the evening of November 24, 1936. In a double wedding ceremony with his younger sister, Miss Grace Ethel Babcock Brown and her fiancé, Russell Greene Spears, the two couples were married by Clerk John Gentile of the Third District Court in the living room of his home and store at 24 Pierce Street in Westerly, Rhode Island. Each couple served as attendants to the other.

Marriage licenses were obtained prior to the civil ceremony. An hour before the weddings, Ethel Wilcox secured her license from Town Clerk Linton L. Brown at the Carolina town office. Ellison, his sister, and Spears together went to the Westerly town clerk, W. Russell Dower, to apply for their documents. Ellison Brown and Russell Spears listed their occupations as masons on their applications. The brides listed their occupations as housekeepers.

The *Providence Journal*, which ran a story on the weddings on its front page, described the wedding attire. "The bride [Ethel] was dressed in a simple green travelling suit, with a small green hat perched on her dark hair. Brown wore a dark blue suit."[59] The *Journal* reported that Ellison Brown and Ethel were the first of the two couples to offer their wedding vows. "At the completion of the ceremony the couple kissed and then stepped aside for Spears and Miss Brown," the newspaper observed.[60]

As official witnesses of his sister's wedding, Ellison Myers Brown signed his name

> in full. His bride for the first time signed her married name, Ethel Mae Wilcox Brown.
> Also witnessing the ceremonies were Mr. Gentile's wife Clara H. Gentile, Mrs. Betina Gentile [whose relationship was not disclosed] and Arthur Nash of Boston, a salesman for a wholesale beef house, who was at Mr. Gentile's store when the couples arrived.[61]

The *Westerly Sun* ran an article on its front page under this headline: "Tarzan Brown Olympic Runner Catches Up With Indian Bride." On page two, it ran this item:

MARRIED
SPEARS-BROWN — In Westerly, R. I., Nov. 24, 1936, at 24 Pierce Street, by

Ellison and Ethel Brown. Rhode Island, Autumn, 1936 (AP/Wide World Photograph).

Court Clerk John Gentile, Mr. Russell Greene Spears of Westerly and Miss Grace Ethel Babcock Brown of Alton.

BROWN-WILCOX — In Westerly, R. I., Nov. 24, 1936, at 24 Pierce Street, by Court Clerk John Gentile, Mr. Ellison Brown of Alton and Miss Ethel Mae Wilcox of Westerly.[62]

The *Providence Journal* alluded to a honeymoon trip. "The four Narragansetts … crowded into the one seat of Brown's coupe after the ceremony and set out for a wedding trip. Where they were going they would not say."[63] The newspaper assured its readers that Tarzan Brown's running shoes were packed "in his suitcase in the back of his car." Ethel Brown told the author that neither couple had the means for a honeymoon and that no honeymoon was ever taken.[64]

The peace and happiness of the newlyweds was abruptly disturbed with the news that Clifford Brown, an older brother of Ellison's, was involved in a fight that resulted in serious injury, and was being held by police as a result. Clifford, age 28, and Charles Monroe, age 33, Clifford's best friend and a fellow Narragansett, had been drinking at Clifford's second-floor residence on Monday afternoon, November 23. About the time his brother and sister were planning to go into town to get their marriage licenses for their weddings later that evening, Clifford and Charles became engaged in an argument that got increasedly heated. At some point the argument turned violent. Around 5 p.m., Charles Monroe, unconscious, was taken to South County hospital in need of emergency medical care. He died as a result of his injuries early the following morning. The unreleased preliminaries of an autopsy reportedly showed a fractured nose and head wounds.

The *Providence Journal* reported that after the fight, Clifford Brown had left his second-floor tenement. He allegedly went to a neighbor's "and ordered his wife to return home" which she did. Back at home, reportedly Clifford Brown "became abusive to his wife, Chief McNulty said, and she sent her brother, William Harry, 16, who had been in the house during the afternoon, for help. When Chief McNulty went to investigate, he said, Brown threatened him at the door of the stairs leading to the tenement, and Chief McNulty locked him up."[65]

Clifford Brown was held at the South Kingston police headquarters. His brother Ellison Brown visited with Clifford "and gave him cigarettes," the *Journal* reported.[66] After it was determined that Monroe was deceased, Clifford Brown was charged with murder in the Wakefield Office of the sheriff of Washington County. He had no attorney to represent him. Only his brother Frank, who had visited with him, stayed with him during that unusual nighttime proceeding. On Wednesday night of November 25, a special session of Second District Court was convened. "Judge Steven J. Casey found Brown probably guilty of the murder charge and ordered him held without bail for the February session of the Washington county grand jury. Brown was committed to Providence County Jail," reported the *Providence Journal*.[67] Both the *Providence Journal* and the *Westerly Sun* newspapers claimed that Brown pleaded guilty to the murder.[68]

Monroe's body was delivered to the Avery funeral home in the town of Wakefield. He was reportedly survived by his mother, two sons, a brother and two sisters. In a final paragraph, the *Journal*, without elaboration or explanation, stated that "Police said there was no connection between the quarrel in which the two men engaged and the marriage of 'Tarzan' Brown later on Monday."[69]

The busy year of 1936 had seen a lot of firsts for young Ellison Brown: his first B. A. A. marathon win, his first stage show extravaganza, his first brand new suit of clothes (with collar and tie), his first dedicated holiday given to his people in his honor, his first visit to the governor's office, his first legislative proclamation, his first meeting with the Rhode Island Assembly, his first voyage on a sailing ship, his first trip on an overnight train, his first international Olympics sporting event, his first race he could not complete, his first (and the running world's first) consecutive marathon victories, his first electric refrigerator (which he could not use), his first major surgery, his first (and only) marriage, and his first experience of murder within his own immediate family. The year in which Ellison Brown had firmly established himself in the eye of the public came to a close with Tarzan Brown in need of healing.

14

"Full of Real Heart" — 1937

A two-mile race held in Providence, Rhode Island, in the second week of March 1937, attempted to supersede the North Medford classic that year as the first running event of the new season. In that event, Ellison Brown competed against the venerable Leslie Pawson and other athletes anxious for winter to fade and for the running season to get underway. Although neither Pawson nor Brown managed to win the Providence event, at least one Boston newspaper observer, Will Cloney, assessed that Pawson "looked very, very good" but that "Brown looked terrible — heavy, almost fat, and hip-draggy."[1] No mention was made of his operation of a few months earlier or the status of his medical recovery. It was not an auspicious start for Brown.

The sixth annual North Medford twenty-mile race, the usual start of the distance-running season, took place March 20 under blue skies and ideal weather conditions. The reigning champion of the event, Johnny Kelley, did not disappoint in the 1937 edition. He won his fourth straight Medford victory, and he broke his own record while setting a new mark, 1 hour, 52 minutes, 59.4 seconds. Walter Young, the Canadian snowshoe champion at three and ten miles, finished second. Pat Dengis was third. The ostensibly ageless Clarence H. DeMar, a recent father of twins, finished in eighth place. (Actual age: 49.)

Neither Pawson nor Brown appeared in Medford to compete despite expectations to the contrary. Pawson did not show because his wife was about to deliver a baby at any moment.

Will Cloney, for one, did not expect Brown's participation in the North Medford race, and explained that "the disappointment about Brown was really the fault of the officials for the Tarz never really said he would run, as far as could be learned."[2] Cloney continued with this dark premonition: "His failure to show was taken as an indication that his running career is ended, for the time being, at least."[3]

Skipping the Medford competition was presumably the prudent suggestion of his trainer, the *Westerly Sun* implied. "Neither [Pawson nor Brown] was in shape for the long event, and while Brown was anxious to compete he was urged to remain out until he reached running prime."[4] That someone was in the role of trainer and could impel Brown to miss the Medford race was itself in doubt, as this item by Bob Dunbar in the *Boston Herald* revealed:

> It will be interesting to see who handles Tarzan Brown in today's race. Most people think the Indian is on his way down from the top, and his fair-weather trainers apparently have deserted him. His case is a real object lesson, but he has a chance to change the tune. A victory would do that.[5]

No victory was possible since Brown never competed. But he did have a trainer. His name was Charlie Anderson, of Boston. They called him "Chick." Ethel Brown, nearly seven decades later, recalled Anderson, "a great big tall guy. He was married to my husband's cousin."[6] In his role as trainer, "he used to rub my husband down," Ethel said. Chick would "follow behind him in the car" when Brown was training.[7] Along with Chick Anderson, Ellison had acquired an assistant trainer as well, named Joe Finster.

With an eye toward the B. A. A. Marathon on Monday, April 19, Brown trained in earnest under Anderson's watchful supervision. For two weeks in April, Ellison Brown worked out, but did not run long distances. He was finally permitted to run twelve miles on successive days, with just over a week to go before the marathon. Following that latest workout, Tarzan Brown announced with confidence, "I feel fit and light as a feather, my legs don't bother me and I feel good in every way."[8] His feet, though, were tender. To remedy that, he was "soaking them in brine to toughen them for the long grind" to come, the *Westerly Sun* reported.[9] Brown's wife, Ethel, years later, disputed the *Sun's* report. According to Ethel, Ellison never soaked his feet in brine or did anything of the kind.[10] She agreed that Brown's physician, Dr. John Shibilio, was consulted, and oversaw the conditioning and progress of his feet when needed. Trainer Anderson's main concern, according to reports, was to keep Brown from working too hard, from exerting too much energy, from applying too strenuous an assault on his leg muscles. A plan was in place, consisting of a diet of nourishing foods, a regimen which included plenty of rest, only short-distance runs, and a restriction on automobile driving until after the marathon was over. Not until the Wednesday before the marathon would Brown run any significant distances.

Unlike the previous year running under the auspices of the Providence Tercentenary Committee, this year the local civic entity, the Westerly Chamber of Commerce, was his sponsoring organization along with its president, Mr. John B. Findlay. Brown made a stop there to officially thank chamber president Findlay for the support, and promised to do his best. He was wished good luck by the Westerly well-wishers on hand to bid him farewell. Tarzan Brown then left Rhode Island for Boston with a few days before the marathon, and stayed at the Anderson residence. In Boston on Saturday he "completed the final stages of his short preparation for the race ... with a ten mile glide over Wellesley Hills, the toughest part of the Boston course. He will rest today

[Sunday] and tomorrow morning at 10 o'clock will report at B. A. A. head-quarters in Hopkinton for a physical examination."[11]

Little in the way of strategy was disclosed publicly. But monitoring his progress during the final waves of training, Anderson "pointed out ... that if Brown shows the least signs of weakness he [the trainer, Anderson] will yank him but the Indian has displayed courage in the past and it is likely that he will finish out the race no matter how far behind the leader he is."[12]

The Boston press had no faith in Brown's ability to overcome the remnants of his surgery in time for the marathon. Bob Dunbar, for example, wrote in one column: "Tarzan Brown now is officially entered in the B. A. A. marathon, but unless he has some trick inside his running shoes, he will be just another runner among the large field on Patriot's Day. No one is giving the Tarz even an outside chance this year."[13] In another column two days later, he added, "Tarzan Brown took a 15-mile hike through the woods yesterday. Unless he springs a surprise, he will not be out of the forest by the 19th."[14]

On the day Brown's official entry was announced to *Globe* readers, Nason also revealed his dim evaluation for Brown's chances, due to the runner's shortened timetable for training and getting into shape. Nason wrote:

> It is the consensus of opinion among the fraternity that Tarzan Brown will be no factor in next Monday's race. Operated on for hernia late last year ... Brown resumed training only last week.
>
> Nine pounds over his running weight, the speedboy from Bradford, R. I., faces the almost impossible task of regaining his peak in ten days after a long layoff. Unquestionably the fastest man on the North American continent for 20 miles, the Narragansett benedict was never exceptionally long on endurance, anyway.
>
> ... Yet Tarzan is as unpredictable as the April weather itself. One cannot possibly ignore him. He has abnormal speed, and has inherited the splendid physique and strength of his Narragansett ancestors. The lifting of a doctor's competitive ban last week saw Tarzan leap right into training, although he fully realizes the proportions of the obstacles in his path.
>
> It can never be said that Brown isn't of the stuff champions are made. He says he won't pass over his B. A. A. laurels without first making active defense.[15]

Where Nason evinced understanding, such was not universal in the Boston press. There was deep-seated anger, almost a sense of betrayal, underlying some of the prognostic writings discounting Brown's marathon chances. An example in the *Herald* was accusatory:

> [There] ... is the Tarzan himself, the Narragansett Indian who won himself a European trip last year, who ruined his magnificent body with an organ-grinding program of racing last summer, who has recuperated silently this winter, and who makes a final bid tomorrow.
>
> Only a handful expect Tarzan to win and very few of the experts expect him

to finish. He has not entered any competition this year, nor has he done much scientific training. Apparently past his usefulness as a prize winner (and a demander of expense money), the Indian has been more or less shunned by his fair-weather friends. Disillusion has not necessarily impaired his running ability, but the steps leading to that disillusion may have broken his body so that it cannot meet the demand of 26 long miles.[16]

Aside from the erroneous submission that Brown had not entered an event up until the B. A. A. marathon (he ran in Providence in March), the passage was less a factual account than a diatribe against his past handlers, his inadequate training methods, a suggestion that he (or they) had improperly insisted on expense money over and above what he (or they) should have been allotted, and the positing of a negative state of mind that could cripple or deter his stamina. Where or how this point of view developed is not expressed.

Runner and overall favorite to win John Kelley was not so sure how to assess his rival in this personal comment he made for the *Globe* a day before the marathon:

> Tarzan Brown, the 1936 winner, has been somewhat of a puzzle. As he is one of my best personal friends, I hesitate to predict what he will do. I know that if anyone is the superman it is Tarzan Brown, because of my seven-week association with him on the Olympic trip. Naturally, I hope to win, but I personally trust Brown has recovered from his operation and contributes a good performance.[17]

Kelley, the sportsman, spoke the words like a gentleman.

The temperature was high on Patriots' Day that year, the warmest marathon day since 1931. This likely contributed to the huge number of spectators, estimated at possibly one million strong. Vehicular traffic on the course "was, by far, the worst in history."[18] Kelley ran a strong race but faltered by Coolidge Corner, with roughly two miles to go before reaching the finish line. He drank a lot of water, became ill at one point, vomited, and valiantly continued his efforts. He had set a vibrant pace for himself but his calculations were slightly off. Taking advantage of Kelley's miscues was Walter Young, a twenty-four-year-old, unemployed Canadian, who dueled Kelley for twenty-three miles, swapping the lead with him sixteen times. The "long-legged, awkward-gaited"[19] runner-up to Kelley a month earlier in the North Medford race was able to make up a 200-yard deficit and put nearly six minutes between his first-place finish and Kelley's second-place results by the race's end. (Young's time was 2:33:20.) Young's hopes of getting hired as a policeman back home in Verdun were fulfilled with his victory. Course recordholder and new baby holder Les Pawson finished third, yet he was over eight minutes in back of the winning Young. In a strange run, Pawson ran twenty-three miles alone, in the third spot, with no one close by either in front or in back of him with whom he could chat. Jock Semple was a sensational ninth, Leo Giard tenth, and Clarence DeMar fourteenth, with an even 2 hours, 53 minutes. A limping Mel Porter was sixteenth. Pat Dengis was forced to drop out after fourteen miles, his bladder once again competing against him.

Ellison Brown, who wore number 1 in honor of his being the defending title holder, managed valorously to cross the line at Exeter Street. The *Herald*, perhaps signaling a change of its own heart, reported "the courageous Tarzan Brown, manifestly out of condition but full of real heart, finished 31st."[20] His time was 3 hours, 7 minutes, 4.8 seconds. The *Westerly Sun* reported that Brown "limped past the Auburndale Station far in the rear carrying one of his shoes."[21] It had subheadlines that read: "Westerly Man Has Foot Trouble/Carries Shoe." There was no further elaboration or clarification about the condition of Brown's feet. But the first thirty-three athletes to cross the finish line were awarded prizes, and Ellison Brown's thirty-first-place finish qualified him for one of those coveted prizes.

Ellison Brown had suffered sharp "stomach pains at the point where he was operated upon several months ago," the *Westerly Sun* reported a few days later.[22] The debilitating pains had forced the runner to walk for several miles in the marathon.

There is another explanation for the poor performance time registered that day, according to the Tarzan Brown and Boston Marathon lore that continues to flourish to this day. The story goes that on a very warm day such as was the case on that Patriots' Day 1937, Tarzan Brown decided on the spur of the moment upon seeing Lake Cochituate, or, by some accounts, Fiske Pond, in Natick, to have an impromptu swim.[23] Not placing the demands of winning above all else, he impulsively but naturally chose to take a dunk in the cool, inviting waters.

His wife, Ethel, remembered the moment:

> He really did swim in Lake Cochituate, in 1937, I think. And he climbed out and finished the race! That's the kind of man he was. When he was tired he slept, when he was hungry he ate.[24]

Whether the episode occurred or not in 1937 must be left to the folklorists. The reporters at the time never mentioned it, though it is inconceivable they would have avoided reporting it had they observed it. That in itself places some doubt on the event occurring that year. It is possible the incident may have taken place the following year, in 1938, or in 1941, or possibly in 1942, if it actually happened at all. As legends go, it may be more a case of embellished fiction than fact.

Incidentally, Jerry Nason, in the course of his coverage of the marathon results in the morning after's edition of the *Globe*, referred to "Heartbreak Hill" by name. Nason wrote that Kelley "finally passed him [Young] on Heartbreak Hill, that frame-wrenching twister that runs up and up from Center

St. almost to Boston College itself."[25] This may have been his first utilization in print of the name generally accorded to have been christened by him.

The local office of the National Reemployment Service came to the employment rescue two days after the B. A. A. Marathon was over. A position for Brown was secured as part of the federal WPA project. The job involved making improvements on a bridge in Carolina, Rhode Island, near his Alton home. The construction-site work would enable him to earn money, and at the same time, "keep in the open air and harden himself for future running tests."[26] It seemed like an ideal match between job and employee. Brown, reportedly "all primed to go," started on April 21.[27]

A ten-mile race was held around Lake Quinsigamond, at the state park of the same name, which forms a border on the east side of the city of Worcester, Massachusetts. Sponsored by the St. Margaret Mary Church, the event took place on May 15. Ellison Brown, along with fellow Olympic marathon teammates Johnny Kelley and local boy favorite Biddie McMahon, assembled to compete with running powerhouses Les Pawson and Jock Semple, and fifty-three other athletes.

Pawson led the pack the first two miles. Kelley stayed right behind him. Shortly thereafter, Kelley assumed the front-runner's spot and never deemed it necessary to look behind him. He crossed the finish line 200 yards ahead of George Durgin, another popular hometown athlete,[28] who managed to beat Pawson for second place, overtaking him at the midway point of the course. Pawson held on to earn third-place honors. Fourth place belonged to Walter Ray. Tarzan Brown finished in fifth place.

The *Boston Globe* reported on May 20, 1937, that Tarzan Brown and Paul DeBruyn were officially entered in the upcoming Lawrence-to-the-Sea Marathon scheduled for Memorial Day, May 31.[29] Announced as expected entrants along with these two B. A. A. Marathon winners were two even earlier former B. A. A. Marathon champions, Clarence H. DeMar and "Bricklayer" Bill Kennedy. The race went on as scheduled but Brown never did appear in the event. He was in a recuperating mode, but now he had to recover from more than just last fall's surgery.

On Saturday, May 22, Ellison Brown and his wife, Ethel (and their dog, Teddy,[30] in the rumble seat) were driving on their way to complete the second half of a solemn errand. They had purchased flowers to place on their deceased mothers' graves. The couple had accomplished the task at Ethel's mother's burial site and were on their way along Route 3 to the First Hopkinton Cemetery where Ellison's mother was buried. Just after 7 o'clock, less than a mile from the Hopkinton graveyard, they were involved in a serious collision, in front of the parking lot of the Lantern Glow Inn.[31] A heavy sedan with a driver and three passengers in it crashed into the passenger door of the Brown's much-lighter roadster. The impact forced the Brown car to spin 180 degrees and buckle up against a telephone pole, but because it had been hit so hard, it continued to careen forward. The battered car with the Browns in the front and Teddy sealed shut inside the now-closed rumble seat "bounced and twisted along the shoulder of the road for more than 50 feet" before finally coming to a halt.[32] The car was demolished. Customers came out of the Lantern Glow establishment at the sound of the accident, and the police were summoned. The Browns were "extricated from the wreckage," according to the newspaper account.[33] They both sustained multiple injuries in the ordeal and were in need of medical assistance. Ellison suffered "contusions and abrasions of both hands and arms, a laceration of the scalp, a severe bruise of the calf of the right leg and numerous lesser cuts," according to the *Westerly Sun*.[34] Ethel fared much worse, due to the fact that she was on the side of the vehicle that received the point of impact. The *Westerly Sun* reported a "severe body contusion" as her main injury. A doctor who happened to be a patron inside the Lantern Glow at the time of the collision, a Dr. F. B. Agnelli, offered his medical services at the scene. Ethel and her husband were delivered to his office a few miles away, on Narragansett Avenue in Westerly, by Mr. Francis E. Armone, a sanitation worker who volunteered to transport the couple from the accident scene. Dr. Agnelli treated the couple and released them, ordering Ethel to remain in bed for several days. Ellison's cuts were bandaged. The *Sun* reported the doctor's summation of Ellison Brown's situation: "Dr. Agnelli said that while [Ellison] Brown's injuries are not serious they will be painful and it will be at least several weeks before he will be able to resume training for a racing comeback."[35]

Oliver A. Phillips, age 42, was identified as the operator of the sedan that hit the Browns. His car received minimal damage, and he and all three of his passengers were unscathed, suffering no injuries. Chief of Police William L. Kay of Hopkinton and Rhode Island state police investigated the accident, taking note of tire marks on the road surface. They determined that Phillips was fully responsible for the accident. In attempting to turn into the Lantern Glow parking lot, he had turned squarely into the Brown vehicle instead. He was cited on one count of "operating a vehicle so as to endanger," ordered to appear in Third District Court, and allowed to go on his way.[36] Whether "his way" included a needed stop at the bar of the Lantern Glow is unknown.

The Browns were taken back to the scene of the accident, despite their injuries, to answer questions by the police and to retrieve Teddy, who was fortunate not to have suffered any injuries of his own in the accident. The scared dog refused for over an hour to allow himself to be removed from the car. Ellison Brown was given a summons to appear in court. His driver's license had expired and had not been renewed. He was thus cited for operating with an expired driving license.

The next Friday both Ellison Brown and Oliver Phillips appeared in Third District Court before Judge M. Walter Flynn. In the Phillips' case, a plea of not guilty to the charge of operating so as to endanger was submitted by his attorney, Judge John J. Dunn. The case was ordered continued for two weeks.

Brown pleaded guilty to his charge of operating after his license had expired, without assistance of counsel. Judge Flynn continued his case two weeks for sentencing.

In the midst of those two weeks, on May 31, the Lawrence-to-the-Sea marathon took place. Canadian Walter Young, the year's B. A. A. Marathon winner, won in crippling heat with temperatures soaring to nearly 100 degrees. The remarkable forty-nine-year-old veteran Clarence H. DeMar took the second-place prize. Leo Giard finished third, and Jock Semple finished tenth. Paul deBruyn dropped out after eleven grueling miles. Ellison Brown, although expected by the Lawrence race officials, did not show, nor did Bill Kennedy. Brown, who was now making two separate recoveries—from his surgery and from his automobile accident—was not at home resting. He was at a different event, one closer to his home.

The national 15-K race held in Norwich, Connecticut, on May 31, 1937, was a highly anticipated event featuring John Kelley, Leslie Pawson, and Tarzan Brown in competition with each other out of a total field of 32 runners. That Memorial Day was scorching hot, but it did not deter Johnny Kelley from winning the battle to the finish line and thus the title with a time of 51 minutes, 1 second. The *Globe* mentioned that "His time was slow because of the heat which forced several starters to drop from the race."[37] Brown was one of those casualties. He called it quits just beyond the midpoint of the race. That proved to be a better showing than the defending champion, Canadian Scotty Rankine, who threw in the towel before even reaching the halfway mark. Eino Pentti finished second, a quarter of a mile behind Kelley. His time was 52 minutes, 18 seconds. Pawson, who finished in third place, was a full minute behind Pentti. The newspapers did not pay much attention nor devote much copy to the event. No details about Brown or his physical condition were provided.

Brown appeared in the Third District Court facing Judge M. Walter Flynn as a result of the Hopkinton accident. The local newspaper did not report the results of that hearing, but he was fined the usual but substantial $10 and assessed court costs, standard court procedure. Brown's judicial woes would have ended there had he not been arrested yet again, charged with the same offense following another car accident, this time in Ashaway, Rhode Island.

Brown was back in the Third District Court facing Judge M. Walter Flynn once again on the morning of June 18. The *Westerly Sun* reported the proceedings under the headline: "Eight Fined For Violations of Auto Laws, Third District Court Hands Out Penalties Totaling $87."[38] In the first case on the docket, Ellison Brown "was fined $10 and costs" for what the newspaper reported to be "his second offense of this nature within ten days." With another vehicle, Brown had managed to get involved in another accident. This time Brown had been arrested and no other driver was reported cited. The second accident occurred on Nooseneck Hill Road in Ashaway. No injuries were reported. Brown once more paid the fine.

Brown did not run the National A. A. U. Marathon held in Washington, D.C., on June 12, which was won by Mel Porter. Pat Dengis was runner-up, earning second-place honors and the remarkable, durable DeMar was fourth.

The *Westerly Sun* reported that June 14 had been officially proclaimed "Indian Day" by the Rhode Island Assembly and that Governor Robert E. Quinn had signed the proclamation. There was no mention of Tarzan Brown, not in the proclamation itself nor in the journalistic accounts of it. The proclamation said, in part:

> Whereas it is well for the people of this State to recall those historic events which have contributed to the enrichment of the story of the founding and progress of Rhode Island, particularly the lasting friendship between our founder Roger Williams and the sachems of the great tribes from whom the initial purchase of this land of ours was made....[39]

What was supposed to have been a celebratory day for the tribe(s) originally proposed in recognition of the great success of Ellison Brown now became a more ordinary day of recognition. The change of date from the originally selected April date was not explained. Of course, no rebuttals to the state's version of history were either permitted or sought.

The 1937 edition of the Bradford ten-mile race, in its third annual run held in Haverill, Massachusetts, and sponsored by the Sacred Heart parish, listed Tarzan Brown as an entrant, along with William McMahon, who was grist for the rumor mill that he was retiring from distance-running competition altogether. The announcement was made a week before the scheduled June 25 event.[40] On the day of the race, Brown and Pawson were both given handicaps and ran from scratch. Pawson crossed the finish line ahead of the pack, but was not awarded the first-place win, for his corrected time (adding 6½ minutes to his actual time of 52 minutes, 7 seconds) gave him a fourth-place finish with a corrected time of 58:37. Brown ran strongly. He finished right behind Pawson across the finish line with the second actual best time of the day. His elapsed time, however, figured to be 1 hour, 12 seconds, which put him eighteenth in the competition. It hardly seemed fair, the handicapping being obviously based upon past performance and not taking into account recent (and current) conditions. Lewis Young of Cambridge won with a corrected time of 57 minutes, 26 seconds.

The *Westerly Sun*, providing some detail, wrote this encouraging line at the finish of its article describing the event: "Brown ran a pretty race, and his handlers were satisfied that he is regaining the form which made him a champion a year ago."[41] Strangely, the *Providence Journal*, which covered the event in its pages, made no mention of Brown at all. And, McMahon's participation (or lack thereof) could not be found in any newspaper reports.

The first Myles Standish 10-mile run, held in Duxbury, Massachusetts, on Plymouth Bay, was held on July 3 to celebrate the town's first three hundred years. This was another handicap contest and the race officials required that Tarzan Brown be held back six minutes after the start. He was the last of all 59 runners to advance from the starting line, which was located at historic Plymouth Rock. Tough competitors like DeMar and Leo Giard were already on their way by the time Brown was permitted to begin. Despite that difficult situation, he "put up quite a race," observed the *Boston Globe*.[42] He had to weave his way through a narrow course replete with competing fellow athletes inadvertently serving as obstacles hindering his path. For eight miles Brown was impeded from going full throttle, but he battled onward despite the frustration. Usually astutely aware of his distance covered and how much he had left ahead at any point in a race, such was not the case that afternoon due in part to the crowded conditions on the course as he sought to negotiate his way along. With two miles to go to the finish line, he was heard to ask how much further he had left to go. Apparently nobody could or would supply an answer. At that point, he sprinted as fast as he could, still having to work his way around straggling, tiring runners. Ellison Brown crossed the finish line in fourth place. Brown won the time prize for the race with the best actual elapsed time from start to finish, 56 minutes, 44 seconds.[43] Brown's fourth-place corrected time, with the six-minute handicap, was 62 minutes, 44 seconds, by the *Herald's* arithmetic. The winner, a twenty-three-year-old Brockton ice dealer named Michael Mansulla, won the race with a corrected time of 60:41. It had taken him nearly a minute (fifty-seven seconds) longer to go from the starting line to the finish line than it had taken Brown. Ted Sturgios, a twenty-three-year-old who worked as "a counterman in a Providence restaurant," finished in second place. He had come to the race directly following his early 5 a.m.-to-1 p.m. shift at the diner.

Clarence H. DeMar finished seventh. He addressed the crowd at the prize presentation ceremony after the race, where he stated, "To finish seventh makes me feel old, but I will try again next year, and hope to do better." The elder marathoner was the "recipient of enthusiastic applause."[44]

A quick two days later, Brown, DeMar, and Sturgios were again competing, this time in a five-mile run in Whitinsville, Massachusetts, a small town midway on a line between the cities of Worcester and Woonsocket, Rhode Island. The first annual N. E. A. A. A. U. 5-Mile Road Race, as it was billed, sponsored by the American Legion post, mapped out a course from Whitinsville to Uxbridge and back to Whitinsville. A field of twenty-five runners competed. The race became a two-man dual, as Ellison Brown and Frank Mann of Sherborn went head to head in the final half mile. With one hundred yards to go, Brown, with the old familiar, powerful burst of speed, managed to pass Mann for good to win the contest by a distance of sixteen yards. His time was 26 minutes, 2.4 seconds. Mann placed second; Ted Sturgios of Providence was third; Clarence H. DeMar finished 14th.[45]

The New England A. A. A. U. 15-K championship race in Dedham was scheduled to take place on the evening of July 17. The year before, the event was held the second week in September, and Brown had beaten Kelley in a memorable race, their first competition against each other since their return from the Olympics. Hawk Zamparelli, who held the course record for the race from 1935, had dropped out with cramps in the 1936 edition. This year, the race was receiving much excited attention in the press. Bob Dunbar of the *Herald* wrote: "The championship 15-kilometer run at Dedham tonight is definitely a three-man race, with defending titlist 'Tarzan' Brown given only a slight chance to ward off the threat of Johnny Kelley and Hawk Zamparelli. Kelley is reported to be in top condition, and Zamparelli, still disturbed at the A. A. U. officials for not sending him to the national championships, is anxious for an 'I'll-show-you' win."[46] Had Les Pawson, a last-minute entrant, submitted his papers earlier, the newspapers in all probability would have trumpeted his possibilities in what would have been touted as a four-man race. Presumably, each of the forty-three starters that evening (of the fifty-eight entries) hoped to make it a one-man race.

When the starting gun for the roughly 9½-mile run was shot, quickly out at the head of the pack was Ted Sturgios, followed closely by two men, Tarzan Brown and Johnny Kelley. After the first mile Sturgios relented the lead, slipping out of the limelight as he sunk back into the ruck. Kelley and Brown then led the pack, running side by side "together eight or 10 yards ahead of Pawson, with Zamparelli another 20 to the rear."[47] After another mile, Ellison Brown suffered a severe stitch, which temporarily sidelined him and reduced his movement to a slow walk. Kelley accelerated his pace, as Pawson picked up the chase but he could not stay with Kelley for very long. Zamparelli passed Pawson just beyond the three-mile mark and he too made a valiant attempt to catch up to Kelley. He managed to bridge some of the seventy-five-yard gap, closing in almost to within forty yards of the leader, but Kelley would not be denied. He was smashing the course record Zamparelli, his closest pursuer, had established.

Ellison Brown, meanwhile, recovered from the painful stab in his side. He had fallen from the front of the herd to a distant fifth. Once revitalized, Brown "came back with a grand drive near the end,"[48] which put him in a pitched battle with Pawson for third place, just behind Zamparelli, with less than one mile to go. When it was all over, Kelley had set a new record with the victory, his time 49 minutes, 52.6 seconds. Hawk Zamparelli finished 46.4 seconds behind Kelley, and 22 seconds ahead of Tarzan Brown, whose time was 51 minutes plus 1 second. Pawson, who finished fourth, was 48 seconds behind Brown, with 51:49.

Both Kelley and Brown were surprised to learn that the pacing had been so rapid — below fifty-one minutes, the *Herald* reported.[49]

Jerry Nason wrote this positive assessment after watching Brown run: "The performance of Tarzan Brown was by far the most impressive since his hernia operation, and the Narragansett seems definitely on his way back."[50] Art Walsh had the following observations:

> Brown won last year in 51:04 and beat that time by three seconds yesterday, so he wasn't going too slowly, despite his stitch, cramp, or whatever you choose to call it.
>
> Brown declares he is rapidly approaching the form that carried him to Unicorn triumph in 1936. He feels stronger with each race and definitely is pointing to that B. A. A. classic next April.[51]

Not withstanding the optimistic reports of Brown's improving condition, Johnny Kelley meanwhile was quietly enlarging his collection of victory trophies. The fourth annual St. Mary's Parish Worcester-to-Jefferson 10-Mile Road Race, held July 31, was another stop where Johnny Kelley could effectively demonstrate his *modus operandi* for winning these shorter runs: off to a quick start, jump to the head of the pack, set a blistering pace, take first prize, and establish a new course record. The aforementioned race was another all-Kelley affair. His winning record time was 55:05. He led the whole way. Les Pawson, two-time winner of the event and co-holder of the old record, finished in second place, two minutes behind the Arlington winner. Ellison Brown did not even rate a descriptive sentence in the newspaper account of the race.[52] The only clue that he appeared at the event was the inclusion of his name on the list of finishers. (Had he not managed to cross the finish line, his name, in all likelihood, would not have been visible in the article at all.) He completed the race, finishing fourth, his time an even 58 minutes. Incidentally, DeMar had participated in the run as well. He finished in eleventh place, an even five minutes behind Tarzan.

In running events from the beginning of August through the remainder of the year, Tarzan Brown was virtually invisible in the newspapers. One exception was October 12. Ellison Brown returned to the Port Chester, New York, marathon, the scene of the first part of his tremendous two-wins-in-two-days effort one year before. The 13th annual edition of the marathon featured a strong field of forty-nine,[53] with five former Port Chester winners competing — Leslie Pawson, Pat Dengis, Frank Lalla, Clarence H. DeMar, and Ellison Brown — as well as other formidable runners including Paul Donato, Leo Giard and Jock Semple.

Tarzan Brown and Les Pawson jointly set the early fiery pace, with Donato hanging tough behind the Rhode Island pair. They led the pack for five miles. Louis Effrat, reporting for the *New York Times*, observed the proceedings at that stage and wrote, "Brown dropped back after that and it was evident that he was not in the best of shape."[54] For most of the first ten miles

Pat Dengis had remained back, steadily running in the fifth position. Then, he came charging to the fore. He seized a hold on the front-runner's position and never relinquished it. Pawson, his position behind Dengis maintained though the gap between them increased to a mile, followed Dengis across the finish line.

Tarzan Brown's defense of his title took a different turn. He experienced sharp abdominal cramps and was forced to give in to them. In this race they would not subside. With equal parts disappointment, frustration and dissatisfaction, he dropped out of contention at the halfway mark. It may have been his last competition of the 1937 season, closing with pessimistic overtones.

Dengis, who had won Port Chester three years earlier, back in 1934, repeated his success, with a slightly slower time this year of 2 hours, 33 minutes, 44.9 seconds. The *Times* noted Dengis' achievements, "In six Port Chester attempts Dengis now boasts a remarkable record, including two firsts, two seconds and two fourths."[55] Pawson took second-place honors with a registered time of 2 hours, 39 minutes, 35 seconds, nearly six minutes behind Dengis. Philadelphian William Wilson was third. Clarence H. DeMar finished seventh, in 2 hours, 48 minutes, 48 seconds. The undaunted Semple rounded out the top ten, finishing tenth, in 2 hours, 51 minutes, 9 seconds. Donato and Giard were thirteenth and fourteenth, respectively, finishing just under the three-hour mark.

Pat Dengis' running season was not over, although it was over for Ellison Brown. Dengis went on to win another New York marathon one month later — the Yonkers Marathon.

15

"A Running
Enigma" — 1938

When the 1938 season opened up with the 7th annual North Medford run, the sportswriters wondered in print who might beat Johnny Kelley for a change, for Kelley had won the last four in a row. Ellison Brown was not entered and did not participate in the March event. On a course dangerous and heavy with vehicular traffic, Kelley did not disappoint his legions in the area that bet on his triumphant effort.

Ellison Brown did not enter the Presentation Run on April 2. Les Pawson won the time prize and Frank Brown, a milkman from Medford, won his first notable race. All reporters were characteristically making picks and speculations about the Patriots' Day marathon, scheduled for Tuesday, April 19. Nason wrote an article in the *Boston Globe* on the day the entries of Ellison Brown and "Bricklayer" Bill Kennedy were announced by the B. A. A. These two former winners represented the youngest and oldest past victors prepared to tackle this year's event. Nason characterized Brown for his readers:

> Tarz Brown is a running enigma. After his 1936 victory he broke down in the Olympics, later underwent a hernia operation, and since has displayed none of that wonderful speed of 1936. Some feel his training is poorly directed; in fact, he has no trainer at all. In his own crude way he has prepared for this race; and feels he will win. Whether he does or not, we want to go on record as saying that Tarz Brown is as game a kid as ever came down from Hopkinton afoot.[1]

The regular cast of B. A. A. marathoners was signed up: Kelley, Pawson, Dengis, and DeMar, along with Durgin, Giard, Semple, Porter, and the Canadians Dave Komonen and Gerard Cote. The 1937 champion, Canadian Walter Young, who had lobbied and won a job on the police force after his victory, was unable to get time off from the force to participate and defend his title. William McMahon was also absent from the starting line as a runner, but was there dressed as a spectator. He was taking his rumored retirement seriously.

One participant was having a bitter dispute with race officials. The disagreement was such that it threatened to keep him from running the marathon for the first time in twenty-eight years. Johnny "Cigars" Connors was told by the local registration committee of the B. A. A. that he could no longer use his nickname, which he had copyrighted, on the official papers and programs. In other words, sign in as "John Connors" or do not participate. A controversy arose after Connors had participated in a show at the Chicago World's Fair, sponsored by Mr. Ripley's Believe It or Not. The A. A. U. expressed doubts about Connors' amateur status, although no one seriously took Connors to be a bona fide athletic competitor in any of his previous twenty-seven Boston runs. Connors wrote a letter to Victor O. Jones of the *Globe* "in which he blasts the two members of the registration committee who took the 'Cigars' out of his name. I'd like to print the letter, but can't, what with the laws of libel being as they are," quipped Jones.[2] Jones went on to present the letterhead that Connors used. On it was printed the following:

The Wonder of Wonders,
the One and Only Original
That Inimitable and Versatile, the Wizard —
Johnny "Cigars" Connors
Walking, Smoking, Real Smoke Stack
And Human Torch

The most publicized cigar smoker of all times. World's champion cigar smoker and holder of every and all known cigar smoking records. Famous and colorful, known all over the world for 35 years. The irrepressible, the only living person who can smoke cigars in his mouth, nose, ears and eyes at one time. Only person in the world who can smoke 20 cigars at one time. The first and only cigar-smoking Marathon runner in captivity — Cigar-a-Mile Connors — veteran of more than 300 Marathons. Star attraction at the Chicago World's Fair, 1935. Seven times a feature of Robert L. Ripley's Believe It or Not cartoons in 400 different newspapers.

Smoked 2000 cigars in 48 hours without sleeping, eating or drinking.
Holds the record, 8 minutes flat,
for running up and down the Custom House stairs, Boston, Mass.,
26 flights of stairs.
Rolled a peanut with his nose — Boston to Worcester, Mass.
— 44 miles in 46 hours.
Smokes 100 cigars a day and 700 a week.
Has already smoked 8,000,000 cigars in more than 35 years, enough to go around the world and back twice.[3]

Kelley, Pawson, Dengis, Cote — in any newspaper at any given time up until race day you could find one of these names as the likely winner. But Jerry Nason, stepping outside the box from his fellow sportswriters, made an unusual selection in that he picked a little-known Canadian, Duncan McCallum, as his dark horse special. No one gave Ellison Brown much of a chance or bothered even to say as much. On April 19, the morning of the big event, the *Globe* repeated Nason's pick of McCallum in an article that included this oh-so-brief mention of Ellison Brown:

Brown is being virtually ignored in the pre-race roundups because, one suspects, of the hernia operation he underwent a year ago. The Narragansett personally feels he has regained his speed which sent him driving down the course shattering all records as far as Coolidge Corner in 1936.[4]

According to the word in the locker rooms and on the streets, the older runners liked the temperature to read high up on the scale, the higher, the better. April 19 turned out to be that kind of day, as the temperature rose into the upper-mid-60s by noon on its way up to the mid-70s. The starting pistol was brandished for the very first time by George V. Brown's son, Walter, because the father had passed away. When Walter, future president of the B. A. A., owner and manager of the Boston Garden, founder of the Boston Celtics basketball team, and president of the Boston Bruins of the National Hockey League, flexed his index finger to squeeze the trigger, the runners were off.[5] At the gun's crack, young Oneida Native American Russell George jumped to the forefront; Walter Hornby was second and Nason's pick, McCallum, was third. Kelley and Pawson, nearly arm in arm, followed after. Two miles in, by Ashland, George exchanged places with McCallum and Hornby held onto second place, as Cote pushed his way to fourth. Tarzan Brown was running in sixth place. Behind him were Willie Wilklund, Mel Porter and Lou Gregory. The pace was slow, unusually so, and the order was soon to change. Just before Framingham, Brown was slipping. He "developed engine trouble within the first four miles and started walking,"[6] not a good sign. By Framingham, Pawson, and Kelley right behind, had both advanced, moving into the third and fourth berths behind McCallum and Hornby. Lou Gregory, Russell George, Simons and Porter continued strongly, and Brown and Cote "allowed themselves to fall back off the pace."[7] Cote was in eighth place and Brown was out of the top ten for good.

Kelley and Pawson created an informal formation, and the pair continued most of the race neck in neck. Just before Natick, Kelley and Pawson had exchanged places with McCallum. By Natick, it was recorded as Kelley, Pawson and McCallum. The Wellesley checkpoint, roughly halfway, had the same top three. Cote pushed back into contention, registering sixth in Wellesley. By then, Brown was falling way back. He never regained a competitive position in this one. Dengis, off to a slow start, was in 20th place, but with a concerted effort began making inroads.

As the marathon was underway, two vehicular accidents occurred. In one, marathon officials traveling on the marathon course in a large beach wagon were struck by a car head-on. The driver of that vehicle, Alexander Campbell Jr., driving with his father and mother, lost control of his car and careened across the road and forcefully hit the passenger wagon directly. The occupants of that car were thrown from the vehicle onto the road, sustaining serious injuries. Five men were taken to the Framingham hospital for medical treatment. Alfred Lil, former president of the N. E. A. A. A. U. and once president of the national A. A. U., received multiple cuts to his head. So did Joe Nutter, sportswriter for the *Providence Journal*. Ike Sheehan, famous athlete of an earlier era, suffered cuts and a possible fractured skull. George Hatfield, an official and judge of the ongoing marathon, had a shoulder injury. A fifth passenger, Coach Magee, injured his back. Drivers of both vehicles, Alexander Campbell Jr. and Owen Howe Jr., who drove the marathon officials, were shaken up but did not require medical treatment.

A second accident involved the marathon runner Leo Giard less than two miles from the Hopkinton starting line. An errant motorcyclist somehow collided with the runner, sending him sliding across the pavement, mostly by way of the skin of his knees. Badly bloodied, he retired to the side of the road, where he received some quick treatment, and, courageously, continued his quest along the marathon course. Giard pulled into the Wellesley checkpoint in ninth place despite the delays he was forced to endure, and he held onto the tenth spot at the next check in Auburndale (17 miles). Eventually unable to keep it up, he had to accept his finish at fifteenth overall.

It was Pawson and Kelley engaged in a tight two-man race as the two friends approached Newton Lower Falls. At this point Kelley, seemingly out of the blue, was able to subsume a twenty-five-yard lead for Pawson had to slow down with a keen case of indigestion, probably due to a hamburger he ate around 10:30 that morning before beginning the marathon. As Nason told it, the hamburger "began to voice its protest."[8] For a short spell Pawson fell behind. He later said, almost philosophically:

> Maybe it was the hamburger, and maybe it wasn't. I have always felt that any runner has one bad moment in a race and perhaps that was it. At any rate, I'll never eat so close before a Marathon again.[9]

Pawson also had this to add: "Losing the lead to Johnny at that stage of the race wasn't a catastrophe, I knew. I feel that any time you are within 100 yards of the leader you are better off than being up front."[10] Though Kelley was ahead and hauling downgrade, Pawson, having rather quickly regained his digestive equilibrium, was back in the struggle for victory, and, despite the heat, had caught up to Kelley. They were just about to begin the ascent of the Newton hills.

Meanwhile aircraft plant mechanic Pat Dengis had stepped up his speed to a near-supersonic pace, having blasted past runners from twentieth to fifth position by the time he reached Auburndale. As he overtook Cote he pantomimed the gesture of a kiss blown to the French Canadian. They both chuckled over it afterward. "It's good publicity,"[11] said Cote, who had been dropped to sixth place during the kiss. With Kelley contending with the hills, Dengis was making up ground. As Pawson and Kelley reached the crest of the hills and began the slight descent to Lake Street, Dengis had passed Porter and McCallum to assume third place behind Kelley. Dengis later recalled:

"Those hills were the easiest part. They just seemed to evaporate under my feet. I was over them in a jiffy."[12] In a matter of four miles, Dengis had managed an extraordinary feat; he had caught up to Johnny Kelley. Where Kelley was tired and in need of more and more water, Dengis was still remarkably fresh and full of vigor. Kelley had to stop three times, while he administered water to his face or took a drink, and Dengis rushed by. The two athletic adversaries patted each other on the back as Dengis took second place for his own, now in pursuit of the leading Les Pawson. Pawson slowed down momentarily, but the familiar voice of his wife shouting encouragement entered his consciousness. He fell into strong-legged stride mode once more.

McCallum was in fifth place and steadily making track with just two miles to go when he apparently fainted. He was assisted off the hot pavement and so could not finish. Incredibly, Clarence DeMar, just shy of his fiftieth birthday, had found a way to gain some ground, registering in eighth place behind Dengis at the last checkpoint, Coolidge Corner. Between there and the finish line, he managed to move up another place, finishing seventh. Dengis had gone from seventh at that checkpoint to second, but could do no better for Pawson did not give an inch. Pawson triumphed, winning his second B. A. A. Marathon. He did not break the standing record he had personally set in 1933 under completely different weather conditions.

Tarzan Brown, with a time of 3 hour, 38 minutes, 59 seconds, finished a full hour behind the first three finishers: Pawson (2:35:34), Dengis (2:36:41), and Kelley (2:37:34). It had taken him a half hour longer to complete the marathon than it had taken him the year before, despite a full year more of recuperation time since his surgery. His final position in the 1938 B. A. A. Marathon was 54th.

A possible explanation for his poor time registered that day may be the quick-dip-in-the-lake episode according to the Tarzan Brown and Boston Marathon lore. Patriots' Day in the year 1938 was indeed a warm one, with the temperature reaching 75 degrees F. Tarzan Brown may have decided on the spur of the moment to hop the guardrail and take a plunge into Lake Cochituate in Natick (on the left-hand side), or Fiske Pond (on the right), both situated approximately halfway into mile 9 along the course. Some versions of the tale say Tarzan contentedly waved to all the hot-footed, sweat-drenched runners as they passed by, that he abandoned the rest of the run after his swim. The official marathon results of 1938 do not square with this telling of the story, since he did officially complete the marathon, albeit 54th. Without a doubt, it would have been possible for Tarzan to begin the marathon, stop for a cooling dunk, and return to the running competition at hand, and his time in the 1938 race would accommodate just such an interlude.

Journalist Bill Rodriguez, writing in 1981, selected 1938 without any question or doubt as the year in which Brown "waved so-long to spectators toward the end of the race and dove into an enticing pond."[13] He did not cite any source(s), and without such attribution the reason and accuracy of his date selection for what is essentially an episode of lore as opposed to an episode of fact cannot be assessed. A careful reading, however, of his wording might be telling. Rodriguez's use of the phrase "toward the end of the race" would seemingly rule out Fiske Pond, which, at just beyond mile nine, is nearer to the Hopkinton starting line than the Exeter Street finish line. There are other swimmable waters along the course (the Charles River and the Chestnut Hill reservoir are examples) but there are no other "enticing ponds."

Author Michael Connelly also accepted the reality of the episode as fact though he chose the waters of the lake rather than the pond, and, like Rodriguez, he too contended that it occurred in 1938. He wrote:

> It was here in 1938, with the temperature approaching 80 degrees, that past winner Tarzan Brown surrendered his lead in order to take a swim in the refreshing waters of Lake Cochituate. After finishing his dip, Brown returned to the race and finished in fifty-first place. Later asked about his decision to sacrifice a shot at the first place trophy, he retorted, "Sooner or later, they (trophies) get black and you have to throw them out."[14]

Connelly unfortunately offers no argument or evidence for his contention, nor does he cite any source(s). Perhaps his source was Rodriguez.

One further item of interest concerning Jerry Nason's *Boston Globe* coverage of the 1938 B. A. A. Marathon deserves comment. Nowhere in his reporting of the 1938 event can be found the name "Heartbreak Hill," the landmark he is presumed to have christened in 1936, and employed in his commentary in 1937. The closest Nason came to using the term this year was in the following sentence, in which he wrote, "Heading into Auburndale past the Woodland Golf Club, where begins the four-mile stretch of Newton's *heartbreaking hills* that have killed off so many contenders in the past, Pawson and Kelley were still engaged in their dogfight" (emphasis added).[15] Other references to the same point in the course were not as closely connected to the cardiac-disabling connotation. For example:

> That heart-rending rise of macadam, which reaches its peak at Boston College, broke up the two-man battle, and it was the smaller Kelley, victimized by this mountain last year, who yielded the struggle.... [Pawson] plugged up the hill, passing the summit where the spires of the college crown the top of the Marathon mountain.[16]

Here was an opportunity to reasonably employ the proper nouns "Heartbreak Hill" at this point in the narrative describing the race, especially with Kelley involved in the reference, but Nason chose not to utilize the designation in his 1938 coverage.

The National A. A. U. 15-kilometer race, scheduled for the afternoon of Memorial Day, May 30, and sponsored by the Elks club at Elks Field, was a highly anticipated event. The *Westerly Sun* delineated the depth of the entertainment planned for the day: "The championship run will feature an all-star bill that will include an hour of motorcycle racing, six acts of vaudeville, an air show by the Conn. National Guard air fleet, [a] concert by [the] Elks Band and other features."[17] For the race, runners from a wide area — New York City and New York state, the far reaches of Pennsylvania, and greater New England — entered, creating the largest field ever for the event, over seventy contestants.

Johnny Kelley was the defending champion, intent upon retaining his title. Despite his efforts, that was not to be. After the race had gotten underway Kelley established himself second behind the leading runner, New Yorker J. Errol Vaughn. Eino Pentti was running right behind Kelley. It remained that way for thirteen laps. Ellison Brown reportedly "ran up with the pack all the way," but the results proved otherwise.[18] Kelley pushed himself, driving ahead of Vaughn to the front of the pack at lap fourteen. Two laps later, New Yorker Victor Drygall, making inroads, edged past Kelley and filched his front-runner's role. Drygall remained there until the finish. His first-place finish was completed in 49 minutes, 45 seconds. Kelley was passed by Pentti as well, who finished in second place but made a strong bid for the first-place victory. Pentti crossed the finish line only two seconds behind Drygall. Kelley's time was 49 minutes, 59 seconds, which earned him the prize for a third-place finish.

After those three came Vaughn, Joe Sullivan, Bill Steiner, Frank Darrah, Robert Campbell, Lou Gregory, W. Keene Frick, and Roger Labonte, in that order. And then, in twelfth place, came Brown. No reason for his uncharacteristic finish was offered.

Ellison Brown, with Tippy Salimeno's help, acquired the assistance of a trainer charged with the supervision of the daily workouts between races. Edward "Smokey" Woodmansee of Hopkinton, Rhode Island, came aboard to pay attention to quotidian training matters. Positive results were immediate.

A series of shorter races were held over the summer throughout New England, and Ellison Brown participated in his share. A few received newspaper coverage, such as the one that took place on a hot June 19 in Brooklyn, Connecticut. It was held as part of the celebratory events commemorating the 300th anniversary of the settling of people of Finnish heritage on the American continent. The eleven-mile course was drawn from the eastern Connecticut-Rhode Island border to the Brooklyn Fairgrounds. It finished with a lap around the fairgrounds track, where three thousand spectators eagerly awaited the first glimpse of the approaching runners.

This was Ellison Brown's afternoon. After the starting gun was fired, Brown found his way to the front of the small field of fifteen. Only one man among them, Dave Fagerlund of the Finnish-American A. C. of New York City, was able to give Brown any kind of a challenge, and although he valiantly tried his best, he was plainly no match for the swiftly running Brown. Fager-lund, "cracked at the halfway mark,"[19] leaving Brown to snap the tape at the finish line a full mile ahead of Fagerlund. As he sprinted around the track in front of the stands, Brown received "a great ovation" from the mostly Finnish-American crowd.[20] They were clearly an audience steeped in the tradition of old-fashioned sportsmanship, for they cheered and showed their apprecia-tion based upon the merit of the athlete, not his nationality, on an occasion created for the celebration of one particular nationality to which the victor, Brown, did not belong. Brown deserved the adulation — his time was 67 min-utes, 31 seconds. Quite a few minutes later Fagerlund began his final track lap, eventually winning second place. He was seven minutes, forty-nine sec-onds behind Brown. His final time: 75 minutes, 20 seconds.

One handicap race held on Saturday, June 25, 1938, a "tar-melting" hot summer day in West Roxbury (a part of greater Boston), was the third annual Holy Name 10-mile run. Of the eighty-two participants scheduled, John Kel-ley, Tarzan Brown, Leslie Pawson Clarence H. DeMar and Hawk Zamparelli, no longer an enrolled student at Northeastern University due to a shortage of money, provided the organizers with marquee name runners. With the exception of DeMar, they were given handicaps of 5½ minutes each in appre-ciation. Perhaps out of respect, the fifty-year-old DeMar was still handi-capped — fifteen seconds.

The *Herald's* Will Cloney, rather unusually, described some of the sar-torial details. Kelley wore a uniform with the name of his employer, Boston Edison, emblazoned across his chest. Cloney reported that Tarzan Brown sported "a terrific cerise muslin suit that appeared to be home-made."[21] The apparel of Pawson and Zamparelli apparently did not merit inclusion in the *Herald's* sports pages.

Kelley waited five and a half minutes before being allowed to go and then made his way past all the runners in front of him, one by one. By the time he had traversed eight miles, he had assumed the lead over the large field. Kel-ley really never faced any opposition. He finished in 54:14, somewhat slower than his record for the course but more than adequate considering the swel-tering heat. Pawson, running his second race in 24 hours (along with Hawk Zamparelli), finished officially in fifth place, though his actual time (55:47) was second to Kelley's. Tarzan Brown, despite his brilliant costume, was sev-enteenth. His time of 59:09, just nine seconds behind Ryder (who was the second-place runner) with the 5½ minutes added, was 64:39. DeMar did bet-ter than that, finishing in thirteenth place. He ran (63:58) but his time was adjusted by only fifteen seconds, to 64 minute, 13 seconds. Hawk Zampar-elli could not finish in the heat.

A July 5 banner headline atop the *Westerly Sun* sports pages proclaimed, "Tarzan Brown Wins Twice in Holiday Races."[22] Under that was a subhead-line with the optimistic message: "Westerly Indian Shows Definite Comeback Signs In Great Wins."[23] Ellison Brown, back to his iron-man ways, won back-to-back races against strong, challenging fields in both events, the first taking place in Worcester, Massachusetts, and the second in Burrillville, Rhode Island.

On Sunday afternoon, July 3, Brown shared the wait at the scratch line with Les Pawson. They had a 5½-minute holdup as the rest of the field, including the veteran Clarence H. DeMar, got started in the ten-mile race. In fact, DeMar, in uncharacteristic fashion, led the pack for much of the race. When finally allowed to commence, Brown wasted no time making up the deficit the scratch delay had created. It required seven miles of vigorous, hard running before he could catch up to DeMar. Brown dutifully yet respectfully passed him. Brown sped to the finish line without a challenge thereafter, crossing the end line more than a quarter of a mile ahead of Pawson and the rest of the field. His time: 56 minutes, 15 seconds.

One afternoon later, on Independence Day, Brown and DeMar were both at it again under the hot sun. Little Lloyd Anderson attempted to give Brown a run for his money, challenging him all the way until the final mile. There, in a burst of acceleration, Brown staged an incredible sprint which separated him from Anderson by over a minute in time at the finish line. Brown finished first, setting a record; his time over the course was 47 minutes, 52 seconds. That incredibly fast mark sounded the alarm bells. The course was later measured by A. A. U. officials, who determined that the length was only 8.9 miles, more than a mile shy of the advertised ten-mile distance. In this event, however, Brown's strategic efforts were not adversely affected by the deficiency of the course length and the incompetence of the race officials.

In that 1938 Burrillville race, Anderson officially finished in second place. "The best Clarence H. DeMar could do was 16th," the *Westerly Sun* observed.[24] No other names or final positions were reported.

A race called the Irish-American Civic Club's 12-mile Road Race was held on July 10 in New Bedford, Massachusetts. The famed trio of Brown, Pawson, and Kelley (the Irish-American of the three) competed against each other on a very warm afternoon, and for the first four miles no runner attained the upper hand (or foot) over any other. Then, Brown and Kelley transformed the three-of-a-kind into a pair of aces as the two men together raised the pace up a notch or two. Pawson did not answer the call, and fell back slightly. For the next five miles, Kelley and Brown matched each other stride for stride. With three miles to go, earlier than his customary point to do so, Brown fired up the reserves and blasted in no uncertain terms ahead of Kelley to the finish line alone.

Brown's time over the twelve miles was 1 hour, 5 minutes, 7 seconds. Kelley finished a minute and seven seconds behind, garnering second place. Pawson was third in one hour, nine minutes even. A steadfast DeMar completed the course in thirteenth place.

The following day the *Westerly Sun* told its readers that Brown "looked better in yesterday's race despite the heat than he had at any stage of his fine comeback try."[25] The *Boston Chronicle* carried a front-page photo of Tarzan Brown and Johnny Kelley running on a busy, automobile-laden city street in New Bedford. The title above the photo read: "CLINCHING HIS THIRD STRAIGHT IN COMEBACK ACT." The caption below the picture read: "TARZAN BROWN is shown outdistancing Arlington's Johnny Kelley who was favored to win the 12-mile marathon at New Bedford on Sunday, July 10. This was the Indian's third straight victory within 2 months."[26]

Another duel between Pawson and Brown took place on a very windy and wet July 24 in the Notre Dame A. C. Handicap 12-Mile Run in Central Falls (and Providence). This time, it was Pawson who captured the time prize by the slimmest of margins—a single second over Brown. "So close was the duel between Pawson and his Indian foe that they seemed to be running as one over the water-logged course," reported the *Westerly Sun*.[27] Pawson's time was recorded as 1 hour, 2 minutes, 38 seconds. In addition to the time prize, Pawson finished second and received that prize as well. Brown finished in third place. The weather conditions and handicapping probably did not play a role in Brown's time-prize battle with Pawson, but it probably did affect the outcome of the race in general.

Lloyd Anderson, who won first place, had been granted an extremely generous handicap of 5 minutes, 15 seconds. Other finishers included Linden Dempster in fourth place, an unknown Pat Supree of Foxboro in fifth, and Andrew "Hawk" Zamparelli in sixth place, now affiliated with the John C. Carr club. Zamparelli's time was listed as 1 hour, 5 minutes, 10 seconds.

Four nights later, on July 28, Somersworth, New Hampshire, was the site of the annual 10-mile road race sponsored by the Holy Trinity Church. Kelley, Pawson, and Zamparelli competed in the hotly contested race. Brown ran the first five miles in the back of the pack. In the second half of the race, he spurted ahead to the forefront, withstanding the powerful recurring challenges of Kelley as well as the strong probes of Hawk and Pawson. In the end, it was not close as Brown beat Kelley by fifty yards (and thirty-five seconds). Brown's winning time was 50 minutes, 15 seconds. Kelley placed ahead of the third-place Hawk. Pawson finished fifth.

A contest a few days later on July 31 received brief mention in the *Boston Globe*, an article with few details included. A 12-mile scratch race was held for the second year in a row in Webster, Massachusetts, sponsored by the St. Joseph's Athletic Club. In that event on an extremely warm day, Tarzan Brown won handily, running the course in 1 hour, 3 minutes, 13 seconds. Andrew "Hawk" Zamparelli took second place, running nearly two minutes behind Brown. His time was 1:05:10. Showing in third place was Andre Brunelle of the North Medford Club. He finished a minute and two seconds in back of Hawk.[28]

Four days later, on August 4, Brown and Hawk were at it again, this time at an evening race in Providence, Rhode Island, under the auspices of St. Vincent de Paul parish.[29] Despite the evening hour for the start, the heat of the day was still uncomfortable for rigorous athletic activity. Nevertheless, the competition for the 10-mile run included Les Pawson and Clarence H. DeMar among the thirty-four starters joining in the fray. It made no difference to Tarzan. What started out as "strictly a two-man affair between Pawson and Brown"[30] where they ran shoulder-to-shoulder, nearly evenly matching step for step, changed after two-thirds of the course had been covered. At that point, Brown uncorked his unpatented rapid-fire jets and zoomed to the finish line, to the deafening cheers created by the thousands of spectators packed along the finish line area.

Tarzan Brown won the race, beating Pawson by a full minute and four seconds. Brown's time was 52 minutes, 5 seconds. Les Pawson finished in 53 minutes, 9 seconds. Hawk Zamparelli was third; his time was 55 minutes, 7 seconds. Fourth-place honors went to local runner Lloyd Anderson, his time, 56 minutes, 12 seconds. Six men did not finish, but DeMar did. He crossed the finish line in fifteenth place.

Brown emerged in just five minutes from the dressing rooms, while some runners were still just approaching the finish line. Brown stepped purposefully toward the table where the winners' prizes were on display. The *Westerly Sun* recorded his words and what followed:

> "I want the bowl," he declared. "I got plenty of those others." He was referring to statues and trophy cups. "I'm a married man now, and I can use that one."
>
> The prize he pointed to, originally intended for the third-place winner, was a bronze, pedestalled bowl of some size. The committee held a hurried consultation. Tarzan got the bowl.[31]

Whether Pawson, the second-place finisher, received the available first-place trophy and how the plan to disperse the other prizes was reformulated was not reported.

Abe Soloveitzik, in his sports column, felt compelled to comment on the excitement Ellison Brown was generating in recent weeks with his successes. He wrote:

> Tarzan Brown is certainly kicking the daylights out of those fellows who said he was all through. Seven wins in his last nine starts has again boosted him to the fore as the nation's best distance runner. He's eyeing the Boston marathon run next year and hopes to make the Olympic team in 1940.[32]

Six days later, on August 10, Ellison Brown traveled to Maine to run in the Old Orchard Beach 10-mile road race. So did Hawk Zamparelli, Les Pawson, and Clarence H. DeMar. Famous comedian, radio voice and motion picture star Fred Allen, taking the afternoon off from his vacation in Maine, served as one of the race's official judges. A field of thirty-six men readied at the starting line, aiming to qualify for winners' prizes.

First across the finish line was Tarzan Brown, running the ten miles in 51 minutes, 18¾ seconds.[33] At the finish, Brown was 300 yards ahead of the next-in-line runner, Zamparelli, who finished in 52 minutes, 4.6 seconds, and one hundred yards ahead of Pawson, who finished third. DeMar finished eleventh.

Brown "jogged eight miles"[34] on August 18 in preparation for the National A. A. U. 25-K race set for August 20 in Newport, Rhode Island. Brown was scheduled to rest August 19. Since toiling under the close scrutiny of his trainer, Ed "Smokey" Woodmansee, Brown had been on a winning tear, registering eight victories in his last ten races.

Brown, Pawson, DeMar and the defending title holder Johnny Kelley were on hand less than two weeks later to compete for the title of the National A. A. U. 25-kilometer championship race sponsored by the Newport Chamber of Commerce. An account by the AP wire service, bereft of detail or description, was carried by the *Boston Globe*.[35] But the succinct headline told the whole story: "TARZAN BROWN WINS 25-KILOMETER GRIND."

First in a field of sixty-four[36], Tarzan Brown's winning time of 1 hour, 26 minutes, 18 seconds, beat Johnny Kelley by three and one-half minutes. Kelley finished second, and Jean Berthelot of Newark, New Jersey, was third. The steady-rolling Leslie Pawson finished in fourth place. George Durgin of Lynn, Massachusetts, finished in the fifth spot. Mel Porter of New York was ninth and veteran plodder Clarence H. DeMar, plying his running trade with dogged determination all summer, crossed the finish line in eighteenth place. Lou Gregory, who usually put up a staunch challenge, did not finish in the top ten.

A little over two weeks later, another title was at stake: the New England A. A. U. 20-kilometer championship. Taking place on the afternoon of September 10, the road race was the prominent feature of the 101st Infantry Association (VFW) convention, and, as such, commanded attention. Needless to say, with Tarzan Brown, Johnny Kelley and Leslie Pawson going head to head in a starting field of 51, interest in the event was huge.[37] Ethel Brown had accompanied her husband from Rhode Island to Waltham, the watch city, to be on hand to watch Ellison run.

The approximately twelve-mile course began at the Waltham City Hall and wound its way through the streets of Waltham, Watertown, Newton and Auburndale (just west of Boston, Massachusetts) and even included a section of the famous B. A. A. Marathon course. The course concluded with a final lap around the Waltham Athletic Field.

Arthur Duffey ticked off these details at the race's beginning: "Scarcely had the start been made ... than the Indian, running in fine form, swung into the lead, passing Fred Brown of the North Medford Club. Not far behind was Kelley, while George L. Durgin of Beverly and Linden Dempster were next, Les Pawson fourth, and the rest of the field strung out along the road."[38] At the three-mile mark, the *Post* reported Brown and Kelley "running almost shoulder to shoulder" with Pawson third.[39] The *Herald* saw it differently. Rather than side by side or shoulder to shoulder, it observed that Kelley constantly trailed Brown by twenty yards. It reported, "Tarzan took the lead at the two-mile mark, and from that point maintained his 20-yard advantage over Kelley."[40]

Hawk Zamparelli flirted with fourth place. Roger Labonte, Linden Dempster, and George Durgin — even Jock Semple and Clarence DeMar — hung in tough, but it was apparent to everyone present that the three stars of the B. A. A. were in a contest of their own. Duffey wrote, "Coming into Watertown square, it was plainly evident that the race was among Brown, Kelley and Pawson, each watching the other carefully."[41]

As the three front-runners sped through Newton Center it was Tarzan Brown and Johnny Kelley, one and two, followed closely by Les Pawson, content to keep the pair right where he could see them. By Newtonville, Brown had opened up a short lead of about twenty yards. Nobody seemed too concerned; certainly no one had cause to panic. The three runners leading the pack remained in these seemingly fixed positions, as they swept toward the Woodland Golf Club. It was here that Kelley attempted to test Brown's resolve. Duffey reported, "Going by the Woodland Golf Club and on to Grove street, Brown appeared worried, as Kelley began to force him, but it was only for a while."[42] Brown refused to yield any ground, and Kelley, still firmly in second place, would have to come up with another strategy. That may not have been a possibility. As they made their return to Waltham, Brown, Kelley and Pawson, though leg (and arm) muscles were toiling to the highest degree, were in a balanced but immutable state. None of the three could cause any shift in their positions. It was a different story behind them. Zamparelli had faltered. He joined twenty-three others who were forced to drop out of the competition.[43] Labonte was fourth but could not make any gain on Pawson. Dempster, Tony Medeiros, and Durgin were in fifth, sixth and seventh places, respectively. Semple was a third of the way back of the entire field. DeMar was about two-thirds of the way back.

Duffey described the heavily populated scene at the athletic field where the finish line was drawn:

> At the Waltham High Field, one of the largest crowds flocked around the entrance, the Indian hardly being able to get in. He started to finish his last lap around the track as Kelley came into the park, 20 yards behind. The last lap was a sizzler, but there was no question about Tarzan being the class of the field.[44]

According to all reports, Brown made a dashing sprint to the finish line, breaking the tape after running hard for 1 hour, 12 minutes, 58 seconds. Kelley registered his finish just four seconds behind; his official time was recorded as 1:13:02. Those four seconds translated into a Brown advantage over Kelley of perhaps twenty yards. Pawson was third across the finish line, behind Brown by nearly one hundred yards. He finished in 1:14:19.

Among the rest of the field, Labonte finished fourth, a full two minutes and nine seconds behind Pawson. Dempster was fifth, Medeiros sixth, and Durgin finished in seventh place. There was no dispute that Italo Amicangioli finished eighth but there was confusion over his time. A misprint in the *Herald* had him tied in time with the ninth-place runner, Andre Brunelle. Brunelle's North Medford teammate, Dave Murphy, took the tenth-place prize. Eleventh place was seized by Jock Semple, only seven seconds behind the tenth-place Murphy. Not listed in the newspaper compilation of finishers and their times was the name of the venerable veteran Clarence H. DeMar, who received the most rousing applause of the day, especially as he entered the park for the final lap before crossing the finish line. DeMar was a finisher once again; this time he was the twentieth man to cross the finish line.

The *Post* ran a beautiful photograph with the title, "The Victor and His Prizes," along with its coverage of the race. The caption to that photo read: "One of the first to greet Ellison (Tarzan) Brown, Narragansett Indian and former B. A. A. Marathon winner, was his beautiful wife and Mayor Arthur A. Hansen of Waltham at the Waltham Athletic Field, after winning the New England A. A. A. U. 20 Kilometer championship held by the Veterans of Foreign Wars."[45] In the picture, Brown, still clad in his racing attire, has one arm around the waist of his wife, Ethel, and one hand around his newly acquired trophy. His honor, the mayor, grasping his fedora by his side, smiles with obvious pleasure at the camera.

That bright and breezy Saturday afternoon, Ellison Brown had run "one of the greatest races of his career," Arthur Duffey fervently told his readers.[46] Brown was now the concurrent proprietor of a pair of championship titles: the recently captured national 25-K title and the just-obtained New England 20-K title. The victory in Waltham, of note for the title crown, was also noteworthy for another reason. According to the *Herald*'s calculation, "it was his 10th straight distance win this summer."[47] The *Westerly Sun* figured this latest victory to be "his eleventh in thirteen starts since June 19."[48]

Six days later, the *Herald*'s Bob Dunbar had this heads-up item in his column of September 17:

> Somewhat lost in the shuffle of the school football openings will be the 15-kilometer run at Dedham today. The field of 48 includes such stars as Johnny Kelley, Hawk Zamparelli, Tarzan Brown, and Francis Darrah. The Tarzan has found new life this year and once more is a leading marathon threat.[49]

Dunbar's complimentary remarks about "The Tarzan," the only runner given supplemental commentary, stood out in the press because very little ink was being devoted to runners and the results of the running game at this point in time in any of the newspapers, so it seemed.

"Tarzan Brown Astonishes Fans with Eleventh Win," trumpeted the *Chronicle*'s sports headline on September 24, 1938. The New England A. A.

U. 15-kilometer title was decisively taken by Brown over the second-place Kelley and the third-place Pawson. The weekly paper, which did not offer detail or description, gave its mostly minority readers this title roundup:

> By winning the title here Saturday the Indian adonis completed a brace of wins which now includes the New England A. A. U. [sic] championships at 15, 20, and 25 kilometers.[50]

The *Herald* devoted only three paragraphs to the story with no byline, under the headline: "RECORD PLOD WON BY TARZAN BROWN." Any short race with Brown, Kelley and Pawson competing with all cylinders firing had the potential to be close and thrilling, and this 15-kilometer event, sponsored by the Oakdale A. C. at Dedham, Massachusetts, held September 17, 1938, was no exception. John Kelley, defending both his title and the course record he had set the year before, began the race up front along with Brown, Pawson and local running club member Frank Mann. The four were "running neck and neck and pull[ed] away from the rest of the field of 45 starters," the *Globe* reported.[51] After four miles, Brown and Kelley were intensely legging it alongside each other upon the difficult course as they began the taxing ascent upon "meeting two steep hills on High st., at the Westwood line."[52] Pawson had fallen back, about fifteen yards, but was determined to keep in third place. Mann accepted the fourth slot, just slightly behind on Pawson's heels. Sticking together, Kelley and Brown reached the halfway mark. Duffey reported, "At the five-mile distance, Kelley managed to get a lead over the Indian and started to pull away but it was only for a while."[53] By mile six, Ellison Brown took over the lead from Kelley and never gave it back, no matter how single-minded Kelley was to retake it. Pawson doggedly held onto his position. Mann had slipped to eighth at race's end. His fellow club member, Roger Labonte, took the fourth-place honors.

Tarzan Brown was ahead by approximately twenty yards at the finish. The time listings showed he finished only *2.2 seconds* ahead of Kelley. Brown's time was reported in the *Post* to be 48:42.6 to Kelley's 48:44.8.[54] By the *Herald's* account, Brown had shaved a full minute and ten seconds off Kelley's 1937 time in establishing a new record. Kelley's time the year before was reported by all newspapers to be 49 minutes, 52.6 seconds. That being the case, the *Herald* here was on the money. The *Post*, in one of its disagreements with a competitor, reported that Brown "broke Kelley's record of a year ago by 50 seconds."[55] Why the paper gave this erroneous, mathematical discount of 20 seconds is unknown.

Kelley had finished 1 minute, 7.8 seconds faster than the year before, thereby also breaking his own set record. Pawson, who took the third-place prize, finished in 49:32, fifty seconds in back of Brown. He also joined Brown and Kelley in finishing under the year-old course record, by 20.6 seconds. This year's pace was hot indeed!

The newspapers were at odds on other points as well. The view expressed in the *Boston Globe* headline, "TARZAN BROWN WINS DEDHAM RUN EASILY," really did not square with the facts, for Brown won by a margin of only two seconds over John Kelley, nor was it shared by the rival sportswriters. The *Post*, for example, called it "one of the hardest fought battles ever held in the New England A. A. A. U. 15-kilometer championship races." Another disagreement yet emerged.

The *Herald* reported that "the victory was his [Brown's] seventh straight in road running competition this summer," despite its own statement the week before that the previous race had been his tenth straight.[56] By *Post* sportswriter Arthur Duffey's calculation, Brown "scored his 11th straight triumph."[57] (The *Globe* did not venture into the computational mire on that one.) Although there were some differences of opinion on that issue, nobody disagreed with Duffey when he stated, "Tarzan ran a well judged race from start to finish." On that point, all present, newspapermen and runners alike, could easily concur. Brown had acquired another major running title, his third championship within the space of four weeks.

Heavy rains, winds and higher-than-usual seas combined in the days leading up to September 21, but no one in southern Rhode Island was prepared for the overwhelming imminent destruction on the way that day. Forecasting in 1938 was in its infancy. Still, many disregarded official orders for mass evacuation when the orders were issued. The familiar choice to "ride out the storm" was as popular though foolhardy an option then as it is in our times. Just how many lives could have been saved if the calls to evacuate were heeded will never be known. In the Narragansett community, situated on the Rhode Island coast, the damage was extensive. Buildings were leveled, rooftops were uplifted, windows shattered, and crops and landscape destroyed. During the afternoon of the 21st the land and everything on it was battered by the high force of winds and the crashing blow of a twelve- to fifteen-foot tidal surge. The especially high eighteen to twenty-five-foot-high tides that were present were due, in part, to the gravitation pull and the nearness of the autumnal equinox. Amidst the devastation, boats were destroyed, the coastline eroded and fishing, so important to the native peoples for sustenance, was disrupted for weeks. Fires were rampant throughout the region as well. When it was all totaled, the damage was wide-ranging, estimated to be "at least $306 million in damage, which would equal about 3.5 billion in today's [1999's] dollars."[58]

Early on, Ellison Brown was watching the rough, high seas with much interest and wonder. According to Ethel,[59] he returned to the house to take her down to the beach to show her the violent surf he had been observing. Packing their son along, the three faced the angry, explosive waves. Ethel became frightened, frightened for herself, her son and her husband. The family returned to their fragile dwelling, picked up a few items, got in their automobile, and drove inland toward Hope Valley, about twelve miles from the coast. In that vicinity, an immediate crisis developed, and developed quickly. In a flash, they became trapped by two huge trees, one which fell across the road directly in front of them obstructing their way forward, and the other which came crashing down right behind them, blocking their way as they attempted to go in reverse. Utterly stuck but unscathed, they abandoned the immovable vehicle, fearing what fate had in store. Ethel recalled that a policeman appeared in the rain-soaked, dark road, similarly unable to drive his patrol car. Decked out in a slicker, he was screaming and running for his life, offering no visible assistance to anyone. The Browns spotted a nearby building with obvious signs of life, and they headed toward that shelter. It turned out to be, Ethel was soon to discover, an undertaker's funeral parlor. The Brown family, wet and cold, huddled in a part of the building shaped like an "ell" along with a number of other wayward souls caught in the full fury of the massive hurricane. They began to wonder how long they might have to remain there, and what the chances were of getting something to eat, especially for their child, when, in a violent gust — like an explosion — the roof of that ell-shaped enclosure was ripped right off from over their heads, leaving splintered debris and rain plummeting down upon them. They were shuttled off to a cellar area, where innumerable caskets were stacked. Ethel was not sure if they were empty or "occupied." The family received little in the way of consolation.

As time passed, the hurricane traveled north on its path toward the province of Quebec, in Canada. When the weather permitted, men with large saws, both of the hand and the powered variety, appeared on the roads, ready to saw the massive trunks and open up the thoroughfares, so critical to getting the rescue teams in and the needy to assistance, medical and otherwise. The Browns, fortunately, were able to survive the hurricane of 1938 without injury, a massive storm which took six hundred lives, over half of those in the state of Rhode Island alone.

Brown was hired to work with the Rhode Island State Division of Roads and Bridges in an emergency clean-up crew. The clean-up operation took many weeks. Brown managed to train only sparingly for an upcoming 30-kilometer title race. The national race was hosted on October 12, in Greenfield, Massachusetts. Greenfield, situated twenty-two miles south of Brattleboro, Vermont, and about one hundred miles west and north of Boston, saw the assemblage of a strong field of distance runners, including Brown, Kelley, and Pawson along with Canadian Gerard Cote. An AP report with little detail appeared in the *Westerly Sun*.[60] The headline, "Leslie Pawson Is Winner of Title Run At Greenfield," essentially told the story. Pawson's time was given: 1 hour, 48 minutes, 54 seconds. George Durgin finished second — not a tight race at all — in 1 hour, 54 minutes, 25 seconds. Cote was third, Paul Donato was fourth, and Jean Berthelot finished fifth. Sixth place belonged to Brown; his time was listed as 2 hours, 4 minutes. Kelley took ninth place, finishing in 2 hours, 5 minutes, 22 seconds. There was no additional commentary on the results, the race, the travel, or the condition of the area in the aftermath of the hurricane.

On November 6, the National A. A. U. Marathon title was at stake at the annual Yonkers, New York, marathon. Featured was a highly talented field ("the best field assembled for a marathon this year"[61]) including Brown, Cote, Dengis, Donato, Evans, Heinicke, Kelley, Pawson, Porter and Young. For the second time in two years, Pat Dengis beat everybody to the finish line. He finished a quarter mile ahead of Gerard Cote, taking the lead ahead of Cote at twenty miles and never looking back. His time to the finish line was 2 hours, 39 minutes, 38 seconds. The Quebecois' time for the second-place prize was 2 hours, 43.5 minutes. Third place belonged to Mel Porter, completing the marathon thirty-five seconds behind Cote. Fourth, over five minutes later, was Dengis protégé Don Heinicke. Pawson finished fifth; his time was 2 hours, 50 minutes, 7 seconds. Paul Donato; the three Canadian runners, Lloyd Evans, Walter Young, and Fred Bristow; and Augustus Johnson of East Port Chester, New York, filled out the top ten finishers. Johnny Kelley finished thirteenth. Journalistic accounts of the race did not list Ellison Brown among the first twenty-five finishers. There was no way of knowing if he indeed finished at all.

The final race of the season was held on Thanksgiving Day in Berwick, Pennsylvania, despite the worst weather conditions in the twenty-nine-year history of the event. The race was run in the midst of a heavy snowstorm along a snow-covered, rough-surfaced, 9-mile, 257-yard course. In a very close race, the trio of Tarzan Brown, New York Millrose A. A. member Lou Gregory and Penn State running star Pete Olexy from Lansford, Pennsylvania, battled each other the entire distance. According to the AP dispatch, "not more than 10 yards separated the three at any point on the last four miles."[62] At the finish line, it was Olexy, beating Lou Gregory by just one second, a matter of five yards. Olexy's time for the course was 51 minutes, 25 seconds. Tarzan Brown came in third, having literally slipped back in the final moments. Brown's time for the race was 51 minutes, 33 seconds— six seconds behind the winner and five in back of the second-place Gregory. Les Pawson finished thirty-three seconds behind Brown, for fourth-place honors. Unknowns Joe Clark of Germantown and Toronto runner Lloyd Longman finished behind Pawson. Next came Johnny Kelley, in 53 minutes, 13 seconds, for a seventh-place finish.

The inclement weather and snow accumulation had made it a difficult run for all participants, and contributed to the difficult travel back to New England.

16

"I Give Him a Ride and He Gives Me a Beating"—1939

It was a cold, bracing, sweeping wind that blew through the greater Boston area on Saturday, March 18, 1939, as the eighth annual North Medford 20-Mile Road Race jump-started the new running season. A March snowstorm the previous weekend had dropped snow on the region, catching unwary weather forecasters and consequently most of the public by surprise. A week later, snow still lined the route, and parts of the course were icy, but "the mid-week rain and the customarily heavy vehicular traffic combined to clear most of the ice and snow away," Will Cloney of the *Herald* reported.[1]

Johnny Kelley, winner of the last five consecutive North Medford runs, decided not to compete but instead to watch from the sidelines, conserving his strength for the upcoming B. A. A. Marathon, which once again was to serve as a U. S. Olympic team tryout. Kelley's decision not to enter the North Medford contest must have been a relief for the sixty-six of seventy-nine entrants who showed up for the competition. Among the hopefuls were Les Pawson, winner of the first two North Medford races (before Kelley's string of wins) as well as current champion and still record-holder (from 1933) of the B. A. A. Marathon. In addition to those running credentials, Pawson had recently run a different kind of race, and won that as well; he was elected alderman from his home town of Pawtucket, Rhode Island. The thirty-four-year-old Pawson was a Democratic candidate in a chiefly Republican district, yet he had won by a landslide.

Ellison Brown, coming off a mostly lackluster couple of seasons, shared the starting point with (among others) Canadians Gerard Cote and Walter Young, New Yorker Mel Porter, and Jock Semple, who had a new club affiliation: the B. A. A. Semple had disbanded the team at his former employer, United Shoe Machinery of Beverly, and reformed at the club with the icon of the Unicorn. Locally, this was big news.

When the race commenced, a swarm of athletes headed out in a flurry.

For the first mile most of the veterans were content to stay in the background, letting the less-experienced runners go forth. After a few miles, Pawson, sporting "mittens knitted in all the colors of the rainbow,"[2] and Cote, wearing gloves, had established themselves near the front, running side by side, which they did for most of the race. Jean Berthelot, a French-born pastry chef employed at Jack Dempsey's restaurant in New York City, "wearing a pair of blue-wristed milk man gloves"[3] and "long underwear under his regular uniform,"[4] joined the two front-runners. Young was in a second grouping, which stayed up close to the front. Tarzan Brown, somewhat hindered by a slow start, tirelessly worked himself into fourth place.

At Malden Square, a short freight train threatened to disrupt some of the runners. With the warning gates lowered, Pawson, Cote and Berthelot hunched under the striped barriers. The three crossed the tracks and just got past the oncoming train safely, without any apparent delay. Brown was forced to stop as the train was passing. According to Will Cloney, Tarzan Brown was only "held up for a few seconds by the train, but he was not seriously hindered."[5] Whether the train was responsible for enough of a delay to any of the runners to affect the race's outcome was not established, nor did the newspaper accounts suggest as much. A pelting of snowballs thrown by some attention-seeking juveniles also did not impede the racers nor apparently cause a change in the final results.

At the nine-mile mark, the order of the top five runners was Pawson, Cote, Berthelot, Brown, and Young. Cote took his gloves off, literally and figuratively. By the thirteenth mile, Cote had surged ahead of Pawson, breaking up the threesome that had led most of the way. He pulled ahead of Berthelot for good a mile later. Cote was on his way, and he picked up his pace. He pulled his gloves back over his hands. Brown was still fourth, and Young fluctuated between the fifth and sixth places with Paul Donato. Mel Porter led the next small cluster of competitors.

Gerard Cote continued to blaze ahead in the cold air. But as leader with no one to follow, he got momentarily confused and took a wrong turn off the course near the end. He "was shooed back"[6] and resumed his beeline to the finish line.

About the fifteenth mile,[7] Tarzan Brown caught a stitch in his side. The pain caused him to halt. Within a matter of eight minutes, he had slipped from fourth to ninth place, and was unable to curtail the pain. He could only stand by and watch the rapidly deteriorating race results. But as soon as he was able, he pressed onward to the finish line.

Gerard Cote won by 500 yards. Will Cloney gave this description and interpretation of the twenty-five-year-old winner: "Cote ran a confident race throughout, his very style indicating his frame of mind. He ran with a sort of strut, his broad shoulders squared and his chest thrown out, and he never was in trouble."[8] In his post-race celebration, "the fashion-plate who looks more like a professional dance partner than a marathoner" with his slicked down black hair and his natty gabardine suit, lit a big victory cigar.[9] It was this unemployed man's trademark when he won (and when he lost.)[10] His time was 1 hour, 54 minutes, 53 seconds, the second fastest time for the course. Jean Berthelot was the second to finish, two and a half minutes behind Cote, in 1:57:22. Les Pawson was third with 1:58:04. "Pawson was not disappointed at his showing," the *Boston Post* reported, "but he expected to win."[11]

Ellison Brown registered a rather hollow 2:07:28 in a ninth-place finish. Of Brown's work that wintry afternoon the *Post* had this to say, "Ellison (Tarzan) Brown finished 10th [*sic*] and looked good during the race until the last six miles."[12] There was no elaboration of his physical condition in any of the principal newspapers.

In addition to the legitimate race, the afternoon had seen some subterfuge. Nason reported:

> An unknown entitled Walter Marshall of Rhode Island came bolting into sixth position like Jesse Owens in a furlong.... The checkers didn't have his number (71) at any stage of the final 10 miles and he was scratched from the results.... None of the boys could recall being passed by him.[13]

Cote, who had finished with a second-place finish the year before, had come very close that time but had not been able to prevail over Kelley in Medford. Now he enjoyed his victory, even though he still had not beat Kelley in Medford. A respectful John Kelley had observed Cote's accomplishment with admiration. "That's a remarkable performance on an afternoon as cold as this," he said.[14]

All watched as Gerard Cote accepted a gold wristwatch from the Honorable John Carr, mayor of Medford, for his victory.

The eighth annual Presentation Literary and Social Association 10-mile Handicap Road Race was held on Saturday afternoon, April Fool's Day. There were 116 names on the official entry list that morning, including such luminaries as Leslie Pawson, Hawk Zamparelli, George Durgin, Fred Brown and Jock Semple. (John Kelly, as was his custom, chose not to run competitively that close to the B. A. A. Marathon, and so was not entered.)

Before leaving his Pawtucket, Rhode Island home for the race in Brighton, Massachusetts, Les Pawson got word that Tarzan Brown was requesting a ride to the race. Unlike Pawson, Brown was not entered in the event. Nevertheless, Pawson gladly agreed to give his friend a lift. Club members and spectators were surprised but delighted to see Tarzan Brown's appearance when Pawson arrived. As Pawson made his prerun preparations, Tarzan Brown explained his racing intentions to the race officials and convinced them to allow him to be a "post entry," meaning he could compete in the run. He was duly assessed the harshest handicap, the scratch position. He'd get to start, but he'd share with Pawson the privilege of being the last runners to leave the starting line. Pawson's designation to run from scratch was based on his well-known past performances. He held the record for the Presentation's ten-mile course. He was the only man to win the race from the scratch position, and he was the only man in its history to win both the race and the time prize simultaneously. That occurred in 1933, the same year he later won the B. A. A. Marathon and set a new record for it, a record which was still in place.

One hundred runners[15] awaited the starting gun, under ideal weather conditions for running. As Brown and Pawson watched, ninety-eight runners, sent off in relays based upon their handicaps, commenced the athletic contest. What seemed like a long interval — a full five minutes— transpired and the two Rhode Islanders were finally allowed to start. Having been held back that long, they had some serious catching-up to do.

Brown and Pawson determinedly pursued the pack. For the first half of the course, the resolute pair applied strides of near mechanical precision as they ate up distance, yard by yard. Where the course shared some of the same roadways with the B. A. A. Marathon course — the Newton Hills stretch and Lake Street — Ellison Brown and Leslie Pawson made noticeable headway, as other perspiring individuals ahead of them began to tire, wither, give in, give out or give up. Pawson eked out a lead over Brown. He kept at it, and that lead increased in turn, at one point reaching upward of one hundred-fifty yards. As they continued to move amongst the top ten runners, the two intent scratchmen never let up.

With less than two miles to go, things changed dramatically. Brown picked up his pace. He began to sprint with such velocity that he quickly wiped out the distance between Pawson and himself, and all the while, Pawson hadn't slackened his pace. As Arthur Duffey described the action: "Finally, one mile and a half from home, Pawson and Brown turned on full steam with the Indian gradually gaining the upper hand. Dashing into Tremont street and heading for the Presentation clubhouse, the Indian managed to gain some 20 yards on the Pawtucket champion and crossed the line with yards to spare."[16] Yards to spare! It was really a matter of seconds—four seconds to be exact. Brown broke the finish-line tape with the third fastest time in the race's history, and one second faster than his own 1936 time when he won the time prize. His corrected time: 55 minutes, 57 seconds. Brown won two prizes— the day's time prize and the first-place award, the second man ever to do both. Pawson, the other one to accomplish that feat, finished in second place, only four seconds behind Brown. Pawson's record for the course was still intact, by twenty-seven seconds. The always gracious, record-holding gentleman had this to say:

> "Now what do you think of a guy like that," kidded Les before ducking into a shower. "I give him a ride up here and he gives me a beating. But all joking aside: Tarz ran a beautiful race. I'm perfectly satisfied with my own performance."[17]

Tarzan Brown chimed in with a response to his fellow competitor and man responsible for his ride home. He revealed a bit of his strategy, and he sounded like a man in control:

I jes' let you go out over those hills and kill those other fellows off, Les. When you started pouring it on I let you go to it. I didn't want any part of that business. Comin' off the last hill I was feelin' great.[18]

Tarzan Brown, the man who signed in late for the event, turned heads that afternoon. Jerry Nason, who had championed the runner in the past and had seen hundreds of athletes do amazing things, wrote, "Veteran curbstone critics marveled that Brown could yield to a man of Pawson's superlative speed as much as 100 yards on the Commonwealth av. hills, then retrieve the yardage so effortlessly."[19] Will Cloney was one of those veterans of whom Nason spoke. Cloney was equally impressed. For one thing, he had discerned a different sort of strategy employed by Brown than he had recognized in past performances. Of this he wrote:

Yesterday he adopted unusual and amazing tactics…. Tarzan permitted Pawson to discourage the opposition on the long Newton hills while he himself plodded along carefully and saved himself for a swooping descent off the heights. That flight pulled Pawson back rapidly, and a mile from the finish line the Tarz was out front.[20]

Based on what he had witnessed, Cloney was looking ahead. He wrote, "The Tarzan right now is in the middle of a comeback that may very well culminate in a trip to Finland next year."[21] Finland was the planned site of the XIIth Olympiad.

Gerard Cote, still glowing from his North Medford victory, was on hand to watch the Presentation run. He was undeniably awed by what he saw. Standing with him was fellow Canadian contender for the upcoming B. A. A. Marathon, Walter Young. Young too was suitably impressed by Tarzan Brown that afternoon. He expressed these words of compliment: "That was great running by Brown today."[22] If the Canadians on hand (and other marathon hopefuls) did not hear Ellison Brown's optimistic words directly from the runner's mouth after the race, the odds are good they pondered them after reading them in the next day's newspaper.

"Next week I'll run a 17 mile race in New York," said Tarz, "then lay off races until the Boston Marathon. I'm trainin' hard for that. I'm faster now than I was three years ago."[23]

Tarzan Brown wasn't just talking. On April 8, 1939, he traveled to upstate New York for the Chittenango-Syracuse Marathon, a 16.4-mile running event, with a field of athletes mostly from the state of New York and the province of Ontario, Canada. Youthful Russell George, of whom sportswriter Jerry Nason complained had been "reported to be an Oneida Indian one year and

Tarzan Brown (left), and Leslie Pawson are in good spirits as they pose for photographers after running the eighth annual 10-Mile Handicap Road Race of the Presentation Club. Brown won both the first-place and the time prizes. Pawson was the second-place prize winner. Brighton, Massachusetts. April 1, 1939 (courtesy of the Boston Public Library, Print Department).

an Onondaga the next,"[24] had set the record when he won the race the previous year.

At the starting gunshot, George took to the forefront. Tarzan Brown followed deftly behind George, who led all runners for the first half of the race. Robert "Scotty" Rankine, former Canadian Olympic star, ran, for the most part, in the third position. When Brown showed signs of making his move into the lead at the midway point, there was nothing the others could do about it, try as hard as they might. They kept on running, but Brown was simply stronger and much faster, running "at a tireless pace that killed off competition."[25] Neither George nor Rankine (nor anyone else involved, for that matter) was capable of containing Brown's speed, or contesting his leader's status. He led from the halfway point all the way to the finish line.

Brown finished first, setting a new course record of 1 hour, 28 minutes,

43 seconds. Rankine finished in second place two hundred yards behind the winner, and Russell George finished in third place. In their pursuit of Brown, both men had also beaten George's course record. Of further note: fifty-two-year-old Clarence H. DeMar ran and finished, placing fifteenth.

17

"To the Welcome Relief of the Finish Line" in Record Time — 1939

The week before the 43rd annual B. A. A. Marathon, the prognosticators were sending mixed signals. The competing athletes, an influential force in the opinionated, prerace guessing game, seemed mostly unimpressed with Brown's chances. Will Cloney of the *Boston Herald* told the story:

> The entry of Tarzan Brown was announced last night by Director Tom Kanaly. The Tarz, rated one of six co-favorites for the marathon, is not given too much consideration by the runners themselves. Most of them think that he will fold after 23 miles.[1]

The radar of *Post* sportswriter Arthur Duffey was picking up similar intelligence. He wrote:

> If Tarzan is going to win the B. A. A. Marathon, he does not seem to be worrying Les Pawson, Walter Young or Gerard Cote in the least. These three all believe that the Redskin will not be able to stand the gaff for the full distance. In the meantime Pawson is keeping an eye on Young and Cote and the Canadians are watching Pawson. You'll undoubtedly find the winner among this latter trio.[2]

Jerry Nason reported former winner Walter Young's rather harsh assessment—fighting words, really—in the *Globe*'s sports pages. Young, in a manner the television wrestlers fifty years into the future would admire, slung his arrows at Pat Dengis first:

> "Dengis has no speed at all," says Young, disposing of a two-time national champion. "If Kelley was made to run the course without all his brothers, aunts and uncles helping him out he wouldn't do so well. Tarzan Brown knows nothing about pace judgment at all. But Les Pawson is a beautiful runner all the way."[3]

Pawson certainly had a lot of supporters, among participants, writers and observers. As early as April 5, Nason was writing about Pawson being

184

the early favorite.[4] Seven experts in a straw poll assembled by Nason were all in the Pawson camp. A week later, Nason wrote glowingly of Pawson:

> Pawson is in beautiful condition.... No runner is so respected by his contemporaries as Pawson, for his intelligence, even temperament, mannerliness and competence as a runner. The critics call his style of running the nearest thing to perfection of all the macadam specialists.[5]

When Tarzan Brown registered his decisive victory in the Syracuse run, his stock slowly but surely began to rise among observers. Duffey put in his column what he had been hearing around town, and in the space of a little over a week from his last epistle, he found that the general view had changed. Expectations for a victory by Ellison Brown were increasing and they were widespread. Duffey reported:

> No matter where one went to find an opinion yesterday it was generally to be heard: "I like the Indian to win. How can they beat him?" Then it was Gerard Cote from Quebec, with Johnny Kelley following right up with the rest of them.[6]

Duffey could not dismiss the fact that people were favoring the Rhode Islander. Duffey added the following about the enigmatic runner:

> Tarzan Brown seems to be the runner who has 'em all guessing. Tarzan has been running in such fine form this season, that he will have a lot of followers. Can the Indian go the full 26 miles, 385 yards? That is the question. Tarzan is in condition. He may repeat this year.[7]

Duffey sounded like he was just about to make Tarzan his endorsement, but he ultimately went with most of the print writers and selected Pawson ("rarin' to go") as his pick, giving 2–1 odds to the Pawtucket alderman. Walter Young ("a real threat") was his second pick, with 5–2 odds, and Brown ("looks dangerous") was third in line with probabilities figured at 3–1. Johnny Kelley ("must be considered") was next, by Duffey's oddsmaking, at 5–1, followed by Dengis ("last start good") at 6–1, and Cote ("likes a cold day") next at 7–1 odds.[8]

Though a participant, that did not stop Johnny Kelley from having, and expressing, his own opinion of how the marathon would conclude. In an interview, he put Pat Dengis of Baltimore at the top of his favorites list. Kelley picked Les Pawson to finish in second place. An obscure Canadian runner, Lloyd Evans, was his choice for third. He put his own name in the slot for fourth place. Well-known and respected Canadians Gerard Cote and Walter Young were his picks for fifth and sixth places. And how did he think Tarzan Brown would do? Kelley was unable to say. "He [Kelley] rates Tarzan Brown, the 1936 B. A. A. winner and a fellow Olympian, as the mystery man."[9]

Kelley revised his predictions six days later. In an article under his own byline submitted to the *Boston Evening Transcript*, under the headline, *"Kel-*

ley, in Hideaway, Writes On Marathon," Kelley, writing from Hopkinton, still listed Dengis as the likely winner and Pawson his choice for second. Kelley explained, "The reason I pick Dengis over my pal, Pawson, defender and holder of the course record, is because Pat is such a determined fellow and he has won so consistently for the past two years."[10] Kelley had amended his top seven list, replacing Evans with Cote in the third slot. Unchanged, he listed "myself" for fourth. Heinicke now was filled in for fifth place where Cote's name had been. Walter Young was still sixth, and Tarzan Brown was seventh, perhaps no longer such a "mystery."[11]

And what prognostic marathon ramblings would be complete without Pat Dengis' two cents? Jerry Nason reminded his readers that "the prodigious pen" of "the voluble Welchman [*sic*]" had been forecasting the Boston event for five years, usually with elaborately handwritten submissions. This year, his anxiously awaited evaluations and other literary meanderings nearly failed to arrive on time to get published for the benefit of *Globe* readers. But the April 14 edition of the *Globe* included the sixth annual musings of Dengis, and they began as a direct reply to Walter Young's pointed remarks from the week before:

> I see where one half of the athletic hoboes [Walter Young] who have wasted six weeks training over the Boston course has been popping off regarding the Kelley clan, Tarzan Brown's bad judgment of pace, and my sad need of speed. Heh.
>
> I've taken many a verbal crack at the Kelley clan, but to give 'em their due, every time I saw a Kelley on the course it meant a needed drink of water for me. With regards to Brown, I must say his knowledge of pace is awful; yes, sir, terrible! He shifts into high gear right away and doesn't wait around for anybody else. Something ought to be done about this—I shall write my Congressman right away and have the 40 miles per hour limit strictly enforced from Hopkinton to Boston.
>
> So I need speed, eh, Young? Well, I trimmed Young at Dallas, Tex: ripped 18 minutes off his Salisbury record; shellacked him in his own back yard at Montreal last July 4, and beat him by 14 minutes and 14 years in the national championship at Yonkers.
>
> How did he think I did it ... with mirrors? If I need speed then this bird needs a horse.[12]

Dengis, of course had more to say about all the favorites. He shared his view of the chances of Ellison Brown in the upcoming marathon: "Tarzan Brown will have the race in his pocket for 16 or 17 miles, then it will drop out a hole. I fear the 'Rhode Island Rambler' will not be able to navigate the last five miles without the assistance of a Svengali, a wheel-chair, or Jack Farrington, who pulled him through in '36."[13] With strikingly aberrant shortsightedness, Dengis stated, "There is not a man in the field capable of breaking 2:33 and the first two or three will be the only runners under 2:40 on Wednesday."[14]

Pat Dengis was Pat Dengis' first choice for victor, but out of unusual and atypical modesty, he listed his number one selection with the notation of just three question marks: "? ? ?." (This uncharacteristic humility prompted a parenthetic editorial aside within the confines of the Dengis article, which read: "Ed. Note — Hey, what goes on here? This is the first time Pat has dodged the personal pronoun.")[15] His other selections were ordered as follows: Porter, Heinicke[16], Kelley, Pawson, Donato, Cote, Young, Evans, and lastly, in *tenth* place, Brown.[17] Time would tell.

Mrs. Dengis, asked by Nason to predict the outcome, picked Kelley to win, her husband, Pat, second, then Pawson, Cote, Evans, Young, Brown, Heinicke, Fred Bristow and McCallum.[18]

Nason, waiting until Patriots' Day morning, put Dengis first on his list and Tarzan Brown seventh.[19] Seemingly out of the blue, Nason included this odd item in his discussion of Tarzan. "Matt Haggerty, one of his [Brown's] Rhody supporters, has plenty of wampum ($300, to be exact) that says Tarzan repeats today."[20] Just who Matt Haggerty was and why Nason would publicize this eccentric offer of a high-stakes wager was left to his readers' imaginations.

Will Cloney made his personal selection, and was in agreement with his colleague Duffey from the rival *Post*. It was Les Pawson to win. Cloney, who saw all the major competitors as runners to watch, had this up-to-date assessment of Tarzan:

> Brown, the Narragansett Indian who won an Olympic berth by staggering over the finish line in 1936, is approaching the climax of a remarkable comeback, although considerable doubt exists as to his capabilities over the long route. In 1936, he blasted all intermediate records and then very nearly lost in the final mile. Two weeks ago he showed that he has speed by breaking the record in a 16.4 mile race at Syracuse: today he will attempt to show that he also has endurance by finishing courageously.[21]

Bob Coyne, sports cartoonist for the *Post*, devoted his April 12 page to Brown. In a departure from almost all of the knowledgeable sports beat observers, it was Coyne's belief that Tarzan Brown was "now in top form [and] is picked to repeat his '36 win over the B. A. A. course next Wednesday!"[22]

One final prediction was made the morning of the marathon, in Hopkinton, by the veteran runner Clarence H. DeMar, who, in addition to having observed a lot of runners throughout his career, also had a certain gift for prophetic picks. Getting a feel for the day's weather, he told George Carens of the *Boston Evening Transcript*: "Conditions are right for a record run. I'm picking Tarzan Brown to win, and I think he'll break Pawson's mark. Put the race down at 2 hours, 29 minutes."[23] Only time would tell.

By the way, the 1939 B. A. A. Marathon would not see Johnny "Cigars" Connors smoking down the course. His entry was officially rejected for the second year in a row, continuing the practice newly adopted and enforced only the year before. Connors was again refused the opportunity to be part of the spectacle "because he demanded that he be allowed to use his nickname in the program."[24]

The sportswriters, like everyone else involved, were aware that the weather might be a major factor. With forecasts expecting cold, wet and windy conditions, Will Cloney for one felt that that kind of weather would favor the Canadians athletes, with the province of Quebec runners, Young and Cote, foremost in his mind.[25] That parochial view was based, in part, on a common belief — the assumption that Canadians are necessarily acclimated to raw weather compared with their American counterparts. That Canadian runners can perform in inclement weather with greater success or advantage than other athletes is unsubstantiated. But there was no doubt the weather would indeed be a factor, at least in affecting the numbers of spectators, which had been large in the past few years, due in considerable part to the fan-friendly meteorological conditions on the marathon afternoons.

On the night before the marathon, April 18, Ellison Brown was in bed early, getting plenty of rest. "I slept 12 hours last night," he told reporter Ralph Wheeler.[26] The next morning at 9 o'clock, he had his customary big race day breakfast: "a steak and some toast."[27] Then Salimeno and Brown departed for Hopkinton, Massachusetts.

Wednesday, April 19, 1939, was darkly overcast with a temperature of 50° F, but the dampness made it feel much colder than that. Precipitation in the form of dense mist had hovered over Hopkinton in the late morning hours, but it dissipated slightly as the marathon's noontime starting hour drew near. A vigorous wind from the east was a greater cause for concern. Nevertheless, the runners assembled at the Tebeau family farmhouse, the Lucky Rock Manor, still the mustering locale in Hopkinton for the marathoners. Of the 215 entries, a field of 178 were on hand.[28] Adding to the numbers of bodies present at the manor were a host of newspapermen, doctors, race officials, and plenty of nonspecific interested and disinterested parties. A routine medical checkup was given each runner, and official numbers were distributed. Ellison Brown weighed in at 133 pounds[29] and was assigned number 189.

The Associated Press wire service reported "that Brown was denied admission to the race until a friend paid his $1 entry fee."[30] Tarzan lore tells that Walter Brown, the starter, gladly provided the last-minute entry fee for the former winner embarking on his seventh consecutive B. A. A. Marathon. Fred Lewis, in *Young At Heart*, states flatly, "Walter Brown gave Tarzan the dollar."[31] Like other bits of the B. A. A. Marathon lore, the details — even whether this episode actually occurred — is difficult to determine. Tippy Salimeno, the manager and trainer, accompanied Brown to the marathon that day. One would think the entry fee would have been taken care of before the eleventh hour (literally 11 o'clock), and by Salimeno as a part of his managerial duties. Brown's entry was reported to be officially received on April 16, three days before the marathon. How his paperwork could be formally submitted and accepted without the attendant fee is confounding.

A partial eclipse of the sun, barely noticeable with the thickly overcast skies, was underway in the heavens as runners assembled for their starting positions. The eclipse "reached its height at 11:59, one minute before the start of the race."[32] Promptly at noon, Walter A. Brown pulled the trigger, and groups of runners headed towards Boston.

Les Pawson and Russell George set the pace, leading a group from the starting line to Ashland, two miles from the start. Pawson and George were running side by side. Three yards behind were John Paul of St. John, New Brunswick, running third, and Joseph Blaggie of Cambridge, fourth. Brown, Cote, Young, Kelley and a few others made up a second group, following closely behind. As Tarzan would later recall:

> When the gun sounded I strode along in easy fashion, along with Johnny Kelley, Gerry Cote, Lloyd Evans and some more of the runners. Pawson went out to the front and I let him go. I wanted to have him where I could keep an eye on him. Young stayed in the background and did not want to make any race of it at the start. I felt the same way.[33]

At the first check station, six and one-half miles along the course, at South Framingham, Pawson registered first, about twenty-three seconds longer than his time in 1933, the first year he won the marathon and set the record. Only eight yards behind was George in the number two position, and Cote was third. Brown was fourth, followed very closely by Young. John De Coste, John Kelley, and Michael Mansulla were right behind, in a small pack of their own. A light drizzle developed. Tarzan continued the story from his perspective:

> I think that Pawson was leading at Framingham with Russell George, another Indian, and Cote ahead of me. I was in fourth place and well satisfied. I do not know where Young, Dengis, Kelley or some of the other stars were and I didn't care.
> We were just jogging along when Pawson, the leader, seemed to be coming back to me, although I was hardly running. As we came into Natick the first thing I knew Young came up to me and we ran beside each other while Pawson dropped back into third place.[34]

Catching up to and surpassing Pawson gave Brown two things: the lead, and cause to quickly reassess the situation. He made this on-the-spot evaluation: "I thought that Pawson was licked right there, for he generally keeps right up in front and does not allow anyone to pass him at that stage of the race."[35]

The Natick checkpoint recorded Brown and Young in the one and two spots, followed by Les Pawson, Gerard Cote, Russell George, Don Heinicke of Baltimore, John Kelley, Walter Hornby, Michael Mansulla, and Pat Dengis.

Runners (left to right) Gerard Cote, Ellison Brown, Johnny A. Kelley and Michael Mansulla compete in the B. A. A. Marathon in Boston, April 19, 1939 (courtesy of the Boston Public Library, Print Department).

Ellison Brown was one second under Pawson's 1933 time, and about three minutes ahead of his own record time to that checkpoint station. Both he and Young "refused" to drink any water offered them at that point, according to *Post* writer Al Hirshberg. "Pawson was the only one of the leaders to take any water at Natick," Hirshberg observed.[36]

As the runners approached Wellesley College the drizzle was heavier and steadier. The traditional encouragement provided by the college women was not hampered by the weather, but the *Globe* reported "only half the usual number of glamorous femmes braved the elements to watch the 'parade' go by."[37] The students in colorful raingear applauded and cheered the athletes onward. Walter Young waved to the college women. Tarzan Brown, running with his gaze set to the wet shiny road directly in front of him, "failed to give them even a single glance."[38]

Brown and Young, running hard side by side, passed through Wellesley Center first. Pawson was third, followed by a pack including Cote, Heinicke, and Kelley. Ten yards after came Hornby, Mansulla and Dengis.

Brown and Young approached the halfway point, matching splashy wet stride for stride on the watery pavement. The rain — it was no longer just drizzle by this point — had soaked through the footwear, jerseys and shorts of the runners. The drenched sportswear became appreciably heavier the more infused with water it became, and it clung uncomfortably to the skin. Adding to this annoyance, puddles and potholes had to be attentively avoided. Joe Nutter observed:

Brown looked strong and capable, as he ran with a business-like, stoical expression that indicated his serious intent on making a comeback. If he looked up at any time from the glistening ribbon of asphalt that winds from Hopkinton to Exeter Street, we didn't see it. Eyes glued to the pavement, jaw set, he ran a superb race and fought off all inroads of pain and discomfort with Spartan fortitude while a driving rain beat a steady tattoo on runner and spectator alike.[39]

Tarzan Brown and the twenty-six-year-old Walter Young entered Wellesley Square in first and second place, with Pawson still third, Cote fourth and Heinicke fifth.

Kelley had yielded his fifth-place position which he had held for the first thirteen miles. He later would say, "I felt all right but I couldn't get any-place."[40] Brown recalled that segment of the contest:

At Wellesley square I think that I had a few yards on the Canadian, but not enough to amount to anything. We were both striding along together. At Woodlawn Park it was the same story. I was about a couple of yards to the good.[41]

Brown and Young had reached the moment of reckoning — the Newton hills. The weather had gotten decidedly worse. The skies were opening up and the rain was a veritable downpour. The conditions were perhaps the worst in memory since the marathon back in 1912, when Native American Andrew Sockalexis, cousin of baseball legend Louis Sockalexis, finished second to Mike Ryan in a soggy, stormy, miserably muddy muck.

Brown bore on relentlessly. He left Young behind as he climbed the first incline, astonishingly picking up his pace. He later revealed how he was thinking at the time:

I do not know how Young was feeling, but I decided to give him the works. I began to step on it and I saw Young begin to slip back. I knew I had him. He did not want to give me a race.[42]

Brown put a quick fifty yards between them.

And Walter (Young) said, "Let him go, he'll only last 20 miles." Both Pawson and Dengis said the same thing. Even when Brown had stretched his lead to 100 yards on the next hill, to 200 on the climb to Boston College, to 300 at Lake street, and to 400 at Coolidge Corner, the other contenders were not convinced that the race was his.[43]

It looked like clear sailing for the leader, as he successfully completed the treacherous hills. He was now drinking water, an uncommon practice during most of his runs. Brown was steaming into Lake Street well in front but unusually thirsty. Despite the rain, an attentive Jack Barnwell was able to observe the moment with care:

Within the next half mile however, he beckoned for water on three occasions.

There seemed to be something wrong. The trouble was not eradicated until he reached Cleveland circle at the head of Beacon street where he managed to remove a phlegm clot in his throat.

Once that clearance was made it was all over but the shouting.[44]

Vehicular traffic was heavy on the course, even more so over the last five miles as the course traversed the busy city streets. The cars created a very dangerous situation for the runners, especially in the rain. As John Gillooly, reporter for the *Boston Daily Record*, observed: "At Lake street, you could look around and see nothing but the automobiles carrying the press and the officials. There were 215 entries; there must have been an equal number of automobiles and Brown was well barricaded."[45]

By this time, word had reached some of the most resilient spectators, lining the last five miles of the rain-soaked course between fifty and one hundred deep, that Brown was on track to break the course record. That information was shouted to Ellison Brown as he passed by. Brown did not visually acknowledge the fact, but he had heard it. He would later say:

> Someone, in the meantime, yelled at me that I was ahead of the record. That didn't make any difference to me. I was not thinking of a record. I just wanted to win.[46]

It happened more than once. Tarzan recounted it, "A couple of times on the course I heard somebody say something about a new record, but I didn't pay much attention."[47]

The Coolidge Corner check-in station, the last one before the finish line, had Brown first, Young second, Heinicke third, Dengis fourth, Pawson fifth, and Cote sixth.

Don Heinicke, running with exceptional energy in the late stages of this, his first B. A. A. race, passed Walter Young with just a mile to go to the finish line. Heinicke set his sights on Brown.

Through Kenmore Square and down Commonwealth Avenue, Tarzan Brown had maintained a steady gait. He was on a blistering pace. On the final rain-swept mile, Brown all of the sudden showed signs of faltering. Twice he stopped running; first by the Harvard Club on Commonwealth Avenue for a brief instance, and then for a second time after turning onto Exeter Street and the final stretch. In the first instance, Brown was deprived of the advantage of having his trainer come to his rescue, as Jack Farrington in that capacity had done in nearly the same spot three years before. Tippy Salimeno had been thrown off the course twice by overzealous A. A. U. officials. C. Desmond Wadsworth, known as "Dezzy," an A. A. U. and B. A. A. official described by one Boston sportswriter as "the little man with the big megaphone and choleric countenance," for some unexplained reason had "bellowed himself purple in the face at the newspapermen who were trying to get at the drama of the race" in their attempts to cover the event.[48] *The Daily Record* writer Dave

Egan, having lost the last vestiges of respect he may have had for Wadsworth and the majority of his fellow A. A. U. officials, reported that by "Kenmore square, he [Wadsworth] had succeeded in hounding most of the newspapermen off the course, so that many of them got their story second hand."[49] Egan, who painted himself considerably more assertive than most of his colleagues in journalism — he always referred to himself in the third person as "the Colonel"— held fast and ignored the power-wielding official's directives to get their vehicle off the course. Egan, consequently, was still on the beat, still on the marathon course when Brown first faltered, and was thus able to report what occurred. "The Colonel," who was riding in the *Daily Record* vehicle with fellow reporter John Gillooly and former Rhode Island state senator Edward J. "Hap" Fenelon, described what he considered to be the pivotal moment in the marathon:

> At the Harvard Club ... we had started going hell-for-leather towards the club-house and the finish line, when the Senator looked back and croaked a mighty croak.
> "He stopped," he wept. "He's walking, and looking back. Let me out of this car."
> At that particular moment in his life, Fenelon would have stepped out of a moving airplane. He had marshaled half the town of Westerly to this race, and he had personally hollered himself hoarse, and he would personally see to it that the Narragansett Indian (of which tribe "Hap" Fenelon is the first white chief) obeyed the orders of his chief and broke the record.
> In one step, he was over John Gillooly and the Colonel, and he was out in the middle of the road, and he was talking plain, Narragansett Indian talk to the drooping Brown. The Tarzan picked up his feet, went into his trot, swung into a run.[50]

The following day, "the Colonel" was still marveling at Fenelon's contribution. "The story of the record-breaking effort was written in front of the Harvard Club, only 600 yards from the finish line.... At that point, "Hap" Fenelon hopped out of the *Daily Record* car and swiftly promised orange pop, and forced Brown to lift his leaden legs into the run for the tape; and at that point, a record which may stand forever was written into the books."[51] Edward J. "Happy" Fenelon, the Rhode Island state senator from Westerly who had introduced the resolution in the state senate honoring Ellison Brown after his 1936 B. A. A. victory, was as fervent a Brown supporter this year as he had been before. It was fortuitous that he had been permitted to ride in the *Daily Record* car where, at the moment of need, he was enabled to play such a key role in Tarzan's final efforts.

Providence newspaperman Joe Nutter was on the rain-swept scene 100 yards from the finish line, a point from which no official had been able to make him move. From Joe Nutter's vantage point, he could see that Ellison Brown "halted momentarily as though dazed."[52] It was the second time Brown had stopped. He appeared to stagger, and then right away he managed to walk. Tarzan turned his head as he looked around. He would later explain that this shift down to walking mode was not unintentional. Brown said, "I walked a few steps near the finish to conserve my energy for a sprint to the tape should one be necessary."[53] Will Cloney reported from the spectators' perspective: "For a second, a terrifying second the crowd thought that he would collapse 100 yards from the tape, but the Tarz wobbled for three or four steps, glanced back, rubbed his head absentmindedly, and resumed his victorious course to the welcome relief of the finish line."[54]

Ellison Brown recalled the moment in his first-person account in the *Globe*. Due to the sheets of rain he had gotten slightly turned around on the downtown streets.

> The reason I stopped so near the finish is easily explained. I hadn't looked up for several miles and didn't know I was on Exeter st. I knew I must be near the finish, so I stopped and looked back, figuring that if Young was still close to me I would save a little strength and then outsprint him at the finish.[55]

In a competitor newspaper, the *Post*, Brown gave this supporting firsthand account:

> I just stopped to see if I could see if Young or anyone else was near me. Then I started running again. And when I heard that crowd yelling "Tarzan" I began to sprint.
> I thought I would never get to that finish line. I hardly know what happened after I crossed Boylston street and the crowd surged around me.[56]

Tarzan Brown broke the worsted tape more than a quarter mile ahead of the second-place Don Heinicke. He set a new record time for the course: 2 hours, 28 minutes, 51.8 seconds. This was 2 minutes, 9.8 seconds faster than Pawson's six-year-old course record, standing from 1933. It was also 4 minutes, 49 seconds faster than Brown's own winning time back in 1936. He became the fifth B. A. A. Marathon winner to repeat a victory. His performance time was the first of only seven American record times ever established at the Boston Marathon (Men: 1897–2003).[57]

The *New York Times* reported it to be a new world mark, toppling the world record time set by Kitei Son at the Berlin Olympics in 1936 by 27.4 seconds.[58] The headline in the *New York Times* proclaimed: "Tarzan Brown Runs Fastest Marathon in History to Annex Boston A. A. Race." The *Boston Globe* concurred, stating, "Yesterday Brown smashed all recognized Marathon records for established races held at a known distance of 26 miles, 385 yards."[59] The *Boston Herald* ran this headline on its front page: "Brown Sets World Mark In Marathon, Prefers Job." In its accompanying article, Will Cloney wrote, "Brown's fairy-tale flight over the Newton hills, when he made his principal attack on the record also brought a new world standard that will replace the figure of 2 hours 29 minutes, 19 2–5 seconds established by Kitei Son of Japan in winning the 1936 Olympic marathon title in Berlin."[60]

Tarzan Brown is about to win the 1939 B. A. A. Marathon and set a new course record on Exeter Street in Boston, April 19, 1939 (courtesy of the Boston Public Library, Print Department).

The view that only Son and now Brown had shattered the two-hour, thirty-minute mark was pervasive among area sportswriters. An example was this line from the typewriter of George C. Carens of the *Boston Evening Transcript*: "The Japanese marathoner, Son, was the only other human being who ever broke 2 hours and 30 minutes for the distance and Brown was nearly a half a minute ahead of that record."[61]

The *Providence Evening Bulletin* was in agreement, when it reported: "Only one other runner in all the history of recorded achievements has ever covered an official marathon course in less than 2 hrs., 30 min., and that individual was Kitei Son, the Japanese ace who won the Olympic marathon crown at Berlin in 1936, in 2 hours, 29 minutes, 19.2 seconds."[62] So his readers could better understand how to judge marathon experiences, the *Bulletin's* Joe Nutter added the following: "However, it must be noted that no two marathon courses have anything in common except their full distance, and 'Tarzan's' record must stand on its own merits, and it does that without any fear of contradiction from any quarter."[63] Along the lines of varying baseball parks with idiosyncratic fence heights and lengths or golf courses with their unique designs (as opposed to standardized football fields, for example) marathon courses were very individualized with differing grades and surfaces, making it difficult if not impossible to compare in certain meaningful ways. However, if the distance was officially established and recognized, then the time was usually accepted. But sportswriters, including Joe Nutter uncharacteristically among them, oversold Brown's achievement in one important respect: Kitei Son was not the first or only marathon runner to register a time under the 2½-hour mark. That "first" is accorded to Albert M. Michelsen, who ran to victory in the Port Chester national marathon on October 12, 1925. The 26-year-old Michelsen ran the 26-mile, 385-yard course in 2 hours, 29 minutes, 1.8 seconds. The *New York Times* reported that a quarter of a million spectators witnessed that event. (And who finished in second place in that 1925 Columbus Day sporting event? Why, none other than Clarence H. DeMar, then reported to be "only two years short of 40" years of age, running in 2 hours, 31 minutes, 7.8 seconds.[64])

Whether or not Michelsen was appreciated as the first to break the 2½-hour barrier, Tarzan Brown's mark in the 1939 B. A. A. was faster by ten seconds. He was at the very least the second American to finish an official marathon under 2½ hours, but did he smash the world mark as promulgated by the newspapers following his B. A. A. record-setting win?

American sportswriters, including those of the *Times*, the *Transcript*, and the *Bulletin*, were either unaware or ignoring the results of much more recent marathons in Tokyo, Japan, which took place in 1935. Three runners in three separate events all had run faster than Ellison Brown's 1939 Boston time, according to Martin and Gynn in their *The Olympic Marathon*. Each time registered established the current record at the time. Of the three, the fastest was Kitei Son (Korean name: Son Kee-Chung), the 1936 Olympic marathon winner. In a marathon on November 3, 1935, he took first place with a winning time of 2 hours, 26 minutes, 42 seconds. Another marathon runner, Yasuo Ikenaka, won in Tokyo on April 3, 1935, in which he finished at 2 hours, 26 minutes, 44 seconds. A third Japanese runner, Fusashige Suzuki, was first in a race held March 31, 1935, with a time of 2 hours, 27 minutes, 49 seconds.[65] One can only speculate as to why the newspapers would pay no attention to those accomplishments. One possibility for the oversight is the fact that the Tokyo races of 1935 might not have been officially sanctioned or may not have been conducted to the satisfaction of the international (or, in the least, the American) athletic community. Skepticism as to the distance measurements, always questionable in those days, may have been prevalent among U. S. newspapermen. Another possibility, that the sportswriters were simply unaware of those marathons having taken place, seems less plausible. A further possibility may involve a tendency to discount or disregard Asian achievements over American ones at that time.

Jerry Nason was one American sportswriter who was cognizant of matters marathon in Imperial Japan. Nason was more suspect of the course distances as opposed to the runners' recorded times. He discussed the issue, starting with Tarzan's achievement. Wrote Nason:

> The one thing that struck me more forcibly than anything else in yesterday's eminent foot battle was the time, which was not only a record for this particular race, but the fastest Marathon ever raced by any man over *an established, universally recognized* course of 26 miles, 385 yards.
> Just previous to the 1936 Olympics we received some amazing tales of mighty Marathon feats in Japan. Sonki Tei, a Korean, was credited with a Marathon in 2:26:14. Three weeks later Yasuo Ikanaka ran a race in 2:26:43.
> The chances are these times were accurate, but the chances are the courses were not. Japan later proved its prowess in the Olympic Marathon when Katei Son swept to the finish at Berlin in 2:29:19 1–5, the Olympic record.
> … In other words, on a course *known throughout the world* as a famous Marathon test, the 24-year-old Narragansett Indian ran the fastest Marathon race yet officially recorded[66] [emphasis added].

Nason would not out-and-out say that the Japanese courses were shorter than the official 26 miles, 385 yards. How could he know that with any certainty? But though he seemed to singularly acknowledge the reports from Tokyo, Nason, like his American brethren of the nation's sports pages, did not accept the Japanese results as officially standing. His front page declaration, that Ellison Brown's "new mark bettered all records for recognized marathon races over the regulation 26 miles, 385 yards,"[67] expressed the prevailing view in the American press.

Back to the Boston race, Don Heinicke had been unable to catch Brown, but the rookie runner was proud to register a strong second, especially in light of the big-name talent he had bested that afternoon. His fast time, 2 hours, 31 minutes, 24.6 seconds, nearly broke the course record as well, only 23.4 seconds shy of Pawson's mark. It was only the seventh marathon of Heinicke's athletic lifetime. The young man's running career began after he was forced to forego his favorite sport, baseball, because he had suffered the loss of four fingers on his right hand in an occupational accident with a printing press. Also stricken with tuberculosis (along with his father and brother, both of whom succumbed to the fatal consumptive disease), his physician recommended distance running as a way to strengthen his damaged lungs. Pat

Dengis had taken his fellow Baltimore resident under his wing. Now with the visibility of a second-place finish ahead of such luminaries as Pawson, Dengis, Kelley and Young, Heinicke's marathon career appeared to be well underway. He would return throughout most of the next decade, competitively striving to attain that coveted but elusive victory of the B. A. A. Marathon.

A disappointed Walter Young finished in third place at 2:32:41. The Verdun, Quebec, gendarme told reporters:

> Frankly, I felt sure that I was going to win today, particularly when I was running even with Tarzan at the Newton hills. I was confident that I could run rings around him over the last 10 miles, but it turned out just the opposite. At that, I finished a minute better than when I won the race two years ago.[68]

Fourth place belonged to Pat Dengis. His time was 2 hours, 33 minutes, 22 seconds. He had been burdened with a lingering sore throat and a head cold which the weather may have aggravated, and despite his prerace bravura with the pen, he almost did not participate. It was reported that Dengis "had run seven miles around Hopkinton in the morning" in an effort to "rid himself of a heavy cold that he developed since he arrived in Boston yesterday."[69] As odd a course of action to fight a cold as that may sound — "he was doubled up with coughing fits before and after the race"[70] — nevertheless his performance later that afternoon had been terrific. His time was faster than the times he had registered in 1935 and 1938, the two years he finished second (to Kelley and to Pawson, respectively.) He was magnanimous in defeat, saying, "Tarzan ran a beautiful race. My hat's off to him."[71] For Dengis, "it was his first marathon defeat in a year."[72]

The man whose record was shattered, Les Pawson, finished in fifth place. His time of 2 hours, 33 minutes, 57.6 seconds was better than his winning time the year before. Pawson concisely summed up what went wrong for him when he said, "I figured Tarzan and Walter were going too fast and that they'd fold on the hills — but they didn't."[73]

Paul Donato of Roxbury, sporting a badly bruised, indigo-hued knee from an earlier tumble during training, had been advised by nearly everyone not to run, but run he did. He finished sixth. He endured lots of pain ("I was in agony") during the first three-quarters of the marathon, but he gamely continued onward. He was greatly relieved and grateful to find that "the last five [miles] didn't bother me at all."[74]

Thirty-one-year-old Walter Hornby of Hamilton, Ontario, finished in seventh place, just as he did back in 1933, the year Pawson established his record. Hornby's time this year, in 1939, at 2 hours, 37 minutes, 11 seconds, was faster than his other seventh-place finish time by 4 minutes, 21 seconds.

Gerard Cote finished eighth for the second year in a row. Six minutes, eighteen seconds faster in this latest effort, he was able to remain optimistic despite having been unable to meet his expectations.

"I am ver' disappointed, yes," mourned the French-Canadian snowshoe runner. "I am trouble [*sic*] by stomach cramps all the way, but my legs are perfect. O, well. Some other time, eh?"[75]

Johnny Kelley had really never contended after the first half. His thirteenth-place finish was his worst in six years, but he had given it everything he had, and he had stayed in it. His skin had turned from nearly white to purple due to the wet, cold conditions. He said afterwards:

> I never could seem to get going. But no alibis.... I was tempted to drop out a dozen times. I kept thinking of making a position in the Olympic tryout rankings. That kept me running. Tarzan did a grand job. He's a great runner.[76]

The newspapers had trouble reporting Kelley's time. The *Boston Daily Globe* had Kelley's time as 2:41:03.[77] The *Herald* and *Providence Journal* reported 2:41:30, and in the *Post* Kelley finished in 2:41:31.[78] The *New York Times* reported 2:41:39.[79] Moreover, the *Boston Evening Globe* listed the top thirty-seven names and affiliations, but omitted Kelley. (Michael J. Mansulla of the Boston Y. M. C. A. was thirteenth on the front-page list, substituted in the place where Kelley belonged.)[80]

Jock Semple, running in the B. A. A. Marathon with his new affiliation, the symbol of the unicorn representing the B. A. A., finished in eighteenth place, in 2:45:45. It marked "the first time in several years" that the B. A. A. had club members running as participants.[81] One of those members, George L. Durgin, had the best finish of any B. A. A. runner—fourteenth place, right behind John Kelley. The quick-starting Russell George completed the course in twenty-seventh place, with a finishing time of 2:50:26.

Clarence H. DeMar kept his completion streak intact, by finishing his twenty-first B. A. A. Marathon in thirtieth place, at the age of 50. His time was 2 hours, 51 minutes, 27 seconds. His prophetic morning prediction— that, one, Tarzan Brown would win; that, two, Brown would break Pawson's course record; and, that, three, his time would be two hours, twenty-nine minutes—turned out to be only nine seconds off the mark! DeMar's summary of Brown's afternoon accomplishment was characteristically succinct. He praised it as "well-planned."[82]

18

"This Marathon Business Is Okay But You Can't Support a Family on It" — 1939

George Demeter was at his traditional spot by the finish line on Exeter Street, waiting this time in the heavy rains for the 1939 race winner with the laurel wreath in hand. Immediately after securing the victory, Ellison Brown was "caught, supported, swathed in blankets,"[1] as Demeter reached in and over the bodies to place the laurel wreath upon Brown's head. Photographers took pictures of the winning marathon runner, the flash bulbs reflecting off the raindrops. Brown was "carried" inside to the training quarters of the old B. A. A. clubhouse (which had been transformed into a Boston University building of classrooms) for the postrace medical check, still wearing the laurel. The *Post* reported: "Once inside he quickly removed his crown and said, 'That'll be swell for the young fellow,' meaning young Tarzan, a little over a year old. 'Let's have some orange juice.'"[2] The *Post* newsman apparently missed what happened next. Providence sportswriter Joe Nutter reported that "the doctors who examined him said that he fainted and had to be revived."[3] Not short of duration, "it took five or six minutes to revive him."[4]

Following this chaotic scene, the laurel wreath went missing. Joe Nutter's account, in the *Providence Evening Bulletin*, suggested deliberate theft. He recounted for his readers: "In the commotion that followed the leading of 'Tarzan' into the training quarters, the laurel wreath was disregarded and some pilferer lifted it. George Demeter, the Bay State representative who had had the wreath brought from the Marathon Valley in Greece, promptly offered $100 as a reward for its recovery."[5]

The Associated Press reported the disheartening loss: "The laurel wreath with which George DeMeter [*sic*] of Boston crowns Boston marathon winners was stolen from Brown shortly after it had been placed on his brow, it was learned tonight. DeMeter offered $100 reward for its return."[6]

The medical examination included a close inspection of the runners' feet. Dr. Hugh Gallagher of Somerville examined Brown's feet, and the *Post* reported that the doctor found them "in fine condition."[7] "Only three tiny toe blisters" were reported on either foot.[8] But that was not the full extent of what the doctor found. The *Post* noted that "there were two injured blood vessels on his right foot but nothing alarming."[9] Apparently Ellison Brown's right shoe had undergone a beating during the marathon, for the upper part had separated from the sole resulting in a four-inch tear, "located in the region of the first metatarsal."[10] On that foot was a bruise.

Ardent and impatient reporters caught a glimpse of Brown as he momentarily appeared from behind the closed door of the makeshift examination room. "He [Brown] emerged from that room finally, and found his way to a warm shower, where he remained for almost a half-hour. He showed no disposition to leave the comforting warmth of the shower."[11] "Newspaper photographers and reporters ... sought to corner him in the privacy of his shower," the *Herald's* Ralph Wheeler reported.[12] They ultimately left him alone but grew more impatient as the minutes passed. Eventually, Brown left what little peace and privacy he had in the shower and met a heated and annoyed Tippy Salimeno for a needed rubdown. The press no longer considered this any kind of privacy zone, and began to ply their journalistic practices, while, at the same time, Salimeno, now wearing the hat of primary rubdown trainer, began plying the muscles on Brown's durable body. All the while Salimeno was telling whoever would listen about how he had been mistreated on the marathon course by a few obdurate A. A. U. officials.

Salimeno had operated his automobile to assist his runner during the run. The Salimeno vehicle did not display the official banner, a prerequisite unheeded by the Westerly manager for unreported reasons. According to *Globe* sports contributor Herbert Ralby, "Tarzan's new manager," Salimeno, was duly

> shunted off the course just below Coolidge Corner because his car didn't have an official flag. Undaunted, the "merry" maestro hopped an A. A. U. car to Kenmore sq., where he was again tossed out.... He finally reached the clubhouse frothing mad and squawking about the way the race was conducted.[13]

On the same subject of Salimeno's complaints, the *Providence Journal* reported that the manager-trainer had been able to assist his client and give advice for twenty-two miles before his run-in with a few intractable marathon officials. After twenty-two miles

> Salimeno said he was ordered by officials to get off the course. He said he tried to follow in official cars, but was twice removed and put back with the crowd. As a result the Indian finished the last four miles without his trainer's help.[14]

As a compliant Brown lay upon the table engaged in Salimeno's rubdown treatment, listening with a sympathetic ear but remaining silent himself, the

Salimeno venting was eventually interrupted as the table was first approached by Les Pawson. Pawson, reaching out a congratulatory hand with which to shake the newest recordholder's hand, proudly stated (loud enough for the press to hear), "Well, we've still got the record in Rhode Island." Upon hearing this, "'Tarzan' beamed for the first time."[15] The two Rhode Island runners shook hands. It was the kindly Pawson's way of congratulating Brown personally and simultaneously publicly showing his respect to and for his friend and fellow competitor. Brown understood. A picture of the moment graced the front page of the Thursday edition of the *Boston Daily Globe* under the mini headline "No Hard Feelings Over a Record." The caption under the photograph identified the two men, and stated, "The holder of the old record congratulates the man who set a new one."[16] The unstated, underlying message was that it all transpired in the spirit of gentlemanly, good-sportsman-like, healthy, athletic, American competition.

Pawson pointed out (to the members of the press thirsty for copy) that Brown had beaten a very strong field of runners, one loaded with trophy collectors from many contests, including the B. A. A. Marathons of years gone by. In particular, Pawson underscored how, in the late stages of the race, these superior runners were still giving it that extra competitive expense. In view of the competition, Brown's victory was certainly all the more impressive. "'I never saw so many strong runners in the final stretch,' Pawson declared. 'Tarzan played the bid just right, saved something for the end, and then finished in good shape.'"[17]

Ellison Brown soon dressed, then had to stand still as "some 20 photographers exploded a hundred or more flash bulbs in his face"[18] in their commercial efforts to preserve his image. He then engaged in conversation with reporters in the clubhouse, answering their questions and offering his own observations.

On the subject of comparison of today's victory to his first Boston victory, he said, "This race ... was much easier for me than when I won in 1936, although I ran five minutes faster today. I am in better condition."[19]

Oddly, only in the *Boston Post*, in a piece with the byline of *Ellison M. "Tarzan" Brown as told to Arthur Duffey,* were views expressed by Brown contrary to those reported in all the other news outlets. For example, Brown's sentiment that this year's race was easier than his first win was contradicted in the *Post*, wherein Brown purportedly stated, "The Marathon this year was the toughest race I ever had, harder than when I won the run in 1936."[20]

How was he feeling? Better? "Yes, I feel much better than I did when I won the 1936 marathon run, principally because I know more about pace than I did then. I tried to maintain a steady pace all the way this afternoon, feeling sure that I could kill off the rest of the field by so doing."[21]

Nason made the observation that Brown

didn't, as he so impetuously attempted when he won in '36, try to blind the field in the early miles. This time the Tarz spread his speed over the full 26 miles and rocked the record off the list.

"That may be so," admitted the Indian somewhat reluctantly. "I know I felt much stronger passin' through Kenmore sq. this time. I think the reason for the record was not my judgment of pace so much as my condition.

Three years ago I weighed 139 pounds in this race. Today I weighed 133, and lost only two of them. I gave no thought to the record. I was out to win. It is true I didn't go out front as fast as in 1936, but my idea was still the same: to kill off the field."[22]

Patriots' Day in Boston had not encountered rain, especially heavy at the end of the race, in an estimated twenty-seven years. What effect did the rain have on his running, some of the assembled reporters wanted to know. "'It was slippery going for the last couple of miles,' he explained, 'but I refused to be bothered by it for I was determined to win.'"[23]

This B. A. A. Marathon was the first of three Olympic trials for the still-scheduled 1940 games in Finland. (The other two were the national marathon in Yonkers, scheduled for November, and the next B. A. A. Marathon, to be held the following April 1940.) Brown was asked a number of questions about this centerpiece topic. He surprised the gathering with this mixed response:

> Right now, I do not intend to run in the next Olympics, but I may change my mind before then. I can't see any future in marathon running and I certainly won't let my boy follow in his father's footsteps, which have covered quite a little territory, as you must agree.[24]

To the *Globe* readers he tried to clarify his feelings on the subject:

> Sometimes I am anxious to make the Olympic team, then again I am not. If I could go to Finland a month before the games and train — well I would be anxious to go, provided I could train myself. Then, on the other hand, it would be hard to leave my wife and son; Ellison Meyers, Jr. is 1½ years old now. They were one reason why I ran so well today. I had more to run for than three years ago.[25]

There were two issues (and two special individuals) on his mind. If he were to compete in the games in Finland, certain things would have to be put in place on his behalf. To prevent a repetition of his unsuccessful efforts in Berlin, Brown would require plenty of time to train adequately. Toward this end, getting to the Olympic site a month earlier would be warranted, to enable a satisfactory training schedule, if he were persuaded to go. However, whether he would make the trip did not depend entirely on whether it could be agreed that he could train early and adequately. He would have to decide independently whether he wanted to participate. That would depend primarily upon whether he could adequately provide for his family (*viz.* if he had a job between now and then), and how they were likely to get along during his absence for that period of time. His family's welfare — that was the primary issue.

Ellison Brown poses with his son, Ellison Brown Jr. ("Sonny"), one week after winning the Boston Marathon, Rhode Island, April 26, 1939 (*Providence Journal* photograph).

In the *Providence Journal*, Joe Nutter reported Brown's reaction, again with emphasis on his apparent ambivalence:

"Well, yes and no," was his laconic answer when questioned on his Olympic aspirations.

"I might be interested, but I don't know. I wouldn't want to leave my family to make any ocean trip," replied the native son of the forests and fields, who was surprised and a trifle chagrined when he belatedly discovered that one had to cross the ocean to participate in the Berlin Olympic meet in 1936.[26]

Tarzan's wife, Ethel (right), and son, Ellison Jr. ("Sonny"), listened to the radio to hear of his B. A. A. Marathon victory at the Rhode Island home of Ellison's aunt, Mrs. Charles E. Johnson (left), Charlestown, RI, April 19, 1939 (*Providence Journal* photograph).

Actually, though he climbed the ship's exterior all the way up to the smokestacks to try to get a good view of Germany before the S.S. *Manhattan* set sail, Brown thoroughly enjoyed his ocean voyages, by all accounts. The concern he was expressing was the demands of leaving his new young family. In contrast to his situation back in 1936, things were now different — he was now a husband and father.

The account in the *Post* was once again antithetical to the other reported accounts of Brown's ambivalent feelings toward being selected for the Olympic team. There he purportedly stated:

> I am going to keep on Marathoning. I guess it is in the blood and I could not stop if I wanted to stop.... So I'll be seeing you in the next Boston Marathon and I hope the Olympic committee will select me to be one of Uncle Sam's

representatives in the next Olympic Marathon. What could be more appropriate than to have an Indian, an American Indian, wear the colors of the Stars and Stripes in the next Olympiad.[27]

His immediate concern, of greater concern, was securing work so he could provide for the new family. He spoke about it, and Nason captured Brown's words for his *Globe* readers: "I haven't a job at the moment. I certainly hope I can get one."[28] The *Herald's* Ralph Wheeler captured the same sentiment as did his colleague: "No, I haven't got a job but I certainly would like to know where I can get one. This marathon business is okay but you can't support a family on it."[29] The expressed desire for employment was included in the *Post's* pages—no disparity on this point. Brown told Duffey:

I hope that my victory in this run will get me a steady job. Walter Young got a job as a policeman after he won the marathon a couple of years ago. I would like to do the same.[30]

About this time, two young boys of Micmac descent, Carl Pin Jr. and his brother Lionel, were ushered in to meet the Marathon champion and shake his hand. Their introduction to Brown was captured on film by a *Globe* photographer, and the picture was printed in the April 20 edition of the newspaper.

Salimeno and Brown were ready to depart the inner locker room sanctum for the presentation of prizes. No journalistic accounts of the presentation seem to exist. But this brief item in a column by George Carens the day before the marathon took place is of interest. It begins with C. Desmond "Dezzie" Wadsworth, the A. A. U. official who received the brunt of "The Colonel" Dave Egan's wrath for having Salimeno and a number of newspapermen autocratically cleared from the course. Carens wrote:

Dezzie Wadsworth in his dynamic fashion has overlooked no detail to make the race perfect. He even has promoted a new medal for the winner—the Edward E. Babb Memorial, which E. E. Jr., will give annually to the winner. This is to be a gold medal with a diamond, and it will perpetuate the name of a former A. A. U. president and one-time B. A. A. athletic committee chairman.[31]

Whether Ellison Brown was the first recipient of the Edward E. Babb Memorial gold medal is unknown.

After the awards ceremony, Salimeno and Brown planned to eat and then hightail it straight to Rhode Island. Unlike 1936, there would be no night out on the town for this husband and father winner, although "he could have had two tickets for a show."[32] Brown, however, did agree to delay his return home in exchange for an exciting experience new to him; he would be a featured guest on the radio that evening, on "Secony's Names-in-the-News" program.

As he gathered his things and prepared to leave the clubhouse, most accounts have Brown leaving without the missing laurel wreath. In keeping with this scenario, an AP story, printed in the *Boston Globe* under the headline "LOSS OF WREATH AFFECTS INDIAN," claimed that Tarzan Brown and "his youthful wife, who will soon present her husband with their second child, ... bemoaned the loss of the wreath." Ethel, unnamed in the report but described as "very pleased about Tarzan's victory," was portrayed as upset about the incident. As she was attending to her family's laundry chores, she was reported to have remarked, "It was a dirty trick to steal it."[33]

The United Press reported that the wreath was returned on April 21, two days later from when it "vanished." In the UP story, which was printed in the *Providence Evening Bulletin*, it described what happened: "Chairman C. Desmond Wadsworth of the B. A. A. athletic [*sic*] Committee found the wreath in a package on his desk. Office attaches said an unidentified youth had left the wreath, which will be forwarded to Brown, a Narragansett Indian residing in Westerly, R. I."[34]

A somewhat similar account was written in a brief front-page item in the *Evening Globe*. A few added details of the mysterious matter were provided. Wadsworth found the package containing the wreath as soon as he arrived in the morning. The "young man had asked for Mr. Wadsworth," by name before leaving the package. He did not allow himself to be identified or offer any information on himself, the contents of the package, or the circumstances of how he had taken possession of it.[35]

No further details were ever provided, so whoever was responsible for absconding with it and whoever returned it remained unknown. No claim for Demeter's $100 reward was publicly reported to have been submitted.

The *Boston Post*, its reports inexplicably so often contrary to its competitors' in its 1939 B. A. A. coverage, once again reported an incident very differently. In an April 20 item under the headline "TARZAN MISPLACES WREATH AFTER RACE" the following appeared: "Tarzan Brown got a scare after the race when he misplaced the wreath which goes to the Marathon winner every year. He missed it several hours after the race, and, just as plans were made to offer a reward for it, the laurel was discovered in the locker room of the old B. A. A. Clubhouse, where Tarzan had left it in the excitement."[36]

Ellison Brown arrived at the radio studios of WNAC, a part of the Yankee network. On the "Names-in-the-News" program, Brown was interviewed by *Boston Evening Transcript* sportswriter George C. Carens. Scheduled along with Brown on the program was new author Wells Lewis, the son of Sinclair Lewis, who was there to promote a just-published first novel. A photograph showed the two young "newsmakers"—author and runner—meeting and shaking hands.[37] In the photograph, Tarzan is dressed in suit, collared shirt and tie, with a large laurel wreath adorning his head. That wreath was a substitute given to him by the *Boston Daily Record*. "The *Boston Daily Record* had a laurel wreath made up in a hurry" following the discovery that the authentic one was missing.[38] They gave Tippy Salimeno the honors of placing it upon Brown's head at the radio studio. A photo of that moment appeared in the *Daily Record*. Its caption reported Brown's reaction at the presentation: "He was all smiles."[39]

All that remains of the radio interview are partial, transcribed comments from Brown's responses used in Caren's own column, "The Pulse," featured in the *Boston Evening Transcript*. Brown took that broadcast opportunity to reach a large audience and hammer home his most urgent message, that of his desire for employment. This was right out of the Walter Young playbook, for Young had parlayed his 1937 B. A. A. win into a well-publicized quest for a job, and the ploy had worked wonderfully for him; he joined the Verdun, Quebec, police force, a position he kept for four decades. Tarzan Brown was a true disciple of Young in this respect. He kept reiterating his search for a job every chance he got. His meeting with reporters in the locker room after the marathon had been his first chance to spin his job search as the new marathon winner. The radio interview was the next opportunity. Tarzan Brown's segment began with the newly twice-crowned marathon winner (his second Boston win, his second laurel wreath of the day) talking jobs. "'I'm a jack-of-all-trades,' began the 25-year old Tarzan. 'I'm looking for a job to support my wife and little boy.'"[40] At the conclusion of the radio program, Salimeno, Brown and at least one reporter (likely to be *Post* writer Arthur Duffey) left Massachusetts for Rhode Island. *The Post* reported Brown's late-night arrival under the headline, "HOME TOWNERS GREET TARZAN" with the follow-up subheadline, "Eats Huge Sandwiches, Hopes to Land Job." It said:

> Amid a throng of home town well wishers Tarzan Brown arrived at 11:15 tonight. Tarzan was accompanied home by Thomas "Tippy" Salimeno, his manager and two others who made a fast motor car trip from Boston.
> Asked how he felt, Tarzan said, "Fine, but I am hungry." He at once started eating huge salami sandwiches and washed it down with plenty of soda water.
> Salimeno, his manager, was indignant at the treatment he received at the hands of the A. A. U. officials who twice put him off official cars. Turning again to Tarzan, Tippy asked him what he was going to do now. Tarzan said, "I am going home to my wife and child and tomorrow I hope to land a job." With that statement he headed home.[41]

One last time on that long, eventful day, Brown had utilized his public platform to its fullest extent to get the word out about his need for employment. Now, finally, a full but fatigued Ellison Brown was headed home to be reunited with Ethel and their son, the end of an exhausting but historic day.

The *Providence Evening Bulletin* reported that the very next morning he and his small family were up a little before ten o'clock. His breakfast consisted of only a glass of grape juice. When a reporter feigned surprise, Brown offered by way of elucidation, "But, boy, am I going to store away a big dinner."[42] Claiming to feel good, he got behind the wheel of a borrowed car and drove to Westerly. He acquired all the newspapers he could find to read about his heroic exploits. As reporters dropped by to get a story, Brown picked up on the Young tactic and put his need of a job again squarely in the newspaper-reading public's eye, like this example from the *Providence Journal*: "'I'd like a road job with the State,' that was his supreme wish. His Westerly friends were prepared to say he would be given such a job, probably today."[43]

The *Boston Daily Record* reported that Edward "Hap" Fenelon, who had assisted Brown in the critical last mile of the marathon, "and other [unnamed] fellow townsmen, assured Tarzan they would soon land him a position."[44] Brown must have had mixed feelings about his chances when, the next day, the *Daily Record* was still reporting a job possibility, not an offer, in the works. Sportswriter Rolly Hill reported, "It was made known that Brown may soon find employment with the state in a very short while with influential political allies taking his part."[45] On the one hand, the time frame was good news, for if true, it meant that employment was imminent. On the other hand, unlike the report in the previous day's paper, this time, no source was given and the "political allies" were all unidentified. Fenelon's name was now conspicuously missing from the article. Despite what must have seemed like a real possibility—particularly considering the connections people like Fenelon must have acquired having been a state legislator, and the fact that he was reading it in the newspapers—Ellison Brown still wasn't taking any chances. He would continue his public appeals for work in every forum that came his way.

As for "Hap" Fenelon, he had reportedly "set a new worrying record for 26 miles, 385 yards" while riding in the *Daily Record's* vehicle during the marathon, closely monitoring Brown's progress along with reporters Dave Egan ("the Colonel") and John Gillooly. His assistance to Brown during the race had been a contributing factor in Brown's breaking of the record. Of that at least the Colonel, for one, had no doubt. The Colonel described Fenelon's support method: "He would lean his noggin out the door of the car into the rain at sporting intervals, and cup his hands, and tell Tarzan that nobody was in sight, and the Tarzan would say, 'Okeh, Hap, I'm comin.'"[46] The former senator had come through before, during the race; he certainly should be able to dependably do so again, after the race. In the meantime, as reporters and photographers came by to get more copy and more photographs of the B. A. A. winner, a very cooperative Brown talked running, shook hands, and posed so his image could be displayed across the country. And then, keeping up his Walter Young act, he would say:

> "Really fellows, I like all this, but a job would be so much nicer." That was Brown. Every newspaper that hit Westerly carried scores of pictures, his name in blazing print. His reaction was "So what? I haven't got a job."[47]

Providence Journal reporter Leonard Warner cast a critical eye on the people who derived satisfaction in claiming Brown as their own local star. No behavioral nuance escaped the observant, socially aware eye of Warner, who wrote: "Westerly folk got quite a kick out of opening a paper — any paper — and seeing Tarzan's picture and then telling every stranger who came to town 'I'm a good friend of his.' But nobody came through with a job."[48] However, somebody did actually come through with something, something tangible. Warner informed *Journal* readers: "The only 'real' thing he [Brown] received yesterday — something that he could eat — was $10 worth of groceries from Matt Haggerty, Westerly's printing press owner, who said he won $300 bet [sic] on Brown's victory. Haggerty is planning a victory dinner for Tarzan next Tuesday night, and Frank Sullivan, president of the Westerly Chamber of Commerce, said his bureau may honor the runner."[49] It was Matt Haggerty and his proposed wager whom Jerry Nason had casually mentioned the morning of the marathon. Apparently Haggerty had found a taker. Three hundred dollars was a considerable sum in those prewar years. Having won the bet, the presumption was that he was acting honorably by giving the Brown family a piece (3.3 percent) of the winnings, in the international currency — groceries. Incidentally, Haggerty wired Nason to make sure the news of his win had not escaped Nason's notice. Nason recorded Haggerty's vaunting message for his readers. Referring to himself in the third person, Haggerty gloated, "Tarzan won the race and Haggerty won the bet." Without a glint of modesty, he continued, "Any future predictions you want I will make them for you."[50]

Life was back to normal but the kitchen coffers were not in the usual condition by any means, thanks in large part to Haggerty's gamble. Arthur Duffey gave a picture of the Brown household, the day after the marathon.

> It was just another day. They [Ellison and Ethel] were just planning how they could keep the game of life going.... The house is now stocked with plenty of groceries and everything is well in the Tarzan Brown family pro tem [sic].[51]

Duffey allowed Brown space at the tail end of his article so that Brown could directly address the sportswriters and indirectly address the A. A. U., and ultimately speak through the *Boston Post* to the citizenry at large. It was a platform, the access to which under normal circumstances was tightly guarded, access that did not come easily or often to most if any Native Americans. Brown did not mince his words. He said:

> There is one thing I would like to impress on you sports writers as a final remark. Why doesn't the A. A. U. or the officials give us something or other than medals and cups. Why don't they give us some serviceable articles of furniture, something we can use. I have a stack of medals and cups — but what good are they?"[52]

Brown had expressed to Leonard Warner a similar thought. Warner transcribed the runner's words:

"I wish you"—and he was looking straight at his interviewer—"would say something about these marathon awards. Why don't they give us something we can use to buy something with?"

Brown, an unemployed stone mason who has been supporting his family on WPA wages, said that if he were as good in boxing as he is in running—"I'd clean up."

"But just because running is the ugly duckling of sportdom, I get nothing but medals and you can't eat those."[53]

It was tough talk, and there was pain behind the words. Brown was a natural runner and a survivor, but the powers that be in the racing game were not making life any easier for distance runners. These were not, by and large, college men with bright futures running in organized track meets; these were, for the most part, the unemployed or low-wage earners in a continual, endless struggle to make ends meet, while providing entertainment (spectators), employment (journalists, overtime for police details, etc.), revenues (for the towns holding such events), and potential patriotic glory (Olympic competition) freely to others. Yet, for many of the athletes in these still remarkably tough times, to which Brown could easily attest, it always seemed to take a scheme to pawn cups, trophies, and medals in exchange for dollars to use for the purchase of foodstuffs and to maintain shelter. That $10 worth of groceries from Haggerty was very real to the Browns. On the other hand, the $290 left in the printing press owner's pocket was invariably certain to be nothing but pure disposable income.

Salimeno's complaints concerning his treatment at the hands of marathon organizers and officials rankled not only those A. A. U. men in authoritative positions but also the marathon winner himself. Neither Brown (nor Salimeno) claimed to know the real motives for these actions although they had hunches. Both men understood that barring Salimeno may have had a real effect on Brown's chances at victory. They found it plausible that the barring incident demonstrated an attitude shared by some of the A. A. U. officials, an attitude consistent with actions taken intent on trying to impede Brown's efforts to win. Ellison Brown spoke out about it, and was not silenced. The newspapers covered his dissent, as did the *Globe* which reported this comment: "'Why, it seemed they didn't want me to win the race,' Tarzan declared, 'but the crowd surely was with me.'"[54] The more sensationally styled Hearst organ, the *Boston Daily Record*, carried the emotionally inflammatory headline, "Tarzan Blasts A. A. U. Chiefs." The article, by Rolly Hill, said:

Still quite happy over his record-making victory in the B. A. A. Marathon Tuesday, Ellison "Tarzan" Brown nevertheless took time out yesterday to send a slight slap winging at A. A. U. officials who patrolled the course during the running of the grind.

Brown's remarks were directed at officials who ordered his trainer, Tippy Salimeno, from the course within the last four miles of the run for no apparent reasons.

"It seemed to me that they weren't very eager to have me win the race," Tarzan stated. "It bothered me at the time and it still does but I knew that the crowd was with me," he went on.[55]

In good old newspaper fashion, what constituted a "blast" from Brown in the headline was nothing more than "a slight slap" in the article underneath the headline, but the charge itself, a rather serious one, is the point. No public response to it from the officials appeared in the papers, nor was a private response received by Salimeno or Brown. Surprisingly, there did not appear to be any obvious backlash against the athlete for raising the charge in public. Brown's reputation was not marred for his publicly outspoken comments. The loss of the laurel, another episode troubling to Brown, may have garnered the marathon champion a little more sympathy than one would otherwise expect him to receive under more regular circumstances. Slowly yet undeniably, Tarzan Brown, often regarded as taciturn, was starting to be seen as someone who spoke his mind. The sportswriters were encouraging about it; it kept them happily busy, supplied with material. The officials may not have been so glad to see this side of the runner. From the standpoint of a portion of the public at large (and it cannot be ascertained in estimated percentages), the new outspokenness and bluntness was attributable to the lack of socializing controls and lower grade of civility associated with the native peoples. Yet there must have been some more progressive members of the public at large who regarded Brown's words as nothing other than the frank expression of his personal feelings, voiced no differently than any other public figure.

Other words of candor reported from the marathon champion were creating cause for concern and may have ruffled some feathers. The Olympic issue, arising from Brown's "somewhat contradictory"[56] comments to sportswriters, beginning with the very first encounters with reporters after his locker room shower, was repeatedly hashed over by the print media. Brown had shown both interest in going to Helsinki, Finland, on the one hand, and inscrutable indifference on the other. The press and as much of the public as it could stir up, were confused. Brown tried on numerous occasions to explain himself. At the end of the day, it essentially boiled down to the job issue. Leonard Warner wrote that Brown "was still insistent that a job was far more important than a place on the 1940 Olympic team which will go to Finland for the international games." Warner quoted the athlete's succinct explanation, "We can eat what I get from a job, but not what I get from the Olympics."[57]

If he were selected to go— and by no means was the committee's selection process such that his record-smashing B. A. A. victory in what was publicly deemed to be an Olympic trial guaranteed the certainty of his selection — the notion of traveling to Finland early enough to allow ample training time was not finding a receptive audience where it mattered, that is, among A. A. U. officials. In spite of the less-than-stellar results of U.S. Olympic Marathon teams in the recent past, Brown's suggested plan was actually considered controversial. Brown's expressed view about it, labeled "the same old demands for an early getaway to the next Olympics," and now referred to in some papers as "Brown's Bleat," was culling responses from interested parties.[58] One in particular, Edward S. Parsons of Northeastern University, the man who devised the new three-pronged system of trials to get appointed to the U. S. Olympic team, was quick to point out that he (in his role as chairman) and the rest of the American Olympic selection committee would disregard "Brown's Bleat" when the committee convened to do its work. Parsons, like an attorney trying to maintain the mantle of fairness, was quoted as saying, "It isn't our job to consider when and how a Marathoner shall go to Helsingfors. We pick 'em; they send 'em."[59] However, when asked his personal opinion as to which runners of the just run B. A. A. Marathon impressed him, he had this to say: "'Speaking solely for myself,' said E. S. P., 'I was delighted with the power and precision of Brown's running; I felt Don Heinicke did a grand job for a youngster in his first B. A. A. race, but the fellow who impressed me most of all was Pat Dengis, who finished fourth.'"[60] On hearing this, sportswriter George C. Carens, barely hiding his exasperation, editorialized: "On a day the world record was broken for a full Marathon course, Parsons was most impressed by the fellow who finished fourth — 4½ minutes behind the winner. Incredible!"[61] This was not a good sign; after all, Parsons was chairman, not just a member, of the selection committee and would presumably hold some sway over others.

Without much doubt the printed statements of Ellison Brown exuding indifference toward going to Finland had reached most of the ears of the selection committee members. With the games still very much scheduled to take place, despite Europe's increasing military buildup, two more marathon trials would have to transpire before the committee would have to convene and work out its selections.

It didn't take long for the House of Representatives in Providence to pass a resolution honoring the Rhode Island resident and marathon hero. Brown's victory in Boston took place Wednesday afternoon. On the very next day, on Thursday afternoon, April 20, 1939, Representative Ronald C. Dove of Westerly introduced this resolution of congratulations:

> Resolved, That this General Assembly now bestow upon Ellison Myer [sic] (Tarzan) Brown the tribute of official recognition congratulating him, the town of Westerly and the State upon this outstanding achievement in the world of sport; directing the Secretary of State to transmit to him a duly certified copy of this resolution with sincere wishes for his success in future races which shall try his sinews and present other challenges to fibre and to spirit.[62]

Later that evening, the Westerly Town Council moved to officially honor

Ellison Brown. The *Providence Journal* reported the Council's action, pointing out that

> Nothing was said about the job which the runner is so earnestly seeking. Judge Herbert W. Rathbun, Town Solicitor, was instructed to draw a resolution to be entered in the records complimenting Brown.
>
> Councilman Charles J. Butler suggested that since Brown was the best of advertising the town has had in many years, he be given the council's $500 advertising account. There were few comments but no action.
>
> The unemployed runner was voted $10 last night, however, by the Westerly Dart Baseball League.[63]

The suggestion of Councilman Butler, offered in true civic spirit, was a clever if unorthodox way the council could give the Brown family some money without appearing to stoop to an outright handout of charitable assistance. Brown would be, after all, an advertising tool the city could utilize, and he could be paid for whatever publicity the city could draw upon for the purposes of enhancing prosperity. Brown would not be receiving a gift; he would be working for the City of Westerly, thereby "earning" his remuneration. Councilman Butler's informal motion did not receive a second. Although the city was not prepared to offer a job to its most famous athlete at that meeting, behind the scenes, in its department of transportation, the wheels, rumor had it, were literally turning. Brown would have to be patient and wait a little longer.

There was no explanation as to what prompted the Dart Baseball League to offer the donation to Brown or whether he ever received the pledged ten dollars.

In the WNAC radio interview the evening of the marathon, Ellison Brown brought up an interesting sidelight to his Boston experience, an anecdote that until his victory had not been told. He had said he had mailed a letter to an unnamed Boston sportswriter, a letter he did not sign, telling the recipient to expect a major surprise since he was announcing his prospective victory in the B. A. A. Marathon and the setting of a new course record. Radio listeners heard Brown say:

> "I knew I was ready for a miracle run," Brown declared. "I wrote a Boston sportswriter that he had a shock coming in this race. I said the record would be broken. I didn't sign the letter, because I wanted it to be a surprise when I ran so well."[64]

Dave Egan, in a sensationalized, tabloid-styled article under the headline, "Letters Reveal True Story of Tarzan Win," printed the Sunday following the marathon, attempted to tell the story, with Brown's help.[65] A photograph in the *Boston Daily Record* (on Friday, two days before) showed Ellison Brown in a suit and tie, sitting at the typewriter, fingers covering the keys. A caption under the photo said: "Ellison 'Tarzan' Brown, winner of the B. A. A.

Marathon, shown batting out some notes on typewriter for his life story by Dave Egan, which will appear in next Sunday's *Advertiser*."[66]

Tarzan Brown had purportedly become quite the pen pal for he wrote and sent not one but two separate postcards, one signed and one anonymous, to not one but two different Boston sportswriters, near the end of his time of training while staying with his aunt in Pawtucket. To Arthur Duffey of the *Post*, he allegedly sent an unsigned message, which stated, "There will be a miracle man in the race on Wednesday. His name is Tarzan Brown."[67] The second postcard, with his signature affixed, was sent to the Colonel, Dave Egan. It said: "I am at my aunt's. Her name is Mrs. William Steele, 179 Mineral Springs avenue, Pawtucket, R. I. I will win."[68] Both cards confidently announced a victory in advance. Whether either of these *postcards* was supposed to be *the letter* mentioned on the radio is difficult to determine. But Egan, not to be outdone, revealed the existence of a letter as well. It was handwritten in pencil, written not to a Boston sportswriter but to the *Westerly Sun's* sportswriter, Abe Soloveitzik. Egan made a point of explaining that this letter, distinguished from the postcards, was written much earlier although he offered no specific date. He wrote: "When he [Brown] wrote his postcards to the good Duff and me, his training was over, and he knew what he could do. He wrote this [letter] to Abe when he was a discredited Marathoner, with not too many friends in the world—only Abe, and his trainer, 'Tippy' Salimeno, and ex-Senator "Hap" Fenelon, and half dozen more."[69]

Before presenting the lengthy letter in its entirety, Dave Egan implored his readers "to read this [letter] with respect," warning his audience that the words were extremely heartfelt and emotion-filled; this letter to Soloveitzik was nothing to "sneer over" or "feel superior to."[70] Whether the letter was presented verbatim as the marathon champion had purportedly composed it is unknown, but it nevertheless is an interesting document, one that offers the reader a glimpse, however authentic, into the mindset of Tarzan Brown (or perhaps those around him.) The letter:

Well, Abe, I told you that I would give you a story. Well, here it is. You don't have to publish it until I make good again, and I am going to do it this April. You see when I went to the hospital for the operation I was the American Champ, but after I came out and had been out 2 months I tried to run and I found out I couldn't without ruining myself completely, so I never tried again and all I did was drive my car and my legs and body wasn't getting no exercise, but it was in me to run again, so two weeks before the Boston Marathon last year, I let you know that I was going to run and still I hadn't done no other training.

I knew I didn't have a chance in a million to win, even finish in the first ten, but I new [sic] that if I could finish that some day I would be a greater runner than ever before.

Now I will tell you how I trained for the race. With only 10 days to go, my first day of training I ran 20 miles, the first 20 miles I ran since getting out of the hospital. The next day I ran 15; the third day I ran 15; the fourth I ran 10 and then my leg muscles tightened. That's the truth. That was all the training I did before I went in the race and not even a shell of my old self. I finished in 55 [sic] place. After I got beat, the people I thought was my best friends began to make wise cracks. They said I was done, washed up. Married life ruined me. But they didn't know what was going on in my mind. I kept saying to myself, some day, boy, you are going to the top [to] stay, and the thing that is going to make me champ again is a memorie, [sic] as you read in my other book The King of Kings. [Ed. note: Brown has written an autobiography, which has been read only by his wife and the Westerly sports editor. It is titled "The King of Kings."]

Now I am going to tell you how I can win the Boston Marathon. I don't know if Westerly will help me or not this year, but if they do, this is what I will have to do. I can leave my wife and baby at my aunt's house, and I will have to get on some farm where I can take long walks, do plenty of exercise, and eat good solid food. After three weeks of that, I will be a new man.

In March, I can try the 20-mile race at Medford, and if I finish in the first 10, I will win the Boston Marathon. (Ed note: he finished ninth.) I will still have a month to get in twice as good shape, but if I don't finish in the first 10, I will give up the running game, and I have too much at stake to give up now.[71]

No surviving drafts of *The King of Kings*, if it ever indeed existed in a physical form beyond the realm of ideas, to this date can be found. Ethel Brown insisted, over sixty years later, that her husband wrote no such thing nor did anyone else, that it never existed.[72] Why Brown (or Egan) refers to it as "my *other* book" is another mystery. In the substance of the letter to Soloveitzik, the letter writer seems to blur or conflate the 1937 and 1938 seasons in a way Brown would be unlikely to do. It was in the 1938 B. A. A. Marathon that Brown had his disastrous finish, in 54th place, not 55th as stated in the letter — a patently uncharacteristic mistake in every respect, incidentally, for Brown to have made.[73] But from the letter, it sounds as if the 1938 marathon took place the very next year following his hospitalization for his hernia operation. That, however, would be 1937, the year in which he finished 31st.

The possibility exists that sportswriter Dave Egan was planning to create a work on the life of Brown, perhaps in collaboration with the runner, a sort of "as told to" account of Brown's life up to the present, through the 1939 marathon victory. If so, Egan, in an attempt to generate or gauge interest in the project, may have created or at least greatly embroidered the letter for the newspaper audience.

A search through the newspaper coverage of 1939 does not produce a definitive usage of "Heartbreak Hill" as the proper noun designation of the Newton rise before Boston College. That point in the course had a decisive impact on the outcome in 1939, as it so often does, for it is popularly understood to be "where the story of the race is almost always told."[74] Brown, who had been running evenly with Walter Young for a major portion of the marathon, had distanced himself from Walter Young at the onslaught of those Newton hills, and Young never was able to recover. Brown went on to record his victory.

Boston Daily Record reporters John Gillooly and Dave Egan, in writing about that point in the marathon, referred to that locale with the words "the heartbreak" but not as a proper noun. Gillooly wrote: "Presently he [Brown] and Walter Young took over the top position and they ran practically arm and arm all the way to the turn into the home stretch which brought them upon the Newton Hills, *the heartbreak* on the highway, where Marathon races are always won and lost" (emphasis added).[75]

Much closer to the Nason term was this Dave Egan description of the same general moment: "The red-skinned robot threw Walter Young aside like an old Indian blanket on the first of *the heartbreak hills*, and then he chugged along, his white-shod feet beating a rhythmic patter in the rain, his dark arms swinging back and forth, his lips always drawn down in a sulky line" (emphasis added).[76]

A third mention in the *Daily Record*, this one without the benefit of byline, used the slightly different, and hyphenated, wording: "Like a torch of victory they beckoned him on, over *heart-breaking hills* and foot-blistering pavements, through drenching rain and roaring crowds to the finish and the laurel crown which awaited him" (emphasis added).[77]

A variant of the locution, in the phrase "the famous heartbreak mountain," found its way onto the front page of the *Boston Evening Globe*, not by Jerry Nason but by his colleague Tom Fitzgerald.[78] Jerry Nason's own 1939 marathon coverage did not use the name for which he is credited with originating. "On the first of the twisting Newton hills," Nason wrote, "the Indian sped away from his harried rival and from that point on had the course record at his mercy."[79] Nason never referred to the last of those hills, the specific one he named. In the newspapers, multiple references to the grades were used without the "heartbreak" modifier, from "the trying Newton hill section,"[80] to "Newton's straining summits."[81] The designation "Heartbreak Hill," so it seems, had not yet caught on as the name of the last of the Newton hills, though it was named, according to the lore, three years earlier, back in 1936.

In the *Post*, this intriguing application appeared in a sentence composed by Jack Barnwell, and it utilized the uppercase lettering as the Nason expression would do when its usage eventually became widespread. Barnwell wrote, "When the test came at *Heartbreak Curve* in Newton, Brown had what it takes" (emphasis added).[82] "Heartbreak Curve" as a formulation, with its capitalized first letters, seems to be the nearest thing to Nason's celebrated "Heartbreak Hill." The Barnwell phrase never really came into common parlance as the advantage of hindsight of modern B. A. A. history informs us, but in 1939, neither had Nason's "Heartbreak Hill" yet become embedded in the Boston marathon vocabulary. In 1939, even Johnny Kelley had not yet adopted the usage of the name "Heartbreak Hill," as an article he penned for the *Boston Evening Transcript* confirms. In that first-person commentary written two days before the 1939 marathon, Kelley recounted the 1936 encounter through Newton that legend claims inspired Nason's origination of the "Heartbreak Hill" moniker. Of that race Kelley concluded, "I licked myself in 1936 by climbing the Brae-Burn hill too fast in overtaking Tarzan Brown."[83] Further along in the passage, Kelley recalled the more recent 1938 contest, another in which that Newton hill again proved to be a crucial turning point in the marathon. Wrote Kelley, "Last year, Pawson had one of his good days, and after Les and I had battled evenly to the top of the Brae-Burn hill he went away and although I was still second at Carlton street in Brookline, Pat Dengis came like the wind and beat me by 54 seconds for second place."[84] "The Brae-Burn hill," as Kelley referred to it, was not of popular usage as far as sports-writers were concerned. Yet Kelley's employment of it as if it was understood or known to be the name of that particular grade is beguiling.

The Rhode Island Chiropodists Society, meeting at their third annual Foot Health Congress at the Biltmore Hotel in Providence, had a plaque designed with a three-dimensional figure of an athlete running upon a plat-form, his back attached to the wooden escutcheon. The words "TARZAN BROWN, PRESENTED BY CHIROPODIST SOCIETY" were engraved on metal and attached to the shield's surface, just above the runner's head. The presentation of the plaque by the president of the society, Dr. Albert Kumins, was scheduled to take place April 23, 1939.[85] The timing was colored with irony; Ellison Brown's feet were actually in painfully poor condition at the time the foot specialists were celebrating foot health.

The three-man Westerly Highway Commission through its Chairman C. Palmer Chapman announced late on the afternoon of April 24 that it had agreed to hire Ellison Brown for a job with the Westerly Town Highway Department. The chairman stated, "We'll put him to work tomorrow morning."[86] The commission's decision to hire Brown was unanimous. The commission refused to spell out any of the specifics about the position being offered. William Schofield of the *Providence Journal* reported: "The commission declined making any statements about 'Tarzan's' pay or his exact duties. 'He'll work with the gang,' was the only explanation."[87]

The outdoor job was with the road-building division. This was the news Tarzan Brown had been hoping and waiting for. "'Swell!' was his reaction last night to the knowledge of a job. 'That makes everything swell! Now I can earn my own way and take care of my own family.'"[88]

The timing was less than ideal. Brown's feet were in bad shape, so bad, in fact, that he would be unable to begin the job for which he had so relent-lessly lobbied. He could accept the job but would have to delay his first day until the condition of his feet improved, allowing him to stand and work for long lengths of time. The newspapers kept track of the story. The *Globe* ran the headline, "AILING FOOT KEEPS 'TARZAN' FROM JOB."[89] A story in the *Providence Evening Bulletin* provided details to the story, under the headline, "Tarzan's Feet Decline to Work Before Monday, Marathoner, Overjoyed by Prospect of Westerly Road Job, Finds Blisters Will Force Slight Delay."[90] The *Bulletin* reported that Brown had been examined by a physician who ordered him to stay off the job so his feet could have time enough to heal. His feet had never been in such a dreadful state after a race, but the rain-soaked running shoes and socks had combined to cause painful and damaging blisters. The original newspaper reports about his feet directly after the marathon did not convey the severity of the blistering.

A photograph carried in the *Providence Journal* showed Brown sitting with his young son by his side. Ellison's pant legs were rolled up to his knees, allowing his feet to soak in an old-time washtub. The lengthy caption, oddly capitalized like a title, read: "Still Blistered and Sore from Their Jaunt Through the Boston Marathon, the Feet of Ellison Myer 'Tarzan' Brown of Westerly Balked Yesterday at Carrying Him to Work at His New Highway Job. So 'Tarzan' Sat in the Sun and Soaked His Toes in a Tub, the Better to Walk — or Run — to Work Next Monday."[91]

On Thursday afternoon, April 28, Ellison Brown traveled to Pawtucket, Les Pawson's hometown, where his feet were examined and parts bandaged by a chiropodist. He was also measured for new shoes, all free of charge. A front-page article in the *Providence Journal* that covered the visit included this deeper probe of a perverse situation:

> For years "Tarzan" has sought steady employment. No luck. Victory in the marathon last week prompted Westerly officials to give him a job with the town highway department. And here is the paradox:
> The feet that brought him this recognition are keeping him away from the job — because of their blistered condition.[92]

At one point the chiropodist applied a bandage to a sore, blistered toe. The foot specialist saw beyond the terrible blisters and bloody cuts to recognize the soles' architectural beauty. He remarked aloud to Tarzan, "Do you know that you have perfect arches?" Tarzan replied with a knowing smile.[93]

The following Monday was the prospective new starting day for the new job. Thanks in measure to the chiropodist's efforts, Brown's feet were sufficiently healed by then, ready for paid work and for more running.

19

"A Question of Fairness"— 1939

On an unseasonably cold Saturday, May 13, 1939, an unemployed 23-year-old hitchhiked his way from Rockland, Maine, to Boston's North Shore. As he had done two times before, Bruno Mazzeo arrived just in the nick of time to enter the (fourth) annual Major-General Clarence R. Edwards Point of Pines 12-mile handicap road race in Revere, Massachusetts, a race he had won in 1936 and 1937. This year he was running against seventy-seven other athletes, including stars Tarzan Brown, Johnny Kelley, Clarence H. DeMar, and Hawk Zamparelli. Mazzeo, who had spent most of the last twenty-four hours making slow but steady progress toward his Boston-area destination, took full advantage of the *eight-minute* delayed start imposed upon Brown, Kelley and Zamparelli. Mazzeo, who for a majority of the race hardly went noticed in the rear ranks, made a speedy sprint to the finish line in the last twenty yards to take first place.

Tarzan Brown, in his first competitive run since the B. A. A. Marathon, was the fastest runner of the race overall. His elapsed time of 1 hour, 7 minutes, 29 seconds won the time prize for which he received the Howard C. Davis trophy cup. He missed breaking the course record by just 29 seconds, a record set the year before by Pawson, who chose not to participate this year. Due to the handicapping, eight minutes was added to his time, which gave Brown a corrected time of 1:15:29, earning him the official possession of a sixth-place finish.

Arthur Duffey of the *Boston Post* reported that Brown "ran a good race. He had not had a shoe on since the B. A. A. race."[1] Duffey clearly meant a running shoe. It must have been fortuitous news for Ellison Brown that his feet did not show any signs of a lingering problem or new blister condition by race's end. On account of his recent foot troubles, he had not trained for this race. In fact, his last training had been for the marathon. Although the *Herald* touched upon this point, it really did not clarify to any extent: "Brown, questioned before the race anent his possibilities of winning said he thought his training for the longer B. A. A. race might effect his chances over the shorter distance. He was coming fast at the end, however, as he was not listed among the first 15 at the three-quarter mark."[2] It was, as it turned out, nearly an impossibility to overcome the obstacle of the eight-minute deficit. Still, Brown was the only scratchman to finish in the top ten. Kelley finished eleventh, suffering nausea after the contest. Zamparelli, the other scratchman, having one of *those* days, finished way back in twenty-ninth place.

Incidentally, DeMar finished two in back of Zamparelli. Commented the *Herald*: "Clarence De Mar [*sic*], veteran Keene, New Hampshire plodder, ended in the 31st position. He was happy at the finish, however, and with his characteristic enthusiasm, inquired, 'Where's the clam chowder at?'"

A special ten-mile road race was held in Westerly, Rhode Island, on May 20. The *Boston Herald* reported the event as being "staged in his honor," referring to the local running hero, Ellison Tarzan Brown.[3] The race was sponsored by the Catholic Youth Organization of the Immaculate Conception Church, and conducted by A. A. U. officials. The ten-mile run generated a lot of excitement. Over 7,000 of the area citizenry lined the Westerly, Rhode Island, and Pawcatuck, Connecticut, streets that made up the course, an unusual looping course that included some taxing, sloping terrain. For many, this was their first opportunity to witness a road race. Moreover, it was the first chance many of them had to see the famous local running champion, Ellison Brown, in competitive action. They would not be disappointed.

Two clients managed by Tippy Salimeno, Tarzan Brown, and his original running inspiration, Chief Stanton, were among the notable entries, along with such prominent athletes as Les Pawson, Johnny Kelley, Hawk Zamparelli, Clarence H. DeMar, and the Point of Pines winner from the week before, Maine resident and star hitchhiker Bruno Mazzeo.

Former state senator, local pol and Brown supporter "Hap" Fenelon was given the honor of starting the runners on their way with a crack from the starter's pistol. A small crowd of seven runners led the larger pack after getting underway, and that group remained together during the first mile. That assemblage included Brown, Pawson, Kelley, Zamparelli, Francis Darrah, James McCafferty and Mazzeo. By the time they reached beyond the first mile marker, at the Stillman Avenue bridge, this once-cohesive running horde had broken up, and Tarzan Brown moved into the forefront, with Pawson, Kelley and Darrah holding fast. Hawk Zamparelli and Bruno Mazzeo were now five yards back, creating a secondary formation. A third group consisted of Linden Dempster and John Riley of Roxbury, Massachusetts, Lloyd Anderson of Providence, and Bill Carrigan of Boston. The *Westerly Sun* reported the action of the front-runners: "The leaders moved farther in front and the pack split widely when the runners hit Granite Street. Brown took over a 30 yard lead with Pawson and Darrah running together in second place and Zamparelli and Kelley bringing up the rear in the front group when they reached the top of the grueling Granite Street hill."[4]

The Granite Street hill turned out to be the most difficult part — the tipping point, so to speak — of the entire course. Referred to as "a stumbling block to most of the runners," in the *Sun's* view, "Brown stood the test better than the others."[5] About this time, Kelley dropped back a bit, fatigue showing in his stride. In vivid contrast, "Brown was running easily and without apparent strain."[6] That's how it may have appeared to onlookers, but Brown would later tell a different story. "That grind up Granite Street took the pepper out of me,"[7] he would say the next morning.

Running along East Avenue, well-lined with spectators, Brown pushed his lead by accelerating noticeably. ("I got straightened out on East Avenue."[8]) He passed by Wells Street, where his wife, Ethel, and the Browns' little boy, Sonny, stood along the sidelines cheering. Tarzan Brown now had a sizable, forty-yard advantage. But no lead was safe with these formidable athletes, especially on a short-distance course. Pawson was coming on strong, and very soon was making a serious challenge to Brown, for he was running a close second — and getting closer with each passing second. Darrah, suffering a stitch, fell back, but Zamparelli refused to let the leaders get too far in front of him. Kelley, feeling recharged with some newly found energy, was right back in the thick of it, just steps behind Hawk.

Brown was not about to let this one get away from him, especially in front of the home folk. "I didn't feel good at the start," he would later reveal, but fortunately for the runner, "during the last three miles I was just beginning to hit my real form."[9] That would be decisive.

The *Sun* witnessed those final miles during the final minutes, reporting for posterity the racing action as it proceeded along the local avenues, avenues whose names ring with an atavistic familiarity to most Americans with small-town roots:

> The runners came over Grove Avenue, Railroad Avenue, and Canal Street to the Stillmanville bridge. The Indian runner started his finishing drive there. Pawson attempted to match his spurt but Brown pulled steadily ahead. He went out in front by more than 200 yards after crossing the bridge and kept up the killing pace along Stillman Avenue and Liberty Street. Rounding Liberty to West Broad and with the home stretch ahead Brown sprinted to the finish line for a convincing victory.[10]

A crowd four thousand strong cheered wildly as Brown crossed the finish line in a dash that suggested he had plenty of jet fuel left in his reserve tanks.

Over the last four miles, an official vehicle carrying the mother of Les Pawson drove on the course close to her son. She could be heard voicing support for him, who was helplessly unable to catch up to Brown but was content to take second place. Brown's winning time was 54 minutes, 27.6 seconds, "one of the fastest times ever recorded at that distance."[11] Pawson finished in 55 minutes, 19 seconds. The third-place prize was awarded to Hawk Zamparelli. Johnny Kelley, in the last half mile, passed the slowing

Darrah to seize fourth place, while the slipping Francis Darrah, in the exchange with Kelley, ended up fifth. Brunelle and Dempster took prizes for sixth and seventh places, respectively. The next man to cross the finish line, Mazzeo, had experienced some difficulty:

> Bruno Mazzeo finished in eighth place with blood streaming from a cut on his forehead. An over zealous helper in throwing water on the Rockland, Me., plodder struck him with a glass. He had the wound treated after the race.[12]

Running could be a dangerous sport, Mazzeo discovered that afternoon. He made a complete recovery.

Clarence H. DeMar, 52 years young, finished eleventh, registering under one hour with three seconds to spare, at 59 minutes, 57 seconds. An exuberant throng responded boisterously to the running veteran. As the *Sun* observed, "The crowd cheered the shuffling daddy of long distance runners for two full minutes after he had finished."[13] Following the extended ovation, DeMar changed clothes quickly, and attended the prize ceremony along with the other prize winners. After being presented with his award, he took the opportunity and gave an impromptu address to the Westerly citizenry, relating an earlier visit to the area a dozen years back. "'I talked in Westerly twelve years ago in a church group,' DeMar said, 'and only thirty turned out. I see several thousand here today and evidently they would rather see me run than listen to me talk.'"[14] DeMar could tell it like it is.

Chief Stanton "received almost as fine an ovation as Tarzan Brown."[15] His 28th-place finish was the second best finish of any local runners. First best, of course, was his protégé.

After the race, Ellison Brown paid a visit to Dr. John Shibilio "for treatment of several blisters on the balls of both feet," the *Sun* reported.[16] The newspaper, despite its own medical report, insisted to its readers that the blisters were not a serious concern, and that Brown was "in the best condition of his career at the moment."[17] In fact, he and Tippy Salimeno, who was still functioning as his working manager according to the *Sun*, were already looking ahead to the 15-K championship race in Norwich, Connecticut, scheduled for Memorial Day, May 30, ten days away.[18]

If it were up to Pat Dengis, though, Brown and Salimeno would be preparing for a longer run, a full-length marathon, held at the same time as the Norwich run. Dengis publicly challenged Brown to compete in the Lawrence-to-the-Sea marathon. On May 27, Dengis told the *Globe*, "I want another crack at that Indian and want it bad."[19] Dengis, the holder of the Lawrence-to-Salibury, Massachusetts, course record, from a competitive standpoint had not gotten over Brown's record-breaking victory in Boston the month before and wanted another opportunity to race that distance against him. He attempted to depreciate the value of the B. A. A. win in his challenge. Dengis said:

> Nothing would be more to my liking than to tangle with Tarzan at Salisbury. In fact I have issued a challenge to him to race there and not go into moth balls till next November. If he thinks he can beat me, let him come up to a real Marathon course (Salisbury) of the full 26 miles, 385 yards and not an undersized roller coaster course like that at Boston.[20]

Although the Hopkinton-to-Boston course had not always measured an accurate distance of 26 miles, 385 yards (as was purported to be the case due to construction between 1951 and 1956, for example), there was no known dispute about its distance during the late thirties, and especially not in the year 1939, the year Brown set a new course record. Dengis was just blowing smoke to enhance his bluster. But he did sweeten his offer as an enticement to get Brown to consider the Lawrence race. The *Globe* reported:

> Not content with the mere formality of a challenge, Dengis is prepared to stake Tarz to a pink and white basinet and other nursery essentials if he, Pat, fails to whip the romping redskin on Memorial Day.
>
> "A gossip columnist tells me the stork has been flying around the reservation down at Westerly, R. I., lately and I'll provide a complete layette for the new papoose if Mr. Brown will race me at Salisbury Beach. That's a genuine offer," insists Dengis, "and if the stork calls twice, I'll double that offer."[21]

Dengis was thorough as he combed through the psychological armory choosing ego-dismantling armaments with which to battle and goad Brown into running in Lawrence. Dengis' transparent resorts to psychological assault — the side bet (nearly bribery), belittling, bullying — to persuade Brown proved to be ineffective. Even the material offer, of infant bedding "and essentials" thrown into the pot apparently had little sway. Dengis had one parting public stab: "I'll bet my last dime that sea-going redskin will dodge another race with me on Memorial Day and will, instead, go looking for some soft touches in eight and 10-mile sprints."[22]

There were probably very few who would concur with Dengis and describe such athletes as Leslie Pawson, Lou Gregory, or Eino Pentti as "soft touches" in any footrace, no matter what length the course. While Pat Dengis was handily beating Johnny Kelley (2nd), Gerard Cote (3rd), Clarence DeMar (6th), and Don Heinicke (7th) to take his second straight victory and establish a new course record at the Lawrence-to-the-Sea marathon in Massachusetts, Ellison Brown was in Norwich, Connecticut, setting his own new course record while competing for the national 15-Kilometer title against Pawson, Gregory, Pentti and Darrah. An Associated Press dispatch carried a headline in the *New York Times* that announced: "BROWN IS FIRST IN RUN — Indian Sets Record With 51:53 in National A. A. U. Event."[23]

A postentry permitted to compete by a quickly convened consultation of A. A. U. race officials, Brown ran near the back of the pack for the first four laps, letting others up front set the pace. From the fifth to the seventh lap, he steadily passed the competition as he supplanted one by one each runner ahead of him. From the eighth to the eighteenth lap, Brown battled it out with Joe McCluskey, the former Fordham University running star, his toughest opposition in that day's contest. McCluskey, a once-formidable collegiate track star, was sprinting hard, giving it everything he had. He had managed to build a twenty-yard lead over Brown at the start of the eighteenth lap. By the end of that lap, Brown had caught and overtook McCluskey, who was fully exhausted and now limping. McCluskey would not finish in the first ten (if at all.)

In the lead, Brown took the liberty to stop to remove his shoes, which were causing him much discomfort. He resumed the contest, as he "pounded his way around the dirt track, whipping down the final 100 yards with a sprinter's drive."[24] He reached the finish line forty seconds ahead of the second-place Les Pawson, who in turn finished ahead of the third-place finisher, Lou Gregory, by just seven seconds.[25] Brown's record time had sheared "about two minutes" off the title record. No report on the condition of his feet was available. Pentti finished sixth and Darrah finished seventh.

New holder of the national 15-K title, Brown and manager Tippy Salimeno wasted no time planning to secure the national 20-K title as well, in a race scheduled for June 10 in Endicott, New York. Brown, Salimeno and rookie assistant trainer Eddie Murano drove together to Endicott. Little information about the trip or the event could be uncovered. What was reported is that Brown trailed in the race for eleven miles, then pushed to the front of the field. With less that a half mile to go, he "jockeyed for the lead with the runner-up [unnamed] and then sped across the finish line with a remarkable burst of speed to win by 10 yards," as reported by the *Westerly Sun*.[26] Running the 15-kilometer distance under one hour and eight minutes, Brown pruned four minutes off the winning course time from the previous year, although his time did not set a new record for the distance.

The three successful sportsmen — the manager, the athlete and the assistant — returned to Westerly the next day. They discussed the possibilities, considering his successes, of Brown entering the Olympic trials for the shorter-distance Olympic events in addition to the marathon event. No conclusion was reached. Ellison Brown was back with the road crew at work bright and early on Monday, June 12.

In his first return to Boston to race since he annihilated the B. A. A. Marathon course record in April, Ellison Brown was "a surprise entry" in the Bunker Hill 10-mile modified marathon from Stoneham to Charlestown.[27] The race was scheduled to take place in the afternoon on Bunker Hill Day, June 17. Only Brown was assigned to run from scratch, having to wait 6½ minutes before being permitted to run.

When the starting gun reported, Brown stayed put. After 6½ minutes, he finally commenced his afternoon's work.

He was forced to plod almost four miles before he caught sight of the first of the contestants. He found the going very difficult, for traffic was heavy, and he had to dodge in and out of automobiles. Up front, police were clearing a path for the leaders.[28]

Still, he had paced himself extraordinarily well for the ten-mile run, in the view of all observers. Brown had managed to catch up to a majority of the field with a few miles to go. He was less than 300 yards in the rear and was expecting to make his signature, rapid-fire sprint to the finish line. This time, there was a problem with that modus operandi — the race was over; he was already at the finish line, and he had registered a twelfth-place finish. Brown, who had finished in the incredible time of 47 minutes, 15 seconds and had won the time prize, had run out of course before successfully passing the runners in front of him. He reportedly had been running with a wristwatch, like DeMar often did, so as to judge his pace carefully. "Brown thought he had at least a mile to go, judging from the time he kept with his watch," the *Herald* reported.[29]

He understood immediately what the problem was — the course was not the ten miles in length it was advertised to be. He protested immediately and forthrightly to unsympathetic A. A. U. race officials. He argued that the course was short; the officials at first denied it outright. He pointed out that if the course was a full ten miles long, he was the fastest human being alive, since "the world's record is somewhere around 51 minutes, and I can't run that fast."[30] At 47:15, he would have shattered that mark by an overwhelming margin. Yet he was hardly breathing heavy by the finish. Additionally, the world record, actually 50:15 set by Finland's Paavo Nurmi, was made on a course in nearly ideal conditions, whereas the course conditions this day, what with the heavy traffic and all, were decidedly unfavorable, making a record time even more unlikely. "I ran a good race today, but I certainly wasn't that good," Brown countered.[31] In fact, James McCafferty, the twenty-one-year-old foundry worker who finished in first place in 51:04, under these same conditions was also suspiciously close to Paavo Nurmi's official world mark. And so were some of the other runners.

To make him run from scratch in a nine-mile race, against handicaps allotted for a 10-mile race, was patently unfair, and it was a question of fairness. There was no way anybody, not even Tarzan Brown, could make up 6½ minutes on so short a course. This argument reached only deaf official ears.

A nervy suggestion was put forth. Maybe, instead of sticking to the middle of the officially designated course, the runners, including Brown, had themselves shaved the distance by cutting corners, straying from the course when possible, running on the opposite side of the street from the one measured, and in other devious ways had deliberately run a shortened length — in other words, cheated. Al Hirshberg of the *Post* wrote:

Unfortunately the Tarzan heard him.

"I didn't do any cutting across," quoth he. "I followed the road. So did everybody else I saw, and I saw about everyone else, because I passed most of the field. Maybe they don't mind running only nine miles. But I came all the way from Westerly to run 10. Something ought to be done about it."[32]

Only the *Globe* reported that "the race committee later agreed that possibly the course was a bit short, a new route having been laid out for this year."[33] But none of the Charlestown committee members volunteered to own up to measuring the course personally, nor would any of them say who else might have. The official referee of the race, Frank Facey, claimed not to know who measured the course. Sam Scanlon, the general manager of the race, "wasn't sure but he figured that maybe the A. A. U. officials did the measuring. Scanlon said that the race was short last year, so, by rerouting it around by Bunker Hill street, he thought sure that it should make up the difference."[34] It was suggested that the police had asked that the course be redirected so the runners would not travel through Stoneham square. Nobody would assume responsibility.

Someone commented that Ellison Brown should be satisfied since he was getting the time prize. Still upset, he was quoted in the *Post* with this response, although the language sounds suspect, perhaps having been reconstructed:

Who wants the time prize? I finished 12th. Imagine me finishing 12th? Does that look right to you? I have to come all [the] way from Westerly to finish 12th against this crowd? A fine thing! A pretty pass! No sir, Tarzan Brown doesn't finish 12th in a fair race. Somebody made a mistake.[35]

The awards ceremony went on as scheduled. Prizes were awarded in accordance with the results posted. Brown received a stickpin for his twelfth-place finish and a watch for the time prize. Al Hirshberg did not give any description of the stickpin but did describe the timepiece as "incidentally, a not-too-bad looking watch."[36]

Still dissatisfied with the way the event was handled, Brown devised an immediate solution. He offered to take another handicap — 6 minutes, not the preposterous 6½ — and race any and all comers back to Stoneham, the starting point. He would risk his two prizes, but the others would not be required to — they could keep everything. Alas, there were no takers. Wrote Hirshberg: "It was too much of a risk for the committee or anyone else to take. Besides, everyone else was tired and it was getting near lunch time.[37]

Back home the next morning Ellison Brown was still bothered by the Bunker Hill race and what might have been. He spoke to the *Westerly Sun*:

"I was in the best condition of my career, and I ran my most perfect race." Brown said, "I paced myself for a 10-mile race and I know that I could easily have won the race if it went the full distance. If I had known it was as short as it was I could have opened up earlier, for I never felt better in my life."[38]

Some of the newspaper sports reporters, buoyed by the slightest controversy, were elated to have once again a very vocal Tarzan Brown in their midst to cover. Headlines such as the *Globe's* "Tarzan Brown Protests Defeat After Bunker Hill Road Race"[39] gave opportunity to portray the Indian as a complainer. The *Post*, in a twist, offered an unusual slant in its headline, "INDIAN DISCOVERS TONGUE AT LAST," followed by this subheadline, "Tarzan Talks Fast at Charlestown When '10-Miler' Turns Out to Be Nine — McCafferty Wins."[40] The *Post* led with a description of the transition of Brown from taciturn to talkative. "Tarzan Brown, the stoic Narragansett Indian, who has never been known to say more than 17 words over the average conversational distance, finally found out what he was saving his breath for yesterday. The winner of the B. A. A. Marathon angrily held court at the Charlestown Y. M. C. A., the finish of the Bunker Hill '10-mile' road race, and sarcastically pointed out exactly how he had been done dirt."[41] That Brown was angry was incontrovertible. That he enveloped his complaints in sarcasm was unsupported; it certainly was not borne out by the reportage. Brown's protestations about the length of the course were voiced firmly but respectfully. The failure of race officials to take responsibility for the shortcomings in the measurement of the course was more reprehensible than the comportment of Brown, the complainant. Yet, if the messenger was taking the hit for the message, and doing so with the eager assistance of some sportswriters, that was fine as far as race officials were concerned. But not all sportswriters were on board: The *New York Times* headline showed sympathy for Brown's grievance and, above all, its legitimacy: "TALE OF A MISSING MILE: Tarzan Brown Finds Course Cut Short in New England Run."[42] The *Herald* took an altogether different tact. It looked to the consequence of Brown's run under the presumption that the race officials had properly measured the course. "BROWN SHIVERS NURMI 'RECORD'" its headline proclaimed.[43] Surrounding the word *record* in quotation marks suggested something irregular. In the very least, it alerted the reader of the need to take a closer look, to go deeper into the accompanying article — an important function of any newspaper headline. But, unlike the *Times*, the *Herald* without sympathy exploited the controversy as this insensitive line from its article indicated: "So the battle of Bunker Hill was staged over again with a redskin supplanting the redcoats."[44]

The *Herald* described Brown as being "surrounded by managers and handlers" (that's "*managers*" in the plural, mind you) yet no report (in any of the papers) gave any account of these managers and handlers making any protestations or complaints. Only Brown alone presumably spoke up for himself. But certainly, if Tippy Salimeno had been present among the managers and handlers (and there is no firm indication one way or the other), he would have insistently pressed Brown's case. And it is very likely that the press would have published the extended copy, at least that fraction of it fit for a family newspaper.

On June 18, two championship A. A. U. races, a six-mile and a three-mile run, were held in Newport, Rhode Island. Hawk Zamparelli forged an impressive win in the longer event, beating Johnny Kelley, who came in second, and Les Pawson, who finished third. Zamparelli, appraised by Jerry Nason in what was meant to be complimentary, "look[ed] very businesslike in the process."[45] That Sunday afternoon, Pawson did double duty; he also ran in the three-mile race and finished second in that one. Ellison Brown's absence was conspicuous.

Jerry Nason had stood firmly with Tarzan Brown on so many occasions and the sportswriter was, by all accounts, genuinely in his corner. That was all the more reason why what was usually a routine kind of article to preview a race stood out so strikingly. One purpose of the June 23 item was to promote the next day's running of the Roxbury Holy Name 10-mile road race, and the expected homecoming of sorts on the scratch line of Brown, Pawson, Kelley and Zamparelli. Those four in competition together always created the potential for a tremendous athletic contest. Although indeed pure vintage Jerry Nason prose, this, however, was no ordinary Nason sports page contribution, although the first four paragraphs began innocuously enough. An exception, perhaps, was the Nason-formulated new title for Brown and his unidentified support crew. Nason wrote: "Tarzan Brown Inc., accompanied by his new management and complete entourage, is advertised to appear in West Roxbury tomorrow at 5:30 p.m. to toe the scratch line.... Brown is considered to be the very hottest of the American distance runners at this moment, as his six straight road conquests and a 'world record' in the abbreviated Bunker Hill Day race suggest."[46] As The *Globe* sportswriter continued, the tenor of the piece shifted, taking on the chilling language more akin to that of a big-shot racketeer making a veiled threat. Wrote Nason, "The word is around, however, that the eminent Indian may have a chance to cool off shortly if he doesn't embrace more tact in his declarations about this and that and the other thing."[47]

Nason explained:

> The town fathers at Newport were very upset last Sunday because the Tarz demanded something rather substantial in the matter of expenses to compete in the New England A. A. A. U. meet down there, not far from his own wigwam.
>
> The Cunninghams, et. al. are in position to make such requests of the A. A. U. daddies, but the case of a road racer seeking access to the amateur treasury to compete in a championship meet is almost without precedent.
>
> Diplomatic relations between Tarzan Brown, Inc. and the A. A. U. are some-

what strained, then.... The Indian was staying out of the municipality of Newport on Sunday....[48]

Undisclosed were the names of Brown's new handlers and "complete
entourage." To the central point, just how excessive was the request for
expense money? Whatever Nason had heard, he wasn't saying. Was it legitimate for a runner to ask for what he felt was proper, and then freely decide
to accept or refuse the (final) offer, based on his own calculations of fairness,
or after a close look at the ledger sheet? Even for a race in Newport, situated
about fifty miles from the Westerly area, the costs of training, transportation, and food were not negligible. As Johnny Kelley remembered (and it
applied to all the runners): "Running cost us money. We had to spend money
to go to races. For bigger races, we'd get money for gasoline — for expenses,
maybe $20.00 or $25.00, but a lot of times you'd spend more than what they
gave you by the time you got home."[49] Incidentally, "the Cunninghams, et.
al" mentioned by Nason referred to champion short-distance sprinters of
university training (i.e. white-collar athletes.) A double standard openly
existed. When it came to (lowly) blue-collar (or *no*-collar) athletes, asking
for expense monies was a highly questionable action, but quite all right for
the Cunninghams et. al. to ask for and get it. They "were in a position," as
Nason explicitly wrote, quite distinct from Tarzan, Kelley et. al.

Two weeks later, in the name of balanced journalism, Nason revisited
the issue in the second half of his *Globe* opinion column, this time including
the view from the Brown camp. The passage of time, though short, apparently had not lessened the level of passion on both sides. Nason:

> Brown's popularity among the A. A. U. people has waned considerably because
> of his failure to compete in the New England championships at Newport last
> month.
> The Newport committee claims the "Tarz" asked for expenses. Brown's
> manager replies to the contrary.
> "We did not ask expenses," he declared somewhat heatedly, "because we
> never intended to enter, not being aware until a few days before that the meet
> was being held. Since Tarzan was already entered in the Bunker Hill race the
> day before we couldn't withdraw him to run at Newport, and certainly I
> wouldn't let him run two days in a row.
> "There's been a lot of talk about Tarzan asking for expenses, and hints that
> I'm making money out of handling him. Say for me that I haven't taken one
> red cent from Brown; rather I have paid money out of my own pocket more
> than once to help defray his expenses.
> "Also mention that if Tarzan doesn't get his expenses he can't run in these
> races. Everybody everywhere is asking him to run in their events. This kid
> loves to run, but he can't travel around to all these places if they don't pay his
> expenses!"[50]

The manager, who went unnamed without explanation, disputed the
Newport committee's claim that the Brown camp had made any overture for

expense money, let alone a request for "rather substantial" (read: excessive) expenses, as Nason initially framed the charge. The manager's argument was concise: We did not intend to run in Newport. We were not entered to run in Newport. Without an intention to participate, by definition, we wouldn't need any dialogue concerning expenses, for there would not be any issue of expenses. Therefore, we would not be making a request — a request of any size — for expense money. It was a lock-tight rebuttal to the Newport race authorities.

Without cross-examination, there was no way to know what the Brown camp would have regarded as a reasonable request if they had intended to enter the Newport race instead of committing to the Bunker Hill run. Did they demand unreasonable amounts of expense money for the races they did enter? All amateur-ranked runners seemed to be accused, at one time or another, of trying to make money in the pursuit of their sport through higher-than-appropriate expense fund demands. Clarence DeMar, Jock Semple, Johnny Kelley, Les Pawson, Jesse Owens, and Tarzan Brown — all complained of being shortchanged by athletic association officials in their expense reimbursements at some point in their careers, and often at multiple points. The tension between the disbursers and those submitting requisitions was a byproduct of the system as it had evolved. The definition and underlying conception of an amateur athlete was inherently confused and the lines, always somewhat blurry, could not be drawn with precision. The awarding of prizes, even if not in the form of currency, was additionally problematic and incongruent with the nonprofessional concept.

Prizes were difficult to acquire but once acquired, were fairly easy to valuate (or appraise). Expenses, on the other hand, were easy to acquire but once acquired, were fairly difficult to valuate (or assess). Assigning and bracketing training expenses, for example, to just one particular racing event (in the midst of a series of them) was a complicated task. While transportation costs were fairly transparent and computable (but not in all cases), training and food expenses could be less definite. Add permit fees, entry fees, management commissions, trainer expenses, athletic wear needs, telephone costs, postage, etc., and the whole edifice became an enterprise that needed financial support to survive. How to separate legitimate individual event expenses from the costs associated with maintaining a viable competitive athlete — that was a difficult but crucial question to answer, and the squabble between the Newport A. A. U. committee and Ellison Brown's manager was not aimed at approaching a solution to it.

Brashly asserting one's integrity in the face of rumors to the contrary ("*I haven't taken one red cent from Brown.*" Brown's unidentified manager — -"*I'm not a crook.*" U.S. President Richard Nixon) often has the opposite effect on the listener than the speaker intended and hoped for. However these statements were received, it may be unusual in the world of sport but Brown did have a few scrupulous managers working with him during his early career. Tippy Salimeno and Jack Farrington were two who clearly had an interest in Brown's success and welfare, not in stealing his money. (The fact that he had none doesn't change the picture of their individual integrity.) Other managers who came along here and there may not have been so altruistic. Generally on the up and up, there were some elements in the A. A. U. and the racing establishment that were unscrupulous in some circumstances. As an athlete, one had to have one's eye wide open in all directions. An age-old situation persisted: the athlete so often found himself in a perilous position, between a shark for a manager on the one hand, and an autocratic, often corrupt organization in operation and control of the sport on the other. A conflict clearly existed; both entities had little real interest in the welfare of the athlete. The powers that be might recognize a priority to protect and promote the athlete if so doing coincided with its opportunities to increase its own wealth. Prizefighters at all levels and fans of pugilism would recognize and understand this microcosm.

While the manager mentioned in Nason's passage was deliberately unidentified, he could very well have been Tippy Salimeno, who was still serving as Brown's primary trainer during most of 1939 and kept an interest in him throughout his career. In a May 21 article in the *Westerly Sun,* Salimeno was firmly at the helm as "manager."[51] In a July 11 article, also in the *Sun,* Salimeno was identified as "Brown's trainer."[52] Yet, in between those dates, on June 23, Nason refers to Brown's "new management and complete entourage."[53] The usually astute Nason or the staff at the *Westerly Sun* may have been confused on this point. One can only wonder why.

Lastly, there was no mistaking the message of Brown's manager which came through loud and clear at the end of Nason's column. The manager's own veiled form of a threat was in direct response to those in charge of promoting races in Newport and meant for all other promoters as well: *Tarzan Brown was a red-hot commodity. No expense money, no Tarzan.*

20

"The Greatest Attraction in New England"— 1939

A field of fifty-eight hopeful starters converged on Robert Street by the Roslindale Railroad Station, the site of the starting line for the Holy Name A. A. handicap road race. Among those challenging each other and the course record were Brown, and Kelley, who had set the course record in 1934, and Pawson, Zamparelli, DeMar, Jock Semple, and James McCafferty, the victor in the previous week's mile-deficient Bunker Hill run. Brown, Kelley, Pawson and Zamparelli plus the unfamiliar Robert Campbell were assigned the scratch position, all required to endure a 5½-minute wait before being allowed to venture forth into the fray. (No explanation was offered as to why Campbell was harshly assessed the scratch position along with the B. A. A. Marathon past and present winners.)

Five different runners led at various segments of the race, "a novelty in itself"[1] for a race of ten miles but a factor in creating a high level of excitement. One of those fronting the pack, beginning at the four-mile mark and blazing ahead for over a mile, was the veteran runner Clarence H. DeMar. The fifty-one-year-old was in unusually strong command of his powers and, although he ultimately finished twelfth, "was always a factor in the race until the closing miles,"[2] to the crowd's delight. The race was run at a tremendous pace, and when it was all over, Kelley's old record was crushed, first by Brown, then by Pawson, Kelley, and Campbell, all scratchmen. Due to the handicapping, they finished fourth, sixth, seventh, and fifteenth, respectively. Tarzan Brown had bested the field in winning the time prize, running the ten miles in 52 minutes, 14 seconds flat. Les Pawson crossed the finish line just *four* seconds behind Brown, and thirteen seconds later, Johnny Kelley joined him there.

The official first-place winner was James McCafferty, his second consecutive first-place victory. To win, he had to bear down and sprint hard over the remaining four hundred yards to the finish line to decisively pull ahead of Andre Brunelle. The 37-year-old Brunelle, a "Somerville chain-store worker,"[3] had held steady matching strides with the eventual winner from just beyond the halfway mark until that final quarter mile. Only an interval of seven seconds ultimately separated the number-one and number-two runners.

Tarzan Brown, according to the *Herald*, "came up with a driving finish that brought him into fourth place a few steps behind Ryder," who finished third.[4] The *Post* disputed the perception of that "driving finish." Instead it claimed that "had he [Brown] not stopped and looked around coming into the finish line he would have broken the record by a greater margin."[5] Despite the discrepancy in reporting, Brown no doubt ran a strong race. In the view of Arthur Duffey, Brown "was in superb form."[6] He was presented with two of the twenty-two prizes[7] at stake for his afternoon performance — one, the time prize, for registering the fastest time, and another for his fourth-place finish.

Hawk Zamparelli, one of the scratchmen, did not seriously exert himself in the race, having decided to conserve his strength for the national 10,000-meter competition scheduled to take place the following week in Lincoln, Nebraska. The university dropout-turned-automobile salesman, despite withholding his utmost, "was quite surprised to learn he'd missed the old mark himself by only 19 seconds."[8] Due to the peculiar arithmetic of the handicapping system, Zamparelli's time put him officially nineteenth. Jock Semple finished fourteenth.

Just four days later, on June 28, Brown, Pawson and DeMar were competing in another ten-mile race, this time in Cranston, Rhode Island, under the auspices of the Cranston Young Men's Republican Club. The race was held in the evening to avoid the high daytime temperatures. At the gun Hawk Zamparelli darted out front at a furious pace and kept it up for two miles. Brown and Pawson ran together, keeping the pushing Zamparelli within close sight. After two miles, Zamparelli gave up the pacesetting role, and he bowed out of the contest. His interest in this run, like the Roxbury race, had been only for the advantageous real-time workout he was able to derive from it, for the benefit of his preparation for the national track meet the next week. The fallout from the slashing pace he had set in the first fifth of the race for Brown and Pawson continued unabated until the finish line.

Pawson and Brown ran a feverishly quick, furiously rapid two-man footrace, taking over the lead seamlessly where Zamparelli exited. Other runners in the race were, for all intents and purposes, invisible, offering no challenges or resistance to the two swiftest, most resolute leaders. For the remaining eight miles, as they had done during the first two miles, Brown and Pawson battled stride for stride, fighting "each other over every step of the course."[9] The two fiercely competitive but staunchly friendly speedsters "were never more than a few strides apart,"[10] according to the *Boston Globe*. To the *Westerly Sun*, "there was never more than a dozen yards between them."[11] A few strides or a dozen yards over the eight-mile haul — the race was extremely close and the prodigious pace was spectacular.

Somebody had to win. Leslie Pawson "ran the fastest ten miles of his career"[12] and it wasn't fast enough — by *two* seconds. (In the previous race he was defeated by *four* seconds—this qualified as progress.) The official timer clocked Tarzan Brown at 50 minutes, 15 seconds. Brown's 50:15 tied the great Finnish athlete Paavo Nurmi's all-time 10-mile world record, established in Germany on October 7, 1928. Unlike the Bunker Hill run, there was no question whatsoever on this evening over the accuracy of the course's distance.

Taking third place was Norfolk Y. M. A.-affiliated Roger Labonte. He crossed the finish line over three and one-half minutes after Brown and Pawson had stepped over it. His time was 53:49. B. A. A. team member William Simon finished fourth, his time 54 minutes, 3 seconds. Andre Brunelle, a North Medford club constituent, was fifth. In 16th place with a registered time of 57 minutes, 37 seconds, Clarence DeMar had notched another finish to his long list of athletic accomplishments. He was the deserving recipient of "a great ovation" as he completed the run.[13]

Ellison Brown eventually returned home proudly in possession of both the first-place prize and the time prize to show to Ethel, his wife. He was immensely prouder when she showed to him their new infant daughter, Ethel May (called Sis), who had set foot into the breathing world at about the same moment her father had set foot across that Cranston finish line.

Despite the intense summer heat, another four-day interval separated yet another grueling ten-mile athletic battle. Leslie Pawson, Clarence DeMar, Roger Labonte and Anthony Medeiros, who had all fought hard in a futile attempt to beat Brown in Cranston earlier in the week, were now assembled in East Somerville, Massachusetts, for the first annual St. Polycarp's Men's Association handicap road race. They were joined by a fresh Johnny Kelley, James McCafferty, Robert Campbell and Jock Semple, plus fifty-one[14] other able-bodied harriers. Everyone understood who the hot man to beat was.

Tarzan Brown "the Indian expected to win the race beforehand for, as he said, he wanted to bring the prize home to his squaw, Mrs. Brown, and the little papoose," Arthur Duffey wrote.[15] The newspapers covered the will-win-it-for-the-new-baby-at-home angle. The urban course, however, laden as it was with its heavily congested traffic, would be a difficult one for any runner to expect to conquer. On top of that, the victory would be doubly difficult to achieve when John A. Kelley, in prime condition with an appetite and a determination to win, was among the participants.

To no one's surprise, Brown, Kelley and Pawson were designated the three scratchmen. At 6:30 p.m. the other runners were sent on their way from the starting line on Temple Street in front of St. Polycarp's Church in a series of relays, and the scratchmen were held back; they were the very last to get started, 6½ minutes after the first band of runners had headed out. When finally given their chance, Brown, Kelley and Pawson shot off the starting line like three of the famous Blue Angels Navy jet fighters with full throttle open yet in perfect formation. Running elbow to elbow to elbow, the three all but left a trail of smoke as they blazed forward, dodging the numerous four-wheeled vehicles, their only impediments at this early stage. The triumvirate had plenty of fuel and plenty of resolve.

Up front, one Somerville runner who had been allotted a generous handicap, Bill Lanigan, commanded the lead position for most of the first mile before being overtaken by another local hopeful, William Malloy. After a couple of miles under his leadership, durable B. A. A. member Jock Semple pounded his way to the forefront, and led from Porter Square into Davis Square. Continuing along the slight but consequential, steady incline of College Avenue connecting Davis Square to Powder House Square, there was a shakeup of the leadership once more. This time Semple was relieved of the front-runner's role by a veritable running institution, Clarence H. DeMar, who had been "always up among the leaders and finally led the procession at the five-mile mark near Dilboy Field."[16] As the runners passed by the campus of Tufts College, DeMar was first amongst the many and going strong.

Meanwhile Kelley had burst ahead of his two rivals as they greeted the third mile mark. "Pawson faded out of contention mid-way through the race, and Brown conceded the battling Irishman a sound 50-yard margin from the third to the seventh mile," Jerry Nason observed.[17] As Kelley made gains on the majority ahead of him, Brown maintained a steady gait, but had not yet found his groove. In Duffey's view, "Tarzan was nowhere in the first five or six miles of the chase."[18] But that was soon to change, "once he got into his winning stride."[19] John Kelley relentlessly worked his way toward the front, and, by now, Ellison Brown was hot on his heels. As they moved up to the eight-mile mark, along the Fellsway West roadway, things shifted. Tarzan Brown picked up his pace noticeably and the gap that Kelley had engineered behind him started to shrink, and shrink quickly. DeMar still ahead, Kelley could feel Brown coming strong. In a matter of minutes, a fierce two-man race was underway — Kelley and Brown stride for stride once more. But it would be short-lived. Ellison pressed, edging ahead of Kelley by only a yard or two. His sights had already turned toward the veteran DeMar, fifty yards ahead.

> Kelley held on. When Brown flashed by DeMar to take over the lead, Kelley was only five strides back. The race wasn't definitely won as the redskin swooped down Fellsway West for the last mile of running.[20]

The two-man battle was in earnest as Kelley chased Brown over the last mile. This was a full-out sprinting competition, despite the previous nine miles of exhausting effort. Brown reached deep down for that climactic burst of speed he had demonstrated so many times before. It would not let him down on this sultry evening. Nason narrated for his readers: "'Tarzan's' finishing prowess stood him in good stead again, for Kelley hung on game as a bulldog, right to the wire. The Indian's winning margin was roughly 55 yards, marking a significant chapter in twosome racing off the scratch mark."[21] Both the *Herald* and the *Boston Sunday Advertiser* reported an even-tighter margin between Brown and Kelley, only 20 yards.[22] The time difference was beyond dispute — just nine seconds separated the two. Brown's finishing time was 53 minutes, 21 seconds; Kelley's was 53:30. Remarkably for a scratch runner, Brown had earned both the time prize and first prize.

Roger Labonte, who had come on vigorously in the final minutes to successfully pass DeMar for control of third place, finished 22 seconds behind Kelley. Clarence H. DeMar, in a magnificent run, held off a surging Robert Campbell to capture the fourth-place honors, crossing the line just *one second* ahead of Campbell. Behind Campbell was Pawson, who on this evening could manage only a sixth-place finish. Jock Semple had a good day, 23 seconds behind Pawson for sole possession of seventh place. James McCafferty, who had created a clamor lately, had his string of wins halted at two; he came in eighteenth. The team prize went to the Norfolk Y. M. A., primarily through the joint efforts of Labonte and Campbell.

A beautiful *Globe* headline summarized the event: "Three-Day-Old Daughter, Dogged Race by Johnny Kelley Provide Incentive As Tarzan Brown Wins."[23]

The *Globe*, the *Herald*, the *Post* and the *Westerly Sun*— the four shared a jointly held consensus that Tarzan Brown, with this victory, had successfully achieved his eleventh win of the season. (Winning the time prize in a handicap race counted as a win.) Three of the newspapers touted the victories as being eleven *straight* wins; the exception was the *Herald*.

The ten-mile Burrillville Rangers A. C. second annual road race took place on a scorching Tuesday afternoon, Independence Day. Brown would be running on just three days' rest. A small field of twenty runners braved the broiling afternoon temperatures to run the course which was less than ten miles in distance but without controversy.

Lloyd Whitey Anderson, his entire ninety pounds put to work in the effort, led the pack from the start. Brown followed in second place, a good fifty yards behind Anderson for the duration of the first half. Running a very close third was Andre Brunelle. Not long after passing the midway point the heat got to "the midget runner,"[24] and as he "wilted" Brown rushed in to fill the leadership vacuum. Sticking close to Brown was Brunelle. The *Westerly Sun* reported that Brown and Brunelle ran "for more than seven miles ... side by side, and the thousands of spectators who lined the course cheered wildly as the two shared drinking and dousing water."[25]

In time it became incumbent upon Brown to write the proper ending to the ensuing drama unfolding on the sun-baked pavement. With one mile left to go, he turned on the jets and in a blaze of speed quickly left Brunelle fifty yards behind. Before it was all over, Brown had downshifted from a sprint to a jog as he snapped the tape to win first prize. His time was 49 minutes, 56 seconds. Brunelle finished sixteen seconds later, registering a time of 50 minutes, 12 seconds. Little Lloyd Anderson, who had burned so brightly in the first half, had not burned out in that conflagrant start; he recovered to finish third in an even 51 minutes.

The *Boston Globe* reported on DeMar, a fan of the warm weather. It said, "Clarence DeMar, who traveled by bicycle most of the way from Keene, N. H., arrived two minutes before starting time and then proceeded to finish fifth in 52 minutes, 50 seconds."[26] Two remarkable feats, both performances of endurance — the bicycle ride from New Hampshire to Rhode Island and the 10-mile run — all in one sweltering day, one would think, would get one's name in all the papers, especially one of such celebrity. The *Westerly Sun* did not mention DeMar by name or his presence despite his exceptional fifth-place finish!

A specially constructed trophy, named the Governor William H. Vanderbilt Cup, became the newest addition to Ellison Brown's collection of prizes. That collection, incidentally, was growing fast, for Brown had scored "a triumph in every race he has entered in the past three months."[27]

Ellison Brown runs to his 12th consecutive victory in the 10-Mile Burrillville, Rhode Island, Rangers A. C. second annual road race on a hot Fourth of July. Burrillville, Rhode Island, July 4, 1939 (*Providence Journal* photograph).

The *Sun* reported that Tippy Salimeno, serving as Brown's trainer, divulged "that the Indian was far from being in the best condition for the race. He had spent a sleepless night Monday night, while he ministered to his wife, who only last Wednesday became the mother of a baby girl."[28] There were no other details about the health of Ethel, the baby, the son, or the runner's feet.

The *Sun* reported that Brown had returned to his Westerly Town Department highway crew on July 5. Notwithstanding having to work laborious road construction under a hot July sun, in just five days' time Brown would be running in competition again: next stop, New Bedford, Massachusetts. The harsh effects of the summer heat, the muscle and foot wear-and-tear on the sizzling road surfaces at races and on the day job, the supersonic pace— set within the races themselves, and in the number and frequency of events— these considerations underpinned a *Sun* summary of the nearly superhuman runner at this moment in time:

> Brown has shown few effects of the road grinds and right now is in better shape than at any time of his career. He has broken records in almost every one of his starts, and has set such speedy paces that very few of the races have been more than workouts for him after the first few miles.
>
> While the summer heat naturally takes its toll on all runners, Brown, thus far, has been maintaining his sensational pace. He may rest after the New Bedford run for several weeks before entering his next competition, but at the moment he is the greatest attraction in New England and few sponsors dare run their races without asking him to enter.[29]

Tarzan Brown defended his title won the year before as he repeated a victory at the second annual Irish-American A. C. 12-mile road race which took place on Sunday, July 9, in New Bedford, Massachusetts. The afternoon race had originally attracted one hundred entrants, but only fifty dared to actually show up to run due to the extreme heat of the day, and of those fifty, only twenty-five could withstand the intensity of the blistering sun to endure the entire twelve miles of the course and reach the finish line.

To two strong-willed runners none of that mattered. This was nothing less than a two-man race between John Kelley and Tarzan Brown from start to finish, despite the involvement of other able athletes, including Hawk Zamparelli, Clarence H. DeMar, Jock Semple, Lloyd Anderson, Jean Bertholet, Roger Labonte, George Durgin, Anthony Medeiros, and Paul Donato. Les Pawson, though entered, did not show.

When the trigger was pulled on the starting gun, Johnny Kelly, Tarzan Brown, and everybody else took off in a compact hustling herd of humanity and heat. Within the first mile, Kelley had found his way to the front side of that already perspiring pack, and Brown seemed to grant Kelley permission to set the pace as to his preference. Brown tracked right behind, his eyes alternating from the pavement just ahead of him to Kelley's back, over and over.

As another heated mile receded behind, so too did the slowly disassembling pack of other runners. Kelley and Brown galloped for nine burning miles, with Kelley positioned one stride ahead of Brown the whole while. Kelley was drenched with a mixture of his own perspiration combined with the water he had poured over himself in his attempt to reduce some of the incredible body heat his extreme exertion was creating. But he did not let up his break-neck pace.

Brown, in order to win, would have to summon more velocity, for he could determine that Kelley was not going to relent on the pace he had established and maintained. As they reached into the deepest regions of the heart inside that final mile, this would be the closing make-or-break moment.

With his body reacting to mental commands quicker than they could be consciously expressed, Tarzan Brown unearthed that incredible bit of more, that reserve, which he formulated into an amazing spurt of speed that he needed to pass ahead of Kelley. Suddenly, it was over.

Both men had put up an intense effort. This had been more than an athletic endurance match — this bordered on physical self-destruction. Under the sweltering July sun, Brown had beaten Johnny Kelley over twelve miles to the finish line by nine seconds. Brown's time was measured as 1 hour, 4 minutes and 55 seconds.[30] Kelly's time was 1:05:04. Hawk Zamparelli, who finished third, was a ways back; his time was 1:08:07. Semple had beaten DeMar to the finish line, also by just nine seconds, taking thirteenth place ahead of DeMar. Their times were 1:13:44 and 1:13:53 respectively.

It was Ellison Brown's third victory within eight days.

When Monday morning rolled around, Tarzan Brown was absent from his highway department job, "taking a needed rest," according to the *Westerly Sun*.[31] He reported for work the very next morning, refreshed and recovered from the physical stress his body had undergone on Sunday.

Tippy Salimeno, recognizing the wear and tear his runner was enduring, recommended taking the rest of July off, a three-week layoff. Important races in the fall required easing up during these days of extreme summer heat. Salimeno reasoned that conserving energy and physical condition in the less important races now would pay off dividends later in the year when the titles were at stake. Additionally, it would preserve Brown's feet from the harm the hot ground conditions of this summer's racing would cause. Brown appeared to agree with the manager-trainer's judgment.

The layoff did not extend to the first of August as it was originally conceived. Perhaps the St. Vincent de Paul 10-mile road race in Providence was too close in proximity to Westerly to be ignored, or the hiatus had, by now, become too much for the restless runner to bear. Tarzan Brown had gotten Salimeno to enter him in the July 27 contest, which advertised stars Pawson and Zamparelli, and many second-tier, less-prominent but just as hopeful athletes as Anderson, Darrah, Dempster, Labonte and Maderios, young men who were increasingly determined to gain notoriety in defeating Brown and ending his streak.

Both Pawson and Zamparelli had unexpectedly withdrawn without explanation but twenty-one runners were on hand to challenge Brown as the evening race commenced. Brown followed his reliable personal strategy of letting other runners take to the front of the pack and expend their valuable but finite energy setting a pace using unsound judgment based in part upon inexperience. At the midway point, Brown then decisively overtook the lead, and put the pace-setting responsibility into his own capable hands (and feet.) Frank Darrah of the Norfolk Y. M. A. managed to stay close enough to the front-runner throughout miles eight and nine to be within striking distance of overtaking Brown should he falter. But he did not falter. Instead, Brown "turned on the heat in a drive to the finish line"[32] that left a forty-four second gap between Brown and Darrah, finishing in 51 minutes, 22 seconds.

Without providing detail, the *Westerly Sun* observed that Brown's time would have been substantially even faster had he not been impeded over the last several hundred yards by the exuberant crowds there to watch the event. In what manner they interfered with Brown or the outcome was not specified in its sports pages. Whether they hampered only Brown also was not made clear. The *Herald*, which carried a brief single paragraph AP wire account of the race, made no mention of the attendant crowd at all.[33]

By the time Darrah had crossed the finish line, in 52 minutes even, to secure a second-place prize, Roger Labonte, affiliated with the Methuen, Massachusetts A. C., and the Providence runner Anderson had nearly caught up to Darrah but both had run out of gas or run out of course or some combination of the two. Labonte finished six seconds shy of Darrah, in 52:06, and the little, light, local Lloyd Anderson was only a second behind Labonte, registering 52:07.

Three days later, on Sunday, July 30, Brown was entered to run a 12-mile afternoon event from Southbridge to Webster, Massachusetts, part of the third annual track meet sponsored by the St. Joseph's A. C. Included in the field of thirty-six were Labonte and Anderson, back for another shot at the champion Brown, along with the always-challenging Lou Gregory of the Millrose A. A., the national 10,000-meter champion.

Ellison Brown suffered "a slight cramp" in the early going that affected his performance. The stitch, not given a focal point as being abdominal or in a leg muscle by the *Westerly Sun* that reported it, persisted for "more than four miles before it eased."[34] When it did subside, Brown did not make an immediate move to the front but remained back, biding his time. At the nine-mile marker, with three-quarters of the distance behind him, Brown deemed the moment appropriate and without haste adeptly preempted the lead for himself, with only Lou Gregory offering any serious challenges. Brown, in the last three miles, was in firm command, but Gregory kept knocking. Brown responded to each of Gregory's solicitations with an even more powerful surge of his own. During the last mile, Gregory did not let up, but Brown was able to fend off each potentially position-altering attempt. By the time the finish line was in sight, Ellison Brown had forged ahead with a final rapid spurt that increased his lead over Gregory to half a minute. Brown reached the finish line in 1 hour, 1 minute, 35 seconds. Gregory was second, thirty-five seconds behind the winning Brown, with a time of 1:02:10. Third place belonged to Francis Kelley from Philadelphia. Roger Labonte and Lloyd Anderson failed to make the most of their rematch with Brown. Labonte finished in sixth place and Anderson, by the *Boston Globe's* calculations, finished seventh.[35]

In the estimation of the *New York Times*, "Brown, the tireless Indian runner from Rhode Island, continued his domination of New England road racers" with the victory.[36] The victory was his fifteenth consecutive in 1939.

Following the race, Brown's feet were once again in need of attention, the result of painful blisters encountered over the twelve miles of running. While returning to a layoff would have given his feet the resting regimen they may have needed, Brown would hear nothing of it. From a competitive stand-point, he was highly looking forward to the ten-mile race scheduled for Sat-urday, August 5, in Boston. The ten-mile road race feature event of the 86th annual Scottish picnic and games of the Boston Caledonia Club at Caledon-ian Grove, West Roxbury, was an invitational, allowing only ten of the lead-ing distance runners to compete in the event. It would be another chance to go head-to-head with Johnny Kelley and Les Pawson. From another perspec-tive, however, the event was a cause for some concern. It was not a feet-friendly surface; it was a rutted, oval track of cinders and dirt. Each mile consisted of eight laps around the track.[37]

Arthur Duffey, in his opinion column "Sport Comment," could hardly contain his enthusiasm, especially about Brown. He wrote:

> If there are four better 10-milers in the country today than Tarzan Brown, Lou Gregory, Johnny Kelley and Les Pawson, who are they? I cannot recall any bet-ter. The Indian is the greatest runner from 10-miles to the full Marathon in the country. The four meet over the modified Marathon route at Caledonia Grove, West Roxbury, this afternoon. I'm stringing along with Tarzan — but don't sell any of the other three too short.[38]

Tarzan Brown was the strong favorite. "Not only is Tarzan expected to spread eagle the field," anticipated the *Boston Post*, "but to establish a new 10-mile record on the local track."[39] Johnny Kelley, Lou Gregory, Les Paw-son, Hawk Zamparelli, Bob Campbell, Roger Labonte, Linden Dempster, Warren Dupree, and the Rev. Carlos M. Whitlock of Barre, Vermont, might have something to say about that.

Under clear bright skies on an extremely hot afternoon, things got a lot more heated for the A. A. U. race officials when Tarzan Brown finally arrived at the track. He entered the contest at the last minute, "per usual," according to Duffey.[40] This may have set off the officials, for they subsequently had a problem with Brown's attire. The officials adamantly refused to allow him to run wearing "a half sort of running jersey."[41] The "shirt, which did not reach to the top of his running pants, ... was lighter than the usual running raiment."[42] Brown had hoped to wear the lighter, less-burdensome garment for some relief in the tremendous heat. The inflexible officials would not bend, especially for Brown. In their estimation the jersey did not conform to the A. A. U. rules.

A different take was presented by Frank Conway in the *Boston Sunday Advertiser*. As Conway saw it, the problem with the shirt for race officials was that it was torn.

> Just as the slick-running Indian was about to take his place at the starting line, the A. A. U. authorities noticed a large tear in the front section of the jersey just above the trunks. They immediately requested him to replace this jersey, informing him that it was a strict A. A. U. rule to wear a full track uniform in all A. A. U. sponsored races.
>
> Brown informed the officials that the tear wasn't made intentionally, and the jersey was the only one he had in his possession. He was then told that he wouldn't be allowed to run unless he procured a new jersey.[43]

Brown was quickly issued an ultimatum: put on another top or be barred from running in the event. It did not take long for Ellison Brown to make up his mind. He chose to disengage entirely from the event, as he was, to say the least, not real warm to the idea of conforming to the constraints of an A. A. U.-imposed ultimatum. As word circulated that Brown was withdrawing, other runners stepped forward to urge that he reconsider. Conway wrote, "The quiet-spoken Indian decided he wouldn't run at first, but he changed his mind when running colleagues Johnny Kelley, Leslie Pawson and Lou Gregory and other [*sic*] begged him to remain in the race."[44] A fellow athlete offered Brown a regulation jersey to put on. As George M. Collins reported to *Globe* readers, "He [Brown] went away mad as a hatter, but another jersey was secured and, with a grim look on his face, Tarzan went to the mark."[45]

At the start, Kelley, Gregory and Brown each took turns heading the fast-moving runners, without anyone taking real possession of the lead. At the second mile Kelley did do so, but it was short-lived. By mile three, Brown again was steering, but Gregory was sporadically switching out front for short spells. "Pawson was the first to feel the effects of the grind and dropped back at the end of four miles and Kelley's threat was wilted at the five-mile mark."[46] Gregory and Brown ran what developed into a two-man duel. Beyond the midpoint of the seventh mile, Brown had gained a respectable advantage over Gregory and the rest of the pack. The *Westerly Sun* estimated that lead to be one hundred yards. Then, at the eighth mile, Brown "suddenly stopped, sat down on the edge of the track and peeled off his shoes and socks."[47] As he was removing his shoes, Gregory closed the gap. As Tarzan took off his wrinkled socks with care, Gregory soared past where Brown was sitting. Gregory had increased his own new lead to about seventy yards[48] in the minute or so it took Brown to discard his shoes and socks and get down to bare feet. Ellison Brown was not through. He got up, and started to sprint barefoot, and in a very short period of time he was on Gregory's heels.

Brown, his unprotected soles rapidly touching down and lifting off of the burning hot cinders of the track, passed Lou Gregory by with a mile in laps to go. Brown poured it on, separating himself from Gregory by a full twenty-five yards as his chest forcefully broke through the finish tape.[49] Four thousand spectators present jumped to their feet, generating "a rousing cheer for Brown."[50]

"It was easily one of the most sensational 10 miles ever run and it was one of the fastest run in this country," wrote Arthur Duffey.[51] Brown finished in 54 minutes, 52.7 seconds; he set a new mark for the soft-dirt track and the meet despite the unforgiving heat and the need to run the last two miles barefoot.

Gregory finished in second place; Kelley finished a distant third. The newspapers did not devote much space to Kelley, nor report his words after the race as they so often did. Les Pawson finished fourth; Warren Dupree was fifth; Linden Dempster was sixth; and Rev. Carlos Whitlock was seventh. Robert Campbell dropped out of the event after struggling for six miles. Hawk Zamparelli did not run any of the race. He withdrew before the start, indicating to the race officials "that he had sprained his leg."[52] No word was given of Labonte's results.

Ellison Brown's victory over the limited field of highly skillful runners extended his winning streak to sixteen straight.

On the morning of August 12, 1939, Ellison Brown, Johnny Kelley, Hawk Zamparelli, Lloyd Anderson and Clarence H. DeMar traveled northeast to Old Orchard Beach, Maine, to compete in the second annual baby marathon, an afternoon ten-mile handicap race. Tarzan Brown was the defending title holder, having won the initial edition of the event the year before. For that achievement (and his reputation), he was rewarded with the scratch position, obliged to yield the start to the whole field of forty-nine challengers before being given the chance to get into the fray.

Fred Allen, the celebrity entertainer, was vacationing in the Pine Tree state and was again tapped to be an honorary judge in the event as he was the previous year, along with Maine residents James C. Oliver and R. H. Hazard. Despite a blazing sun, high temperatures, and very little discernable ocean breeze, several thousand spectators were on hand to witness the event.

Little, light Lloyd Anderson of Providence, the 97-pound marathoner, was given a 2½-minute handicap, and he took it for all it was worth, utilizing it to the fullest. That head start enabled him to keep ahead of everybody, including Brown, for the entire course, from start to finish. Try as he might, Brown could not catch up to the speedy twenty-year-old flyweight perambulator. Neither could Kelley, Zamparelli, nor DeMar, for that matter.

When all was said and done, Anderson chalked up the first-place victory with a reported time of 57 minutes, 4–10 (*sic*) seconds, and Brown finished second, an estimated fifteen yards behind, in 58 minutes, 4–5 (*sic*) seconds.[53] Hawk Zamparelli finished third, just ahead of Kelley, who had to settle for the fourth-place prize. DeMar, who last year finished eleventh, improved his showing this year with a seventh-place finish. Of the forty-nine entrants, only twenty had the staying power to withstand the heat and make it to the finish line.

The *Globe* headline read, "TARZAN IS DEFEATED BY 97-POUND RUNNER."[54] The newspaper, like its rival, the *Post*, did not clearly convey that Brown had indeed won the time prize, Tarzan having run the course in the quickest time. The elapsed time reported in the *Globe* was not "corrected" with the subtraction of the scratch wait of two and one half minutes. Only the *Westerly Sun*, reporting on their local man, pointed out Brown's "win," its headline proclaiming, "Brown Wins Time Race At Old Orchard/Westerly Runner Races Ten Miles Under 2½ Minute Handicap/17TH VICTORY/Johnny Kelly Finishes Fourth and Clarence DeMar Seventh."[55] The *Sun* attempted a brief explanation, using language that may have resembled Orwellian Newspeak to the uninitiated:

> Although he finished second, Brown was actually the winner of the race, negotiating the course more than two minutes faster than Anderson and keeping intact a 17-race stretch which has seen him in the most sensational winning streak in racing history. During the string of victories, dating back to last April, no runner has been able to outspeed Brown over any distance ranging from 9 miles to 26 miles, 385 yards, the full marathon distance, and he has won time prizes in every event in which he has been entered.[56]

Tarzan Brown had been suffering a chest cold and sinus condition, which, according to the *Sun*, had pestered him for a full week. No excuses by or for Brown were being offered and "no alibis for failure to steam through in first place" would be put forth.[57] Nevertheless, during the race, Brown's perdurable feet had capitulated to bloody, painful blistering. As soon as he had returned to Rhode Island, he sought treatment from his physician, Dr. John Shibilio. In the opinion of the medical doctor, the runner's feet were deemed to be in "tough shape."[58] By August 20, however, the doctor felt that Brown probably would be ready to mount a defense of his national title at the A. A. U. 25-kilometer championship race in Newport. Even Dr. Shibilio understood that if Brown had his heart firmly set on competing in that title run, no person alive could dissuade or keep him from doing so; not even the condition of his own two feet, however gruesome, could or would deter him.

Jerry Nason reported the existence of a letter sent from the famous actor and former Olympic swimmer Johnny Weissmuller[59] to Ellison Brown in the summer of 1939. In the letter, according to Nason although he did not quote it verbatim, Weissmuller, who though the first was but one of a number of actors who played the Edgar Rice Burroughs' character "Tarzan of the Jungle" on the silver screen, complained at some length about Brown's use of the name "Tarzan," which Weissmuller believed belonged rightly and exclusively to himself. "Weismuller [sic] issued a subtle warning" to the Rhode Island runner, Nason wrote, backed by the presumptive threat of some legal action.[60] Nason pointed out, however, that the "Tarzan" moniker had been attached to Ellison Brown before Weissmuller ever played the role, or as Nason put it, "long before Weismuller ever let his hair grow for the purpose of keeping his back warm while leaping around in the cinema foliage."[61] Weissmuller's first Tarzan film was *Tarzan the Ape Man* which was released in 1932. No litigation was pursued, nor did Brown cease to be called "Tarzan," as he was addressed that way by nearly everybody.

21

"Tarzan Brown's Thunder" — 1939

On the morning of the National A. A. U. 25-kilometer race day, Arthur Duffey reported in the *Boston Post* that the A. A. U. race officials still had not received the entry of Ellison Brown.[1] Already upset with Brown for shunning two June 18 races, the Newport officials were probably not predisposed to cut him any slack if he or his manager missed the deadline for signing up. Entered for the August 20 event was a stellar field, including some of New England's finest runners. The pride of Arlington, Massachusetts, Johnny Kelley, was ready to get back into his winning ways, along with Les Pawson of Pawtucket, Hawk Zamparelli of Medford, Jock Semple of Boston, Roger Labonte of Norfolk, Francis Darrah of Roxbury, George Durgin of Boston, Anthony Medeiros of Medford, Lloyd Anderson of Providence, and Bruno Mazzeo of Maine. From the Millrose A. A. of New York, Lou Gregory, Mel Porter, and Paul Berthelot hoped to make the national title Newport race more than just a New England affair.

Despite that *Post* report, on time with his entry and ready to run was Tarzan Brown, last year's winner and the course recordholder. With a projected 2:30 p.m. starting time, the field of fifty runners assembled around the staging area of the starting line. When the skies opened up with a sudden rain shower, the event was delayed for almost fifteen minutes. Soon thereafter, the rain had let up enough for the race to get started. In a light drizzle, Newport mayor Henry S. Wheeler pulled the trigger of the starting pistol, and the national title 25-K race was underway.

In the first pack charging forward, Brown, Kelley, and Gregory set the pace in the wet and heavy ocean air along Ocean Drive. "Tarzan and Kelley were out in front up to the twelve mile mark when Gregory made his first bid and took a wide lead. Evidently Brown and Kelley allowed the Millrose runner to take a longer advantage than they intended and when Brown did turn on the usual spurt in the last mile Gregory was to [*sic*] far out front to catch."[2]

Lou Gregory had a five-hundred-yard lead over the second-place Brown when he crossed the finish line in Freebody Park, according to the *Westerly*

247

Sun.[3] Brown actually slowed as he entered the park, seeing that he had no opportunity to overcome the margin Gregory had amassed. Gregory had finished the roughly 17½-mile run in 1 hour, 28 minutes, 28 seconds. Brown placed second in 1 hour, 29 minutes, 51 seconds; he had been "bothered by cramps along the route."[4] Kelley registered a third-place finish; he bound across the finish line in 1½ hours plus fifteen seconds. Darrah was fourth, Berthelot fifth, and Pawson sixth, followed by Durgin, Medeiros, Labonte, and Dempster filling out the top ten. Jock Semple was nineteenth. Mel Porter did not crack the top twenty-five.

Brown still held the course record; it was safe from Gregory's (or anybody's) challenge by two minutes, ten seconds. That was of little consolation. His magnificent succession of seventeen victories was halted. "The setback was the first in 18 races for Brown and cracked one of the longest and most brilliant winning streaks in long-distance running annals. Since last April the Indian runner has competed regularly in runs ranging from 10 miles to the full marathon distance of 26 miles, 365 yards, without suffering defeat," extolled the *Westerly Sun*.[5] Succinctly stated the *Globe* headline: "'Tarzan' Brown 2nd at Newport."[6]

There was no postrace commentary in the papers, but Arthur Duffey inserted this item in his "Sport Comment" column:

> Lou Gregory, after giving Tarzan Brown one of his worst beatings in the national 25-kilometer championship race at Newport, R. I., returned immediately to Cornell after his victory. Lou is taking his A. M. degree at Ithaca this morning. He will return to New England Labor Day for the American Legion 10-mile race at Manchester, Mass. If the soldier committee is wise they'll bring the Indian and Gregory together again in that race. Tarzan is pretty sore over his defeat at Newport and wants to get even.[7]

Ellison Brown took the next two weeks off from competition. He had almost successfully gotten the upper hand over a persistent sinus condition and summer cold that had been affecting his breathing passages for almost a month. The *Westerly Sun* reported that he "has taken things easy for the past two weeks,"[8] but did not provide any details.

The half-mile circular track at the Kingston, Rhode Island, fairgrounds was the site of a ten-mile race held as one of the featured events of the Kingston Fair on September 2, 1939. Tarzan Brown was the defending champion, and in this third annual edition of the race he faced a challenging field, which included Les Pawson, Lou Gregory, Hawk Zamparelli, and Lloyd Anderson, all of whom had competed in a 12-mile race in Providence the day before. Gregory had won that one. The Saturday afternoon Kingston race would provide the first opportunity for Brown to rematch with Gregory after Gregory's Newport win. The thirty-four-year-old Gregory was on a winning roll of his own.

Brown was not willing to let Gregory get out front with a lead and repeat the disastrous results of Newport. When the gun fired in Kingston signaling the start, Brown assumed the front-running position in the early going, and set a torrid pace. "Gregory stayed on his heels and they ran in that fashion until the 14th lap," the *Westerly Sun* reported.[9] Pawson was running third, with Labonte, Zamparelli, Dempster, and Anderson bunched tightly together, about a minute behind Pawson.

Brown in time managed to open up a fairly sizable advantage of twenty-five yards. That propitious margin soon evaporated, as the persistent Gregory erased it with an accelerated spurt in response. Lou Gregory, breathing heavily, managed once again to get within a step of the leading Brown and seemingly was preparing to stay there forever. After nine miles, Tarzan Brown had had enough of Lou Gregory's game. "Brown put on his famous finishing burst on the last lap and pulled steadily ahead with Gregory unable to match it."[10] Brown crossed the finish line seven seconds ahead of Gregory, his time, 53 minutes, 58 seconds. In doing so, he "clipped three full minutes off his previous mark in winning the 10-mile race."[11] It was a satisfying victory in front of many hometown friends and supporters.

A justifiably fatigued Pawson, who took third-place honors, was two minutes, 18 seconds behind Brown. His time was 56:16. Labonte held on to fourth place, in 56:53. Zamparelli was fourteen seconds behind Labonte, and Dempster was just five seconds in back of Zamparelli. Lloyd Anderson was seventh, his running time 58 minutes, 19 seconds.

A week later, in a contest for the New England A. A. A. U. 15-kilometer title held in Lexington, Massachusetts, for the first time, Johnny Kelley handily beat his close friend and running rival Les Pawson by three hundred yards in a highly charged race. Kelley's victory time was 50 minutes, 19.6 seconds. He finished 4.6 seconds shy of a full minute ahead of Pawson, who came in second in 51:15. George Durgin of the B. A. A. was third, and his fellow club member, the venerable Jock Semple, finished in twelfth place.

Clarence H. DeMar was present in Lexington that September 9 afternoon, but chose not to enter that 15-kilometer race. Instead, he elected to compete in another of the track and field events held that afternoon — not a running competition but a walking race, the one-mile walk. DeMar finished third in that seven-minutes-plus contest. Ellison Brown was absent from Lexington that day, with good reason.

On the following afternoon, Ellison Brown found himself competing in a race that took place in a vastly different-looking fairground from the one in rural Kingston, Rhode Island, the scene of his most recent race. Brown appeared at the site of the internationally famous 1939 New York World's Fair for a 15-mile road race sponsored by the *New York Journal-American*. The race's course was adroitly devised by planners with much playful ingenuity to take the runners "over all parts of the huge fairgrounds and at times almost into the middle of the many attractions."[12] Yet for all the cuteness associated with the design of the course, the race itself was far from frivolous; this was a real sporting event.

Sixty men comprised the field of runners. The starting gun was fired and the race got underway as, across town in the Bronx, another September race was in the midst of being all but over. At Yankee Stadium, the first-place New York Yankees, with a monstrous 17½-game lead over the second-place Boston Red Sox, were on their way to winning the first game of an eventual sweep of a doubleheader over the hapless Washington Senators.

Ellison Brown wasted no time getting in front of the large pack of runners as the World's Fair visitors, many from foreign countries, looked on in amazement. Tarzan Brown maintained "a good lead" over the others and "ran easily most of the distance."[13] In and around the fairgrounds, past pavilions and pedestrians, Tarzan Brown led a parade of runners on a circuitous route but straight to the finish line. His time for the fifteen-mile run was 1 hour, 24 minutes, 39.6 seconds. Jean Berthelot of the Millrose A. A. of New York was second, and Robert Cooper, unattached, was third.

"Tarzan Brown Wins World's Fair Run."[14] The headline in the *Boston Herald* told the story but it did not tell the whole story. As soon as the prize ceremony was completed, Brown quickly commenced his travel back to New England. Like the Yankees, he was on his way to completing a doubleheader of his own. Destination: National League Field, known colloquially as the Beehive, the home ballpark of the Boston Bees, in Boston, Massachusetts.

Like his iron-man stunt three years earlier following his return from the Olympic Games, when he ran and won two marathons on successive days, Brown was once again in the middle of an iron-man event of his own making. He had just completed a victory at the World's Fair run in New York City; that was part one. Next, as in 1936, he had to travel overnight to New England, to compete in a second running event the very next day.[15]

Boston mayor Maurice J. Tobin's second annual charity Field Day at National League Field was a six-hour affair beginning at noon on September 11. A 10-mile road race with a field of just over a dozen invited athletes (including Johnny Kelley, Les Pawson, and Lloyd Anderson) was the feature event to which Brown was headed. Over fifteen thousand spectators converged on the ballpark for the day's events. Along with the main feature of the day, the ten-mile race, other planned events included the marching bands of the Boston Fire Department and the Boston Police Department; the Coconut Grove orchestra; firefighters' displays of daring rescues and ladder-climbing exhibitions; three baseball games including a three-inning baseball game between firemen (the "Smokies") and police (the "Coppers"), and a game between a team of city pols ("the City Hall nine" which included the mayor's personal participation) and a team of Massachusetts state politicians ("the Statehouse nine," what else?); a four-inning softball game pitting Boston sportswriters against the Boston Olympets hockey club; a separate men's and women's hundred-yard dash; a baseball-throwing competition (men's and women's); a forward pass competition; boxing and wrestling matches; a vaudeville presentation by local theater and radio performers; a singing contest; a jitterbug group; and "a nerve-shattering act in which a boy was shot out of a cannon."[16]

On a track around the inside perimeter of the baseball park, Johnny Kelley, showing no signs of wear from his Lexington exertion two days before, took the early lead and led after the first mile, with Pawson, the previous year's winner, running second and Brown third. Frank Darrah, winner of the Pike's Peak race in Colorado, was among the leaders during the first half. At various points, each of the front four briefly led the others, but no runner could acquire an early edge. When Brown led, he hiked the pace up a few notches, but, according to the *Westerly Sun*, "appeared content to let the other runners move up front occasionally as long as they did not go too far ahead."[17] The runners completed lap after lap. The surface of the track consisted mostly of grass, with some areas of dirt. The *Herald* reported that "both Brown and Kelley ran barefooted, making their machine-like pace all the more amazing."[18] Kelley may have started out wearing shoes—"flimsy shoes," as George C. Carens suggested, but "these wore away gradually."[19] Running without shoes may have been an advantage, as the pair made a slight gain away from the third-place Pawson and the rest of the pack. Howell Stevens of the *Post* reported this assessment after five miles: "At the halfway mark Brown was about four yards in front of Kelley. Pawson was running third and Darro [*sic*] had dropped back to fourth. Lloyd Anderson of Providence, who weighs only 95 pounds and proved a great favorite with the crowd, was eighth at this point."[20]

By the sixth mile, the race was a two-man, classic Boston duel; Johnny Kelley and Tarzan Brown running stride for stride, with Brown holding a slight two-yard advantage for most of the laps making up mile six. The spectators (and other performers) were completely engrossed in the unfolding drama. Pawson, feeling some residual effects of his Lexington run, slipped nearly thirty yards in back of Kelley, but was still ahead of the rest of the runners. Lloyd Anderson had advanced to sixth place by the end of the sixth mile.

As Brown and Kelley blazed their way upon the opening laps of the seventh mile, there appeared some discernable movement. Brown suddenly forged his largest lead of the day but it would not last long. Howell Stevens observed, "Tarzan opened up a 10-yard gap on the seventh mile but Kelley closed it and the Indian was only a yard ahead at the start of the eighth mile."[21] Now Kelley tried. Kelley managed to pull ahead of Brown as they made their way to the close of the eighth mile, and Kelley actually opened up three yards of daylight between them. He led with that slight margin over the laps comprising the ninth mile and through the first four laps of the final mile. But try as he might, he could not sustain his margin, because he could not control Tarzan Brown. Stevens of the *Post* reported the endgame: "Just as the final lap started, however, Tarzan leaped to the fore and broke away from his persistent adversary by a blinding burst of speed. Kelley tried desperately to hold the Indian within striking distance, but was unable, Tarzan crossing the ultimate line about 23 yards ahead."[22]

Brown had reached deep once again and unleashed a tremendous reserve of power, jetting along that final lap and accelerating all the while. A loud, thunderous ovation from the crowd in the stands and those on the field filled the ballpark as he and then Kelley made their concluding laps around the field to the finish line. Pawson, still running third, about three hundred yards in back of Kelley, also enjoyed the boisterous cheers and applause. Little Lloyd Anderson of Providence finished in fourth place, as the people voiced their uproarious approval.

The victory was Tarzan Brown's second in two successive days, his third straight since August 20, his twentieth win of the year of twenty-two contests entered. He finished with the exceptionally fast time of 54 minutes, 16.2 seconds. His feet appeared to be in relatively good shape, despite the barefoot run, the accumulated wear and tear of the two back-to-back races combined, and the general bad state they had been in most of the summer season. Kelley, on the other hand, came out of the Mayor's Day race with both feet in a most painful, miserable condition. "The skin was completely worn off Kelley's feet" by race's end, Stevens reported.[23] George Carens discussed the beating Kelley's feet endured from the ordeal. He first described how the year before, Kelley had finished second to Pawson while punishing his feet on the cinders of Fenway Park, where the event was held. This year, was a replay, in that

> it was Kelley again who poured on the pace to make it a most interesting 10-mile race, and again his lot was the runner up position, due to Tarzan Brown's hurricane last-lap efforts.
> This time there were no cinders to bother Johnny at National League Field, but he donned flimsy shoes to traverse the grass course. These wore away gradually and he discovered that a white boy's feet cannot stand the punishment an Indian's feet can take. For Tarzan Brown came through unscathed, while Kelley lost the bottoms of his big toes.[24]

Sportswriter Carens' racial views notwithstanding, the fact was sores, lesions and sore feet from running were equal opportunity afflictions, ones that crossed all racial, social and economic lines. The runners all understood this, learning the lesson at one time or another from painful direct experience. Carens mistakenly believed that Ellison Brown, being of Native American heritage, had super feet that did not suffer damage in footraces to the extent of Caucasian runners' feet. Where was Carens just a few short weeks ago, when Brown had to postpone his first day of employment? Without much evidence, too often Caucasian sportswriters, like the *Boston Evening Transcript's* George Carens, were quick to chalk up advantages and disadvantages to racial distinctions rather than athletic efforts, training methods, proper gear, personality or habit.

On the morning of October 12, Our Lady of Mount Carmel H. N. S. in East Boston provided an opportunity before the end of the year for Kelley, Pawson, Gregory and Brown to compete against each other (and others) in yet another ten-mile race. The four would be assigned scratch positions. Also signing up to compete among the list of seventy-seven were Donato, Darrah, and Zamparelli. Last but not least, the *Post* reported the intentions of the remarkable man from Keene: "Clarence H. De Mar [*sic*], the veteran of all Marathon runners, was an 11th-hour entry last night. De Mar, despite his 52 years of age, is still running in good form. He will be one of the most closely watched runners in the race."[25]

The next day's headline in the *Post*, "KELLEY IS VICTOR IN 10-MILER," was deceptive if one did not delve further into the accompanying article, since Arlington's Johnny Kelley never did make it to mile three. He dropped out of the race at some point shortly after mile two. The headline was not inaccurate, however, as it meant to trumpet the success of Kelley — that is, Newton resident *Gene* Kelley. The young Newton Y. M. C. A.-affiliated runner had been given a five-minute handicap, and had taken full advantage of it. He was first across the finish line, winning the first-place prize. But his time was not the fastest.

Leslie Pawson, who had competed in the Port Chester marathon the previous Saturday, like Johnny Kelley, failed to live up to expectations, but unlike Kelley, was not brimming with disappointment. He finished in twelfth place. Tarzan Brown did somewhat better, finishing tenth, two places and fifteen seconds ahead of Pawson, but he had to overcome a rough beginning to manage even that. As Arthur Duffey reported, "the Indian was slow to get into his running in the opening miles, but made up much ground in the closing two miles. He won the second time prize," running the course with the second fastest time of all the participants save Lou Gregory.[26] Gregory finished second and won the first time prize, a very good result for the scratchman. Gregory, who "was not in the race for the first six miles, ... gradually overhauled his competitors," showcasing "a fine sprint" in the final mile but fell short by three seconds to catch Gene Kelley at the finish line.[27] Gregory's actual time for the ten-mile race was 53:48; Brown's was 54:37; and Pawson's was 54:52. First-place winner Gene Kelley's time was a much slower 58:45. DeMar's finish and time was not reported. He was not listed among the top twenty finishers.

In his opinion column, Arthur Duffey extolled the virtues of Gregory's athletic prowess and offered a reason for his failure to overtake Gene Kelley for first place in the East Boston race. As Duffey saw it, it was Gregory's "unfamiliarity with the course [that] undoubtedly proved his downfall."[28] The senior *Post* sportswriter provided no wider explanation or clarification. In the speculative realm, it may have been that race officials were not adequately stationed along the congested course route to sufficiently direct the late-starting Gregory (and perhaps other runners as well) through the narrow, nonparallel East Boston streets, with which he, a New York resident, would have been utterly unacquainted. If Gregory had indeed lost his way, even momentarily, he did a magnificent job reaching the finish line when he did. Duffey expressed an additional opinion. In his view, Gregory was "about the most consistent runner we have seen in New England and seems to be grabbing much of Tarzan Brown's thunder."[29] The first component of this conjunctive opinion, Gregory's consistency as a runner, could have been legitimately argued with support from racing statistics, although in my view, he was quite the opposite, however much success he was enjoying recently. The second part, however, was offered without explication, and one could hardly imagine where to look for evidentiary support. Arguably, "Brown's thunder," especially in light of the way he performed throughout all of 1939 up to this point, was hardly something any other athlete could steal. Or purchase. What was Arthur Duffey thinking?

The national A. A. U. Marathon championship at Yonkers, New York, formerly simply the Yonkers Marathon but now a bigger deal with its newly national affiliation and importance, was the second marathon event by which runners could qualify for selection to the U. S. Olympic marathon team. (The first was the 1939 B. A. A. Marathon which Ellison Brown had won in no uncertain terms. The third of the three trials was the B. A. A. Marathon set for April 1940.) By November, the likelihood of the games going forth in Helsinki, Finland, was extremely slim. Russian forces were battling for control of a lane to the sea through the Scandinavian country as the war widened. Despite the good chance the next summer games would never take place, the qualifying marathon trials would still take place as planned and the U. S. Olympic team members would be selected.

The *Globe* reported twenty-three runners from New England entered in the Yonkers marathon, with Kelley and Pawson heading a list that included Donato, Durgin, Medeiros, Brunelle, and Semple. As for Ellison Brown, the newspaper gave this conflicting stance: "In the list mailed out by the N. E. 3-A. U. the name of Tarzan Brown does not appear, although he is advertised as being among the entries at Yonkers. Brown, by virtue of his record-smashing B. A. A. win in April, heads the Olympic standing."[30]

Brown planned to run in that autumn race but he did not appear in the event. Perhaps he or his manager was unclear of the Olympic team selection process. In contrast to the arrangement in place in 1936, this time a first-place victory in one trial was not sufficient for placement on the team. A mathematical system was devised that required participation in all three, no matter what the outcomes. Brown, having been required to run only one of two trials in 1936, may not have recognized the changed requirements, nor did many of the sportswriters at that time. This discussion continues in greater depth following the 1940 B. A. A. results in the next chapter.

Pat Dengis was widely considered "the favorite at Yonkers, having won four of his five races this year, losing only in Boston,"[31] and he did not fail to live up to the billing. Dengis shattered that marathon's four-year-old record, set in 1935 by Johnny Kelley, by nearly five minutes, with a time of 2 hours, 33 minutes, 45.2 seconds. He took the national title crown for the second straight year, his third national championship win. His was an incredible performance, for he set a blistering pace and finished five hundred yards ahead of Canadian Gerard Cote, who finished in second place, also coming in under the wire of the old course's standing record. Cote's time was 2 hours, 35 minutes, 33 seconds. Third place belonged to Johnny Kelley who also finished under the record time he himself had set. Kelley stepped across the finish line an estimated three hundred yards behind Cote, in 2:37:08. Les Pawson was fourth, almost four minutes behind Kelley, followed a minute later by Mel Porter, who had been the odd man out in the Olympic selections process back in 1936, having been forced to settle for being the officially designated alternate, which he still viewed as a source of deep disappointment. Wicklund finished sixth, Heinicke seventh, Durgin eighth, Frank Kelley ninth, Donato tenth, and Semple finished twelfth.

Arthur Duffey had a conversation with Dengis following the Baltimore resident's record-smashing win at Yonkers. In his column Duffey wrote:

Pat Dengis, the mechanic-Marathoner, was in a very reminiscent mood after winning the recent Yonkers Marathon, against one of the strongest fields ever. The race was for the American Marathon championship, a race every plodder wanted to win. "Well, it is just my luck," said Pat. "Here I have won about every conceivable Marathon except an Olympic Marathon and a B. A. A. Marathon. When I began to point for the Olympic race at Finland in 1940, a war comes along and cancels it.

"At that I am going to keep plugging along. I have won about a half a leg on the right to represent the U. S. A. in the next Olympic Marathon, if it is held, and I want the B. A. A. title next April 19." Incidentally Dengis was a little peeved that Tarzan Brown wasn't in that same Yonkers race for Pat felt sure he would have licked the Indian.[32]

Tarzan did show up (but Dengis did not) to compete in the 30th annual Thanksgiving Day race held in Berwick, Pennsylvania, a long, tedious drive from Rhode Island. Brown and Les Pawson were both unable to complete the nine-mile, 175-yard run. The AP reported that "Brown went out at the top of the mile-long Foundryville hill," but did not explain where along the course that hill was located.[33] In a fascinating magazine feature piece on Brown in *PIC* Magazine, a six-picture sequence of photojournalism told the story. The

1. In the 30th annual Berwick, Pa., marathon on November 23rd, "Tarzan," the Indian iron man, got a cramp in the first mile of the race.

2. Trainer Tip Salimeno drove ahead, borrowed bicarbonate from a farm wife, hurried back to give the soda to his gas-pained young runner.

3. "Tarzan" crept up on the field of 48 racers, and it began to look as if he might be able to surge to the front despite the time he'd lost.

4. At the end of the fourth mile the cramps were back. The Indian tried desperately to continue anyway, but Tip convinced him he should stop.

5. Back at the car, the Narragansett boy watched the backs of others disappear from sight. He'd trained, schemed, planned to win the event.

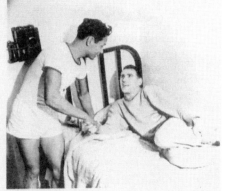

6. The cramp was a tough break, but "Tarzan" accepted it stoically. Back in Berwick, he hastened to congratulate Lou Gregory, winner of the race.

This six-photo sequence of the 30th annual Thanksgiving Day race in Berwick, Pennsylvania, appeared in *Pic* Magazine. Berwick, Pennsylvania, November 23, 1939. Photographs by Sam Andre (courtesy of Larry Hirsch; *Pic* Magazine is the property of The Condé Nast Publications).

words "He Got a Cramp" accompanied the initial photograph showing Brown, wearing a white running outfit, striding on a flat rural road. The caption reports that Tarzan Brown "got a cramp in the first mile of the race." Picture number 2 shows Tippy Salimeno, in a dark suit and fedora, apparently jogging in motion alongside Brown, handing the athlete a bottle. The caption explains: "Trainer Tip Salimeno drove ahead, borrowed bicarbonate from a farm wife, hurried back to give the soda to his gas-pained young runner." In the third picture, Brown appears to be listening to his trainer as he rubs his stomach. Spectators and automobiles can be seen in the background. The caption reads: "'Tarzan' crept up on the field of 48 racers, and it began to look as if he might be able to surge to the front despite the time he'd lost." The next picture in the sequence, the fourth, shows Brown doubled over in pain on the side of the road. Salimeno's hand grasps the back of Brown's neck. The caption: "At the end of the fourth mile the cramps were back. The Indian tried desperately to continue anyway, but Tip convinced him he should stop." The fifth photograph in the sequence shows Brown and Salimeno at an automobile. "Back at the car, the Narragansett boy watched the backs of others disappear from sight. He'd trained, schemed, planned to win the event," the caption states. The final picture in the sequence appears to have been taken in a very modest rooming house room with only an old model, dialless telephone adorning the wall. There New York runner Lou Gregory lies on the bed, holding onto his left shin with one hand and shaking Ellison Brown's hand with the other. Reads the final caption: "The cramp was a tough break, but 'Tarzan' accepted it stoically. Back in Berwich[*sic*], he hastened to congratulate Lou Gregory, winner of the race."[34] Lou Gregory took first prize, with Canadian Lloyd Longman finishing second about one hundred yards behind Gregory. Two hundred yards behind Gregory was Johnny Kelley, who finished the race in third place.

On December 2, the announcement that the Olympic Games had been "called off entirely" was made from Brussels by Count Henri De Baillet-Latour, president of the International Olympic Committee. "Finland, now at war with Russia, yesterday returned its commission to organize the games under a regulation which provides that a nation at war automatically loses the right to act as host."[35] Finland had spent over $10,000,000 preparing for the international event, it was also reported. In the following months, there would be a number of reports that the games were on, were off, were back on, and so on. In the United States, the trials for team member selection were ordered to continue despite the overwhelming prospect that the Olympics were not going to take place.

Pat Dengis, on the heels of his success at Yonkers, would not see his selection to the Olympic team realized, but not because of the calamity the German army was inflicting upon Europe. A tragedy closer to home occurred Sunday, December 17. The thirty-seven-year-old marathon runner and airplane tool designer and mechanic, along with Richard Sohn, a twenty-one-year-old pilot, both employees of the Glenn L. Martin Company, a Baltimore airplane manufacturer, were killed in an airplane crash. An obituary appeared in the *New York Times* and other newspapers, reporting the tragic loss.

Ellison Brown, Johnny Kelley, and Les Pawson, accompanied by Tippy Salimeno, departed on December 19 at 7 p.m. by automobile (Pawson's), beginning an overnight drive of 350 miles to attend the afternoon funeral in Baltimore the following day. The *Westerly Sun* reported that the four great marathoners, Brown, Kelley, Pawson and Dengis, had "last ran together in the Boston Marathon in April."[36] The *Sun* sportswriter and columnist Abe Soloveitzik eulogized the Welsh athlete in a beautiful piece. He discussed the three fellow marathoners who traveled to the funeral of Pat Dengis:

> He [Dengis] had company yesterday when they lowered his body into the grave, company who came a long way to pay respects to a fellow marathoner.
>
> Three runners, who often plodded along hardpacked roads with Pat; who passed him their water bottle when his throat was parched; who urge[d] him to keep on when their own pain-racked bodies could no longer stand the grind of the torturous race; who celebrated with him in victory and who condoled him in defeat.
>
> They were Ellison Tarzan Brown, Westerly's brilliant runner; Johnny Kelley of Arlington, Mass., and Leslie Pawson of Pawtucket.
>
> Three plain, day-in and day-out young fellows who work by the sweat of their brows to keep fodder in their pantries; who gave up a valuable day's pay to be in at the final services of a great pal.
>
> Mr. Sporting Public won't miss Pat Dengis but Tarzan and Johnny and Leslie will. They'll miss his cheery greeting at the start of the Boston Marathon next April. They'll miss his big smile and hearty handshake at the finish. They know that Pat has gone on to a world which holds more than bursting bomb-shells and tragedies and injustices.[37]

The Westerly sportswriter continued with this anecdote that took place with Brown, meant to give the reader a glimpse of Dengis as a man with true sportsmanlike character. He wrote:

> I met him [Dengis] just once, on the occasion of Brown's sensational victory last April. It was more than three hours after the finish and Tarzan was crossing Exeter Street, from the Lenox Hotel.
>
> A slightly-built man, his face widened in a broad smile, came running up the sidewalk to meet him.
>
> He threw his arms around Tarzan and hugged him.
>
> "Gee," he cried, "you were great. I am tickled that you won the race and broke the record. It was great going."
>
> "Yup," said Tarzan.
>
> Then he hugged Tarzan again and hustled on.
>
> "Who was that?" I asked Tarzan.
>
> "That was Pat Dengis. He finished fourth today," Brown replied.
>
> And that is the kind of a fellow that Pat Dengis was. He didn't win. He

didn't break any records but his friend won and he was glad and he really meant it when he said so."[38]

Johnny Kelley told the *Globe* that he, Brown, and Pawson had made a pact. Kelley explained, "The three of us have agreed to place the wreath on Pat's grave should one of us win it next year."[39] That was the race Dengis wanted to win above all others, but was never successful in doing so. "'No runner ever tried harder to win at Boston or more clearly deserved victory,' said Kelley, one of the three New Englanders who defeated Dengis to win the race."[40] It was a gesture in the good-hearted spirit of the distance runners of that golden era. The most vocal of the four, in print if not in person, was now silenced. The Christmastime cheer that would normally permeate the daylight-deprived days of late December could not diminish the empty feeling that the premature Dengis demise had stamped upon the marathon athletes' lives as the year 1939 gave way to a new, war-wrought decade.

22

"The Fastest Thing in Floating Foot Power America Has Ever Known"— 1940

With freezing temperatures in the low twenties coupled with artic, driving winds, the annual North Medford Club 20-Mile road race was more than just a running contest; in 1940 it was a test of survival. The March 23 race, the traditional season opener in its ninth edition, featured a prominent lineup of talent among the seventy-one[1] endurance athletes who competed. Les Pawson, winner of the first two races beginning in 1932, and Johnny Kelley, five-time winner, lined up at the starting line with Canadian Gerard Cote, the defending champion; Tarzan Brown; the "3-D" runners Francis Darrah, Paul Donato, and George Durgin; Canadian Lloyd Evans; Donald Heinicke, the late Pat Dengis' protégé from Baltimore; the undaunted B. A. A. stalwart Jock Semple ("no race ... would be complete without Johnny the Scotsman Semple"[2]); and sixty-one other hardy, hopeful athletes. A slew of winter gloves and mittens, knitted hats, earmuffs or bands, long johns, thick wool stockings and socks, and heavy sweatshirts and sweaters lined up with them, enveloping the runners in futile attempts to ward off the chill of the inescapable wind amidst icy conditions.

In a preview, sportswriter Arthur Duffey, perhaps due to restlessness over the winter racing hiatus, seemed to elevate the North Medford race, treating it more like the B. A. A. Marathon, by making prerace predictions. On that score, he picked Don Heinicke of the Stonewall Club of Baltimore to win and Girard Cote to come in second. Of all the athletes, Cote had most recently been involved in competitive action, having won a grueling winter snowshoe marathon in his native Canada, where he beat Walter Young, the 1937 B. A. A. Marathon winner and a former snowshoe racing recordholder.

Following Cote, Duffey had Ellison Brown picked to finish third, with these words: "There are also such runners competing as Tarzan Brown, the greatest of 'em all, if right. Tarzan never set the woods on fire in his preview of the Boston marathon, but down Westville [sic] way they say he will do."[3]

Clarence H. DeMar's absence on race day fomented the rumor that he had decided to finally retire once and for all from the running game. That wasn't the case. The bitter cold and biting winds had helped convince the veteran to postpone the start of his perambulatory season. As a runner who always preferred the warmest days for running, he would get involved when the weather was a bit more to his liking.

The fifty-one-year-old athlete had endured a difficult year. DeMar, who taught printing, was dismissed because the Keene Normal School decided to end the course. After searching, he landed a position with Winchendon High School, Winchendon, Massachusetts, twenty miles from his home in Keene, a distance he would make on foot each way every school day. His contract was abruptly voided by Winchendon school officials after six months, not even allowing him to complete the school year. Winchendon officials claimed the two sides had reached a mutual agreement for his departure, and offered this reason for DeMar's discharge: "on the grounds that he failed to maintain discipline."[4] According to DeMar, he "was fired to make room for cheaper instruction."[5] When the local newspaper presented the official version of their mutual separation as opposed to an outright sacking, DeMar was furious at the dishonesty and distortion. Only Jerry Nason presented the circumstances as DeMar saw his immediate dismissal, noting, "Clarence DeMar never quit a race, so why should he quit a good job?"[6] No recourse was available to DeMar to challenge the decision.

As the North Medford race commenced, Pawson, Kelley, Brown, Cote, Heinicke, and Evans quickly formed a six-man battalion and battled the wind and cold as much as each other. Four miles along, that initial group "had been split in two and Kelley, Cote, and Pawson were out front."[7] Following Pawson closely in a car were his wife and their daughter, Joan, who was celebrating her third birthday. Mrs. Pawson offered runners hot tea. Brown, Heinicke and Evans hung together a short distance behind. Durgin ran fifth throughout the last three-quarters of the race. Approaching mile six, Pawson and Kelley pushed ahead of Cote, and the good friends ran side by side until mile sixteen. "The last 1000 yards of their tandem effort carried them across the waste expanses cut by Mystic avenue, and the wind that previously had only plagued them turned into a merciless foe," Will Cloney observed.[8] As the wind gusts hammered down, the men resiliently forged forward. Pawson was pushed to the shoulder of the roadway a number of times, interrupting the rhythm of his stride. Kelley, with his lighter frame, was at moments prevented from keeping up with Pawson when lengthy blasts of cold air battered against the front of his body mass. Kelly "pulled his blue stocking cap down until it covered his eyes and almost reached the top of his sweater in back. He lowered his head and kept his pipe-stem legs churning, but his feet wouldn't go where he directed them and he staggered along as though he were plowing through a snow storm."[9]

Ellison Brown had run third or fourth for sixteen windswept miles. He had successfully "zig-zagged through a maze of cars in Malden square and barely made it,"[10] reported the *Herald,* but he had courageously kept going. The vehicular traffic, though, wouldn't be the cause of his undoing, or a sharp sideache such as he suffered the year before at mile fifteen. This year the elements were to blame, especially that ferocious wind. Brown "seemed to wilt in the wind," wrote Duffey.[11] With less than a quarter of the way to go, he called it quits. Brown would cite the cold on his legs, which had caused them to be "not tied up, but just frozen right through."[12] Despite Cloney's observation that "only Heinicke and Donato were barelegged,"[13] Jerry Nason of the *Globe* reported that "the frost penetrated his [Brown's] bare legs" and soon thereafter he was forced to withdraw, whereupon "he clambered stiffly into a car."[14]

Pawson, who "was never in trouble,"[15] went on to victory, his third in the history of the race. The thirty-five-year-old runner's time for the run was 1 hour, 56 minutes, 2 seconds. Pawson beat by well over four minutes the eventual second-place man trailing behind him, and was only three minutes from the course record despite the wholly inhospitable weather. Nason wrote, "Under the trying conditions which existed, it was a magnificent performance, comparable to anything the alderman-papa has ever done."[16] A photograph of his daughter, Joan, giving her daddy a birthday kiss on his cheek for the victory completed the proud father's happy and successful day.

Kelley's afternoon was not so fortuitous; he could not hold onto second place in the final four miles, sliding to sixth place at the finish. Don Heinicke, showing a burst of speed right near the end, edged ahead of Cote to secure second place, in 2 hours, 21 seconds. Cote, third, finished in 2:00:55. Donato, "the Roxbury strong boy,"[17] was fourth and Durgin of the B. A. A. came in fifth, two minutes ahead of a weather-battered Johnny Kelley. Semple finished thirteenth, but his B. A. A. won the team prize.

The William A. Reddish A. A. committee of Jamaica Plain, Massachusetts, shifted the schedule of their 30th annual 10-mile race in hopes that it would attract more of the star running talent of the area. In years past, the race, traditionally held two weeks prior to the B. A. A. Marathon, was considered by many runners to be too close to that historic marathon to make sense to enter. Now, with the race moved up on the calendar, Clarence H. DeMar, for one, was signing up to enter, marking his season debut. Tarzan Brown and Les Pawson had competed the previous year in the Presentation Run (held the first week in April and set for the following week this year). They were both entered in this handicap contest and would be scratchmen, looking for a victory against defending champion Hawk Zamparelli. So too were eighty-four other optimistic "cobblestone compatriots."[18]

With threatening, darkly shaded rain clouds overhead, the two Rhode Island scratch runners had to stay put until all of the other runners were given their marching orders, some granted as much as a six-minute head start over the scratchmen. When finally allowed to go, Pawson charged ahead, ultimately taking the time prize while finishing in seventh place. Sportswriter Will Cloney wrote:

> His [Pawson's] scratch-mark companion, the unpredictable Tarzan Brown, stayed with Leslie for only half the race. The Narragansett Indian then pattered pleasantly along, crossed the line in 23d place and skipped up three long flights of steps without drawing a short breath.
>
> Brown, who may very well be playing possum as part of his schedule for the B. A. A. race, was clocked in 53:12, which gave him sixth place in the matter of actual time.[19]

Cloney's use of the word "possum" was unfortunate, yet at that time it went without saying that Native Americans could be sneaky: this Caucasian viewpoint required no expository support. Just how any act of "possum" could assist or benefit Brown was left without explication. Nason too failed to discern the fiercely competitive persona in Brown, the usually all-serious-business athlete. He wrote, "Tarzan Brown, the Injun [sic] runner, started from scratch with Pawson, fell back on the first hill and finally finished in 23d position. He was not the least perturbed."[20] Despite his 23rd place finish, only five runners—Pawson, Darrah, Durgin, Campbell, and Zamparelli—actually ran the course faster than Ellison Brown did. Arthur Duffey, though he mistakenly attributed to Brown the third fastest time overall, perhaps understood better than his colleagues how to read the situation. Duffey wrote, "In justice to the Indian, it should be said that Brown did not over-exert himself, for he is centering all his attention on the coming B. A. A. race."[21] In his view, there was no trickery involved. Instead, Brown was just following a sensible plan for prioritizing events, conserving his strength, and getting the most out of a premarathon "practice" run.

Twenty-two-year-old Fred McGlone, a Boston and Maine Railroad maintenance department employee and noted golfer, took first-place honors, grabbing the lead with just a little more than a half mile left to go. He beat the second-place finisher, Bob Wallace, a San Francisco art student, by one hundred yards when it was all over. Before that, he had managed to collide with not one but two photographers poised near the finish line, knocking into them and their gear, sent tumbling in multiple directions. McGlone managed to remain on his feet, and continued his quest to reach the finish line. Where the *Herald* saw a hockey-styled play against a pair of photographers, the *Post* saw a different type of athletic move—closer to a hurdle event—as McGlone made it to victory "in spite of having to dodge and jump over a motorcycle at the finish line."[22] The *Post* headline told the story: "M'GLONE WINNER OF REDDISH RUN, Comes From Behind and Jumps Over Motorcycle at Finish to Lead the Field at Jamaica Plain."[23] Whether McGlone had to overcome the obstacles of two photographers, a motorcy-

Ellison Brown, who finished 23rd, talks with veteran runner Clarence H. DeMar (left) who finished 34th, after completing the 30th annual William A. Reddish A.A. 10-Mile handicap road race in Jamaica Plain, March 31, 1940 (courtesy of the Boston Public Library, Print Department).

cle, or all three, in any event, no sooner had McGlone done so when rain clouds opened up and a spring shower soaked the spectators and participants.

Zamparelli finished in ninth place. DeMar, running with a five-minute handicap, finished in 34th position to boisterous cheers from the attendant crowds. As Nason pointed out, "At that, he [DeMar] whipped more than half of the 87 starters."[24]

One last local competitive tune-up presented itself to the athletes before the Patriots' Day marathon — the ninth annual Presentation 10-Mile Handicap Road Race, which shared the difficult Newton hills segment of the course with the longer, world-famous B. A. A. Marathon. An immensely strong field of ninety-four (*Post*), ninety-five (*Globe* and *Herald*), or one hundred one (*Providence Journal*) participated. "Right up front will be Leslie and Ellison," Bob Dunbar predicted to his readers of the April 6 event.[25] Advertised to appear in two places at the same time, Ellison Brown was reported to be attending the first annual Annapolis-to-Baltimore Pat Dengis Memorial marathon, according to its race officials. As it turned out, Brown ran the Brighton-Newton run, sharing the scratch line with Pawson and Girard Cote.

All other runners were given varying handicaps, but none more than that of five minutes, the scratch time allocation.

The 1940 edition of the Presentation race was really two races, a veritable double feature, a race within a race. To most observers, the race consisted of the general ten-milers and their attempts to finish — win, place, show or otherwise. Imbedded within that race was another contest, to be played out amongst the scratchmen going for the time prize. This other match transformed into a fabulous two-man contest between Brown and Pawson, for Cote, not wanting to exert too much strenuous effort before the B. A. A. Marathon, never committed much to it, and finished 25th.[26] Tarzan Brown and Les Pawson, running within five yards of each other solidly for nine miles, trailed, caught, and surpassed all but four from the entire field by the time the two scratchmen had reached the end of the tenth mile. Only in the final mile did Brown manage to create a ten-second advantage between them, a spacing of "less than 50 yards" or "a matter of 60 yards," depending upon the source.[27] "Brown was really trying today," an AP wire writer reported,[28] and his time of 56 minutes, 17 seconds, earned him the time prize, and what turned out to be a fifth-place finish. Pawson, finishing 56:27, finished ultimately in sixth place. The reason for the lack of a definitive placement was due to an unusual disqualification. Runner Fred McGlone, who had finished in fifth place, was eliminated from the results for cutting a corner in the first mile of the course. Race officials "claimed that McGlone disregarded the warnings of three different inspectors and deliberately ran off the course," the *Herald* reported.[29] "It is alleged he cut across somebody's lawn about a mile along in Newton Corner," Jerry Nason reported with care, legalities clearly in mind.[30] Despite a heated, "vigorous" protest that lasted two hours after the event was history, the ruling for disqualification was not altered. That moved Brown into fifth place, Pawson into sixth, and so forth.

McGlone's (and his team's) protest, by the way, did not result in newspaper coverage painting him (or them) as a chronic complainer or uppity or any other unflattering trait, despite what must have been a rule violation on his part, leaving out the issue of his intent. In contrast, the Bunker Hill run that Ellison Brown protested the previous year for its incompetently measured length resulted in widely unfavorable press for the runner, in spite of the fact, importantly, that no infraction whatsoever on the runner's part was alleged: the charge is a double standard.

The Norfolk Y. M. A., McGlone's team, won the team prize despite his disqualification from fifth place due to the success of its other team members. The team, however, refused to accept the team prize in protest of referee Richard Walsh's upheld decision on McGlone. This was done in order "to exhibit its sincerity."[31]

First place, incidentally, was captured in an exciting display of speed and determination by Anthony Paskell of Cambridge, a repeat of his 1937 victory in the event. The 32-year-old kitchen worker's time in victory was 60 minutes, 38 seconds, and he had been granted the assistance of a five-minute handicap. Only one second separated him from the second-place runner, Maurice Charbonneau. A 22-year-old machine shop worker from Lynn, Massachusetts, who was reportedly expecting to lose his place of employment the following week, Charbonneau enjoyed a five-minute head start as well. For the most part, Charbonneau led the field, and he and Paskell battled head to head. Charbonneau was stronger on the downgrades of the formidable Newton hills, and Paskell was dominant on the upgrades. With a half mile to go, Paskell opened up a small lead and nearly lost it in the final few yards as Charbonneau made one last attempt to overtake him. "Pounding Tony just happened to look back in time to save his skin,"[32] reported Nason, for he saw Charbonneau gaining and he made a last-ditch effort to forestall his losing hold of the lead. "The Cambridge veteran became all arms and legs, however, and flailed across the finish effectively rather than smoothly," observed Cloney.[33] The difference was one second in time. Frank Darrah, meanwhile, was coming on strong, and might have passed them both, if he had not run out of course. Darrah, a construction worker, settled for third place, with the third fastest time of the day. He had actually partaken of the "two" races, running in between the leaders and the scratchmen in the finale, making a strong bid for winning either or both.

Nineteen-year-old George Daniels was fourth; Hawk Zamparelli finished seventh; Andre Brunelle was eighth; Bob Wallace, who nearly won the Reddish race the week before, was ninth; "and young Dick Cleveland got 10th because veteran Bob Campbell, his Norfolk associate, refused to pass him at the finish."[34]

Paul Donato of Roxbury was not entered in the Presentation event. He was running the B. A. A. course, practicing for the April 19 marathon. Oddly, he was traversing the Newton hills about the same time the Presentation leaders were on that same section of their course. Donato could be seen running on the right-hand side of Commonwealth Avenue as Paskell and Charbonneau ran along the left side. "Although he'd already traveled 16 miles neither 10-miler could catch him," Nason matter-of-factly observed.[35]

As attention turned toward the B. A. A. Marathon, little by little the sports pages began simmering their yearly stew of predictions, historical tidbits, updates and innuendos. One of the earliest concerning Ellison Brown was a quotation featured in Arthur Duffey's column: "'I only fear Les Pawson in the Boston Marathon,' quotes Tarzan Brown. Pawson was never so hot as this year and when he's hot it is a tough spot for everyone else. Don Heinicke of Baltimore ought to be another contender that Tarzan should keep in his book."[36]

Two days later, an almost startled Arthur Duffey reported that Ellison Brown's entry had been received and officially announced by B. A. A. officials.

The extraordinarily timely entry, so stunningly unusual from the Brown camp, led Duffey to read deep into the circumstances for meaning. His conclusion: "The entry of the Indian at such an early date means that Brown is out for a win this year more than ever. As a rule the Redskin is among the last to enter."[37] Where was the insight? Had Brown ever entered the B. A. A. Marathon not to finish first?

Jerry Nason reported Brown's prompt entry for his *Globe* readers.

> What comes as a shock, if not a disappointment, is the fact that the noble Narragansett got around this early to enter the thing. It is not his habit. Last year he was the last celebrity to enter and the first to finish.[38]

Nason added some interesting personal commentary.

> What I always admired the guy for was finishing 31st (in 1937) and 54th (in 1938). He could have quit any time at all and spare himself the humiliation, and it is humiliation to finish 31st and 54th once you're a Marathon champion and still in the throbbing prime of competitive life.
> Nobody questioned Tarzan's gameness before or after.[39]

Nason continued. He portrayed Ellison Brown as sharply and accurately as any two sentences ever written by any sportswriter ever could. "Tarzan is like the little girl with the curl and the trouble is nobody can guess whether he is going to be very, very good this year or not. If he is he will kiss the boys goodbye, because the Indian at his best is just about the fastest thing in floating foot power America has ever known."[40] As great a runner as Ellison Brown was—and he had been awarded plenty of cups, trophies and prizes in his day—that quality that made him a question mark before each race was pure Tarzan Brown. With his physical prowess, he certainly was capable of winning any race he entered, but he didn't — no one did; not Kelley, not Pawson, no one did. In part it was the nature of the sport. But on any given day, at any given racing event, Brown's chances of success were certainly as good as anybody else's, and better than most.

But there was another element, an element of the unexpected, associated with Tarzan Brown and no other runner. There were stories, a part of the Tarzan lore, of occasions when Brown would deliberately avoid crossing the finish line to win first place in a race in which he was (literally) minutes ahead of all other runners. In these instances, according to the lore, Brown would choose to wait inches from the finish line until another runner finally caught up, crossed the line, and took the first-place win. At that Brown would then follow over the finish line for the second-place honors. Why? Brown had seen the prizes in advance. A standard trophy cup was earmarked for the first-place winner. To the second-place winner was allocated, say, a pocket watch, much easier to sell for cash, and for more money than the cup would bring. In a race where Brown was comfortably ahead of the competition going down the final stretch and sprinting to the final line, a spectator never knew for certain with Brown that the predictably obvious outcome was going to obtain, due to that rarely seen but existent element of the unexpected.[41]

Returning to Nason, he concluded his words about Brown with this quotation from the runner and a remark:

> "Looks like that record of mine is goin' to get busted on April 19," said Tarzan recently.
> He neglected to say by whom. We suspect he meant by Ellison Meyers [sic] Brown.[42]

Brown entered one last footrace before the Patriots' Day marathon, the 30th annual 10-Mile Handicap Road Race of the Cathedral A. A., held on Saturday, April 13. His was an eleventh-hour surprise entry in the race known simply as "the Cathedral," the oldest living ancestor of all preliminary races to the B. A. A. Marathon, and one usually avoided in recent times by marathon-bound athletes due to differences in training concepts from those of earlier decades. On the morning of the run, Arthur Duffey had written:

> Tarzan Brown is going to be a closely watched runner in the race today. The Indian is going a little out of his way in tackling a 10-mile race with the B. A. A. Marathon less than a week away. "I think I am going to need plenty of speed to win the race this year," said Tarzan in entering the run. "I know I have the stamina but my speed is what's worrying me." The Indian believes that Pawson is the man to beat in the Boston run.[43]

A strong field of eighty-six[44] ten-mile runners, including Andrew "Hawk" Zamparelli, Anthony Paskell, Lloyd Anderson, Linden Dempster, Fred McGlone, Maurice Charbonneau, and the hitchhiking Bruno Mazzeo from Rockland, Maine, participated in the South End-to-Castle Island-and-back competition. An atypically flat course lacking any of the challenging hills that would give a scratchman a fighting chance to win, the Cathedral race usually featured brisk, windy conditions, especially out by Castle Island, and this year was no exception, as the entire "course was wind-blown all the way."[45]

First-time contestant Ellison Brown was the only runner assigned to start from scratch, a five-minute holdback. In previous editions of the race Zamparelli had been the one designated to a scratch start. Despite that impediment, he had won the time prize the year before, and had captured that prize successively in 1935 and 1936 as well. With Brown's participation this year, Hawk Zamparelli would not be consigned to the scratch wait, but would be granted a generous minute-and-a-half handicap instead. That should make a big difference, mentally if not physically, on his race results, but it would likely have little bearing on his safety. "The Hawk has a colorful record in this race," Will Cloney of the *Herald* reminded, "for in addition to winning numerous prizes he also won a trip to the City Hospital a few years ago when he lost an argument with an automobile on Old Colony boulevard."[46] He recovered fully. From that day forth, the car salesman and newly appointed constable was more keenly alert to the many dangers inherent in running races in cities.

Bowdoin College coach John Magee, who had founded the race three decades earlier in 1909, ceremoniously fired the starting gun at three o'clock that set the runners on their way. Fifty-two minutes and forty-two seconds later, Tarzan Brown crossed the finish line, taking the cup for running the distance faster than anybody else while establishing a new record for the ten-mile course. He was only twenty-five seconds behind Zamparelli, despite the 26-year-old's charitable handicap. Zamparelli won first place, but another runner's error enabled him to do so.

Rhode Island native Walter R. Jarvis, an eighteen-year-old carpenter's apprentice, had led the race from mile three, running with an abundance of vigor and spirit. When he reached the halfway mark in the course, confusion set in over the direction of the course. The course, having been found shy of ten miles in the past, had been extended this year to circle around the historic Fort Independence on Castle Island. Unfortunately for Jarvis, no race officials or members of the press were there at that location at the precise moment he needed assistance. "At this juncture events are somewhat hazy" explained Nason, "because the press and official cars were well snarled in the traffic far back on the course."[47] Jarvis did not have time to spare waiting for answers. Rather than lose any valuable time deliberating, he quickly chose to follow "his police escort."[48] "If he followed the law, reasoned Walter, he'd be okay," wrote Nason.[49] That strategy did not pay off. The leading Jarvis speedily left Castle Island for the South End without having run the circle around the fort. With two miles to go, he was told he had missed a portion of the course, but by then "all he could do was keep running, and he finished with loads of power."[50] He arrived at the finish line with an estimated half-mile lead, a lengthy margin that inevitably raised questions.[51] That half-mile advantage was equal to the distance he had missed around the fort. Nason reported: "Everybody was properly sorry for the incident, chiefly because the debutant from Rhode Island banged away in remarkable fashion all the way. He finished fast and strong and there is at least a shred of doubt that Zamparelli could have caught him even had the youngster run the right course."[52]

Walter Jarvis was officially disqualified, but race officials felt he should be rewarded nonetheless. As Will Cloney noted, "He definitely would have been in the prizes, even if he had run the right course."[53] Cathedral officials promised to send him a special prize, a set of bronze bookends, "the personal contribution of the Rev. Harry O'Connor."[54]

Zamparelli finished about seventy-five yards and seventeen seconds ahead of John Coleman of Worcester, who captured the second-place prize. Brown, eight seconds later, took third place. Fred McGlone, a recent victim of disqualification, trailed Brown by five seconds when he reached the finish line. Other notable finishers included Daniels in fourth place, Medeiros in fifth, Dempster seventh, Charbonneau in eighth, Paskell fifteen, little Lloyd Anderson sixteenth, and Rockland, Maine, hitchhiker Mazzeo twenty-second overall.

In this final tune-up for the upcoming B. A. A. classic, Brown's speed seemed to be well intact. Observed Nason, "The Indian appeared to be running well within himself all the way. He caught a full dozen of the panting palefaces in the last mile."[55] Duffey, too, relished what he saw, and offered this evaluation based upon a color scale: "The Tarzan looked in the pink."[56] Looking ahead to the next athletic encounter, the *Post* sportswriter averred, "The Indian still looks formidable to repeat his former B. A. A. triumph of a year ago."[57]

23

Bad Cramps, Bad Socks — 1940

On the day of the forty-fourth B. A. A. Marathon, Friday, April 19, Arthur Duffey on the front page of the *Boston Post* picked Ellison Brown to win. In a distancing third-person, passive voice, he conveyed his choice to his readers. He wrote: "Tarzan Brown, long limbed aborigine of the Narragansett Indians of Westerly, R. I., is slightly favored to win the 44th Boston Marathon.... Despite the fact that rarely does a champion repeat in the long run ... the Indian is expected to be the first to cross the finish line on Exeter street in a field of 195 runners."[1] Duffey went on to say it would not be easy, and that Brown would have to be at the very top of his game, but that was just what he was expecting to see. The *Post* sportswriter added, "He is admitted to be the greatest Marathoner of all time when at his best."[2] His choice for second place was Don Heinicke, the previous year's runner-up in the rain, and most recently the winner of a memorial marathon held in the late Pat Dengis' honor thirteen days earlier. Les Pawson, a major favorite this year after such strong early season showings, was Duffey's third-place pick. In 1940 both Pawson and Brown would be going for their third B. A. A. Marathon victory. John Kelley was Duffey's predicted fourth-place finisher. Kelley, it seemed, "was almost ignored in the pre-race estimates."[3] The thirty-two-year-old Kelley had finished thirteenth the year before, but was taking this year's race very seriously. He was a man now doubly engaged: engaged fully from a psychological standpoint in the marathon and all it would require of him to achieve a rousing victory, and, engaged to Mary Knowles, a woman he planned to wed the following week; all the more incentive to win, one might think.

Jerry Nason, like his fellow press colleague Arthur Duffey, also predicted an Ellison Brown victory but labeled Pawson a "co-favorite." Separate from his own personal selection, Nason reported the results of what was actually a focus group made up of B. A. A. race officials, judges, inspectors, referees, and runners — seventeen in all. Describing the members of this predictive body and their presumptive expertise, Nason wrote, "They are, all of 'em, gents who see the racers week in and week out."[4] In the preference poll, the men assigned numerical values to their preferences, the marathon contestants they expected to do the best. An overall consensus, based on the individual rankings of preference, was calculated. It had Les Pawson winning, Tarzan Brown second, Don Heinicke third, Paul Donato of Roxbury fourth, Canadian Gerard Cote fifth, John Kelley sixth, Canadian Lloyd Evans seventh, George Durgin of Beverly eighth, Fred McGlone of Roxbury ninth, and Frank Darrah of Manchester, New Hampshire, tenth. These results were published in the *Globe* five days prior to the marathon, accompanied by this caveat by Nason, "Picking a Marathon winner is about as easy as sorting cracked corn from green peas with boxing gloves on. But if anybody can come close these folks ought to."[5]

Not to be outdone, the *Herald* too had a focus group and results to report. Will Cloney reported a "*Herald* Board" comprised of seventeen "road-racing experts," including some runners, some officials, and some observers, both partial and impartial. Runners on the panel included Hawk Zamparelli and Paul Donato, who were not allowed for the purposes of the poll to vote for themselves. Results of this board showed Pawson with a 156-to-147 point edge over Brown, and 135 points for Heinicke. Paul Donato received the fourth highest number of points, 110. (Points were calculated out of a possible 170, although the methods used were not fully explained.) Only one expert picked Kelley to finish first, but he made everyone's top ten list. Cloney wrote, "If pass [*sic*] performances (of both runners and experts) mean anything, then Pawson, Brown, Heinicke, and Donato will be in the first five on Friday. It will be fun to see how the thing turns out."[6] The consensus of the "*Herald* Board" for the first four marathon runners, it may come as no surprise to find out, matched the *Globe* panel's consensus for those positions with a corresponding precision only polling efforts before the Truman-Dewey presidential campaign could confidently provide.

Jock Semple, a member runner in the B. A. A. Marathon (and so many other races) and one of the seventeen members of the B. A. A. Marathon board reported by the *Globe*, publicly picked Pawson to win, with a weather proviso. Said Semple to Nason: "My money is on Leslie Pawson. Brown was only able to stand up because of the cold and especially the rain last year. Give Pawson a good day on Friday, no head wind, and you'll have a 2 hours 27 minutes record and Pawson a three-time winner!"[7] Nobody, it was safe to venture, was putting any money on Semple.

Six former B. A. A. Marathon winners with a total of fourteen[8] victories in their collective possession were Brown, Pawson, Walter Young (a late, last-minute entry,) John Kelley, and the two senior veterans, 51-year-old Clarence H. DeMar and 55-year-old "Bricklayer" Bill Kennedy. Other members of the field included runners with the, by now, familiar names of Brunelle, Campbell, Cote, Darrah, Donato, Durgin, Evans, Giard, Mazzeo, McGlone, Paskell, Porter, Rankine, Semple, and Zamparelli.

Marathon runners were instructed to take the 7:55 a.m. B. & A. train, "the Albany-Mohawk Special," from Boston's South Station out to Hopkinton. If that train was missed, the B. A. A. warned, the athletes were on their own to get transportation to the Lucky Rock Manor. By nine o'clock the Lucky Rock Manor was opened for the athletes. They began assembling, and could be found in their usual state of affairs and partial dress. The associative scents of rubbing alcohol, witch hazel, wintergreen and other oils, and various liniments, some familiar, some strange, combined with the collective smells of men and men's bodies; the mix of odors pervaded every inch of the indoor space.

Present at Lucky Rock Manor was Eva Dengis, widow of Pat. She was accompanied by Bill Schlobohm, a race official associated with the Yonkers Marathon. "Mrs. Dengis seemed visibly affected by the bustling scene in which Pat had formerly been one of the most colorful and popular figures," the *Globe* reported.[9]

At 10:30, Paul and Humbert Cerafice, in charge of race logistics in the Tebeau family residence, began to shout out runners' names as they were called to the basement for their required physical examinations. Of those assembled, two runners failed to pass that qualifying exam, consequently disallowing them to compete. One, "a white-haired plodder from Clinton, Albert Mintel," was the first to be rejected. "Augustus Johnson, a better-than-average hiker from Port Chester, N.Y., was also declared ineligible by the official examiners. Johnson," the *Globe* reported, "is a husky-looking Negro chugger [*sic*]."[10] All others made it from the Manor to the starting line with a clean bill of health and an official marathon number. DeMar was heard to say, "Listen. I paid a buck for the number and got no diaper pins."[11] Presumably he meant pins needed to attach the number to his running jersey.

A rather wide assortment of fashion styles and colors adorned the marathon runners. Tarzan Brown's trunks, in particular, received special mention in at least two of the major Boston dailies. The *Herald's* Bill Rae took the opportunity to razz good-naturedly at Brown's expense, when he reported that Tarzan "did his bit to set the world on fire — with a pair of cerise shorts to blind the eye. The verdict was unanimous that they were the shorts heard 'round the world."[12]

By the noontime hour, a bright sun had created a warm day for the runners; ideal weather for the spectators, of which "upwards of a half million persons" were reported.[13] A field of one hundred sixty-six eager runners was poised to go when Walter A. Brown, at the starting line, prepared to pull the starting pistol trigger.

The Reverend Charles Whitlock of Barre, Vermont, bolted to the front of the starting pack when the gunshot was heard, "but got lost in the shuffle thereafter."[14] Whitlock, sprinting, had led for one hundred yards. The running cleric's short-lived sprint led Tom Fitzgerald of the *Globe* to wisecrack,

"At least, the reverend will have a concrete example the next time he chooses as his text, 'The first shall be last, etc.... ' "[15] The Presbyterian Church pastor who had initially led the flock finished not last but eighty-sixth.

Soon thereafter, Gerard Cote, the reigning snowshoe champion of the province of Quebec, took over the lead. He would later say, "At first I was not too keen to set the pace, but the runners did not seem to be running fast enough for me so I just swung into the lead."[16] Running second was Lloyd Evans. Pawson, Kelley, Rankine and Heinicke were all right there, hanging in with them. It was a fast-paced start. Robert "Scotty" Rankine would recall, "This rip-tearing stuff at the start isn't my style of running. Don't know why I banged it out so fast at the start."[17] Rankine, a shoe cutter by trade, was unfamiliar with the particulars of the B. A. A. Marathon, having never run it before, despite his ten years of competitive running. Just teetering in back of the first bunch were Donato and Willie Wicklund, a perennial early starter. Ellison Brown "was running about 10th, with Tony Paskell over the first three miles. He [Brown] was following his original plan of not going out too fast."[18] Two miles in, Cote, with Evans running second, had put almost seventy-five yards between himself and the first pack of runners in positions three through nine. After five miles, Cote was still leading and a little surprised that he was. Cote would later say, "I still was in front when we came into Framingham. No one seemed to want to take the lead."[19]

The order of the runners behind him had changed somewhat. Brown shared the identical sentiment Cote had experienced minutes before; the pace was not fast enough to his liking. "Tarzan couldn't stand the lethargy, however, so he worked up gradually and was second, 50 yards behind Cote at South Framingham, first checking station. Rankine, Wicklund, Pawson, Heinicke, and Kelley were jammed together in third."[20] The *Globe* gave this accounting of the first check-in: Cote first, Brown second, Kelley third, Rankine fourth, and Pawson fifth.[21] Lloyd Evans had fallen off the pace. A shift took place.

Heading into Natick, Cote still led. As he recalled:

> At Natick, I was a little in the lead over Kelley and Pawson and Rankine, but it was not enough to rave about. They all seemed to be running well within themselves and rarin' to go anytime. Then I heard someone say Tarzan Brown was in fourth place.[22]

Heinicke was sixth checking into the Natick station. Wiklund was seventh, but fading. McGlone had managed to get into the eighth spot, a position he would maintain for the rest of the marathon and the position in which he would eventually finish. Ninth place belonged temporarily to Mansulla and tenth was in the possession of Donato.

Just before the runners made their approach to Wellesley College and the traditional cheering college women, Tarzan Brown assumed the front-

Tarzan Brown (left) and Don Heinicke run in the 44th B. A. A. Marathon, Patriots' Day, 1940. Brown wears Number 1 and Heinicke wears Number 2 based upon their finishes the previous year. Boston, Massachusetts, April 19, 1940 (courtesy of the Boston Public Library, Print Department).

runner's position, as Cote dropped back to run with Rankine and Pawson. Kelley had slipped into second place, staying a dozen or two yards—sometimes much fewer—behind Brown, and a dozen or two—again, sometimes much fewer—ahead of Rankine, Pawson and Cote. Tarzan Brown, who customarily did not appear to acknowledge people lining a course, did not even seem to notice the Wellesley College women and their spirited cheers. Al Hirshberg of the *Post* jotted down some notes as he observed the marathon from the course sitting in the firm leather seat of a shiny new Mercury convertible donated for the day by Morley Motors, Inc., in return for promotional visibility. The reporter Hirshberg wrote:

> Tarzan running as if he were asleep. His eyes are half-closed and his pace is steady. Out where the girls gather at Wellesley he looks like a winner. That's what the girls think.[23]

Johnny Kelley, on the other hand, turned his head and smiled, even waved to them as he passed by, encouraging an even more boisterous spectator response. The leaders, apparently, did not garner the most response from the college women. They instead

> got polite hand-clapping from Wellesley's fairest, but when 'Donis Heinicke comes by, they stampede the course. 'Donis doesn't notice them. He is feeling badly, and he never does get going until it is too late.[24]

Don Heinicke, who had held steady, checking into three consecutive checkpoints (Wellesley, Auburndale, and Lake Street) in the sixth position, would later reveal his bout with nausea. "'I was a little bit sick to my stomach back in the first 10 miles,' said Don, 'but that did not hold me back too much.'"[25] Heinicke could see Brown, with Kelley and Rankine in a grouping up in front with Pawson and Cote in a two-man posse trailing the leaders. It was all visible ahead of him.

Cote was keeping close visual tabs on the front-runners as well. As the runners approached Newton Lower Falls, at mile 16, on their way to the Woodland Country Club and the Auburndale check-in station, Cote edged ahead of a flagging Pawson. After the marathon was over, Pawson would offer this description of his situation then: "I felt fine until the 14th mile was reached. Then my legs seemed to crumble up a bit and it took me a couple of miles to straighten 'em out again."[26] Despite his leg trouble, Pawson would remain positioned behind Cote at Auburndale and along the upcoming Newton hills to the Lake Street checkpoint, all the while trying to keep Heinicke, directly behind *him*, from gaining any ground.

Al Hirshberg recorded that Tarzan Brown "slips badly" at the Woodland golf course.[27] Cote would later state his observation of a change he discerned in Ellison Brown, a change he could detect although he could see only Brown's backside from his vantage point running on the course:

> I noticed Tarzan from behind and he was not running well. His legs seemed to be tying up.... Just as I was thinking about the Indian, along came Scotty Rankine, full of running. Then I began to perk up. Scotty had beaten me over the full Marathon in Canada and I knew he was good.
>
> As we came into Auburndale Johnny Kelley and Rankine were leading, with Tarzan Brown third, and I was fourth. I do not know what became of Les Pawson but someone said he was running in sixth place just ahead of Paul Donato.[28]

Donato, seventh at Auburndale and still seventh by Lake Street, trailed Heinicke, who in turn trailed Pawson.

Ellison Brown was seized by some muscle cramping, first in one leg, then in the other. Running third, he decided to try to work through it, slowing temporarily but not allowing himself to break out of the rhythmic lope he was maintaining. The right calf muscle was especially tight, and Brown reluctantly had to stop.

> Opposite the 13th green at Woodland Golf Club he signaled to following cars and stopped right in the middle of the street. He reached down, rubbed the calf of his right leg, accepted a jug of water from an official car, and set out again, but by that time he had lost 50 yards to the leaders. Cote was about 200 yards back, Pawson a little more behind.[29]

In less than two miles, he had another immediate physical concern demanding his attention.

Brown experienced gripping abdominal pain at mile eighteen. It slowed him considerably, but he refused to allow it to govern him to quit. Meanwhile, Kelley and Rankine were embattled in a pitched struggle as they started up the first grade of the notorious Newton hills. Sportswriter Jack Barnwell of the *Post* filed this battlefield dispatch:

> Rankine's troubles were triple as he tried to negotiate the hills. Johnny Kelley was battling him stride for stride—and he didn't expect it. Tarzan Brown was supposed to be the plodder he had to beat and Rankine frequently looked over his shoulder at the trailing Indian. The third and costly one was hunger which hit him in the pit of the stomach. He partook of two ice cream bars. Illness followed and Cote was the lone contender in the front ranks to battle for the honor and glory of the Maple Leaf.
>
> Sad-faced Brown wasn't looking too well as they started the hills. Rankine and Kelley were shoulder to shoulder for all practical purposes and passing water to each other from official cars at frequent intervals.[30]

Brown had managed to endure despite a stabbing stomach stitch. While his leg muscle tightness had subsided somewhat—perhaps his attention to the stomach pain had really only diverted his awareness of the leg muscle problem—within the next two miles his feet were becoming more and more uncomfortable. Ellison Brown was forced to hold up, stop, sit momentarily and remove his socks. He put his shoes back on, choosing not to go barefoot. He was just beyond mile twenty, on the Newton hills. After making the adjustments, he continued onward, and by the Lake Street check-in, he was running fifth. In front of him were Rankine, Kelley, Cote, and Pawson, who "had some trouble with his shoes along the way."[31]

Kelley had managed to edge ahead of Rankine on the rising grades of the hills along Commonwealth Avenue in Newton, but history, insistent on repeating itself, had its own requirements. Kelley had burned a lot of energy on his way over the hills, and found his arms sore and weighty, and some stiffness was setting in. Mentally, though, he was in very good shape. Over the crest of the final hill where some joy might be expected, Kelley had a new pain signaling a newly developed physical ailment with which to contend. He "was suffering from a tendon pull to his left leg [that occurred] on the downgrade."[32] That created the opportunity Rankine desperately needed; he appropriated the front-runner status for himself, and registered first at the Lake Street station. Kelley was now second, twenty-five yards behind Rankine, but not ready to concede anything. In fact, he shortened the gap between them. Cote, in the meantime, was ready to make a move. He still felt fresh and energized. As he saw it, Rankine and Kelley had fatally wounded each other, and it could work to his benefit. He started running hard, accelerating in his pursuit of Rankine and Kelley. He had some 200 yards to offset in order to catch what appeared to be an exhausted, vulnerable pair. Cote methodically closed that gap, first coming upon Rankine just beyond Cleveland Circle, and then, bustling up Beacon Street at a furious pace, overhauling the leader Kelley where Dean Road intersects. The finish line was four miles away.

By Coolidge Corner, Cote had opened up a 25-foot lead. At this juncture, the 5 foot, 5¾-inch athlete, with his compact frame, was leading the entire pack with over two and a half miles to go, running more than one minute, six seconds behind the record.[33]

The vehicular traffic was thick, especially around him now that he led. The *Globe* described the course as "the traffic-clogged highway" and added: "It seems the B. A. A. was overly generous in handing out official flags this year.... There were more official cars than there were runners and when Cote started to pour it on in his final burst the race began to look like the Indianapolis Speedway [*sic*]."[34] Gerard Cote ran the last two miles, with the exception of the last 200 yards, in a very rapid pace, chasing no one. He increased his lead over Kelley; it now measured over one hundred yards at Audubon Circle, due to his energetic sprint and "because Kelley was stopping every two minutes to walk a few steps."[35] A fatigued and fading Rankine was dropping back as Heinicke, Pawson, Donato, and Brunelle surged by. Cote was too far ahead to challenge. Cote would recall his final spurt:

> My legs were working like pistons. I then saw I was in front. I felt like waving to all the crowd who were urging me on. I hardly remember a thing until I reached Exeter street and saw that finish line. It sure was a fine feeling to hit that tape a winner.[36]

The men, women and children along the sidelines leading up to the finish line shouted loudly as the smiling, sweat-drenched runner passed by. Over the final two hundred yards he reduced his sprint to a jog, not because of exhaustion, but so the congenial Quebecer "could salute the jammed ranks of spectators along Exeter Street. He crossed the line with the broadest of grins."[37] A couple of gold teeth visible because of his wide smile flashed with reflected sunlight.

Cote finished in 2 hours, 28 minutes, 28.6 seconds. Cote broke by 23.2 seconds the course record set the year before by Ellison Brown, and simultaneously set a new world record for the marathon. He won by one of the largest margins. He broke the worsted 3 minutes 35 seconds and nearly 900 yards ahead of the second-place Johnny Kelley. "Not until 10 minutes after the finish did he [Cote] know that he had broken the record," Will Cloney revealed.[38] He could have sliced even more time from the record had he not waved and blown kisses to the crowds while jogging the final quarter mile; even then Cote still had plenty of energy and sprint left in him, by his own account. (He spent that night dancing, celebrating, and carrying on until two in the morning at the Statler Hotel.) His eye had been focused only on the victory. Had he known the course and world records were on the line, it is not likely his behavior near the finish would have been much different. He wanted to win. What he wanted even worse was the attention and acclaim, however fleeting, victory in the B. A. A. Marathon bequeathed upon its laurel possessor. Cote wanted to absorb it all, every bit of it; he didn't want to hurry by the adulation. He exulted in every glorious moment, each step of the way toward victory, during that last 200 yards.

"The rest of the way, I just ran, with no thought for the record, but only to win," Cote said after winning his first marathon in the United States.[39] It would take Cote a while after receiving the laurel wreath to locate a celebratory cigar to smoke, as was his custom. Unusually, he "didn't have one handy this time," observed Nason.[40]

For Kelley, the battle with Rankine had been bruising. Outlasting that skirmish, Kelley began to entertain the thought of being first to reach the Exeter Street line. Said Kelley:

> Rankine ran beautifully as far as Lake st. When I got by him there I thought I had the race won. Then Cote came out of nowhere. He was flying. I couldn't hold him. At Coolidge Corner they (it was Carl Linder, 1919 winner) gave me a piece of maple sugar. It saved my life. What a lift it gave me.[41]

Kelley helplessly watched as Cote sped past. In the shape he was in, Kelley could not hope to catch up to him. Still, he was able to admire what he was witnessing. "Cote's finish was a remarkable piece of running," Kelley would later say, his high-level sportsmanship perspicuously showing through.[42] As he headed into Kenmore Square, Kelley was forced by fatigue to stop running, to break down into another walk pattern. After the briefest of intervals, Kelley gamely took back to running again, revived perhaps by the candy. He was able to stave off a strong belated challenge by Heinicke, and finished in 2 hours, 32 minutes, 3 seconds, his fastest B. A. A. Marathon time to date, and four seconds faster than his time in 1935, the year the laurel was placed upon Kelley's head. Cote was wearing it now.

Eighteen seconds behind Kelley, Don Heinicke finished the 1940 marathon in third place. His time of 2:32:21 was 57 seconds slower than his time the previous year, when he finished second to Ellison Brown.

Heinicke could not conceal his disappointment. He felt compelled to offer an explanation for his showing. Don Heinicke believed his participation in the Dengis Memorial marathon thirteen days before had harmed his chances in the Boston race. "O, there's no doubt about it. My running and winning that Baltimore Marathon two weeks ago did not help me any, especially the way these fellows were flying today. You can't run two marathons in that space of time and give your best both times," he said.[43] This sentiment, unquestionably sound in Heinicke's case, was not the case for one Ellison Brown, who won successive back-to-back full marathons in October 1936. Heinicke evidently was not up-to-date on marathon history. In fairness to him, the author points out that Heinicke had just completed a grueling marathon when he spoke those words. He told the *Herald*, "I'm about 10 pounds lighter than I should be."[44] Undoubtedly he could have been heavier had he not plied his efforts so strenuously in the event honoring his mentor.

Fourth to finish was Leslie Pawson. Will Cloney wrote: "Pawson, who never offers an alibi, found the hills too tough yesterday. He stopped and walked several times and thought that his lack of endurance work this spring probably was the reason."[45] Pawson, the epitome of good sportsmanship and magnanimity, said, "I want to give Cote all the credit for winning. He ran a swell race."[46]

Paul Donato filled out the top five. "It was his third appearance in three years among the first 10, but as his head banged wearily on the rubbing table, he reiterated his decision to withdraw from competition."[47] Was the Roxbury foundry hand really going to give it all up?

> "Yes, this is my last Marathon," grinned the black-eyed, oft-styled Vest Pocket Hercules. "Why stay in it? I've finished fifth twice now, and sixth in another try. It isn't worth the time and trouble any more. I'm quitting now, and having some fun for a change. Say, what do you have to do to win this race now — run the course in 2:20?"[48]

That question might have been rhetorical, but it rang loudly through the din. (Until 1953, no B. A. A. Marathon winner finished at or under 2:20. Only Kelley, Cote and DeMar of the 1940 participants would compete in that one thirteen years later.)

Sixth place belonged to thirty-eight-year-old Andre Brunelle, the North Medford grocery warehouse worker. His was an incredible performance. In South Framingham, he was 27th, but he persevered, steadily working his way toward Exeter Street, passing many formidable runners along the way. Seventh place was thirty-year-old Scotty Rankine, who gave Brown and Kelley a real contest. The strong hunger he quelled by quickly consuming two ice cream sandwiches did not help his effort to finish higher up. He may not have had a firm grasp of the complexities of hunger pangs during athletic events, despite being the reigning Canadian marathon champion. Said Rankine, "[I] ate two ice-cream sandwiches in the last couple of miles, but I could have eaten a steak!"[49] Lack of accessibility along with pressing time constraints may have worked in the runner's favor, preventing an even larger gastric disaster. There was plenty of clam chowder available to the athletes after the race.

Fred McGlone, eleventh at the first check in South Framingham, ran eighth all the rest of the way. He nearly finished in seventh place, for he was only five seconds behind the Canadian champion, Rankine. A photograph showing McGlone's sister, Margie, running alongside him in Natick, very demonstrably goading him onward, appeared in the *Globe*.[50] What effect

Margie's exhortations had on the runner cannot be assumed or determined. What definitely had an impact upon the runner was an injury to his metatarsal arch of his left foot. He ran hard despite the considerable pain.

It was the first top-ten finish for "fair-haired" George Durgin, a thirty-year-old stockroom clerk, who landed in ninth place. The tenth spot was Frank Darrah's.

Whether Augustus Johnson was ruled ineligible by doctors at his physical examination in Hopkinton or not, Johnson ran a terrific race, finishing eleventh. The *Herald's* Will Cloney reported Johnson's flamboyant finish, seeing humor where others might not:

> Biggest laugh at the finish line came when Gus Johnson, Port Chester Negro, sprinted the last 20 yards into 11th position. Just before he exploded, Gus turned to the portly state policeman who had been following him and said, "Want me to turn the heat on?" The copper nodded, and Gus did. Incidentally, he never is a contender for first place but he seldom is out of the first 15.[51]

Joe Blaggie[52] of Cambridge finished a half minute after Johnson, in 2:44:31. Fourteen seconds later, Ellison Brown crossed the finish line. It had been a difficult race for him. He had experienced his share of difficulties after a strong start, including a stomach stitch; a leg cramp; problems with his socks, which had bothered him, requiring their removal; and bunions, perhaps fomented by the socks.

> Tarzan Brown, co-favorite with Pawson, was another disappointed champion in the dressing room. The Tarz looked good when he took the lead at the 16-mile distance and you could have bet all the tea in China that he would have won. A cramp in the legs and a few bunions caused the Indian to sink from the top position, to finish 12th in the race.[53]

Brown offered insight into his thirteenth-place finish. Reporter Joe Nutter presented this synopsis:

> Brown felt after the race that he could trace his failure to two factors. He was short on work, his training having covered only six weeks, and he went into the event weighing 133 pounds, whereas now he feels that he should have been up around 140. His early pacing efforts seemed to fit in well with his plans for the race, but his legs tightened, and he had stomach cramps at the 18-mile mark. His strength fading, he dropped back and then lost additional valuable time when he stopped to remove his socks, six miles from the finish.[54]

Brown's training of six weeks—basically, the full spring racing schedule plus two weeks of preparation before the traditional first race in North Medford—was not unusual for him. In fact, he had run what could be considered an additional speed race one week before the marathon. If an explanation of sorts was needed to explain his difficulty in the marathon—a superficial exercise that may not fundamentally make much sense—one place to look might be the shifted date of the Presentation race, which had created a new set of conditions on the spring training schedules of the athletes. Pawson, for one, felt the effects of the date change on him. Making no excuses, Pawson told Nason:

> You see, in the past the Presentation race in Brighton comes about the first of the month. I run it for speed work, then I take a full practice run over this course. This year the Presentation event was held later and, consequently, I missed out on my usual run over the course. Yes, I guess I didn't do enough work for this race.[55]

Pawson missed out on some long-distance endurance road work. It's not clear what Brown may have missed. His stated concern in the final two weeks leading up to the marathon was his speed, and he concentrated on strengthening that aspect of his running game. Lower leg cramps, stomach cramps — these can crop up, as they so often will do, under even the best of conditions.

Clarence H. DeMar finished, and he did so in under three hours: 2 hours, 55 minutes, 32 seconds. The people lining the course at all points along the twenty-six miles saved their most vociferous cheers and applause for the intrepid New Hampshire veteran. The man, soon to be fifty-two in June, finished in 27th place, and was heard to say, "And I'm very disappointed that I didn't do better in my 81st full marathon."[56] Although it took him four minutes longer this year than in 1939 to reach the finish line, DeMar's 27th place finish was actually an improvement; the previous year, he was 30th. "'Come to think of it,' he added, 'I finished 27th in the Olympics at Amsterdam, too.'"[57] That was back in 1928, at age forty.

After the marathon the veteran may have seemed to some a bit obstinate and incompliant, but it could not simply be attributable to his age or personality: these days there always seemed to be somebody wanting something from him. As the *Globe* reported, "Clarence DeMar refused to pose for photographers holding a glass of milk as the cameraman wanted him to.... 'What's the use? I don't use that stuff before a race, anyhow,' said Mr. DeMarathon."[58]

Clarence DeMar did not return to Keene but stayed in Boston, where he had contracted work in the *Herald* composing room, setting advertising type. The labor required that he stand on his feet seven and one-half hours, working well into that Patriots' Day night.

Other finishers included Jock Semple at twenty-ninth and Leo Giard at thirty-fifth. Two former B. A. A. Marathon winners, Canadian policeman Walter Young and "Bricklayer" Bill Kennedy, persevered despite a plethora of reasons, excuses and opportunities to drop out, finishing in fortieth and eighty-fourth places, respectively.

On April 19, 1940, the *Boston Daily Globe* ran these headlines on page 17 of its sports pages. The largest read: "Cote's Fresh Finish Too Much for Kelley and Fading Rankin[e]." The next largest in point size and prominence to appear on the page, situated at the top left, read: "First Man to Lead Pack Soon Faded to Rear." The subheadline, nearly inconspicuous without the boldface lettering of the other two, stated the following: "Heartbreak Hill Fatal to Dark Horse Rankin[e], Who Caught Kelley."[59] Here was the second printed case of the Newton hill being called "Heartbreak Hill" as its proper name, and put forth as if it was the commonly used, well-known name of that landmark on the course. In the accompanying article with no byline (unusual if the writing was Jerry Nason's), the reader had to drop down forty-four lines of copy in the column farthest to the left before arriving at the following paragraph printed in boldface type on the page:

> Heartbreak Hill is aptly named make no mistake. It was here that "Scotty" Rankin[e] overhauled Kelley and then ran himself into the ground making the race made to order for the St. Hyacinthe flyer, Cote, who closed with the speed of a Glenn Cunningham from Cleveland Circle in.[60]

There was no explication or elucidation in that article, as if the name were, if not commonplace, then at least familiar. While the article continued with two-thirds yet more to go until its final sentence, the name (or the subject) did not reoccur.

On the same page in a column that constituted the continuation of a first-page article, one other utilization of "Heartbreak Hill" can be found, and this appearance does have, if not exactly an explanation, at least a geographical marker along with it. The occurrence of the name, far down the page in the third column (from the left), fourth paragraph up from the bottom, could be found as follows:

> Up a nasty grade to the Brae Burn C. C. where the course flattened out for a mile run to the Newton City Hall, where another tough hill confronted them, went the duelling [sic] leaders. Another level stretch of about 300 yards and then up Heartbreak Hill, a mile-long climb upwards where many a prospective winner has wilted and either dropped out or [been left] far behind.
>   It was up this hill from Center st. to Boston College that Kelley and Rankin[e] battled it out....[61]

That "mile-long ... hill from Center st. to Boston College" was definitely and irreversibly referred to by the name it would be known by in future generations—"Heartbreak Hill."

Johnny Kelley, it seems evident from this 1940 coverage, played a central inspirational part in the hill's christening, in partial accordance with the B. A. A. Marathon lore as it has passed (and continues to pass) from one generation to another. What does not concur with the orthodox canons of the lore as popularly put forth is the year and Kelley's counterpart in a struggle that comes to a tipping point somewhere up along that hill; it could be argued, with evidence here from the 1940 *Globe* coverage, that it was Kelley's battle *with Rankine in 1940* that inspired the name, and not the famous Brown-Kelley battle (and "pat") which took place in the marathon of 1936, the version widely and fondly remembered and countless times retold since as the inception of the name.

"Heartbreak Hill" as a name, which may not have taken hold in print until 1940 (and even then not used widely — it is not found in competing newspapers' accounts in 1940 — only in the *Globe,* Nason's outlet), was purportedly born over the display of Kelley's disillusionment in losing to Brown, in 1936, after catching up to him after an exhaustive expenditure, Kelley giving it everything he had and more, ultimately in vain. That seminal moment, taking place at Heartbreak Hill, may indeed have given birth to the name. Only, the name may have remained in a sort of incubation until 1940, when Kelley again was at the mercy of that formidable Newton hill. And then, it just may be that the name derived from an odd sort of blending, one part current and one part retrospective. In any case, one thing seems hard to deny: inevitably, that elevated rise along the marathon course, at *some* point, was going to *need* a name, and a relevant one, considering the prominent role it almost invariably seemed to play in influencing and sometimes outright determining the outcome of the world's greatest continual marathon.

The 1940 B. A. A. Marathon was the third of three Olympic trial events for selection to the U. S. marathon team. The other two, the 1939 B. A. A. marathon, and the 1939 Yonkers marathon, had already taken place. According to *Herald* sportswriter Will Cloney, "The winner of the Unicorn classic automatically qualifies for a spot, but his two mates will be chosen from the runners who have the best averages in three tests— Friday's race [the 1940 B. A. A. Marathon] plus the Yonkers and B. A. A. races of 1939. This selection plan was devised a year ago last December and was well publicized at that time."[62] The so-called plan, however, was fraught with inherent problematic concerns. Even the math was not beyond question and interpretation. And contingent issues, such as the death of Pat Dengis, impinged upon the results.

Ellison Brown, for example, won the 1939 B. A. A. Marathon but did not compete at Yonkers. "The Tarz has never explained why he didn't comply with the rules and run in the New York race, but he automatically eliminated himself," asserted Cloney.[63] Of course, at the time, by all accounts Brown's record-breaking win in Boston had all but officially put him on the team.

Without explanation, Cloney wrote that "the committee has decided to postpone the compilation of points until after Friday's race [the 1940 B. A. A. Marathon] particularly because numerous difficulties have already arisen."[64] If the 1940 marathon race was one of three trials of an already established process, one might wonder how the committee could make its selection decisions without yet having the results of that third trial at hand. Why would deliberations need to be postponed *before* all the results were in?

In Cloney's view, the deceased "Pat Dengis, the Welshman who was more patriotic than most native-born Americans, tops the list for the first two races because he was third in Boston and first in Yonkers."[65] Cloney was correct in stating that Pat Dengis had won the Yonkers marathon, which he did right before his untimely death, but the prominent sportswriter was mistaken in claiming Dengis had finished third in Boston in 1939. Dengis had finished fourth. Walter Young had finished third, but, as a Canadian citizen entertained no claims to selection for any United States Olympic team. From a mathematical standpoint, was it proper to give the nonqualifying, non-American athlete's results to the American athlete who finished next after him? Acceptance of that methodology would yield one set of results. The chances are good that the utilization of another computational system would deliver a very different set of results.

Cloney continued:

> Of course, the committee will drop Dengis' points out of the reckoning entirely. It also will eliminate the Brown points in the B. A. A. race last year and the points of Frank Kelly (Philadelphia) and John Anderson (Roxbury) in the Yonkers race because those runners did not compete in both races.[66]

In other words, as the *Herald* sportswriter understood the process, if an athlete failed to compete in all three contests, he would not — make that, he *could not* qualify for the team. If this interpretation was correct — and by all means it may have been — then a sportswriter at the competing *Globe* was hopelessly confused. In that paper, in a piece that ran the day after the marathon, it was stated, "Tarzan Brown needed a victory to make the team since he didn't compete at Yonkers last year."[67] But, under Cloney's interpretation, how Brown finished — first, fortieth or four hundredth — could make no difference in his hopes to be selected since he had no result whatever to offer from the Yonkers trial. Having missed that trial, his chances were nil.

The methodology "would follow the system now used in determining winners of the team prize. All men not eligible for the choice will be dropped out of consideration, and the remaining candidates will be judged according to their relative showing," Cloney wrote in making another attempt to explain the complex selection mechanism. This did not make any clearer the process; team prize selection methods frequently induced heated argument. Another runner with particulars perhaps having some bearing on Brown's predicament was Mel Porter. The sole Olympic team alternate in 1936, Porter was ill and had to miss the 1939 B. A. A. marathon. He was officially "excused" from that event.[68] He ran fourth at Yonkers. Though his entry was received for the 1940 marathon, his quest for employment in Panama prevented his timely return. A no-show, his results, too, were voided.

The day after Patriots' Day, both the *Herald* and the *Globe* ran items that stated, as a result of the completion of the third trial, Pawson, Heinicke and Kelley were chosen to be the three U. S. Olympic team members. No computations or explanations of the arithmetic involved were offered. The *Herald*, which did not include any mention of Ellison Brown, provided the names of the athletes it figured to fill the three alternate placements: Paul Donato, George Durgin, and Fred McGlone. The *Herald* obligingly pointed out that nothing had been decided officially.[69]

In the publication entitled *2004 U. S. Olympic Team Trials — Men's Marathon Guide Supplement*,[70] a clarification of the process can be found, but not an explanation. Three lists naming the top six finishers and their times in the three trial races—1939 Boston, 1939 Yonkers, and 1940 Boston — are given. A fourth list, called the 1940 Final point list is also provided, which shows the points given for each finish and their totals. (The lowest points correspond with the fastest finishes.) What is not stated but can be gleaned from a study of all four lists is that a runner, to be included in the final tallying Point List, must have a marathon finishing position for each of the three trial races. In other words, one must have competed in, and presumably finished in, all three events to qualify for arithmetical consideration. That finishing position, one can see, need not be in the top six (as in the cases of Kelley, Heinicke, Donato and McGlone).

Boston *19 April 1939*	AAU Yonkers *12 November 1939*	Boston *19 April 1940*
1. Brown	1. Dengis	1. Cote
2. Heinicke	2. Cote	2. Kelley
3. Young	3. Kelley	3. Heinicke
4. Dengis	4. Pawson	4. Pawson
5. Pawson	5. Porter	5. Donato
6. Donato	6. Wicklund	6. Brunelle

1940 — Final Point List

	'39B	'39Y	'40B	TOT
1. Heinicke	2	7	3	12
2. Pawson	5	4	4	13
3. Kelley	13	2	2	17
4. Donato	6	10	5	21
5. Durgin	14	8	9	31
6. McGlone	11	14	8	33

In the Final Point list Kelley was erroneously awarded a second-place finish (2 points) despite officially finishing third in Yonkers. A corrected total of 18 would not have affected the standings. With the benefit of historical hindsight, all things being equal, one can figure that Ellison Brown would have had to finish the Yonkers Marathon in first, second, or third place in order to beat Kelley for selection to the Olympic team. (The sum of his combined 1939 and 1940 B. A. A. Marathon results, 1 plus 13, totaled 14 points.)

It all turned out to be a moot point. The 1940 Olympics, scheduled to be held in Helsinki, Finland, were, by this time, well in doubt of taking place due to the war in Europe. The deadline, April 1, had been moved back again and again. Officially declared canceled by the International Olympic Committee in December 1939, it was extremely unlikely that the games would go on. Still, an occasional item would suggest otherwise. The world famous Finnish runner, Paavo Nurmi, had been in the United States raising money for the Finnish Relief Fund in March 1940. As late as March 23, 1940, Nurmi assured the press that the Olympic Games would be held as scheduled. Said Nurmi from a stop on his fund-raising tour in Detroit, "I know what I'm talking about when I say that they're already going ahead and making plans for it [the Olympiad] at home. They will be held and you can bet every penny on it."[71] Few if any lost money taking on that wager. Nazi military forces in April were in the midst of their attempt to occupy Norway. The Russian army had not been prevented from overtaking neighboring Finland.

Still, the Olympic selection committee, headed by Ed Parsons, director of athletics at Northeastern University, was determined to comprise a team. Perhaps there would be competition somewhere other than in Europe. The future was incredibly unstable and unpredictable in April 1940.

24

"Three Races to Every Two"—1940

The Point of Pines fifth annual General Edwards Memorial 13-Mile handicap road race was held on the afternoon of May 11 in Revere and through parts of Lynn, Massachusetts. Among a field of 120 starters were Ellison Brown, Johnny Kelley, Clarence DeMar and Jock Semple, along with Darrah, Dempster, and Durgin, Anderson, Charbonneau and McGlone. Brown and Kelley were assigned to run from scratch, starting five minutes after the rest of the field.

Ellison Brown and John Kelley ran hard side by side, "together practically the whole distance."[1] Copiously pouring it on right up until the final moment, the formidable pair managed to come onto Revere Boulevard in sight of the leaders and the finish line but unable to make up the handsome handicap advantages granted the front-runners. They had made tremendous gains, and had nearly caught up with the third-place runner, Ted Carpenter. Running tight as can be with Kelley until the very last moment, Brown crossed the finish line sandwiched one second behind the third-place finisher and one second ahead of Kelley. Brown won the Edwards Time Prize, as well as the prize for fourth place. His corrected time for the run was 70 minutes, 12 seconds. Kelley's was 70 minutes, 13 seconds.

The first-place winner, running with a generous 3-minute, 45-second handicap, was the five-foot, four-inch Linden Dempster, of the Norfolk Y. M. A. Twenty-seven seconds after Dempster claimed first place came Frank Darrah, his teammate. Ted Carpenter of Melrose completed the trio ahead of Brown and Kelley.

Clarence H. DeMar, who finished in fourteenth place, had run in fine form until just after the course midpoint when he "lost a shoe. In spite of his hard luck he kept gamely on," Arthur Duffey reported.[2] The undaunted Scotsman Jock Semple finished nineteenth. He received one of four special prizes for being one of the top-four North Shore athletes to finish; the other three were Maurice Charbonneau (sixth), George Durgin (twelfth), and Walter Emery (fifteenth).

The Braintree Tercentenary 10-Mile road race was held May 25 in a steady drizzle and mist. A field of forty-one runners competed but only 32 completed the course distance. Started at scratch with a huge, hindering six-minute hurdle placed upon him, Ellison Brown nevertheless overcame that yoke, speeding forth to assume third place with one mile to go in the race. By race's end, he had seized the time prize "by almost two minutes" and finished in third place, behind Robert Campbell, the first-place winner, and Ed Cook, Jr., who finished second, only one second behind Campbell. Brown's time to traverse the ten-mile course was 51 minutes, 51 seconds.

Les Pawson had a difficult afternoon, managing to finish but without much satisfaction, in sixteenth place. Clarence H. DeMar finished in twenty-first place, ahead of Hawk Zamparelli.

The fourth annual Lawrence-to-the-Sea Marathon, also called the Salisbury Marathon for the finish line on the sands of Salisbury Beach, was a heavily hyped event. The media saw the star-studded event as a collection of intertwining matches or feuds between athletes with grudges to avenge. The marathon was touted as a battle between the Olympic teams of the United States (Kelley, Pawson and Heinicke) and Canada (Gerard Cote, Fred Bristow and Harry Wingfield); a personal duel between Gerard Cote and Ellison Brown, this year's B. A. A. Marathon winner and record breaker vs. last year's winner and record breaker; an athletic setting whereby grudges and resentments could be contested and at least fifty percent of them laid to rest; and a forum where "I'll-show-you's" could be publicly registered.

Cote's umbrage at being beaten the week before by Scotty Rankine for the Canadian Marathon title (why did that not get Rankine a place on the Canadian Olympic team?) was but one case. Ellison Brown's presumptive rancor as a result of being overlooked as a selection to the American Olympic team was allegedly another. Despite the imagination of the press digging deep into these storylines, the marathon itself, with its field of fifty-five highly talented distance runners, including the veteran DeMar, on its own merits promised to be an exciting running event and one highly anticipated by the spectators.

Ellison Brown, usually a participant in the nearer-to-home Norwich, Connecticut, 15-kilometer National A. A. U. run held annually on Memorial Day, chose to face off with the strong field over the longer-distance course. He was given number ten to wear. Number one was reserved in honor of Pat Dengis in absentia.

The sun was burning with intense heat and so was the road surface as the athletes assembled in front of the Lawrence City Hall for the 12:45 p.m. start. The three American Olympic team members, Johnny Kelley, Les Pawson, and Don Heinicke, "were decked out in pretty new white suits, appropriately trimmed with red and blue and starry shields," as Jerry Nason reported.[3] Brown had on "his regular running rig, consisting of a white jersey and a pair of pants that looked like a cerise sunset."[4] Along with these high fashion statements were the Canadians, the veterans Clarence H. DeMar and "Bricklayer" Bill Kennedy, and Jock Semple, and many others, including Paul Donato, who had sworn himself to retirement from the marathon business after his fifth-place showing in Boston on Patriots' Day. The blast from the handgun set them all eastward on their way.

Leading the pack the first few miles was the recently designated new world marathon recordholder from St. Hyacinthe, Quebec, Girard Cote. Cote's lead in the marathon was short-lived. Nason narrated:

> Tarzan put the pressure on right away. He put Cote behind him with a terrific pace to the five-mile mark. Kelley, Pawson and Heinicke hung on grimly as an "Olympic" triumvirate while the romping redskin started to tear the late Pat Dengis course record to shreds.[5]

Tarzan led until the ninth mile of the course. There, Kelley and Pawson let it be known of their intentions to take over the lead spot of the high-paced pack. Heinicke and Cote made up the rear flank of this speedy group. For a short distance, less than a mile, Brown allowed the pair of Olympian teammates to front the contingent, but he quickly resumed his lead role by mile ten, bursting with stockpiles of energy. In the city of Haverhill, Brown maintained the lead as he kept up the torrid pace. Kelley, Pawson, and Heinicke managed to hold firm in staying with him, running just behind but keeping Brown right where they could see him. Next followed Cote, running fifth, with runners Italo Amicangioli of the B. A. A., Andrew Brunelle (unattached), and Tony Medeiros of the North Medford club a bit further back. After them could be seen a host of runners, including DeMar, causing a great commotion from the large crowds all along the route.

Leaving Haverhill, Kelley decided the moment was right to make a move to the front, and he did. Again, Brown seemingly let Kelley dabble with the front-runner's position. Soon thereafter Brown again proposed to take over, without much perceivable opposition or challenge to that notion. He spurted to the head of the pack, and at Merrimac, Brown expanded his lead over Kelley by over one hundred yards, and Kelley in turn stretched his own margin ahead of Pawson. By the town of Amesbury, with about six miles to go, Brown pressed on smoothly, running "better than ever."[6] Only once more did Kelley offer a challenge for the front spot, but he could not sustain it. Brown this day was too strong, too fast, too determined to win. Ellison Brown crossed the finish line in record time, winning the time prize and the first-place cup.

Tarzan Brown established a new record for the course and at first appeared to have set an unprecedented new world mark for the marathon distance. "Brown Breaks World Record," proclaimed the *Globe* headline.[7] His time of 2 hours, 27 minutes, 29.6 seconds, raised immediate concerns about the length of the course. After an investigation the course was indeed found to be short. The *Post* reported that the course lacked nearly one mile "owing to excavation work being done in Amesbury."[8] The *Globe* discovered that "some street construction near the start in Lawrence" resulted in "about 400 yards being whittled off."[9] The *Providence Journal*, in attempting to clarify the distance muddle, looked into the issue and reported that "race officials began checking distances and found this year's race to be a quarter of a mile short of last year's and neither of them within a mile of being the full marathon route of 26 miles 385 yards."[10] The Lawrence-to-the-Sea Marathon had a history of having been sloppily measured. Brown would easily have set an unprecedented marathon time, but the officials had been delinquent once again in their measuring conscientiousness and their capability and the resultant lack of accuracy. As it was, in Nason's estimation, "Brown even on the original course would have broken the record."[11]

One hundred yards behind Brown bounded Johnny Kelley to seize second-place honors, running his all-time fastest race with a time of 2:28:18, "ten seconds under Cote's B. A. A. record."[12] Over three minutes later followed Don Heinicke to the finish line, in 2:31:39. Pawson, with a time of 2:32:17, completed the American Olympic contingent to the finish line. Next came the first Canadian team runner, Cote, over seven and one-half minutes behind the fourth-place Pawson — a full twelve and a half minutes and 0.4 seconds *after* Ellison Brown had broken the tape. Cote's time was an even 2 hours, 40 minutes. His Canadian teammate, Fred Bristow, finished sixth, in 2:46:21. The third Canadian team member finished seventeenth, behind DeMar and Semple, who were fourteenth and fifteenth respectively.

Einno Pentti, James Rafferty and Frank Darrah were relieved to find that Brown was in Massachusetts beating up on Kelley, Heinicke and Pawson, leaving them to take the top prizes in the Norfolk title race.

The annual New England A. A. A. U. 20-kilometer championship race was held in Pawtucket, Rhode Island, on June 8, sponsored by the Pawtucket Elks Club. An incredibly strong field was entered, including Kelley and Pawson, along with Hawk Zamparelli, Bob Campbell, Durgin, Dempster, McGlone, Anderson, and Jock Semple. Ellison Brown had undergone the removal of the nail of his right big toe on Monday, June 3, for an undisclosed reason. What would seem a grim, possibly debilitating procedure apparently was not taken too seriously by the runner or the print media. Brown decided to compete in the New England title race despite lingering nagging pain still bothering him five days later. A headline read, "Sore Toe Fails to Stop Tarzan."[13]

George Durgin led the field in the earliest going but that would not continue beyond the first mile. Two miles into the approximately 12½-mile course, which snaked through the cities of Pawtucket and Central Falls, Brown opened up a short lead over Kelley, running second, and Pawson, running third. The runners held this formation for nearly seven miles, "never more than 50 yards apart, and frequently separated only by a few strides."[14]

Kelley challenged Brown a half mile from the finish line, catching up to Brown, and then passing him. Kelley actually managed "a short lead" but it was a momentary, fleeting state of affairs, as Brown "started his sprint and won easily."[15] Brown's time of 1 hour, 6 minutes, 40 seconds showed that he crossed the finish line only nine seconds ahead of the second-place Kelley, about twenty-five yards in distance. Pawson finished third, eight seconds behind Kelley, nearly the same distance of twenty-five yards back.

The usual names of Campbell, Zamparelli, Durgin, McGlone, Demp-ster, Medeiros, and Charbonneau filled out the top-ten list of finishers. Jock Semple finished thirteenth in this one. Clarence H. DeMar completed the race in the twentieth position. The finish enabled him to receive an official award, as prizes were distributed among the top twenty runners. Not unusually, DeMar received the greatest applause from the throng of spectators.

In the formal pomp of the awards presentation ceremony, Ellison Brown was presented the Governor William H. Vanderbilt Trophy and the New England Association A. A. U. gold medal by former Representative Robert Mulligan, and he received a literal pat on the back from Elks exalted ruler John Buchanan. A photograph of the moment, complete with wide smiles on the victorious runner and the two officials, was published in the *Providence Journal*, along with the photo title, "Another Big Day for Rhode Island's Tarzan."[16] The victory was reported in the *New York Times*.[17]

The National 20-kilometer run, held in Endicott, New York, June 15, was a near replay of the New England 20K race of the week before, featuring another closely contested effort by the three New England marathon giants, Brown, Kelley, and Pawson, in a field of forty-five contestants. The early pace was set by Brown, Kelley and Lou Gregory. Gregory eventually was forced to give up his effort, dropping out of the competition halfway through, the reason undisclosed. Like the run the previous week, Kelley and Brown ran closely together for a majority of the course, from just a stride or two apart to a distance of never more than fifty yards apart. Pawson ran third for most of the second half, but not as close to Kelley's heels as Kelley was to Brown's. Leading the thirty-eight finishers across the line was Brown, who did so in 1 hour, 8 minutes, 44.2 seconds, finishing for the second time in two races about twenty-five yards ahead of the second-place finisher, Johnny Kelley, "after a thrilling duel."[18] The AP reported that Brown's victory was his second straight win in the event.[19] Kelley's time was 1 hour, 8 minutes, 47 seconds, a closer finish than the week before, but a second-place finish nonetheless. Pawson, repeating his third place showing, registered a time of 1 hour, 10 minutes, 14 seconds. Over two minutes behind him were Fred McGlone and Peter Olexy, filling out the top five prizewinners.

Only two days after winning the national 20-kilometer title crown, Brown was in Charlestown, neighbor to the city of Boston, to compete in the annual Bunker Hill Day 10-mile run. The course was closely measured and its length was verified to be the full ten miles as specified, in light of the controversy caused the year before by the short distance. The road race's "General Manager Sam Scanlon made sure that it was O. K. this time," reported Will Cloney.[20] Jerry Nason, however, reported that "the course measures 10 1-10 miles."[21] That single tenth of a mile, it appears, was considered of no consequence. What was of consequence was the very heavy vehicular traffic, going in both directions along nearly the entire course, creating a greater burden on the one scratch runner — you guessed it — Tarzan Brown.

Sixty starters were sent off from the starting line as Brown was held for six minutes, which was, all things considered, a reasonable improvement over the previous year's 6½-minute delay. After the required wait, Brown forged his way through a giant obstacle course of fume-belching cars and smoky commercial trucks, while dodging errant drivers, some most assuredly inebriated in respect for the local holiday, but nearly all deserving of the notorious Boston-driver reputation that has marked the area's motor vehicle operators to the present day. Brown suffered some exceedingly close calls that would undoubtedly have resulted in injury, in some cases serious injury. Despite the impositions Brown was set on a herculean effort to catch up to and pass the runners released ahead of him on his way to the finish line. At one point, a fellow road racer had become a human impediment, not intent upon heeding the sportsmanlike rules of the distance runner or, quite possibly, hearing impaired. Said Brown later, "He kept staying in front of me and I thought I'd have to hang a Joe Louis on him."[22] Fortunately for that young athlete, Brown got by him before changing sports and transforming from frustrated distance runner into angry pugilist.

As Ted Carpenter, nineteen-year-old Faneuil Hall Market meatpacker, went from second place after seven miles to a first-place victory at ten with the aid of a three-minute handicap, Brown was still slicing his way through a maze of obstructions but doing so with an incredible velocity underfoot.

Thirty-three seconds after Carpenter captured the first-place honors, Brown, in a fiery burst of swift motion, held the third-place-running Frank Ryder at bay as he broke the blue worsted strung up at the finish line in City Square for second place one second ahead of Ryder. Completing the course in 54 minutes, 39 seconds, Brown snared the time prize and set a new course record. Fred McGlone, who had competed along with Brown in Endicott, New York, finished seventh, and Hawk Zamparelli eighth.

Nason was ecstatic in his praise, writing, "Tarzan Brown was red hot again yesterday. His 54:39 for the course suggests that he is close to being in the best condition of his checkered macadam career."[23] A shirtless Brown stared straight into the camera lens, looking directly out from the newspaper page to a Tuesday morning readership, an expression of annoyance palpable.

Two days later Nason again felt the need to extol the virtues of Brown's athletic powers while publicizing the upcoming West Roxbury Holy Name 10-Mile Run scheduled for Saturday evening, June 22. Nason provided a summary of Brown's 1940 achievements, as he wrote:

> Nobody had made much of it, but this guy Brown has been mopping up the macadam and Kelley and Pawson and everybody else with it.
>
> Barring the Boston Marathon, which he was supposed to have won but didn't, Tarzan the Terrible has been pinning their ears back right and left. Offhand, he has either won outright or snared the time prizes in the Presentation, Cathedral, Edwards, Braintree and Bunker Hill handicaps, knocked 5 minutes off the Salisbury Marathon record, won the New England 20 and national 15 [sic] and 20 kilometers championships.[24]

For the record, Nason, in his zeal, had gotten carried away when he ascribed the 1940 national 15-kilometer title to Brown. Brown, who held that title the year before, had passed on the opportunity to defend and retain that one when he chose to compete in the Salisbury Marathon (also known as the Lawrence-to-the-Sea Marathon) instead. About *that* marathon, Nason had more to say, as he continued, "The fact is, Tarzan ran the race on Memorial Day that he was supposed to have run on Patriots' Day, when he walloped vengefully through Essex County in 2 hours, 27 and a fraction minutes for a 26-mile marathon. He was super-sensational that day."[25]

Nason called forth to the stand an expert for some corroborating testimony. "'When the Indian is right,' says Al Hart, the long-distance official and member of the disbanded Olympic marathon committee, 'he is the greatest runner we will ever see over the distances.'"[26]

Nason lamented the harsh, cruel luck runners such as Kelley or Pawson must have had for appearing in the same epoch with the inscrutable Brown. Wrote Nason, "So it is unfortunate for Kelley and Pawson, great endurance anklers themselves, that Tarzan happened along in their era, otherwise they'd have been cleaning up the prizes between them instead of viewing the romping Redskin almost constantly from the rear."[27] He emphasized Kelley's "phenomenal" skills and the remarkable paucity of victories they have garnered for him. After offering a laundry list of second-place finishes by Kelley in 1940, Nason squarely placed the blame. "Johnny," he wrote, "is getting to be a regular All-America second on account of Tarzan."[28] Nason's was a harsh but truthful indictment.

When the fifth annual Holy Name A. A. 10-mile participants assembled at the starting line in the twilight of June 22 awaiting gunman Bill Prendible's commencement shot, three scratchmen had five minutes, plenty of time, to sit by as the seventy-nine other runners, in relays, headed out on the streets through West Roxbury, Roslindale and Jamaica Plain. The three, Ellison Brown, Les Pawson, and Frank Darrah, were supposed to be joined by a fourth party, Johnny Kelley, but he and his new bride were in New York City, visitors to the World's Fair, and reportedly did not return to Boston in time.

Two booming sound trucks were meant to keep the crowds lining the course informed as to the status of the various runners. At times the roar of the trucks nearly canceled out each other's pronouncements, creating a cacophony of words but no understandable information. It was an experiment that would require some fine-tuning and logistical foresight to better serve future events.

As soon as their five-minute waits were up, Brown, Pawson and Darrah began the long chase after the field and the finish line. Brown wasted no time, sprinting at a very rapid pace. Pawson did his best to stay with him. So did Darrah.

Jock Semple, after a mile or two near the front of the ruck, took a lead position and set the pace for most of the run. Semple, running without an assigned handicap, led the field up until the ninth mile. By then Brown had managed to pass nearly every runner in sight on that course. In the final mile, Tarzan Brown flew by Semple and the runners in the Scotchman's wake. Brown jetted past, followed by an entourage of the low-handicapped runners. In a matter of just two minutes, eighteen runners crossed the finish line behind Brown, causing a major accounting headache for the race officials. (They were able to handle it without any reported complaints.) The runners bunched so tightly together, especially at the end, created an extremely close squeaker of a contest. Ellison Brown finished first, breaking his own record for the race; his time for the ten miles was 52 minutes, 6 seconds.

Brown was followed across the finish line by Medford milkman (Bernard) Joe Smith, just six seconds separating them. Smith, thrilled with what he had done, was bursting with excitement. "'Imagine finishing that close to Tarzan,' exclaimed Joe. 'He must have had an off day.'"[29]

Next came little Lloyd Anderson, thirteen seconds later, taking the third-place prize. Les Pawson, who otherwise "ran a magnificent race, covering the course in 52:29 to finish fourth," was runner-up to Brown in the time prize category, twenty-three seconds slower overall.[30] Fifth place belonged to Edward Cook. One second later, Hawk Zamparelli finished, registering sixth. His time was the fourth fastest. Frank Ryder, son of the Boston College track coach and recent third-place finisher at the Bunker Hill Run, finished in seventh place, four seconds ahead of Jock Semple, who finalized his run in eighth place, running the ten miles in 57 minutes, 56 seconds. Filling out the top ten was Tony Medeiros and Rhode Island youngster Walter Jarvis. The third fastest time was Darrah's, the third scratchman, but he finished in nineteenth place. Semple's B. A. A. team won the team prize.

A photograph in the *Globe* depicted what looked to be a friendly scene, as the bespectacled Rev. Edward F. Ryan, D. D., pastor of the Holy Name parish of West Roxbury and a strikingly large man, sporting a light-hued, flat-crowned straw hat with a dark cloth hatband upon his large head, shook the winner Ellison Brown's hand as the grinning number two and three runners, Joe Smith and Lloyd Anderson, looked on with glee.[31]

It was raining hard on Friday evening June 28, when the Haverhill Massachusetts Tercentenary 10-mile road race got underway despite the miserable, uncooperative weather. Kelley, Pawson and Brown were on the scratch line along with Darrah as an emboldened field splashed forth from the starting point. The four scratchmen, after being held for 5½ minutes, jointly pursued the field amidst driving sheets of rain, slick surfaces, and considerable wind. At the halfway point, Pawson found he had the speed advantage and asserted it as he advanced ahead of the other three and pushed onward past all but six of the entire field of athletes. Pawson, with a time of 52 minutes plus 1 second, finished in seventh place, but took the time prize. Kelley and Brown "came driving down the final 50 yards of the course side by side, and Kelley found enough kick left to cross the finish line less than six inches ahead of Brown," the *Globe* reported.[32] The two finished fourteenth and fifteenth, respectively.

For an exasperating second time in recent races, a discrepancy in the course length was reported, this time attributed to a Haverhill policeman's error. "Officials said the motorcycle escort leading the runners crossed the wrong bridge into Bradford," creating a shortened total distance, the *Herald* reported.[33] In the meantime, race officials went about their official race business, awarding prizes based on the data they had at hand with a suggestion that they would look into the question of distance accuracy in the future. Bob Wheaton, a Putnam, Connecticut, resident running under the auspices of the North Medford club, was declared the first-place winner, and his fellow club mate, Joe Smith, the milkman, finished second. Other finishers included Campbell fourth, Durgin tenth, Semple eleventh, and scratchman Darrah nineteenth. All in all, it was not a particularly endearing event for Brown, and he planned to make up for it with two races on the same day on the upcoming July 4 holiday, just six days hence. He was hoping for better weather and further hoping for better (i.e., more competent) race course supervision.

Dozens of Independence Day road races were held in cities and towns as part of their July 4 holiday observances. The City of Warwick, Rhode Island, sponsored a morning 10-mile road race as part of its civic festivities. Tarzan Brown arrived early to compete with speedster Bob Campbell, and runners Ed Cook, Fred McGlone, Lloyd Anderson, Walter Jarvis and others making up a small field totaling twenty.

A 10:25 a.m. start was signified by Warwick mayor Albert Ruerat's handgun shot. Immediately Campbell sprung to the front of the pack and set the pace, leading for the first six miles. Brown never let Campbell get too far ahead of him. They traversed Greenwood, Hillsgrove and Lincoln parks, and by the latter, at Jefferson Street, Brown inched ahead of Campbell. Brown kept the narrowest of leads to the very end. The race for the top three positions was extremely tight with only five seconds separating the three runners. Brown crossed over the finish line just one second ahead of Campbell, who beat out Cook for second place by a mere four seconds. Brown's time of 50 minutes, 57 seconds "was said by N. E. A. U. officials to be fast for the course," the *Providence Journal* noted.[34] Cook finished third; McGlone was fourth, ten seconds behind Cook. Little Lloyd Anderson finished fifth, rounding out the top five.

The prize trophies, all named for the politicians who donated them, were handed out in a formal ceremony after the event by Mayor Ruerat. The mayor and three of the runners, McGlone, Campbell, and Anderson, sported jackets and ties for the occasion. Cook wore a sports jacket over a T-shirt. Brown, the only casually dressed prizewinner at the awards table, had on a light-colored, hooded sweatshirt (with the hood down). Ellison Brown received the largest trophy for his first-place victory, another Governor William H. Vanderbilt Trophy for his collection. Campbell was awarded the U. S. Senator Peter G. Gerry Trophy for his second-place finish. Upon Cook was bestowed the Mayor Ruerat Trophy. The fourth-place McGlone was presented with the Senator Sweeney Trophy, and Lloyd Anderson took the Congressman Risk Trophy, which looked more like a cup.

Despite managing to nail down the victory, Brown had pulled a leg muscle in that morning 10-mile contest. That contingency did not keep the Rhode Island resident from pursuing his intention of competing in a second 10-mile running event that same day. After collecting his victory trophy in Warwick, Brown traveled sixty miles to Springfield, Massachusetts, to run in a 10-mile handicap race that afternoon. Two other runners who also ran in Warwick that morning, Lloyd Anderson and Martin Geary, followed in Brown's footsteps, so to speak, to Springfield for the iron-man challenge. It was a relatively small-scale event; the field of runners totaled twenty-one.

This second effort of the day did not go according to Ellison Brown's master plan. According to the *Providence Journal*, the "pulled leg muscle caught up with Tarzan Brown," and forced him to drop out after the first mile.[35] As Jerry Nason saw it,

> The Narragansett nobly attempted a holiday double.... Tarzan's ambition, it commences to be apparent, is greater than even his vast racing resources. This super-man of the highways shirks nothing in his macadam ventures. Innumerable times in the past he has raced distance events on succeeding days. Four years ago he raced and won two 26-mile marathons on successive days.
>
> But tackling two races the same day, same being 60 miles apart, is pretty close to being the most daring effort by the Indian. Obviously, it was folly.[36]

It may not have been across the judgment boundaries into folly for Anderson (and perhaps for Geary too) although Nason did not mention them. Anderson, who had finished fifth in Warwick, succeeded in finishing eighth in Springfield, and also won the third time prize. Geary, less successfully, finished eighteenth in the morning competition and twentieth in the afternoon race. Amesbury native Pat Polleto finished first in the Springfield race. Al Menard of Fiskedale was second, fifty yards behind. Third place was taken by Frank Darrah, who also won the time prize.

Nason emphasized that Brown, unlike his fellow star competitors Johnny Kelley and Les Pawson, seemed less proficient at pacing himself over the summer running schedule than over an individual racing event. In second-person exegesis, Nason wrote:

> Brown probably has put in three races to every two for Kelley and Pawson this season. This gives you an idea of the amount of mileage the Indian has put under his arches. It also gives you an idea of how fast Tarzan burns up the remarkable energy that is his. Lately events have caught up with him. His defeat at Haverhill by both his big rivals came 48 hours after he had competed in another event of lesser import. You might have noticed that Pawson and Kelley have used better judgment by picking their spots on a heavily-loaded Summer racing schedule.[37]

At the St. Polycarp's 10-mile handicap run on the evening of July 6, Ellison Brown, the course recordholder, attended the Somerville event but was not entered. He viewed the sport along with the sportswriters and spectators. He "showed up with one calf taped as a result of a muscle strain."[38]

Hawk Zamparelli, automobile salesman and constable, took full advantage of the five-minute delay imposed upon scratchmen Johnny Kelley and Les Pawson (and his own three-minute head start) and Brown's sidelining, and managed to pull out a first-place win. He also registered the third fastest time of the evening. Pawson, who finished fourth but won the time prize, failed to break Brown's record for the course by twenty-nine seconds. Second place belonged to Charlie Regan, a former boxer-turned-runner at his new bride's insistence. Frank Ryder finished third. Johnny Kelley, thirty-one seconds behind Pawson, won the second time prize but finished eighth.

Brown planned to give his leg (and body) time off from competition. When the opportunity arose ten days later for another iron-man two-race day, Brown was ready, willing, and hoped to be able.

25

"Winning Most of the Silverware" — 1940

Undaunted at unsuccessfully competing in two races on July 4, Ellison Brown attempted the feat again on July 13. The first of the two events occurred in Lynn, Massachusetts: it was the first Young American Club 10-mile handicap marathon run. Another three-man scratch battle among Brown, Kelley, and Pawson, this time it was Kelley's to win. He won the time prize with a time of 55 minutes, 14 seconds. Pawson was second in the time prize contest, running the course in 55½ minutes flat. Brown, who finished third in that trio to win the third time prize, was five seconds behind Pawson; his time was 55:35. The field of eighty-three created a problem for all three scratchmen, for they "had all they could do with dodging among the stragglers."[1] Adding to the obstacle course-like conditions, many of the runners were running in tight bunches, making them extremely difficult to pass. An indication of the crowding and the grouping could be discerned from the summary of how the runners finished. Even at the finish line, five runners, including Pawson and Brown, crossed within seven seconds of each other.

The race's first-place winner was twenty-year-old Maurice Charbonneau, a member of the club sponsoring the event. He benefited from a generous three-minute handicap. The little-known Donald Porter of the same club finished thirty yards behind Charbonneau to take second place. Jock Semple finished third, running with a one-minute, thirty-second handicap.

After the Lynn race, Ellison Brown, a glowing Jock Semple, and a surprising number of other athletes (but not Kelley nor Pawson) made their way the twenty or so miles to the northeast to Gloucester, Massachusetts, out on Cape Ann to compete in the Bay View Brotherhood's annual five-mile road race held that evening.

Brown's results were nearly a repeat performance of his iron-man attempt in Springfield. He and Hawk Zamparelli, the defending winner from the year before, both suffered pains in their legs and could not continue beyond the second mile. They dropped out. There was no elaboration over the injuries or comments from the two athletes in the sports pages. The warning offered by Nason to pick events more judiciously, as did Kelley and Pawson, had gone unheeded by Brown.

Bob Campbell, who led after the first mile, won handily, crossing the finish line over one hundred yards ahead of the second-place Frank Darrah. In third place was Ted Carpenter. Jock Semple, incidentally, finished ninth in that evening race, 4 minutes, 17 seconds behind the first-place-winning Campbell. All in all, it had been a fantastic day for Semple.

A small field of twenty runners participated in the New Bedford (Massachusetts) Marathon Association's 10-Mile handicap road race on a rainy Sunday, July 21. Local club member Ed Cook, Jr., with a four-minute handicap, finished first in the race. Ellison Brown finished second "about 200 yards behind Cook," taking the time prize.[2] Walter Jarvis, having no trouble finding his way along the rain-soaked course, was third. Unusually, no times of any of the runners were disclosed in the local newspaper accounts.[3] Over in another part of the state, at about the same time, Johnny Kelley was seizing first-place honors in the Duke of Abruzzi East Boston-to-Danvers 16-mile road race. Clarence H. DeMar managed to finish eighteenth in that one.

Nearly arriving too late in the early evening of July 25, Ellison Brown was permitted to file a late on-the-spot entry and barely had enough time to put on his running shoes for the St. Vincent de Paul 10-mile road race, held in Providence and sponsored by the Knights of Columbus. The race, held in the evening because of the extreme heat of the day, turned out to be essentially a two-man contest between Brown and Pawson but it was not close; Brown ran the full ten miles in an astonishing 51 minutes, 40 seconds, the fastest time ever recorded for the distance, according to sportswriter Joe Nutter.[4]

In the very early going Les Pawson led all twenty-four runners, with Frank Darrah and Frank Ryder challenging. Brown kept close to Pawson. A short time later, Brown put himself in front and never trailed.

At one point about halfway along the course, Darrah, right up front with the leaders, was struck by an automobile ("the little Norfolk Y. M. A. runner was cut down by a machine," Joe Nutter reported[5]). The vehicle made contact with Darrah's right leg, and the impact knocked him to the hot pavement. Darrah managed to break his fall with his hand, and even made a brave attempt to get up and resume the competition but he found he was unable to do so. In addition to the spot where the vehicle had banged into him, his leg muscle had started cramping with excruciating pain. Darrah had to reluctantly take himself out of the running. He hoisted himself onto the seat of an official car and rode back to the starting point on Regent Avenue, the only member of the field who failed to finish.

Brown, in the meantime, was sailing. He had opened up a lead of fifty yards at Chalkstone Avenue, and had steadily but rapidly built it into a huge quarter-mile ahead of Pawson and the rest of the pack. A short respite wherein he removed his shoes because of the heat had no noticeable effect upon his margin of victory or his record time. He sprinted barefoot to the finish line over the hot street surfaces, beating the second-place Pawson by over a minute and a half. In third place was Ted Carpenter, forty-eight seconds in back of Pawson. Tony Medeiros of North Medford finished fourth, local boy Lloyd Anderson was fifth, and Frank Ryder was sixth.

A photograph in the *Providence Journal* under the title "Surveying the Damage" showed a postrace scene with Pawson and a shirtless Brown looking at Darrah's leg injury with others looking on. Darrah, seated on a blanketed cot, and Pawson were both pointing at the spot on Darrah's calf where the bruise was located.[6]

Joe Nutter included this testament, putting the victory in the context of very recent history:

> Brown was superb as he sped over the course leading almost the entire journey....
>
> The race was another noteworthy triumph for the Westerly Indian. He had suffered severe leg cramps after attempting to fathom two marathon runs on July 4, and had suffered a recurrence of those cramps in running as late as last Sunday. He felt that he was ready for a great race if his legs held up, and they held up well, so that he set his own pace in the testing portions of the grind.[7]

Brown showed no caution in selecting his next running event. The very next day, he competed in the Marshfield, Massachusetts, Tercentenary handicap 10-mile race under the sanction of the A. A. U., an event held in the afternoon despite the blistering July summer heat. Twenty-two runners attempted to defy the heat and compete, but only ten survived the high temperature and the torrid pace to complete the distance to the finish line. Among the athletes involved were Brown, Lou Gregory, Clarence H. DeMar, Fred McGlone, and Hawk Zamparelli. (Johnny Kelley had officially entered and been advertised to appear. If he did so, he did not finish.)

It was not Brown's afternoon. Lou Gregory resisted the heat as he took both the time prize and the first-place winner's prize. His corrected time was 57 minutes, 50 seconds. He and Brown had been held back for a lofty 6½ minutes as scratch runners, allowing everyone else a handicap of some amount, before being permitted off the starting line and onto the course. Despite the poorly calculated assessments, Brown was not sharp. He finished two seconds shy of four minutes behind Gregory. That put Brown fifth across the finish line. Hawk Zamparelli was sixth, twenty-two seconds behind Brown. Hawk had been assessed a 5½ minute wait at the start, which, though oppressive from perhaps a number of standpoints, was a full minute's advantage over Gregory and Brown.

Joseph Morgan of the Norfolk Young Men's Association, the team prize winner, led until the eight-mile mark, where he was overtaken by the heat and by Gregory. He managed to finish second behind Gregory, collapsing upon crossing the finish line. Morgan was treated for "heat prostration."[8] Filling out the top five were Ralph Holland, who finished third and by doing so contributed to the Norfolk team win, and Italo Amicangioli of Newton, who took fourth place. Amazing veteran Clarence H. DeMar, an enthusiast for running in hot weather, was among the top-ten finishers, taking the tenth-place prize. As an indication of the unsatisfactory job of the race officials in levying and assigning handicaps, it is noteworthy that even the fifty-two-year-old DeMar had been assessed a wait at the line — a flattering forty-five seconds.

Ellison Brown took a whole day off from competition. The next day, Sunday, July 28, his late entry was accepted for the fourth annual Webster, Massachusetts, 12-mile road race, the feature event of the N. E. A. A. A. U. track meet sponsored by St. Joseph's Athletic Club. In this one, Tarzan Brown put himself up in front of the pack as the echoing blast from the starting gun could still be heard reverberating by the lake. Brown took charge. He ran the twelve miles in 1 hour, 8 minutes, 8 seconds. He crossed the finish line one hundred yards ahead of the next competitor to finish, Al Menard. Andre Brunelle claimed the third-place prize.

Sixty early entrants were advertised as planning to attend Russell Field in Cambridge, Massachusetts, on Saturday, August 3, for the Elks Club-sponsored 10-mile race, as reported in a short item in the *Herald*.[9] The headline proclaimed, "DeMar to Run in Cambridge Race." It went on to say, "Opposed to DeMar will be Johnny Kelley and Tarzan Brown, who have been winning most of the silverware offered for gallops over the cobblestones lately."[10]

Race day was another scorcher of a day with very high temperatures. Brown and Kelley were held at the sun-baked starting line for 6½ minutes as designated scratchmen. (At least the race officials saw fit not to hold DeMar back for any amount of time, with all due respect.) When finally allowed to lunge forward, the two old foes, Kelley and Brown, battled each other head-to-head for the time prize. Brown finished thirty-seven seconds ahead of Kelley to win that time prize. Brown's corrected time for running the ten miles was 52 minutes, 35 seconds. Despite finishing thirty-seven seconds behind Tarzan, Kelley still beat the rest of the field with the second fastest time, for which he was awarded a second time prize. Kelley's time was 53 minutes, 12 seconds. Brown finished fourth overall in the race, and Kelley finished seventh.

The heat seemed not to have any negative effect upon Anthony Medeiros, described in the *Herald* as "a 27-year-old husky who tosses scrap metal around in the Boston and Maine car shops for a living."[11] Medeiros, affiliated with the North Medford Club, abrogated Phil Leslie's lead position in the final half mile and registered the victory. His corrected time was 53 minutes, 57 seconds. Norfolk team members Ralph Holland placed second and the wilting

Phil Leslie just barely managed to hold on to finish third, but the team could only muster a second-place team prize. North Medford took that honor due to the intriguing computational point system involved; its members held first, ninth and twelfth places, respectively. Norfolk runners finished second, third, and fourteenth.

Citizens of the state of Maine as well as vacationing out-of-staters were anticipating another exciting edition of the Old Orchard Beach 10-mile handicap road race scheduled for Saturday, August 17. Last year's winner and course recordholder, tiny Lloyd Anderson, was back to defend his record and reputation against Tarzan Brown, John Kelley, Jock Semple, Clarence H. DeMar, and others making up a total field of fifty-two. Six and one-half minutes of constraint — that is what Brown and Kelley were obligated to endure as the other athletes left the starting line at the square in segmented relays and worked their way up West Grand Avenue on the fairly flat course.

Despite that heaping six-and-a-half minute scratch burden, Brown and Kelley knew what they faced, and burned their way past the stragglers first and the more serious contenders soon thereafter. Brown, for his part, ran rapidly; he passed every harrier in the event. *Every* one. When he was finished, he had shattered Anderson's course record. Moreover, he broke the standing record for a ten-mile run, period. He burst across the finish line in a blur, 51 minutes, 32 seconds from the time he was let loose to go. In a handicap race he did the difficult; he overcame that oppressive duration of scratch time as he broke the tape to capture the first-place cup as well as the time prize. Kelley ran fast too, but he was just not quite as quick as Brown — nine seconds slower overall to be exact. Kelley's time, 51 minutes, 41 seconds, earned him the second fastest time and third place. Second place belonged to a John Coleman of Worcester. The B. A. A.-affiliated Coleman may have had a four minute and thirty seconds handicap advantage, as the *Boston Globe* reported, or he may have been "running without a handicap," as the *Herald* claimed.[12] Listed fourth following Brown, Coleman and Kelley across the line was Andrew Maderio from Boston by the *Globe's* account and Ed Merdeiros by the *Herald's*. Taking fifth-place honors was Rockland, Maine's, favorite son's brother in the running field, David Mazzeo, brother to Bruno. Whether he chose to hitchhike from Rockland to Old Orchard is not known. Other finishers included Joe Smith, the Medford milkman, who finished eighth; Maurice Charbonneau, the tenth man; Hawk Zamparelli, the twelfth-place finisher; Fred McGlone, fourteenth; and "'the Grand Old Man' of road racing, Clarence DeMar,"[13] who finished a very impressive fifteenth, his time, less than an hour — 57 minutes, 16 seconds.

The very next day offered an opportunity for the athletes to get five more miles of roadwork in, at a race sponsored just a few miles farther northeast in nearby Portland. Johnny Kelley, Hawk Zamparelli, Joe Smith and others accepted the challenge. Ellison Brown did not stay overnight to compete in that short-distance, five-mile race. Kelley won it, in 25 minutes, 12 seconds. Zamparelli finished second, fifty-two seconds behind Kelley.

A hearty field of thirty-five runners, including Tarzan Brown, Les Pawson, Lloyd Anderson, and Maurice Charbonneau converged on Kingston, Rhode Island, at the Kingston State Fair to compete in its annual ten-mile race. Prize watches were part of the lure for the first eight finishers. Medals were awarded to the next ten, runners nine through eighteen.

This race proved to be another Brown-Pawson head-to-head battle, at least up until the eighth mile. According to the *Globe*, Brown led all the runners around the oval track for the first 3½ miles.[14] Pawson followed closely, running second. Then, Pawson pushed ahead of Brown. He seized the lead position and set the pace for the next half mile. His front-runner status was short-lived. In the fourth mile, Brown commandeered the leadership position once more, set a dizzying pace and would not be forced to yield. Pawson reluctantly slowed slightly, slipping to the third spot. But McGlone and Anderson were closing in. Pawson was able to find fresh reserves, and he managed to regain the second slot. It mattered not to Brown, who tore across the finish line in a veritable blur, finishing in 54 minutes, 50 seconds, a new record for the fair's annual run. Pawson finished second, but it took him a minute and two seconds longer than Brown to reach the end of the course. McGlone finished third, Anderson was fourth and Italo Amicangiolo fifth.

Labor Day, Monday, September 2, was not a holiday of rest and relaxation for Ellison Brown. The day offered the daring, aspiring runner another chance to test (or show off) his iron-man endurance and stamina. Brown was officially entered in *three* competitive running events on that same day. That in itself might cause one to wonder about Brown's personal judgment concerning the limits of his own physical gifts which were, by any standard, so obviously extensive, a subject upon which Nason had digressed on more than one occasion. Brown's desire to run three races that same day, even if wildly preposterous in reality, offered a vivid indication of his self-esteem as an athlete. Furthermore, it allowed a rare peek into his private mental state, exposing his near-reckless, "undisciplined wild streak that sometimes overtook him."[15] In any event, as Joe Nutter quipped, "he had hopes of making a real Labor Day of it for himself by participating in at least two of the races, possibly three."[16]

A 12-mile handicap race over the city streets of Providence, Rhode Island, was the first of three competitions, and it began that morning. The weather, which reportedly was favorable, thankfully cooperated early in the day.

A six-and-a-half-minute, constraining scratch designation greeted a disbelieving Brown at the starting line in front of City Hall, and he openly expressed his unhappiness at that oppressive wait. Nutter wrote that "before the race started, Tarzan admitted that he had no hopes of capturing the actual

Eventual winner Tarzan Brown (right) battles Leslie Pawson, who finished fifth in the Providence 12-mile road race in Providence, Rhode Island, on September 3, 1940 (*Providence Journal* photograph).

first place, the time prize was his only quest."[17] Some impositions were just too large, he knew from experience, and could not be overcome.

Brown, it turned out, was not alone with that hefty 6½-minute assessment; Les Pawson, ready to challenge, shared the same scratch burden. Lloyd Anderson and Frank Darrah, both with five-minute handicaps, and Fred McGlone with a four, along with some other speedy harriers, were planning to make the most of their beneficial advantages of getting started that far ahead of Brown and Pawson. The busy streets of the capital, filled with vehicular traffic, pedestrians, and hundred and hundreds of spectators, added to the challenge of the scratchmen when finally they were allowed to get underway.

Frank Darrah was not fooling around; he was hustling toward the finish line with everything he had. Hawk Zamparelli also started out strongly, but he was not feeling one hundred percent that morning. Brown kept focused, percolating with a rapid but rhythmic pace, and it was slowly beginning to pay off. He made inroads on the pack, his view of which was limited to backs, backsides, and backs of legs. Three miles from the start, Brown began to get ahead of Pawson as he continued his long march forward on the trail after Darrah. Despite the obstacles he had to dodge along the course — and there were many to add to his frustration — he was shortening the incredible advantage Darrah had built up and parsimoniously hoped not to squander.

A few miles farther, a point came where Brown, always adept at appraising in real time his momentary position in a contest, found himself two hundred yards in front of Pawson and nearly an identical two hundred yards in back of Darrah. In an amazing display of muscle power, a determined Brown opened up his stride, and in a matter of minutes, had barreled alongside Darrah. Both men were furiously blazing their way ahead of the pack, following the lead not of competitors but of some police and race officials. Zamparelli called it quits, jumped into an official car, and rode comfortably to the finish area, but Pawson kept the leaders in sight. Anderson, light and quick, was tireless that morning, sustaining an especially rapid pace to the cheers of the crowds strewn along the sidewalks. Fred McGlone, still strong in the final mile, had managed to flank Pawson; the two ran with a matching even gait.

In the last two miles, Brown "flashed forth with his greatest speed,"[18] as he opened up first one, and then two hundred yards of city pavement between himself and Darrah. Brown, "chalking up his 18th victory of the season,"[19] had run the twelve-mile course in 1 hour, 6 minutes, 55 seconds, breaking the finish line tape a half minute before Darrah finished with a claim on the second-place trophy. Lloyd Anderson, "said to be the lightest marathon runner in captivity," crossed the line next, a strong third and fourth in overall time. Fourth place belonged to Fred McGlone, who had succeeded in edging ahead of Pawson, the local star, in the final stretch.

After the prize ceremony, it was time to ride, not run, up Route 1 to Boston.

The six-mile handicap race of the Boston Caledonia Club, one of the high points of the afternoon along with the bagpipe competition in the 83rd annual Scottish Highland Games and athletic contests, was a Labor Day classic taking place at its traditional location, the Caledonia Grove in West Roxbury. In addition to the planned spectacle, entertainment and competitions set for the daylong event, there was a practical, serious purpose this year. Money would be raised and contributed to support a fund for the Scottish branch of the British Red Cross, so sorely needed during the prolonged air bombardment of Great Britain by the German air force.

Generating much excitement, the six-mile race, in forty-eight laps around the grounds, showcased a strong field, as it customarily did. The *Post* labeled "Brown [the] leading entry in [the] attractive event" and warned that "the Redskin will have to be at his best for he meets such contenders as Eino Pentti, the Finnish-American star from New York, ... [and] the present 15-kilometer champion."[20]

The *Post* had been right on target to put the spotlight on Pentti, who ran well and ended up winning easily. His run was made all the easier when, after just three and one-half miles, Brown was forced out with a sore toe. With Brown out of the running, Pentti's principal worries vanished.

Hawk Zamparelli, who had been unable to complete the morning run in Providence, started out in the front of the pack with George Durgin and Bob Campbell, Brown and Pentti loosely behind them. For the second time that day, Hawk was required to throw in the towel. Campbell took over. *Post* sportswriter Arthur Duffey wrote, "The Indian remained right at his heels until just after the half-way mark was reached when Brown stopped. With the Indian out of the race Campbell and Pentti carried on."[21] Eventually, Campbell faced fatigue at the pace and Pentti proved his short-distance expertise. The fund-raising Finnish-American's time for the six miles was 32 minutes, 56.4 seconds. "There were no phenomenal times," Nason wrote in his *Globe* coverage. "They weren't expected for that matter. The track is notoriously slow."[22]

Brown's unexpected sore toe quickly dispelled any plans he might have had to enter a third event. The weather, which, in the afternoon had been threatening rainstorms, slowed the start of the third race, the Reddish A. A. 10-Mile Run, which featured forty starters and twenty finishers. Johnny Kelley took the time prize, running the ten miles in 1 hour, 1 minute, 8 seconds. Al Menard finished first, John Coleman second, Leo Giard third, Frank Ryder fourth, and Jock Semple fifth. Johnny Kelley actually finished in sixth place. The B. A. A. earned the team trophy, to the joy of Semple.

Many footraces were held on that Labor Day in 1940 and one other which received coverage deserves a mention. The AP reported a six-mile race held in Brewer, Maine, and the *Boston Post* published the wire story with this headline: "DeMar Wins First Race In Six Years."[23] His winning time was 35 minutes, 51 seconds. It was back in 1934, according to the AP article, when DeMar had last won a first-place prize. That event was the New England championship marathon at Manchester, N. H. Unusually, the grandmaster of the marathon's age was not included in the article.

Hawk Zamparelli was literally running the national 25-kilometer race but not in the usual manner. This time he was working with the host organization, the Parkway Club of Revere, as the man in charge of putting on and running the event. Zamparelli had lined up a field of good talent for the Sunday afternoon, September 22, N. A. A. U.-sanctioned race. Some of the stellar names signed up for the Everett, Massachusetts, event included, in alphabetical order, Ellison "Tarzan" Brown, Bob Campbell, Linden Dempster, Lou Gregory (who won the 25-kilometer event the previous year held in Newport), John Kelley, Leslie Pawson, and Jock Semple. A field of seventy-five runners in all was officially on hand at the starting line when the approximately 15-mile, 900-yard race commenced.

When the gun blasted its signal for the athletes to start, Brown, Kelley and Gregory wasted no time getting going. Though not decisive, that jackrabbit start turned out to be very advantageous, because, as the *Herald* reported, "another group of runners was hopelessly held by a pack of 'official' cars going over the route."[24] Included in this obstructed grouping were Pawson, Dempster, Campbell and Peter Olexy. Also affected to some degree were all the other runners, however far behind them.

Kelley and Gregory established a quick tempo. Brown stayed closely behind. The *Herald* reported that Brown "had planned his race carefully and was content to let Kelley and Gregory set the pace."[25] After five miles, Brown pulled ahead of Kelley and Gregory. The three ran to Malden Square ahead of the rest of the pack, with Brown leading, Kelley up close, and Gregory a number of steps behind. Pawson, Campbell and Dempster were over a minute behind, in a second, tightly bunched pack. Behind them were McGlone, Semple, Al Menard, Lloyd Anderson, Maurice Charbonneau, Jack Ryder, and a large field of others. Things remained relatively stable for the next five or six miles.

Gregory attempted to seize the lead, as he passed Kelley and closed in on Brown with just about two miles left to run. Gregory was "at Brown's elbow."[26] Gregory appeared energetic as he moved "ahead of the Indian but it was only temporary," Arthur Duffey observed.[27] Brown "refused to relinquish his lead."[28] Instead of succumbing to Gregory's challenge, Brown accelerated. A two-man battle developed down the stretch. Kelley, running third, had hopes that Brown and Gregory would cause each other to burn out before the finish line in time for Kelley to overtake them. That scenario would not play out. Instead, Brown, with three hundred yards to go along the Revere Beach parkway, spurted ahead of Gregory with a fiery burst of speed and Gregory could not answer the call when it mattered most. It was enough to get Brown to the finish line three seconds ahead of Gregory, winning by an estimated three to five yards — down to just a few strides. Brown's winning time was 1 hour, 22 minutes, 37 seconds. Gregory was second in 1 hour, 22 minutes, 40 seconds. Johnny Kelley took third place, in 1 hour, 23 minutes, 9 seconds. Les Pawson finished fourth, coming in with the second pack of runners, in 1 hour, 25 minutes, 12 seconds. Campbell and Dempster followed Pawson closely. Semple finished twelfth, in 1 hour, 31 minutes, 40 seconds, with light, lithe Lloyd Anderson ten seconds behind Semple.

Ellison Brown had won back the national 25-kilometer title he had once held. In the prize-awarding ceremony, he was presented "a solid gold medal and watch."[29] All runners finishing in the top twenty received prizes. The Parkway Club provided the entire field of 75 athletes plus the race officials, some press members and quite a few others with a generous quantity of food and beverage. With the one exception of the obstruction by official vehicles early on, Zamparelli's promotional efforts had been considered a grand success.

Brown, Kelley and Pawson came together in Pawtucket, Rhode Island, on October 12, to compete in the New England A. A. U. 25-kilometer championship race, held in commemoration of the sesquicentennial of the city, on what turned out to be an unusually hot day for mid-October.

Mayor Thomas P. McCoy fired the pistol that set in gear the twenty-one runners at the starting line in front of City Hall. Brown began far back of the pack in the early going, and slowly worked his way to the front. There was a short duration, on Pawtucket Avenue, when Brown led the field, but he was overtaken by Kelley, and shortly thereafter, Kelley was overtaken by Pawson. The three—Brown, Kelley and Pawson—finished in succession in that order but not in the first, second and third places. Pipefitter Frank Darrah, resident of Manchester, New Hampshire, had seized the front-runner's position with three miles to go and doggedly held on for the first-place victory and the New England title. He had reason to be proud. He broke the tape ahead of "Brown, the Westerly Indian, by almost 150 yards, completing the event in 1 hour, 24 minutes, 7 seconds."[30] Filling out the top ten finishers in the championship run after Pawson were Campbell, Dempster, McGlone, Anderson, Stanley Tibbetts, and Menard.

A commercially minded civic group calling itself the Arlington Trade Associates decided to sponsor a ten-mile race in native son John Kelley's honor. It was their intention to create an annual event that would continue "long after Kelley has passed out of the active running picture."[31] The Arlington Trade Associates sought and were granted the official sanction of "the New England A. A. A. U. under the direction of 'Doc' McCarthy, the track coach at Arlington High School."[32] For the initial Johnny Kelley Road Race, scheduled for "Johnny Kelley Day," Saturday, October 26, Johnny Kelley the man was present as an entered contestant.

Frank Darrah, the recently crowned New England 25-kilometer champion, spoiled the obvious climax to the Kelley race by unleashing a burst of speed in the last mile to beat Johnny Kelley to the finish line by a hundred yards. Darrah was clocked at 50 minutes, 14 seconds. He finished ten seconds ahead of Kelley. The headline in the *Herald* read, "KELLEY DEFEATED IN 'OWN' RACE."[33]

Pawson came in third, one minute and twenty-one seconds behind Kelley. Linden Dempster and Michael O'Hara were next, then Ellison Brown, in sixth place, with a time of 53 minutes, 39 seconds. Brown, who had run alongside Darrah in the first mile, may have intentionally dropped back. It is possible Tarzan may not have wanted to rain on Kelley's parade. Other runners included seventh-place finisher Ted Carpenter, Joe Smith in eighth place, Frank Ryder, ninth, and Jock Semple in the tenth position.

The 1940 edition of the Yonkers National A. A. U. Marathon saw Gerard Cote finally achieve the success that had eluded him in that event after four years of finishing as the runner-up. Conspicuously absent from the starting line were two influential competitors. The nonappearance of the defending champion, the late Pat Dengis, was self-explanatory. Tarzan Brown did not run in the race. He arrived at the Empire City Racetrack forty minutes too late. He had mistakenly confused the day of the race, thinking the marathon was scheduled for the following day. Somehow Brown realized his mistake around 10:30 that morning, the morning of the competition. He jumped into his Chevrolet and sped from his home in Rhode Island to Yonkers, New York, a distance of 130 miles, in 2.5 hours, a near record in itself considering the roads, the traffic and risks. He arrived too late to compete.

The Canadian's chances for victory buoyed in part by Dengis' and Brown's omission from the field, Cote beat back a strong challenge from Lou Gregory, winning in what was reported to be "one of the closest finishes in years."[34] Pawson finished third in what must have been a difficult week. On the previous Tuesday, Election Day, the incumbent had failed to get reelected to the post of alderman in his home city of Pawtucket. Now he was finishing behind Cote and Gregory. Fred McGlone finished in fourth place behind Pawson, and Frank Darrah finished fifth behind McGlone. Baltimore's Don Heinicke, who attempted to take over the mantle from his late mentor, Dengis, had to settle for sixth place. Johnny Kelley was seventh. Jock Semple finished ninth. Fifty-seven-year-old "Bricklayer" Bill Kennedy was the twenty-eighth man to cross the finish line; his time was 3 hours, 29 minutes, 40 seconds. A "victory dance" was held after the marathon, sponsored by the Chippewa Running Club. It was there that the prizes were awarded to the runners, along with meals, drinks, speeches and good times.

The long drive to Berwick, Pennsylvania, from Rhode Island for the 31st annual Thanksgiving Day race, usually an endurance competition all its own, was an ordeal due to a combination of difficult conditions, including inclement weather, poor road surfaces that were icy in spots, and, in some instances, snow covered, highway construction, and an ailing automobile.

The course, like the ride out, was snow covered and slippery, and featured traffic and road construction. The runners chose to run in the tracks created by automobile tires where the course was over paved road though under considerable snow cover. Where there was no vehicular traffic, the runners were forced to cut a path through unplowed snow, having to navigate fairly deep drifts in places. On the return leg, most of the runners resorted to the easier, more manageable car tracks and faint foot traces through the snow. Despite the obstacles, Tarzan Brown ran the 9-miles-plus course most of the way at the head of the twenty-two man hoard, with Pawson at his heels from starting line to finish line. When Brown snapped the worsted line to win, Pawson was only fifteen yards and a mere five seconds behind. Brown completed his victory run in 50 minutes, 35 seconds.

Filling out the top ten: third place belonged to Edward Blackwell of Philadelphia, who crossed the line twenty-five seconds after Pawson did. He had trailed Pawson by fifty yards in the last mile. Johnny Kelley was fourth; his time 51 minutes, 27 seconds. Filing in after Kelley were Joe Kleinerman, Joseph Clark, William Steiner, Don Heinicke, Henry Klalka (*sic*), and, in tenth place, Gerard Cote, (among his many titles) the snowshoe champion of St. Hyacinthe, Quebec, registering a finish in 54 minutes, 10 seconds.[35] Given the conditions, it might have made some sense for Cote to have had his trusty snowshoes on in this one. Lou Gregory, the defending title holder from the year before, could not make it to the finish line this time.

"I really trained for this race," Tarzan said after winning. It was the same theme he had told reporters before the race. Then, he had said:

> "I trained for two and a half weeks, especially for this race," he had declared after his arrival Wednesday evening. "It's the first time I ever trained for the Berwick race, and I find nothing but snow when I get here. It will be tough going but it will be just as tough for the rest of them."[36]

It was tough, but fortunately not too tough to pull out a win. Ellison Brown received a diamond ring for his victory in Berwick. The victory over Pawson, Kelley, Heinicke and Gregory was sweet indeed, a most gratifying finish to the 1940 running season.

26

"He Has Everybody Guessing" — 1941

The 20-mile North Medford road race in its tenth edition took place on Saturday, March 22, 1941. Les Pawson, now age thirty-six and defending champion, and Johnny Kelley, winner of a string of five straight annual victories starting in 1934, were on hand to run and get the 1941 running season off to a good start. So was Gerard Cote, who had worried that the Canadian military, engaged with Great Britain in the widening war with Germany, would not allow him the time off to travel to the States to participate. The Quebecois must have had difficulty reading his military superiors. Not only did they happily permit the record-holding B. A. A. Marathon winner to compete in the Medford 20-mile race but Cote was granted permission to remain in the States so he could train for and compete in the B. A. A. Marathon a month later.

Besides Kelley, Pawson and Cote, also on hand for the start were Andre Brunelle, Bob Campbell, Paul Donato, Fred McGlone, Jock Semple, and Joe Smith. Don Heinicke of Baltimore, unexpected because of his war-related chemical plant work, was given the Saturday off so he could come to Boston to run. Friday evening directly after his shift he caught a night train to Boston, and showed up at the starting line at the last minute, a post entry — a play right out of the Ellison Brown playbook. Unfortunately, Brown did not run that play himself. "Tarzan Brown has not been heard from," Jerry Nason noted.[1] There was no word and no surprise appearance, prompting Will Cloney to wonder, "No one seems to know where the fabulous Indian is hibernating."[2]

The distance running season's debut, notwithstanding Brown's absence, nevertheless began punctually in its North Medford incarnation, at 2:30 p.m. sharp. When it was over, John Kelley, 33 years old, had notched another North Medford victory, his sixth, despite a difficult set of obstacles hurled in his path, any one of which should have invariably cost him the first-place victory or resulted, in all probability, in an early withdrawal. Kelley, for starters, was the hapless recipient of an icy snowball which hit him hard on the hip at the seven-mile mark, according to the *Herald*.[3] The *Globe* placed the incident much earlier in the race, "along about four miles," and described ground zero as being Kelley's left thigh, not the hip. "It was a nice, hard, icy projectile" thrown by "a juvenile snowball pitcher," the *Globe* reported, causing an immensely painful bruise.[4] It hardly mattered which report was the more exacting since in either case Kelley withstood the pain and gamely kept his sights on his competitive mission. However, if the *Globe* account had the corner on accuracy on this occasion, Kelley suffered the effects of the impact for a considerably longer duration of the race; a difference of three miles (*Globe* vs. *Herald*) translated into roughly fifteen minutes. Next, in a rendering of the proverbial addition of insult to literal injury, Kelley was accidentally "doused with a pitcher of ice water at an inopportune moment,"[5] creating added physical (and mental) discomfort in the cold, windy conditions along the course. Last but not least, Kelley's naturally anxious racing countenance was taxed to the limit by what he perceived to be the reckless driving of the automobile escort, operating much too closely behind him, creating an unsettling sense of impending danger. The disturbing yapping sound of a persistent barking dog hot on that vehicle's trail enhanced the lack of serenity in what felt like just a matter of steps behind the runner Kelley's heels. Yet Kelley persevered. He finished in 1 hour, 55 minutes, 51 seconds.

Leslie Pawson suffered stomach cramps on two separate occasions during the race which took him out of leading contention, but he managed despite being slowed to finish second, in 1 hour, 56 minutes, 18 seconds. Fred McGlone, age 23, and Joe Smith, age 26, were side by side as they approached the final stretch with 150 yards to go. At McGlone's suggestion, "rather than sprint madly,"[6] they synchronized their steps, and, in the final yard to the finish line, raised their adjacent arms in the air and clasped hands, crossing the finish line together, intent on sharing third place with a tie. The racing judge was not receptive to that brotherly display of camaraderie, and declared McGlone the sole third-place winner and Smith fourth. McGlone's sister Maggie, a runner in her own right in female racing events and a big supporter of her brother, had followed him along the course in a car, offering valuable assistance in the form of water, fruit pieces, and positive verbal goading. How she felt about her brother's orchestrated finale with Smith is unknown. Smith, new father and local (Medford) milkman judged to be fourth, had no complaints with the final scoring. After the race he openly accepted that McGlone could have beaten him to the line if they had run the final 150 yards in a fair competitive showdown. As it was, Smith registered his finish in 1 hour, 54 seconds, 21 seconds,[7] more than a minute ahead of the fifth-place Cote, who, like Pawson, suffered from abdominal cramps. Don Heinicke finished sixth in 2 hours, 3 minutes, 26 seconds, four seconds shy of a full four minutes in back of Cote. Finishing out the top ten were Donato, Campbell, Semple, and O'Hara. Jock Semple, thirty-seven years old, had found new employment as a night watchman. The night hours did not appear to negatively affect his running time; in fact, quite the opposite apparently obtained, as it was his best finish in the North Medford run in seven tries. "He didn't run like a guy who needed any sleep," jibed Nason.[8]

Semple, who always placed importance on the running team and its team achievements, and as captain of the B. A. A. team had a large emotional investment in its inconsistent recruiting efforts, portrayed himself as a bit miffed at President Franklin Roosevelt and his military draft policies. Complained Semple:

> Sure I voted for him [FDR] and what does he do? Well, first he takes George Durgin; then he nabs Johnny Fitzgerald; and just last week he carried off Italo Amicangioli. How am I ever going to get a winning team together if this draft keeps up?"[9]

On Monday, March 24, the following headline appeared in the *Herald*: "Missing Indian Most Discussed Person at North Medford Run."[10] Under that was this subheadline, also in boldface: "Whereabouts of Tarz Brown Topic For All, Source of Worry for Kelley."[11] Will Cloney began with the question, "Has anyone here seen Tarzan Brown?"[12] Answering his own rhetorical question, he reported that neither Pawson nor Kelley had heard from their esteemed colleague. Cloney wrote Pawson's reponse first:

> Tarz probably hasn't much incentive to run anymore. He has a job, a wife and family, and may not have any time. Then again, no long Olympic trip is in prospect. Of course, there's no telling, though. Tarz has his own ideas.[13]

Strangely, the set of conditions that Pawson proposed for Brown's lack of incentive obtained in his case as well: job, wife and family, and lack of time. Pawson had complained, in fact, that he was only able do his "long training," workouts designed to improve his distance stamina, on Saturdays and that stormy weather falling on many of those Saturdays had pulled him off his schedule. As far as the Olympic incentive was concerned, Brown had been to the Olympics and certainly wanted to return, a chance to redeem himself. Pawson, due to the wartime cancellation of the 1940 Olympic Games in Finland, never had run in an Olympic marathon. From his perspective in 1941, the next Olympic games were scheduled for 1944, and the trials would probably take place in 1943 at the very earliest, and in 1944 as well, if (and it was a big "if") the war ended. If Olympic trials were an incentive to compete in a race for Brown (or anyone else), then there would effectively be no incentive until 1943, two years hence. Did Pawson expect Brown to lie low for two years? Only Ellison could answer, as Pawson clearly understood.

Johnny Kelley's reaction to Brown's absence was characterized in terms of Kelley's anxiety. Recorded Cloney:

> Kelley, elated at what he termed a completely unexpected victory, found time to worry about the Indian. "I just wish I knew what he is doing. I'll bet he's

laying low, training hard for the B. A. A. I want to win that one for my wife, but he might show up at the last minute and fool us all."[14]

Ellison Brown still mattered. He was still a factor. He was newsworthy even in absentia.

The *Globe* scooped the competition with this March 25 item, under the heading: "Tarzan Brown Opens 1941 Road Campaign Here This Saturday."[15] The unsigned article is presented:

> Tarzan Brown, legendary legman, will make his first road-racing start of 1941 on Saturday in the annual Reddish A. A. 10-miler in Jamaica Plain.
> The Indian thus tears the shroud of mystery from himself. Not even his intimates in the macadam set have heard from him in weeks. He did not, as has been his custom, compete last week in Medford. Conflicting rumors had it that he had hung up his racing shoes, that he was training in secret for the Boston Marathon race.
> His official entry has been received, however, by the Reddish race officials.[16]

Two days later, the *Herald's* Bob Dunbar got wind of the story. Dunbar wrote, "Promoters of road races are anxious to get the best runners possible, so the Reddish A. A. authorities are bowing right and left because Tarzan Brown has signed for their event. Like all officials, however, they will keep their fingers crossed until they see him at the starting line."[17] The Reddish race promoters must have slightly relaxed their white-knuckled, crossed fingers or breathed a little bit easier after reading Nason's March 28 contribution to the *Globe* sports pages. Not only did the lengthy piece confirm that Brown was indeed intending to participate in their ten-mile race, but the coverage also presumably enhanced the stature of the event and, at the same time, intensified spectator anticipation and interest, precisely the same ends Brown's participation was supposed to realize. Nason's typewriter could barely contain the alliterative, stereotypical Native American pejorative terms he unleashed:

> The panting palefaces will be hustling along with a little extra zest in Jamaica Plain tomorrow p.m., because the dull throb of the war drums can be heard in Westerly, R. I.
> Ellison Myers Brown, the brown blitzkrieger of the macadam, the fastest and the noblest of the Narragansetts, the trotting tribesman who has Indian-ized more palefaces since One-Eye John was scaring the early residents of Sudbury half out of their wits— Tarzan, in short, has daubed on the war paint again.
> Last week in Medford all the highway headliners except the romping redskin showed up for the road-racing inaugural. Tomorrow in the Reddish A. A. handicap all the celebrities except Brown will be absent.
> What goes on here: A sit-down strike?
> Not exactly. It happens that the Indian makes his seasonal debut in a race which contemporary big shots like Les Pawson and John Kelley and Gerard Cote decided would not be especially beneficial to their Marathon prepara-

tions. They claim they do not need speed work so much as endurance and the Reddish race, being a handicap and only 10 mile[s] long, is a speed test.[18]

Nason went on to explain why the promoters of the Reddish race should not fret that Brown's other celebrity colleagues had not signed on to their event. The passage reveals the high level of regard with which Brown was seen, both by the public and the sportswriters. Nason, in comparing Brown to two of the most popular and respected icons of the era, one in the realm of animation, the other in the distance running field, was rendering a tribute. This was not hyperbole; this was the language of open praise. Nason wrote:

> Fortunately for the promoters Brown is a whole show in himself. The Indian is the greatest single drawing card in the game today. You might call him the Mickey Mouse of the macadam popularity polls. He's the equal of the personality plodder of yesteryear, Clarence Harrison De Mar [sic].[19]

DeMar, a most remarkable sportsman, achiever of the highest level, and still active (and tough-as-nails competitor), in a straightforward sense, had no equal — not on any level. But DeMar was that rare athlete, recognized and revered in his own time, for what he had done, for who he was, and for what he represented. Nason was attempting to inform all of the community he could reach that Ellison "Tarzan" Brown had the gifts, that he belonged in that same caliber, the one reserved for very special, once-in-a-generation, talented individuals with all of the potential to reach the heights of the running realm that had been established by DeMar in his, an earlier, era. Consequently, a Brown performance should not be casually viewed or dismissed, win or lose. Did I say "lose?"

> Unpredictable Tarzan can be a full-fledged flop, like he was last April 19, or the marvel of Marathon, as he was last May 30. In that period of roughly six weeks last year the Indian, with revenge in his heart and determination etched on his grim lips, came from a disastrous 13th in the Boston Marathon to ruin the world record at Salisbury Beach.
> O, yes, indeedy, the brown brave from Westerly paid off a lot of old scores on the sylvan sands at Salisbury. At Boston the estimable M'sieu Cote whipped him by 16 searing minutes. Kelley, Heinicke and Pawson all finished better than a mile ahead of him, but he ground 'em all into the road in May.[20]

It looked like forty-six runners including Tarzan Brown, assembled in front of the Lowell School on Centre Street in Jamaica Plain, would make up the field for the long-standing 31st annual Reddish A. A. Road Race. Minutes before the 2:30 start, a forty-seventh man, who had finally made up his mind at the eleventh hour to enter the race, was frantically filling out the required forms three flights up inside the Lowell School building. Desperately trying to get officially entered, the race officials acquiesced just in time and allowed 39-year-old Andre Brunelle that last-minute post-entry opportunity. As things unfolded, Brunelle, who had won this race seven years ago in 1934, must have been doubly glad they did.

Brown was assigned the scratch line start. As Cloney pointed out, that in itself created "a terrific task, because the race runs through congested areas like Roslindale Square, Forest Hills, and Jamaica Plain. A good day brings such crowds that even pedestrian traffic has trouble moving."[21] Everybody else began the race at some point in time before Brown, including Brunelle, who, having been granted a two-minute handicap, got to start four minutes before Brown was allowed to begin. A determined Brunelle, little by little, worked his way to the head of the pack. It took him five miles, by the midway point, to get up front, where he staved off any and all challenges to be first to the finish line. Meanwhile Ellison Brown would later say he couldn't get it going until that midpoint, but he did not lay blame on the size of the gallery or any impediments they may have spawned.

Over the second half of the race, Brown was more satisfied with his running performance, but it was not vintage Tarzan Brown. "The Tarz couldn't get warmed up for nine miles, felt like himself for the last one, and finished 18th in actual order, seventh according to the clock," observed Will Cloney.[22] The 18th place-finish had a positive and negative aspect to it, Nason pointed out. "He was 18th, which was five places higher than he finished a year before, but his time was more than a minute slower."[23] In light of the press buildup for his debut, the results, ten miles in 54 minutes, 56 seconds, were regarded as something of a disappointment.

The time prize was won by Joe Smith with a time of 53 minutes, 22 seconds. Afterward the milkman told the assembled members of the press, "I had a charley horse when I started, and I didn't know what I could do.... Funny thing, but this year I'm finishing races without being a bit tired; last year I was bushed."[24]

John Coleman, who in 1940 had come so close to victory, having had it snatched away from his grasp in the final moments, again found himself in nearly the same boat, but with slightly less drama since the final stretch to the finish this year was not as close a contest. Running fast and in the middle of contention at the six-mile mark, by the end, in actuality, fifty yards separated Brunelle and Coleman. Brunelle simply sprinted faster when it mattered to reach the finish line first. George Daniel, a Norfolk team member, was fourth, Jock Semple was magnificent with a fifth-place finish, and Fred McGlone, also a Norfolk teammate and the pick of many curbside observers, finished just one second behind Semple.

Ellison Brown spoke with Jerry Nason. Brown told Nason he had been chopping lots of wood in the past two months for physical conditioning, but had not done much road work of late. To make up for that, would Brown enter any of the scheduled short races before Patriots' Day and the B. A. A. Marathon? Nason got his answer. Brown told him he would skip the 10-mile runs like the Presentation Race in Brighton the following week. "'Guess I better go out and run 50 miles instead!' said the imperturbable Indian."[25]

In the past, Brown would explain how he wanted to improve his speed capacity. For that reason, he would run the handicap races as a prelude to the April 19 big marathon, concentrating on increasing his sizzling pace. At this point in his running career Brown's view about his need to concentrate on improving his speed had undergone a change. He talked about it with the *Globe* sportswriter, and Nason passed along the information to his readers:

> "I'm not worryin' about speed like I used to," confesses the flying warrior. "I got natural speed. It was born in me, I guess. I been gettin' tired in the last few miles of the Marathon, so what I need's strength."[26]

For a regimen to build up his strength, Brown resorted to chopping wood with an ax, the kind of outdoor work familiar to him in past days of training for big races. After two months Brown "doesn't dare estimate the cords of wood he's chopped," wrote Nason, who described the results of Brown's ax wielding. "His big hands are fringed with callouses (*sic*) and Tarzan is not especially fond of chopping wood. But every time his ax bites into a pine knot the Indian feels he's that much closer to victory on Patriots' Day,"[27] only three weeks away. Brown offered this, "I'm goin' to be stronger than I ever been in the Marathon race."[28]

Ellison Brown had put a lot of thought into the past 1940 B. A. A. Marathon, and had carefully dissected the cause of his lack of success in it. Looking back after a year, he spoke about that race to Nason, who in turn disclosed to his readers the essentials of Brown's reflections:

> "My stomach turned weak," he reminisces grimly. "Don't know why. I was in good condition. 'Long 'bout Wellesley I took the lead, feelin' good. I says to myself: 'I'll go right out all the way in and break the record again.' That's how good I felt. Then my stomach got weak. I been figurin' it out and that's why I been choppin' wood. I'm not goin' to have no weak stomach this year."[29]

The Reddish race showed him that he needed to improve his leg strength. It also revealed that he had developed greater upper body heft and power, along with improved abdominal muscles, the perceived Achilles' heel of his weakness. Brown had faced his body-strengthening needs head-on. He was also hoisting his confidence levels.

The two intervening ten-mile races before the B. A. A. Marathon — the Presentation in Brighton and the Cathedral Road Race in the South End — took place without the participation of Ellison Brown. Les Pawson was rumored to be planning a run in the 10th annual Presentation Race but did not do so. Honore St. Jean, thirty-two or thirty-nine years old, depending on the source[30], worked the night shift at a cotton mill in Manchester, New Hampshire. He worked the night before the race, operating textile-weaving machinery. Getting out at seven o'clock in the morning, he then hitchhiked to Boston, getting to Oak Square in Brighton in time to run the Presentation Race, which he won without the benefit of a night's sleep. It was his first major win. Joe Smith, who finished second, won the time prize.

Pawson did show for the 31st annual Cathedral Club 10-mile road race, and won it handily despite some difficulties brought about by the race officials at both ends of the course. At the start they sent Pawson, the only scratch runner, into the fray a minute too early by mistake. If that hadn't happened, it was agreed that Paul Donato would have won, but Donato had no intention of protesting the results, partly in deference to Pawson. "'This is all supposed to be sport,' said Donato."[31]

At the course's end there was no literal finish line painted. This caused innumerable problems with the close finishes, of which there were quite a few. Adding to that complication and of greater impact, the officials botched the timekeeping. Their inability to tabulate the runners' times with any accuracy led to the stunning but impossible conclusion that seven runners had broken Brown's record.[32] One race official, Joe Lewis, it was discovered, had kept his stopwatch in its set position, enabling the bumbling officials to calculate the approximate correct times. Following their computational session, it was determined that Pawson, who had won the time prize, had established a new record to replace the one set by Tarzan Brown the year before by forty-four seconds.

In the race, Pawson beat Donato by a margin of 125 yards at the finish. Donato finished second, ahead of McGlone, Ryder, and Cook respectively. Pawson's strong showing had the pundits picking him for victory in the upcoming B. A. A. Marathon.

In fact, Nason reported the results of the loosely organized annual poll he conducted on the marathon predictions. The consensus, reported April 15, 1941, was that Pawson would finish first, Cote second, and Kelley third. Heinicke and McGlone were predicted to fill out the top five. Tarzan Brown's name was not to be found on the list. According to Nason:

> Most of the boys shied away from Tarzan Brown, the unpredictable Narragansett brave. He has everybody guessing. Harold Goslin pitched him the only first place vote he got. Otherwise, the Indian didn't fare so well in the poll.[33]

Cloney likewise reported his straw poll of expert picks. A headline reported the consensus of the *Herald* group, that Cote would finish first.[34] Actually the group evenly divided over Cote and Pawson as a first-place choice, but when the total preferences were all scored and tabulated mathematically, Cote led, with Kelley and Pawson following closely. Two of the experts selected Tarzan Brown as their predicted winner, but none of the others had much in the way of expectations; Brown's total points placed him ninth overall. Ahead of him were the three mentioned above followed by Heinicke, Donato, Smith, McGlone and Rankine. Brunelle was cast in the experts' consensus for a tenth-place finish.

Ellison Brown's officially submitted entry was announced on April 15. In the *Globe's* announcement, an unnamed sportswriter included this description and a little history:

> Brown is the mystery man of the Marathon. He has raced only once this Spring and looked only so-so in his single outing. He won the race in 1936 and again three years later, when he put the record down to 2:28:58.
>
> But last April, when Gerard Cote broke his record, the Indian fell far back to 13th position after leading the pack to Wellesley. A month later he came back to break the world record in the Salisbury Beach Marathon.
>
> "Nobody knows what Tarzan will do," said one of his macadam contemporaries the other day, "not even Tarzan."
>
> At his best the Indian probably can run the course well under the present record of 2:28:28 3–5, held by Cote.[35]

Nason, the day before the marathon, wrote:

> The entry who has 'em all stymied is Ellison (Tarzan) Brown, the Indian. Twice a winner when hardly anybody gave him a chance, the Narragansett is the same old mystery man. He threatens publicly to ruin the record, so privately he must be training hard.
>
> Brown in Grade A first-class, No. 1 condition will run all over anybody in his way. What everybody seems to be afraid of is that he will be in Grade 2 [*sic*] second-class, No. 2 condition. Then he won't figure.[36]

Dave Egan, "the Colonel," wrote the following column which was published on the morning of the marathon. Despite his respect for Brown as an athlete, the words he employed to characterize the man contributed to a demeaning tone. He began with a referral to the *Westerly Sun* sports editor:

> Our Westerly representative, Mr. Abe Soloveitzik, has been hurrying and scurrying around in our behalf down that way. He has beaten the bushes and discovered the forest home of Tarzan Brown, who has been living the life of the legendary Riley on baked squirrel, baked rabbit, clams, and oysters hard by the sight of King Phillip's Great Swamp fight.
>
> The Peter Pan of the pavement retired from his highway job in Westerly, probably on the ground that he did not wish to be an enemy of the highways 365 days a year, and he plunged back into the woods many months ago, with his wife and his two children and his gun. He has been employed as a woodchopper until recently, but in the past six weeks, he has also abandoned that career in order to prepare for the Marathon. He has run a total of 230 miles over the rugged roads of southern Rhode Island, and maybe that will give you a vague idea of the punishment those top-flight Marathoners inflict upon themselves in advance of the race.
>
> Oh, yes, there is one more thing which must be reported about our favorite road-racer. He believes that he will cover the course in two hours and 26 minutes. That, chums, would mean merely a new world record for the Marathon distance, so you may see for yourself that the Peter Pan of the pavements believes that he is ready for his annual effort.

He will run a different type of race, this year, than he has in the past. Tarzan, in other years, has run as fast as he could as long as he could. He has swung his way to the front, and whippeted over the roads and asked the rest of the boys to catch him if they could.

This time, however, he is running to set a record that will live forever. He plans to let the others set the pace for the first 17 miles. He plans to do his running in the last eight miles. With an equal share of the racing luck, he is great enough to carry out his plan, and you may see something today which you will not soon forget. You may see a wild Indian come whooping down the stretch.[37]

The "life of Riley" context is utterly repugnant in light of the reality of the living conditions of the Narragansett in what were still the Depression years in their community. Life and times were difficult, and no one was taking it easy. That Ellison Brown was of a type that could not hold down a steady, regulated job for a sizeable length of time was due to the unique traits upon which his personality was built and the makeup of the world in which he grew up — not irresponsibility, laziness, lack of ambition, or in a most highly volatile word, shiftlessness, as the white world so easily could and would attach as a descriptive label. It was simpler to suggest that people of color as a group (Native Americans were so classified in Rhode Island for many years and the dark skin tone confirmed the classification for political purposes) were outright unable or unwilling to hold onto steady employment (despite its scarcity) and not naturally smart enough to recognize the peril of that course of action. An "enemy of the highways," in a time of growing military conflict overseas (Pearl Harbor was still less than eight months away) was a form of ridicule of the lowest sort.

The "Peter Pan" connotation suggested to most readers, I suspect, a person on the level of a child. Additionally it may have been meant to invoke a person living in the realm of fantasy. That in itself I find to be way out of line, both inappropriately racist and mean-spirited. Whether Brown ever stated that he intended to shatter the standing course record, a feat he had accomplished two years before, is unknown. While he may have confided such a prospect to Soloveitzik, though I have uncovered no evidence that he did, Brown most certainly never stated that intention directly to Egan. Moreover, Brown's running strategy should not have been revealed beforehand for the other runners to read, no matter how reckless it might have been for Brown to confide it to some person, an unproven supposition. The integrity of the marathon itself, like any sporting event, demands some discretion. Somewhat equivalent to stealing signs in baseball, it is the kind of thing that all parties acknowledge occurs to some degree, but, despite its unethical, unsportsmanlike bearing among players, never should it be assisted by members of the sports press.

Egan's final reference to seeing "a wild Indian," while despicable, is on a par historically with other journalistic coverage of those prewar times. The Rhode Island-born Egan claimed a partiality to Ellison Brown and called him "our favorite road-racer"; imagine the column he would have produced had he no affection for the talented Brown.

27

Injury — 1941

Saturday, April 19, 1941, Patriots' Day in Massachusetts, started out as an overcast morning with pleasant temperatures, but the skies soon turned azure and the temperatures began to soar as a bright sun rose higher in the sky. By noontime, the mercury was approaching the seventy-degree mark. It would rise four more degrees over the afternoon; it was very warm, the way Clarence DeMar preferred it.

A field of 124, the smallest in recent memory ("a new low," according to Will Cloney[1]), the results of intensive recruitment efforts and conscription to build up the United States military, assembled at the Lucky Rock Manor in Hopkinton for the premarathon preparations, under the watchful eye of the gracious Mrs. Alice McHale Tabeau. At 10:30 a.m. the weigh-in and physical examinations began, administered in quick fashion by the medical team of Dr. M. A. Cohen and Dr. George Gaunt. They were carried out routinely without any apparent hitches. Well before 11:45, the aggregation of athletes proceeded to the starting area corral, where the runners were "checked by Clerk of Course and Starter Walter A. Brown."[2] At noon, Walter Brown stood poised, armed with the same gun his late father, George Victory Brown, had used to start the runners. "This most punctual of all sporting events"[3] lived up to its reputation as usual, as a myriad of bells in church steeples, some near, some farther away, could begin to be heard signaling the midday hour when Brown momentarily interrupted the ringing cacophony with his firing of the historic handgun.

Two *Globe* sportswriters, riding in the same complimentary touring automobile, a new 1941 Buick Special Sedan (complete with "dual horn control, adjustable cigarette lighter, triple-threat synchro-mesh brakes, shatter-proof side walls, automatic upholstery, fluid-drive trunk-rack, freewheeling ash trays and two-tone glove compartment"[4]) sharing the same vantage point, got very different impressions of the early going. Jerry Nason reported that Hawk Zamparelli, now in the service but on short leave from the 211th Coast Artillery at Camp Hulen, Texas, seized "the immediate lead," followed closely by the trio of Johnny Kelley, Gerard Cote and Lou Gregory.[5] Tom Fitzgerald put Ellison Brown in the pristine leadoff spot. Fitzgerald wrote: "In a strange contrast to other years, it was one of the real contenders who took the lead at the start. Tarzan Brown, the Narragansett tribesman, who is such an enigma to his fellow plodders, was out there on top and keeping him company in a little group a few yards back were such celebrities as Andrew 'Hawk' Zamparelli, the soldier man from Medford and schoolmaster Lou Gregory."[6]

Two miles along, in Ashland, Hawk, running on a painful bandaged knee, had moved to the front of the pack. Behind him, Gregory, Kelley and Cote ran in a tight formation, followed by Don Heinicke, Joe Kleinerman, Paul Donato, Les Pawson, Scotty Rankine and Joe Smith. Ellison Brown, Fred McGlone, Andre Brunelle, Jock Semple, and the marathon veterans Clarence H. DeMar, age 52, and "Bricklayer" Bill Kennedy, age 57, were in hot pursuit on the searing pavement, and it was really heating up. "It was plenty hot," wrote Cloney. "In fact it was so hot that the runners appeared to be running in cellophane panties."[7] That mental picture had to be left to the newspaper readers' imaginations since Cloney did not explain or offer further clarification.

At Framingham, the first checkpoint, Gregory led, with Kelley second, and Cote third. Kleinerman had moved into fourth place, with Heinicke and Pawson close behind him. Hickey and Rankine were next. Tarzan Brown was ninth, and Hawk was now trailing Brown. Four miles down the course, at the second checkpoint, in Natick, Gregory still led, but Cote and Kelley had swapped positions behind him; Cote had moved up into the second slot and Kelley had slipped back to third. At this juncture Medford milkman Smith had supplanted Heinicke for the fourth spot as Heinicke began to falter, though only temporarily. The fifth spot belonged to Pawson. Checking in sixth was Rankine. Filling out the first ten were Heinicke, Kleinerman, McGlone and Brown, who was not running comfortably yet. Zamparelli had dropped back considerably.

Large throngs lined the course, from Natick to Exeter Street in Boston. As the runners neared Wellesley College, Pawson attempted to challenge the leaders. He passed the two men directly ahead of him, positioning himself behind Cote. When Pawson surged ahead of Cote, Cote found he was powerless to do anything about it but "spread his hands in dismay as Pawson sped past him,"[8] a gesture meant to depict futility. Pawson kept on rolling. He caught up to Kelley's 120 pounds of flesh and bones and determination. Instead of passing him, Pawson ran alongside Kelley. The two friends, in this competitive predicament of matching strides as they had done so many times before, shared water, with Pawson conveying it from its source from car window on one side to his fellow runner on the other. Senior *Globe* writer Victor O. Jones commented:

> Each time Pawson doused himself, he immediately reached up for another container and passed it over to Kelley.
> Now you may think it's a pretty simple stunt to grab a container of water from a car moving along beside you while you run. But I watched Pawson do

this stunt maybe 100 times on Saturday. Each time he had to turn his head, take his eyes off where he was going. Also he had to half turn his body. And he had to break the smooth rhythmic swing of his arms to get his right hand up to the container. Each time he went through his dousing, he broke his stride perceptibly.

But if getting water for himself was a chore, getting it for Kelley was even more complicated. Because to get the container to Johnny, Pawson either had to reach his right hand across his chest, or he had to transfer the container from his right hand to his left hand before giving it to Kelley. Sometimes he did it one way, sometimes the other ... for some eight miles.[9]

Of course, all the while, each man assessed the other's condition as best he could with mostly sideward glances.

Leaving the raucous cheering coeds behind on the way to the Wellesley check-in station at mile thirteen, Pawson decided the time was right to bolster forward and, just like that, he overtook Kelley, but only by the slightest of margins. The Wellesley checkpoint recorded Pawson, Kelley and Cote, followed by Rankine, Heinicke, and Smith, followed by a fading Gregory, Kleinerman, Ellison Brown, and McGlone.

Four miles later, at Auburndale, the two Canadians, Rankine and Cote, exchanged positions. McGlone had also switched his position with the man in front of him — Ellison Brown, who checked in eighth. Kleinerman and the thirty-nine-year-old Brunelle filled out the top ten, Gregory had fallen back, out of the top ten, and very soon would be physically forced to give in to the heat and the tough competition. It was grueling and he reluctantly called it a day. With the Newton hills stretch approaching, Pawson hoped to leave Kelley behind him, for good. But Kelley, no stranger to this arduous uphill segment of the course, figured he might finally be able to shake Pawson. At that moment, the pair enjoyed a three hundred-yard advantage over Rankine, the man in temporary possession of third place and the nearest contender.

On the first hill neither Pawson nor Kelley visibly appeared to forcefully challenge the other. Pawson later revealed the reality of the situation. He said, "We [Kelley and Pawson] were fighting all through the Newton hills, trying to make each other crack. I tried to get away from him on the first hill, but I couldn't."[10] By the final grade, now known as Heartbreak Hill, Pawson "seemed a little more determined. Les cocked his head a little to the left, squinted up through the lane of holiday spectators, and appeared to put on a little more pressure. Then up the grade they went, and Kelley still was with him at the top."[11] Kelley, gamely or stubbornly, seemed to be holding fast.

After checking into Auburndale in the eighth position, Tarzan Brown found his body unable to adjust to the torturous grind, out of harmony with the competitive task at hand. Cloney wrote, "The unpredictable Tarzan Brown, who stayed in the first 10 for 17 miles,... disappeared — but completely.

He wasn't in the clubhouse after the race and checked out of his hotel immediately."[12] Along with his rapid retreat from the marathon environs went any
opportunities the sports reporters otherwise may have exploited for obtain-
ing a personal explanation or procuring quotations. Brown, never loqua-
cious, clearly did not feel like talking or facing anybody, especially the press.
A mix of feelings including disappointment, frustration, and some embar-
rassment must have accompanied him on the silent ride back to Rhode Island.

On the initial descent from Lake Street, Pawson and Kelley were still running side by side, "the margin was still unchanged and the field lagged even
further back in their wake."[13] Onward to the Coolidge Corner check station,
Pawson intensified his movements, accelerating ever so slightly. Kelley was
unable to match the increase in velocity. Pawson created a two hundred-
fifty-yard gap as he soared along the final stretch. Kelley would not give up,
but his hopes rested on the chance that Pawson might fail to continue on his
new pace. Kelley did not slow to take water. For the first time, he did not shift
into walking mode.

Amazingly, Pawson did, first stopping dead in his tracks on Beacon
Street, then resorting to a walk. He would later tell reporters: "I wasn't in
trouble. I had a little knotting of a muscle well up on the thigh of my left leg.
I get it off and on in training. So I stopped and walked three or four steps to
relax the leg and set off again."[14]

Pawson recovered very quickly and in enough time, amazingly, to hold
onto his lead. He resumed his machine-like striding as he continued to hus-
tle his way through the streets packed along the sides with noisy crowds to
the finish line and his third victory. His time, 2 hours, 30 minutes, 38 seconds, was faster than his previous two winning times. Kelley, for his part,
continued on for another of his second-place finishes—his fourth—breaking the tape and slumping first in the open arms of his father and then over
to embrace his wife. His time of 2 hours, 31 minutes, 26 seconds[15] was his
own personal best time ever for the course. He had reached the finish line
over four minutes ahead of Heinicke, who finished third. More than four
miles back, at Lake Street, Heinicke had checked in third ahead of Cote, and
he finished that way—in third place, ahead of Cote.

Cote, still the course recordholder, had suffered a cramp near Wellesley. After crossing the finish line, he lit up a cigar just as he would have had
he won the marathon. "'I lose so many races I don't mind losing another,' he
said cheerfully."[16] The former newspaper distributor had parlayed his fame
from his 1940 victory into acquiring "Gerry Cote's Grill, a dine and dance
establishment in the center of St. Hyacinthe, Que."[17] The twenty-seven-year-
old, always dapper, reigning snowshoe champion had secret plans to marry
a woman from Montreal as soon as he returned to Quebec. He spoke to
reporters who always got a kick out of listening to his patois.

"I am not too disappoint [*sic*]," observed the Quebec fashion plate, taking his defeat with a grin and good grace. "I am in good condition, yes. I am as good as last year when I win. But this day is not mine. This day belongs to Pawson and he is not to be beat."[18]

Joe Smith, who had run in sixth place from Natick to Coolidge Corner, managed to gain a position on Exeter Street to finish in fifth place. He and McGlone had run together for seven miles and could have finished as they did in the Cathedral race, deliberately at the same time. They actually discussed it en route while running. They decided about the time they approached Kenmore Square not to repeat that stunt, but to make an honest race of it. There they shook hands. A ways later Smith found a second wind, and in the last fifteen yards, sprinted past McGlone, finishing twelve seconds ahead. McGlone may have been distracted; his sister, Margie, ran the final ten yards with him.

Brunelle, the 39-year-old grocer, finished seventh, one place back from the previous year. The heat had gotten to him. "'I didn't have any lift at the end,' confessed Andre."[19] Jock Semple, 37, finished eighth to a thunderous ovation; his time, 2:47:26. Semple was elated. Back in 1930, eleven years earlier, he had finished seventh, the same year Clarence DeMar won for his record seventh time. "'So, I am too old, now eh?' howled Jock in his finest Scot's burr, as he literally leaped across the line. 'Mon, O, mon, it's gude ta be in the mooney, ageen.'"[20] Paul Donato, 23, finished ninth. It was his fourth consecutive top-ten finish. Joe Kleinerman, a 29-year-old post office clerk from New York who had positioned himself amongst the top ten runners throughout the entire twenty-six miles of the marathon, held on for a tenth-place finish.

Clarence H. DeMar finished twentieth, but might have done a bit better had he not taken the time to punch not one but two spectators in the face. The two men, in separate incidents, had come onto the course and had penetrated too far into DeMar's personal space. The first occurred at Woodland Park, just before the Auburndale check station and the Newton hills. There the hapless spectator, unaware of proper marathon-watching decorum, stepped out onto the course to request from DeMar his autograph. Instead of a handwritten signature, he received "a well-placed right hand" fist to the face.[21] "I just gave him one good punch and ran," DeMar would later say.[22] In the second incident, which took place at Cleveland Circle, with roughly four miles more to go, a clumsy but perhaps well-meaning individual spilled water all over DeMar, especially onto his running shoes. Regardless of the intent, it was not received as a welcomed gesture. The right fist once again squarely found its mark, as the runner kept on moving, his carefully timed stride hardly noticeably interrupted.

DeMar was unsatisfied with his time: 3 hours, 5 minutes, 37 seconds. Said DeMar, "I'm proud of having finished my 23rd B. A. A. marathon, but

I'm ashamed of having taken more than three hours. That's my worst time ever."[23] His three children for the first time got to see him run a part of the B. A. A. Marathon. The two brothers, ages 7 and 10, and their older sister, 11, had a commanding view from which to watch their daddy; a window from a room in the Lenox Hotel. Later that evening, Clarence H. DeMar went to work in the composing room of the *Herald*. His children were photographed at his work station admiring their father, who was adorned in white shirt and tie covered with a printer's apron. The photograph, which ran on the front page of the newspaper, depicted DeMar commencing that very night's work, most of it up on his feet for the duration of his night shift.[24]

The white-haired "Bricklayer" Bill Kennedy, who had won back in 1917 and finished 85th the previous year, succeeded once more in finishing the race, in 24th place — his 27th finish in his twenty-eighth B. A. A. Marathon appearance. After the ordeal, he was spry and willing to converse.

> "Sometimes they ask me why I don't give up marathoning," he cracked. "I always tell 'em I'd rather give up brick-laying. Honest, I get more tired laying bricks than I do running these things." He skipped off smartly toward the shower room.[25]

Pvt. Andrew "Hawk" Zamparelli, who had traveled all the way from Texas despite a sore knee, courageously tried to make a race of it for as long as he could. He knew it was just a matter of time before he would have to bow out. But Hawk did not bow out. He was determined to finish and he did — in agony, four minutes and twenty-three seconds behind DeMar, and just ahead of Bill Kennedy, in 23rd place.

George Demeter, in his traditional role, was waiting at the finish line with the laurel wreath.[26] This year the wreath was not imported from the Olympic valley in Greece, due to the expanding war in Europe. Wrote Will Cloney, "It was a home-grown specimen, because the laurel picking in Greece isn't so good these days."[27] He was not simply being facetious, despite his style. The *Globe* headlines for the day after the marathon, Sunday, April 20, stated the grim news: "NAZIS GAIN IN GREECE: Waves Push Southward at Terrific Cost."[28]

Marathon winner Les Pawson, who had been defeated in his reelection bid for alderman last November, had been a mill hand until recently. He was currently employed as a foreman of a public park, but he was hoping to land a better job, and following in the footsteps of Walter Young and Ellison Brown, used his short period of high visibility to get the word out. His wife, Betty, was expecting a second child soon.

Pawson was asked to assess his performance. He modestly replied:

> I am 36 years old, an age when most athletes are washed up, but I can honestly say that this was my best Marathon race. The time itself proves it. It is faster than when I set the record in 1933 and at no time during my other two victo-

ries was I as strong as in this race.... I feel that my race today would have been under the record, perhaps better than 2 hours 27 minutes had it been a cool day.[29]

No one doubted Pawson's factual basis or his sincerity; he was never known to boast. He had a few more points to express:

I was after this one. This is a race I wanted to win and badly. A three-time winner of the Boston Marathon! There are only two of us. Clarence De Mar [*sic*] and myself. Now I suppose Tarzan Brown will come back next year and win his third Marathon. You never can tell what Tarzan will do.[30]

Ellison Brown was the athlete that came to mind when Pawson considered another runner that could achieve three B. A. A. Marathon wins. That was high praise.

The 1941 marathon would make a good candidate as the one from which Tarzan Brown paused to take an invigorating plunge in cool water, though this is pure speculation. On the one hand, the best supporting reason for ascribing the incident to 1941 would first and foremost be the temperature that day — a hefty 74° F and lots of brilliant sunshine. Moreover, Brown did not make an official finish that year. On the other hand, at least one newspaper account of the marathon counters the likelihood, or at least gives reason to suggest that the watering holes were not the lake or pond in Natick. The *Herald* reported that Brown stayed in the running for seventeen miles, which is seven miles beyond Lake Cochituate and Fiske Pond.[31] A seventeen-mile run would take Brown by Newton Lower Falls, where the course spans the Charles River. A version of the story exists that says Tarzan Brown jumped into the Charles.

It is possible that, like so much of the lore surrounding the man, the incident has grown into legendary status but never actually transpired. This view is supported by author Tom Derderian. Derderian ostensibly pinpointed the purported source of the story, which he traced to one Fred Brown. Fred Brown, no relation to Ellison Brown, was a competitive runner from a whole family of runners, the chief organizer of the North Medford running club for many years, and the bitter rival and nemesis of Jock Semple, as both men competed to recruit new running talent to their respective athletic organizations. According to Derderian, Fred Brown related this story to Nason, and the rest, as they say, is legend. According to Derderian: "With tongue in cheek, Fred told Nason that one year during the race Tarzan had jumped into Lake Cochituate in Natick and liked the cool water so much he stayed. Although it never happened, it was considered plausible and it made a good story. Nason told it and retold it."[32] Derderian attached no specific year to Fred Brown's story nor did he give the year Brown told it to Nason. Exactly which year Tarzan Brown *did not make* his mythic plunge is indeterminate. Derderian did not cite any source(s), not did he give any evidence for the conclusion he reached — that "it never happened."

In the newspaper accounts of the 1941 B. A. A. Marathon, no use of the term "Heartbreak Hill" can be found. Tom Fitzgerald of the *Globe* came closest, when he wrote, "The cruelest test of this premier of all marathon races comes at the *heart-breaking slope*, which is crowned by the spires of Boston College" (emphasis added).[33] Jerry Nason, by consensus the father of the phrase, also did not employ the term that year, though the opportunity came up. Wrote Nason, "Pawson won his race at Lake st., at the backslope of *the last big hill*" (emphasis added).[34]

Interestingly, in the premarathon writing in 1941, in a discussion of Kelley's marathon history Nason recounted the 1936 race, the year lore holds he invented the "Heartbreak Hill" sobriquet. Returning to the moment that gave rise to the name, Nason wrote:

> When he [Brown] hit the hills in Newton he must have led Kelley by nearly a mile.
> So what does Kelley do? He decides to go after the Indian and on the hills at that. Nobody every put the watch to him, but Johnny must have set an all-time record racing over the hills from Auburndale to Boston College that afternoon.
> It was right near the crest of *the last big one* that he caught the wobbling redskin. It had been a pulsating pursuit, but a tactical blunder, for Kelley left all of his running on the hills (emphasis added).[35]

Nason referred to that specific ultimate elevated piece of Newton real estate in the very context of which (and when) he is alleged to have devised its proper name, but curiously did not employ its use on the occasion. Nor did Nason refer to heartbreak of any sort in connection with Kelley's marathon fortunes.

The fifth annual Salisbury Beach Marathon, also called the Lawrence-to-the-Sea Marathon, held May 30, 1941, was a star-studded affair, with Cote, DeMar, Heinicke, Kelley, Pawson and Semple competing. The late entry of Ellison Brown added to the excitement.

The year before, Brown had smashed the course record and it was widely reported and accepted at the time that he had set a new *world* record for an official marathon as well. This year, that triumphant achievement was unceremoniously downgraded. "Road construction caused a change in the course last year and deprived the flying Brown of a new world mark of 2:27:29," Herbert Ralby of the *Globe* explained.[36] What turned out to be a shortened course had corrupted the results. Thus, the swift 1940 performance by Brown, just like that, was dismissed, though the responsibility for the miscalculated distance was obviously not his. The 1939 record for the course set by the late Pat Dengis, 2:34:54.4, was reestablished as the mark to beat. Dengis' ability to bait Tarzan, in one sense, had not been constrained by his untimely death.

At 12:45 the marathon commenced in front of the Lawrence City Hall. From about the fourth mile onward, Kelley and Cote assumed the roles of dual leaders. They ran alongside each other for nearly thirteen miles, to mile seventeen. Pawson, meanwhile, followed closely behind, characteristically keeping them in view. The *Globe* reported that "Ellison 'Tarzan' Brown, who won the race a year ago in sensational time, ran well for a few miles, but then dropped back and finally out of the race shortly after the 10-mile mark." [37] No information about his condition was publicly forthcoming, but Brown was suffering from an undiagnosed pulled tendon in his right leg. He was mum about the injury and began the race thinking it was healed.

Kelley began to show signs of fatigue and Pawson took that opportune moment to exchange places with him. Cote also saw an opportunity, to take sole possession of the front-runner's position. This he did, putting a two-hundred-yard gap between the second-place Pawson and himself. Cote's new bride, on honeymoon with her husband, rode in an official car behind him on the course. The Canadian, most observers agreed, was running with power and appeared ready to secure the victory. Pawson, however, was not ready to concede.

At mile twenty-three, Pawson made his challenge, passing Cote and seizing the lead. Now it was Cote who was called upon to respond. He was not about to lie down. He reached into his reserves, and found what he needed. Cote spurted by Pawson and then some, putting fifty yards between them. But he was expending too much energy in that exhausting effort. Pawson, running smoothly, calmly made another bid for Cote's position. With the finish line about a mile and three-quarters away, Pawson surpassed the tiring Cote. Pawson continued his sprint, unchallenged, to the finish-line tape, building up a 500-yard advantage. His time, 2 hours, 31 minutes, 28 seconds, without any doubt broke the Dengis course mark. Cote followed Pawson over the line, two minutes, four seconds later, for a second-place finish. Don Heinicke, Dengis' protégé, finished third behind Cote, in 2 hours, 36 minutes, 51 seconds. Kelley was fourth, a whopping 6 minutes, 17 seconds behind Heinicke. Clarence H. DeMar, incidentally, finished the grind, taking twelfth place. He went over the three-hour mark, to his unmatchable dissatisfaction, finishing in 3 hours, 1 minute, 17 seconds. Semple finished next, in 3 hours, 2 minutes, 31 seconds.

Cote took the results good-naturedly, though he was filled with disappointment to fail in the midst of his honeymoon. He later "blamed his collapse in the late stages of the race on the fact that he hadn't eaten his usual hearty meal before the grind and as a result weakened in the final miles."[38] He managed to find consolation; the taste of a good-smoking cigar.

Tarzan Brown passed on a majority of the racing events that summer, including the 1941 Bunker Hill Day handicap race and the several Independence Day races that were annually held. Without his participation, those annual road races that took place, despite a dwindling number of civilian runners available to participate, offered real chances for other runners to win the top prizes, although Kelley and Gregory seemed to have filled the void left by Brown's absence. Still, the hiatus of Brown from running enabled other, less-successful runners to increase their levels of confidence, an important ingredient in winning running performance.

The sporting event that had captured the greatest part of the public's imagination and interest that summer was not in the running realm but in major league baseball. New York Yankee centerfielder Joe DiMaggio's consecutive hitting streak — 56 straight games — came to an end on July 17, a record that has withstood serious challenge since that summer of 1941.

The 15-kilometer Road Race in Fall River, a part of the feature events on behalf of the American Legion's state convention, was held on the night of August 21. Brown, hopeful his troublesome tendon problem was in the past, was eager to determine that it was no longer a factor and get back to winning races. He, Kelley and Pawson were on hand on the Massachusetts South Coast to compete in the event, along with McGlone, Smith, Coleman, Cook, and others. A raucous 20,000 spectators watched as Johnny Kelley beat the field in 52 minutes, 19 seconds. Kelley led the entire way. John Coleman of the B. A. A. club was second, 41 seconds behind Kelley, in 53 minutes flat. Ed Cook took show. Pawson (54:53) and Brown (54:58) finished fourth and fifth, respectively. The newspapers did not give a detailed account of the event, nor any explanations for Brown's continued difficulties. How much Brown was bothered by the tendon is not known.

The Kingston fairgrounds annual 10-mile race around the half-mile oval dirt track took place ten days later, on Saturday afternoon, August 30. Ed Cook of New London led for over three-quarters of the distance, and then Les Pawson, not to be denied, at the end of the eighth mile seized the lead and captured the first-place honors, beating Cook by twenty-five yards; his time, 53 minutes, 17 seconds. Third-place winner Clayton Farrar, also of New London, finished in 54 minutes, 1 second. The familiar names of Joe Smith, Fred McGlone, and Linden Dempster were the next runners, respectively, to cross the finish line. The *Providence Journal* reported, "Tarzan Brown of Westerly, who started in spite of a pulled tendon, was forced to drop out at the end of six miles."[39] This was the first public word of Brown's injury.

The fourth annual Providence 12-mile handicap road race, held on Labor Day, September 1, was touted as another Brown, Kelley and Pawson free-for-all, but in actuality, the event turned out to be a rather tepid affair; for the most part, it was all Johnny Kelley's. Of a total field of only 35 runners, the four scratchmen — Brown, Kelley, Pawson and Gregory — were assessed enormous seven-minute delays. For Brown and Pawson, those outrageously figured sanctions did not make a whole lot of difference, for after completing four miles, both Brown and Pawson abandoned their efforts; the former because of his painful tendon and severe leg stiffness and the latter due to a sharp stitch in his side. The *Westerly Sun* carried the condensed story under the headline, "Brown Drops Out Of Both Holiday Races."[40] No details or particulars about Brown's condition were provided.

Kelley, when able to start, steadily and with determined certainty made up ground, as he passed first one and then another runner ahead of him. It took him ten miles to reach the front of the pack. He held on for the last two miles with no visible letup, increasing his lead to a full quarter mile, ensuring victory. Kelley received the time prize and the first-place prize. He finished nearly two minutes ahead of the second-place winner, the University of Connecticut student Charles Robbins, who was entered in only his third competitive race. The third-place prize went to fellow scratchman Lou Gregory. Gregory had done some serious road work recently, both on his feet and behind the wheel, having competed in three marathons, in Schenectady, Syracuse and Toronto, all within an eight-day span. It was, to say the least, Tarzan Brown-like in its conception.

Clarence H. DeMar, incidentally, managed an eleventh-place finish, completing the course in 1 hour, 20 minutes, 1 second. Jock Semple finished seventeenth.

It became clear to Brown that the tendon would need more time to heal, and that the risk of reinjuring it could jeopardize missing more races, including next spring's B. A. A. Marathon. The best thing to do, Brown concluded, was to stop running competitively for the remainder of the year. This would allow the tendon to strengthen, even though Brown could not avoid depending upon it completely, for chores connected to basic survival, such as woodchopping, harvesting, and a host of other tasks still required his efforts and the leg and tendon's constant use.

Johnny Kelley, without Brown to challenge him, took the New England 25-K title in Somerville, Massachusetts, and the National 25-K title in Everett, both in September. The attention of the sporting world turned to major league baseball once more, as Ted Williams finished the regular season with an astounding .406 batting average. Fearlessly and gamely, he had chosen to play in both scheduled games of a doubleheader on the final day of the season rather than sit out the competition with a batting average that would have been arithmetically rounded upward to .400. On that final day, the Red Sox leftfielder went 4 for 6.

On October 2, Kelley finished second to Fred McGlone in the Salem-to-Lawrence 30-K Run. In the middle of that race, Les Pawson was hit by a car, sustaining injuries to his leg muscle and arm, serious enough to need to be rushed to the Middleton Clover Hill Hospital. No broken bones were found during X-rays, but the bruises were grave, more serious than at first perceived to be. A slice deep into his calf muscle caused what would be a constant source of discomfort, especially during prolonged activity. It would take a lot longer than Pawson originally was led to believe for it to be fully healed.

None of the newspaper reports at the time of the incident disclosed the identity of the driver or a description of the vehicle, or gave the suggestion that such information was even known. Six months later, in a *Providence Journal* report on the B. A. A. Marathon, sportswriter Joe Nutter mentioned that Pawson "was struck down by *an official's* car" (emphasis added) in the course of the race.[41] This was a previously unreported detail. No corroborating word, detail or more precise identification of the person responsible for the accident could be found in the press.

On the tenth day of October 1941, a second daughter, Marlene, was born to Ethel and Ellison Brown. In time she would be given the Narragansett name Mish-Na-Nah, or Red Cedar.

The National Marathon Championship at Yonkers, held November 10, was won by (Bernard) Joe Smith, the 6'2" milkman from Medford. Thirty-three runners from an initial field of fifty-four survived a downpour and a hailstorm to finish the marathon, the last four miles of the course featured inside the Empire City racetrack. Smith ran most of the marathon from the back of the pack. Before entering the racetrack, he had charged forward to catch up to Heinicke and then Cote, the defending champion. Passing them by, Smith then caught the leaders, Kelley and McGlone, running together, matching stride for stride. All three runners— Kelley, McGlone and Smith — entered the Empire City complex running three abreast. After two miles, Kelley faltered some, and Smith and McGlone battled each other for the title. McGlone challenged Smith three times "in the last three-sixteenths of a mile, but to no avail," the *New York Times* reported.[42] Smith beat McGlone by fifty yards and 9.8 seconds, finishing in 2 hours, 36 minutes, 6.8 seconds.

In the traditional Thanksgiving Day run in Berwick, Pennsylvania, the 32nd annual edition, Johnny Kelley placed second to Lou Gregory, who completed the run in 48 minutes, 25 seconds, and beat Kelley by twenty-five seconds.[43] Coleman was third, Kleinerman fourth, Cooper fifth, McGlone sixth, Pawson seventh and Heinicke eighth in that one. Pawson had tried to ignore his injuries and run the Berwick race. He experienced much more pain than he expected in his leg, and was compelled to decide that it would be best to take a break from competitive distance running for the time being. His expectations at the time were to be ready for the North Medford 20-mile race in mid-March.

Ten days later, on December 7, Japanese military planes bombed the United States fleet at Pearl Harbor in Hawaii. Twenty-three hundred deaths resulted and nineteen ships were sunk or damaged in the early morning attack. The next day, the United States declared war on Japan. Three days later, on December 11, the United States declared war on Italy and Germany in response to their declarations of war on the United States. Against this backdrop, running footraces seemed a somewhat trivial matter.

28

"Indian Comet" Along the Comeback Trail — 1942

The eleventh annual North Medford 20-Mile Road Race nearly did not take place. The North Medford Club over the winter had decided against sponsoring the race. Four club members, all runners — Joe Smith, Andre Brunelle, Fred Brown and Lou Young — formed a committee and conducted the event themselves. Runners were clearly their primary focus; they purchased twenty-five trophies to offer as prizes instead of the usual ten and double the usual five medals. The race was scheduled for the afternoon of March 21, 1942.

Tarzan Brown's name was listed[1] among the sixty-one entries, at number 60, but he did not show up. Neither did Les Pawson, a three-time past winner, who was still feeling the effects of last fall's car accident on his leg muscles. He had begun training at the beginning of March, "and thought he had gained his usual tip top condition until he stretched his distances beyond 20 miles. Then he discovered his bruised leg muscles couldn't stand the strain. They started to pain so he had to quit."[2] The 37-year-old Pawson had a new occupation, despite the injuries sustained in October. He was now a defense plant guard, assisting the war effort on the home front.

Quebecois Gerard Cote, winner in 1939, could not make the trip to the States. Johnny Kelley, the defending champion and winner of six of ten editions of the race, did make an appearance, but was forced to drop out after seventeen miles, suffering the ill effects of a head cold. The winning runner was John Coleman, a twenty-year-old insurance clerk from Worcester. Fred McGlone was second, and Heinicke finished third.

Other young racers were stealing their share of the first-place prizes in the races which traditionally were held in advance of the B. A. A. Marathon. Eighteen-year-old newcomer Joe Morgan won the Reddish 10-miler. The Presentation 10-Mile Road Race, looked upon by some as a B. A. A. Marathon barometer and sharing in common some of the course, was won by twenty-one-year-old Charley Robbins, the former University of Connecticut cross-country captain. The time prize was won by Coleman.

Ellison Brown had not been heard from nor had he entered any of the early spring races. An April 9 article in the *Westerly Sun*, under the headline, "Indian Runner May Seek Third Victory In Historic Hub Grind," was mostly noncommittal in terms of what could be expected from Brown, but it did include the fact that he "has been working out regularly for several weeks."[3] The *Sun* went on to warn that Brown's training lacked the element of competition and that that "may hurt his chances" for success in the Hopkinton-to-Boston marathon.

As late as April 16, the absence of Brown's name on the official entry list confounded the sportswriters on the marathon beat. Fred Foye's writing represented the typical comments:

> ... no word of his (Brown's) 1942 condition has been received by even those closest to him from Westerly, R. I.
>
> Abe Soloveitzik, sports editor of the *Westerly Sun*, was asked about Brown today and he answered: "You fellows up in Boston know almost as much as I do."
>
> Soloveitzik then made local contact with one Tom Salimeno, known about Westerly as Tarzan's "manager" and it was learned that Brown has been in training since mid-February and that when last seen four days ago he was still planning to enter the marathon.[4]

Would Brown enter, and would he make the deadline for doing so? One new complication could cause difficulty. April 19th, Patriots' Day, by the calendar was scheduled to fall on a Sunday. The usual policy in the land of blue laws on such an occasion was to hold the marathon the next day, on the Monday following. The marathon had never been conducted on a Sunday in its entire history. Wartime and its attendant preparations demanded special considerations. In the interests of creating as little interference as possible with the national defense industry, Governor Leverett Saltonstall of Massachusetts recommended in a letter to B. A. A. Marathon chairman Dezzy Wadsworth that the marathon take place on Sunday, when the most people could view it and not miss any valuable weekday work time in the defense plants. The plan was readily approved by Wadsworth on April 13, just six days before Patriots' Day. The *Boston Traveler* reported that same day that "every entrant was notified by mail today. And official notification, too, went to all police heads along the race route and to any official connected with the staging in any way."[5] The *Westerly Sun* carried an AP report of the date change in its sports pages on April 13 as well. Would Brown read or hear of it in time to be in Boston on Sunday, not Monday? Sportswriter Fred Foye and marathon race officials might have been wondering the same thing, for Foye added, "Post entries aren't supposed to be accepted but B. A. A. officials will be more than glad to accept the late entries of Leslie Pawson, Tarzan Brown or Canada's Gerry Cote, all of them champions of recent years who are not included in the field to date."[6]

Clarence H. DeMar was a late entry because one of his children was "dangerously ill with rheumatic fever and [he] hesitated about running."[7] He was given the number 1 to wear in the marathon, usually reserved for the defending champion. Pawson, the 1941 winner, would have been the defending champion, but he would sit out the 1942 marathon, unable to defend his title due to lingering soreness mainly in his calf muscles sustained in that automobile accident in Lawrence. Unless DeMar's son's condition deteriorated, DeMar stated his plans to be in Hopkinton in time for the start.

It was reported that Paul Donato had been inducted into the Army between the time he sent in his entry and race day. Stationed at Fort Devens, in Massachusetts, there was a chance he might make it to the marathon. As of April 17, he had not received his superior's permission.

As the clock ticked off the minutes to the Sunday noon start, as of late Saturday, April 18, Brown's entry still had not been received, nor had race officials heard a word from him or from Tippy Salimeno on his behalf. Joe Nutter, in the *Providence Sunday Journal* the next day, April 19, the morning of the marathon, stated straight-out that Rhode Island contenders Pawson and "Ellison Myer [*sic*] 'Tarzan' Brown, the Narragansett Indian from Rhode Island's South County, will not run."[8] Nutter offered this account:

"Tarzan" is living in Charlestown, R. I., and is working now as a farmhand for Tom Browning. He trained to some extent during the winter months, but dropped his running around mid-March. He said last night he had decided to pass up the marathon this year, but that he would continue to keep himself in shape with the hope of getting back into the B. A. A. race in 1943. He felt that he was not in the proper condition to make a credible showing in today's grind."[9]

Springtime was an extremely busy time for farm workers, and Brown had little free time to train. It made some sense that he forgo the marathon if not in good athletic condition.

If being on a fellow athlete's list as a favorite for winning the marathon made any difference in actuality, Fred McGlone, the twenty-seven-year-old[10] freight train brakeman, would have won the 46th edition of the B. A. A. Marathon with ease. He was the number one choice of Pawson, the 1941 winner; of Cote, the 1940 winner and course recordholder; of Johnny Kelley, the 1935 winner and four-time runner-up; of Joe Smith, the National Marathon (at Yonkers) winner; and of Don Heinicke, the third-place finisher the past two years. McGlone was also the majority choice of the *Globe* board of selection experts. The *Globe's* own marathon scribe, Jerry Nason, differed, however; on Saturday, the day before the race, Nason picked Johnny Kelley to win it.[11]

The next morning, on Sunday, Nason had a scoop. Under the subheadline, "Indian Comet Seeks 3d Win," he presented his *Globe* readership with the following tale: "Yesterday afternoon at about 2 o'clock a man named

Tippy Salimeno stepped into a pay station in a Westerly, R.I. café, dropped some change in the slot, and in a two-minute telephone conversation turned today's big Marathon race completely upside down. This was the dramatic, last-minute entry of Ellison (Tarzan) Brown, the fabulous Indian foot racer, because Tippy Salimeno was the agent through whom the 'Romping Redskin' declared himself in on today's pavement pageant and sent the experts scurrying for cover."[12]

Marathon manager Thomas Kanaly accepted Brown's late entry, the 145th (and last), despite the rolls having officially closed by the deadline of the past Wednesday. The exception for Brown was made "because of his former exploits in the race," Nason reported.[13] Although he did not alter his pick with Brown now entered in the competition, Nason concluded his piece with this hedge: "Once more, due to dramatic late developments, it would surprise nobody should a Brown start the race (Walter) and another finish first (Tarzan)."[14] In 1939, Brown had submitted an eleventh-hour entry into the marathon, and proceeded to shatter the course record. If this fragment of history were to repeat itself, Nason's conclusion could be right on target.

Sunday was a gray overcast day with temperatures in the low forties and no significant breeze. Ellison Brown "again lived up to his title of mystery man," Joe Nutter observed, "by stalking into the Lucky Rock Manor at Hopkinton shortly before noon and a few moments later took his place at the starting line in a dramatic bid for another title."[15] At the crack from Walter Brown's pistol, just 113 hopeful starters set out in an eastward direction as young sprinter Johnny Barlong dashed ahead to lead the pack. Shortly thereafter he was relieved by another short-term front-runner, Joseph Meo. By then the quartet of John Coleman, Johnny Kelley, Fred McGlone and Charlie Robbins emerged as a unified pacesetting formation. They checked into the first two stations—Framingham and Natick — as the top four. In contrast, Tarzan Brown, "the Indian, failed to put on his usual starting burst and was left in the pack as the runners started the long grind," according to the *Westerly Sun*.[16] The newspaper did not mince words when it stated that from a physical standpoint, "Brown's condition was actually pitiful."[17] On this most observers agreed. What they could not agree upon was just where Brown bowed out of the race — that was a matter of some dispute. By the *Sun's* reckoning, Brown "ran a little better than ten miles"[18] before throwing in the towel, which would have put him just beyond the Natick check station approaching Natick Center. Over four months later, it revised that estimate, stating that "he failed to go more than eight miles."[19] The *Providence Journal* contested even that much performance, claiming Brown "was never even a remote contender for the honors in this race. He was out of the race before the first checking station." If so, Brown would not even have reached 5.3 miles. The *Herald's* John English put Brown's departure at the midway point of the marathon, in Wellesley.[20] Tom Fitzgerald put Brown's exit point the furthest along of any of the observers, at mile sixteen. He wrote that Brown "found the pace entirely too much for him," and then continued with this exclusive claim, "so he dunked himself in the river at Newton Lower Falls and hopped into a waiting car."[21] Fitzgerald's account cannot be verified, nor was it corroborated by any other reporter at the time. But there is some reason to doubt it. The weather that afternoon was overcast and 44° F, not necessarily the kind of day where an instant cooling-off is an imperative. Moreover, on the day after the marathon the *Herald* ran a small item the length of one paragraph, entitled "Anybody Here Seen Ellison T. Brown?"[22] The whereabouts of Brown on the marathon course, according to the piece, were "a deep, dark mystery."[23] The *Herald* recounted that Brown "was checked in 14th position at South Framingham and 25th at Natick square. Thereafter he was missing."[24] If Brown had stayed in the marathon all the way to Newton Lower Falls as Fitzgerald alleged, there ought to have been a check of Brown at the station after Natick, which was Wellesley, at 12.5 miles. If the *Herald* piece was accurate, no record of Brown existed beyond the Natick station. How Brown could have reached Newton Lower Falls and the waters of the Charles River without being recorded at the Wellesley station first is a puzzle. (Wellesley station is encountered more than two miles before Newton Lower Falls along the course.) Or, if one of the other accounts is right and Brown had dropped out of the race at a point much earlier along the course, at least before the Wellesley checking point, is it reasonable to think he would have continued to travel another three miles or so along the course until he reached Newton Lower Falls so he could take a dunk in the river? If he dropped out at Newton Lower Falls, it seems plausible that he would jump into the river there. If he dropped out somewhere else, it seems unlikely that he would then travel to the river to make a splash.

In any case, Brown did not show up at "the Exeter street building, as far as could be learned, but apparently was picked up by his manager, changed his clothes in the car and went directly home," the *Herald* surmised for its readers.[25]

At Auburndale, the checkpoint before the start of the Newton hills, it was Coleman, McGlone and Kelley in the one, two, three positions; Lou Gregory hailed fourth; Joe Smith, fifth; and a rather quiet Gerard Cote was running sixth. On the way up the first grade, Coleman made a bid with a burst of a sprint to leave McGlone and Kelley behind. Coleman constructed a thirty-five yard lead, as Johnny Kelley weakened, ready to break into a walk. McGlone, on the other hand, pursued Coleman with everything he had and reached him by Center Street. On the final grade, McGlone led the field, and Coleman, now burned out, was soon to drop out completely. Gregory and Smith were not burned out, having conserved their energy behind the fast-paced trio. Up Heartbreak Hill Gregory flew and reached a leg-worn McGlone near the peak at Boston College. Gregory assumed front-runner status just

prior to reaching the Lake Street check-in station, but very close behind him
was Medford milkman Joe Smith. McGlone and Kelley, both slowed by the
earlier pace for which they were in large part responsible, were still third and
fourth, respectively. Before Coolidge Corner, Smith had overtaken Gregory,
subsuming the lead, and the two ran in rapid record pace to the Exeter Street
finish line, both runners snapping the worsted under Cote's course record, a
record they managed to conquer by their speed over the final two miles. Smith
set a new world record, 2 hours, 26 minutes, 51.2 seconds, as he finished
about two hundred yards ahead of Gregory. Gregory, with a time of 2 hours,
28 minutes, 3.6 seconds, bettered Cote's old mark by nearly a half minute,
even as he placed second. Carl Maroney of North Medford, finished in third
place, about a mile behind Gregory. Fourth place belonged to Don Heinicke,
who had managed to improve from the ninth spot as recently as Lake Street
and had checked in sixth at Coolidge Corner. An exhausted Johnny Kelley,
forced to walk a number of times, held on for fifth place. Cote was sixth at
Wellesley, the halfway point, and sixth at the end.

The ordeal of Fred McGlone, who had been many observers' marathon
favorite, deserves mention. McGlone had gamely run the Newton hills but
the battle with those inclines compounded with the grueling pace of the first
ten miles took a disastrous toll on his leg muscles and his energy reserves.
McGlone lost his footing and toppled to the pavement three to six times in
the last mile.[26] Flat on the pavement within eyesight of the finish line, police
and spectators provided unrequested assistance in helping the runner to his
feet. McGlone, according to sportswriter Herbert Ralby, "was too weak to
more than half-heartedly brush them off,"[27] and he was officially disqualified
from the race by marathon referee Dan Ferris for having received assistance
in violation of the racing rules. McGlone's seventh-place finish behind Cote
was expunged, which moved up each finisher behind his, starting with Bill
Steiner, who had finished eighth but would now be accorded the seventh-place
prize.

It was doubtful, in Bob Dunbar's view, whether McGlone "actually
benefited by the actions of the crowd or the policemen."[28] Boston mayor Maurice Tobin sided strongly with McGlone against the disqualification. The
mayor claimed he saw McGlone ward off the arms of aid extended to him.
The athlete had also voiced objection to the help though his vocalizations were
unduly feeble due to his weakened physical condition. It was ultimately
decided and announced by Walter A. Brown that McGlone should share a
duplicate seventh-place prize for his courageous effort, since he had no control over the acts of others at the time in the physical state he was in, and
since the assistance had made no consequential difference to the outcome of
the competition. Dan Ferris had been effectively overruled.

No comparisons to Ellison Brown's disqualification in the 1936 Berlin
Olympics were presented in any of the newspapers, though some including

the *Globe* recalled an earlier Olympic incident, the Johnny Hayes victory following Dorando Pietri's collapse and assistance in 1908. Dorando, unlike McGlone, was actually carried over the finish line with the intention of helping him snag the victory. That incident could not serve as a precedent in this circumstance.[29]

At the finish line, Smith was crowned with a laurel wreath from California, not Greece, but it was offered ceremoniously by Costas Kotsias, the mayor in exile from Athens, Greece, with George Demeter's blessing. The Providence newspaper recorded the mayor's words: "'The Battle of Marathon marked the defeat of the barbarians,' said the refugee Mayor in making the presentation. 'In historic Boston, the Athens of America, this event symbolic of victory, promises that in the near future a triumphant soldier will arrive announcing to the American people and the world once again a victory over the barbarians.'"[30] Boston newspapers glossed over the exiled official's pronouncement.

Jock Semple finished fourteenth, in 2 hours, 49 minutes, 3 seconds, ahead of Brunelle, Donato, Robbins, Giard, Wicklund, DeMar and Fred Brown. Semple was now a member of the United States Navy. After Pearl Harbor, he had gone down to the Navy recruitment storefront to sign up. Semple, in his inimitable manner of speech, related the circumstances of that first encounter with a desk sergeant who initially refused to allow him to join:

> "Can't come in," said the sergeant at the desk.
> "Why not?" I said.
> "Flat feet," he said.
> I looked down, and by God he was right!
> "Aren't you Johnny Semple, the marathon runner?" asked the sergeant behind him?
> "I want to join the Gene Tunney program," I said. "I want to be in the Navy. These dogs have run almost a hundred marathons and they have carried me around the world the equivalent of two times. America's in the war now, and I want to fight, and I won't take No. Besides, who's going to see my feet?"
> "Let him in," said the second sergeant. "He looks like the kind who plans to die with his boots on anyway."[31]

Jock Semple served honorably in the Navy during the war years but always managed to find a way to make it to Hopkinton in time for the start of the Patriots' Day marathon.

Clarence H. DeMar finished his 88th full marathon, coming in under three hours; in 2 hours, 58 minutes, 14 seconds. He finished in 25th place, which was moved up to 24th following McGlone's disqualification. DeMar was content with his performance on that cool afternoon.

It was the *Globe's* Tom Fitzgerald, not Jerry Nason, who utilized the expression "Heartbreak Hill" in his reportage of the 1942 B. A. A. Marathon. Referring to the point in the marathon where John Coleman withdrew,

Fitzgerald wrote: "With the Kelley-Coleman-McGlone domination disrupted, Gregory and Smith promptly took over. It was the schoolmaster [Gregory] who gained the advantage first, churning strongly up 'Heartbreak' Hill which stretches up to the spires of Boston College."[32]

Only "*Heartbreak*" was surrounded by quotation marks, though *Hill* was also given an uppercase "H." In case anyone found the name unfamiliar, Fitzgerald aided the reader by giving its location. No other sportswriters employed the term in the coverage of the marathon that year.

The *Westerly Sun* reported in September that Brown had competed in only that one race that entire 1942 season, the Boston Marathon. It was news, then, when Brown began to train diligently again "in daily workouts" under the careful scrutiny of Tippy Salimeno in July with an eye toward "the comeback trail."[33] The Pat Dengis Memorial Marathon, which took place September 12, was the first competitive run Brown would enter. He and Salimeno headed to Baltimore together on Thursday afternoon, September 10. The course's start and end was at Homewood Field, with the intervening hilly miles careening through the northern suburbs of Baltimore.

Lou Gregory, in late June, had undergone hospitalization for an appendectomy. Though still recovering from the surgery and in some discomfort, the school principal entered the marathon mostly in the spirit of honoring his friend, Pat Dengis. This was his first competition since the operation. Little did Gregory expect to finish first, which he did in 2 hours, 40 minutes, 19.5 seconds, over nine minutes ahead of the second-place finisher, Fred McGlone. The immediate result of Gregory's exhausting expenditure of energy, just after crossing the finish line, was that "he was taken violently ill." An on-site trainer, Jimmy Benson of Johns Hopkins, prepared to have Gregory taken by ambulance to the nearest hospital emergency room, but Gregory "rallied considerably," and that trip was spared.[34] Gregory's major fear was not his immediate medical condition but that his enlistment in the U.S. Navy would be jeopardized if word of his postrace circumstance reached them.

Ellison Brown finished fourth in that marathon, in 2 hours, 58 minutes, 35 seconds, behind McGlone and William Jones. Brown had a little trouble at the very end of the race establishing his official finish. The *Baltimore Sun* devoted the last paragraph of its coverage to Brown, describing what occurred:

Ellison (Tarzan) Brown of Westerly, R. I., almost missed that [finish] line. He charged down the track, saw the open gate leading to the showers and ran headlong into the building behind the stands, failing to finish by some six feet after racing 26 miles, 383 yards. Officials quickly sought him out, had him complete the race and but for a few seconds added to his time, there was no damage, for no one come [*sic*] in between and he held on to fourth place.[35]

Well-known local runner Don Heinicke was the defending two-time champion, the only winner the Pat Dengis Memorial Marathon had had since its inception. This year Heinicke could complete only twenty-two miles of the course before dropping out.

The Indian Citizenship Act, enacted June 2, 1924, had granted citizenship to all Native Americans born within the national borders who were not yet citizens. This act provided the legal foundation for conscripting native-born American Indian men into the United States military service for the first time, notwithstanding the fact that in every one of the United States of America's military conflicts, including the Second World War, Native Americans volunteered to enlist in the highest percentage of any other subgroup of citizens. By the end of August 1942 the *New York Times* was able to report, "Of the 60,000 Indian males in the United States and possessions between the ages of 21 and 44, approximately 8,800 are serving in the armed forces of the nation. Army officials maintain that if the entire population was enlisting in the same proportion as Indians there would be no need for selective service."[36] Indeed among eligible male Native Americans, compliance with the draft registration was "more than 99 per cent complete," according to the Office of Indian Affairs' own statistical records.[37]

Like other male citizens, Brown was required to register for the draft. Both his age and role as a father mandated under regulations then in place that Ellison Brown was ineligible for induction into the army, but there was plenty to do to support the war effort on the home front. Ellison started new employment, working for the C. B. Cottrell Company, which operated an iron foundry in Westerly, Rhode Island, and had taken on defense contracts as did many other companies at that time. And, like a number of other firms, Cottrell sponsored a host of organized athletic activities for its employees. Two leagues—a baseball league named the New England Victory League, and a softball league called the Industrial Softball League—were examples of organized sports newly established and supported by defense industries, designed for the participation of their workers. Ellison Brown joined C. B. Cottrell's running club, and was no longer "unattached," but ran races under the colors of Cottrell. His wife, Ethel, also found new work. She worked "for a short while" in a fabric dye manufacturing and processing concern in Bradford, Rhode Island, all the while continuing to oversee and raise her growing family. When it became impossible to continue the schedule of employment and maintain reliable childcare, she was forced to give up working there.[38]

On his second effort along his comeback trail, Tarzan Brown competed in the Pawtuxet Valley road race, held September 20 in central Rhode Island, against Johnny Kelley, John Coleman, Ed Cook, Lloyd Anderson, Ted Vogel and eighteen other speedsters. Of forty-one entrants, only twenty-four showed up at the starting line on race day, a prevalent condition during the war years. Starter Bill Mailliux fired the pistol and sparked the runners to action. Kelley and Coleman battled the entire distance with Brown on their heels. By the last mile, the three were not bunched together. Kelley had found his high gear in the last half mile to win. He crossed the finish line in 46 minutes, 33 seconds. Coleman finished second, in 48 minutes, 2 seconds. Brown was third, fifty-three seconds behind Coleman. He won a third-place prize and a second trophy, one presented to the first Rhode Islander to finish. In an unusual twist to prize disbursement, the top ten finishers had their choice of prizes, beginning in order of their finish. The next ten received medals. Norfolk Young Men's Association runners Cook, Danials, Anderson, and Brunelle finished 4–7. Vogel, B. A. A. affiliated as was Coleman, finished eighth.

Back on June 6, Mary Kelley, Johnny's wife of two years, had died suddenly after just three days in the hospital. Cancer was the cause. Kelley was crushed, but running helped steady the emotional upheaval. One unforeseen consequence of his wife's death was his reclassification by the draft board. Unmarried, he became eligible for the service, and on November 4, 1942, Johnny Kelley, age thirty-five, was inducted into the army according to an AP dispatch.[39] Kelley was sent to Fort Devens, in Massachusetts, for six weeks of basic training and then was transferred to Fort McClellan, Alabama, where he was enrolled in Special Services. Throughout his military service, Kelley managed to continue his running and conditioning, mostly in the evenings.

Within a week of his induction, Kelley received permission to run the National A. A. U. Marathon in Yonkers, New York, which took place on November 9. Kelley led the entourage of forty-four runners going into the second of the final four laps inside the Empire City racetrack. With two laps to go, Fred McGlone passed Kelley to take the lead and went on to win, finishing in 2 hours, 37 minutes, 54 seconds. Kelley, forced into a walk to the finish line, managed to hold on for second place. No word of the identities of the other competitors was given, and it is unknown whether Ellison Brown was among the starters.

On November 22, Pvt. John Kelley retained his New England A. A. A. U. 15-kilometer title in Franklin Park, in Boston. He overtook Ed Cook, who led for the first six miles, to successfully defend his title, in 48 minutes, 48 seconds. Cook finished second, Coleman third. Kelley headed straight to Berwick, Pennsylvania, for his ninth undertaking in the 33rd annual nine-miles-and-change run held each year on Thanksgiving Day. The *Herald* reported that Ellison Brown, who won Berwick in 1940, would participate in that event in 1942, along with Lou Gregory, who was after his fourth win, and McGlone, Coleman and Cook. McGlone did not make it to the event.

The Berwick Marathon was won by John Kelley in 48 minutes, 55 seconds. It was his first win of the event, coming on his ninth attempt. He beat out the second- and third-place finishers, Norman Gordon and Curtis Stone, by sixteen seconds and twenty seconds, respectively. Tarzan Brown finished in eighth place; his time was 51 minutes, 14 seconds. Twelve seconds later came Don Heinicke, for ninth-place honors. Lou Gregory, the defending champion, failed to finish, forced out by a stabbing sideache. Coleman finished fifth and Cook was seventh. At the end of the day, Canadian Scotty Rankine's course record was still in force. He was unable to appear.

Ellison Brown's September-through-November brief campaign on the comeback trail in the fall of 1942 did not yield any first- or second-place victories. That was not exactly how he envisioned it would be. He would decide over the winter months whether he wanted (and was able) to continue the struggle back into both competitive and physical condition.

29

"The Prettiest Thing I Ever Saw in Action"—1943

Racing against such stalwarts as Ellison Brown, Lou Gregory, Don Heinicke, and the veterans Clarence H. DeMar and Jock Semple, Leslie Pawson came roaring back into the competitive running arena to win the North Medford 20-mile run for the fourth time in twelve years, his body sufficiently healed from the automobile accident that put him on the sidelines for the 1942 season. Pawson, thirty-seven years old,[1] father of two, and newly employed as a ship rigger at the Kaiser-Powers shipyard at Providence, swiftly completed the traditional premier race of the running season in 1 hour, 56 minutes 11 seconds, and he ran with extra poundage, weighing in at 142 instead of his usual 135. Pawson, the race's original winner in 1932, beat the second-place Gregory, the Cleveland, New York, school principal scheduled to enter the navy, by a quarter mile. Don Heinicke finished in third place. Clayton Farrar of the Coast Guard was fourth.

Tarzan Brown did not fare well. He finished sixteenth, in 2 hours, 21 minutes, and 29 seconds. The AP dispatch in the *Westerly Sun* did not mention his participation in the race.[2] Bob McGarigle, working for the *Herald*, did. He wrote:

> Tarzan Brown, Westerly, R. I. Indian, finished 15th [*sic*] and was not the least satisfied with the effort. "I'll need more training," said Tarzan. "You can bet I'm going in for it, too. I intend to win that B. A. A. run. It will be my last attempt. It'll be do or die."[3]

Les Pawson said after the race, "I really didn't expect to do it."[4] His wife, Betty, admitted that she had bet one dollar that her husband Les would not win. She did not reveal with whom the wager was made. The good-natured Pawson had a laugh over it and remarked, "Well, that's about all the confidence I really had in myself at the start."[5] The Pawson confidence, a major factor in holding down the competition, by the finish appeared to be back at nearly full strength.

DeMar, who customarily did not start his running season so early, finished "but just about did. Warn't in shape at all," he shrugged.[6] Jock Semple, in the navy, was stationed in Sampson, New York. He described what he had to go through to get to Medford for the race. Semple said, "Well, I started out at midnight from my station, hitchhiked the 60 miles to Syracuse and got there just in time to catch my train at 2:30 in the morning. What would I have done if I had missed my train? Oh, well, I didn't even dare think of that."[7] Semple finished sixth in a field of over fifty runners, his time a respectable 2 hours, 9 minutes, 46 seconds. By his own accounting, Semple had now logged a total of 24,020 miles in his quarter-century of road racing.

The 35th annual William A. Reddish A. A. Ten-Mile handicap road race was held April 4. Arthur Duffey of the *Post* wrote that "Tarzan Brown, the Narragansett Indian and the most colorful of all the Marathon runners" was currently "working in a defense plant in Providence."[8] Duffey posited that Brown was using the Reddish race for an opportunity to work on his running speed for the B. A. A. Marathon two weeks away. The *Herald's* McGarigle shared that view, writing:

> Tarzan Brown obviously is using this event as a sharpener for the coming B. A. A. classic which he vows will be his last effort at long distance racing. He's been an in and outer throughout his career, spectacular at times, extremely sluggish often. It has been a long time since Tarzan has tasted the fruits of victory.[9]

Four runners out of a field of thirty-two were assigned to the scratch line—Ellison Brown, Gerard Cote, Fred McGlone and Eddie Cook. All were held, saddled with a six-minute delay. When the six minutes had passed, Brown made a "brash dash" from the starting line that must have directly caused a terrible stomach cramp, adversely affecting his chances of winning the race and, what was even worse, giving him no chance to tune up his speed capabilities.

Twenty-one-year-old shipyard electrician Ed Shepard and twenty-year-old Lloyd Bairstow, both current residents of Maine, took the first two prizes. Though they had never met until just before the start of the race, the men discovered that they had ridden the same passenger train out of Portland to Boston. Moreover, Shepard and Bairstow had each been corresponding with Jock Semple, who had urged them to train together. Semple himself was unable to make the journey from upstate New York. Speedster Ed Cook took home the time prize. Clayton Farrar finished ninth. Experienced runners McGlone, Cote and Brunelle finished tenth through twelfth, respectively. Tarzan finished fifteenth, with a corrected time for the run of 56 minutes, 29 seconds. Nason observed: "After he ran himself out of a bad cramp the Indian finished with a lot of fire. 'I'm coming along fine,' said the Tarz. And he ain't kidding, chums!"[10]

Ellison Brown ran in a third preliminary springtime race held ahead of the B. A. A. Marathon, the 33rd annual Cathedral 10-mile run on Saturday afternoon, April 10. In this one, Brown finished thirteenth, but had the sixth fastest time overall; his corrected time was 52 minutes, 54 seconds for the distance. Ed Cook, repeating his feat of the previous week, took another time prize, in 50 minutes, 25 seconds. First place belonged to seventeen-year-old Ted Vogel of Watertown, a very promising start to an illustrious running career.[11] Vogel's mother, Sally, accompanied her son to the race but did not watch him run. Instead, while "the pink and freckle-faced Vogel" was charging full steam for the finish line, she was inside the cathedral, praying fervently for his victory.[12] Her prayers, she believed, were answered.

Louis Young, a member of the North Medford club, was second, fourteen seconds behind Vogel. Charlie Robbins, currently helping the war effort working at United Aircraft in Hartford, finished third. In fourth place was Gerard Cote, fine-tuning himself physically for a shot at a second win in the upcoming B. A. A. Marathon. Cook, the time prize winner, was fifth, Thomas Crane from Springfield was sixth, and McGlone, Farrar, Shepard, and Fred Brown filled out the top ten.

So far, Ellison Brown's early racing season had been inauspicious at best. His official entry for the B. A. A. Marathon had arrived in time to be announced April 15. The *Westerly Sun* reported that the local running hero was seriously devoted to training:

> Tarzan, who will be running under the colors of the C. B. Cottrell Plant, has been tuning up faithfully for this [most] important of all road races and is now rapidly rounding out into top form.... The Indian star is really serious about this race as he has been running over local country roads nightly and is working hard to attain the same precision like gait which carried him to fame in other years.[13]

Arthur Duffey saw some significance to the fact that Brown's entry to the B. A. A. Marathon was submitted unusually early this year. He wrote:

> As a rule he waits until the very last minute before entering. Perhaps he may have something there. At any rate, Tarzan believes this is his year. As he recently put it at the Cathedral run, "I have been letting down my followers too much lately. It is about time for me to get back on the top of the heap." And don't think the Indian doesn't mean it.[14]

Jerry Nason, always with one ear aimed at the runners themselves and the other monitoring his own original alliterative constructions for a lasting contribution to marathon jargon, wrote the following piece under the headline, "'Jitters Day' for Marathoners" and this subheadline, "Angry Tarzan Brown Out After Record." In it he concisely provided a litany of Brown's athletic strengths, and the fact that the other runners were well aware of them. Nason began:

> In the parlance of the pavement pounders, this is "jitters day"—two days before the Marathon race.

Along about bedtime tonight all of the hot-shot candidates for the laurel wreath on Sunday will commence worrying themselves dizzy about Tarzan Brown.

In the banner bunion field he is more worrisome than all the rest combined, and they know it. The Indian is a macadam conundrum and always has been. He may break the record, as he threatens to do, or he may blow up.[15]

Gerard Cote, who ought to know, confirmed Nason's sentiments. He would tell the *Post's* Al Hirshberg about Brown instilling worry in him and others:

Now, you know who the most dangerous man in a Marathon is? Tarzan Brown. You never know what is going to happen with him. Sometimes I worry about one man, sometimes I worry about another when I run, but I always worry about Tarzan Brown. He is either very good or very bad. When he is very good, he is [a] hard man to beat. When he is very bad, it's something else again. But he is [a] natural runner and if he feels good, he gives everyone worry.[16]

Nason looked closely at Ellison Brown's attributes, both positive and negative, and offered this descriptive assessment: "The romping redskin has more natural ability and takes less care of it than any runner in the field. He has more speed, more ability, more imagination and less will power than any other potential winner."[17]

Tarzan Brown announced that the 1943 marathon would be his last, and that he wanted to retire from the event having left a sturdy time record with his name emblazoned upon it, one that would withstand the challenges of others for a number of years to come. The record for the marathon he had established, in 1939, had not survived. Gerard Cote had installed his own replacement record for it the very next year, in 1940. Reported Nason:

This is the self-announced finale for the Narragansett brave. He is 29, has three children and expects a fourth papoose under the Brown lodge-pole soon. "This is the last try for ol' Tarz," says the Westerly, R. I. warrior. "I'm getting no younger and it's time I settled down. I want to quit by leaving a real record for the boys to shoot at. That's what counts: the record! ... They haven't reached the bottom yet," says Brown. "I figure it can be done in about two hours, 24 minutes."[18]

Nason next tackled the issue of whether Brown was in good physical condition, always a concern of the sportswriters and the other runners. No one really knew, Nason was the first to admit, except the individual concerned. "Only Tarzan knows. He likes his beer and his idea of preparing for 26-mile races is considered unique, if not fantastic."[19] But Brown was reassuring on that score. He felt he was on the track for success after competing in the preliminary spring races, the results of which, clearly, did not appear to bode well to the untrained novice observer. Still on the subject of Brown's condition, Nason reported on the glories of Brown the athlete when in top form. He quoted an expert on the subject, marathon official Al Hart, who offered his opinion in appreciation: "When Tarzan Brown is in shape," says Al Hart, the referee of Sunday's macadam derby, "he is the prettiest thing I ever saw in action. He has the most graceful long-distance stride I've ever seen. He simply sneaks along."[20]

With two days to go until the race, rumors of an athlete's condition heatedly circulated, but the subject of those rumors was not Brown but Cote. Word was out that Cote had strained his Achilles tendon during training, and that the injury would affect his chances of winning, which, up until then, had been considered by most as superb. Now his chances "had taken a nosedive," it was reported, and Cote was viewing "Sunday's race through a veil of gloom."[21]

Before the race, Arthur Duffey of the *Post* and Jerry Nason's *Globe* board of experts favored Pawson to win, though he was after his fourth victory. Of Brown, the *Post*, in its characteristically racist language, had this to say:

> Lo, the poor Indian! Tarzan Brown of Westerly, R. I., the best Marathoner of them all when at his best, is back again for his third win this year. He won the race in 1936 and 1939 and says that he is back to scalp the White man over the local course. "Tarz" looks better than he ever did. His work in a defense plant, where he has been pushing a truck, has made him stronger than ever.[22]

Nason's experts had selected Pawson but in the *Globe* on the morning of the marathon Nason personally picked Tarzan Brown to win, stating, "Your old curbstone scrivener is hereby selecting the romping redskin to win. It is the kiss of death, but Tarz won for me in 1936, and I guess maybe in his finale he will be a good Indian boy (Boy? He's 29, father of three) and run the panting palefaces into the road again for me."[23] He was the lone supporter in the two-time winner's corner.

Walter Brown, the marathon starter, was currently *Maj.* Walter Brown and on active duty in the service during the spring of 1943, in the middle of World War II. So it was that his brother, George, Jr., would fire the traditional starting pistol to get the runners underway at high noon in Hopkinton for the 47th B. A. A. Marathon, held for the second consecutive year on a Sunday, this one being April 18. A war-reduced field of just eighty-nine starters (of 113 entrants) assembled first at the Tebeau Farm and then at the starting corral in Hopkinton. Former winners Brown, Cote, DeMar, Kelley and Pawson were suited up to run. The most recent winner and course record-holder, Joe Smith, new member of the Coast Guard, was also on hand but chose to ride the course on his backside in the *Boston Post* station wagon rather than run it on his legs.

The 1943 B. A. A. Marathon began mostly as a contest between Sergeant Cote, Private Kelley and Pawson. Ellison Brown did not figure substantially in the race or the results. Pawson led the first half of the course through Wellesley, and then army allies Cote and Kelley fought their own two-man contest the second half. Kelley, on special leave from Fort McClellan in Alabama, was once again defeated by his trek over the Newton hills, especially the last one, Heartbreak Hill. Cote gained a small lead at Boston College by the peak, but Kelley managed to pull even on the always-crucial downgrade. Kelley actually checked in first at Lake Street, ahead of Cote. Pawson fell back to check in fifth there as both McGlone and Lloyd Bairstow surpassed him. During the final four and one-half miles from Lake Street through Coolidge Corner to the finish line, a speedy, hustling Cote emerged with a lead that Kelley could not overcome. McGlone, Bairstow and Pawson would remain three, four and five at the finish. Heinicke, sixth at Lake Street, was sixth at Exeter Street.

Cote ran remarkably well despite two considerable obstacles, a sore ankle[24] injured in a pothole while training the past Monday and a forcefully strong head wind. His time was 2 hours, 28 minutes, 25.8 seconds, the third fastest time in the history of the race. Afterward, Cote described the pain he had endured while running. He said:

> "Every step from the start it hurt," said Cote. "Each time my foot come down — ouch! But the pain is ver' bad most of all in the last mile. I am glad when I get to the finish."[25]

The next day Cote was still discussing his sore ankle and how it affected his marathon run. Said Cote:

> Everyone says that they worry about me on account of my leg. I worry about me, too. I don't think I am going to win after that happen running to Wellesley and back last week…. I run differently yesterday on account of that strain. I run flat-foot, like this."[26]

He then demonstrated the flat-footed approach he was forced to adopt compared to his normal gait for *Post* reporter Al Hirshberg.

Johnny Kelley had notched his fifth second-place finish in the B. A. A. Marathon with an even 2.5 hours. Reporter Harold Kaese captured the thirty-five-year-old army private's disillusionment immediately after the race when he wrote, "Throwing himself on a cot, he said chokingly, 'Second, second, second again.'"[27] Kelley would later express these too-familiar thoughts with an understandable degree of sadness:

> I planned to stay with Cote on the hills and then out-spurt him over the flat during the last six miles but that last climb in Newton took too much out of me…. I'm just a bridesmaid again as far as this race is concerned…. This is the fifth time I thought I could win it but those hills beat me again.[28]

For Private Kelley, it was a depressing storyline and it was getting old.

Clarence H. DeMar finished in seventeenth place. Before the marathon he revealed his day's expectations: "I'm planning to run this course in about three hours today."[29] He managed to finish under that — in 2 hours, 57 minutes, 58 seconds. As he made his journey east of Hopkinton, all along the route throngs offered the grand master a rousing ovation. Few spectators probably realized that while they still slept earlier that morning, DeMar had awoken at 5 to milk his dairy cows at his farm in Reading. Then, with little time to lose, he found his way out to Hopkinton. After running the twenty-six miles, he returned to his farm where he had to milk the cows again. DeMar's day was still not half over. He next headed back to Boston where he went to work composing print at the *Herald* on the night shift.

Before he had left the dressing room after the B. A. A. Marathon, he was asked by a reporter if he would now consider retiring from competition. DeMar snapped back with a question, "Why should I?"[30]

Ellison Brown finished in 3 hours, 1 minute, 52 seconds, which was six seconds shy of a full four minutes behind Clarence H. DeMar, for a twenty-first-place end result. No commentary or further information was recorded or offered by any of the various print reporters. The results over the entire spring of 1943 were extremely disappointing, to say the least.

The usage of "Heartbreak Hill" figured in Nason's morning-of-the-marathon coverage, as he described the course to his readers. He wrote, "From Cleveland Circle it is a dead straight run to Exeter st. with Heartbreak Hill behind and only Misery Mile ahead."[31] No quotation marks surrounded either notable course icon's name, but upper case *h*'s and *m*'s were printed. The next day, Nason's *Globe* colleague, Tom Fitzgerald, opted to use the term in the following descriptive passage:

> Then they [Cote and Kelley] settled grimly for the alpine passage over those Newton hills which wrecked the hopes of so many seekers of George Demeter's laurel wreath before this.
> Cote got ahead by maybe a stride as they bent over in the drive up the slope to the Brae Burn Country Club. It was only a stride and he couldn't increase that advantage. Then for the big one — the famed "Heartbreak Hill" which is crowned by the spires of Boston College.[32]

Ellison's father, Otis Byron Brown, passed away in April 1943, at his daughter's home in Peace Dale, Rhode Island. Two months later, Ethel gave birth to her fourth child, the couple's second son, whom they named Norman but called "Thunderbolt" or "Bolt" for short.

The Holy Name eighth annual 10-Mile Handicap "Race of Champions" was held on an extremely warm Saturday evening, on June 26, despite the wartime restrictions on gasoline, rubber (tires), certain foodstuffs, and "dim-outs" of electric streetlamps. An optimistic Ellison Brown was there to compete against an eminent cast of runners, including Campbell, DeMar, Giard, Heinicke, McGlone, Medeiros, Shepard, Vogel and Young. A five-minute delay was assigned four scratch runners: Ellison Brown, Frank Brown, Bob Campbell and Fred McGlone. Other runners received more victory-friendly handicaps.

Ted Vogel led for the first half of the race, when Tony Medeiros took over the lead and finished first overall, also taking the time prize by four seconds over McGlone, who finished in third place. Medeiros' North Medford teammate, Lou Young, finished second. "Tarzan Brown, after plodding along deep in the ruck for miles, came up fast to land sixth position," the *Post* reported.[33] Brown had the third fastest time overall, after Medeiros and McGlone; his time for the ten-mile course was 1 hour, 36 seconds. (Medeiros' time was 59 minutes, 21 seconds.) Heinicke, traveling from Baltimore by train to make the competition, finished in fourth place. "Vogel, who folded badly in the late stages, [finished] fifth."[34] Giard was seventh, followed by DeMar, Sheppard, and Frank Brown.

Just as Tony Medeiros crossed over the finish line, he collapsed into the arms of spectators, visibly in a dazed condition. His receivers helped him down onto a grassy area where he stayed prone for forty-five minutes, muttering incoherently. Dr. Eugene F. McDonough, on hand at the finish line and taking charge, examined the runner on the spot and would not allow Medeiros to be moved for nearly an hour. Then the Lowell, Massachusetts, native was taken to Faulkner Hospital where he spent the night at the physician's directive. Medeiros was diagnosed as suffering from heat prostration. His wife, Mildred, frightened at the time, noticeably "brightened up" when assured by the doctor that her husband would be all right. "Tony's attractive strawberry blonde wife," as the *Post* referred to her, "later went to the municipal building to accept his prizes."[35] She told reporters that her husband, age 29, "didn't have any time to train for the race, as he works in a defense plant seven days a week."[36] A consensus was that the heat and that lack of training were the dual causes of Medeiros' medical complications.

The Independence Day 15-Kilometer championship race in Fall River, Massachusetts, featured a field of twenty-eight hopeful runners. Straight from the Iowa City, Iowa, Pre-Flight School in the United States Navy, Lt. Lou Gregory was on hand to compete against Tarzan Brown, Bob Campbell, Pvt. Ed Cook, Clayton Farrar, Don Heinicke, Fred McGlone, Anthony Medeiros, Charlie Robbins, Ed Shepard, and others.

Two miles into the just-over-nine-mile run, Gregory seized an opportunity to take the lead when Tarzan Brown unexpectedly "pulled a tendon in his leg and dropped out," according to an AP dispatch.[37] The *Providence Journal* reported that Brown withdrew earlier, at 1.5 miles, "when he developed a charley-horse."[38] Gregory, unchallenged for the pacesetting front position by any other contestant, went on to finish in record time, in 50 minutes, 50 seconds.[39] Nearly a full two minutes behind Gregory, Charlie Robbins took the second-place prize. McGlone, Cook and Heinicke finished third, fourth and fifth, respectively. Twenty-six of twenty-eight starters crossed the finish line.

The journalistic record in general is spotty in its coverage of the running events that took place in 1943, and in particular is even less complete to the extent of Ellison Brown's competition that season. Certainly there were fewer racing events held in cities and towns as the war claimed more and more of the hours of its citizenry for defense labor. Virtually no weekday events were scheduled, as had been the case in previous years. Joe Nutter of the *Providence Journal* would refer to that time and the paucity of racing events as "a summer of almost complete inactivity."[40] When races were held, the fields for those running events were markedly smaller with many participants out of the area serving their country, although many servicemen, it may surprise the reader to find out, had little trouble receiving permission for leaves to attend the higher-profile title events. The military authorities understood that allowing and enabling these events to take place, despite the ongoing war, was good for morale among the troops and the citizenry and therefore to be encouraged.

Brown, no doubt, ran less in 1943, in part due to time constraints from family and job. There did not seem to be enough time for training. He could no longer ignore the fact that in order to compete, within the unfamiliar parameters of working with an older body subject to strains and muscle pulls, training and conditioning were absolute prerequisites for winning the top prizes. This revelation was not immediately obvious at the time, and perhaps a certain degree of denial had to be overcome. In addition, the competition, especially in the last couple of years, was gradually transforming, as younger athletes appeared on the scene and started gaining experience. These spirited and highly trained athletes were making names for themselves, and crossing finish lines with quicker and quicker times.

Johnny Kelley had been honorably discharged from the army on August 28, along with most other men over 35 years of age. He returned to Arlington and his old employment with Boston Edison, but changed departments, from working security to working in maintenance.

Barely home a week's time, Kelley entered the National A. A. U. 20-K race held in Providence on Labor Day, September 6, 1943. Ellison Brown did not enter. Pawson and McGlone both had officially made notification of entering the event but did not make the start. On the day of the race, Les Pawson suffered an upset stomach. The night before the race Fred McGlone, attending a swimming party, sustained a deep cut on one of his feet. Without the three, Kelley's chances of winning were markedly improved and he did not fail to take advantage, although with the way he was running at that point in his life, he did not need any breaks. Kelley took the title that day, on his thirty-sixth birthday.

The National A. A. U. Championship Marathon at Yonkers was held November 7, and was won for a second time by Gerard Cote, capping a very successful year for the Canadian sergeant. Kelley ran Yonkers that year, but, like a rerun of Boston in April, could not outrun the speedy Quebecois to the finish line. Kelley, who had battled Cote valiantly, in the end faded and had to settle for fourth place. Less than two minutes separated the first-place Cote and the fifth-place Pawson, with Fred McGlone, Clayton Farrar and Kelley in between. Tony Medeiros, Don Heinicke and Jock Semple followed Pawson in, finishing sixth through eighth. Brown was not listed among the top twenty finishers nor mentioned in any of the coverage; it is unlikely he took part, though not a certainty.

The Berwick, Pennsylvania, race, held each Thanksgiving, featured a reduced field of only a dozen starters in 1943. Johnny Kelley made the journey to that Pennsylvania town, but there is no indication that Brown did.[41] Kelley took the lead in the opening mile and never looked back, traversing the rugged nine-mile, 200-yard course in 48 minutes, 47 seconds, to take first place for the second consecutive year. Kelley finished a half-mile ahead of L. A. C. B. Morton of the Royal Canadian Air Force. Third place was won by Maine resident Ed Shepard, now working for the Todd Shipbuilding Corporation in Gorham, Maine. All three received diamond ring prizes. The 1943 season was officially over.

30

"An Ungovernable Tear" — *1944–1945*

When entries to the North Medford 20-Mile Run were being received, none was forthcoming from one Ellison Brown. There was an undernourished expectation that he would show up as a postentry just as the starting pistol trigger was about to be squeezed. That scenario did not take place. There was no word from Brown or Salimeno. Speedy Coast Guardsman Clayton Farrar took the top trophy in that season opener.

When entries to the Reddish A. C. race were being processed, none was received from Brown. Again, although some half expected him to show up at the blast of the starting gun, that did not happen. There was no word from the Brown camp. Once again, Coast Guardsman Farrar flew to the finish line, taking the top prize.

When entries to the Cathedral Ten-Miler were being sorted, none bearing the name of Ellison Brown was announced. A few officials may have expected him to appear at the starting line, but that did not come to pass. For the third time in three races, it was Clayton Farrar who finished first.

It was a surprise, then, when, five days before the 48th edition of the B. A. A. Marathon was slated to take place, the Boston Athletic Association announced via newspapers throughout New England the marathon entry of Tarzan Brown. The *Westerly Sun* reported the news of Brown's entry submission along with this update: "Tarzan, who has run in the B. A. A. on many occasions, has been working out for the past two weeks in preparation for the big race and claims to be in top shape for the Patriot's Day race."[1] The *Boston Globe* ran a Jerry Nason piece under the headline: "Tarzan's Marathon Entry Wrinkles Hot Shots' Brows."[2] Nason announced to his readers that Brown had officially and "unexpectedly entered the race he vowed a year ago never to run again,"[3] creating a most puzzling and more troubling task for the expert forecasters. Without having participated in any of the springtime preliminary runs, there was no telling what condition the athlete was in and therefore no way of proffering an educated guess as to how he might do. Still,

Nason repeated his oft-stated contention that "when he is in any kind of condition, Tarzan is a terror in this event."[4] Nason continued:

> He's gone to the starting line fit and ready only twice. Both times he won in a gallop. At 29, the Indian should really be at the peak of his running. At 29, a father of three little Browns he has found it increasingly harder to concentrate on training and he never was a stickler in that department.
> In our estimation the Tarz is the best of 'em all when he wants to be.[5]

It was hard to argue with Nason on any of the points he expressed.

Both Ellison Brown and Gerard Cote would be seeking their third B. A. A. Marathon victory. Kelley was trying to nail down that elusive second win. On the day before the Wednesday marathon, Nason reported that "the curbstone betting is even that Johnny Kelley will be 1–2-3."[6] Nason's panel of experts had selected Fred McGlone. As far as Brown was concerned, Nason maintained that "Tarzan Brown, as usual, has all hands mystified. The romping redskin hasn't raced since last year, when he flopped (21st).... But the highway heroes know that when the Tarz is in shape he might run them right off the course, as he did in '36 and '39."[7] No one was picking Brown, but no one was ignoring him either. Nason's personal pick, his "hat box special" (not a "blue plate special" this year) was Don Heinicke.[8]

Many pundits chose Cote, the Canadian army sergeant, to repeat his performance of the previous year and win. A picture of the victorious Cote from 1943, smoking his cigar, feet up, imbibing port wine and beer, along with reports of his postmarathon nightlife, dancing and whatnot out on the town in Boston, did not sit well with his Canadian army superiors nor with the families of his uniformed fellow comrades. This was too much merriment, no matter how much athleticism, during wartime to tolerate. The suggestion that Cote was using military funds for travel expenses fueled the anger of the Canadian officers. A ban was issued to curtail all participation by Canadian servicemen in athletic events not conducted under the Canadian military's jurisdiction. The ban, in place in the early spring of 1944, was expected to keep Cote from the 1944 B. A. A. Marathon, but it did not succeed. Cote's personal interpretation of the edict enabled him to run in Boston. He reasoned that when he was on furlough he was as free as any other citizen to do as he pleased. He buttonholed a restaurateur and sports fan by the name of Frank De Rice, described as "Montreal's Howard Johnson," to accompany him to Boston and pay the freight.[9] Cote would face the military music—win, lose or draw—after the marathon when he made his return to Quebec province.

Clarence DeMar chose to sit out the 1944 marathon. He claimed he was unable to provide the amount of time needed to properly prepare for the marathon. His defense work during the days, nights at the *Herald*, dairy farm chores and young family consumed too much of his time, but he planned to be on hand. Instead of participating on foot as a runner, DeMar, employed to work in the role of reporter and marathon analyst for the *Globe*, would ride the course in an automobile. There were no objections. Fortunately no one attempted to make the case, as ruling Olympic autocrat Avery Brundage in the Eleanor Holm Jarrette situation in 1936 had done, that DeMar, by taking on such a journalistic assignment, should be required to forfeit his amateur athletic status (which would affect him should he decide to run competitively again.)

On the morning of the marathon, Nason reiterated the story of how Jack Haggerty of Westerly had offered to bet $100 on Brown in 1939. On the eve of the 1944 marathon, the same fellow Haggerty had again made contact with the *Globe* sportswriter. Haggerty's message was not identical to the one he had sent Nason five years earlier, though it was just as hope filled. Haggerty supplied some training data heretofore unknown by the Boston print media. Nason relayed it to his readers:

> "We have hopes," scribbles he [Haggerty]. "Tarzan has been doing all right in training. He had a slight injury to his ankle, but I think he will be in there just the same.
> "He did a nice 20 miles last Sunday, in fine time. Tell Always Wrong Egan [the Colonel at the *Daily Record*] to watch Tarz!"[10]

How serious the ankle injury was, there was no one saying. How slight was "slight" was anybody's guess. Of course, Nason was quick to point out that Haggerty, this time, did not accompany his epistle with a cash-on-the-barrelhead wager on Brown.

Tarzan Brown failed to appear for the marathon. Henry McKenna of the *Herald* wrote, "Tarzan Brown didn't show, which wasn't a surprise."[11] The Boston press displayed a lack of journalistic curiosity and seemed rather uninterested to find out what was up with the Rhode Island runner. Only the *Westerly Sun* offered an explanation along with its report of Brown's absence from the race. It said, "The reason Brown gave for not reporting was that his injured ankle had not healed enough to stand up under the long 26-mile grind."[12] No details were offered.

Despite Brown's omission from competing, the 1944 B. A. A. Marathon was an extremely tight contest, as Cote and Kelley fiercely battled each other from the Newton City Hall, roughly mile nineteen, up and over the usually decisive Newton hills, clear through Kenmore Square to the tape on Exeter Street. Just seven hundred yards from completion, Cote made a final push forward that Kelley, who had given it all he had and had nothing left to tap, could not match. In the end, only 12.6 seconds, or an estimated forty-five yards,[13] separated Cote the victor from Kelley the runner-up. The thirty-year-old Cote's winning time was 2 hours, 31 minutes, 50.4 seconds. It took six and a half minutes after Kelley registered his sixth second-place finish for Charlie Robbins to cross the finish line for third-place honors.

On both ends of the course this year Cote had to struggle to avoid personal disaster. Before noon, he was running late getting to Hopkinton before the start, arriving with a bare twelve minutes to spare. He was checked in by marathon officials and checked out by marathon physicians adjacent to the starting line. On the other end, with a strong challenge from Kelley on his hands—"the fiercest fight any Marathon has known,"[14] Nason labeled it— Cote had no time for blowing kisses to the spectators lined along the course as he had in 1940 and 1943, and he was not flashing his gold teeth in a wide-stretching grin this time either. He was seriously engaged in a scrap that required his full effort and attention. He gave it; he gave it his all.

Kelley had tried a new tactic of running from behind the leader rather than attempting to be the leader himself, a workable strategy he found he liked and regretted not having employed in previous races. Although Kelley's altered approach caused Cote a certain amount of consternation, overall, it did not end up making enough of a difference to get the result Kelley had desperately sought. The thirty-seven-year-old marathon warrior was teary-eyed after another second-place finish, especially a race in which victory appeared so attainable. Nason captured a glimpse of Kelley's deep-seated anguish, as he recorded Kelley lamenting. "'It is a terrible thing to be so close that you can watch the winner actually finish,' said John, resolutely choking back a sob, as an ungovernable tear fell from the corner of each eye."[15]

In other results, William Wiklund, age 36 and employed at the Wright Aircraft plant in Patterson, New Jersey, finished fourth. Canadian runner and snowshoe racer Lloyd Evans of Montreal finished in fifth place. Don Heinicke, who experienced stomach cramps which forced him to alternate between walking and running over the last four miles, crossed the line sixth, over four and one half minutes behind Evans. Bruno Mazzeo of Maine finished seventh, followed by Lou Young, Jock Semple and Clayton Farrar. Ted Vogel finished in fifteenth place. Fred McGlone dropped out at Newton Lower Falls after first suffering a stabbing stomach pain and then encountering severe and painful blistering on one of his feet.

Clarence H. DeMar summed up the race in the opening two sentences of his maiden *Globe* report with the words, "The best man won the 48th annual B. A. A. Marathon. Kelley was good—very good, but Cote was better."[16] DeMar managed to assail with his fingers on the typewriter keys rather than with his fists across a spectator's jaw, but the attack no less struck its target. He addressed a major peeve of his in his *Globe* piece. Wrote DeMar:

> Cote's lead on Kelley at Lake st. was less than 50 yards. Here some loud-mouthed spectator yelled, "Go it, Johnny, he's only a quarter of a mile ahead!" That guy was a pain to Kelley. We runners do wish that excited spectators would either tell approximately the truth on distances, time and positions, or else shut up![17]

Though a rookie reporter, it was vintage DeMar.

Incidentally, Nason did not use his designation, "Heartbreak Hill," in his 1944 marathon coverage, nor did any of his colleagues. The closest Nason came was in a passage where he wrote once again of Johnny Kelley placed in that very familiar vicinity: "It was the greatest Marathon race of modern times. It was 5 minutes away from the record, but time had long since been forgotten when Kelley reached *the dreaded Newton hills, monument to many a broken heart* and blister, only 100 yards behind Cote" (emphasis added).[18]

Ellison Brown stayed out of the racing limelight for the duration of 1944, a limelight greatly diminished by wartime activity. Over the summer very few cities and towns devoted resources to race sponsorship, and even fewer sports pages were devoted to covering those limited racing events. With American military involvement in every part of the globe, the public, it was suggested, had little attention or time to devote to foot racing. Furthermore, the defense industries that so many workers were a part of offered their own leagues for team athletic competition, including leagues of softball, baseball, and basketball, games that, it was argued, a much greater majority of weekend athletes could play and enjoy. Attendance at college-level sporting events was also encouraged, especially during the football season, and the sports pages devoted lots of ink and space to the coverage of them. Boxing, baseball, hockey, golf, and tennis all captured more of the sportswriters' ink than did (nonschool) running events. With the exception of a few unshakable annual events such as the spring's B. A. A. Marathon and the fall's Yonkers and Berwick races, the blue-collar plodders were disappearing and so too were the venues where they could ply their trade.

Late in the fall, on November 12, Navy hospital attaché Charlie Robbins won the national marathon at Yonkers. Heinicke finished second, Medeiros third and Kelly fourth, followed by McGlone, Wicklund, and Semple. In Berwick, Kelley won his third victory in a row, edging out Scotty Rankine of the Royal Canadian Air Force by fifteen seconds. Rankine, who was competing in Berwick for the first time after a seven-year absence, was denied his sixth title in that nine-mile, rugged race.

With few racing events to enter in 1944, it may have seemed like a temporary, war-related dry period, but with a few exceptions, money-seeking promoters understood the insurmountable difficulty — perhaps a near impossibility — of charging marathon spectators any sort of admission charge. Events that took place in stadiums, arenas and ballparks were the ones that could require the public to pay to pass through a turnstile at the entrance. Like the argument against solar power — that you couldn't meter the sun — sports promoters were quick to understand that they hadn't found a viable way to put a turnstile on a city sidewalk.

For the first time since its initial run in 1932, the North Medford 20-Mile Road Race failed to take place in March, as the traditional race marking the opening of the 1945 running season. During the second week in April the Reddish A. A. Ten-Mile Handicap Race was held. Charlie Robbins, who had finished third behind Cote and Kelley in the 1944 B. A. A. Marathon and holder of the national marathon title from his November victory at Yonkers, beat the small field in Jamaica Plain. Johnny Kelley, who finished second at the finish line, incredibly won the time prize. Ellison Brown did not appear.

The buildup to the B. A. A. Marathon as witnessed in the newspapers was very quiet, very subdued in April 1945, in part because of the death of Franklin D. Roosevelt during that time and because the long-running war was not yet over. Last year's champion Gerard Cote was stationed in England, a move believed to be in retaliation for his violation of the spirit of the commanding officer's order proscribing competition in sporting events conducted outside the Canadian military. He would not be running in Boston, defending his title. Ellison Brown would not be competing in the marathon either. This year, he did not even enter. Also staying out another year was Clarence H. DeMar. He would repeat working the marathon beat for the *Globe* a second year.

Nason did not neglect to stir the pot and make his pick. Though he listed Kelley and Robbins as favorites, he personally selected the Canadian Scotty Rankine to win. Rankine had not been seen competing locally in a number of years.

The marathon provided Johnny Kelley with the opportunity he had been desperately seeking since 1935, another first-place finish. In the smallest field in the marathon's history—only 67 starters of 90 entered—Kelley ran a masterful race, running with a strong steady pace and a lot of patience. He let Farrar, Heinicke, Robbins and Bairstow do their thing, and he steadfastly did his. Until the Newton hills, he stayed back, within himself. It was there that Farrar burned out, and Bairstow replaced him as front-runner. With just over three miles to go, Kelley grasped the lead and was never seriously challenged. He was beaming as he completed the final mile, and, taking a page out of the Cote playbook, blew kisses and waved to the enthusiastic though limited spectators. ("The crowd was the smallest I have ever seen," observed DeMar.[19]) Kelley crossed the finish line in a very respectable, and quick 2 hours, 30 minutes, 40 seconds, which was 1 minute, 27 seconds faster than his winning time ten years earlier. Bairstow, running second, was 2 minutes, 10 seconds behind Kelley at the Exeter Street line. Heinicke finished third, Rankine fourth, Evans fifth, and Robbins sixth. Lou Young, Medeiros, and the undaunted Jock Semple were seven, eight, nine. Morton from Toronto filled out the top ten.

Nason mentioned "Heartbreak Hill" in his coverage of the marathon in two separate editions of the paper. In the earlier one in the April 19 *Globe*, Nason wrote, "But Farrar, while he fled over the first of the Newton hills, left a lot of his running there and before he reached Heartbreak hill, longest ascension on the course coming up to Boston College, he was slowed down to almost a walk."[20] Nason's usage in this instance was in accordance with the term's regular usage as commonly used and understood today. The lowercase *h* in the word *hill* matched the manual-of-style conventions of the day, such as *Kenmore square* and *Beacon st.*

There is a difference to be noted in Nason's usage of the term the following day. He wrote: "Meantime, Farrar galloped grimly as far as his fuel lasted. And that was exhausted, along with Farrar, at the very bottom of Heartbreak Hill, the long, twisting, tortuous lift from Newton Center to B. C."[21] The sentence is ambiguous. The phrase "the long, twisting, tortuous lift from Newton Center to B. C." may be construed as an appositive, modifying "Heartbreak Hill," giving information on its shape and location. If so, the location element is too sweeping. The base or start of Heartbreak Hill is commonly understood to be at the beginning of Mile 21 of the course. Newton Center, reached a mile before, in Mile 20, is where the *second* Newton hill (of three) is encountered. (At the end of the second hill, midway through Mile 20 is the intersection with Centre Street.)[22]

Nason said Farrar finally ran out of gas by the time he reached the start (the bottom) of Heartbreak Hill. If so, Farrar had used up his energy on the long, twisting, difficult, *second* grade before confronting Heartbreak Hill, the Boston College hill, the last hill in the series. Nason's descriptive phrase, by that interpretation, would not modify Heartbreak Hill but the terrain preceding it.

Notice that Nason applied uppercase *H*'s to both *Heartbreak* and *Hill* in his usage the second day. Aspects of its usage were still not firmly established with any continuity by 1945.

For the second straight year, Charlie Robbins won the Yonkers marathon and retained the national marathon crown. Kelley, six hundred yards behind, finished in second place. He was followed by Rankine and Heinicke, Morton and Gregory. Semple was tenth. If Ellison Brown competed, he failed to finish or garner any newspaper mention.

Brown, the 1940 winner, was reported by the AP to be officially entered in the 1945 Berwick race, along with the current champion, Johnny Kelley, who was after his fourth straight win, and previous winners Rankine and Gregory. They comprised the field of 35, "the largest in the history of the Berwick Marathon foot race."[23] For the 36th edition of the annual Thanksgiving Day event, the AP reported four special prizes offered for the top winners: a gold watch and three diamond rings.

Fighting against an unrelenting, gusting headwind, Kelley won the race; his time was 49 minutes, 16 seconds. An Oklahoma runner named Forest Efaw finished in second place, 46 seconds behind Kelley. No other runners' names or their final placements were reported in the AP dispatch. There was no word on whether Brown had shown up to run in the race, or how he fared if he did take part.

31

"Surprises by Finishing 12th" in Final Comeback — 1946

Ellison Brown came out of his self-imposed racing retirement to compete in 1946. His emphasis was on winning his third B. A. A. Marathon title as Pawson and Cote had done, and as Kelley was intent upon doing. Employment in the defense industries was drying up following the end of the war. Prolonged strikes now dotted the American labor landscape; that April striking miners were leading the charge of organized labor. Ellison found himself once again without gainful employment as was the case through so many intervals during his life. It was his hope that a successful showing in Boston would enable him to connect to an employer. There was, of course, some room for doubt at the arduous task ahead of him. He was a realist when it came to running. He had a strategy. All he would say ahead of time was, "Maybe I can win the Marathon, maybe I can't. But I'll tell you this much — if I'm up there at twenty miles nobody's gonna beat me."[1]

The 15th annual North Medford 20-Mile run, back to its traditional last-week-in-March schedule, took place Saturday, March 23. Columnist Bob Dunbar of the *Herald* had been churning the early spring copy and the results were not peaceful. An example, this one of Tarzan Brown, appeared the morning of the North Medford race:

> It must be pretty hard for a man who has been hailed in the headlines as one of America's greatest athletes to reconcile himself to menial tasks in order to keep his family together. That's the situation with Tarzan Brown, the Indian who represented the United States in the Olympic marathon and at one time held the B. A. A. record. He's running at North Medford today in the hope that he can regain popularity and land himself a good job.[2]

Dunbar had expressed a sentiment that rang true, not only for Ellison Brown, but for many of the old-time marathoners, many of whom had suffered chronic spells of unemployment or were forced to accept difficult or dangerous employment or employment that paid less than a living wage. By 1946, with the wartime economy about to switch back to a peacetime one, jobs were becoming temporarily scarce as a surplus of workers returned to snap them up.

Clarence H. DeMar had also sent in his entry to compete in the North Medford run. Dunbar got in a flap with the fifty-eight-year-old, no-nonsense veteran. Wrote Dunbar:

> The return of Clarence DeMar to the road-racing scene in the annual North Medford Club 20-miler tomorrow is truly amazing. Clarence won't have any delusions of grandeur because he hasn't a ghost of a chance of winning, but he'll still get more applause than the winner. It's difficult to understand why Clarence bothers, however, for in recent years he has become very cynical about such intangible rewards.[3]

Dunbar's words provoked an angry, in parts cryptic reply from the veteran, some of which the *Herald* sportswriter shared with his readers:

> Writing to take exception to a recent note here that he has become cynical about such intangible rewards as applause, marathoner Clarence DeMar pens, "Don't like the note! How do you know what I'm cynical about? Just because the windbags of A.A.U. lied to protect each other and parasites and tried to get rid of me in 1937 on Texas trip doesn't mean anything to those who regard the truth. Not applause but other intangible things much worth while."[4]

DeMar had on more than one occasion been publicly at odds with race officials and the controlling forces at the Amateur Athletic organization. The man did not suffer hierarchies, bureaucrats, reporters—in general terms he did not suffer fools well at all. Bob Dunbar took advantage of his access to the sports pages and purported to offer a rephrased version of his original point. His reworded one actually said something quite different:

> Okay, let's put it another way. Too bad a man like DeMar, who in his prime won seven B.A.A. marathons and sundry other titles, doesn't let well enough alone so that people will remember him as the greatest American marathoner of all time. If he keeps running and finishing 30th, as he did at North Medford last Saturday, the memory will be clouded considerably.[5]

Bob Dunbar could not have been any more mistaken. Every additional effort DeMar made on the competitive roads only added to his legend and admiration. The man's competitive drive, his endless strong-willed determination, and his ability to keep physically competitive year after year were lauded by the people of New England and elsewhere. DeMar, in his day, but especially more so in his later years (including the time of Dunbar's warning of DeMar tarnishing his image) was regarded in the highest esteem by the sports public. DeMar did not get the opportunity to respond to Dunbar's rephrased opinion in print. Whether the marathon master wrote a reply to the sportswriter or not is unknown. How the atmosphere inside the *Herald* newspaper building where both men worked was transformed due to the tiff on the sports pages can only be imagined.

Despite the anticipation of Brown at the North Medford race, he did not appear. Kelley did appear, but only as a spectator, choosing to conserve his energies for a shorter race the following week. Gerard Cote, a civilian again, won the 15th annual race, on a blustery, roaring and gusty day, running the last seven miles alone and ahead of what was left of an original field of fifty-five starters. Will Cloney observed that Cote "finished strongly and had showered and dressed before the 10th man had hit the finish line."[6] Don Heinicke finished second. The Baltimore resident had recently switched employment, taking a meatpacking job after giving up his position in a chemical plant. Clayton Farrar was third and Charlie Robbins was fourth, despite an unexpected delay. They were "cut off by a passenger train that had stopped across the street, so they pushed alighting commuters aside, clambered up the steps on one side and down the other, and resumed the race."[7] That daring feat earned them their own mini headline in the *Herald*, which read, "Marathoners Run Right Through Train."[8]

David Mazzeo finished in fifth place. His experienced brother, Bruno, the expert hitchhiker, also competed, but stubbed his toe after leading the first eight miles, and had to settle for a fourteenth-place trophy. White and Durgin were sixth and seventh, followed by the still-competitive Jock Semple, who finished eighth, and Tony Medeiros, who finished ninth.

Clarence H. DeMar finished; he crossed the line in thirtieth place, earning one of the prizes which were generously awarded to the first thirty-three finishers. Cloney reported on DeMar's apparel, noting with detail, "His costume was bizarre — worsted trousers, a striped street shirt, and an off-white sleeveless pull-on."[9]

When the Reddish A. A. race, its distance upped to fifteen miles, was held the next Saturday, March 30, Johnny Kelley took no prisoners, crossing the finish line in 1 hour, seventeen minutes flat. The remarkably rapid run drew the ugly but inevitable questions about the accuracy of the length of the course. Will Cloney wrote of Kelley's time: "Since that clocking is almost three minutes faster than the accepted world record for the distance, the accuracy of the measuring may be questioned, but irrespective of the actual mileage, Kelley was tremendous yesterday."[10] Robbins, Medeiros, Farrar and Bruno Mazzeo followed Kelley in, filling out the top five.

Jock Semple managed to run and finished fifteenth, despite having been the recipient of very sad news from overseas. His parents, he had just learned, "had been asphyxiated in a household accident."[11] The son, who had dutifully written a letter to them "every week for the last 23 years,"[12] found a measure of solace in running.

Passing over the North Medford and Reddish races, Ellison Brown decided to tackle the Cathedral Club 10-mile road race for debut of his 1946 comeback campaign.

Now that he no longer worked at Cottrell, he was unattached, but Brown found a way to get affiliated, affiliation which provided small but not negligible support for racing, including the covering of entry fees, the securing of expense money, and other tangible benefits. And, at the same time, Brown was in the vanguard of breaking down an old barrier, though far from intentionally doing so. The *Herald* published the headline on April 9: "'Tarzan' Brown Runs As Girls Club Entry." The never tongue-in-cheek *Herald* reported:

> Ellison "Tarzan" Brown, former B. A. A. marathon record holder who will be making a comeback attempt this year, will be entered officially from the Red Diamond A. A.–which is news because that organization consisted solely of girl athletes until Tarzan was allowed to join.
> Al Hart, sponsor of the club, decided it would do no harm to befriend the lonesome Redskin. He went one step better and bought Tarzan a complete uniform, including custom-made shoes. Tarzan will warm up in the Cathedral race on Saturday.[13]

The generosity that benefactor Al Hart extended to Brown certainly was a help to the runner and could make a significant difference in how he fared. The new running shoes were especially appreciated.

The Saturday before the B. A. A. Marathon, sixty-five runners lined up for the 3 o'clock start of the 36th annual Cathedral race in Boston's South End. Though there was some negotiation extended over whether Brown should be a scratch starter, he chose to do so, refusing any handicap assistance as a knock against his pride and skills. He regarded the run primarily as a tune-up for the upcoming marathon and exactly how he finished was not of great concern to him. Seeing how his leg muscles felt after testing them in competition was his essential concern.

First place belonged to Ted Wood, age 22, a poultry farm worker. The *Herald's* Will Cloney reported, beyond the need of his readers to know, that Wood had "been training only six months, following his discharge from three-months' service in the Army Air Force for a nervous breakdown."[14] Ten seconds after Wood crossed over the finish line came Lloyd Bairstow, who also won the second time prize. The first time prize for the fastest runner was won by Clayton Farrar; he finished in 50 minutes, 27 seconds, but ended up in sixth place. Another notable perambulator, Tony Medeiros, finished third. Jock Semple took the ninth-place prize, and his B. A. A. team won the team prize. Wrote Cloney of the gruff but lovable Scot, "Capt. Semple was like a mother hen fussing over her brood — in this case, Bairstow and Wood."[15] Charlie Robbins, the third fastest in time, finished twelfth. Stylianos Kyriakides, the Greek champion in America to win the B. A. A. Marathon for a larger purpose than the purely athletic one, "was highly pleased with his showing. He's not a speed runner yet he looked very good," observed Cloney.[16] He was sixteenth, but fifth in time, with a registered time of 51 minutes, 40 seconds.

Tarzan Brown's actual time for running the ten miles was an even 54 minutes, but the scratch-delayed start contributed to his failure to make a prize-winning finish. He completed the course in 26th place. His weight was of concern. Brown weighed in at 150 pounds, "about 10 pounds heavier than his best weight," according to Cloney.[17] The B. A. A. Marathon was scheduled for Saturday, April 20, just a week away.

The fiftieth B. A. A. Marathon was a reunion of sorts for four athletes who had missed the competition the year before. In 1945 Brown did not enter or show. Cote had missed the marathon, having been purposefully ordered overseas. Lou Gregory, in the navy, had not been able to make it. And Clarence H. DeMar, who had been present but had spent the last two marathons in a vehicle writing for the *Globe*, was back this year as a running competitor. Why not? he figured; he was still a young man at fifty-seven. The large starting field of 101 included the defending champion, Johnny Kelley, New York principal Lou Gregory, the veteran runner and navy man Jock Semple, as well as the familiar cast: Bairstow, Heinicke, Robbins, Vogel, Young, Medeiros and Evans. In addition to the Canadians, the marathon was truly an international event as Kenneth Bailey of Great Britain and Stylianos Kyriakides of Greece took part.

Kyriakides, like Brown and others, wanted to use a victory in Boston in order to gain a platform from which he could make a public appeal, not for personal employment but for relief aid for his war-torn homeland nation. Kyriakides, thirty-six, ran a shoulder-to-shoulder race with Johnny Kelley for almost twenty-five miles. He had "hurled three challenges at Kelley before the latter wilted, almost in sight of the finish line," the *New York Times* reported.[18] With a strong spurt to the finish line, Kyriakides completed his missionary drive in 2 hours, 29 minutes, 27 seconds. He almost was prevented from competing by the B. A. A. physician in Hopkinton because of his appearance; he looked in poor physical condition. George Demeter, the Greek-American restaurateur and laurel wreath proprietor, intervened on Kyriakides's behalf, reportedly saying, "He's a representative of Greece, and Greece will take responsibility for him. He's going to run."[19] Demeter's word was unquestionably good enough for B. A. A. race officials.

Just before the race began, Kyriakides was handed a paper note from Demeter to carry with him on the marathon course. In Greek writing, the note contained the ancient Greek motto: "With it, or on it," a message meant to suggest the warrior returns victorious carrying his or her shield, or dead, carried upon it. On the other side of the note were Pheidippides' historic words, "We won."

Demeter, supportive in the political quest of Kyriakides, was equally overjoyed with his victory, and was pleased to place the laurel wreath on the Greek runner's brow. The runner first emotionally embraced a disappointed Kelley, and then spoke effectively to reporters about the conditions in his native coun-

Longtime friends Johnny Kelley (left) and Ellison Brown together, circa 1945 (courtesy of the Boston Public Library, Print Department).

try, the plight of his countrymen, and his intentions to tour the United States in a concerted effort to raise donations of desperately needed money, medical supplies, food and clothing. The message was passed to the public through the print media, reported worldwide, and marked what in reality became a newly international era for the B. A. A. Marathon. Nason would later recall, "Word of it went all over the world and the Greeks did get some help."[20]

The selfless cause to which Kyriakides struggled took the sting out of another second-place finish for Kelley. Kelley listened closely to the athlete he had met first back in 1936 at the Berlin Olympics. From Kyriakides' humanitarian appeal, Kelley could appreciate the gravity of the political situation the Greek athlete described. Said a tearful Kelley, "He wasn't running for himself, he was doing it for his country."[21]

Cote, who finished third, had to overcome severe abdominal cramps midway along the course. Gregory, who led early, held on for a fourth-place finish. Tarzan Brown "surprises by finishing 12th," the *Westerly Sun* proclaimed in a subheadline.[22] Brown's time from Hopkinton to Exeter Street was 2 hours, 48 minutes, 47 seconds. He was preceded over the finish line by Morton, Kernason, Evans, Robbins, Vogel, L.Young, and Medeiros. It would be Ellison Brown's final B. A. A. Marathon.

Clarence DeMar finished 9 minutes and 55 seconds over the three-hour mark, in thirty-second place. Despite the adulation of the spectators, DeMar was not happy about his results. He matter-of-factly declared, "It was my slowest B. A. A. race, but I'm sure I'll do better next year."[23] Later that evening he made his way to the *Boston Herald* building for a nightshift mostly on his feet in the composing room.

1946 was the last year, according to Nason, that automobiles were permitted along the B. A. A. Marathon route during the race. The decision was made in response to the deplorable conditions Nason described during the close contest between Kyriakides and Kelley. Said Nason:

> He [Kyriakides] and old Johnny Kelley have this terrific battle all the way. Terrific. But nobody ever saw it. They were surrounded by these automobiles—and vaguely, in this blue haze of gas fumes, you could see two guy in white uniforms, running. How either one of them finished, I don't know.[24]

The following year the press and race officials were assigned to travel on one official bus. In addition to putting an end to the pollution and danger, the race within a race of the competing newspapermen in their automobiles also came to the end of an era. "Right away the times [of the runners] picked up noticeably," Nason noted. "The runners didn't have the cars impeding them and they didn't have to suck up those fumes into their lungs."[25]

In one sense the employment situation worked itself out and in another sense it never did. The scheme to win the marathon and get a job obviously did not pan out in 1946. But, in his usual, somewhat haphazard way, Brown worked—at masonry and shell fishing, odd jobs and agriculture, clearing brush, chopping wood and digging wells—whatever could be done depending upon the need or the season, usually for exceptionally meager compensation. After the war, Ethel continued to work, and did so her whole adult life.

After the 1946 marathon in Boston, Ellison Brown had enough evidence to come to the realization that his days of competitive running were now behind him. All athletes at a certain point in their career are forced to come to grips with that reality, and Brown was no exception; for aging athletes it was a difficult decision and one hard to face squarely. He did not give up running altogether, and would, on occasion, compete in local races or take up an individual racing challenge. Late in life Ellison Brown told Jerry Nason, "In my heart I always felt, if I was in shape, I could beat any man living up to 50 miles. I quit running before I ever ran my best race or even knew how to train for it."[26] Regrets notwithstanding, in the sporting world of his day, Ellison Brown had a great run.

32

"Time and Marathoners Fly"— *The Postwar Years*

On the first of October in 1949, Tarzan Brown fired up his "Silver Streak," a ragged truck with its name proudly written on one side of its silver hood. The vehicle was lacking such safety inspection-required parts as headlamps, taillights, fenders, and windshield wipers. "The cracked windshield was bound by clothesline as was the one door," the *Providence Journal* reported.[1] The dilapidated truck was registered as a farm vehicle and had special farm license plates, under which is was illegal to be operated on state roads beyond a two-mile limit of the farm for which it was presumably in use, or after dark.

One day, with supper on the stove, on a spur-of-the-moment whim, Ellison Brown hurriedly rounded up Ethel and the kids, "to take the kids for a ride."[2] Despite mild protests voiced by Ethel, the family climbed aboard the "Silver Streak," and Ellison headed the rattling, puffing truck with its leaking radiator in the direction of Providence, where Ethel's brother resided. Tarzan took the sparsely populated back roads, and "stopped at every bar along the way"[3] for a thirst-quenching refreshment.

When they reached the city limits of Providence they were pulled over by Patrolman Joseph T. Fitzpatrick of the Providence police, who ordered the vehicle immediately impounded. A reporter and photographer from the *Providence Journal* were summoned to the inner confines of the police station where the truck, Ellison Brown, and his two sons were photographed. Along with a photograph, Brown's words were given space in the newspaper:

> "I'm not no millionaire," Tarzan said. "I use this truck for mason work and to go two miles from the house I built to get water and groceries. I wanted to give my wife and four children a good time today and brought her here to visit her brother ... for an outing.
> "I set a nice record and I don't see why they want to make any trouble now. I don't like the idea of them impounding my [registration] plates. I'm an Indian and I want that put down."[4]

According to the *Journal*, police officers advised him to junk the vehicle, or

Left to right: Ellison Brown and his sons, Ellison Jr. ("Sonny") and Norman ("Thunderbolt") sit with the impounded "Silver Streak" in the Providence police station garage, Providence, Rhode Island, October 2, 1949 (*Providence Journal* photograph).

get it towed back home. Ellison hoped to "accept the offer of a friend to install lights on it here in Providence."[5]

Personal items in the vehicle at the time were confiscated when the truck was impounded, including a special gold Browning automatic firearm. (Brown, incidentally, was an expert marksman. According to John A. Hopkins, Sr., "he could put a .22 shell on a mound of dirt and hit it at 50 yards without raising any dust."[6]) He never got the truck or his belongings taken from the vehicle back. He was not even allowed to pay a levy or fine to get those possessions returned.

The Brown family, rescued by Ethel's relations in Providence, inevitably made it back to their home, while the "Silver Streak" episode gained some snickers along with some good-natured ribbing following the publication of the *Journal*'s photograph in the newspaper.[7]

It was during the 1951 B. A. A. Marathon that a nineteen-year-old survivor of the atomic bomb blast that destroyed Hiroshima, Shigeki Tanaka, won the marathon with the third fastest time over the course. (He did not break the record set by Yun Bok Suh in 1947, failing by 2 minutes, 6 seconds.) It was in that marathon, according to the *New York Times*, that the eventual fifth-place finisher, the 26-year-old bespectacled Shunji Koyanagi of Japan, set a grueling pace over the midsection of the course, as he "threatened to make a runaway of the race. He led at every checking point and broke Tarzan Brown's 1936 course records at Woodland Park (16.8 miles) and Lake Street (21.2 miles)."[8] (Koyanagi led for 22 miles before fading.) The *Times* failed to remark that Brown had surpassed his own Lake Street record during his 1939 record-setting run. In 1936, at Lake Street he registered 1 hour, 59 minutes, 43 seconds. Three years later, he set a new record there; his new time was 1:57:47. The Brown records at those checkpoints had survived throughout the decade of the 1940s.

From 1932 to 1949, the North Medford 20-Mile road race was held, sponsored by the North Medford Club. In 1950 and 1951, the race was held under the sponsorship of the Dilboy American Legion Post.[9] After that, it was discontinued.

In the last week of March 1955, on the 26th, a 12-mile handicap race was held in Cambridge, Massachusetts, on a rainy, cold, raw afternoon. It was the sixth annual run sponsored by the Hyde Shoe Company, makers of athletic footwear including ice skates. It must have felt like one of those old North Medford races to Ellison Brown, as he surveyed the makeshift runners' locker room at the Kelly School on Willow Street, adjacent to where the starting line was drawn. Brown saw the preparing runners and overheard the race officials in a discussion over the handicapping times assigned to the different runners entered. The sights, sounds and smells may have been familiar but the role Brown played that day was new. This March he was father to the runner, and as he cast a hopeful eye upon his son, he must have momentarily felt some long-dormant feelings resurfacing in him.

The newspapers had anticipated the entry of Ellison Brown, Jr., called "Sonny" at home and "Tarzan Brown, Jr." in the sports pages, with delight. The *Boston Post* noted, "Nineteen-year-old Tarzan Brown, Jr., son of a former record breaker in the B. A. A. Marathon, is entered and may surprise. He is said to be every bit as good as his dad was at the same age."[10] Just what age "the same age" was meant to specify was not cut and dried; there was confusion as to Sonny's correct age at the time. In the next day's edition, the *Post* reported his age as 17, two years younger than what it gave the day before.

The *Globe* shared the *Post's* confusion. John Ahern, writing in the *Globe*, stated:

> It is unlikely it will happen, but no one with memories of past races would squawk if Tarzan Brown Jr. were the boy to do it [win big]. The 19-year-old son of the former marathon record holder is entered in this one and if his entry doesn't scare the rest of the large field, it certainly makes a lot of us feel old.
>
> This young gent, who was an infant when his father set the record in 1938 [*sic*], has a better potential than the great Tarzan had at the same age, accord-

ing to Len Malagrino, a neighbor of the Browns at Westerly, R. I. If that is the case, then the boy to watch in a year or two will be this youngster.[11]

Along with that race preview was featured a photograph from 1939 of father Ellison, elegantly dressed in a suit and tie, holding his namesake toddler in his arms, under which the lengthy caption read, "TIME AND MARATHON-ERS FLY — This photo, taken two days after Ellison (Tarzan) Brown, Rhode Island Indian, broke the world record in the Boston Marathon in '39, comes back to haunt the marathoners. Tarzan Jr., held here in his father's arms, makes his road-racing debut tomorrow in the Hyde Shoe 12-mile race, Cambridge. He is now 17 and trained by his father."[12] In the caption, Sonny's age was 17; in the accompanying story of the same paper, he was 19. The *Herald*, in its preview, played it safer when it reported, "Tarzan Brown Jr. of Providence will make this his first race."[13] It did not venture to provide his age.

The race featured some strong runners, trying to beat the record for the course set the year before by John J. Kelley (the younger), who could not defend his title. He was a member of the United States Army track team, on tour in South America. His record time for the course was 1 hour, 3 minutes, 42 seconds. Incidentally, the perennial competitor of distance running, John A. Kelley (the elder), still a force to be reckoned with in the 1950s, had won the time prize two years before!

When it was decided that Sonny, wearing number 67, would be assigned the kind of scratch assessment Tarzan might have received in his heyday, the father's anger would not subside quickly. It was patently unfair to saddle a 17-year-old son with impediments based upon his father's past achievements, yet that was exactly what the Hyde race officials were doing.[14] Protesting the process and the method employed fell on deaf ears.

Needless to say, Sonny — his Narragansett name is "Strong Bear" — admirably finished the course from start to finish, but due to the overly stringent assignments allocated to the runners, crossed the finish line in 36th place. It was his first formal organized racing experience. According to the *Post*, Ellison Brown, the father, "was satisfied" with his son's debut. "'This kind of weather would suit me fine,' said the veteran, 'but the lad was chilled to the bone out there today. But you will hear from him later.'"[15] The optimistic sentiment, the strong and immutable paternal pride, and the faith he had in his son were conveyed in the *Globe's* report as well.

> Little Tarz, starting his first race, was a confused youngster, but he managed to hang on and get home in 37th [*sic*] place.
> That's okay for a start," the road racing celebrity claimed, rubbing his boy's head in admiration. "He'll do okay. By Summer time he'll be showing these guys something. I'll go out and run with him and I might come back myself. But he's gonna be as good as the old man."[16]

Although the boy's finish was given as 37th in the *Globe* account, the *Herald*

Ellison Brown and Ellison Jr. ("Sonny") stand in the chilly air at the completion of the fifth annual Hyde Shoe 12-mile race in Cambridge, Massachusetts, March 27, 1955 (courtesy of the Boston Public Library, Print Department).

and the *Post* concurred that Ellison Jr. finished 36th. "The boy did all right (36th), but got cold," the *Herald* quoted the father. Perhaps Brown then got taken with nostalgia, for he said, "I got the urge to run again. Who knows, if I take a little weight off, I might get out there again. I'm only 41."[17] It was mostly fanciful thinking, caught up in the moment.

The inclement weather was an obstacle to the participants during the race but it was not the only hindrance; official misdirection was also a problem. It seems Rene Doiron, who had taken the lead at four miles, headed into a traffic circle at the Fresh Pond parkway, situated at the midway point of the race. Doiron followed the wrong police cruiser out of the rotary, not the official lead car, and ran a half mile in an errant direction. When he was eventually reached and redirected, he had lost a good deal of time and all of his advantage. The doubling back cost him dearly; that effort put him in 24th place behind new leaders, but he battled back still to finish 17th overall. Lee Chisholm, who had been granted a six-minute handicap, grabbed onto the lead shortly after Doiron's miscue at the Fresh Pond circle, and finished eight seconds ahead of the second-place finisher, Donald Fay.

Joe Kleinerman, of the Millrose A. A. of New York, finished third and had the third best time overall. Kleinerman, and the tenth-place finisher, Tony Medeiros, of the North Medford club, had the double pleasure of competing against both Ellison Brown the father and Ellison Brown the son. The two had raced against the father innumerable times, including another rainy, cold spring day sixteen years earlier when he shattered the record of the B. A. A. Marathon in 1939.

In mid-April 1955, a recently discharged ex-paratrooper, Albert T. Jordan, age twenty-two, was drinking in a busy tavern in his hometown of Peace Dale, Rhode Island. The topic of the moment was the upcoming B. A. A. Marathon. Tarzan Brown happened to be present in that tavern. "We were just down there having a little fun," he would recall later.[18] The impetuous young ex-serviceman, reduced by the consumption of alcohol to bravado, boasted that he was in better shape than "some of the runners around here," that they were "too old and fat to run."[19] It didn't take long before he directed a challenge personally at Brown, stating that he could easily beat the former marathon champion in an impromptu race. Tarzan reiterated Jordan's insulting gibe: "He said us old-time marathon runners were all washed up — just has-beens."[20] It was a challenge to his reputation and it was personal. Brown agreed to meet it then and there.

A course of a distance of 2½ miles was proposed and it was agreed to by both men. It "began in the Peace Dale flats, followed Kingstown Road to Columbia Street, to River Street, then to Wakefield's Main Street and up High Street to the starting point."[21] The disdainful ex-serviceman, a good twenty years younger than Brown, bullheadedly put up his new and expensive, beautifully crafted "leather jacket that 'Tarzan' had admired against the Indian's" own worn jacket.[22]

The boy had poorly assessed his elder adversary. Tarzan Brown, despite wearing inflexible work boots, quickly and with relative ease won the match and the jacket. In "13 or 14 minutes" Tarzan Brown completed the 2½ mile course from start to finish. According to the *Journal*, "the youngster never finished;" Jordan "walked in about 15 minutes later."[23] A caption to a photo of Brown holding the jacket read, "Not a laurel wreath but a prize just the same."[24] Charles Quinn of the *Journal* reported that Brown had actually employed a strategy in meeting the informal challenge. Wrote Quinn: "'Tarzan' said his most recent exploit was 'as far as I've run in about ten years.' He [Brown] 'went right out fast' and ran the younger man 'into the ground the first mile' to tire him out."[25] It worked like a charm.

Such challenges came Brown's way once in a while, like the older gunslinger sought after by a new generation of trigger-happy newcomers with something to prove. In many instances, Brown would race the cocky challengers as he immediately found himself — in work boots or hip high fishing boots, sober or not — it made no difference. In fact, it hardly ever mattered.

No one remembers Tarzan Brown on the losing end of any of these local, small-time challenges.

Ellison Brown holds the leather jacket he recently won in an impromptu footrace challenge. Wakefield, Rhode Island. April 14, 1955 (*Providence Journal* photograph).

In many of the multiple accounts of these numerous incidents, Brown, with either abundant generosity or an extremely imprecise, poor calculating ability, would allow his challenger what seemed to be a way-too-liberal head start. Such positing must have worked to his advantage, for he rarely failed to beat the bewildered opponent. Many locals remember or claim to remember races in which Brown, leading at the time, would make a stop midway along the course for a stool at the bar of an open tavern. After a few drinks and witnessing (or being told of) his challenger's progress (as the by-then usually arm-flailing, huffing, perspiring, muscle-aching, energy-depleted runner would be spotted passing by), Brown would calmly pay his tab, step out into the fresh air, and continue the race. He would invariably win.

33

Untimely Death: The Final Years

The Road Runners Club of America's American Long Distance Running Hall of Fame, created in 1970,[1] in only its third year of inducting runners into its ranks (at only five per year the first four years), selected Tarzan Brown in its 1973 panel of candidates for the honor. Brown was inducted along with *Boston Globe* sportswriter Paul "Jerry" Nason and runners Victor Drygall, James "Hinky" Henigan, and Peter McArdle. The 1973 slate joined the initial slate of 1971 (Bob Campbell, Clarence H. DeMar, Leonard "Buddy" Edelen, John J. Kelley, and Browning Ross) and the 1972 slate (Ted Corbitt, Fred Faller, Louis Gregory, John A. Kelley, and Joseph Kleinerman) in the hall of fame honors. In 1974, the year after Brown's induction, Pat Dengis, Les Pawson, Mel Porter, Charles Robbins and Fred Wilt, contemporaries who competed with Brown at some point in his career, were selected.

In November 1973, it was announced that Ellison "Tarzan" Brown was inducted into the American Indian Athletic Hall of Fame, located at Haskell Indian Nations University in Lawrence, Kansas, for his distance-running achievements. Tippy Salimeno, Brown's manager and lifelong supporter, had been instrumental in getting the runner recognized by the selection committee in Albuquerque, New Mexico. According to writer George Falcone, Brown received the news of his induction "very humbly, expressing sincere gratitude to his former manager in racing, Thomas 'Tippy' Salimeno of Westerly."[2]

A year later, a grand testimonial banquet was held to honor Ellison Myers Brown for his running achievements, his induction into the National Indian Athletic Hall of Fame, and his contributions to the Narragansett people. Taking place at the Charles Towne Lounge, at the intersection of Routes 2 and 112 in Charlestown in southern Rhode Island, the event was attended by more than four hundred well-wishers. Seated at the head table with Brown were his wife, Ethel; Sis, his eldest daughter; running luminaries Leslie Pawson and John A. Kelley; Brown's longtime supporting manager Thomas "Tippy" Salimeno; and Mr. and Mrs. Jock Semple on behalf of the Boston Athletic Association. Also in attendance were Brown's other children, his two sisters, relatives, fellow tribe members, town officials, B. A. A. winner and eight-time national marathon champion at Yonkers John J. Kelley (the younger), scores of friends and supporters, and members of the news media.

The *Westerly Sun* reported the event on its front page, noting: "Toastmaster Ferris B. Dove, known in the tribe as Chief Roaring Bull, opened the evening by introducing Chief Red Fox, Chief Sachem of the tribe, who extended the welcome to the audience. Mrs. Valcena Thomas spoke a prayer before the meal of chicken, potatoes, and vegetables was served."[3]

A biographical sketch and brief history of Ellison Brown was presented to the assembled guests. This was followed by introductions of his family. Jock Semple was introduced and addressed those in attendance. He referred to the guest of honor as "one hell of a runner," spoken in his thick Scottish brogue.[4] Semple presented a gift from the B. A. A. along with his verbal tribute.

In a heartfelt personal tribute to Tarzan, "John Kelley spoke of the comradeship, respect and admiration" among the community of runners for Brown, one of their own. Kelley told the listeners how his feelings of kinship with Brown were such that "he felt as though he had run right alongside of 'Tarzan' in the thirties."[5]

Leslie Pawson stood and recited some of the memories he treasured from many competitive runs with Tarzan. "He recalled the fellowship that they shared either in the locker room or on the race course."[6]

Salimeno praised Ellison Brown as "a world champion in the running game" and saluted the three great marathoners of that era, all present — Brown, Kelley and Pawson — as "three of the best runners in the world."[7] Tippy Salimeno had been on a mission, a mission to get Brown some of the recognition he deserved, in the annals of distance running and in the local community. On the former score, one step in his mission had been accomplished, and Salimeno was very pleased about the hall of fame induction of Brown. Ethel Brown remembered the evening vividly and Salimeno's chastisement of the local community for its shameful neglect of the world-acclaimed athlete living in its midst. Ethel recalled of Tippy, "he always said Westerly never treated him [Brown] right. He got right up at my husband's banquet and told everybody that."[8] Salimeno "finished by saying that they [he and Brown] never made any money running but they had memories that can't be forgotten or taken away."[9]

George Falcone, concluding the testimonial portion of the evening, talked about how he and Salimeno had worked since the summer of 1973 for the cause of getting Brown inducted into the Indian Athletic Hall of Fame. He expressed his delight and satisfaction in knowing that Brown "was given a place in the museum next to the immortal Jim Thorpe," what Falcone termed a most "fitting honor."[10]

After a few friends offered more warm expressions, Tarzan Brown, the center of attention, thanked everybody for their kind words and generous praises. At one point he looked over the large assemblage of exuberant guests with a panoramic sweep of his eyes, and then said, "I'm not a politician but I'm gonna get into it." It was the only quotation the *Providence Journal-Bulletin* reported.[11]

John J. Kelley remembered back thirty years to that evening. "Tarzan was in great social form, playing host to everyone and obviously relishing every minute of 'his night.'"[12] "As he was preparing to sit down, Chief Red Fox presented him with a check representing the donations that each member of the tribe had given as a way of recognizing the man who had brought honor and recognition to the Narragansett Indians," the *Sun* reported.[13] The check, the sum of which was reported in the *Journal-Bulletin* to be $500, had been an unexpected surprise to the family.[14]

Following the tributes, the guests were urged onto the floor, to dance to the music of the Inkspots, described as "Tarzan's favorite musical group."[15] John J. Kelley, who made a tardy appearance to the event, had this anecdotal recollection from that night:

> I had had to teach a class between 7 pm and 9 that evening and was therefore a late arrival. No problem. Tarzan took me and a young running friend in immediate tow, ordered us each a large glass of whisky and surveyed the tumult on the dance floor below the balcony where we stood. A rock band was blasting. "Boys," he said, "Pick a girl. I'll cut in for you." Young Mark and I decided to sip our drinks instead.
>
> Now, Johnny A. Kelley, Tarzan's 1930's nemesis, had traveled all the way from Massachusetts, and, being a strict early-to-bed guy, took his leave as I entered. Again, no problem. With Johnny "the Elder's" departure, Tarzan simply escorted me onto the stage and introduced me as his old pal of the roads, "Johnny Kelley."[16]

It wouldn't have been the first time there was some confusion over two runners named John Kelley, but it might have been one of the few times that the confusion was deliberate.

The *Westerly Sun* carried two striking photographs of Tarzan at the banquet on two successive days. On its front page, it ran a picture of a very dapper Ellison Brown sporting a formal black bow tie and a carnation on the lapel of a fashionable vertically-striped dinner jacket, standing next to his wife, Ethel, their daughter Sis, and Tippy Salimeno. The caption read: "A NIGHT TO REMEMBER — Long-delayed acclaim was accorded Ellison 'Tarzan' Brown, the great Marathon runner and a one-time member of the U.S. Olympic team, at a testimonial dinner Friday night at Charles Towne Lounge. In this photo with 'Tarzan,' are (from left) his first manager and trainer, Thomas 'Tippy' Salimeno, his daughter Sis, and his wife, Ethel."[17] The next day, the *Sun* ran a photograph of Brown flanked by Kelley and Pawson. The caption for that picture read:

THREE OF A KIND — There was a lot of class at the testimonial dinner Friday night at the Charles Towne Lounge for Ellison "Tarzan" Brown, a Narragansett Indian from Charlestown, who twice won the famed Boston Marathon. With Tarzan (center) are John J. [*sic*] Kelley (left) and Les Pawson, a couple of "pretty fair" runners in their own rights, who are numbered among the BAA champions. This trio dominated the U.S. long distance field in the early 1930's. The occasion was in recognition of Tarzan's recent induction into the National Indian Athletic Hall of Fame.[18]

Brown is standing between the two friendliest but fiercest competitive runners he ever beat (and occasionally was beaten by), his arms around them. Kelley, smiling broadly, is adorned in a loud plaid, unbuttoned sports coat and striped tie. Pawson, also smiling for photographer Charles Thibeault, is dressed formally in a gray-toned suit with a dark-hued shirt and a tie of patterned design.

It was a proud and treasured night for the Brown family. For Ethel, there was something else that contributed to an indelible memory of that evening. In the car on the way to the Charles Towne Lounge, Ethel, behind the wheel, looked over at her husband and momentarily was overcome by a strangely eerie though transitory sensation. Perhaps it was the look on Ellison's face or a look in his eyes that inspired it. Like many long-time married couples, she could often discern what was on his mind, especially if something was troubling him. This was altogether different. Seeming to sense her momentary dread, Ellison looked over at his wife and spoke in an unusually hushed tone, saying that it would soon be over, that he was going to be killed, that they were going to kill him. And he told Ethel not to do anything about it, warning her for her own safety. He did not say any more or explain as they rode in a wordless silence dispelled by the sounds of their automobile tires turning along the loosely packed rural road, a dark ride to a bright, festive occasion with guests excitedly anticipating their arrival. Ethel would never forget that night, November 8. "That was the night he told me that he was going to be killed. And I didn't pay any attention to it at first, until I just see the way he was acting."[19]

Summer nights in southern Rhode Island and eastern Connecticut bring large crowds of young people out to the stretch of coastline at Misquamicut, Rhode Island, where Rhode Island's beaches are located. For many years during the summers, the bars and restaurants that line Atlantic Avenue, the road that parallels the shoreline, attract hundreds, sometimes thousands of drinking-aged revelers, especially in the evenings after the sun has set and most of the families have left the beaches until the daylight of another day. In the early-to-mid-seventies, when drinking ages were lowered to eighteen in many states at the time and awareness of the dangers of drinking and driving were not yet a politically hot topic, incredible amounts of liquor were consumed in a short period of time in many of the establishments in Misquamicut. Certain come-ons and drinking promotions were also popular for a time, such as "beat the clock," where drinks started at the price of a quarter, and increased 25 cents every fifteen minutes. The steadily increasing price hike created an incentive to pound down as many drinks as possible early on while the prices were low. Obviously, getting deeply drunk (or "hammered" or "cocked"), if not the goal, was nevertheless an end result. The volatile combination of alcohol along with a scene of widespread recreational drug use, coupled with people in crowds—well that could, on occasion, lead to rowdy or dangerously violent behavior. Huge muscle-toned bouncers were on hand at most of the bars to keep things from getting too far out of hand, and a fairly large contingent of police usually created a ubiquitous visible presence, especially patrolling the roads to and from the beach area, where frequent cars and motorcycles would be pulled over for all too easily exceeding the 25 miles-per-hour posted speed limit. All the ingredients for serious trouble were in Misquamicut and that, in part, no doubt was what attracted the partying, hard-drinking crowds to go there.

It was in this atmosphere that Ellison Brown and his nephew, Russell Spears, age 35, found themselves on the warm, sticky night of August 23, at a bar called the 'Wreck.' At closing time the customers were being routed out of the bar following "last call." The parking lot surrounding the building filled with pedestrians, many struggling to walk on unsteady legs, and little attention being paid to safety if at all. As cars' engines were being started and headlights turned on, a chaotic situation in the parking lot ensued, as anxious drivers attempted to find their way out of the poorly lit and indefinitely marked lot area amidst the slow-moving, some still-imbibing revelers.

Phillip K. Edwards, age twenty-six, was at the Wreck Bar that night. It was after 1 in the morning, in a crowd of people and cars in the parking lot, that he must have found his way to his parked van. The Middletown, Connecticut, resident managed to get the key into the ignition and crank the engine. Like most vehicles parked in close proximity to the nighttime ocean breezes, a filmy fog covered the surfaces of his windshield, both inside and out, creating less than full visibility. The engine was too cold for the defroster to be of much use yet. Exactly what transpired next may never be known, but the result was the death of Ellison Brown. The *Westerly Sun* reported that Brown was struck by that van, and that "fifteen minutes later in The Westerly Hospital he was pronounced dead by a team of doctors who had tried to save him."[20]

Credible reports and information of Tarzan Brown's last day alive and the legal system's response are remarkably difficult to come by. At the time of the accident, it was widely reported that Brown was run over following an argument with Edwards. There was a lot of disparity in the reports and a paucity of detail. The AP dispatch in the *New York Times*, for example, had Brown "arguing with Edwards and two passengers in the vehicle."[21] The *Globe* reported that "police said the incident occurred after Brown and Edwards had an argument."[22] Once the story — another Indian killed after an argument in a bar — was disseminated, it was very difficult to alter, correct, or altogether change the picture of what happened the night Ellison Brown was killed. That account was accepted without question, for example, by author Peter Nabokov in his historical work entitled *Indian Running,* where he wrote summarily of Brown's later years: "He went through a series of odd jobs, sold his trophies to pay for groceries and medical bills for foot injuries stemming from his running, and was killed by a car after an argument in a bar."[23]

That Brown was a party to an argument with Edwards before his death was (and continues to be) vigorously denied by family members Ethel Brown and daughter Sis and was rejected by Tippy Salimeno, among others. Mother and daughter "insist that Tarzan had merely been there [at Misquamicut] to meet some people so that he could get a ride home. Both the police and the man's [Edwards] lawyer confirmed that Tarzan was an innocent bystander, that he had no words with the young man who, frightened by some rowdies who were banging on the side of his van, plowed through the crowd."[24] In another account, writer Colman McCarthy confessed his personal relief to hear Tippy Salimeno

> debunk the myth that Brown died in a barroom brawl. On August 23, 1975, Brown was in a parking lot in Misquamicut when a van, driven by a 26-year-old Connecticut man, plowed into him. That Brown was an innocent bystander — and not a rowdy participant in a fight that got out of hand — was confirmed by police accounts.... [25]

Russell Spears had accompanied his uncle Ellison Brown to Misquamicut, but his role that night was not investigated nor was he required to give a deposition. According to an account of the night which he related to *Globe* reporter Michael Madden, Spears and Brown were not even in the Wreck Bar that night. His recollection of events began with the contention that Ellison was very tired at the time. Brown found a spot on the beach and took a nap, "out back of the Blue Sands bar." Spears left his uncle to snooze while he went into the beach recreation hall with some other unnamed family members. At some point thereafter two rival groups of youths, divided along state lines (one from Connecticut and one from Rhode Island), began provoking each other into fighting. As the tension and the crowd increased, so too did the noise level. Madden presented Spear's version of events:

> The noise of the fight awoke the 61-year-old Indian from his slumber, Spear theorizes.
> The young men from Connecticut were getting the worst of the battle. "I remember thinking, 'Their only hope is to make a run for it,'" recalled Spears. Which they did, running to their vehicle and rushing to hurry away from danger. The 61-year-old Indian, still half groggy, walked down the road toward where his nephew and other family members were.

"He probably heard the noise and he was walking down the road to see what it was, said Spears. "That's when it happened."

The young men sped off in their vehicles. The Indian was run over. "He wasn't dead when they first ran him over," Spears thought then. "But the kids panicked, they backed up and ran him over again. That's what killed him."[26]

In Madden's article, there was no mention of Spears's charge later from that night that Spears was also hit at that time by the van that struck his uncle.

Phillip Edwards was apprehended and taken into custody. Ethel Brown received a telephone call, uncertain from exactly where it originated (maybe from the hospital), telling her to get to the emergency room of the Westerly Hospital as quickly as possible, where her husband had been hurriedly transported. Ethel arrived from Charlestown too late to see her husband alive. He had already been pronounced dead.

Initial newspaper reports claimed that the "Westerly police charged Edwards with assault with a dangerous weapon, a motor vehicle, and driving to endanger, death resulting."[27] The *Sun* further reported that Edwards had a preliminary hearing before Justice of the Peace John F. Lallo on Saturday, August 23, and was released on $3,500 surety bond. According to the *Providence Journal*, that first hearing took place at police headquarters.[28] At that time an arraignment was scheduled for the coming Monday in Fourth District Court, in Westerly, before Judge Francis M. Kiely.

The headline on the front page of the *Westerly Sun* on Monday evening, August 25, 1975, read: "Connecticut Man Charged In Tarzan Brown's Death; *Police Say Truck Is Murder Weapon*."[29] Appearing for his 1 o'clock hearing, Phillips K. Edwards was formally arraigned on three felony charges and one misdemeanor charge; "on charges of first degree murder (felony); driving so as to endanger, death resulting (misdemeanor); and two counts of assault with a dangerous weapon, an automobile (two felony charges)."[30] The two charges were the result of two men allegedly being struck by Edwards' van, Ellison Brown and a Richard Baker. The complaint by Russell Spears, the 35-year-old nephew of Brown, of also being struck by the van did not result in any charges.

With two attorneys representing him, James J. Longolucco and F. Thomas Lenihan (of the Westerly law firm Longolucco, Parrilla & Lenihan, located at 16 Canal Street), Edwards was advised not to make a formal plea to the three felony charges, only to the misdemeanor charge. "He entered a not guilty plea to the misdemeanor charge of driving so as to endanger, death resulting."[31] When Edwards, his parents and his attorneys had their first opportunity to express their sorrow to Ethel over what had happened, none chose to do so. A brief look at the defendant's mother's face, according to Ethel who had just lost her husband, revealed a glint of commiseration and an acknowledgment of the horror of what had taken place, but that was not overtly expressed then, nor was it ever. No sympathy or apology was ever extended to Ethel or the rest of the Brown family.

A graveside service for the slain runner was held in the woods of Charlestown. Charlestown, Rhode Island, August 26, 1975 (photograph by William K. Daby/*Providence Journal* photograph).

Bail was set by Judge Kiely at $6,000 surety and a District Court hearing was scheduled for September 12. "Edwards was remanded to the Adult Correctional Institution on the murder charge pending a bail hearing to be held in Superior Court at West Kingston," the *Westerly Sun* reported.[32]

On Tuesday, August 26, funeral services for Ellison Brown were conducted at the Harvey W. Buckler Funeral Home at 121 Main Street in Westerly. The Reverend Lloyd Frederick, pastor of the Central Baptist Church, led the services. More than five hundred mourners were in attendance, which overflowed from the funeral parlor onto the lawn and sidewalk, and continued to the lawn of the Pawcatuck Seventh Day Baptist Church across the street. The *Sun* observed that "there was a sprinkling of Indian costumes and headdresses in the crowd, but most of those attending the services wore suits and dresses."[33] Rev. Frederick selected a passage from the 19th Psalm for the occasion: "The heavens declare the glory of God and the firmament shows his handiwork ... and rejoiceth as a strong man runneth a race."

The Westerly service was followed by another one in Charlestown, at the cemetery where Brown's final resting place was dug "beneath clusters of oak and maple trees in a family burial plot deep in the woods of Charlestown."[34] A photograph of the final farewell ceremony appeared in both the Westerly and Providence newspapers. According to the *Westerly Sun*, "the services here were only symbolic because the body was *ordered returned* to Providence for *another* autopsy. This was necessary," the newspaper offered by way of brief explanation, "because a murder charge has been brought" (emphasis added).[35] This was not altogether accurate. Apparently no autopsy had yet been performed on the body. It was returned to the Medical Center in Cranston (not Providence) so state medical examiners could perform the autopsy, at the official request of the chief medical examiner, Dr. William O. Sturner. Sturner explained why the body was recalled a second time: "When the body was first brought to the Medical Center on Saturday, no autopsy was performed because it was believed Mr. Brown was the victim of an accident. We don't always get exact, reliable, total information at the time of death."[36] It was truly unfortunate that Dr. Sturner did not contact the Brown family to explain why the body could not be buried at the time of the graveside service. Very little sensitivity was shown to the family in their time of grieving by state officials.

After the burial grounds service, many of the mourners headed over to the Narragansett tribal longhouse on Route 2 for a buffet lunch, to share remembrances of Ellison Brown, and to comfort each other.

The body was returned from the Medical Center morgue to the Buckler Funeral Home, according to the *Providence Journal*, and was scheduled to be interred on Thursday morning, August 28.[37]

In the judicial realm, on September 4, 1975, Judge Anthony A. Giannini of the Providence Superior Court set $5,000 surety bail for Edwards during a morning hearing. Afterwards, Edwards was returned to the state's detention center. The September 12 District Court hearing was still scheduled to take place, according to the *Westerly Sun*.[38] Though not reported, Edwards was released on bail. A grand jury was convened.

In Superior Court in West Kingston, Washington County, a convened grand jury issued a formal indictment on October 6, 1975, which said, in part:

> That Phillip Edwards, with force and arms, at Westerly in the aforesaid county of Washington did operate a vehicle in a parking lot, to wit, Wreck Bar parking lot, so-called in the said town of Westerly, in reckless disregard of the safety of others, the death of one Ellison Brown, on the twenty-third day of August in the year of our Lord one thousand nine hundred and seventy-five, ensuing as a proximate result of an injury received by said operation of said vehicle, wherefore, in accordance with the provisions of §31–27–1 of the general laws [*sic*] of Rhode Island, 1956, said Philip [*sic*] Edwards, alias John Doe is guilty of "driving so as to endanger resulting in death."[39]

On November 24, 1975, the defendant Phillip K. Edwards appeared with counsel and was arraigned. A plea of not guilty was entered. On $1,000 personal recognizance, the defendant's cash bail was released. Five days later, on November 29, the defense counsel made a standard series of legal motions in court, which included a motion for a bill of particulars, a motion to be furnished with evidence favorable to the accused, a motion to be furnished with names of state witnesses, a motion to inspect statements of state witnesses, a motion to be furnished with the criminal records of the state witnesses, and a motion for discovery and inspection by the defendant of the prosecution's evidence. The motions were duly filed and, with the exception of the motion seeking the criminal records of the state witnesses, were recorded on a single sheet in the defendant's case file, number 75–184.[40] The next entry after the November filing of motions was March 12, 1976. On that date, a judgment and disposition was rendered in Superior Court in Washington County. With a plea entered of nolo contendere, the offense of "driving to endanger, death resulting" was ultimately finalized with a guilty judgment. "It is adjudged that defendant be placed on probation for two (2) years without supervision. Costs remitted."[41] Entered under "COSTS" was the figure "45.00" alongside "Grand Jury."[42] No other fees or charges were listed. The justice of the Superior Court signed off on the document three days later, on March 15, 1976. The maximum sentence for the single charge under the law that Edwards could have received was three years. He was given two years of unsupervised probation on the misdemeanor charge. There was no mention of the final results of the case or a reference to its disposition in the newspapers.

The felony murder charge which created the need for the autopsy back in August and the two other felony charges of assault with a dangerous weapon (motor vehicle) were quietly dropped sometime well before the March disposition of the driving-to-endanger case. The date those charges were removed was not noted in the defendant's case file. No other charges were adjudicated. No other charges appeared in the defendant's case file, but there was one reference to the murder charge that could be found. A two-sentence letter written by Chief Hearing Officer B. D. Filliatreault of the Rhode Island State Registry of Motor Vehicles, to the Clerk of the Superior Court, dated March 26, 1976, stated: "Our records indicate that the above subject (Edwards) was prosecuted by the Westerly Police for 'Driving As to Endanger' and 'Murder,' stemming from an accident that took place August 23rd, 1975. We would appreciate any dispositions for our record."[43] No copy of a response is included in the file.

In tribute to the memory of Ellison Brown, a tree and granite stone marker were dedicated in Wilcox Park, located in downtown Westerly, Rhode Island, closest to its Albin Gate entrance.[44] The inscription in stone reads:

This tree planted in memory of
Ellison "Tarzan" Brown
Winner of Boston Marathon
1936 and 1939
US Olympic Team 1936

A beautiful tree, in a park filled with an incredible diversity of tree species, grows by the stone marker, a living monument to the man. I inquired of park director and historian Alan Peck as to the variety of Tarzan Brown's tree. "Its botanical name," he responded, "is *Eucommia ulmoides*," known as the "Hardy Rubber Tree," a rather apt arboreal shrine.[45]

Top: Stone marker in memory of Ellison Brown has been placed in Wilcox Park, Westerly, Rhode Island, April, 2003 (photograph by M. Ward). *Left:* A tree of the species *Eucommia ulmoides* was planted in Ellison Brown's memory in Wilcox Park, Westerly, Rhode Island, April 2003 (photograph by M. Ward).

34

A Final Look

Ellison Brown's athletic years are told in the preceding chapters. In the years after the races, life was continuously difficult as money was always scarce. Like a proverbial diamond in the rough, there were multiple facets that comprised the man. He was, despite the contradictory sound of the description, a simple man of complexities.

On the one hand there was Ellison Brown, "a deep-hearted man"[1] with love in his heart for his family and his surroundings. His family was most familiar with this man. This was the man to whom children would relate easily. A superb storyteller, he could hold the attention of his listeners. He loved to introduce people, especially young people, to the many natural wonders that flourished around them. He was friendly to and understanding of animals and could communicate with them in ways that seemed at times supernatural. Speaking of the supernatural, Tarzan Brown could seemingly vanish into thin air all of a sudden. One moment he'd be visible, the next he could be gone, seemingly without a trace. For an explanation of this ostensibly supernormal ability, one would have to take a look at his utilization of his incredible speed to instantaneously move out of visible range, understand the existent lighting, the angle of ... — but why attempt to explain? Brown was, on some levels, a magical sort of person with extraordinarily unique abilities and ways.

In more earthly endeavors, he liked music and liked to make music. He was able to play the guitar and the accordion (or could make do with whatever was available), and had a good ear for music and lots of natural ability. Brown may have been happiest when he was able to spend time, sometimes hours at a time, by Charlestown Pond, one of his favorite places. There he would fish for oysters in winter, or just enjoy the ever-changing seasonal beauty of that outdoor spot. He loved the woods his entire life, and would take long walks, lasting from a few hours to a few days. He would gather nuts, find berries, beach plums, mushrooms or other wild edibles. Ethel recollected, "Sometimes he'd say, 'No work today,' and we'd pack a lunch and go fishing."[2] Ellison Brown, in the truest sense, communed with nature. He had an unspoken appreciation for being a part of nature and the natural order.

On the other hand, that Ellison Brown had a taste for alcohol cannot be denied nor should it be. It was a side of the man many residents of the Rhode Island towns near to where Brown lived who may not have known him well found most recognizable. Folks from the area to this day can recall barroom encounters with the runner when his running days were behind him, days from the sixties and early seventies, when Brown would take up any challenge. On more than one occasion he would chew a beer glass to win five dollars and a free round on a dare. Arm-wrestling matches and other competitive games were commonly the subjects of bets.[3] When

Ellison Brown contemplates the only trophy retained from his athletic past. Rhode Island, April 4, 1959 (*Providence Journal* photograph).

things got overly noisy or rowdy, and at times they would, Brown and companions would head to another drinking place. Jerry Nason recounted Brown telling him, "Maybe you heard I get in trouble sometimes. Maybe I do. Somebody takes a poke at me and my trouble is, I poke them back."[4] To many locals—and it is truly unfortunate—Brown fit the stereotypic image of the hard-drinking, trouble-making Indian.

The tragedy of a grave problem—alcoholism in the Native American community—and its underlying sources should not be glossed over. The disease, along with all the political and economic ramifications that contribute to its stubborn persistence, goes well beyond the scope of this book, but that certainly is not meant to indicate any lessening of its magnitude or seriousness. Alcohol consumption itself has a complicated history in the life of the whole nation. In spite of the tragic dimensions associated with its abuse, the attitude of the public has ranged between the admonishment of and the admiration for the functional high-capacity drinker. An example of the latter is the following, from Fred Brown Sr., runner and longtime member and leader of the North Medford running club. He related this anecdote from an athletic event he shared with Tarzan Brown and Johnny Kelley in "a Legion race weekend in Fitchburg," Massachusetts, in an unspecified month and year.

"We [both Browns and Kelley] got there the night before

and Tarzan settled right in at the Post bar," Brown recalled. "Johnny liked to go to bed early and he got after Tarzan for getting drunk and told him he ought to get some sleep so he could put on a good show for the people. Tarzan told him to get lost and closed the bar. You know who won the race the next day don't you? Tarzan! In record time!"[5]

Fred Brown could barely contain his admiration.

Not until the year of Brown's death, in 1975, would the Narragansett tribe — a legally incorporated nonprofit group since 1934 — be in a position to make a legal bid for the return of their native tribal lands, property seized generations earlier. A lawsuit for the return of 3,200 acres was filed with the State of Rhode Island, and in 1978 a settlement to that suit, known as the Rhode Island Indian Claims Settlement Act, resulted in the return of about 1,800 acres. Signing on to that settlement, however, had wide-reaching, and in some instances, unforeseen legal ramifications, some of which came to light in 2003 during a dispute over the obligation to collect state sales tax on cigarette sales on tribal land. The state attorney general of Rhode Island would claim that the tribe, by signing the 1978 settlement, agreed to "subject itself to the civil and criminal laws" of the state from that date forth. This would be disputed by the tribe, which, because it has sovereignty, recognized only the federal government's jurisdiction and still adheres to that position.

In 1979, the tribe petitioned the federal government for tribal recognition, and was granted that federal status on April 11, 1983. Ellison Brown did not live to see that happen.

Epilogue

Ethel Brown, wife and widow of Ellison Brown, still resides at her home on King's Factory Road in Charlestown with her daughter, Sis. The two women keep up with family and world news, along with tribal concerns. They continue their vigilant watch to prevent, in their view, Ellison Brown's exploitation in both name and memory. The sons Ellison Jr. (Sonny) and Norman (Thunderbolt) still live nearby although both men suffer health problems. Daughter Marlene is raising a grandson, Jordan Scott Monroe, and visits Ethel's home with regularity.

Avery Brundage, who ruled the amateur sports world of the United States with an iron fist for over forty years, died May 5, 1975. He served as president of the A. A. U. from 1928–1935 and as the head of the United States Olympic Committee from 1929–1953. He also was a force on the International Olympic Committee from 1952–1972. According to John Franch, archival assistant at the University of Illinois at Champagne where the papers of Avery Brundage are archived, there exist no references to Ellison "Tarzan" Brown whatsoever in the Brundage papers. His name could not even be located on a list of passengers that traveled to Berlin upon the S. S. *Manhattan* on July 15, 1936.[1]

Clarence Harrison DeMar passed away at his Reading, Massachusetts, farm on June 15, 1958, at the age of 70. He was a victim of intestinal cancer. He was fondly remembered for his limitless determination and no-nonsense demeanor. No one ever remembered DeMar dropping out of a race. At age 66, he ran his last B. A. A. Marathon, in 1954, finishing 78th in a field of 133. His time was a minute and a half under four hours. His last known competitive run took place the year before his death, in May 1957, when he ran in the New England 30-K championship race. He finished twenty-first in that one, his time reported to be 2 hours, 39 minutes, 30 seconds. A man who disliked authority and authority figures—even coaches—he never forgave the State of New Hampshire for taking his Swanzey farm by eminent domain to build an airport.

John Adelbert Kelley died Wednesday, October 6, 2004, at the age of 97. Obituaries were printed on page 1 of the *Boston Globe* and page 2 of the *Boston Herald* and Kelley was the subject of editorials in both papers. The

New York Times printed an obituary as well.[2] His death reportedly came three hours after he was moved from his home in East Dennis, Massachusetts, on Cape Cod to a nearby nursing home. The embodiment of the B. A. A. Marathon which he first ran in 1928 (at age twenty when Calvin Coolidge occupied the White House), Kelley dropped out of his first two attempts, in 1928 and 1932. From 1933 on (except for hospitalization that kept him out in 1968) he took part until 1992. His accomplishments in that marathon institution included his two first-place victories (in 1935 and 1945), a record seven second-place finishes, eighteen top-ten finishes and 58 finishes overall. In 1958 a fifty-year-old Kelley finished ninth, in 2 hours, 52 minutes, 12 seconds.[3] His last run in the B. A. A. was at the age of 85, when he finished in 5 hours, 58 minutes, 36 seconds.[4] He was selected to the United States Olympic team three times. The man who ran an estimated 1,500 races (including 112 marathons) was, by Jerry Nason's count in 1948, the winner of 604 prizes including 90 watches and 15 diamond rings.[5] By the end of his life, those totals had increased to a reported 115 watches and 22 diamond rings but no money.[6] Kelley, like his fellow runners Ellison Brown, Leslie Pawson, Clarence H. DeMar and Pat Dengis, was a lifelong amateur athlete. Unlike Brown and Pawson, he kept possession of a majority of his prize trophies, cups, medals and medallions. He was survived by his fourth wife, Ginger DeLong.

William Thomas "Will" Cloney made a name for himself as a sportswriter for the *Boston Herald* (until 1953) and then was lured over to the *Boston Post* (where he worked until the newspaper folded just three years later). Cloney was also on the faculty at Northeastern University where he taught English and journalism classes. In addition to that employment, beginning in 1947 he took control of the management of the B. A. A. Marathon, serving in the unpaid role of race director until 1984. One of the decisive changes he instituted was the limiting of vehicular traffic along the course. He required the print reporters covering the marathon to ride a bus, ending their automobile race within a race of which he had taken part for a decade. He presided over the inclusion of women in the marathon, in 1972, after a considerable amount of resistance to the move. Another significant change by Cloney was his opening up of the marathon to allow the wheelchair competition in 1975.

John "Jack" Farrington, the Rhode Island A. A. U. racing official that assumed the training duties that contributed to Brown's 1936 B. A. A. Marathon victory and sailed to Berlin to assist the runner in the Olympics, dropped out of the picture and could not be traced. It was rumored that Farrington remained in Berlin, allegedly involved romantically with his landlady of the apartment he rented during the Olympics. (He was not permitted access to the Olympic Village.) The story could not be confirmed.

Paul E. "Jerry" Nason was the sportswriter most closely associated with the B. A. A. Marathon. Nason's journalistic career at the *Boston Globe* began when he was hired as a copyboy in 1927. A prolific reporter, by 1942 he was appointed the *Globe's* sports editor, a position he held until his retirement in 1974. Even following his "official" retirement, Nason continued to write about the marathon for the *Globe* and other publications. He was an internationally recognized expert on marathon competition. Nason was a major supporter of Ellison Brown during his athletic career in New England. Nason, who believed Brown did not train adequately if at all and thus never reached his full racing potential, nevertheless recognized the sheer talent, astounding athleticism, and abundant grace of the runner. Nason famously chose Brown to win the 1936 marathon, a 100-to-1 shot, and is credited with giving name to Heartbreak Hill following Johnny Kelley's disappointing, failing effort to beat Brown after catching up to him and tapping him on the backside following a ferocious tear over the Newton hills in pursuit. Despite employing racial epithets liberally in his writing, Nason recognized Brown's greatness. Nason died June 19, 1986, at the age of 77.

Joseph William Nutter, who spent twenty-five years writing about sports (and track, his specialty) for the *Providence Journal* and *Bulletin*, died on February 15, 1948, at the age of 47. Jerry Nason of the *Boston Globe* credited Joe Nutter for being the first to alert him to the up-and-coming talents of then-rookie racer Tarzan Brown.

Leslie Samuel Pawson, the three-time B. A. A. Marathon winner, died October 13, 1992, at the age of 87. According to his obituary in the *Globe*, by the time Pawson had been selected to the 1940 United States Olympic team (which did not compete in Finland), he had already given up possession of his medals and trophies; he had "sold them all for badly needed cash during the Depression. They fetched $75."[7] A testimonial banquet was held in tribute to the gentleman sportsman in April 1983.

Thomas "Tippy" Salimeno, the Westerly, Rhode Island, trainer, manager, fight promoter, and proprietor of the Ritz Café, was best known as the man who first "discovered," trained, and assisted Ellison Brown, elevating the runner to national prominence. Salimeno befriended the teenaged Brown when they first met, and remained a friend and supporter of the runner throughout their lives. Salimeno died at the age of 87 on May 30, 1987.

John Duncan "Jock" Semple, runner, trainer, B. A. A. official, author, and among the greatest boosters to the sport of distance running that ever breathed, died on March 9, 1988. Semple competed in 90 marathons; he won three consecutive New England A. A. U. titles from 1933 to 1935. He served as co-director of the B. A. A. Marathon from 1952 until 1982, personally conducting the increasingly growing operation mostly by telephone from the "Salon de Rubdown," the training room inside the Boston Garden where he worked as masseur and trainer to the Boston Celtics and the Boston Bruins. Semple was perhaps best known for the 1967 incident when he tried to remove female marathoner Kathy Switzer's official number from her body to prevent the participation of women in the B. A. A. Marathon. She had signed her application "K. Switzer," an act Semple regarded as subterfuge.

Abraham "Abe" Soloveitzik, sportswriter and the sports editor of the *Westerly Sun* from 1930 until appointed city editor in 1957 (a post he held until his retirement in 1975, the year Brown was killed), championed the local hero Ellison Brown in the sports pages throughout Brown's running career. Soloveitzik passed away June 11, 1979.

"Chief" Horatio S. Stanton, Jr., marathon runner in the 1920s and '30s and the original inspiration for the young running Ellison Brown, died at the age of 84 in June 1981.

Notes

Historical note

1. Kenneth R. Shepperd, "Narragansett," in the *Gale Encyclopedia of Native American Tribes, Volume 1*, p. 173.

2. *Ibid.*, p. 175.

3. *Ibid.*, p. 174. Also, William S. Simmons, *Spirit of the New England Tribes* (Hanover, NH: University Press of New England, 1986), p. 29.

4. Ruth Walden Herndon and Ella Wilcox Sekatau, "The Right to a Name," in *After King Philip's War* (Hanover, NH: University Press of New England, 1997), pp. 126–127.

5. From the "Third Annual Report of Commission on the Affairs of the Narragansett Indians made to the General Assembly at its January Session, 1883."

6. *Providence Journal*, "The Narragansetts, in contest," September 28, 2003.

7. *Boston Post*, April 21, 1936, p. 18. Ethel, Ellison's widow, would not and could not confirm this widely reported story. It was, if it indeed occurred, a very early instance of a running event involving a mismeasured distance at a cost to the athlete involved.

Prologue

1. Tippy Salimeno, quoted in Colman McCarthy, "Tarzan Brown: Rhode Islanders Remember the Legendary Indian Runner," The Runner, January 1982, p. 86.

This tale, now a part of the "Tarzan Lore," was related on numerous occasions by Salimeno. It survives in several sources, including John Kelley, "John Kelley On Running: Tarzan Brown's Legend Survives," Hartford Sports Extra, November 15, 1979, p. 15; Colman McCarthy, "Tarzan Brown: Rhode Islanders Remember the Legendary Indian Runner," The Runner, January 1982, p. 86; Bill Rodriguez, "The Best Racer of All," Providence Journal-Bulletin Sunday Journal Magazine, April 19, 1981; and Jock Semple, *Just Call Me Jock* (Waterford, CT: Waterford Publishing, 1982), pp. 47-48.

2. Jock Semple, *Just Call Me Jock* (Waterford, CT: Waterford Publishing, 1982), p. 48.

3. Tippy Salimeno's recollection of Chief Stanton's words, quoted in John Kelley, "John Kelley On Running: Tarzan Brown's Legend Survives," Hartford Sports Extra, November 15, 1979, p. 15.

Salimeno's recollection also quoted in Colman McCarthy, "Tarzan Brown: Rhode Islanders Remember the Legendary Indian Runner," The Runner, January 1982, p. 86.

4. Tippy Salimeno, quoted in Bill Rodriguez, "The Best Racer of All," *Providence Journal-Bulletin Sunday Journal Magazine*, April 19, 1981.

5. Salimeno, quoted in Colman McCarthy, "Tarzan Brown: Rhode Islanders Remember the Legendary Indian Runner," The Runner, January 1982, p. 86.

6. Colman McCarthy, "Tarzan Brown: Rhode Islanders Remember the Legendary Indian Runner," The Runner, January 1982, p. 86.

Chapter 1

1. Tarzan's three brothers all met violent deaths, their lives cut short. Original source: Byron Brown, telephone conversation with author, December 18, 2002. Secondary source: John Hopkins, *Westerly Sun*, April 18, 1999, p. 24.

2. *Boston Post*, April 21, 1936, p. 19. Chief John Tortes Meyers, whose surname was spelled with two e's (unlike Ellison's middle name despite being named after him), was a Dartmouth-educated Cahuilla Native American from California. He was the catcher on the pennant-winning Giants of 1911, 1912 and 1913. An exceptional player, he batted .332, .358, and .312 during those winning seasons. He played in 18 World Series games with a .290 average in the post-season. A lifetime .291 hitter, Meyers was the first major league catcher to hit for the cycle (against the Cubs, on June 10, 1912). He was a battery-mate of the great Christy Mathewson.

3. *Providence Journal*, April 21, 1936, p. 8. The Brown children attended a one-room schoolhouse for grades 1-8, reported Michael Madden, *Boston Globe*, April 14, 1996, p. 65. Author Falls wrote, "I did some more checking into Tarzan's background

and found-surprisingly-that he was a very well-spoken man for one who never got out of the seventh grade" (Joe Falls, *The Boston Marathon*, p. 45).

4. Grace Spears, in Michael Madden, "Tarzan Brown Narragansett Indian Found Fame on Heartbreak Hill But Never Fortune," *Boston Globe*, April 14, 1996, p. 65.

5. *Boston Post*, April 21, 1936, p. 18.

6. *Boston Sunday Globe*, April 23, 1939, p. 6.

7. Joe Nutter, *Providence Journal*, April 21, 1936, p. 8.

8. *Boston Globe*, April 14, 1982, Sports section. (http://infoweb.newsbank.com/iw-search/we/InfoWeb?p_action=doc&p_docid=0EB97553...)

9. *Ibid.*

10. The Patriots' Day race is offiicially named the Boston Athletic Association Marathon, or the B. A. A. Marathon, but it is widely known as the Boston Marathon, or simply The Boston (or even more simply, just Boston). Patriots' Day is an observed state holiday in Massachusetts and Maine, originally April 19, but modernized to fall, despite the date, on the third Monday in April.

11. Ellison Brown ran his first B. A. A. Marathon in 1933. Apparently that is disputed. Some obituaries omitted that first run: "He ran his first Boston Marathon in 1934," says The *Boston Herald American* (August 26, 1975, p. 3). "Brown, 61, ran his first Boston marathon in 1934," says the *Boston Globe* (August 26, 1975, p. 34). Yet, in an obituary printed two days earlier in the *Boston Globe*, one finds, "He competed in his first Boston marathon in 1933...." (August 24, 1975, p. 91). Jerry Nason, a *Globe* sportswriter and resident expert in marathon matters, must have suffered from faulty recall in 1985 when he wrote, "a few nights before the 1935 Boston race, Brown's first Marathon." in *Sportscape*, April 1985, p. 8.

12. Jock Semple, *Just Call Me Jock* (Waterford, CT: Waterford Publishing, 1981), p. 45.

13. Hal Higdon, *Boston: A Century of Running* (Emmaus, PA: Rodale Press, 1995), pp. 80, 83.

14. Semple, p. 41.

15. Semple, pp. 47-48.

Chapter 2

1. The Leader, October 11, 1934, p. 12.

2. *Ibid.*

3. *Ibid.*

4. *The Leader*, October 12, 1934, p. 1.

5. *Ibid.*

6. *New York Times*, October 13, 1934, p. 21.

7. The AP, carried in the *New York Times*, *Ibid.*

8. Clarence H. DeMar, *Marathon* (Sherburne, VT: New England Press, 1937, 1981) p. 142.

9. *Ibid.*, pp. 142-143.

10. *Ibid.*, p. 151.

11. Ellison Brown, as quoted in Semple, *Just Call Me Jock*, p. 48.

12. *The Leader*, October 12, 1934, p. 2.

Chapter 3

1. John A. Kelley, quoted in Frederick Lewis and Dick Johnson, *Young At Heart* (Waco, TX: WRS Publishing, 1992), p. 22.

2. *Boston Traveler*, March 21, 1935, p. 19.

3. The Longboat record held until 1911, when Clarence H. DeMar successfully dismantled it.

4. *Boston Globe*, March 24, 1935, p. 27.

5. *Boston Globe*, March 24, 1935, p. 27.

6. *Westerly Sun*, March 24, 1935, p. 6.

7. *Boston Herald*, March 24, 1935, p. 27.

8. *Boston Traveler*, April 12, 1935, p. 42. DeMar was a seven-time winner, not eight. No other person has won more times.

9. *Boston Globe*, April 12, 1935, p. 30.

10. John J. Kelley, "On Running," *Hartford Sports*, November 15, 1979, p. 15.

11. Ethel Brown, interview with author, July 31, 2004.

12. Jerry Nason, *Sportscape*, V. 5, No. 3, April 1985, pp. 8–9.

13. Jock Semple, in *Just Call Me Jock*, spells the English name "*Ritchings*" on page 55 and "*Richings*" on page 56. Robert Playfair spells it "*Ritchings*" in the *Boston Globe* (April 20, 1936, p. 9). Hal Higdon, in *Boston: A Century of Running*, leaves the "g" off, spelling it "*Ritchins*" in the text (p. 73) but "*Ritchens*" in the index (p. 241).

14. *Boston Evening Globe*, April 18, 1935, p. 26.

15. Recalled by Samuel Ritchings, in an interview with Robert Playfair, *Boston Daily Globe*, April 20, 1936, p. 9.

16. *Westerly Sun*, April 21, 1935, p. 2.

17. *Ibid.*

18. *Boston Post*, April 7, 1936, p. 17.

19. *Boston Post*, April 18, 1935, p. 18.

20. *Boston Traveler*, April 20, 1935, p. 12.

Chapter 4

1. Jock Semple, in a clipping from John A. Kelley's scrapbook, Boston Public Library — not dated.

2. *Westerly Sun*, June 9, 1935, p. 6.

3. *Westerly Sun*, June 27, 1935, p. 8.

4. *Ibid.*

5. *Westerly Sun*, July 1, 1935, p. 8.

6. *Ibid.*

7. *Ibid.*

8. *New York Times*, July 15, 1935, p. 15.

9. The *Globe, Post* and *Herald* reported a field of 56 runners. The *New York Times* counted 63.

10. *Boston Herald*, August 25, 1935, p. 35.

11. *Boston Globe*, August 25, 1935, p. 25.

12. *Westerly Sun*, August 25, 1935, p. 6.

13. *Boston Globe*, August 25, 1935, p. 25.
14. *Boston Herald*, August 25, 1935, p. 33.
15. The *New York Times* reported a field of only fifty (September 3, 1935, p. 28). The *Westerly Sun* reported fifty-two starters (September 3, 1935, p. 8).
16. *Westerly Sun*, September 8, 1935, p. 2.
17. *Westerly Sun*, September 16, 1935, p. 6.
18. *The Leader*, October 10, 1935, p. 16.
19. *The Leader*, October 11, 1935, p. 10.

Chapter 5

1. *Boston Globe*, March 20, 1936, p. 1.
2. *Boston Globe*, March 21, 1936, p. 11.
3. *Ibid.*
4. *Ibid.*
5. *Boston Herald*, March 22, 1936, p. 33.
6. *Ibid.*
7. *Boston Post*, March 22, 1936, p. 20.
8. *Ibid.* Jerry Nason, in the *Globe*, gave his readers the same prognosis, but reported it as issued from a completely different doctor attending to Kelley in the makeshift dressing room in the Roberts Junior High in Medford. According to Nason, it was a Dr. John J. Manley giving Kelley treatment after the race. (*Boston Globe*, March 22, 1936, p. 31.)
9. *Boston Chronicle*, March 28, 1936, p. 6. Whether the *Chronicle* considered Brown "colored" due to his Native American heritage or his skin tone is unclear.
10. *Boston Herald*, March 22, 1936, p. 33.
11. *Ibid.*
12. *Boston Herald*, April 10, 1936, p. 41.
13. *Boston Chronicle*, March 28, 1936, p. 6.
14. *Boston Sunday Post*, April 5, 1936, p. 18.
15. *Boston Herald*, April 5, 1936, p. 35.
16. *Boston Globe*, April 5, 1936, p. 30.
17. *Boston Chronicle*, April 11, 1936, p. 8.
18. *Boston Traveler*, April 6, 1936, p. 36.
19. Les Pawson, quoted in the *Boston Traveler*, *Ibid.*
20. Fred Foye's reporting, *Boston Traveler, Ibid.*
21. *Ibid.*
22. *Boston Herald*, April 5, 1936, p. 38.
23. *Boston Traveler*, April 6, 1936, p. 36.
24. *Boston Herald*, April 5, 1936, p. 38.
25. *Boston Globe*, April 5, 1936, p. 30.
26. *Boston Traveler*, April 6, 1936, p. 36.
27. *Boston Herald*, April 5, 1936, p. 38.
28. *Boston Chronicle*, April 11, 1936, p. 6.
29. *Ibid.*, p. 8.
30. *Boston Herald*, April 5, 1936, p. 38.

Chapter 6

1. The marathon was held on Monday, April 20, in 1936. If April 19, Patriots' Day, fell on a Sunday, the marathon was usually held the next day in observance of the Boston blue laws. This changed during the World War II years of 1942 and 1943 when the marathon was deliberately held on Sunday to keep disruption of the labor in defense industries to a minimum.
2. *Boston Post*, April 9, 1936, p. 14.
3. A part of Bob Coyne's cartoon in the *Boston Post*, April 9, 1936, p. 14.
4. Coyne, *Ibid.*
5. *Ibid.*
6. *Ibid.*
7. *Ibid.*
8. *Ibid.* Boston's National League team, the Braves, was rechristened the Boston Bees after the 1935 season (with a dismal record of only 38 wins and 115 losses) and near bankruptcy. New owner Bob Quinn submitted team nickname choices chosen by fans to a panel of sportswriters who picked the Boston Bees. The new name was supposed to help transform the luck and fortunes of the team, but the name reportedly never caught on — even Quinn never got used to using it. The team resorted back to bearing the name "the Boston Braves" in spring training in 1941. The Boston Bees finished sixth (1936) and fifth (1937) under manager Bill McKechnie, and fifth (1938), seventh (1939) and seventh (1940) under manager Casey Stengel. Incidentally, after the 1952 season, the Boston Braves team was moved to Milwaukee, Wisconsin.
9. Ellison Brown, quoted in the *Boston Traveler*, April 10, 1936, p. 23.
10. Jock Semple, *Just Call Me Jock.* (Waterford, CT: Waterford Publishing, 1981), p. 47.
11. Semple, p. 48.
12. Jerry Nason, *Yankee Magazine*, 1981, p. 101.
13. Ethel Brown, quoted in John Kelley, "On Running," *Hartford Sports Extra*, (November 15, 1979), 15.
14. *Boston Post*, April 7, 1936, p. 17.
15. Arthur Duffey, *Ibid.*
16. *Ibid.*
17. Jack Farrington, quoted in the *Boston Post*, *Ibid.*
18. Ellison Brown, quoted in the *Boston Post*, April 21, 1936, p. 19.
19. *Boston Post*, April 21, 1936, p. 19.
20. *Boston Herald*, April 21, 1936, p. 27.
21. *Boston Post*, April 21, 1936, p. 19.
22. *Ibid.*, p. 18.
23. *Westerly Sun*, April 21, 1936, p. 2.
24. *Boston Evening Globe*, April 20, 1936, p. 9.
25. *Boston Post*, April 21, 1936, p. 19.
26. *Ibid.*
27. *Boston Herald*, April 21, 1936, p. 27.
28. *Ibid.*
29. Jack Farrington, quoted in the *Boston Globe*, April 21, 1936, p. 24.

30. *Boston Post*, April 21, 1936, p. 19.
31. Duffey, *Boston Post*, April 7, 1936, p. 17.
32. Duffey, *Boston Post*, April 15, 1936, p. 20.
33. *Ibid.*
34. Providence Tercentenary Committee, *Ibid.*
35. Duffey, *Ibid.*
36. Bob Dunbar, *Boston Herald*, April 15, 1936, p. 21.
37. *Boston Globe*, April 16, 1936, p. 20.
38. Pat Dengis, *Ibid.*
39. *Ibid.* Destinations of Lynn or Salem would have meant another twelve to sixteen miles tacked onto the course.

Chapter 7

1. *Boston Herald*, April 20, 1939, p. 20.
2. *Boston Herald*, April 21, 1936, p. 26.
3. *Boston Globe*, April 20, 1936, p. 9. The next day, the *Globe* reported that Dengis "was the only runner who did not submit to a physical examination before the race." (April 21, 1936, p. 25.) The *Westerly Sun*, in an AP story, reported, "Dinges [*sic*] showed up at the start only seconds before the gun cracked. Officials did not have time to weigh him or give him the routine examination, but he was allowed to start." (April 20, 1936, p. 1)
4. *Boston Traveler*, April 20, 1936, p. 1. Author Tom Derderian claims that at the marathon the following year (1937), George V. Brown started his 39th race, which would make the 1936 start his 38th, not his 31st as the *Traveler* reports. See Tom Derderian, *Boston Marathon: The First Century of the World's Premier Running Event* (Champaign, IL: Human Kinetics, 1996), p. 159. The *Westerly Sun*, concurring with the *Traveler* regarding Brown's thirty-first starting duties, reported George O. Brown, not George V. Brown, as the triggerman. (April 20, 1936, p. 1)
5. According to the *New York Times*, April 21, 1936, p. 30. The *Boston Evening Globe* gave the number of runners as 186 in an article by Paul V. Craigue (April 20, 1936, p. 9) and as 182 in another edition of the same date (April 20, 1936, p. 9). The *Westerly Sun* had the figure as 183 on April 20, 1936, p. 9, but corrected it to 184 in the following day's edition (April 21, 1936, p. 1.). The *Boston Traveler* (April 20, 1936, p. 34) reported 188 starters, as did the *Boston Herald*, which put the number at 188 in this humorous contribution by Bill Rae: "Starter George Brown fired the gun out at the Tebeau Farm takeoff and very well may be subject to investigation, for of the 215 scheduled to start, only 188 were seen to come down the hill after the shot." (April 21, 1936, p. 26.)
6. *Providence Journal*, April 21, 1936, p. 8.
7. *Boston Traveler*, April 20, 1936, p. 34.
8. *Boston Globe*, April 21, 1936, p. 25.
9. *New York Times*, April 21, 1936, p. 30.
10. *Boston Post*, April 21, 1936, p. 18.

11. *Boston Post*, April 21, 1936, p. 18.
12. *Boston Evening Globe*, April 20, 1936, p. 9.
13. *Boston Evening Globe*, April 20, 1936, p. 9.
14. *Boston Globe*, April 21, 1936, p. 25.
15. *Ibid.*
16. *Boston Globe*, April 21, 1936, p. 25. This is an early journalistic usage from a historic point of view, as far as I have been able to determine, of the designation "*native American*."
17. *Boston Evening Globe*, April 20, 1936, p. 9.
18. *Boston Post*, April 21, 1936, p. 18.
19. *Boston Post*, April 21, 1936, p. 18.
20. *Providence Journal*, April 21, 1936, p. 8.
21. Frederick Lewis, *Young At Heart* (Waco, TX: WRS, 1992), p. 39.
22. *Boston Herald*, April 21, 1936, p. 26.
23. Joe Falls, *The Boston Marathon* (New York: Macmillan, 1977), p. 178.
24. Hal Higdon, "Start to Finish" online article (www.runnersworld.com/events/boston/boston96/facts.html) p. 4.
25. *Boston Globe*, April 22, 1936, p. 23.
26. Jerry Nason, *The Story of the Boston Marathon (From 1897)* (Boston: *Boston Globe*, 1966), p. 25.
27. Jerry Nason, quoted in Joe Falls, *The Boston Marathon*, p. 41.
28. Ellison Brown, quoted in the *Boston Globe*, April 21, 1936, p. 24.
29. Ellison Brown, quoted in the *Boston Post*, April 21, 1936, p. 19.
30. John Kelley, quoted in the *Boston Globe*, April 22, 1936, p. 23.
31. *Boston Post*, April 21, 1936, p. 18.
32. *New York Times*, April 21, 1936, p. 30.
33. John Kelley, quoted in the *Boston Post*, April 21, 1936, p. 18.
34. John Kelley, quoted in the *Boston Globe*, April 21, 1936, p. 24.
35. *Boston Traveler*, April 21, 1936, p. 26.
36. *Boston Post*, April 21, 1936, p. 18.
37. Otis Byron Brown, quoted in the *Westerly Sun*, April 22, 1936, p. 2.
38. *Boston Herald*, April 21, 1936, p. 26.
39. *Ibid.*, April 21, 1936, p. 26.
40. *Boston Globe*, April 20, 1936, p. 9.
41. Jack Farrington, quoted in the *Boston Post*, April 21, 1936, p. 18.
42. Jack Farrington, quoted in the *Boston Post*, April 21, 1936, p. 18.
43. *New York Times*, April 21, 1936, p. 30.
44. Ellison Brown, quoted in the *Boston Post*, April 21, 1936, p. 1.
45. Art Walsh in the *Boston Herald*, April 21, 1936, p. 27.
46. Ellison Brown, quoted in the *Boston Herald*, April 21, 1936, p. 27.
47. Art Walsh, in the *Boston Herald*, April 21, 1936, p. 27.
48. George Demeter's role in accordance with legend, as recounted by Bill Rae in the *Boston Herald*, April 21, 1936, p. 26.

49. Photo in the *Boston Evening Globe*, April 20, 1936, p. 1, and in the *Boston Daily Globe*, April 21, 1936, p. 24. Caption quoted is from the April 21st edition. The April 20th caption for the same photo reads: "TARZAN BROWN OF PROVIDENCE CROSSING THE FINISH LINE A WINNER IN MARATHON."

50. Ellison Brown, quoted in the *Boston Post*, April 21, 1936, p. 19. This dialogue does not have the ring of authenticity.

51. *Boston Evening Globe*, April 21, 1936, p. 1.

52. *Providence Journal*, April 21, 1936, p. 11.

53. *Westerly Sun*, April 21, 1936, p. 1.

54. *Boston Globe*, April 21, 1936, p. 25.

55. *Boston Daily Globe*, April 21, 1936, p. 24.

56. *Boston Traveler*, April 21, 1936, p. 26.

57. *Ibid.*

58. Ellison Brown, quoted in the *Boston Post*, April 21, 1936, p. 18.

59. *Boston Globe*, April 21, 1936, p. 25.

60. *Boston Post*, April 21, 1936, p. 19.

61. *Westerly Sun*, April 21, 1936, p. 1.

62. *Providence Journal*, April 21, 1936, p. 10.

63. Ellison Brown, as quoted in the *Boston Daily Globe*, April 21, 1936, p. 24.

64. *Westerly Sun*, April 21, 1936, p. 2.

65. *Ibid.*

66. Chief Stanton, quoted in the *Boston Herald*, April 21, 1936, p. 27.

67. *Boston Globe*, April 21, 1936, p. 24. Newspaper photos bear out the polka dot necktie design, despite varying descriptions. To view Brown in sartorial splendor, see *Boston Traveler*, April 21, 1936, p. 26; *Boston Post*, April 21, 1936, p. 19; *Providence Journal*, April 22, 36, p. 9. To the *Post*'s Ruth Bodwell, Brown wore "a gray suit in belted model, a white shirt and white tie with black polka dots." (*Boston Post*, April 21, 1936, p. 19).

68. *Boston Traveler*, April 21, 1936, p. 26. No polka dotted pattern on the necktie is offered here. Instead, "bright-lined" is the adjective attached to the tie.

69. *Boston Herald*, April 21, 1936, p. 27.

70. *Ibid.*

71. Ellison Brown, quoted in the *Boston Daily Globe*, April 21, 1936, p. 24.

72. *Boston Herald*, April 21, 1936, p. 27.

73. *Boston Daily Globe*, April 21, 1936, p. 24.

74. Otis Byron Brown, quoted in the *Boston Post*, April 21, 1936, p. 19.

75. *Boston Post*, April 21, 1936, p. 18.

76. Ellison Brown, quoted in the *Boston Post*, April 21, 1936, p. 19.

77. Jack Farrington, quoted in the *Boston Traveler*, April 21, 1936, p. 26.

78. Ellison Brown, quoted in the *Boston Post*, April 21, 1936, p. 19.

79. *Boston Globe*, April 21, 1936, p. 25; also the *Boston Post*, April 21, 1936, p. 18. *The New York Times*, April 21, 1936, p. 30, placed Dengis' dropout after mile 20, or three miles beyond what the Boston newspapers reported.

80. *Boston Herald*, April 21, 1936, p. 27.

81. Pat Dengis, quoted in the *Boston Daily Globe*, April 21, 1936, p. 24. Washington, D. C., hosted a national marathon, which served as a second Olympic trial.

82. *Boston Herald*, April 22, 1936, p. 27.

83. *Boston Herald*, April 21, 1936, p. 26.

84. Ellison Brown, quoted in the *Boston Daily Globe*, April 21, 1936, p. 24.

Chapter 8

1. Jerry Nason, *Boston Globe*, April 18, 1936, p. 9.

2. Jerry Nason, the *Boston Daily Globe*, April 20, 1936, p. 8.

3. *The Story of the Boston Marathon (from 1897)*, p. 1.

4. Hal Higdon, *Boston: A Century of Running* (Emmaus, PA: Rodale Press, 1995), p. 39.

5. Joe Falls, *The Boston Marathon*, p. 35.

6. Joe Falls, *The Boston Marathon*, p. 36.

7. *Boston Globe*, April 18, 1936, p. 9.

8. *Boston Globe*, April 20, 1936, p. 11.

9. *Boston Globe*, April 21, 1936, p. 1.

10. Jerry Nason's possible share of Native American ancestry related by Richard Johnson, curator of the Sports Museum of New England (Boston, Massachusetts) and editor of Richard Lewis' *Young At Heart*, in a comment to the author, September 19, 2003.

11. Strange as it may seem, disagreements exist concerning whether the Newton hills are three or four in number. One marathon historian, Hal Higdon, saw four (p. 75). Jack Barnwell of the *Boston Post* saw three (April 21, 1936, p. 18). Author Michael Connelly also falls into the three-hill camp. Historian Tom Derderian appears undecided. Derderian described four hills on page 447 ("The hills waited ahead—four of them.") in his book, *Boston Marathon*, and wrote of "the three Newton hills" on page 153 of the same work. No matter how one counts them, Heartbreak Hill has always been the last one of the series the runners had to face.

12. John Powers, *Boston Globe*, April 15, 1988, p. 44. Note the runner's plural use "Heartbreak Hills" (emphasis added). Hal Higdon related that same episode: "When Joan Benoit asked another runner about the location of Heartbreak Hill en route to her first Boston victory in 1979, she was told, 'Lady, you just passed it!'" Hal Higdon, *Boston: A Century of Running*, p. 77.

13. Jackie MacMullan, "In this Corner/Semple Memories Run Their Course," *Boston Globe*, April 16, 1984, Edition: N, Section: Run of Paper.

14. *Ibid.*

15. *Westerly Sun*, April 21, 1936, p. 1.

16. *Westerly Sun*, April 20, 1936, p. 1.

17. *Boston Post*, April 21, 1936, p. 18.

18. A *Globe* editorial in tribute to Johnny A.

Kelley at the time of his death parenthetically reported Nason's authorship as undisputed fact: "The *Globe's* Jerry Nason named Heartbreak Hill after his [Kelley's] struggles in 1936" (Editorial, *Boston Globe*, October 8, 2004, p. A18).

Chapter 9

1. *Boston Traveler*, April 21, 1936, p. 26.
2. *Boston Herald*, April 22, 1936, p. 27.
3. *Westerly Sun*, April 22, 1936, p. 2.
4. *Ibid*, p. 1.
5. *Boston Traveler*, April 21, 1936, p. 26.
6. He returned to the Lenox Hotel according to the *Westerly Sun*, April 21, 1936, p. 2, and April 22, 1936, also p. 2.
7. According to the *Boston Traveler*, April 21, 1936, p. 26, Brown returned to the Waugh residence.
8. *Ibid*.
9. *Boston Herald*, April 22, 1936, p. 27.
10. *Westerly Sun*, April 22, 1936, p. 2.
11. *Providence Journal*, April 22, 1936, p. 9.
12. *Ibid*.
13. *Boston Globe*, April 22,1936, p. 23.
14. *Providence Journal*, April 22, 1936, p. 9.
15. *Ibid*.
16. *Boston Herald*, April 22, 1936, p. 27.
17. *Ibid*.
18. *Ibid*.
19. *Boston Globe*, April 22, 1936, p. 23.
20. *Boston Herald*, April 22, 1936, p. 27.
21. *Ibid*.
22. The version in the *Westerly Sun*, April 21, 1936, p. 1, does not match the one in the *Providence Journal* word for word, the version presented here. The entire first paragraph is omitted in the *Sun's* copy. Alternate words or variations reported in the *Sun* are in brackets, and each word that precedes brackets is omitted in the *Sun*; empty brackets indicate the preceding word, reported in the *Journal*, is omitted without a replacement in the *Sun*; "General Assembly" gets uppercase treatment in the *Sun*, but not in the *Journal*; "Anniversary" gets lowercase treatment in the *Sun*. Brown's middle name is misspelled *Meyers* (with two *e*'s) in the *Providence Journal*, but is correctly spelled *Myers* in the *Westerly Sun*.
23. *Providence Journal*, April 22, 1936, p. 9.
24. *Ibid*.
25. *Westerly Sun*, April 22, 1936, p. 1.
26. *Boston Herald*, April 22, 1936, p. 27.
27. *Providence Journal*, April 22, 1936, p. 1.
28. *Ibid*.
29. *Ibid*, p. 9.
30. *Westerly Sun*, April 22, 1936, p. 2.
31. *Providence Journal*, April 22, 1936, pp. 1, 9.
32. *Ibid*, p. 9.
33. *Westerly Sun*, April 22, 1936, p. 2.
34. *Ibid*.
35. *Providence Journal*, April 22, 1936, 9.

36. Ed Butler, *Westerly Sun*, April 21, 1936, p. 2. The Utter family published the *Westerly Sun*.
37. *Ibid*.
38. *Providence Journal*, April 22, 1936, p. 9.
39. *Ibid*.
40. *Ibid*.
41. *Westerly Sun*, April 22, 1936, p. 2.
42. *Boston Traveler*, April 28, 1936, p. 14.
43. Interview with Ethel Brown, August 2003.
44. An American had not taken the Olympic gold medal for the marathon event in 28 years, when New Yorker Johnny Hayes accomplished the feat in London in 1908. But it wasn't without controversy. Hayes had been closely trailing the leader, Dorando Pietri (sometimes written Durandin), representing Italy, when Dorando in exhaustion slumped to the ground just before crossing the finish line. Immediately bystanders physically assisted him over the line. (The bystanders were probably Englishmen, not partisan Italians, historians believe.) At first Dorando Pietri was proclaimed the winner. After an official protest, he was declared disqualified and the U. S. runner, Hayes, was awarded the first-place prize medal. Dorando was given a consolation prize in the form of a gold cup, presented by Queen Alexandra. The incident inspired Irving Berlin to compose the song, "Dorando, Heesa Gooda for Not." Dorando may or may not have died in Italy in 1942. (See: Red Smith, *Boston Globe*, August 8, 1948, p. 34.)

Chapter 10

1. *Boston Herald*, April 20, 1936, p. 1.
2. *Boston Post*, April 19, 1936, p. 18.
3. *Westerly Sun*, April 19, 1936, p. 1.
4. *Boston Globe*, April 21, 1936, p. 20.
5. *Ibid*.
6. *Ibid*.
7. Ellison Brown, quoted in the *Boston Globe*, April 21, 1936, p. 24.
8. *Boston Globe*, April 22, 1936, p. 23.
9. *Providence Sunday Journal*, May 3, 1936, p. 14.
10. *Ibid*.
11. *Ibid*.
12. *Ibid*.
13. *Boston Globe*, April 22, 1936, p. 23.
14. *Ibid*.
15. *Ibid*.
16. Frederick Lewis, *Young At Heart*, p. 42.
17. *Boston Globe*, April 21, 1936, p. 20.
18. Editorial. *Boston Herald*, June 12, 1936, p. 34.
19. *New York Times*, May 31, 1936, p. 4S.
20. Frederick Lewis, *Young At Heart*, p. 42.
21. Lewis, *Ibid*.
22. *Boston Post*, June 12, 1936, p. 22.
23. *Boston Traveler*, June 11, 1936, p. 20.
24. *Ibid*.

25. *Boston Post*, June 8, 1936, p. 16.
26. *Boston Globe*, June 8, 1936, p. 8.
27. *Boston Herald*, June 8, 1936, p. 6.
28. *Boston Globe*, June 1, 1936, p. 6.
29. *Ibid.*

Chapter 11

1. Susan D. Bachrach, *The Nazi Olympics: Berlin 1936* (Boston: Little, Brown and Co., 2000), pp. 18–25.
2. *Ibid.*, p. 36.
3. Ethel Brown, interview with the author, February 20, 2004.
4. *Ibid.*
5. Ellison Brown, quote in the *Westerly Sun*, July 14, 1936, p. 1.
6. *Westerly Sun*, July 14, 1936, p. 1.
7. *Ibid.*
8. *Ibid.*
9. Richard D. Mandell, *The Nazi Olympics* (New York: Ballantine Books, 1971) p. 92. The *Boston Chronicle* gave the lower figure 372 as the number of athletes on the U.S. team, of which "17 were colored." (July 18, 1936, p. 1)
10. *New York Times*, June 30, 1936, p. 1.
11. John Farrington, quote in the *Westerly Sun*, July 14, 1936, p. 1.
12. Mandell, p. 92. One U. S. athlete failed to board the *Manhattan*.
13. Jock Semple, *Just Call Me Jock* (Waterford, CT: Waterford Publishing, 1982), p. 51.
14. Frederick Lewis, *Young at Heart* (Waco, TX: WRS Publishing, 1992), p. 44.
15. Bill Cunningham, in the *Boston Daily Record*, August 10, 1936, and from Johnny Kelley's scrapbook in the Boston Public Library. Cunningham would use the definite article when referring to Brown by his nickname (i.e. "the Tarzan").
16. John Kelley, quoted in Richard Benyo, *The Masters of the Marathon* (New York: Atheneum, 1983), p. 56.
17. Lewis, p. 43.
18. Mandell, p. 93.
19. *New York Times*, July 28, 1936, p. 12.
20. *Ibid.*
21. *New York Times*, August 11, 1936, p. 26.
22. *New York Times*, August 2, 1936, Section 5, p. 1.
23. *Ibid.*
24. *Ibid*, p. 32.
25. *Boston Post*, June 12, 1936, p. 22.
26. *Boston Globe*, August 9, 1936, p. 23.
27. *Boston Post*, August 9, 1936, p. 17.
28. *Boston Post*, August 9, 1936, p. 18.
29. *Ibid.*
30. *Westerly Sun*, September 10, 1936, p. 8.

Chapter 12

1. *New York Times*, August 10, 1936, p. 12. The figure was reported as "a field of 55" in an AP dispatch, printed in the *Westerly Sun*, August 9, 1936, p. 1. In Frederick Lewis' *Young At Heart* (Waco, TX: WRS Publishing, 1992), the field was considerably larger: "Johnny joined the 74 other competitors on the red clay track." (p. 45.)
2. *Westerly Sun*, August 23, 1936, p. 1.
3. Bill Cunningham, quoted in the *Westerly Sun*, August 23, 1936, pp. 1–2.
4. Ellison Brown, quoted by Jerry Nason, "Born to Run," *Yankee Magazine*, April 1981, p. 94.
5. John Kelley, quoted in Joe Falls, *The Boston Marathon* (New York: Macmillan, 1977), p. 77.
6. John Kelley, quoted in Lewis, p. 46.
7. *New York Times*, August 10, 1936, p. 12.
8. *Boston Post*, August 10, 1936, p. 15.
9. John Kelley, quoted in Lewis, p. 46.
10. *Boston Post*, August 10, 1936, p. 15.
11. *Ibid.*
12. *Ibid.*
13. *Ibid.*
14. *Ibid.*
15. John Kelley, quoted in Lewis, p. 46.
16. John Kelley, quoted in Richard Benyo, *The Masters of the Marathon* (New York: Atheneum, 1983), pp. 56–57.
17. *Ibid.*
18. *Westerly Sun*, August 10, 1936, p. 1.
19. *Ibid.*
20. *Westerly Sun*, August 11, 1936, p. 1.
21. Lewis, p. 45.
22. Jock Semple *Just Call Me Jock* (Waterford, CT: Waterford Publishing, 1982), pp. 48–51.
23. John Christian Hopkins, "1930's Greatest Long Distance Runner," *Westerly Sun*, April 18, 1999, p. 23.
24. Richard D. Mandell *The Nazi Olympics* (New York: Ballantine Books, 1971), p. 276. Mandell's endnote (No. 16, p. 345) cites the admonition: "page 11 of the American Olympic Committee's *Handbook*."
25. *New York Times*, February 2, 2004, p. A23. Gold medal-winning runner Helen Stephens, who grew up on a farm in Missouri, was more representative of the other women on the U.S. team. Stephens said of Jarrett, "She was living a different life from mine…. She was used to drinking champagne for breakfast and I'd never had any of that stuff." In Lewis Carlson and John J. Fogarty, *Tales of Gold* (Chicago: Contemporary Books, 1987), p. 138.
26. *New York Times*, February 2, 2004, p. A23.
27. *Ibid.*
28. In Carlson and Fogarty, *Tales of Gold* , p. 90, Eleanor Holm (Jarrett) says it was the AP that employed her. "Brundage tried to send me home, but he couldn't because the Associated Press hired me, and I had press credentials. It was Allan Gould

of the AP who arranged all this. I had a column and I had some mighty fine writers doing it for me — writers like Paul Gallico, Allan Gould, and Tom Walsh. I had the best time doing my column, and it went on the AP wire all over the country."

29. *Ibid.*, p. 89.

30. Tippy Salimeno, quoted by John Kelley "On Running," *Hartford Sports Extra*, (November 15, 1979), p. 15. Larry Hirsch of Westerly, R.I., a most resourceful former fighter (and later, distance runner) under the tutelage of Salimeno, held the manager-trainer in the highest of regard. He was described as a man of impeccable character, a straight arrow, honest, pure of purpose, and forthright.

31. Conversation with Narragansett native and former prizefighter Domingo Monroe, March 12, 2004.

32. John Kelley interview with author, April 18, 2003.

33. *Ibid.*

34. *New York Times*, August 7, 1936, p. 13.

35. *Ibid.*

36. *Boston Globe*, April 14, 1996, p. 65. (http://infoweb.newsbank.com)

37. In the article, *Globe* writer Michael Madden quotes Ethel Brown, daughter Sis, and Ellison's younger sister, Grace Spears, and her husband, Russell, but not for this specific passage. Where and to whom did Brown make his alleged admission in 1948? Madden does not say in the article. (He was just a child in 1948.) Contacted by telephone (October 2004), the now-retired sportswriter could not recall the specific context from eight years before, but explained that his employer, the *Globe*, had kept boxes of clippings on various subjects that were probably utilized in his research. He speculated that those boxes may have been lost forever with the advent of updated, widespread computer implementation. A daylong search by the author through the microfiche of the 1948 sports pages of the *Globe* did not yield any clues or leads.

38. *Boston Daily Globe*, June 5, 1943, p. 4.

39. *Ibid.*

40. Jerry Nason, "Born to Run," *Yankee Magazine*, April, 1981, pp. 94–97.

41. John A. Kelley's Scrapbook, Vol. II, on microfiche, Boston Public Library.

42. Lewis, p. 45.

43. Tippy Salimeno, quoted by John Kelley "On Running," p. 15

44. John Hill, in the *Providence Journal Bulletin*, July 28, 1995.

45. Jerry Nason, *Sportscape*, (April 1985), p. 9.

46. *Ibid.*

47. Ellison Brown, from a column under his own byline, "Running for Uncle Sam," *Westerly Sun*, September 10, 1936, p. 10.

48. Jesse Owens and Paul Neimark, *Blackthink: My Life As Black Man and White Man* (New York: William Morrow, 1970, p. 198.

49. *Ibid*, p. 200.

50. *Ibid.*

51. *Boston American*, September 13, 1936, p. S-5.

52. *Ibid.*

53. *Boston Herald*, September 25, 1936, p. 45.

54. Jesse Owens with Paul Neimark, *Jesse, a Spiritual Autobiography: The Man Who Outran Hitler* (Plainfield, NJ: Logos, 1978), p. 81.

55. *Ibid*, p. 94.

56. *Ibid.*

57. Owens gives the $114,000 figure in his 1978 book *Jesse* (p. 98). He calls it $55,000 in his earlier book, *Blackthink* (p. 73).

58. Associated Press, in the *New York Times*, July 28, 1936, p. 65. The case for the nonwhite athlete earning his success through hard work, conscientiousness, attitude, etc., (the same as Caucasian athletes) was just beginning to find a voice in the scientific community. At the time very few people viewed Ellison Brown as deserving that same respect for what he put into his efforts.

59. *Boston Herald*, September 25, 1936, p. 45.

60. *Ibid.*

61. The following month she announced her earnings in the entertainment circuit: $2,500 per week and "annuities ... paid up until 1940," big, big money in 1936. (Mandell, *Nazi Olympics*, p. 280) The following year, 1937, she "was getting $4,000 a week." (Carlson and Fogarty, *Tales of Gold*, p. 94) Billy Rose, who produced "the Billy Rose aquacade" spectacles she performed, was doing even better. According to Ms. Holm, "I think he [Rose] used to clear between $40,000 and $50,000 a week. And in those days that was an awful lot of money." She divorced the bandleader-singer Arthur Jarrett in 1939 and became Mrs. Billy Rose. In 1954, that divorce, because of the rancor, was followed in the newspapers as "the war of the Roses." She remarried again, to oil magnate Tom Whalen. Eleanor Holm died of kidney failure on January 31, 2004, in Miami.

62. *Ibid.*

Chapter 13

1. *Westerly Sun*, September 11, 1936, p. 12.

2. *Boston Herald*, September 11, 1936, p. 33.

3. As estimated by the *New York Times*, September 11, 1936, p. 33.

4. *Westerly Sun*, September 11, 1936, p. 12.

5. John Kelley, quoted in Lewis, *Young At Heart* (Waco, TX: WRS Publishing, 1992), p. 67.

6. *Boston Globe*, September 13, 1936, p. 29.

7. *Boston Herald*, September 13, 1936, p. 43.

8. The *Boston Post* reported 53 runners making up the field. The *Westerly Sun* (September 13, 1936, p. 6) had the total at 38. Incidentally, following the *Sun's* first two paragraphs, the entire *Westerly Sun* article is a verbatim copy of Will Cloney's *Herald* article without attribution or byline. The

Globe and *Herald*, unusually, did not report any number of the field.

9. *Boston Post*, September 13, 1936, p. 22.
10. *Boston Herald*, September 13, 1936, p. 41.
11. *Boston Post*, September 13, 1936, p. 22.
12. *Boston Herald*, September 13, 1936, p. 43.
13. *Boston Globe*, September 13, 1936, p. 29.
14. *Boston Herald*, September 13, 1936, p. 43.
15. *Boston Post*, September 13, 1936, p. 22.
16. *Boston Herald*, September 13, 1936, p. 43.
17. *Boston Globe*, September 13, 1936, p. 29.
18. *Boston Herald*, September 13, 1936, p. 43.
19. *Ibid.*
20. *Boston Globe*, September 13, 1936, p. 29.
21. Kelley was forty yards behind Brown at the finish line according to the *Globe's* account, fifty yards according to the *Post*, and seventy-five yards as reported in the *Herald*. How many yards could or did Johnny Kelley purportedly cover in twelve seconds, the elapsed time between first and second place?
22. Results in the three Boston newspapers—the *Herald*, *Globe* and *Post*—did not correspond. The *Herald* listed twenty-five runners, their affiliations and their times. It listed number 22 as Italo Amicangioli of United Shoe Machinery, at 60:17. At number 23 was George Dodge, North Cambridge, 60:32. At no. 24 was William Foster, Norfolk, 63:33. Finishing the list was no. 25, Archie Nelson, North Medford, 64:43. The *Globe* listed twenty-three runners altogether, not twenty-five, omitting Italo Amicangioli and Archie Nelson. The *Post* also provided a list of only twenty-three finishers, but its omissions varied. The *Post* left out Foster and Nelson but included Amicangioli in 22nd place.
23. *Westerly Sun*, October 4, 1936, p. 6.
24. *Ibid.*
25. *Ibid.*
26. *New York Times*, October 12, 1936, p. 30.
27. *Ibid.*
28. *Ibid.*
29. The figure of two hundred yards was given by the *Boston Herald* (October 12, 1936, p. 24). Brown won by the greater margin of three hundred yards by the *Boston Globe's* reckoning (October 12, 1936, p. 20), the *Boston Daily Record's* reporting (October 12, 1936, p. 31), and according to the *Westerly Sun* (October 12, 1936, p. 6.)
30. *Westerly Sun*, October 13, 1936, p. 8.
31. *Boston Post*, October 13, 1936, p. 17
32. *Westerly Sun*, October 13, 1936, p. 8.
33. Durgin was in control most of the marathon, as reported by the *Manchester Leader* (October 13, 1936, p. 12). The *Westerly Sun* (October 13, 1936, p. 8), the *Boston Herald* (October 13, 1936, p. 23), and the *Boston Globe* (October 13, 1936, p. 22) all apparently confused Cecil Hill with George Durgin in their accounts.
34. *Manchester Leader*, October 13, 1936, p. 12.
35. *Ibid.*
36. *Ibid.*
37. *Ibid.*
38. *Ibid.*
39. *Ibid.*
40. *Manchester Union*, October 13, 1936, p. 1.
41. *Manchester Leader*, October 13, 1936, p. 12.
42. Jerry Nason, in *Sportscape*, April, 1985, p. 8.
43. Curt Garfield, quoting Fred Brown; the entire passage in *Middlesex News*: "Boston Marathon History," http://www.townline.com/marathon/history/curt5.htm
44. *Manchester Union*, October 13, 1936, p. 1.
45. *Manchester Leader*, October 10, 1936, p. 8.
46. *Manchester Union*, October 12, 1936, p. 10.
47. *Westerly Sun*, October 13, 1936, p. 8.
48. *Westerly Sun*, October 15, 1936, p. 10.
49. *Ibid.*
50. *Ibid.*
51. *Manchester Leader*, October 10, 1936, p. 8.
52. Jerry Nason, "Born To Run," *Yankee* (April 1981), p. 94.
53. *Boston Post*, October 4, 1936, p. 17.
54. *Westerly Sun*, October 29, 1936, p. 1.
55. The *Westerly Sun* reported that Brown had won seven consecutive races, including three full-length marathons, between his return from Berlin and the day of his emergency hernia operation (October 29, 1936, p.1).
56. *Ibid.*
57. Jerry Nason, "Born To Run," *Yankee* (April 1981), pp. 94–97.
58. The AP wire story, carried by the *Boston Daily Record* and the *Boston Globe* among others, reported Brown's prospective stay in the hospital as "several weeks" in duration (*Daily Record*: October 29, 1936, p. 26; *Globe*: October 29, 1936, p. 27). The *Westerly Sun* reported the length of the runner's hospital stay as "several days" (*Sun*: October 29, 1936, p. 1).
59. *Providence Journal*, November 25, 1936, p. 1.
60. *Ibid.*
61. *Ibid.*, p. 5.
62. *Westerly Sun*, November 25, 1936, p. 2.
63. *Providence Journal*, November 25, 1936, p. 1.
64. Ethel Brown, interview with author, February 20, 2004.
65. *Providence Journal*, November 26, 1936, p. 21.
66. *Ibid.*
67. *Ibid.* p. 1.
68. *Westerly Sun*, November 27, 1936, p. 1.; *Providence Journal*, November 26, 1936, p. 1.
69. *Providence Journal*, November 26, 1936, p. 21.

Chapter 14

1. *Boston Herald*, March 20, 1937, p. 16.
2. *Boston Herald*, March 21, 1937, p. 24.

3. *Ibid.*

4. *Westerly Sun*, March 21, 1937, p. 8.

5. *Boston Herald*, March 20, 1937, p. 16.

6. Ethel Brown, interview with author, July 31, 2004.

7. *Ibid.*

8. *Westerly Sun*, April 11, 1937, p. 8.

9. *Ibid.*

10. Ethel Brown interview with author, August 2003.

11. *Westerly Sun*, April 18, 1937, p 1. The *Westerly Sun* reporter must have meant the hills of Newton, not the Wellesley Hills, as constituting the course's "toughest part."

12. *Westerly Sun*, April 18, 1937, p. 10.

13. *Boston Herald*, April 13, 1937, p. 20.

14. *Boston Herald*, April 15, 1937, p. 29.

15. *Boston Globe*, April 13, 1937, p. 28.

16. *Boston Herald*, April 18, 1937, p. 36.

17. John Kelley, quoted in the *Boston Globe*, April 18, 1937, p. 28.

18. *Boston Herald*, April 20, 1937, p. 20.

19. Jerry Nason's descriptive adjectives, in the *Boston Globe*, April 20, 1937, p. 1.

20. *Boston Herald*, April 20, 1937, p. 20.

21. *Westerly Sun*, April 19, 1937, p. 1.

22. *Westerly Sun*, April 21, 1937, p. 2.

23. According to the Boston Athletic Association's official *Boston Marathon 2004 Media Guide*, the incident took place "In a 1930's race, according to Boston Marathon legend...." p. 25.

24. Ethel Brown, quoted in John J. Kelley, "On Running," *Hartford Sports Extra*: November 15, 1979, p. 15.

25. *Boston Daily Globe*, April 20, 1937, p. 23.

26. *Westerly Sun*, April 21, 1937, p. 2.

27. *Ibid.*

28. George Durgin was listed as being from Worcester in the *Boston Globe*, May 16, 1937, p. 27, but was reported as "George Durgin of Beverly" in the *Westerly Sun*, May 16, 1937, p. 8.

29. *Boston Globe*, May 20, 1937, p. 24.

30. Teddy the dog was referred to as Jingles in the *Westerly Sun*, May 23, 1937, p. 2.

31. The Lantern Glow was still in business entering 2004, nearly a half century later. In the late summer of 2004, it changed hands and was renamed the Milestone.

32. *Westerly Sun*, May 23, 1937, p. 2.

33. *Ibid.*

34. *Ibid.*

35. *Ibid.*

36. *Ibid.*

37. *Boston Globe*, June 1, 1937, p. 24.

38. *Westerly Sun*, June 18, 1937, p. 14.

39. *Westerly Sun*, June 13, 1937, p. 2.

40. *Boston Globe*, June 17, 1937, p. 22.

41. *Westerly Sun*, June 27, 1937, p. 8.

42. *Boston Globe*, July 4, 1937, p. 9.

43. *Boston Herald*, July 4, 1937, p. 11. The *Boston Globe*, in its July 4, 1937, issue on page 9, gave Brown's actual time as 57:01. Discrepancies in the *Herald* and *Globe* reporting gave differing times for both his actual and adjusted times. His corrected time, as the *Globe* computed it, with a 5 3/4-minute handicap added, was 62:46. The *Herald* listed fifth place as belonging to Walter Ray, with the times of 62:46 corrected and 57:01 elapsed, the very figures the *Globe* assigned to Ellison Brown. The *Globe* omitted Walter Ray and his results altogether.

44. *Boston Herald*, July 4, 1937, p. 11. DeMar was erroneously listed as finishing sixth in the *Globe*, due to its omission of Walter Ray in fifth place.

45. *Boston Herald*, July 6, 1937, p. 17.

46. *Boston Herald*, July 17, 1937, p. 9.

47. *Boston Herald*, July 18, 1937, p. 21.

48. *Boston Globe*, July 18, 1937, p. 22.

49. *Boston Herald*, July 18, 1937, p. 25.

50. *Boston Globe*, July 18, 1937, p. 22.

51. *Boston Herald,* July 18, 1937, p. 25.

52. *Boston Sunday Globe*, August 1, 1937, p. 25.

53. *New York Times*, October 13, 1937, p. 33. The AP gave the field total as forty-eight (*Boston Herald*, October 13, 1937, p. 25).

54. *Ibid.*

55. *Ibid.*

Chapter 15

1. *Boston Globe*, April 15, 1938, p. 23.

2. Victor O. Jones, "What About It?" *Boston Globe*, April 14, 1938, p. 22.

3. *Ibid.* Author Tom Derderian contests Victor O. Jones' verbatim copy of Connors' letterhead version of his Custom House achievement, adding thirty minutes to the time for running up and down the tower: 8:30 as opposed to "8 minutes flat." *Boston Marathon*, p. 138. Derderian provided no citation for his source.

4. *Boston Globe*, April 19, 1938, p. 8.

5. Hal Higdon, *Boston: A Century of Running* (Emmaus, PA: Rodale Press, 1995), p. 27.

6. *Boston Globe*, April 19, 1938, p. 9.

7. *Ibid.*

8. *Boston Globe*, April 20, 1938, p. 22.

9. *Ibid.*

10. *Ibid.*

11. *Ibid.*

12. *Ibid.*

13. Bill Rodriguez, "The Best Racer of All," *Providence Journal Bulletin Sunday Magazine*, April 19, 1981.

14. Michael Connelly, *26 Miles to Boston*, (Guilford, CT: Lyons Press, 2003), p. 107.

15. Jerry Nason, in *Boston Globe*, April 19, 1938, p. 9.

16. *Ibid.*

17. *Westerly Sun*, May 25, 1938, p. 9.

18. *Westerly Sun*, May 31, 1938, p. 10.

19. *Westerly Sun*, June 20, 1938, p. 7.

20. *Ibid.*

21. *Boston Herald*, June 26, 1938, pp. 25, 28. Ethel Brown disavowed the report that her husband owned or wore such a loud garment (interview with the author, July 31, 2004).

22. *Westerly Sun*, July 5, 1938, p. 10.

23. *Ibid.*

24. *Ibid.*

25. *Westerly Sun*, July 11, 1938, p. 7.

26. *Boston Chronicle*, July 23, 1938, p. 1.

27. *Westerly Sun*, July 24, 1938, p. 7.

28. *Boston Globe*, August 1, 1938, p. 7.

29. The AP report carried in the *Globe* (August 5, 1938, p. 20) reported this race as a Knights of Columbus-sponsored event. The *Westerly Sun* failed to mention that sponsor, ascribing the race instead as falling "under the auspices of St. Vincent de Paul parish." (*Westerly Sun*, August 5, 1938, p. 11.) In an edition five days later, the *Sun* did refer to the event as "the Knights of Columbus race in Providence." (August 10, 1938, p. 7)

30. *Westerly Sun*, August 5, 1938, p. 11.

31. *Ibid.*

32. Abe Soloveitzik, "Sport Talk by ABE," *Westerly Sun*, August 7, 1938, p. 7.

33. Brown's time as reported by the *Boston Globe*, August 11, 1938, p. 26. The *Westerly Sun* reported Brown's seconds as "183–5" (sic), which being equal to 18.6 differs however slightly from the *Globe's*.

34. *Westerly Sun*, August 18, 1938, p. 13.

35. *Boston Globe*, August 21, 1938. The AP story could also be found in the *Sunday New York Times*, August 21, 1938, p. V-3.

36. The AP reported 64 starters (See note above). The *Westerly Sun* reported a larger "field of 67 starters" and in the same article referred to "the pack of 70 runners" (August 21, 1938, p. 7.)

37. *Boston Globe*, September 11, 1938, p. 27. The field was reported to be "about 39 starters" in the *Boston Post*, September 11, 1938, p. 16.

38. *Boston Post*, September 11, 1938, p. 16.

39. *Ibid.*

40. *Boston Herald*, September 11, 1938, p. 43.

41. *Boston Post*, September 11, 1938, p. 16.

42. *Ibid.*

43. *Boston Globe*, September 11, 1938, p. 27. According to the *Globe*, Hawk Zamparelli was among the 45 percent of the field that did not finish. By the *Post's* figures, roughly 36 percent failed to reach the finish line.

44. *Boston Post*, September 11, 1938, p. 16.

45. *Ibid.*

46. *Ibid.*, p. 15.

47. *Boston Herald*, September 11, 1938, p. 43.

48. *Westerly Sun*, September 11, 1938, p. 7.

49. *Boston Herald*, September 17, 1938, p. 5.

50. *Boston Chronicle*, September 24, 1938, p. 6.

51. *Boston Globe*, September 18, 1938, p. 31.

52. *Ibid.*

53. *Boston Post*, September 18, 1938, p. 20.

54. *Ibid.*

55. *Ibid.* See *Boston Herald*, September 18, 1938, p. 38, for its differing figures.

56. *Boston Herald*, September 18, 1938, p. 38. Its previous statement was published September 11, 1938, p. 43.

57. *Boston Post*, September 18, 1938, p. 20.

58. *USA Today*, November. 18, 1999: http://www.usatoday.com/weather/wh1938.htm, (August 1, 2004)

59. Ethel Brown, interview with author, February 20, 2004.

60. *Westerly Sun*, October 13, 1938, p. 11.

61. *Boston Globe*, November 7, 1938, p. 8.

62. *Boston Globe*, November 25, 1938, p. 11.

Chapter 16

1. *Boston Herald*, March 18, 1939, p. 15.

2. *Boston Herald*, March 19, 1939, p. 28. The *Boston Globe* did not report Pawson's mittens (or gloves—"Pawson wore none at all.") March 19, 1939, p. 26.

3. *Boston Globe*, March 19, 1939, p. 26.

4. *Boston Herald*, March 19, 1939, p. 28.

5. *Ibid.* The *Globe's* Jerry Nason had the exact same assessment: "Brown was held up a few seconds." (March 19, 1939, p. 26.)

6. *Boston Globe,* March 19, 1939, p. 26.

7. *Ibid.*

8. *Boston Herald*, March 19, 1939, p. 28.

9. *Ibid.*

10. "Of his cigar, and a pipe he [Cote] produced from a pocket, he commented: 'Smoking? It does not harm a runner. It is good for the nerves. Cigarettes? No, no. Those I have never smoked.'" In the *Boston Globe*, March, 19, 1939, p. 26.

11. *Boston Post*, March 19, 1939, p. 16.

12. *Ibid.* The *Globe* listed Brown as finishing ninth, and Michael O'Hara in tenth place in 2:07:47 (March 19, 1939, p. 26.)

13. *Boston Globe*, March 19, 1939, p. 26.

14. *Ibid.*

15. *Boston Post*, April 2, 1939, p. 16. "Some 116 were entered with an even hundred going to the starting line." The *Boston Sunday Globe* reported "a field of more than 100 contestants" (April 2, 1939, p. 24) and "a record field of 110 starters," reported the *Boston Herald*, (April 2, 1939, p. 41.)

16. *Boston Post*, April 12, 1939, p. 16.

17. Les Pawson, quoted in the *Boston Sunday Globe*, April 2, 1939, p. 24.

18. Tarzan Brown, quoted in the *Boston Sunday Globe*, April 2, 1939, p. 24.

19. *Ibid.*

20. *Boston Herald*, April 2, 1939, p. 41.

21. *Ibid.*

22. Walter Young, quoted in the *Boston Sunday Globe*, April 2, 1939, p. 24.

23. *Boston Herald*, April 2, 1939, p. 41.

24. *Boston Globe*, April 10, 1939, p. 5.

25. *New York Times*, April 9, 1939, Sunday sports section, p. 9.

Chapter 17

1. *Boston Herald*, April 17, 1939, p. 15.

2. *Boston Post*, April 4, 1939, p. 14.

3. *Boston Globe*, April 7, 1939, p. 24.

4. *Boston Globe*, April 5, 1939, p. 18.

5. *Boston Globe*, April 12, 1939, p. 21.

6. *Boston Post*, April 13, 1939, p. 30.

7. *Ibid.*

8. *Boston Post*, April 17, 1939, p. 13. Arthur Duffey's selection was Les Pawson, 1st, and Walter Young, 2nd. This does not square with Tom Derderian's claim that Walter Young was "the *Boston Post* favorite." (*Boston Marathon*, p. 165.)

9. *Boston Herald*, April 11, 1939, p. 15.

10. *Boston Evening Transcript*, April 17, 1939, p. 5.

11. *Ibid.*

12. Pat Dengis, as quoted in the *Boston Globe*, April 14, 1939, p. 19.

13. *Ibid.*

14. *Boston Globe*, April 17, 1939, p. 9.

15. *Ibid.*

16. Don Heinicke's surname was at times spelled "Heinecke" (e.g.: see Nason, in the *Boston Globe*, April 20, 1939, p. 13)

17. *Boston Globe*, April 17, 1939, p. 9.

18. *Boston Globe*, April 18, 1939, p. 11.

19. *Boston Globe*, April 19, 1939, p. 24.

20. *Ibid.*

21. *Boston Herald*, April 19, 1939, p. 26.

22. *Boston Post*, April 12, 1939, p. 13.

23. *Boston Evening Transcript*, April 20, 1939, p. 5.

24. *Boston Globe*, April 20, 1939, p. 8.

25. *Boston Herald*, April 19, 1939, p. 26.

26. *Boston Herald*, April 20, 1939, p. 21.

27. *Ibid.*

28. *The Boston Globe* counted 215 entries (April 19, 1939, p. 24). So did the *Boston Evening Transcript* (April 18, 1939, p. 4) and the *Boston Daily Record* (April 20, 1939, p. 28.) The *Providence Journal* (April 20, 1939, p. 6) had 216 entries.

29. *Boston Globe*, April 20, 1938, p. 8.

30. *Providence Journal*, April 20, 1939, p. 6. Also in the *New York Times*, April 20, 1939, p. 28, and in the *Boston Globe*, April 20, 1939, p. 8.

31. Fred Lewis, *Young At Heart* (Waco, TX: WRS Publishing, 1992), p. 63.

32. *Boston Herald*, April 20, 1939, p. 20.

33. Ellison Brown, quoted in the *Boston Post*, April 20, 1939, p. 18.

34. *Ibid.*

35. *Ibid.*

36. *Boston Post*, April 20, 1939, p. 19.

37. *Boston Globe*, April 20, 1939, p. 8.

38. *Ibid.*

39. *Providence Evening Bulletin*, April 20, 1939, p. 40.

40. Johnny Kelley, quoted in the *Boston Herald*, April 20, 1939, p. 20.

41. Ellison Brown, quoted in the *Boston Post*, April 20, 1939, p. 18.

42. *Ibid.*

43. *Boston Herald*, April 20, 1939, p. 20.

44. *Boston Post*, April 20, 1939, p. 19.

45. *Boston Daily Record*, April 20, 1939, p. 28.

46. Ellison Brown, quoted in the *Boston Post*, April 20, 1939, p. 18.

47. Ellison Brown, "Tarzan's Own Story," in the *Boston Globe*, April 20, 1939, p. 8.

48. *Boston Daily Record*, April 21, 1939, p. 33.

49. *Ibid.*

50. *Boston Daily Record*, April 20, 1939, p. 28.

51. *Boston Daily Record*, April 21, 1939, p. 33

52. *Providence Journal*, April 20, 1939, p. 1.

53. *Boston Herald*, April 20, 1939, p. 21.

54. *Boston Herald*, April 20, 1939, p. 20.

55. Ellison Brown, "Tarzan's Own Story," in the *Boston Globe*, April 20, 1939, p. 8.

56. Ellison Brown, quoted in the *Boston Post*, April 20, 1939, p. 18.

57. *B. A. A. 2004 Boston Marathon Media Guide*, p. 167.

58. *New York Times*, April 20, 1939, p. 28.

59. *Boston Globe*, April 20, 1939, p. 8.

60. *Boston Herald*, April 20, 1939, p. 1.

61. *Boston Evening Transcript*, April 19, 1939, p. 1.

62. *Providence Evening Bulletin*, April 20, 1939, p. 40.

63. *Ibid.*

64. *New York Times*, October 13, 1925, p. 29. The *Times* spelled "Michelsen" with an "o" as "Michelson."

65. David Martin and Roger Gynn, *The Olympic Marathon*, (Champaign, IL: Human Kinetics, 2000), p. 167.

66. *Boston Globe*, April 20, 1939, p. 13.

67. *Boston Daily Globe*, April 20, 1939, p. 1.

68. Walter Young, quoted in the *Boston Herald*, April 20, 1939, p. 21.

69. *Boston Evening Globe*, April 19, 1939, p. 18.

70. *Boston Globe*, April 20, 1939, p. 13.

71. *Boston Globe*, April 20, 1939, p. 8.

72. *Boston Globe*, April 20, 1939, p. 13.

73. Les Pawson, quoted in the *Boston Herald*, April 20, 1939, p. 20.

74. *Boston Daily Globe*, April 20, 1939, p. 8.

75. *Ibid.*

76. *Ibid.*

77. *Ibid.*

78. *Boston Herald*, April 20, 1939, p. 20; *Providence Journal*, April 20, 1939, p. 6; *Boston Post*, April 20, 1939, p. 18.

79. *New York Times*, April 20, 1939, p. 28.

80. *Boston Evening Globe*, April 19, 1939, p. 1.

81. *Boston Daily Globe*, April 20, 1939, p. 8.

82. *Providence Journal*, April 20, 1939, p. 6.

Chapter 18

1. *Providence Evening Bulletin*, April 20, 1939, p. 40.
2. *Boston Post*, April 20, 1939, p. 19.
3. *Providence Evening Bulletin*, April 20, 1939, p. 40.
4. *Providence Journal*, April 20, 1939, p. 6.
5. *Providence Evening Bulletin*, April 20, 1939, p. 40.
6. Associated Press, in the *New York Times*, April 20, 1939, p. 28.
7. *Boston Post*, April 20, 1939, p. 19.
8. *Ibid.*
9. *Ibid.*
10. *Ibid.*
11. *Providence Journal*, April 20, 1939, p. 6.
12. *Boston Herald*, April 20, 1939, p. 21.
13. *Boston Globe*, April 20, 1939, p. 8. Why Salimeno would be considered a "new" manager is unexplained. Sportswriter Ralby may have remembered Farrington from the 1936 marathon and thought of him as Brown's "old" manager.
14. *Providence Journal*, April 20, 1939, p. 6.
15. *Ibid.*
16. *Boston Daily Globe*, April 20, 1939, p. 1.
17. *Providence Journal*, April 20, 1939, p. 6.
18. *Ibid.*
19. Ellison Brown, quoted in the *Boston Globe*, April 20, 1939, p. 8.
20. Ellison Brown, quoted in the *Boston Post*, April 20, 1939, p. 18.
21. *Boston Herald*, April 20, 1939, p. 21.
22. *Boston Globe*, April 20, 1939, p. 13.
23. Ellison Brown, quoted by Bill King, *Providence Journal*, April 20, 1939, p. 6.
24. *Boston Herald*, April 20, 1939, p. 21.
25. Ellison Brown, quoted in the *Boston Globe*, April 20, 1939, p. 8.
26. *Providence Journal*, April 20, 1939, p. 6.
27. Ellison Brown, quoted in the *Boston Post*, April 20, 1939, p. 18.
28. Ellison Brown, quoted in the *Boston Globe*, April 20, 1939, p. 8.
29. *Boston Herald*, April 20, 1939, p. 21.
30. Ellison Brown, quoted in the *Boston Post*, April 20, 1939, p. 18.
31. *Boston Evening Transcript*, April 18, 1939, p. 4.
32. *Boston Daily Record*, April 20, 1939, p. 30.
33. *Boston Globe*, April 20, 1939, p. 13.
34. *Providence Evening Bulletin*, April 21, 1939, p. 34.
35. *Boston Evening Globe*, April 21, 1939, p. 1.
36. *Boston Post*, April 20, 1939, p. 19.
37. The photograph was published in the *Boston Evening Transcript*, April 20, 1939, p. 5, and in the *Providence Evening Bulletin*, April 20, 1939, p. 40.
38. *Boston Daily Record*, April 20, 1939, p. 30.
39. *Ibid*, p. 31.
40. *Boston Evening Transcript*, April 20, 1939, p. 5.
41. *Boston Post*, April 20, 1939, p. 18.
42. *Providence Evening Bulletin*, April 20, 1939, p. 40.
43. *Providence Evening Bulletin*, April 20, 1939, p. 40.
44. *Boston Daily Record*, April 20, 1939, p. 31.
45. *Boston Daily Record*, April 21, 1939, p. 39.
46. *Boston Daily Record*, April 20, 1939, p. 28.
47. *Providence Journal*, April 21, 1939, p. 5.
48. *Ibid.*
49. *Ibid.*
50. *Boston Globe*, April 20, 1939, p. 8.
51. *Boston Post*, April 21, 1939, p. 18.
52. *Ibid.*
53. *Providence Journal*, April 21, 1939, p. 5.
54. *Boston Globe*, April 20, 1939, p. 13.
55. *Boston Daily Record*, April 21, 1939, p. 39.
56. *Boston Globe*, April 20, 1939, p. 13.
57. *Providence Journal*, April 21, 1939, p. 5.
58. *Boston Evening Transcript*, April 20, 1939, p. 5.
59. *Ibid.*
60. *Ibid.*
61. *Ibid.*
62. *Providence Evening Bulletin*, April 20, 1939, p. 40; duplicated in the *Providence Journal* the following day (April 21, 1939), p. 8.
63. *Providence Journal*, April 21, 1939, p. 14.
64. Reported by George C. Carens, transcribed in "The Pulse," *Boston Evening Transcript*, April 20, 1939, p. 5.
65. *Boston Sunday Advertiser*, April 23, 1939, p. 4-S.
66. *Boston Daily Record*, April 21, 1939, p. 39.
67. *Boston Sunday Advertiser*, April 23, 1939, p. 4-S.
68. *Ibid.*
69. *Ibid.*
70. *Ibid.*
71. *Ibid.* The editor's notes in the letter are Dave Egan's. I have transcribed it as it appeared in the *Boston Sunday Advertiser.*
72. Ethel Brown, interview with the author, February 20, 2004.
73. The newspapers reported his position as 54th. (Example: see the *Boston Globe*, April 20, 1938, p. 22.)
74. John Gillooly, in the *Boston Daily Record*, April 20, 1939, p. 28.
75. *Ibid.*
76. *Boston Daily Record*, April 20, 1939, p. 28.
77. *Ibid.*, p. 2.
78. *Boston Evening Globe*, April 19, 1939, p. 1.
79. *Boston Daily Globe*, April 20, 1939, p. 8.
80. Joe Nutter, in the *Providence Journal*, April 20, 1939, p. 1.
81. Jack Barnwell, in the *Boston Post*, April 20, 1939, p. 19.
82. *Ibid.*
83. Johnny Kelley, in the *Boston Evening Transcript*, April 17, 1939, p. 5.
84. *Ibid.*

85. *Providence Sunday Journal*, April 23, 1939, p. 6.
86. *Providence Journal*, April 25, 1939. p. 1.
87. *Ibid.* p. 12.
88. *Ibid.*
89. *Boston Globe*, April 25, 1939, p. 9.
90. *Providence Evening Bulletin*, April 25, 1939, p. 5.
91. *Providence Journal*, April 26, 1939, p. 14.
92. *Providence Journal*, April 28, 1939, p. 1.
93. *Ibid.*

Chapter 19

1. *Boston Post*, May 14, 1939, p. 16.
2. *Boston Herald*, May 14, 1939, p. 34.
3. *Boston Herald*, May 21, 1939, p. 35.
4. *Westerly Sun*, May 21, 1939, p. 1.
5. *Ibid.*, p. 5.
6. *Ibid.*, p. 1.
7. *Ibid.*
8. Ellison Brown, quoted in *Westerly Sun*, May 21, 1939, p. 1.
9. *Ibid.*
10. *Westerly Sun*, May 21, 1939, pp. 1, 5.
11. *Ibid.*, p. 1.
12. *Ibid.*, p. 5.
13. *Ibid.*, p. 1. The *Herald* reported DeMar's time as 60:18, the time for the runner who finished after DeMar, twelfth-place finisher Michael O'Hara (May 21, 1939, p. 35).
14. *Ibid.*, p. 5.
15. *Ibid.*
16. *Ibid.*, p. 1.
17. *Ibid.*
18. *Ibid.*
19. *Boston Globe*, May 27, 1939, p. 7.
20. Pat Dengis, quoted in the *Boston Globe*, May 27, 1939, p. 7.
21. *Ibid.*
22. *Ibid.*
23. *New York Times*, May 31, 1939, p. 31. The AP dispatch was also carried in the *Boston Herald*, May 31, 1939, p. 17. The *Westerly Sun* reported Brown's winning time as 51:33, twenty seconds faster than the AP reported (May 31, 1939, p., 10).
24. *Westerly Sun*, May 31, 1939, p. 10.
25. Times are according to the AP account. The *Westerly Sun* had Pawson's time the same (52:33) but Gregory's as 52:46, not 52:40.
26. *Westerly Sun*, June 12, 1939, p. 8.
27. *Boston Globe*, June 16, 1939, p. 18.
28. *Westerly Sun*, June 18, 1939, p. 8
29. *Boston Herald*, June 18, 1939, p. 19.
30. *Boston Post*, June 18, 1939, p. 16.
31. *Boston Globe*, June 18, 1939, p. 28.
32. *Boston Post*, June 18, 1939, p. 16.
33. *Boston Globe*, June 18, 1939, p. 28.
34. *Boston Post*, June 18, 1939, p. 16.
35. *Ibid.*
36. *Ibid.*
37. *Ibid.*
38. *Westerly Sun*, June 18, 1939, p. 8.
39. *Boston Globe*, June 18, 1939, p. 28.
40. *Boston Post*, June 18, 1939, p. 15.
41. *Ibid.*
42. *New York Times*, June 18, 1939, p. 70. The *Times* was responsible for the headline; the AP was responsible for the article it accompanied.
43. *Boston Herald*, June 18, 1939, p. 17.
44. *Boston Herald*, June 18, 1939, p. 19.
45. *Boston Globe*, June 23, 1939, p. 29.
46. *Ibid.*
47. *Ibid.*
48. *Ibid.*
49. John A. Kelley, quoted in Lewis, *Young At Heart* (Waco, TX: WRS Publishing, 1992), p. 66.
50. Jerry Nason, "What About It?" *Boston Evening Globe*, July 8, 1939, p. 4.
51. *Westerly Sun*, May 21, 1939, p. 1.
52. *Westerly Sun*, July 11, 1939, p. 8.
53. *Boston Globe*, June 23, 1939, p. 29.

Chapter 20

1. *Boston Globe*, June 25, 1939, p. 25.
2. *Boston Post*, June 25, 1939, p. 16.
3. *Boston Globe*, June 25, 1939, p. 25. "Chain-store" may refer to a franchise retail outlet of the sort familiar today, but more likely in 1939 it meant a commercial location specializing literally in steel and iron chains, industrial or otherwise.
4. *Boston Herald*, June 25, 1939, p. 19.
5. *Boston Post*, June 25, 1939, p. 16.
6. *Ibid.*
7. *Boston Globe*, June 23, 1939, p. 29.
8. *Boston Globe*, June 25, 1939, p. 25.
9. *Boston Herald*, June 29, 1939, p. 22.
10. *Boston Globe*, June 29, 1939, p. 19.
11. *Westerly Sun*, June 29, 1939, p. 22.
12. *Ibid.*
13. *Boston Globe*, June 29, 1939, p. 19.
14. The field consisted of 60 runners, according to the *Globe* (July 2, 1939, p. 4), the *Herald* (July 2, 1939, p. 10), and the *Westerly Sun* (July 2, 1939). The *Post* reported the field to be larger, at 75 (July 2, 1939, p. 14).
15. *Boston Post*, July 2, 1939, p. 14.
16. *Ibid.*
17. *Boston Globe*, July 2, 1939, p. 4.
18. *Boston Post*, July 2, 1939, p. 14.
19. *Ibid.*
20. *Boston Globe*, July 2, 1939, p. 4.
21. *Ibid.*
22. *Boston Herald*, July 2, 1939, p. 10, and the *Boston Sunday Advertiser*, July 2, 1939, p. S-1.
23. *Boston Globe*, July 2, 1939, p. 4.
24. *Westerly Sun*, July 5, 1939, p. 8.
25. *Ibid.*
26. *Boston Globe*, July 5, 1939, p. 8.
27. *Westerly Sun*, July 5, 1939, p. 8.
28. *Ibid.*

29. *Westerly Sun*, July 7, 1939, p. 10.

30. The *Westerly Sun*, July 5, 1939, p. 8, reported Brown's time as 1 hour, 4 minutes, 5 seconds, a probable misprint, and claimed his victory was by a slimmer margin of two seconds, not nine as the *Herald* and *Globe* reported. By not giving Kelley's time, the reader of the *Sun* could not see the error in the arithmetic.

31. *Westerly Sun*, July 11, 1939, p. 8.

32. *Westerly Sun*, July 28, 1939, p. 10.

33. *Boston Herald*, July 28, 1939, p. 15.

34. *Westerly Sun*, July 31, 1939, p. 8.

35. The *Boston Globe* listed Lloyd Anderson as having finished in seventh place (July 31, 1939, p. 7). The *Westerly Sun* put Joseph Plouffe of Worcester in seventh and omitted mention of the Rhode Island resident Anderson entirely (July 31, 1939, p. 8).

36. *New York Times*, July 31, 1939, p. 19.

37. *Boston Post*, August 5, 1939, p. 7. At 8 laps per mile, the race would be 80 laps long. An earlier *Post* article claimed "32 laps for ten miles." (July 30, 1939, p. 19.) The August 6 edition of the *Post*, the day after the race, called the entire ten-mile run "an eight-lap affair." (p. 16.) The *Westerly Sun* reported the track to be "only 220 yards in circumference," which would take eight laps to equal one mile. (August 6, 1939, p. 1.)

38. Arthur Duffey, "Sport Comment," *Boston Post*, August 5, 1939, p. 7.

39. *Boston Post*, August 5, 1939, p. 7.

40. *Boston Post*, August 6, 1939, p. 16.

41. *Ibid.*

42. *Westerly Sun*, August 6, 1939, p. 1.

43. *Boston Sunday Advertiser*, August 6, 1939, p. S-1.

44. *Ibid.*

45. *Boston Globe*, August 6, 1939, p. 24.

46. *Westerly Sun*, August 6, 1939, p. 1.

47. *Ibid.*

48. "Gregory opened up a lead of about 70 yards," according to the *Globe*, August 6, 1939, p. 24. The *Westerly Sun* had Gregory "only 20 yards out front," *Westerly Sun*, August 6, 1939, p. 1.

49. The *Boston Post*, the *Boston Globe*, and the *Westerly Sun* reported a victory by a 25 yard margin (August 6, 1939, p. 16, p. 24, and p. 1, respectively). The *Herald* put the margin in the same ballpark, at "more than 20 yards" (August 6, 1939, p. 31). The *Boston Sunday Advertiser* saw Brown beat Gregory by three times that margin, "by some 75 yards" (August 6, 1939, p. S-1).

50. *Boston Globe*, August 6, 1939, p. 24.

51. *Boston Post*, August 6, 1939, p. 16.

52. *Boston Sunday Advertiser*, August 6, 1939, p. S-3.

53. *Boston Globe*, August 13, 1939, p. 27. Anderson's time was given as 57 minutes and four-fifths of a second in both the *Globe* and *Post* (August 13, 1939, p. 15) but Brown's time of 58 minutes plus a fraction was listed as four-tenths, not two-fifths, in the *Globe* only. The *Post* did not give Brown's

time, nor did the *Westerly Sun* in its much longer article, (August 13, 1939, p. 2.). Furthermore, it is confusing to see that Brown finished fifteen yards behind Anderson but a minute back in time. Brown could customarily cover more than fifteen yards in a full minute, even on the hottest afternoon.

54. *Boston Globe*, August 13, 1939, p. 27.

55. *Westerly Sun*, August 13, 1939, p. 2.

56. *Ibid.*

57. *Ibid.*

58. *Westerly Sun*, August 18, 1939, p. 10.

59. John Weissmuller, born in Romania in 1904, was the 1924 and 1928 United States Olympic medal winner in the 100-meter freestyle and the winner, in 1924, of the 400-meter freestyle in men's swimming. He won a total of five gold medals. Though generally spelled with the double-*s*, Nason used just one *s* in the name. So too did the AP when it reported on the twice-divorced actor-swimmer's third wedding held in "a post-midnight ceremony" on August 19, 1939 (*Boston Herald*, August 20, 1939, p. 2).

60. Jerry Nason, "What About It?" *Boston Globe*, August 18, 1939, p. 6.

61. *Ibid.*

Chapter 21

1. *Boston Post*, August 20, 1939, p. 19.

2. *Westerly Sun*, August 21, 1939, p. 6.

3. *Ibid.* The *Boston Evening Transcript* estimated Brown to be "almost a quarter of a mile behind" Lou Gregory at the finish line (August 21, 1939, p. 6).

4. *Boston Globe*, August 21, 1939, p. 8. The *Globe* reported Brown's second-place time as a minute faster, at 1:28:51.

5. *Westerly Sun*, August 21, 1939, p. 6.

6. *Boston Globe*, August 21, 1939, p. 8.

7. Arthur Duffey, in "Sport Comment," *Boston Post*, August 22, 1939, p. 13.

8. *Westerly Sun*, September 1, 1939, p. 10.

9. *Westerly Sun*, September 5, 1939, p. 8.

10. *Ibid.*

11. *Ibid.*

12. *Westerly Sun*, September 11, 1939, p. 6.

13. *Ibid.*

14. *Boston Herald*, September 11, 1939, p. 17.

15. Ethel Brown traveled to the World's Fair with her husband, but adamantly refused to accept the sixty-year-old newspaper reports that Ellison traveled to Boston for a race the very next day. She had a clear memory of the two of them staying overnight in a hotel and going to the movies in the city that evening. One possibility is that they visited New York City and the World's Fair on two different occasions (Ethel Brown interviews with the author).

16. Howell Stevens, *Boston Post*, September 12, 1939, p. 17.

17. *Westerly Sun*, September 12, 1939, p. 6.
18. *Boston Herald*, September 12, 1939, p. 15.
19. George C. Carens, "The Pulse," *Boston Evening Transcript*, September 13, 1939, p. 8.
20. Howell Stevens, *Boston Post*, September 12, 1939, p. 17.
21. *Ibid.*
22. *Ibid.* The *Boston Herald* reported Brown's margin at the finish line over Kelley as 40 yards (September 12, 1939, p. 15). To the *Westerly Sun*, the race was closer and the margin was half that — just 20 yards (September 12, 1939, p. 6).
23. *Ibid.*
24. George C. Carens, "The Pulse," *Boston Evening Transcript*, September 13, 1939, p. 8.
25. *Boston Post*, October 12, 1939, p. 16.
26. *Boston Post*, October 13, 1939, p. 24.
27. *Ibid.*
28. Arthur Duffey, "Sport Comment," *Boston Post*, October 13, 1939, p. 24.
29. *Ibid.*
30. *Boston Evening Globe*, November 11, 1939, p. 6.
31. *Ibid.*
32. "Arthur Duffey's Sport Comment," *Boston Post*, November 19, 1939, p. 23.
33. Associated Press, in the *Boston Post*, November 24, 1939, p. 20. The AP erroneously listed the 1939 edition of the Berwick Marathon as the 32nd, not the 30th.
34. *PIC* Magazine (circa: January–March 1940) photographs by Sam Andre. Accreditation of the captions is unknown. The pages generously offered by Larry Hirsch, Westerly, Rhode Island, for use from his private collection, 2004.
35. *Boston Sunday Advertiser*, December 3, 1939, p. 1-S.
36. *Westerly Sun*, December 20, 1939, p. 10.
37. Abe Soloveitzik, "Sport Talk," *Westerly Sun*, December 21, 1939, p. 14.
38. *Ibid.*
39. *Boston Daily Globe*, December 19, 1939, p. 7.
40. *Ibid.*

Chapter 22

1. *Boston Herald*, March 24, 1940, p. 20. The *Post* had the field at 89 (March 24, 1940, p. 16).
2. *Boston Post*, March 23, 1940, p. 11.
3. *Ibid.*
4. *Boston Daily Globe*, March 28, 1940, p. 17.
5. *Ibid.*
6. *Ibid.*
7. *Boston Herald*, March 24, 1940, p. 20.
8. *Ibid.*
9. *Ibid.*
10. *Ibid.*
11. *Boston Post*, March 24, 1940, p. 16.
12. *Boston Herald*, March 24, 1940, p. 20.
13. *Ibid.*
14. *Boston Sunday Globe*, March 24, 1940, p. 22.
15. *Ibid.*
16. *Ibid.*
17. *Boston Post*, March 24, 1940, p. 16.
18. *Boston Sunday Globe*, March 31, 1940, p. 23. According to the *Boston Post*, the field was a considerably larger one, with 103 runners (March 31, 1940, p. 16).
19. *Boston Herald*, March 31, 1940, p. 37.
20. *Boston Sunday Globe*, March 31, 1940, p. 23.
21. *Boston Post*, March 31, 1940, p. 16.
22. *Ibid.*, p. 15.
23. *Ibid.*
24. *Boston Sunday Globe*, March 31, 1940, p. 23.
25. Bob Dunbar, "Bob Dunbar's Comment," *Boston Herald*, April 3, 1940, p. 14.
26. The *Boston Herald* put Cote at 24th place (April 7, 1940, p. 38), whereas the *Globe* (April 7, 1940, p. 24), the *Post* (April 7, 1940, p. 16) and the Associated Press (in the *Providence Journal*, April 7, 1940, section III, p. 1) all reported his finish as 25th.
27. According to the *Boston Herald* (April 7, 1940, p. 38) the margin of victory between Brown and Pawson was "less than 50 yards," whereas in the *Globe* (April 7, 1940, p. 24) it was "a matter of 60 yards," a difference greater than ten yards.
28. *Providence Journal*, April 7, 1040, sec. III, p. 1.
29. *Boston Herald*, April 7, 1940, p. 38.
30. *Boston Sunday Globe*, April 7, 1940, p. 24.
31. *Ibid.*
32. *Ibid.*
33. *Boston Herald*, April 7, 1940, p. 38.
34. *Boston Sunday Globe*, April 7, 1940, p. 24.
35. *Ibid.*
36. Arthur Duffey, "Arthur Duffey's Sport Comment," *Boston Post*, April 10, 1940, p. 16.
37. *Boston Post*, April 12, 1940, p. 21.
38. *Boston Daily Globe*, April 12, 1940, p. 22.
39. *Ibid.*
40. *Ibid.*
41. The fact that I was unable to find documentation for a single occasion does not detract from the lore in the least. On a related subject: when asked why Brown did not win some races he seemingly should have won (light competition, in good physical condition, ideal racing conditions, weather, etc.), Ethel Brown said there were times he did not want to win. On those occasions he had planned to compete fully when he traveled to the event but his attitude changed on arrival. He may have been unhappy to find that certain fellow competitors were absent, displeased with certain race officials, just plain obstinate or upset about something, or "just being Tarzan" (interview with author, 2004).
42. *Boston Daily Globe*, April 12, 1940, p. 22.
43. Arthur Duffey, "Arthur Duffey's Sport Comment," *Boston Post*, April 13, 1940, p. 10.
44. *Boston Post*, April 14, 1940, p. 16. Where the

Post reported a field of 86, the *Globe* counted 85 (April 14, 1940, p. 24).

45. *Boston Sunday Globe*, April 14, 1940, p. 24.
46. *Boston Herald*, April 13, 1940, p. 6.
47. *Boston Sunday Globe*, April 14, 1940, p. 24.
48. *Boston Herald*, April 14, 1940, p. 29.
49. *Boston Sunday Globe*, April 14, 1940, p. 24.
50. *Boston Herald*, April 14, 1940, p. 29.
51. *Ibid.* The *Boston Herald* calculated the Jarvis margin as "almost half a mile" (April 14, 1940, p. 29). The *Providence Journal* reported "a good half-mile" (April 14, 1940, sec. III, p. 1). The *Boston Post* figured the estimate of the Jarvis' lead as "nearly a mile" in distance. (April 14, 1940, p. 16.)
52. *Boston Sunday Globe*, April 14, 1940, p. 24.
53. *Boston Herald*, April 14, 1940, p. 29.
54. *Ibid.*
55. *Boston Globe*, April 14, 1940, p. 24.
56. *Boston Post*, April 14, 1940, p. 16.
57. *Ibid.*

Chapter 23

1. *Boston Post*, April 19, 1940, p. 1, 20.
2. *Ibid.*
3. *Providence Journal*, April 20, 1940, p. 8.
4. *Boston Globe*, April 14, 1940, p. 25.
5. *Ibid.*
6. *Boston Herald*, April 14, 1940, p. 29.
7. *Boston Daily Globe*, April 17, 1940, p. 21.
8. Two each to Brown and Pawson, one each to Kelley, Kennedy and Young, and seven to DeMar. By the usually astute Nason's count, the sum was only thirteen (*Daily Globe*, April 18, 1940, p. 25).
9. *Boston Globe*, April 20, 1940, p. 6.
10. *Boston Daily Globe*, April 19, 1940, p. 17.
11. *Ibid.*
12. *Boston Herald*, April 20, 1940, p. 5. The *Globe* remarked of Brown's "scarlet satin trunks." (April 19, 1940, p. 17.)
13. *Providence Journal*, April 20, 1940, p. 8. Tom Fitzgerald of the *Globe* concurred: "The Boston police estimated that more than 500,000 stood in on the biggest free sports show of the year." (April 20, 1940, p. 6.) "The largest spectatorial gathering in recent years," the *Herald* reported (April 20, 1940, p. 5).
14. *Boston Daily Globe*, April 20, 1940, p. 6.
15. *Ibid.*
16. Gerard Cote, as told to Arthur Duffey, *Boston Post*, April 20, 1940, p. 9.
17. *Boston Daily Globe*, April 20, 1940, p. 6.
18. *Boston Herald*, April 20, 1940, p. 5.
19. Gerard Cote, as told to Arthur Duffey, *Boston Post*, April 20, 1940, p. 9.
20. *Boston Herald*, April 20, 1940, p. 5.
21. *Boston Daily Globe*, April 20, 1940, p. 6. According to the *Herald*, Rankine was third, Pawson fifth, and Kelley sixth at South Framingham (April 20, 1940, p. 6).
22. Gerard Cote, as told to Arthur Duffey, *Boston Post*, April 20, 1940, p. 9.
23. *Boston Post*, April 20, 1940, p. 9.
24. *Ibid.*
25. *Boston Daily Globe*, April 20, 1940, p. 6.
26. Leslie Pawson, quoted in "Arthur Duffey's Sport Comment," *Boston Post*, April 20, 1940, p. 9.
27. *Boston Post*, April 20, 1940, p. 9.
28. Gerard Cote, as told to Arthur Duffey, *Boston Post*, April 20, 1940, p. 9.
29. *Boston Herald*, April 20, 1940, p. 5.
30. *Boston Post*, April 20, 1940, p. 9. The final *e* is often left off of Canadian Scotty Rankine's surname.
31. *Ibid.*
32. *Ibid.*
33. Brown's established record for Coolidge Corner was 2:12:39. Cote's time there was 2:13:45. Yet the *Boston Daily Globe* reported that "at Coolidge Corner ... he was running more than two minutes behind the record" (April 19, 1940, p. 17).
34. *Boston Daily Globe*, April 19, 1940, p. 17. Tom Fitzgerald, also writing in the *Globe*, wrote, "There must have been an official car for every runner entered in the race" (April 20, 1940, p. 6).
35. *Boston Herald*, April 20, 1940, p. 5.
36. Gerard Cote, as told to Arthur Duffey, *Boston Post*, April 20, 1940, p. 9.
37. *Boston Herald*, April 20, 1940, p. 5.
38. *Ibid.*, p. 1.
39. *Boston Daily Globe*, April 20, 1940, p. 6.
40. *Ibid.*
41. *Ibid.*
42. *Ibid.*
43. *Ibid.*
44. *Boston Herald*, April 20, 1940, p. 5.
45. *Ibid.*
46. Leslie Pawson, quoted in "Arthur Duffey's Sport Comment," *Boston Post*, April 20, 1940, p. 9.
47. *Boston Herald*, April 20, 1940, p. 5.
48. *Boston Daily Globe*, April 20, 1940, p. 6.
49. *Ibid.* Author Tom Derderian ascribed the ice cream sandwich binge to Ellison Brown, not Rankine, without any attribution (*Boston Marathon*, p. 174). Junk-food binges are a part of Tarzan lore.
50. *Boston Daily Globe*, April 20, 1940, p. 6.
51. *Boston Herald*, April 20, 1940, p. 5.
52. Biaggie or Blaggie, depending on the source or the clarity of the type.
53. "Arthur Duffey's Sport Comment," *Boston Post*, April 20, 1940, p. 9.
54. *Providence Journal*, April 20, 1940, p. 8.
55. *Boston Daily Globe*, April 20, 1940, p. 6.
56. *Boston Herald*, April 20, 1940, p. 5.
57. *Boston Daily Globe*, April 20, 1940, p. 6.
58. *Boston Daily Globe*, April 19, 1940, p. 17.
59. *Ibid.* Scotty Rankine's surname spelled without the final "e."
60. *Ibid.*
61. *Ibid.*

62. *Boston Herald*, April 16, 1940, p. 15.
63. *Ibid.*
64. *Ibid.*
65. *Ibid.*
66. *Ibid.*
67. *Boston Globe*, April 20, 1940, p. 6.
68. *Boston Herald*, April 16, 1940, p. 15.
69. *Boston Herald*, April 20, 1940, p. 5. See also: *Boston Globe*, May 12, 1940, p. 27.
70. *2004 U.S. Olympic Team Trials, Men's Marathon Guide Supplement*, from the U.S. Men's Olympic Marathon Team, Selection Races: 1900–1964, "Updated from the 1996 U.S. Olympic Marathon Trials Media Guide, pp. 85–89," p. 8. http://www.usatf.org
71. Paavo Nurmi, quoted in "Arthur Duffey's Sport Comment," *Boston Post*, March 23, 1940, p. 10.

Chapter 24

1. *Boston Post*, May 12, 1940, p. 20.
2. *Ibid.*
3. *Boston Daily Globe*, May 31, 1940, p. 6.
4. *Ibid.*
5. *Ibid.*
6. *Boston Post*, May 31, 1940, 17.
7. *Boston Daily Globe*, May 31, 1940, p. 6.
8. *Boston Post*, May 31, 1940, p. 17.
9. *Boston Daily Globe*, May 31, 1940, p. 6.
10. *Providence Journal*, May 31, 1940, p. 7.
11. *Boston Daily Globe*, May 31, 1940, p. 6.
12. *Ibid.*
13. *Boston Globe*, June 9, 1940, p. 21.
14. *Providence Journal*, June 9, 1940, Sec. III, p. 1.
15. *Boston Globe*, June 9, 1940, p. 21.
16. *Providence Journal*, June 9, 1940, Sec. III, p. 8.
17. *New York Times*, June 9, 1940, p. S6.
18. The AP, in the *New York Times*, June 16, 1940, p. S8; in the *Boston Globe*, June 16, 1940, p. 24; in the *Boston Herald*, June 16, 1940, p. 35; and in the *Providence Journal*, June 16, 1940, Sec III, p. 2.
19. *Ibid.*
20. *Boston Herald*, June 18, 1940, p. 19.
21. *Boston Daily Globe*, June 18, 1940, p. 10.
22. *Boston Herald*, June 18, 1940, p. 19.
23. *Boston Daily Globe*, June 18, 1940, p. 10.
24. Jerry Nason, *Boston Daily Globe*, June 20, 1940, p. 20.
25. *Ibid.*
26. *Ibid.*
27. *Ibid.*
28. *Ibid.*
29. *Boston Herald*, June 23, 1940, p. 31.
30. *Boston Globe*, June 23, 1940, p. 24.
31. *Ibid.*
32. *Boston Daily Globe*, June 29, 1940, p. 6.
33. *Boston Herald*, June 29, 1940, p. 6.
34. *Providence Journal*, July 5, 1940, p. 11.

35. *Ibid.*
36. *Boston Daily Globe*, July 6, 1940, p. 7.
37. *Ibid.*
38. *Boston Globe*, July 7, 1940, p. 20.

Chapter 25

1. *Providence Journal*, July 14, 1940, p. 5.
2. *Boston Daily Globe*, July 22, 1940, p. 6.
3. Runners' times were not reported in the coverage by the *Globe* (July 22, 1940, p. 6), *Herald* (July 22, 1940, p. 14), or by the *Providence Journal* (July 22, 1940, p. 6).
4. *Providence Journal*, July 26, 1940, p. 7.
5. *Ibid.*
6. *Ibid.*
7. *Ibid.*
8. *Boston Daily Globe*, July 27, 1940, p. 5.
9. *Boston Herald*, July 31, 1940, p. 18.
10. *Ibid.*
11. *Boston Herald*, August 4, 1935, p. 30.
12. *Boston Globe* and *Boston Herald*: same date, same page number — August 18, 1940, p. 23.
13. *Portland Press Herald*, August 17, 1940, p. 9.
14. *Boston Globe*, September 1, 1940, p. 8.
15. John Hopkins, Brown's great-nephew and newspaperman, quoted in the *Westerly Sun*, April 18, 1999, p. 23.
16. *Providence Journal*, September 3, 1940, p. 7.
17. *Ibid.*
18. *Ibid.*
19. *Boston Globe*, September 3, 1940, p. 6.
20. *Boston Post*, September 1, 1940, p. 14.
21. *Boston Post*, September 3, 1940, p. 15.
22. *Boston Globe*, September 3, 1940, p. 7.
23. AP wire story, *Boston Post*, September 3, 1940, p. 13.
24. *Boston Herald*, September 23, 1940, p. 13.
25. *Ibid.*
26. *Ibid.*
27. *Boston Post*, September 23, 1940, p. 15.
28. *Boston Herald*, September 23, 1940, p. 13.
29. *Boston Daily Globe*, September 23, 1940, p. 11.
30. *Providence Journal*, October 13, 1940, p. 7.
31. "Bob Dunbar's Comments," *Boston Herald*, October 11, 1940, p. 23.
32. *Boston Daily Globe*, October 11, 1940, p. 30.
33. *Boston Herald*, October 27, 1940, p. 25.
34. *Boston Daily Globe*, November 11, 1940, p. 7.
35. Associated Press, carried in the *Boston Herald*, November 29, 1940, p. 15, and the *New York Times*, November 29, 1940, p. 29.
36. From the John A. Kelley scrapbook, Boston Public Library collection. Most likely, the clip is cut from the Berwick newspaper, on Friday, Saturday, or Sunday after the Thanksgiving Day race, November, 1940. There are no dates or identifications in the Kelley scrapbook alongside the newspaper clippings.

Chapter 26

1. *Boston Globe*, March 21, 1941, p. 23.
2. *Boston Herald*, March 22, 1941, p. 12.
3. *Boston Herald*, March 23, 1941, p. 31.
4. *Boston Globe*, March 23, 1941, p. 25.
5. *Ibid.*, p. 1.
6. *Boston Herald*, March 23, 1941, p. 31.
7. The *Herald* listed Smith's time as identical to McGlone's, with 21 seconds (1:58:21). The *Globe* put Smith at one second behind McGlone, with 22 seconds (1:58:22).
8. *Boston Globe*, March 23, 1941, p, 25.
9. *Boston Herald*, March 24, 1941, p. 14.
10. *Ibid.*
11. *Ibid.*
12. *Ibid.*
13. *Ibid.*
14. *Ibid.*
15. *Boston Globe*, March 25, 1941, p. 20.
16. *Ibid.*
17. "Bob Dunbar's Comment," *Boston Herald*, March 27, 1941, p. 20.
18. *Boston Globe*, March 28, 1941, p. 24.
19. *Ibid.*
20. *Ibid.*
21. *Boston Herald*, March 29, 1941, p. 7.
22. *Boston Herald*, March 30, 1941, p. 44.
23. *Boston Globe*, March 30, 1941, p. 28.
24. *Boston Herald*, March 30, 1941, p. 44.
25. *Boston Globe*, March 30, 1941, p. 28.
26. *Boston Daily Globe*, April 2, 1941, p. 22.
27. *Ibid.*
28. *Ibid.*
29. *Ibid.*
30. In the *Boston Globe*, April 6, 1941, p. 26, St. Jean was 32. In the *Boston Herald*, April 6, 1941, p. 48, his age was given as 39.
31. *Boston Globe*, April 13, 1941, p. 27.
32. *Boston Herald*, April 13, 1941, p. 28. Will Cloney reported: "Then at the end of the race, the watch readers developed astigmatism or something, cut three minutes off everybody's time, and has [*sic*] seven runners breaking Brown's record."
33. *Boston Daily Globe* (late edition), April 15, 1941, p. 21.
34. *Boston Herald*, April 18, 1941, p. 27. "Cote Experts' 'Pick' To Win Marathon."
35. *Boston Daily Globe* (early edition), April 15, 1941, p. 21.
36. *Boston Daily Globe*, April 18, 1941, p. 22.
37. *Daily Record*, April 19, 1941, p. 37.

Chapter 27

1. *Boston Herald*, April 20, 1941, p. 26.
2. *Boston Daily Record*, April 18, 1941, p. 52.
3. *Boston Evening Globe*, April 19, 1941, p. 7.
4. Automobile description by Victor O. Jones, in the *Boston Daily Globe*, April 21, 1941, p. 7.
5. *Boston Globe*, April 20, 1941, p. 30.

6. *Boston Evening Globe*, April 19, 1941, p. 7.
7. *Boston Herald*, April 20, 1941, p. 26.
8. *Boston Globe*, April 20, 1941, p. 30.
9. *Boston Daily Globe*, April 21, 1941, p. 7.
10. Les Pawson, quoted in the *Boston Herald*, April 20, 1941, p. 27.
11. *Boston Herald*, April 20, 1941, p. 26.
12. *Ibid.*
13. *Boston Evening Globe*, April 19, 1941, p. 7.
14. *Boston Globe*, April 20, 1941, p. 30.
15. The *Boston Herald* listed Kelley's time as 2:31:36, a difference of ten seconds. April 20, 1941, p. 26.
16. *Boston Herald*, April 20, 1941, p. 27.
17. *Ibid.*
18. *Boston Globe*, April 20, 1941, p. 30.
19. *Ibid.*
20. *Ibid.*
21. Robert F. Holbrook, "DeMar Socks Pair of Hecklers," *Boston Globe*, April 20, 1941, p. 30.
22. *Boston Herald*, April 20, 1941, p. 26.
23. *Ibid.*, p. 27.
24. *Ibid.*, p. 1.
25. *Ibid.*, p. 27.
26. According to Will Cloney: "Pawson cracked the tape, bowed under a laurel wreath, posed for photographers, and grinned happily. He was still on hand when Kelley crossed the line...." (*Boston Herald*, April 20, 1941, p. 26.) Contrast with John English's account, also in the *Boston Herald*, where he writes that Pawson was lying on a cot "in the barren basement of Boston University's Soden building, hard by the finish line ... [when] George Demeter came in and placed the traditional laurel wreath on Pawson's brow." *Boston Herald*, April 20, 1941, p. 27.
27. *Ibid.*, p. 26.
28. *Boston Globe*, April 20, 1941, p. 1.
29. *Ibid.*, p. 30.
30. *Ibid.*
31. *Boston Herald*, April 20, 1941, p. 26.
32. Tom Derderian, *The Boston Marathon: A Century of Blood, Sweat, and Cheers* (Chicago: Triumph Books, 2003), p. 56.
33. *Boston Evening Globe*, April 19, 1941, p. 7.
34. *Boston Globe*, April 20, 1941, p. 30.
35. *Boston Daily Globe*, April 17, 1941, p. 22.
36. *Boston Daily Globe*, May 30, 1941, p. 24.
37. *Boston Daily Globe*, May 31, 1941, p. 7.
38. *Ibid.*
39. *Providence Journal*, August 31, 1941, Sec. III, p. 1.
40. *Westerly Sun*, September 2, 1941, p. 8.
41. *Providence Journal*, April 20, 1942, p. 7.
42. *New York Times*, November 10, 1941, p. 25.
43. The AP reported Gregory leading all the way, "never out of the front position, finishing some 300 feet ahead of John Kelley." *Westerly Sun*, November 28, 1941, p. 10 and *Boston Daily Globe*, November 28, 1941, p. 24.

Chapter 28

1. *Boston Herald*, March 21, 1942, p. 6.
2. *Boston Traveler*, April 6, 1942, p. 17.
3. *Westerly Sun*, April 9, 1942, p. 10.
4. *Boston Traveler*, April 16, 1942, p. 25.
5. *Boston Traveler*, April 13, 1942, p. 14.
6. *Ibid.*
7. *Boston Daily Globe*, April 17, 1942, p. 32.
8. *Providence Sunday Journal*, April 19, 1942, Sec. III, p. 5.
9. *Ibid.*
10. The *Herald* (April 19, 1942, p. 46) and the *Traveler* (April 6, 1942, p. 17) reported the Roxbury native as 27 years old. Nason, in the *Boston Globe*, reported McGlone's age as 24. (April 19, 1942, p. 26.)
11. See Jerry Nason, in the *Boston Daily Globe*, April 18, 1942, p. 6.
12. *Boston Globe*, April 19, 1942, p. 24.
13. *Ibid.*
14. *Ibid.*, p. 26.
15. *Providence Journal*, April 20, 1942, p. 7.
16. *Westerly Sun*, April 20, 1942, p. 6.
17. *Ibid.*
18. *Ibid.*
19. *Westerly Sun*, September 11, 1942, p. 8.
20. *Boston Herald*, April 20, 1942, p. 9.
21. *Boston Daily Globe*, April 20, 1942, p. 9.
22. *Boston Herald*, April 20, 1942, p. 9.
23. *Ibid.*
24. *Ibid.*
25. *Ibid.*
26. John English of the *Herald* reported, "McGlone stumbled to the pavement three times." (April 20, 1942, p. 9.) Fred Foye of the *Boston Traveler* reported McGlone "falling about six times." (April 20, 1942, p. 25.)
27. *Boston Daily Globe*, April 20, 1942, p. 9.
28. "Bob Dunbar's Comment," *Boston Herald*, April 20, 1942, p. 9.
29. The reader is referred to endnote No. 44, in Chapter 9.
30. *Providence Journal*, April 20, 1942, p. 7.
31. Jock Semple, *Just Call Me Jock* (Waterford, CT: Waterford Publishing, 1982), p. 70–71.
32. *Boston Globe*, April 20, 1942, p. 9.
33. *Westerly Sun*, September 11, 1942, p. 8.
34. *Baltimore Sun*, September 13, 1942, Sports Section, p. 1.
35. *Ibid.*, Sports Section, p. 2.
36. *New York Times*, August 30, 1942, p. E7.
37. *Ibid.*
38. Ethel Brown, telephone interview with author, September 24, 2004.
39. *Westerly Sun*, November 5, 1942, p. 8. The *Boston Herald* stated that Kelley and Cote "by strange coincidence, entered the service on the same day, November 15, 1942." (April 19, 1943, p. 4)

Chapter 29

1. Pawson's age was given as 37 in the *Boston Globe*, April 17, 1943, p. 6.
2. *Westerly Sun*, March 22, 1943, p. 6.
3. *Boston Herald*, March 22, 1943, p. 12.
4. *Ibid.*
5. *Ibid.*
6. *Ibid.*
7. *Ibid.*
8. *Boston Post*, April 4, 1943, p. 17. He was employed by the C.B. Cottrell Company in Westerly, not Providence, according to wife Ethel Brown, telephone interview with author, September 24, 2004.
9. *Boston Herald*, April 4, 1943, p. 38
10. *Boston Globe*, April 5, 1943, p. 6.
11. Vogel was seventeen years of age in the *Boston Globe* (April 11, 1943, p. 27), and eighteen in the *Herald* (April 11, 1943, p. 44).
12. *Boston Globe*, April 11, 1943, p. 27.
13. *Westerly Sun*, April 15, 1943, p. 8.
14. "Arthur Duffey's Sport Comment," *Boston Post*, April 15, 1943, p. 15.
15. Jerry Nason, *Boston Daily Globe*, April 16, 1943, p. 31.
16. Gerard Cote, quoted in the *Boston Post*, April 20, 1943, p. 16. Cote's assessment of Brown was a postmarathon account.
17. Jerry Nason, *Boston Daily Globe*, April 16, 1943, p. 31.
18. *Ibid.*
19. *Ibid.*
20. *Boston Daily Globe*, April 16, 1943, p. 31.
21. *Ibid.*
22. *Boston Post*, April 18, 1943, p. 22.
23. Jerry Nason, *Boston Globe*, April 18, 1943, p. 24.
24. Cote's injury was described variously as an injured leg, ankle, Achilles tendon, and heel. A Dr. C. Franklin Green, according to Arthur Sampson of the *Boston Herald*, had been treating him for four days prior to the marathon (April 19, 1943, p. 4).
25. *Boston Daily Globe*, April 19, 1943, p. 6.
26. *Boston Post*, April 20, 1943, p. 16.
27. *Boston Daily Globe*, April 19, 1943, p. 6.
28. *Westerly Sun*, April 19, 1943, p. 6.
29. Clarence H. DeMar, in the *Boston Herald*, April 19, 1943, p. 4.
30. *Ibid.*
31. *Boston Globe*, April 18, 1943, p. 24.
32. *Boston Globe*, April 19, 1943, p. 6.
33. *Boston Post*, June 27, 1943, p. 17.
34. *Ibid.*
35. *Ibid.*
36. *Boston Sunday Advertiser*, June 27, 1943, p.1-S.
37. *Boston Post*, July 5, 1943, p. 17.
38. *Providence Journal*, July 5, 1943, p. 22.
39. Lou Gregory's winning time by the AP differed from that reported by the *Providence Jour-*

nal (July 5, 1943, p. 22) and the *Boston Herald* (July 5, 1943, p. 24), both of which listed his time as one minute slower, at 51 minutes, 50 seconds. Neither the *Journal* nor the *Herald* mentioned a new mark for the distance set by Gregory, for if the listing of times each of them reported was accurate, Gregory would indeed not have beaten the old mark of 51:29 set by Navy Lieut. Joe Mc-Cluskey, who, incidentally, did not compete to defend his title that year.

40. *Providence Journal*, September 6, 1943, p. 19.

41. The AP did not provide a list of all twelve contestants; it only mentioned the top three finishers.

Chapter 30

1. *Westerly Sun*, April 14, 1944, p. 8.
2. Jerry Nason, *Boston Daily Globe*, April 14, 1944, p. 15.
3. *Ibid.*
4. *Ibid.*
5. *Ibid.*
6. *Boston Daily Globe*, April 18, 1944, p. 11.
7. *Ibid.*
8. *Boston Daily Globe*, April 19, 1944, p. 20.
9. *Boston Daily Globe*, April 20, 1944, p. 6.
10. *Boston Daily Globe*, April 19, 1944, p. 20.
11. *Boston Herald*, April 20, 1944, p. 19.
12. *Westerly Sun*, April 20, 1944, p. 8.
13. *Boston Herald*, April 20, 1944, p. 1. The *Post's* Howell Steven's observed "a 50-yard margin" (*Boston Post*, April 20, 1944, p. 13). Nason's estimate was greater than his colleagues: "by a mere but mighty margin of 60 yards" (*Boston Daily Globe*, April 20, 1944, p. 1)
14. Jerry Nason, *Boston Daily Globe*, April 20, 1944, p. 6.
15. *Ibid.*
16. Clarence H. DeMar, *Boston Daily Globe*, April 20, 1944, p. 1.
17. *Ibid.*, p. 6.
18. Jerry Nason, *Boston Daily Globe*, April 20, 1944, p. 6.
19. Clarence H. DeMar, *Boston Daily Globe*, April 20, 1945, p. 21.
20. Jerry Nason, *Boston Daily Globe*, April 19, 1945, p. 10.
21. Jerry Nason, *Boston Daily Globe*, April 20, 1945, p. 21.
22. See Michael Connelly, *26 Miles to Boston* (Guilford, CT: Lyons Press, 2003), pp. 176–178, 185.
23. AP, *Boston Globe*, November 22, 1945, p. 39.

Chapter 31

1. Ellison Brown, quoted by Jerry Nason, in Joe Falls, *The Boston Marathon* (New York: Mac-

millan, 1977), p. 43. The suggestion exists that this quotation dates to 1945, not 1946. There is some reason to think Nason was speaking of 1945 from the way the passage is presented by Falls. John Hopkins, for one, accepted the 1945 origination (*Westerly Sun*, April 18, 1999, p. 24.) It is my contention, however, that the quotation is from 1946, based foremost on the fact that Brown did not run Boston in 1945. It was in 1946 that he ran in his comeback attempt in hopes of getting a job.

2. *Boston Herald*, March 23, 1946, p. 4.
3. *Boston Herald*, March 22, 1946, p. 37.
4. *Boston Herald*, March 25, 1946, p. 11. This was one of the earliest instances of a change in the typographical custom of putting a space after each period following a letter in an abbreviation.
5. *Ibid.*
6. *Boston Herald*, March 24, 1946, p. 52.
7. *Ibid.*
8. *Ibid.*
9. *Ibid.*
10. *Boston Herald*, March 31, 1946, p. 55.
11. *Ibid.*
12. Jock Semple, quoted in *Boston Herald*, March 31, 1946, p. 55.
13. *Boston Herald*, April 9, 1946, p. 17. Al Hart served as a marathon official. His admiration for Brown was expressed back in 1943: "The prettiest thing I ever saw in action."
14. *Boston Herald*, April 14, 1946, p. 43.
15. *Ibid.*
16. *Ibid.*
17. *Ibid.*
18. *New York Times*, April 21, 1946, Sec. 5, p. 4.
19. "Forerunners: Kyriakides," from an excerpt of Dabilis and Nikos Siotis, *With It or Upon It*, http://www.greece.gr/LIFE/Sport/forerunnersky-riakides.stm, p. 2. In their book *Running With Pheidippides* (Syracuse, NY: Syracuse University Press, 2001), the quotation presented is a little different. There DeMeter is reported to have said, "He is a Greek! He has a letter from his athletic clubs and Greece is responsible if something happens to him. You cannot keep him out of this race" (p. 177).
20. Jerry Nason, in Joe Falls, *The Boston Marathon*, p. 39.
21. *New York Times*, April 21, 1946, Sec. 5, p. 4.
22. *Westerly Sun*, April 21, 1946, p. 6.
23. *Westerly Sun*, April 22, 1946, p. 6.
24. Jerry Nason, in Joe Falls, *The Boston Marathon*, p. 39.
25. *Ibid.*
26. Ellison Brown, quoted by Jerry Nason, "Born to Run," *Yankee Magazine*, April 1981, p. 101.

Chapter 32

1. John Ward, "Tarzan Brown's 'Silver Streak' No Treat to Providence Police," *Providence Jour-

nal, October 2, 1949, p. 18. (Reporter John Ward no relation to author.)
2. Ethel Brown, interview with author, July 31, 2004.
3. *Ibid.*
4. *Providence Journal*, October 2, 1949, p. 18.
5. *Ibid.*
6. John Christian Hopkins, "1930's Greatest Long Distance Runner," *Westerly Sun*, April 18, 1999, p. 24.
7. *Providence Journal*, October 2, 1949, p. 11.
8. *New York Times*, April 20, 1951, p. 42.
9. "Ask the Globe," *Boston Globe*, September 2, 1984, in "New England Magazine" section.
10. *Boston Post*, March 26, 1955, p. 4. Sonny was born October 26, 1937. He would have been 17. Tarzan Brown was still an unknown at that age.
11. *Boston Daily Globe* (Evening edition), March 25, 1955, p. 27.
12. *Ibid.*
13. *Boston Herald*, March 26, 1955, Sports Section, p. 4.
14. Sonny's unfair handicap and treatment as if he were his father were not reported in the newspapers. The source is Ethel Brown, telephone interview with author, September 24, 2004.
15. *Boston Post*, March 27, 1955, p. 35.
16. *Boston Globe*, March 27, 1955, p. 47.
17. *Boston Herald*, March 27, 1955, p. 56.
18. *Providence Journal*, April 17, 1955, p. 37 (or p. 38, depending upon the edition).
19. *Ibid.*
20. *Ibid.*
21. *Ibid.*
22. *Ibid.* Great-nephew John Christian Hopkins put the incident in 1959, with a navy sailor, in his *Westerly Sun* piece, April 18, 1999, p. 24. In it, he suggests the youngster bet his leather jacket against Brown's $5.
23. *Providence Journal*, April 17, 1955, p. 37 (or p. 38, depending upon the edition).
24. Photograph from the *Providence Journal*, published date uncertain.
25. *Providence Journal*, April 17, 1955, p. 37 (or p. 38, depending upon the edition).

Chapter 33

1. Road Runners Club of America, 8965 Guilford Road, Columbia, MD 21046. http://www.rrca.org/publicat/rrcahof.htm
2. George Falcone, "News," dated November 15, 1973 (Westerly Public Library file).
3. Todd B. Hollis, *Westerly Sun*, November 10, 1974, p. 1.
4. *Ibid.*, p. 2.
5. *Ibid.*
6. *Ibid.*
7. *Westerly Sun*, November 10, 1974, p. 2.
8. Ethel Brown, interview with the author, July 31, 2004.

9. *Westerly Sun*, November 10, 1974, p. 2.
10. *Ibid.*
11. *Providence Journal-Bulletin*, November 9, 1974, p. 6.
12. John J. Kelley, e-mail correspondence with author, January 14, 2003.
13. *Westerly Sun*, November 10, 1974, p. 2.
14. *Providence Journal-Bulletin*, November 9, 1974, p. 6.
15. *Providence Journal-Bulletin*, November 8, 1974, p. A-15. John J. Kelley remembers the music provided by a rock band, not the famed doo-wop group.
16. John J. Kelley, e-mail correspondence with author, January 14, 2003.
17. *Westerly Sun*, November 10, 1974, p. 1.
18. *Westerly Sun*, November 11, 1974, p. 14.
19. Ethel Brown, interview with author, February 20, 2004.
20. *Westerly Sun*, August 24, 1975, p. 1.
21. AP, in the *New York Times*, August 26, 1975, p. 13.
22. *Boston Globe*, August 24, 1975, p. 91.
23. Peter Nabokov, *Indian Running*, (Santa Barbara: Capra Press, 1981), p. 184.
24. Bill Rodriguez, "The Best Racer of All," *Providence Journal-Bulletin Sunday Journal Magazine*, April 19, 1981.
25. Colman McCarthy, "Tarzan Brown: Rhode Islanders Remember the Legendary Indian Runner," *The Runner*, January 1982, p. 86.
26. *Boston Globe*, April 14, 1996, p. 65.
27. *Westerly Sun*, August 24, 1975, p. 1.
28. *Providence Journal*, August 24, 1975, p. A-12. The *Providence Journal* identified John F. Lallo as "bail commissioner."
29. *Westerly Sun*, August 25, 1975, p. 1.
30. *Ibid.*
31. *Ibid.*
32. *Ibid.* The correctional facility was and still is located in Cranston, Rhode Island.
33. Westerly Sun, August 27, 1975, p. 1.
34. *Providence Journal*, August 27, 1975, p. B-1.
35. *Westerly Sun*, August 27, 1975, p. 1.
36. Chief Medical Examiner Dr. William O. Sturner, quoted in the *Providence Journal*, August 28, 1975, p. A-10.
37. *Providence Journal*, August 28, 1975, p. A-10.
38. *Westerly Sun*, September 4, 1975, p. 2.
39. From State vs. Phillip Edward [*sic*], Case Number 75–184, filed November 12, 1975.
40. From State vs. Phillip Edward [*sic*], Case Number 75–184, Case Log sheet.
41. From State vs. Phillip Edward [*sic*], Case Number 75–184, *Judgment and Disposition*, filed March 12, 1975.
42. From State vs. Phillip Edward [*sic*], Case Number 75–184, Case Log sheet.
43. From State vs. Phillip Edward [*sic*], Case Number 75–184, Registry of Motor Vehicles letter, filed March 26, 1976.

44. Wilcox Park was designed by Warren H. Manning on land donated to the city by Harriet Wilcox in memory of her husband in 1898. Manning was an associate of Frederick Law Olmsted, noted architect of the Emerald Necklace system of parks in Boston and Central Park in New York City.

45. Alan Peck, e-mail correspondence with author, May 22, 2003.

Chapter 34

1. Sis Brown, quoted in the *Providence Journal*, April 18, 1982, p. C-2.

2. Ethel Brown, quoted *Ibid.*

3. Danny Cahill, Neil Gouvin, and Tom Mahfood are a few who have shared Westerly area recollections from the late seventies. Despite memories of Brown's proclivities in alcohol use, they had respect for Ellison Brown. Frank Limpert, Trading Post proprietor, had worked as a bartender at the Zoo bar, later the Wood River Inn in Hope Valley, a place where Tarzan and Thunderbolt were welcomed patrons.

4. Jerry Nason, "Jerry Nason Recalls the Marathon — and Tarzan Brown" in Joe Falls, *The Boston Marathon*, p. 44.

5. Fred Brown Sr., quoted in Curt Garfield, "1931–1946: Yankees, Finns, and Tarzan Brown," in "Boston Marathon Scrapbook," *Middlesex News*. (*http://www.townonline.com/marathon/history/curt5.htm*).

Epilogue

1. Franch could not locate Brown's name on the passenger list, but neither could he find the names of Kelley or McMahon. The list in the archives, he posits, "only includes cabin-class passengers." In an e-mail from John Franch to the author, January 21, 2004.

2. *Boston Globe*, October 8, 2004, pp. 1, B-5, editorial on p. A-18; *Boston Herald*, October 8, 2004, pp. 2, 135, editorial on p. 24; *New York Times*, October 8, 2004, p. C-10.

3. Running statistics always seem to create discrepancies. In an AP obituary written by Theo Emery, Kelley's ninth-place B. A. A. Marathon win at age fifty was erroneously put in 1957 instead of 1958. In 1957, Kelley finished 13th, though he ran four seconds faster, finishing in 2:52:08.

4. Barbara Matson, *Boston Globe*, November 5, 1999, p. E-2. According to the obituaries of the *New York Times* and the Associated Press, Kelley was 84 at the time of his last B. A. A. Marathon in 1992. The *Times* gave his 1992 finish time as 5:58:36. The AP listed a flat 5 hours, 58 minutes.

5. Jerry Nason, "Our Olympians," *Boston Daily Globe*, July 19, 1948, p. 10. Not all the prizes containing diamonds contained real diamonds. A prize diamond tie clip, for example, turned out to be adorned with a "stone" of glass. (*Boston Globe*, October 8, 2004, p. B-5.)

6. Frank Litsky, *New York Times*, October 8, 2004, p. C-10.

7. *Boston Globe*, October 15, 1992, p. 59.

Bibliography

Books

Bachrach, Susan D. *The Nazi Olympics: Berlin 1936*. Boston: Little Brown, 2000.
Beagan, Gerry, and Amby Burfoot. *The Guide to Road Racing in New England*. Waterford, CT: Waterford Publishing, 1982.
Benyo, Richard. *The Masters of the Marathon*. New York: Atheneum, 1983.
Calloway, Colin G., ed. *After King Philip's War: Presence and Persistence in Indian New England*. Hanover, NH: University Press of New England, 1997.
Carlson, Lewis H., and John J. Fogarty. *Tales of Gold*. Chicago: Contemporary Books, 1987.
Connelly, Michael. *26 Miles to Boston*. Guilford, CT: Lyons Press, 2003.
DeMar, Clarence H. *Marathon*. Sherburne, VT: New England Press, 1937/1981.
Derderian, Tom. *Boston Marathon: A Century of Blood, Sweat and Cheers*. Chicago: Triumph Books, 2003.
_____. *Boston Marathon: The First Century of the World's Premier Running Event*. Champaign, IL: Human Kinetics, 1996.
Falls, Joe. *The Boston Marathon*. New York: Macmillan, 1977.
Higdon, Hal. *Boston: A Century of Running*. Emmaus, PA: Rodale Press, 1995.
Josephson, Judith Pinkerton. *Jesse Owens: Track and Field Legend*. Berkeley Heights, NJ: Enslow Publishers, 1997.
Lewis, Frederick. *Young at Heart: The Story of Johnny Kelley, Boston's Marathon Man*. Edited by Dick Johnson. Waco, TX: WRS Publishing, 1992.
Mandell, Richard D. *The Nazi Olympics*. New York: Ballantine Books, 1971.
Martin, David E., and Roger W. H. Gynn. *The Olympic Marathon*. Champaign, IL: Human Kinetics, 2000.
Nabokov, Peter. *Indian Running*. Santa Barbara, CA: Capra Press, 1981.
Nason, Jerry. *The Story of the Boston Marathon (From 1897)*. Boston: Boston Globe, 1966.
Owens, Jesse, and Paul Neimark. *Blackthink: My Life as Black Man and White Man*. New York: William Morrow, 1970.
_____. *Jesse: A Spiritual Autobiography: The Man Who Outran Hitler*. Plainfield, NJ: Logos, 1978.
Oxendine, Joseph B. *American Indian Sports Heritage*. Lincoln: University of Nebraska Press, 1988.
Prucha, Francis Paul, ed. *Documents of United States Indian Policy*, 2nd ed., expanded. Lincoln: University of Nebraska Press, 1990.
Semple, Jock, with John J. Kelley and Tom Murphy. *Just Call Me Jock*. Waterford, CT: Waterford Publishing, 1982.
Shepperd, Kenneth R. "Narragansett." In *The Gale Encyclopedia of Native American Tribes, Volume 1*, edited by Sharon Malinowski and Anna Sheets. Detroit: Gale Publishers, 1998.

Simmons, William S. *Spirit of the New England Tribes*. Hanover, NH: University Press of New England, 1986.
Tsiotos, Nick, and Andy Dabilis. *Running with Pheidippides*. Syracuse, NY: Syracuse University Press, 2001.
Wallechinsky, David. *The Complete Book of the Olympics*. New York: Viking Press, 1984.

Monographs

Narragansett Indian Tribe. "Historical Perspective of the Narragansett Indian Tribe." (http://www.narragansett-tribe.org/history)
State of Rhode Island and Providence Plantations. *Third Annual Report of Commission on the Affairs of the Narragansett Indians, Made to the General Assembly at Its January Session, 1883*. Providence: E. L. Freeman & Co., Printers to the State, 1883.
2004 U.S. Olympic Team Trials, Men's Marathon Guide Supplement (http://www.usatf.org)

Newspapers

Baltimore Sun
Boston Chronicle
Boston Daily Record
Boston Evening Transcript
Boston Globe
Boston Herald
Boston Post
Boston Sunday Advertiser
Boston Traveler
Lowell Sun
Manchester Leader
Manchester Union
New York Times
Newburyport Daily News
Portland Press Herald
Press Enterprise (Berwick, PA)
Providence Evening Bulletin
Providence Journal
USA Today
Washington Post
Westerly Sun

Media Guide Publications

2004 Boston Marathon Media Guide. Boston: John Hancock/B. A. A.
2003 Boston Marathon Media Guide. Boston: John Hancock/B. A. A.

Periodicals

PIC Magazine

Video

People of the First Light: No. 4 The Narragansetts. Dan Kain, executive producer.
Reunion of Old Time Boxers at the Westerly, RI Library. Westerly, 1974.
That Golden Distance. Frederick Lewis. Providence, 1985.
WGBY-TV Massachusetts Education Television, Vision Maker Video, 1978.

Index

Numbers in **_bold italics_** refer to photographs

Index